## THE CAMBRIDGE HANDBOOK OF VICTIM ENGAGEMENT IN TRANSITIONAL JUSTICE

How have victims shaped – and reshaped – transitional justice? This volume introduces a novel framework for tracing and interpreting the evolving trajectories of victim-survivor engagement across different phases of grassroots activism, institutional participation, and various forms of resistance. Drawing on a diverse range of empirical case studies from across the globe, the handbook provides both a historical analysis of victims' evolving roles in (formal, informal, and everyday) transitional justice processes and a comparative perspective on the realities of victim engagement today – highlighting increasingly intersecting justice struggles and the porous boundaries of transitional justice. Written for students, scholars, practitioners, and policymakers in transitional justice, human rights, international law, peacebuilding, and social movements, this interdisciplinary resource draws on innovative, situated practices and the protagonism of victims to foster conceptual and methodological innovation for a forward-looking reimagination of victim-led justice after large-scale violence.

TINE DESTROOPER is Professor of Transitional Justice at Ghent University. She has published extensively in various leading journals and recently edited *Transitional Justice in Aparadigmatic Contexts* (with Line Gissel and Kerstin Carlson). Her work has been supported by two European Research Council grants and two Marie Skłodowska-Curie Fellowships, and she was recently a Fulbright Fellow at Columbia University.

ELKE EVRARD is a postdoctoral researcher at Ghent University. Her research on transitional justice has appeared in leading peer-reviewed journals. She contributes to scholarly and public engagement through invited lectures, teaching, and her role as managing editor of the *Journal of Human Rights Practice*. She was recently awarded a grant by the Research Foundation – Flanders.

# The Cambridge Handbook of Victim Engagement in Transitional Justice

Edited by

**TINE DESTROOPER**

Ghent University

**ELKE EVRARD**

Ghent University

CAMBRIDGE
UNIVERSITY PRESS

CAMBRIDGE
UNIVERSITY PRESS

Shaftesbury Road, Cambridge CB2 8EA, United Kingdom

One Liberty Plaza, 20th Floor, New York, NY 10006, USA

477 Williamstown Road, Port Melbourne, VIC 3207, Australia

314–321, 3rd Floor, Plot 3, Splendor Forum, Jasola District Centre, New Delhi – 110025, India

103 Penang Road, #05–06/07, Visioncrest Commercial, Singapore 238467

Cambridge University Press is part of Cambridge University Press & Assessment, a department of the University of Cambridge.

We share the University's mission to contribute to society through the pursuit of education, learning and research at the highest international levels of excellence.

www.cambridge.org
Information on this title: www.cambridge.org/9781009671422

DOI: 10.1017/9781009671378



When citing this work, please include a reference to the DOI 10.1017/9781009671378

First published 2026

Cover image: Niche graves honoring Mayalxil victims of the Internal Armed Conflict, located in the village of Santa Avelina, San Juan Cotzal, El Quiché, Guatemala. Credit: Gretel Mejía Bonifazi

*A catalogue record for this publication is available from the British Library*

*Library of Congress Cataloging-in-Publication Data*
NAMES: Destrooper, Tine editor | Evrard, E. editor
TITLE: The Cambridge handbook of victim engagement in transitional justice / edited by Tine Destrooper, Ghent University; Elke Evrard, Ghent University.
DESCRIPTION: Cambridge, United Kingdom ; New York, NY : Cambridge University Press, 2026. | Series: Hbk Cambridge law handbooks | Includes bibliographical references and index.
IDENTIFIERS: LCCN 2025035505 (print) | LCCN 2025035506 (ebook) |
ISBN 9781009671422 hardback | ISBN 9781009671378 ebook
SUBJECTS: LCSH: Transitional justice | Reparation (Criminal justice) |
Victims of violent crimes – Legal status, laws, etc.
CLASSIFICATION: LCC K5250 .C39 2026 (print) | LCC K5250 (ebook) | DDC 340/.115–dc23/eng/20250805
LC record available at https://lccn.loc.gov/2025035505
LC ebook record available at https://lccn.loc.gov/2025035506

ISBN 978-1-009-67142-2 Hardback

# Contents

# Figures

# Contributors

**Adriana Alas**, born in San Salvador, El Salvador, has a PhD in social anthropology from El Colegio de Michoacán and currently works as a postdoctoral scholar with the Surviving Memory in Postwar El Salvador research initiative at Western University. Her research is focused on competing memory regimes, intergenerational knowledge, and decolonial and collaborative research in rural communities in El Salvador and with the Salvadoran Canadian diaspora. Among other projects, she is dedicated to the elaboration of community-driven books about the memory of the Salvadoran armed conflict in El Salvador's rural communities, with whom she has worked for fourteen years.

**Kim Baudewijns** is a PhD researcher at the Human Rights Centre at Ghent University. In her research in the eastern DRC, she uses participatory research methods to understand the lived experiences of those affected by structural violence and explores how survivors navigate complex ecosystems of transitional justice mechanisms in this context.

**Ram Kumar Bhandari** is an activist and academic practitioner working on issues of the rights of conflict victims, with a focus on the issue of disappearance, victim movements, and transformative transitional justice. He is one of the foremost Nepali advocates for a system of transitional justice that addresses the needs of relatives. Ram comes from a family directly affected by disappearances, with his father having been disappeared during the armed conflict in 2001. He holds a PhD in law and is a research fellow at Kathmandu University and a co-founder of the International Network of Victims and Survivors of Serious Human Rights Abuses.

**Thorsten Bonacker** is Professor at the Center for Conflict Studies at the University of Marburg and serves as the President's Delegate of the European University for Peace, Justice and Inclusive Societies. He obtained his PhD at the University of Oldenburg and held several positions as guest researcher. His research sits at the intersection of sociology and political science, specifically within the field of international political sociology and international relations, and focuses on international administration practices in post-colonial and post-war societies, the role of victims in addressing past mass violence, and atmospheres of violence in conflict and peacebuilding.

**Susanne Buckley-Zistel** is Professor of Peace and Conflict Studies and Executive Director of the Center for Conflict Studies at the Philipps University of Marburg. Her main interests lie in (transitional) justice, memory studies, gender and feminism, as well as spatial and post-colonial analysis. She is the deputy spokesperson and a Principle Investigator of the 'Human Rights Discourse in Migration Societies' interdisciplinary research group (MeDiMi).

**Mauricio Carrasco** works at Chile's national reparations programme PRAIS (Programa de Reparación y Atención en Salud) and lectures in the Department of Sociology at Alberto Hurtado University in Santiago de Chile. His research focuses on transitional justice and human rights violations in post-authoritarian Latin America, with a particular emphasis on enforced disappearance and victim reparations. He played a key role in developing Chile's National Search Plan and was previously a researcher at the National Institute for Human Rights. He holds a master's degree in sociology from Alberto Hurtado University and has extensive experience in human rights documentation and public policy analysis.

**Cath Collins** is Director of the Observatorio Justicia Transicional at the Diego Portales University in Santiago de Chile and Professor of Transitional Justice at Ulster University, Northern Ireland. She divides her time between Chile and Northern Ireland and has been working over the past few years on different aspects of the search for the disappeared in transitional justice settings across Latin America and Ireland. She is a political scientist, community worker, and translator with first and higher degrees from the University of Cambridge, the University of London, and Queen's University Belfast.

**Güneş Daşlı** is a Cara Research Fellow in the Department of International Relations, Politics, and History at Loughborough University. She completed her PhD at the Center for Reconciliation Studies, Jena University, in 2023. Her PhD thesis on transitional justice and Kurdish conflict was honoured with *summa cum laude*. Her research focuses on post-conflict studies, feminist philosophy, restorative justice, and social movements, with a regional focus on the Middle East. Dr Daşlı has consulted on various research projects related to transitional processes, including recent efforts in Iraq. She teaches courses on conflict, gender and peace, and transitional justice.

**Lauren Dempster** is a senior lecturer in the School of Law and a fellow of the Senator George J. Mitchell Institute for Global Peace, Justice and Security at Queen's University Belfast. Lauren's research focuses on transitional justice and her research interests include critical approaches to transitional justice, efforts to address the legacy of the past in Northern Ireland, enforced disappearance, the relationship between transitional justice and environmental harm, and victim mobilisation.

**Tine Destrooper** is a professor at the Faculty of Law and Criminology of Ghent University. She is the Director of Justice Visions, an European Research Council-funded research hub focusing on the roles of victim-protagonists in transitional justice. In 2023 she was awarded a Fulbright Fellowship to undertake research at Columbia University, and a Marie Skłodowska-Curie Fellowship for a research stay at the Institute of Advanced Studies (Paris). She is a co-editor of the *Journal of Human Rights Practice* and the Co-chair of the Human Rights Research Network. Previously, she held positions at New York University's Law School, the European University Institute, Leiden University, Wissenschaftskolleg Berlin, and the universities of Antwerp and Leuven.

**Elke Evrard** is a postdoctoral researcher at the Human Rights Centre of the Faculty of Law and Criminology of Ghent University, where she also obtained her PhD in law. Her work focuses on victim participation, public outreach, reparations, and memory-making in transitional justice contexts, including post-conflict settings and countries confronting widespread historical harm. She has a particular interest in interdisciplinary and mixed method approaches. She is a co-lecturer of an advanced master's course on transitional justice and human rights and serves as the Managing Editor for the *Journal of Human Rights Practice*.

**Pamina Firchow** is an associate professor at Brandeis University's Heller School for Social Policy and Management and the Founding Executive Director of Everyday Peace Indicators, a non-profit organisation dedicated to research and evaluation. In her research, Firchow focuses on the international accompaniment of communities affected by mass violence and the localisation of international development and peacebuilding aid. She has published extensively on participatory approaches to the design, measurement, and evaluation of transitional justice, reconciliation, and peacebuilding initiatives in leading peer-reviewed journals and books. She served as a United States Institute of Peace Senior Jennings Randolph Fellow in 2016 and a Fulbright Fellow in Bogotá, Colombia, in 2020.

**Amanda Grzyb** is Professor of Information and Media Studies at Western University, where her primary teaching and research interests include state violence, genocide studies, social movements, and memory studies. Her edited books, articles, book chapters, public reports, and research-creation projects focus on El Salvador, Nazi-occupied Europe, Rwanda, and Sudan. Dr Grzyb is a founding member of Surviving Memory in Postwar El Salvador, for which she also serves as project director. Supported by the Social Sciences and Humanities Research Council of Canada, the Canadian Foundation of Innovation, and the Ontario Research Fund, Surviving Memory is a community-based research partnership committed to documenting and commemorating the history of the Salvadoran Civil War and preventing future violence.

**Thomas Obel Hansen** is Distinguished Professor in the Department of International Law, Universidad Carlos III de Madrid (UC3M), co-funded by the Spanish Ministry of Science through the Beatriz Galindo programme. He is affiliated with the Francisco de Vitoria Institute of International and European Studies at UC3M. He obtained his LLM (2006) and PhD (2010) from Aarhus University Law School. He is associated with the Transitional Justice Institute, Ulster University (UK), as Senior Research Fellow. His chapter in this volume is an outcome of the research project 'The Standardisation of Transitional Justice: Consolidation, Innovation and Politics', funded by the Independent Research Fund Denmark (grant no. 1028-00206B).

**Maria Hartmann** is a PhD fellow at the Center for Conflict Studies in Marburg and a research associate in the 'Human Rights Discourse in Migration Societies' interdisciplinary research group (MeDiMi). She works on and is politically involved with solidarity in post-migration societies, diasporic memory, and Syrian diaspora in Germany. For her PhD, she is researching encounters of solidarity between dissidents from Syria and the former East Germany. She is interested in the interface between human rights work, participatory research approaches, and transformative methodologies.

**Kevin Hearty** is a senior lecturer in criminology at the School of Social Sciences, Education and Social Work, Queen's University Belfast, and a fellow of the Senator George J. Mitchell Institute for Global Peace, Justice and Security at the university. His research interests include transitional justice, memory studies, and victimology; he previously published work on political violence, police reform, reparations, and victim narratives.

**Mina Ibrahim** is an anthropologist and community archivist from Cairo, Egypt, and a postdoctoral researcher in the 'Human Rights Discourse in Migration Societies' interdisciplinary research group (MeDiMi). His work explores the connections between the recent trials of Syrian regime members in Germany and the everyday understanding of justice among Syrians, particularly former detainees who fled after the 2011 uprising. Since October 2022, he has been part of the Centre for Conflict Studies at the University of Marburg, linking ethnographic fieldwork with oral histories and (absent) paper archives in his research.

**Briony Jones** is Professor of Peace and Justice in the Politics and International Studies Department of the University of Warwick. Her research specialises in the politics of knowledge and claim-making in post-conflict contexts, as well as methodological reflections on inclusive and ethical research practices. She is an affiliated researcher at swisspeace and the Geneva Centre for Humanitarian Studies, and a visiting researcher at the United Nations Research Institute for Social Development.

**Chulani Kodikara** currently works with the Social Scientists' Association and as an independent scholar in Sri Lanka. Her research is on law as a site of women's struggles for equality and justice in Sri Lanka. She is part of the editorial collective of *Polity*, the magazine of the Social Scientists' Association.

**Lisa J. Laplante** is the Director of the Center for International Law and Policy at New England Law, Boston, where she is also a professor of law. Her work in transitional justice began in 2001 as a researcher with the Peruvian Truth and Reconciliation Commission. Soon after, she began to accompany the Asociación de Inocentes Liberados (ARIL), a group of Peruvians who were unjustly imprisoned under President Fujimori's anti-terrorism laws. She continues to support ARIL while they bring their claims for reparations to the Inter-American Human Rights system. Laplante is the author of prize-winning scholarship that appears in top journals and is frequently invited to speak around the world, including by the United Nations and governments.

**Cheryl Lawther** is Professor of Transitional Justice in the School of Law, Queen's University Belfast. Her research interests concern truth recovery and dealing with the past, victims, ex-combatants, reparations, atrocity sites, and the politics of dead bodies. Cheryl's most recent book, *Constructing Victimhood: Beyond Innocence and Guilt in Transitional Justice*, was published by Oxford University Press in January 2025. She is a previous recipient of a British Academy Mid-Career Fellowship, a Fulbright Ireland Scholarship, and an Arts and Humanities Research Council Early Career Grant, amongst other awards. Beyond academia, Cheryl is a member of the Victims' Payments Board and the Victims' Commissioners Advisory Panel.

**Fangyi Li** is a PhD candidate at Edinburgh Law School, researching local conceptions of harm, victimhood, and redress in post-conflict Cambodia and Timor-Leste as alternatives to rights-based understandings of transitional justice. Her research interests include transitional justice, international criminal law, critical theory, and sensory approaches to law.

**Brianne McGonigle Leyh** is Professor of Global Justice Studies with the Netherlands Institute of Human Rights (SIM) and the Montaigne Centre for Rule of Law and Administration of Justice at Utrecht University's School of Law. Her specialisations include human rights law, transitional justice, victims' rights, and documentation and accountability for serious human rights violations.

**Luke Moffett** is Professor of Human Rights and International Humanitarian Law in the School of Law at Queen's University Belfast. He is the author of *Reparations and War* (Oxford University Press 2023) and *Justice for Victims before the International Criminal Court* (Routledge 2014), as well as co-editor of the *Research Handbook on Transitional Justice* (Edward Elgar Publishing 2017 and 2023).

**Marta Paricio Montesinos** is a doctoral researcher at the Centre for Environment, Economy and Energy of the Brussels School of Governance. She is pursuing a joint PhD between the Vrije Universiteit Brussel and the University of Helsinki. Her dissertation focuses on corporate accountability and corporate environmental due diligence obligations in conflict-affected areas. Recently, her work has analysed new legislative developments, such as the EU Corporate Sustainability Due Diligence Directive, and explored the connections between business and human rights and transitional justice, paying particular attention to the role of victims and civil society in advancing corporate accountability in high-risk countries.

**Mina Rauschenbach** is a social psychologist and criminologist, a consultant and a certified mediator, as well as a research associate at the Leuven Institute of Criminology (KU Leuven). She is also an associate general editor for the Elgar series on Transitional Justice. At the nexus between social psychology and criminology, her research interests focus on different justice stakeholders' perceptions and beliefs in the aftermath of serious human rights violations, and how these are shaped by collective understandings of the past and related identity concerns. Her current research addresses the links between recognition and transitional justice, particularly how justice processes and the discourses underpinning these processes can hinder, complicate, promote, or contribute to the recognition of victims and their rights.

**Michael Reed-Hurtado** is a Colombian/US lawyer and journalist with thirty years of experience in the fields of human rights, criminal justice, and humanitarian action, mainly in Latin America. He currently serves as Chief Program Officer at the Guernica 37 Centre. Throughout his career, Reed-Hurtado has strived to combine research and advocacy, to ensure an evidence-based practice and leverage the potential of information technology in documenting atrocities. He teaches and researches at Georgetown University, focusing on state crime, the aetiology of collective violence, denialism and the sociology of lying, and practical dimensions of human rights, transitional justice, and negotiated peace settlements.

**María Helia Rivera Castillo** ('Elida') is a survivor of the Salvadoran armed conflict, a community leader, and a member of the Surviving Memory in Postwar El Salvador research team. Born in the Los Rivera hamlet in the canton of El Sitio in the municipality of Arcatao, she is a member of a *campesino* (peasant) family. She completed middle school and worked as a local health promoter. She also held positions in the municipal government of Arcatao and, later, as head of the Municipal Women's Unit (2012–2024). She is an active member of the Municipal Association of Women of Arcatao and the Surviving Historical Memory Committee of Arcatao.

**Simon Robins** is a practitioner and researcher with an interest in humanitarian protection, human rights, and transitional justice. For the last fifteen years he has combined academic research with a consulting practice focusing on evaluation and programme support with international agencies, including the UN and non-governmental organisations, with an emphasis on states emerging from conflict and violence. He is Research Advisor to the International Committee of the Red Cross Missing Persons Centre and a senior research fellow at the Centre for Applied Human Rights at the University of York.

**Huma Saeed** is a criminologist with expertise in transitional justice. She is a senior transitional justice fellow at the City University of New York and an affiliated senior researcher at the Leuven Institute of Criminology, University of Leuven. A roster expert of the Justice Rapid Response, Dr Saeed has frequently engaged as Senior Consultant with the UN, the International Criminal Court, and other international organisations. She has published extensively on victims' rights, gender justice, economic-state crime, and transitional justice.

**Daniela Suárez Vargas** is an Economic and Social Research Council postdoctoral fellow in the School of Law at Queen's University Belfast and holds a PhD in law and a master of laws from the same university. A qualified lawyer from Universidad del Rosario, Colombia, her research examines how victimhood narratives affect the recognition of experiences of sexual and gender-based violence against women fighters in Colombian transitional justice. Daniela has also practised law and conducted research in transitional justice, international criminal law, criminal law, human rights, victimology, and international humanitarian law.

**Miracle Chinwenmeri Uche** researches victim-oriented justice for victims of international crimes before the International Criminal Court and in domestic and regional mechanisms. Her teaching at undergraduate and graduate level includes public international law, international criminal law, a research module on war and peace, and the criminal law of England and Wales at Westminster Law School. She has worked on refugees' and communities' socio-cultural integration in the Netherlands and Nigeria through Stichting Unity in Diversity, Netherlands. She is currently involved in a research project on fostering resilient communities in Nigeria through sustainable agriculture, with the goal of tackling farming-related intra- and inter-tribal conflicts.

# Acknowledgements

This handbook has its roots in the international conference *Victims and Transitional Justice: Participation, Mobilisation, Resistance*, held in Ghent in March 2024. The conference gathered scholars, practitioners, and activists from around the world, many of whom appear as contributors to this volume. Their presentations, insights, and reflections shaped the trajectory of the handbook in profound ways. We are deeply grateful for the engagement and energy they brought to that gathering and to the broader conversation on victim engagement.

This conference, and the present volume, also mark the closing of an European Research Council-funded research project on victim participation in transitional justice. As such, the handbook is the culmination of several years of research, collaboration, and dialogue. We therefore wish to extend our deepest thanks to the entire Justice Visions team at Ghent University. Throughout this journey, they have been an extraordinary source of intellectual support, encouragement, and companionship. The team, and the Human Rights Centre of which it is a part, have fostered a research environment where critical reflection and theoretical innovation are inextricably linked to a deep commitment to working alongside those who have seen their rights violated. The intellectual, methodological, ethical, and personal contributions of our colleagues have shaped the framework that holds this book together, and, in a more profound sense, how we engage in research.

Many others have supported this work, whether by presenting at the conference, engaging in informal but invaluable exchanges on the complex roles victims play in transitional justice processes, or as part of smaller research projects we have been engaged in. All these insights helped sharpen our thinking, challenge our assumptions, and deepen our commitment to inclusive and impactful scholarship. Also, the conversations that are not explicitly referenced within the covers of this handbook have left their imprint, sometimes in subtler ways, by guiding the questions we ask and the perspectives we foreground. We hope this handbook honours that broader web of engagement and contributes meaningfully to the conversations that continue beyond these pages.

We are grateful to the anonymous reviewers and the editorial team at Cambridge University Press, whose feedback and guidance helped shepherd this volume through to completion. We also thank the European Research Council for their trust in our work and the generous funding they provided (ERC StG VictPart 804154 and ERC CoG GROUNDOC 101171170), and to the Special Research Fund of Ghent University, which funded several projects aimed at sharing research findings more broadly (iBOF/21/031). We are thankful to the Faculty of Law and Criminology at Ghent University, for its open-mindedness regarding the multi-method, pluri-disciplinary – and sometimes unconventional – research that has shaped our work over the past years. The manuscript also benefited from a writing residency at the Paris Institute for Advanced Studies, funded by FIAS through Marie Skłodowska-Curie grant 945408 and an ANR-11-LABX-0027-01 Labex RFIEA+ grant.

We also wish to thank our families, for their support and for facilitating long and frequent periods away from home for fieldwork, conferences, and other exchanges, which have all enriched this handbook – and for the joy of having a warm home to return to after sometimes straining conversations and research experiences.

Most importantly, we acknowledge the many victim-survivors whose experiences are at the heart of this book, along with the stakeholders and victim-protagonists we have worked with since we embarked on this project. More than interlocutors or respondents, many of the individuals and collectives we collaborated with have become a driving force behind our work, inspiring our research agenda, informing our methods, inviting us to reflect critically on ethics and co-creating research outcomes that are relevant to the people and communities involved. We are grateful for the time we have been granted, the spaces we have been invited to, the insights that have been shared with us, and, in several cases, the lasting relations that emerged from this. While this handbook is primarily academic in form, it aims to remain grounded in the lived realities of those who have endured violence and injustice – and who continue to mobilise, participate, and resist in pursuit of justice.

# Abbreviations

| | |
|---|---|
| AFDD | Agrupación de Familiares de Detenidos Desaparecidos (Association of Relatives of the Detained-Disappeared) |
| AFEP | Agrupación de Familiares de Ejecutados Políticos (Association of Relatives of Politically Executed Persons) |
| AHRDO | Afghanistan Human Rights and Democracy Organization |
| AI | Artificial intelligence |
| AIHRC | Afghanistan Independent Human Rights Commission |
| AUC | Autodefensas Unidas de Colombia (United Self-Defense Forces of Colombia) |
| BHR | Business and human rights |
| CAJ | Committee on the Administration of Justice |
| CAJAR | José Alvear Restrepo Lawyers' Collective |
| CAR | Central African Republic |
| CAVR | Comissão de Acolhimento, Verdade e Reconciliação (Commission for Reception, Truth and Reconciliation, East Timor) |
| CELS | Centro de Estudios Legales y Sociales (Center for Legal and Social Studies) |
| CGP | Consultative Group on the Past |
| CIJP | Comisión Intereclesial de Justicia y Paz (Inter-Church Commission for Justice and Peace) |
| CNC | Centro Nacional Chega! (National Chega! Center) |
| CNRR | Comisión Nacional de Reparación y Reconciliación (National Commission for Reparation and Reconciliation) |
| CNVR | National Commission on Truth and Reconciliation (Comisión Nacional de Verdad y Reconciliación) |
| CPN(UML) | Communist Party of Nepal (Unified Marxist-Leninist) |
| CREDDHO | Centre de Recherche sur l'Environnement, la Démocratie et les Droits de l'Homme (Research Centre on the Environment, Democracy and Human Rights) |
| CRSV | Conflict-related sexual violence |
| CSDDD | Corporate sustainability due diligence directive |
| CSO | Civil society organisation |
| CTF | Consultation Task Force on Reconciliation Mechanisms |
| CVC | Conflict Victims' Committee |
| DRC | Democratic Republic of the Congo |

| | |
|---|---|
| ECCC | Extraordinary Chambers in the Courts of Cambodia |
| ED | Enforced disappearance |
| EJI | Equal Justice Initiative |
| EU | European Union |
| FARC | Fuerzas Armadas Revolucionarias de Colombia (Revolutionary Armed Forces of Colombia) |
| FIDH | International Federation for Human Rights |
| FMLN | Frente Farabundo Martí para la Liberación Nacional (Farabundo Martí National Liberation Front) |
| FONAREV | Fonds National des Réparations des Victimes des violences sexuelles liés aux conflits et des victimes des crimes contre la paix et la sécurité de l'humanité (National Fund for Reparations for Victims of Conflict-Related Sexual Violence and Victims of Crimes against Peace and the Security of Humanity) |
| GFA | Good Friday Agreement |
| HRDAG | Human Rights Data Analysis Group |
| HURIDOCS | Human Rights Information and Documentation Systems |
| ICC | International Criminal Court |
| ICD | International Crimes Division |
| ICLVR | Independent Commission for the Location of Victims' Remains |
| ICPPED | International Convention for the Protection of All Persons from Enforced Disappearances |
| ICRIR | Independent Commission for Reconciliation and Information Recovery |
| ICTJ | International Center for Transitional Justice |
| IHD | İnsan Hakları Derneği (Human Rights Organisation) |
| IRA | Irish Republican Army |
| IT | Information technology |
| JEP | Jurisdicción Especial para la Paz (Special Jurisdiction for Peace) |
| JLOS | Justice Law and Order Sector |
| KR | Khmer Rouge |
| LGBTQI+ | Lesbian, gay, bisexual, transgender, queer, intersex, and alternate identities and labels |
| LRA | Lord's Resistance Army |
| LRC | Law Reform Commission |
| LTTE | Liberation Tigers of Tamil Eelam |
| LUCHA | Lutte pour le Changement (Struggle for Change) |
| MONUC | United Nations Organisation Mission of the Congo |
| MONUSCO | United Nations Organisation Stabilisation Mission in the DRC |
| MOVICE | Movimiento Nacional de Víctimas de Crímenes de Estado (National Movement of Victims of State Crimes) |
| NAP | National Action Plan on Business and Human Rights |
| NATO | North Atlantic Treaty Organization |
| NGO | Non-governmental organisation |
| NI | Northern Ireland |
| NPP | National People's Power |
| NSAG | Non-state armed group |
| NTJP | National transitional justice policy |

| | |
|---|---|
| OHCHR | Office of the United Nations High Commissioner for Human Rights |
| OMP | Office on Missing Persons |
| OTP | Office of the Prosecutor |
| PC | Personal computer |
| PIRC | Plan Integral de Reparación Colectiva (Integral Plan of Collective Reparation) |
| PNB | Plan Nacional de Búsqueda (National Search Plan) |
| PNR | Programa Nacional de Resarcimiento (National Reparations Program) |
| PPL | Poderes Populares Locales (Local Popular Powers) |
| PPT | Permanent Peoples' Tribunal |
| QTJ | Quiet Transitional Justice |
| RLP | Refugee Law Project |
| SEFF | South East Fermanagh Foundation |
| SFCG | Search for Common Ground |
| SGBV | Sexual and gender-based violence |
| SHA | Stormont House Agreement |
| SML | Servicio Médico Legal (Forensic Medical Service) |
| TJ | transitional justice |
| TPO | Transcultural Psychological Organisation Cambodia |
| TRC | Truth and Reconciliation Commission |
| UDA | Ulster Defence Association |
| UHRW | Ulster Human Rights Watch |
| UJ | Universal jurisdiction |
| UK | United Kingdom |
| UN | United Nations |
| UNAMA | United Nations Assistance Mission in Afghanistan |
| UNGP | United Nations Guiding Principles on Business and Human Rights |
| UNSG | United Nations Secretary-General |
| US | United States |
| USAID | United States Agency for International Development |
| USD | United States dollar |
| WWII | World War II |
| ZTF | Zonal Task Forces |

# Introduction

## *Tracing Victim Engagement across Different Spaces and Moments in Time*

*Tine Destrooper and Elke Evrard*

Much has been written about victims' myriad roles in transitional justice processes. Many of these writings critique how victims have been involved in formal institutional transitional justice processes, and point to a range of undesirable consequences of how their participation is typically conceptualised. Critical transitional justice studies highlight, for example, the risks of secondary trauma and inadequate psycho-social support, the disconnect between victims' expectations and process outcomes, the dominance of technocratic or formalistic approaches, the instrumentalisation of victim groups, or the hierarchisation of victimisation experiences. The depth and breadth of these critiques frequently extend to challenge the foundational principles of the broader transitional justice project itself. This sense of crisis is exacerbated by the global resurgence of anti-rights politics, the (re-)emergence of regimes with authoritarian tendencies – even in countries that have previously implemented comprehensive transitional justice programmes – and a feeling of crisis surrounding human rights more generally.

In spite of this, victim movements across a range of contexts increasingly harness the principles, language, and mechanisms of transitional justice as a mobilising framework in their various justice struggles, all the while bringing new issues to more formal transitional justice processes. Various dynamics can be observed. First, transitional justice *practices* are increasingly proposed in struggles that have limited affinity with early transitional justice contexts, for example, grassroots actors proposing transitional justice initiatives in contexts of ongoing conflict. Second, transitional justice *language* is finding its way into a wide variety of justice struggles that, at face value, hardly share commonalities with paradigmatic transitional justice cases, from efforts to address abuse within the Catholic Church, to campaigns against extrajudicial killings in the war on drugs, to resistance against oil extractivism. Third, justice actors in paradigmatic cases are increasingly challenging the boundaries between transitional justice and other justice struggles by inserting new *topics* into transitional justice processes, such as the role of corporate actors in human rights violations. This proliferation of transitional justice into a wide range of intersecting justice struggles is genuinely victim-driven. Yet it leaves scholars, practitioners, and policymakers grappling with existential debates concerning the nature and modalities of transitional justice itself, and of victims' roles therein.

This handbook emerges from these debates, but also offers new entry points into them. It provides a systematic investigation of how victims' engagement in transitional justice processes has evolved over time, and of the diverging theoretical viewpoints that have been used to understand and evaluate this engagement. Drawing on this analysis, this introduction develops a future-oriented analytical framework that offers the reader a better historical understanding of victims' evolving roles in (formal and informal) transitional justice processes, as well as providing a comparative outlook on the realities of victim engagement today, acknowledging intersecting justice struggles and the porous boundaries of transitional justice. This framework will be the foundation for a future-oriented re-imagining of victims' protagonism in pursuing justice after large-scale violence.

While both this introduction and several contributions borrow the notion of 'victim' from mainstream transitional justice scholarship, we reject any connotations of passivity or 'idealised victimhood'. Instead, the book builds on the notion of 'victims-as-protagonists', foregrounding victims as drivers of justice struggles, as well as acknowledging the violence they experienced (Méndez 2016; Tuyuc 2024). Importantly, this viewpoint of transitional justice as inherently victim-driven, while seemingly intuitive, should not be taken for granted. Early instances of transitional justice, such as post-World War II tribunals, while responding to the harm suffered by victims, were marked by the conspicuous absence of victims from the actual proceedings.

The centrality and evolution of victims' roles in the consolidation and expansion of the field of transitional justice should thus be understood in the light of several macro-level socio-legal dynamics which are discussed in the next section. These include the emergence of a universalising human rights discourse, which foregrounded the plight of victims of atrocity crimes, and which responded to victims' mobilisation in different localities undergoing political transition. Following this overview, this Introduction reviews the current state of the scholarly debate regarding victim engagement in transitional justice. We then present the handbook's analytical framework, which revolves around the notion of *generations of victim engagement*. Next, we reflect on how the evolution of victim engagement, along with other evolutions in the broader domain of transitional justice, has given rise to a complex ecosystem of intersecting justice struggles covering a wide range of issues; and what this means for how we, as researchers, practitioners, or policymakers, engage with victim-survivors and their justice struggles. Finally, we introduce the logic and structure of the handbook.

## I.1 THE BROADER SOCIO-LEGAL CONTEXT

The developments and debates regarding victim engagement in the domain of transitional justice can be situated against the backdrop of several broader historical and political dynamics. We expand on five interrelated trends: evolutions in the international human rights architecture, the influence of regional human rights systems, the nexus between the formal human rights architecture and the (criminal justice) dimension of transitional justice, developments in the orbit of formal institutions, and broader societal trends.

First, with regards to the formal international human rights architecture, a number of connected trends that have unfolded since the early 2000s have contributed to the growing attention for rights-holders and victims of human rights violations. These include the establishment of the Human Rights Council in 2006 (replacing the Commission on Human Rights) and the consequent introduction of a Universal Periodic Review process, in which civil society and individuals are actively invited to submit information and to participate in the review process, granting them a direct role in the evaluation of a country's human rights performance (O'Brien 2022). Also the expansion of Special Procedures, such as Special Rapporteurs or United Nations (UN) Working Groups, has provided right-holders and victims of human rights violations with avenues to report on human rights abuses and seek redress (Nolan et al. 2017). Additionally, evolutions of the UN Treaty Bodies have furthered the attention for rights-holders and civil society. Here one can think of optional protocols that allow individuals to submit complaints directly to treaty bodies, or the involvement of civil society organisations in the development of their general comments and recommendations (Kissling 2008; Nowak et al. 2019). This has been complemented with the recognition of specific victim groups (such as women and children, persons with disabilities, victims of trafficking and sexual violence), Indigenous Peoples, LGBTQI+ people, and accompanying provisions for their increased participation and consultation (Lundy 2007; Mégret 2017).

Second, evolutions in regional human rights systems have reflected, consolidated and expanded these trends at the international level. The European Court of Human Rights, for example, implemented several elements aimed at accessibility and better handling of individual complaints, and issued landmark rulings advancing victims' rights (van Dijk et al. 2018). The Inter-American Human Rights System has been the most pro-active in terms of increasing its engagement with civil society and victims-survivors, and adopting a victim-oriented approach both in its proceedings and rulings. This is evident in landmark decisions by the Inter-American Court of Human Rights (such as *Barrios Altos v. Peru*) which established ambitious legal standards, including the principle of transformative reparations, also reflected in their comprehensive advisory opinions (Uprimny Yepes 2009). In addition, the work of the Inter-American Commission of Human Rights – in the form of thematic reports, country visits, precautionary measures – considers the perspective of civil society and victims of human rights violations.

Third, growing attention for victims and their active role in justice processes is also rooted in evolutions at the nexus of human rights, criminal justice, and transitional justice itself. The very establishment of bodies such as Truth and Reconciliation Commissions across the globe, have offered victims platforms to share their experiences (Hayner 2011). Similarly, the establishment of international criminal tribunals that incorporate provisions for victim participation, for example in the form of witness testimonies, have contributed to a more active understanding of victims' roles in criminal justice processes (McGonigle 2009). Both trends also reflect an increased recognition of victims' rights in international law (and consequently in national legal systems). This is exemplified by the UN Basic Principles and Guidelines on the Right to a Remedy and Reparation (United Nations General Assembly 2005), outlining fundamental principles for the treatment of victims, such as access to justice, fair treatment, and redress. These principles have progressively been implemented and integrated into international, regional and national legal frameworks, with the Inter-American System also being a norm-leader in expanding victims' rights. These evolutions have been accompanied by a growing acknowledgement of the potential of restorative justice, which has a stronger focus on victims and their communities in criminal justice approaches (McEvoy and Erickson 2006).

Fourth, it is relevant to consider how evolutions beyond the formal human rights and justice architecture have shaped the growing attention for victims' rights and engagement in justice processes. Here it is relevant to highlight the interplay between the previously mentioned evolution and civil society activism. On one hand, these evolutions may be read as a consequence of advocacy on the side of a broad coalition of civil society actors. On the other hand, increased opportunities for access and participation have fed a proliferation of non-governmental organisations (NGOs) and civil society organisations (CSOs) working on victims' rights (Jochnick and Bickford 2016). This has given rise to a dynamic landscape of organisations working in the domain of advocacy, legal representation, psycho-social support, awareness and education about victims' rights, formal representation and consultation at the UN, to name a few. Related to this proliferation of victim (support) organisations, technological evolutions have enabled these actors to mobilise support, coordinate efforts, and raise awareness, sometimes globally, for specific struggles (Gregory 2023; Kingston and Stam 2013; Sorell 2015). These technological evolutions, and the avenues for enhanced collaboration they allow for, have also impacted the development of transnational advocacy networks (Keck and Sikkink 1998). While professionalised NGOs have played a highly visible role in some of this work, the influence of grassroots organisations and social movements in shaping agendas should not be overlooked. Lastly, it is relevant to mention how growing attention for – the participation of – rights holders within the formal human rights system also came to shape approaches in neighbouring domains, as is exemplified in the mainstreaming of a human rights-based approach to development both within and beyond UN bodies (Vandenhole and Gready 2014).

Fifth, these trends emerged in a broader societal context that both shaped and reflected them. From the institutional reforms that have marked the wave of democratisation in the 1990s to extensive media coverage of human rights crisis and the plight of victims, and from growing attention for intersectional harm and inclusive advocacy to programmes envisioning the empowerment of historically marginalised groups, a cultural shift could be argued to have accompanied the aforementioned developments. Of particular importance here are the impact of technology and new media, which have, on the one hand, allowed for the emergence of an entirely new kind of digital activism that relies on social media for mobilising support and advocating human rights. On the other hand, there has been an expansion in the crowdsourcing of information as technology has increasingly allowed for both the collection and dissemination of information of human rights abuses (think, for example, of Forensic Architecture, Bellingcat, or Mnemonics). This has granted a protagonist role to victims in documenting (in real time) human rights violations (Fuller and Weizman 2021).

## I.2 HOW TRANSITIONAL JUSTICE SCHOLARSHIP HAS STUDIED THE ROLES OF VICTIMS

These evolutions constitute the background against which to understand the growing attention for victims' evolving roles within the domain of transitional justice – both in scholarship and in practice. This attention for victims' roles has meant that scholarship focusing on victim engagement in transitional justice has virtually become a sub-field in its own right. To date, however, an overarching analytical model for understanding how victims' diverse roles have evolved over time and across contexts has been missing. Instead, it can be observed that several distinct strands of writing have come to characterise scholarship on the roles of victims in transitional justice, with limited exchanges taking place across these strands. In this section, we survey these strands based on an overview of existing scholarship.

A first strand of writing, which could be described as technical-legal in nature, focuses on examining and evaluating the opportunities for, modalities of, and challenges related to victim participation. It focuses therein on formal, institutionalised transitional justice processes. This strand of writing (implicitly or explicitly) subscribes to the value of both formal transitional justice mechanisms per se, as well as to the importance of victim participation therein (see, for example, Jasini and Phan 2011; Pena and Carayon 2013). Two trends can be identified. On one hand, empirical studies pertaining to this strand have investigated concrete practices and experiences of formal participation, underlining the importance of procedural justice, the dynamics of legal representation, or the barriers that victims face in accessing and participating in transitional justice processes (Byrne 2004; Cody et al. 2015; Stover et al. 2011). On the other hand, normative and legal-doctrinal literature within this strand of writing has focused on theorising and analysing the (expanding) rights and roles of victims in criminal proceedings, truth commissions, and reparation schemes (Doak 2005; Van den Wyngaert 2011). What unifies and characterises these studies is their focus on formal structures and the examination of victims' roles as (individuated) rightsholders therein.

A second, and dominant, strand of writing is rooted in critical transitional justice scholarship and practice. Scholars and practitioners in this paradigm start from a broader critique of formal transitional justice and problematise the so-called 'add victims and stir' approach (Bjorkdahl and Selimovic 2015), whereby victims are simply integrated into existing processes without fundamentally altering these institutions and processes in terms of how they operate or what they should achieve. Within this critical strand too, we can find both empirical studies (de Waardt and Weber 2019; McEvoy and McConnachie 2013) as well as a number of theoretical, methodological, and normative propositions for scholarship and practice (Bundschuh 2015; Ottendörfer 2018; Robins and Wilson 2015). A key characteristic of this strand is its emphasis on a more bottom-up and actor-oriented approach to victim participation in transitional justice. This perspective prioritises victims' needs and agency, explicitly factors in dynamics and relations of power, and considers broader engagement spaces that include grassroots capacity-building, collective mobilisation, and community activism. This body of work also engages with de-colonial and post-colonial critiques of transitional justice (Madlingozi 2010; Mutua 2015; Park 2020), problematising the dominance of Western legal frameworks and networks of experts and expertise, which reflect and reinforce global hierarchies, while marginalising local and indigenous knowledge, practices, and agency. These studies interrogate the meaning-making and epistemologies of transitional justice, rooted in the liberal democratic foundational paradigm, and call for a radical re-politicisation of the field, one that centres survivors and local communities.

A last, more diffuse strand of writing engages with notions such as conscious non-participation, everyday resistance, 'quiet' transitional justice, or studies victim agency in the absence of any formal transitional justice process (Bernath 2018; Clark 2020; Dempster 2020; Thomson 2011). It foregrounds victim agency 'beyond participation', by examining actions or non-actions that typically transcend conventional understandings of the repertoire of victim engagement in transitional justice. This strand gained prominence as the language and practice of transitional justice increasingly started to expand into contexts where no political transition took place or no peace agreements were signed, and where a formal or encompassing transitional justice process is therefore typically not in place. In such settings, transitional justice tends to be mobilised in more ad hoc and experimental ways, often by grassroots justice actors (Destrooper et al. 2023). Like the second strand of writing, this literature tends to challenge dominant or mainstream perspectives on transitional justice, for example by critiquing the preoccupation with highly public, performative, and politicised forms of victim engagement, or by questioning the universal assumptions underpinning victims' justice-seeking behaviours (such as their assumed desire to speak truth or to memorialise violence) (Almeida 2021; Kent 2011; Kidron 2021). This literature is typically rooted in empirical case-bound research, but unlike the first and second strands, it is less unified by a common framework of assumptions or methodologies, drawing attention instead to divergent approaches to pursuing justice and redress.

These various strands of writing highlight significant differences in the study and practice of victim engagement in transitional justice. Yet, owing to their differing orientations and disciplinary roots, they have largely evolved in isolation of, or even in direct opposition to, one another. As a result, despite the depth and breadth of existing scholarship, exchanges across various strands of writing are rare. This means that there is currently no encompassing framework for reading these literatures alongside one another, for tracing the various trends that have shaped the field and what roles victims themselves have played in driving these trends, or for charting where we are heading next. Gaining a clearer understanding of these dynamics is crucial for researchers, victim groups, practitioners, and policymakers who are faced with an increasingly broad and diverse range of justice initiatives that are developed under the banner of transitional justice. Not only is there a proliferation of such initiatives in practice, but many of these initiatives also challenge the existing transitional justice paradigm, underlining the need to rethink and future-proof existing models of engagement. In the next section, we propose an analytical framework, rooted in the day-to-day practices of grassroots justice actors, to facilitate conversations about these topics across the boundaries of different strands of scholarship.

## 1.3 GENERATIONS OF VICTIM ENGAGEMENT AND INTERSECTING JUSTICE STRUGGLES

As the contributions in this handbook set out to demonstrate, each of the aforementioned approaches to conceptualising and studying victim engagement in transitional justice has its merit. What the book also shows, however, is that each of these approaches typically has a different analytical focus, highlighting different spheres of engagement as well as varying forms of agency and intentionality. This explains the scarcity of conversations across these various strands of writing. Scholars exploring the modalities of victim participation in formal transitional justice institutions, for example, may not per se be concerned with individual or collective reasons for non-participation, and those examining grassroots justice mechanisms may have limited affinity with procedural impediments to a more far-reaching type of victim engagements in (semi-) judicial justice processes. Similarly, many critical scholars focus their critique on avenues for victim participation provided by formal institutions, and see those actions victims undertake in the orbit of, or even far away from, the formal transitional justice process as something conceptually different from transitional justice.

This handbook, however, shows that these are all dimensions of the broader justice ecosystems that victims navigate. In doing so, victims themselves often make no categorical distinction between various forums, modalities, or sites of justice, and their justice activism is often characterised by a more trajectorial approach to seeking justice (Evrard et al. 2021). This means that they are often involved across various justice sites and processes, either sequentially or in parallel. This reality underlines the importance of having an analytical framework for victim activism that can capture actions and dynamics developing across these various types of forums. Yet, currently, a framework is missing to understand these different types of actions as part of a multi-faceted struggle for justice. This leads to an unnecessarily fragmented understanding of the justice-seeking efforts and trajectories of victims, who typically navigate multiple spaces, engage in a range of strategies, and operate across diverse timelines. One risk of the absence of a shared analytical framework for assessing the various dimensions of victim engagement is that of conceptual mismatch, which, in turn, hampers the emergence of a comprehensive understanding of victim engagement.

The framework developed in this Introduction and further substantiated throughout the empirical cases in the following chapters therefore proposes a thicker understanding of victim participation. In line with Firchow and Selim's proposal (2022), we will refer to this as 'victim engagement'. This term recognises and accommodates the fluid and interconnected nature of victims' actions across different contexts and modalities. The framework uses the concept of *generations of victim engagement* to distinguish between various types of roles victims have played throughout the lifecycle of transitional justice, tracing the development of victim engagement through three discernible generations: the grassroots activism of victims in the early days of transitional justice, the formalisation of victim participation in institutional processes, and the current phase characterised by diverse and resistance-based forms of engagement. This framework is based on a historical perspective that allows for a more encompassing outlook on what transitional justice is, as well as on how victims' engagement with it has shaped the field.

At the same time, we argue these generational shifts do not follow a linear or successive trajectory in the strict sense. Rather, the concept of 'generations' operates as a heuristic device to trace how, over time, new opportunities, hindrances, and dynamics emerged that impacted victims' roles in transitional justice, as well as the dominant scholarly lenses through which these roles have been analysed and critiqued. But the chapters will also show how, at present, different generational characteristics and forms of engagement often coexist both across and within distinct transitional justice contexts. In any given context, victim groups may be involved across a range of initiatives or spaces that could be interpreted as pertaining to various generations. Indeed, newly emerging modalities or spaces for action often do not render existing ones obsolete, but may be added on to existing action repertoires in ways that result in a dense justice ecosystem, shaped by and contributing to increasingly *intersecting justice struggles*. The dynamics characterising the different generations of victim engagement and their convergence within contemporary, intersecting justice struggles will serve as the central organising framework of this handbook.

A first important contribution of this framework to the literature is that it formally defies the idea that transitional justice started when (inter)national institutions became active in this realm. Instead, it takes as its starting point the activism of victims taking to the streets, for example in Chile and Argentina, to know the fate of their missing loved ones and to demand recognition and accountability. It refers to these victims' mobilisation for justice after large-scale violence as the first generation of victim engagement in transitional justice. This conceptualisation stems from our concern that the currently dominant narrative that equates the beginning of transitional justice with the emergence of formal processes risks perpetuating the invisibility of victims' agency, experimentation, and agenda-setting power, which were foundational to the emergence of what later became known as transitional justice. By acknowledging grassroots justice practices and demands developing in the immediate aftermath of violence, before any formal institutions are in place, as manifestations of transitional justice, we foreground the meaning-making power of grassroots justice actors and their formative importance on early transitional justice. Much of what is referred to as transitional justice today emerged in an ad hoc way, driven by grassroots actors, notably in Latin America, who were seeking truth and justice after military dictatorships (Rowen 2017). Acknowledging their impact on the emergence of the transitional justice paradigm (both historically and to this day), rather than identifying transitional justice's institutionalisation or 'boom' in the late 1990s as the start of transitional justice, is more intellectually honest and acknowledges the agentic role of victims.

Tracing how this activism evolved shows that several demands resulted in the development of what today is typically referred to as the standardised transitional justice 'toolkit' (Gissel 2022). Others were taken forward in other informal or grassroots spaces and processes. While there is a thriving literature critiquing the so-called formalisation and standardisation of transitional justice (Sharp 2019; Turner 2017), the importance of some degree of institutionalisation can hardly be overestimated: the official truth commissions, criminal proceedings, reparations programmes, and institutional reforms that were installed in countries across the globe carried with them a promise of democratisation, non-recurrence, and sustainable peace, but also entailed a formal acknowledgement of the harm that had happened. These mechanisms created highly visible platforms for victims to share their stories, seek (state) accountability, and commemorate loved ones, embedding victims' rights and experiences within state-led transitional justice processes. At the same time, this institutionalisation and formalisation initially side-lined and invisibilised some of the victims' own initiatives, demands, and realities. Even when avenues for victim participation were developed in these formal mechanisms, this participation often failed to meet the expectations of various actors involved, and raised concerns regarding the instrumentalisation or marginalisation of victims' multi-faceted experiences and stories. The handbook refers to this opening of participation avenues in formal transitional justice mechanisms as the second generation of victim engagement in transitional justice. The opportunities and shortcomings of this specific generation has been the focus of much of the scholarship mentioned in the previous section, notably the legal-technical and the critical strands.

Most recently, a third generation of victim engagement has been shaping up. It emerged partly in response to a new set of societal challenges (not limited to political transitions) and partly in response to (the shortcomings of) the second generation of victim engagement. Across the globe, victims of a wide range of injustices are invoking, innovating, and experimenting with the transitional justice paradigm in response to state-led violence, the (re-)emergence of authoritarianism, colonial and slavery legacies, extractivism or environmental harm, racial discrimination, and other forms of historical and contemporary rights violations. Their actions echo the protagonism and agenda-setting power of the first generation of victim engagement, similarly shaped by experimentation and adaptation to context. Yet they differ in that, within this third generation, the element of resistance is central (Jones and Bernath 2017) – not just in terms of using transitional justice to resist violence or a harmful status quo, but also in terms of resisting the injustice inherent in a narrow and exclusionary understanding of what victim engagement in transitional justice is. This resistance encompasses a spectrum of agency and subjectivities and necessitates a fundamental re-imagining of how we understand victim engagement in transitional justice, pushing the boundaries of which actors, practices, and struggles are considered worthy of attention. At the same time, as the chapters (10–14) discussing this third generation of victim engagement show, not all resistance is highly vocal or visible, nor is it necessarily progressive.

The chapters in this book will not only elaborate on the characteristics and modalities of each of these generations, thereby further substantiating this analytical framework. They will also point to the potential coexistence of various generations within one context, and, in doing so, illustrate how the different generations of participation may have emerged at various points in time, but should not be understood as linearly successive. There are, for example, no indications that victims' active engagement in informal processes lessened when avenues for formal participation became available. Neither has formal institutions' attention for victim participation seemingly waned because of the current boom in transitional justice initiatives on the side of civil society organisations. We thus use the notion of generations to mark the emergence of certain types of activism at a certain point in time in a given context, rather than to imply that we have decisively moved on from the one generation to the next. As the chapters will show, while initiatives pertaining to various generations may emerge at different points in time, they typically coexist at present. This generational framework has the potential to foster a deeper insight into why and when certain kinds of engagement emerge and how they evolve. It also allows for a closer examination of the dynamics and intersections between the various types of victim engagement that emerged over time. Such a model, moreover, helps to understand why, in spite of the prominence of critical transitional justice scholarship, the practice of transitional justice is expanding, including to aparadigmatic contexts and often at the initiative of victims themselves (Destrooper et al. 2023).

Both the identification of a third generation of victim engagement that revolves around resistance, as well as the acknowledgement of the coexistence of various kinds of activism pertaining to different generations, moreover, brings to the fore the intersection of various justice struggles in which victims are typically involved and the existence of a dynamic justice ecosystem. For the purpose of this handbook, then, the notion of an ecosystem does not only encompass the manifold justice avenues that victims of gross human rights violations and atrocities crimes pursue to address violent legacies. It also reflects the reality on the ground in which these struggles are increasingly intertwined with other kinds of justice efforts. This means that, on the one hand, the practice and rhetoric of transitional justice are increasingly mobilised in a range of struggles that do not explicitly focus on the direct legacies of authoritarianism or conflict. On the other hand, it also means that an increasingly wide range of injustices are brought into more paradigmatic transitional justice processes (see, for example, Paricio Montesinos, Chapter 17, and Ibrahim et al., Chapter 15). The migration of transitional justice to aparadigmatic contexts and the expansion of its scope in established ones necessitate an acknowledgement of the increasingly porous borders between transitional justice and other justice movements as well as victim-protagonists' critical role in installing and shaping this diverse range of intersecting justice processes. The case studies in the second part of this book demonstrate how these intersecting struggles mark contemporary transitional justice practice, and point to several interrelated dynamics rooted in, and emerging from, these intersecting justice struggles that are likely to characterise the future of transitional justice practice and scholarship.

In the first place, the (explicit or implicit) prominence of resistance in these struggles reconnects transitional justice to its radical roots, where victims' demands were from the outset a call for disruption. While critical scholarship has documented how institutional approaches sanitised these demands, they persist and are regaining prominence (see, for example, Moffett, Chapter 10, and Robins and Bhandari, Chapter 12) – not only to challenge acute violence, but also to resist modes of participation that obscure lived realities, institutional inaction, structural violence, or emerging threats such as anti-rights discourse and democratic backsliding. Moreover, the increasingly intersecting nature of diverse justice struggles highlights how transitional justice is being mobilised alongside, and as a complement to, other justice frameworks, including social justice, human rights, and decolonisation efforts. The chapters show how each of these justice frameworks has its own action repertoire, and how this means that also action repertoires are increasingly mixing under the banner of transitional justice.

This results in a much more complex portrait of what engagement in (transitional) justice struggles looks like, but also of how the complexity of this ecosystem requires us to adopt a more fine-grained approach to thinking about the enabling and constraining effects that various types of actions in the formal and informal realm may have upon one another. Both the complexity and the nature of these intersecting justice struggles make it blatantly clear that current ways of engaging (whether as researchers, practitioners, or policymakers) need to be revisited. Studying victim engagement requires epistemological and methodological pluralism, grounded in a strong ethical commitment to how we research and accompany victim protagonism – including (self-)reflexivity around power dynamics, representation, and positionality. Contributors to this handbook, both implicitly and explicitly, offer handles to guide this reflexivity in research and practice. They emphasise the need to understand and recognise complex intersectional identities, respect diverse justice needs and perspectives, and centre approaches that view victims as agenda-setters and knowledge-holders. Several chapters outline deeply participatory and co-creative methodologies, or offer frameworks for engagement rooted in relationality, trust, mutual recognition, and an ethics of care. Across all contributions, there is a shared commitment to prioritising the safety, dignity, and agency of victim-survivors as central to both transitional justice processes and research.

## I.4 OUTLINE OF THE BOOK

The handbook is divided into two parts, each consisting of empirical case studies from across the globe. The chapters in Part I examine and unpack the dynamics of the different generations of transitional justice. They illustrate how these generations emerged at various points in time and how this shaped their modalities, logic, and aspirations, but also the effect on the afterlives of these 'generations' and how modalities of each generation eventually mix in practice. In doing so, these chapters substantiate the analytical framework proposed in this introduction. The chapters in Part II focus on the current state of practice, highlighting how the coexistence of different modes of victim engagement in intersecting justice struggles challenge the boundaries of transitional justice and push new topics to the centre of the debate. This exploration extends to questions about the implications for how, as researchers and practitioners, we engage in ways that acknowledge victims' protagonism and agenda-setting agency.

Within the first part of the book, three sections cover the dynamics of the three generations. Focusing on the first generation of victim engagement, Mauricio Carrasco and Cath Collins trace victims' self-advocacy and the active (co)-creation of initiatives on disappearance in Chile. They show how, over time, different forms of engagement have appeared but also how justice breakthroughs from 1998 were victim-driven, not state-designed. They highlight the protagonism of victims in bringing about state-led initiatives, rather than focusing only on what happens when victims then 'participate' in these formal mechanisms. In the next chapter, Cheryl Lawther zooms in on Northern Ireland to examine how victim groups can act as moral communities and exercise agency by using their own experiences to leverage change either by demanding a response from government or by installing a range of bottom-up initiatives. Thorsten Bonacker also considers the Northern Irish context, comparing it with Guatemala and Timor Leste to examine how the nature of prior conflicts, including their causes and resolutions, affect both institutional strategies of and decisions on reparations for certain victim groups. In the last chapter illustrating dynamics of the first generation of victim engagement, Güneş Daşlı explores political agency in the context of the Saturday Mothers, the organised relatives of the disappeared in Turkey. She uses the prism of relationality to examine how collective mobilisation can be used to create spaces for imagining different forms of justice and to experiment with action repertoires, even when there is not yet a transitional justice process in place. Jointly these four chapters paint a picture of victim engagement across a range of cases where formal transitional justice was or is not (yet) in place, and where victims are the protagonists in pushing for some form of process to be installed and for justice demands to stay on the social and political agenda.

A second set of chapters focuses on the second generation of engagement in transitional justice. Mina Rauschenbach and Briony Jones draw on their work with families of the forcibly disappeared in Colombia and El Salvador to examine how families navigate their engagement as justice stakeholders within judicial and state-based mechanisms and what types of institutional responses are needed to ensure effective and victim-oriented search processes. Moving beyond this focus on procedural justice, the chapter by Thomes Obel Hansen presents a more sweeping critique of how in Uganda's Transitional Justice Policy, formal 'compliance' with ideas about civil society and victim participation, as endorsed by international standards and guidelines about transitional justice, did not result in an outcome that met the expectations and demands of most local civil society and victim groups. Taking a more solution-oriented approach, Miracle Chinwenmeri Uche explores how the International Criminal Court's Office of the Prosecutor's first Policy on Complementarity and Cooperation, published in Spring 2024, may deliver on the promise of partnership and bringing justice closer to victims. She notably considers whether this new policy may spark victims' interests in other – formal or informal – avenues for redress. In her chapter on Cambodia, Fangyi Li starts from victims' initial justice mobilisation and explores ways of overcoming the risk of big formal initiatives, such as the Extraordinary Chambers in the Courts of Cambodia, pushing alternative justice strategies off the radar. Also, Brianne McGonigle Leyh's work on the US, an aparadigmatic case of transitional justice, addresses the inclusion of various justice repertoires and actors in formal initiatives in the domain of truth, in order to have deeper engagement with and impact among affected communities. Together these five chapters offer a better understanding of key dynamics regarding victims' participation in formal transitional justice mechanisms, as well as proposing ways forward.

The last set of chapters in Part I look at the third generation of engagement, exploring various types of resistance and re-imagining. The chapter by Luke Moffett explores the place of victims resisting the narratives of the State, coercive tactics, and violence against them, in their claims for reparations. It also reflects on the impact of this resistance on victims whose activism can take years, decades, even generations. Through a more micro-level analysis of memoir, the chapter of Lauren Dempster and Kevin Hearty then explores how, in the absence of (access to) formal transitional justice mechanisms, resistance may also lead victims towards other spaces and formats where they can engage in truth practices and narrate their experiences of violence on their own terms. Referring to this as 'quiet' transitional justice, the authors expand the transitional justice imagination far beyond formal mechanisms. Simon Robins and Ram Kumar Bhandari draw on their research with families of the missing in Nepal to demonstrate how both families of the missing's initial mobilisation and their representation in national transitional justice processes intersect with broader forms of resistance both against exclusionary dynamics of these formal processes and against discriminatory trends more broadly. Through a focus on more collective initiatives, Daniela Suárez Vargas examines the ways in which social movements in Colombia wield the political dimension of victimhood as a tool to resist further victimisation, notably in the struggles regarding conflict-related sexual and gender-based violence. In her chapter on the Consultation Task Force on Reconciliation Mechanisms in Sri Lanka, Chulani Kodikara uses the concept of 'archives of desire' to examine whether victims' demand for more formalisation and internationalisation should be taken at face value as a belief in that standardised transitional justice toolkit or instead points towards an underlying dissatisfaction with and resistance against the non-action of national-level institutions. Read alongside one another, these chapters illustrate how various types of resistance have given rise to multiple and innovative initiatives that defy the original moorings of the transitional justice paradigm.

Part II of the handbook explores how this has affected the practice of transitional justice today. A first set of chapters traces several intersecting justice struggles, highlighting both instances where transitional justice is invoked in aparadigmatic justice struggles, as well as instances where new issues and debates are foregrounded in more paradigmatic struggles. The first of these chapters, by Mina Ibrahim, Maria Hartmann, and Susanne Buckley-Zistel, examines how the mobilisation of the transitional justice paradigm by Syrian diaspora constitutes both an aparadigmatic case, but *in concreto* also leads to the interweaving of various struggles, as Syrian diaspora justice actors connect their justice efforts with injustices of living in Germany today – including their status as migrants/refugees. Also Kim Baudewijns' work on the DRC, explores this dual dynamic: on the one hand she describes a non-transitional context in which the transitional justice discourse is mobilised, on the other hand she underlines how a range of justice actors tap into transitional justice language not only with regards to political violence, but also to frame struggles on, for example, youth and democratic participation or environmental harm. In a chapter on Colombia, Marta Paricio Montesinos discusses Colombians' struggle to hold corporations accountable, and argues that victims play a crucial role in pushing for a more encompassing understanding of transitional justice by complementing the initial struggle with new dimensions as they press for the accountability of private economic actors. Taken together, these chapters illustrate how porous the borders of transitional justice have become.

The next set of chapters starts to address some questions regarding how to understand, analyse and 'do' transitional justice in these dynamic and rapidly changing contexts. First, Pamina Firchow and Lisa Laplante set out to develop a theoretical framework that can guide the development and evaluation of participatory reparations programmes. The chapter builds on notions of relational justice to provide both an instrumental and legal justification for inclusive processes in the design, implementation, and evaluation of reparations programmes. The next three chapters foreground innovative methodological proposals regarding how to intervene, both as practitioners and as researchers in this complex and multi-layered context. Huma Saeed's chapter about Afghanistan foregrounds intervention methods rooted in the 'theatre of the oppressed' as a means to understand and appraise multi-faceted justice struggles in the absence of formal transitional justice mechanisms. The chapter by Adriana Alas, Amanda Grzyb, and María Helia Rivera Castillo introduces the profoundly co-creative Surviving Memory project in El Salvador and its contribution to the creation of spaces to promote intergenerational and cross-sector dialogue, and post-war recovery. In the last chapter, Michael Reed-Hurtado examines how, despite many challenges, grassroots actors in Latin America have been experimenting with new technologies, leading to new forms of engagement and novel claims. This set of chapters is only a starting point, but an important one, to re-think how to engage in this increasingly complex justice landscape where transitional justice is one node in a vast and porous justice ecosystem.

While this handbook does not endeavour to offer encompassing answers to definitional questions about what transitional justice today is, what its boundaries are, or what the ideal role of victims is or should be, these chapters offer a framework for understanding how victims have shaped the evolution of the field and continue to shape it, and how adopting an actor-oriented approach can guide our efforts at future-proofing transitional justice scholarship and practice.

## REFERENCES

Almeida, B. 2021. 'The Law and Its Limits: Land Grievances, Wicked Problems, and Transitional Justice in Timor-Leste'. *International Journal of Transitional Justice*, 15(1), 128–147. https://doi.org/10.1093/ijtj/ijaa030

Bernath, J. 2018. 'Political Violence as a Time That Is Past? Engaging with Non-Participation in Transitional Justice in Cambodia'. *Social & Legal Studies*, 28(5), 600–624.

Bjorkdahl, A., and Selimovic, J. M. 2015. 'Translating UNSCR 1325 from the Global to the National: Protection, Representation and Participation in the National Action Plans of Bosnia-Herzegovina and Rwanda'. *Conflict, Security & Development*, 15(4), 311–335.

Bundschuh, T. 2015. 'Enabling Transitional Justice, Restoring Capabilities: The Imperative of Participation and Normative Integrity'. *International Journal of Transitional Justice*, 9(1), 10–32. https://doi.org/10.1093/ijtj/iju030

Byrne, C. C. 2004. 'Benefit or Burden: Victims' Reflections on TRC Participation'. *Peace and Conflict: Journal of Peace Psychology*, 10(3), 237–256. https://doi.org/10.1207/s15327949pac1003_2

Clark, J. N. 2020. 'Finding a Voice: Silence and Its Significance for Transitional Justice'. *Social & Legal Studies*, 29(3), 355–378. https://doi.org/10.1177/0964663919856685

Cody, S., Stover, E., Balthazard, M., and Koenig, A. 2015. *The Victims' Court? A Study of 622 Victim Participants at the International Criminal Court*. UC Berkeley School of Law. https://doi.org/http://dx.doi.org/10.2139/ssrn.2982534

de Waardt, M., and Weber, S. 2019. 'Beyond Victims' Mere Presence: An Empirical Analysis of Victim Participation in Transitional Justice in Colombia'. *Journal of Human Rights Practice*, 11(1), 209–228. https://doi.org/10.1093/jhuman/huz002

Dempster, L. 2020. '"Quiet" Transitional Justice: "Publicness", Trust and Legitimacy in the Search for the "Disappeared"'. *Social & Legal Studies*, 29(2), 246–272. https://doi.org/10.1177/0964663919833027

Destrooper, T., Gissel, L. E., and Carlson, K. B. 2023. *Transitional Justice in Aparadigmatic Contexts. Accountability, Recognition, and Disruption*. Routledge.

Doak, J. 2005. 'Victims' Rights in Criminal Trials: Prospects for Participation'. *Journal of Law and Society*, 32(1), 294–316.

Evrard, E., Mejía Bonifazi, G., and Destrooper, T. 2021. 'The Meaning of Participation in Transitional Justice: A Conceptual Proposal for Empirical Analysis'. *International Journal of Transitional Justice*, 15(2), 428–447. https://doi.org/10.1093/ijtj/ijab013

Firchow, P., and Selim, Y. 2022. 'Meaningful Engagement from the Bottom-Up? Taking Stock of Participation in Transitional Justice Processes'. *International Journal of Transitional Justice*, 16(2), 187–203. https://doi.org/10.1093/ijtj/ijab031

Fuller, M., and Weizman, E. 2021. *Investigative Aesthetics: Conflicts and Commons in the Politics of Truth*. Verso. https://tinyurl.com/45je4c89

Gissel, L. E. 2022. 'The Standardisation of Transitional Justice'. *European Journal of International Relations*, 28(4), 859–884. https://doi.org/10.1177/13540661221120980

Gregory, S. 2023. 'Fortify the Truth: How to Defend Human Rights in an Age of Deepfakes and Generative AI'. *Journal of Human Rights Practice*, 15(3), 702–714. https://doi.org/10.1093/jhuman/huad035

Hayner, P. 2011. *Unspeakable Truths. Transitional Justice and the Challenge of Truth Commissions (second)*. Routledge.

Jasini, R., and Phan, V. 2011. 'Victim Participation at the Extraordinary Chambers in the Courts of Cambodia: Are Retributive and Restorative Principles Enhancing the Prospect for Justice?' *Cambridge Review of International Affairs*, 24(3), 379–401.

Jochnick, C., and Bickford, L. 2016. 'The Role of Civil Society in Business and Human Rights'. In *Business and Human Rights: From Principles to Practice*, edited by Dorothée Baumann-Pauly and Justine Nolan, pp. 181–193. Routledge.

Jones, B., and Bernath, J. (eds.). 2017. *Resistance and Transitional Justice*. Routledge.

Keck, M., and Sikkink, K. 1998. *Activists beyond Borders: Advocacy Networks in International Politics*. Cornell University Press.

Kent, L. 2011. 'Local Memory Practices in East Timor: Disrupting Transitional Justice Narratives'. *International Journal of Transitional Justice*, 5(3), 434–455. https://doi.org/10.1093/ijtj/ijr016

Kidron, C. A. 2021. '"Rebirthing" the Violent Past: Friction between Post-Conflict Axioms of Remembrance and Cambodian Buddhist Forgetting'. *Anthropological Forum*, 31(3), 291–311. https://doi.org/10.1080/00664677.2021.1971512

Kingston, L. N., and Stam, K. R. 2013. 'Online Advocacy: Analysis of Human Rights NGO Websites'. *Journal of Human Rights Practice*, 5(1), 75–95. https://doi.org/10.1093/jhuman/hus036

Kissling, C. 2008. 'The Evolution of CSOs' Legal Status in International Governance and Its Relevance for the Legitimacy of International Organizations'. In *Civil Society Participation in European and Global Governance: A Cure for the Democratic Deficit?*, edited by Jens Steffek, Claudia Kissling, and Patrizia Nanz, pp. 30–52. Springer.

Lundy, L. 2007. '"Voice" Is Not Enough: Conceptualising Article 12 of the United Nations Convention on the Rights of the Child'. *British Educational Research Journal*, 33(6), 927–942.

Madlingozi, T. 2010. 'On Transitional Justice Entrepreneurs and the Production of Victims'. *Journal of Human Rights Practice*, 2(2), 208–228.

McEvoy, K., and Erickson, A. 2006. 'Restorative Justice in Transition. Ownership, Leadership and "Bottom-up" Human Rights'. In *Handbook of Restorative Justice: A Global Perspective*, edited by D. Sullivan and L. Tifft, pp. 321–336. Routledge.

McEvoy, K., and McConnachie, K. 2013. 'Victims and Transitional Justice. Voice, Agency and Blame'. *Social and Legal Studies*, 22(4), 489–513.

McGonigle, B. 2009. 'Two for the Price of One: Victim Participation and the ECCC, a Criminal Court and Reconciliation Commission in One'. *Leiden Journal of International Law*, 22(2009), 127–149.

Mégret, F. 2017. 'The Disabilities Convention: Human Rights of Persons with Disabilities or Disability Rights?' In *Equality and Non-Discrimination under International Law*, edited by Stephanie Farrior, pp. 269–292. Routledge.

Méndez, J. E. 2016. 'Victims as Protagonists in Transitional Justice'. *International Journal of Transitional Justice*, 10(1), 1–5. https://doi.org/10.1093/ijtj/ijv037

Mutua, M. 2015. 'What Is the Future of Transitional Justice?' *International Journal of Transitional Justice*, 9(1), 1–9.

Nolan, A., Freedman, R., and Murphy, T. 2017. *The United Nations Special Procedures System* (Vol. 6). Brill.

Nowak, M., Birk, M., and Monina, G. 2019. *The United Nations Convention against Torture and Its Optional Protocol: A Commentary*. Oxford University Press.

O'Brien, L. 2022. 'Peer Reviewing the World: Increasing Civil Society Participation in the United Nations Universal Periodic Review'. *Political Science Honors Projects*, 93, 1–107. https://digitalcommons.macalester.edu/poli_honors/93

Ottendörfer, E. 2018. 'Translating Victims' "Right to Reparations" into Practice: A Framework for Assessing the Implementation of Reparations Programs from a Bottom-Up Perspective'. *Human Rights Quarterly*, 40(4), 905–931.

Park, A. S. J. 2020. 'Settler Colonialism, Decolonization and Radicalizing Transitional Justice'. *International Journal of Transitional Justice*, 14(2), 260–279. https://doi.org/10.1093/ijtj/ijaa006

Pena, M., and Carayon, G. 2013. 'Is the ICC Making the Most of Victim Participation?' *International Journal of Transitional Justice*, 7(3), 518–535. https://doi.org/10.1093/ijtj/ijt021

Robins, S., and Wilson, E. 2015. 'Participatory Methodologies with Victims: An Emancipatory Approach to Transitional Justice Research'. *Canadian Journal of Law and Society*, 30(2), 219–236.

Rowen, J. 2017. *Searching for Truth in the Transitional Justice Movement*. Cambridge University Press.

Sharp, D. 2019. 'What Would Satisfy Us? Taking Stock of Critical Approaches to Transitional Justice'. *International Journal of Transitional Justice*, 13(2), 570–589.

Sorell, T. 2015. 'Human Rights and Hacktivism: The Cases of Wikileaks and Anonymous'. *Journal of Human Rights Practice*, 7(3), 391–410. https://doi.org/10.1093/jhuman/huv012

Stover, E., Balthazard, M., and Koenig, A. 2011. 'Confronting Duch: Civil Party Participation in Case 001 at the Extraordinary Chambers in the Courts of Cambodia'. *International Review of the Red Cross*, 93(882), 503–546.

Thomson, S. 2011. 'Whispering Truth to Power: The Everyday Resistance of Rwandan Peasants to Post-Genocide Reconciliation'. *African Affairs*, 110(440), 439–456. https://doi.org/10.1093/afraf/adr021

Turner, C. 2017. 'Transitional Justice and Critique'. In *Research Handbook on Transitional Justice*, edited by C. Lawther, L. Moffett, and D. Jacobs, pp. 52–73. Edward Elgar.

Tuyuc, R. 2024. Opening Remarks: When Victims Fight for Justice: A Conversation between Arts, Activism, Academia and Institutions. In *Victims and Transitional Justice: Participation, Mobilization, Resistance*. Justice Visions. www.youtube.com/watch?v=PgXS9zlAbBE

United Nations General Assembly. 2005. Basic Principles and Guidelines on the Right to a Remedy and Reparation for Victims of Gross Violations of International Human Rights Law and Serious Violations of International Humanitarian Law. UN Doc. A/RES/60/147.

Uprimny Yepes, R. 2009. 'Transformative Reparations of Massive Gross Human Rights Violations: Between Corrective and Distributive Justice'. *Netherlands Quarterly of Human Rights*, 27(4), 625–647.

Van den Wyngaert, C. 2011. 'Victims before International Criminal Courts: Some Views and Concerns of an ICC Trial Judge'. *Case Western Reserve Journal of International Law*, 44(1), 475–496.

Vandenhole, W., and Gready, P. 2014. 'Failures and Successes of Human Rights-Based Approaches to Development: Towards a Change Perspective'. *Nordic Journal of Human Rights*, 32(4), 291–311.

van Dijk, P., van Hoof, G. J. H., van Rijn, A. B., and Zwaak, L. 2018. *Theory and Practice of the European Convention on Human Rights*. Fifth edition. Intersentia.

# PART I

# Generations of Victim Engagement

# First Generation

# 1

# Seeking the Missing

## *Relatives' and Activists' Protagonism in the Search for Chile's Disappeared*

*Mauricio Carrasco and Cath Collins*

## 1.1 INTRODUCTION

### 1.1.1 *Modes of Search and Generations of Activism in Chile*

Chile is closely associated with the phenomenon of enforced disappearance, a manifestation of the practice of state terrorism in 1970s and 1980s Latin America. Chile's experience also illustrates the sequencing, coexistence, and intermingling of the three 'generations' of activism in transitional justice politics that this book posits. This chapter traces this lineage, offering Chile's search for the disappeared as an example of victims creating not just outcomes but the very terms and vocabulary of what were later deemed 'transitional justice' concerns.[1] Prompted by a recent step-change in Chile's official efforts to grapple with the legacy of dictatorship-era disappearance,[2] the chapter nevertheless locates the motor of such change outside, and 'below', Chile's state institutions. Chile's relatives' associations have spent five decades crafting, fighting for, and sometimes fighting over, multiple agendas and demands. Their persistence finally prompted the creation, in 2023, of a state initiative to investigate the fate and whereabouts of over 1,000 people who remain disappeared.[3]

Each of the three types of victim engagement in transitional justice addressed in this volume – activism, participation, and resistance – helped drive at least one of four modes of search for the disappeared undertaken in Chile since 1973. These we term, respectively, 'denunciatory',[4] 'administrative', 'judicial', and 'hybrid'. The first arose soon after the 1973 coup, when survivors, relatives, and an incipient human rights movement first detected,[5] then denounced, the practice of disappearance. Early activists had first to set the very terms of the debate, crafting the archetype of the 'detained-disappeared person', the *detenido-desaparecido*.[6]

1 Namely truth, justice, reparations, and guarantees of non-repetition.

2 The National Search Plan (Plan Nacional de Búsqueda (PNB)) officially announced in September 2023.

3 See PNB website for current figures: www.plannacionaldebusqueda.cl/.

4 Elsewhere we describe this mode as 'resistant': here we instead use 'denunciatory', to avoid confusion with the book's usage of 'resistance' to denote third-generation victim activism.

5 Although other actors, including survivors, always featured (Bastias Saavedra, 2013: 180–192), immediate family members of direct victims of disappearance have long been the highest profile group of concerned actors. As in other South American countries, activism against disappearance remains predominantly (self-) organised along these lines.

6 On the emergence of the category, see Bernasconi and Ruiz (2018) or Lira (2015); on its longevity, see Ruiz and Bernasconi (2019). The international-legal category 'enforced disappearance' itself emerged partly owing to Chile's experience: the Ad Hoc Working Group on Chile, established in 1975, was among the first such bodies to be set up by the United Nations (UN) and had a strong focus on disappearance.

This mode of search persists today. Its capacious repertoire includes resort to the street, the courtroom, political spaces, and international fora in pursuit of answers to the deceptively simple question '*¿Dónde están?*' (Where are they?). It also continues to incorporate, though not quite as inflexibly as in neighbouring Argentina, a strong moral stricture against pre-emptively accepting that the disappeared are dead. Expressed in the demand '*vivos se los llevaron, vivos los queremos*',[7] this maxim has over time lost some of its literal quality, finding new manifestations including an insistence on speaking of searching for people, rather than 'remains'.[8]

What this book calls the 'first generation' of 'victim' engagement in transitional justice is, then, the most persistent feature of the struggle against disappearance in Chile. Nonetheless, we contend that for Chile this first generation has always had the 'resistant' quality that the book's premise attributes predominantly to later phases. In Chile, denunciatory search has a prehistory beginning long before political transition and an ongoing reach beyond it. Relatives set the public and international agenda in unimaginably adverse circumstances, first by exposing disappearance, then by demanding truth, justice, and the return of their loved ones. The same people, and/or those who have taken up their mantle, remain at the forefront of new iterations of search-directed action. While novel actors have entered the stage – most notably, sympathetic allies within the state – in this particular arena of transitional justice contention there is still a pervasive tendency to afford special deference to relatives, making it difficult at times for the state to openly take positions that, while appropriately victim-informed, may not be wholly victim-driven.

Importantly, then, while new institutional and civil society responses to disappearance have emerged, the foundational and/or catalytic role of first-generation activism remains central. As one corollary, the language and demands formulated in the early years remain extremely present in today's search and/or other transitional justice debates. Far from representing a historical artefact or phase that has been superseded, denunciatory activism is embedded in present-day search dynamics, influencing victim-led initiatives and state responses alike.

### 1.1.2 *Plan of the Chapter*

What follows provides, first, a brief characterisation of the four modes of search mentioned earlier, each discussed with reference to the generations of victim engagement that this volume adopts as a common frame.[9] The chapter then discusses each mode further, paying particular attention to the first and final modes since this allows us to first establish the self-generated, non-state, and anti-state character of initial search before exploring participation in Chile's most recent, hybrid, mode. As will be seen, early denunciatory search in Chile called forth and has operated alongside other, later, forms, bearing out the book's contention that generations of engagement should be thought of as accretion rather than substitution. At the same time, however, Chile's trajectory (partly) defies the suggestion made in the book's Introduction that

7 Loosely, 'they were taken alive, we want them back alive'.

8 This insistence was ever-present during public colloquia held in 2022 to assist with PNB design. Resistance to forensic epistemologies surrounding search is often traceable precisely to the affective tensions involved in maintaining this insistence over a long period. Rosenblatt (2015) offers examples from Argentina and elsewhere; Garibain (2013) suggests this presumption of life can eventually be experienced as a burden, forcing relatives to 'search for the dead among the living' (29, '*busca[r] a los muertos entre los vivos*', authors' translation).

9 Using the term 'victim' in this context is inescapably contentious. Although our preference is for 'survivor', 'relative', and/or 'activist', here we occasionally use 'victim' to harmonise usage across the volume. The use of 'victim' to refer to relatives and all others significantly harmed by a disappearance is, moreover, consonant with current UN practice.

resistant modes emerge as a 'participatory turn', a critical reaction to experiences of institutionally initiated victim engagement. Rather, search, like the rest of Chile's transitional justice policy agenda, originated in first-principles truth and justice demands formulated then kept alive by victims, relatives, survivors, and their supporters. The design of the current hybrid search effort meanwhile offers evidence that the state can serve to mediate victim engagement, rather than dictating or inducing it.

## 1.2 GENERATIONS OF VICTIM ENGAGEMENT AND MODES OF SEARCH SINCE 1973: AN OVERVIEW

The dictatorship-era phenomenon of denunciatory search in Chile took the form of ever bolder efforts to create a national crisis of conscience about the scandalous practice of disappearance. This mode's early emphasis on legal activism was never abandoned despite later diversification (Bastias Saavedra 2013). A second mode of search, referred to here as 'administrative', emerged after the return to elected government in the 1990s, when post-transitional authorities appeared disappointingly indifferent to the fate of the disappeared. Although a truth commission (the Rettig Commission) collated basic facts, action to trace those still missing was confined to a small, non-specialist follow-up body mainly concerned with administering reparations.[10] Disappointed relatives' associations abandoned political lobbying and returned to denunciatory activism, eventually spurring Chile's third, judicial, mode of search as relatives presented or revived criminal complaints against known perpetrators. In 1998, a judge for the first time admitted one such complaint to the investigation stage. The case included the *detenidos-desaparecidos*, a fact which proved crucial, becoming the grounds for disallowing domestic amnesty (Bustos and Collins 2025). The resultant case universe, analysed in depth elsewhere (inter alia, Observatorio Justicia Transicional 2023, 2024a, 2024b), is still ongoing. In these ways denunciatory, administrative, and judicial modes of search have been layered on top of one another in Chile in summative rather than mutually displacing increments. Victims, relatives, survivors, and activists have driven change and galvanised alternative modes of state response.

Chile's state institutions belatedly opened a new chapter in the hitherto uneventful story of official responsiveness in 2023, creating the non-judicial or non-jurisdictional National Search Plan ostensibly to add complementary expertise, focus, and administrative heft to ongoing judicial activity.[11] The initiative became the 'flagship' human rights policy of a would-be iconoclastic president,[12] but, like its predecessors, it owed much to years of overt and behind-the-scenes pressure from relatives and activists, echoed and amplified by organs of the international and regional human rights systems.[13] Created in sometimes difficult dialogue with relatives' groups, it can also be read, as we will see, as both the logical culmination of the

[10] Though see Lira and Rojas (2022) on remains recovered. By 1996, 1,200 named people were officially classed as detained-disappeared during the dictatorship, with a further 2,000 acknowledged victims of politically motivated execution. Amnesty, however, impeded judicial investigation. See any one of numerous comprehensive treatments of Chile's immediate transitional period (e.g., Rojas and Shaftoe 2022).

[11] That is, activity taking the form of criminal investigation primarily aimed at identifying and sanctioning perpetrators. This mode continues to be active.

[12] Gabriel Boric (2022–2026), elected at the helm of a novel centre-left coalition with anti-establishment components, after an outbreak of widespread social protest.

[13] Viz. UN documents CCPR/C/CHL/CO/7, CED/C/CHL/CO/1, A/HRC/22/45/Add.1, and A/HRC/36/39/Add.3. These last two documents, proceeding from a 2012 UN Working Group mission to Chile, were explicitly taken up by national groups lobbying for the creation of the PNB.

previous judicial mode and an exposition of the latter's limits.[14] Owing to its advent, Chile now presents a hybrid search scenario where administrative and justice-directed initiatives run side by side.[15] This diversification poses new challenges, redolent of the 'third generation' of activism posited in this book, for both state and non-state actors. These include early pressure for the Search Plan to adopt a greatly expanded understanding of participation.[16] The Plan has also had to grapple with scepticism and open criticism from relatives, the political Right, and the general public.[17]

### 1.2.1 *Activism Surrounding the Disappeared during the Chilean Dictatorship*

In the aftermath of the 1973 coup, thousands of people were irregularly detained. The Association of Relatives of the Detained-Disappeared (Agrupación de Familiares de Detenidos Desaparecidos (AFDD)), founded in 1974, became a lifeline for those searching for answers about family members or political comrades who were simply never heard of again (as distinct from those known to have been extrajudicially executed).[18] The AFDD provided emotional and peer support while collating as much information as possible about the missing and providing a conduit to legal and other support services. These were provided initially by the Catholic Church, which also lent a certain level of institutional protection.[19] The ecumenical Committee Pro-Paz (1973–1975), then (from 1976) the Vicaría de la Solidaridad ('Vicaría') provided advice, legal representation, and humanitarian assistance while creating spaces for mutual solidarity (Aranda 2004; Kelly 2015; Lira 2017; Lira and Rojas 2022; Wilde 2015).

Bastias Saavedra (2013) treats the AFDD and sister organisation the Association of Relatives of Victims of Political Execution (Agrupación de Familiares de Ejecutados Políticos (AFEP)) as having a somewhat dependent early relationship with these supporting institutions, characterising AFDD members as 'homemakers … with scant previous political experience' (Bastias Saavedra 2013, 182, authors' translation). This depiction is difficult to square with a pre-coup context featuring high levels of political mobilisation across class and gender divides, but in any case, time and a changed membership profile soon gave the AFDD its own voice and identity. From 1976, the dictatorship's repressive violence targeted traditional parties of the Left. The AFDD accordingly experienced an influx of relatives of disappeared Communist Party activists, many themselves experienced in party, neighbourhood, or union politics. The tireless search for information meanwhile entailed regular rounds of hospitals, morgues, and prisons, leading to the recruitment of new members. Relatives often feared – rightly – for their own physical safety, so hunger strikes and en masse public actions were adopted as collective

[14] For various reasons, the still-burgeoning criminal caseload had reached a plateau in its capacity to generate new finds in disappearance cases.

[15] The PNB explicitly describes itself as hybrid (e.g., PNB Bulletin no. 5, October 2024) in an effort to pre-empt perception of it as de-linked from justice. As authors we use the term 'hybrid' slightly differently – namely, to describe the interplay between judicial investigation, still directed by the courts, and administrative search as carried out by the PNB.

[16] Encompassing co-design and co-execution, rather than mere non-binding consultation or sporadic input via opinion surveys.

[17] Some judicial branch actors have chosen to interpret the creation of the PNB as an insinuation that judicial search has been found wanting. Conversations and off-the-record interviews carried out under the auspices of the Observatorio de Justicia Transicional (2023 and 2024a, 2024b).

[18] Relatives of the latter created their own, separate, organisation: the Association of Relatives of Victims of Political Execution (Agrupación de Familiares de Ejecutados Politicos (AFEP)).

[19] Proceeding from the Church's then central place in national life.

tactics offering a modicum of safety in numbers while making the group's plight and demands visible, including internationally.[20]

Links – sometimes clandestine – were forged with similar associations around Latin America, and with exile and diaspora communities. Cultivating new contacts allowed the AFDD (and AFEP) to develop their own networks and open themselves to radical oppositional strategies,[21] while maintaining efforts to create broad-based support among the general public. To this end hunger strikes were called in 1977 and 1978, and a mass direct legal presentation by female AFDD members took place on the first-ever International Women's Day (in 1977). Actions emphasised the human tragedy behind disappearance, appealing to religious tropes about the sacred duties of motherhood and the anguish of mothers denied knowledge about their children's fate.[22] A year later, an incident often described as the 'first public proof' of disappearance took place: human remains were recovered from a lime kiln in the settlement of Lonquén (Lira 2015). This grim discovery in fact presents something of a paradox, as the victims proved to be people hitherto classified as disappeared. The evidence of their demise therefore rendered them, strictly speaking, no longer *desaparecidos* but *ejecutados*, by extinguishing all remaining hope that they would be found alive. This reclassification of victims from 'disappeared' to 'executed', if and when remains were found, was, however, never done, and the victims of Lonquén continued to be referred to as 'disappeared'. This was in keeping with other manifestations of resistance to categorising the once-disappeared as dead: 1978 saw the AFDD's first street-based public campaign against a law seeking to impose the status of 'missing presumed dead' on the remaining disappeared.

In summary, in the first years after the coup, Chile's then incipient AFDD displayed certain characteristics that are of particular interest. First, a growing sense of identity and agency, accompanied by a gradual influx of members with political experience. Second, a capacity for both imagining and attempting the impossible, cultivating allies wherever they might be found. Third, and most uniquely, a need to navigate the uncharted waters between faith in the possibility of return and concrete evidence of mass killing. The associated binary categorisation of absent victims into the disappeared or the executed has proved notably enduring (Collins 2020, 36–37). Moreover, and eloquently illustrating the conceptual slippage involved, the category of *detenido-desaparecido* – initially associated with the hope, demand, or belief in return alive – was cemented into place by an incident (Lonquén) that actually constituted a tangible testament to mass slaughter. As mentioned, we consider this period and its activism to be the point of origin of a denunciatory strand or mode of search in which relationships with official actors, proposals, and institutions tend(ed) to be absent, wary, and/or oppositional.

### 1.2.2 *Administrative Search in the Early Post-regime Years*

Chile's first post-dictatorial elected president, Patricio Aylwin, proclaimed in his inaugural speech that the 'moral conscience of the nation' demanded 'the truth about the disappearance

[20] On psychological harm, see Castillo Vergara (2013). Bernasconi et al. (2020) describe the dynamic as one of making disappearance *'enunciable'*, or 'speakable' (our translation).

[21] The Vicaría, for example, declined to defend regime opponents (plausibly) accused of violence. By the mid 1980s, when a breakaway faction of the Communist Party came out in favour of armed struggle, this limitation became a substantial point of contention.

[22] Bastias Saavedra (2013). Although in contrast to Argentina's Madres and Abuelas de la Plaza de Mayo, neither the AFDD or AFEP ever had an explicitly gender-specific identity, in practice both were and still are largely composed of women. The gender composition of second- and third-generation relatives' associations tends meanwhile to be notably more mixed.

of persons' (our translation). Promising initial signs, including the truth commission,[23] were, however, followed by stalemate. A 1978 (self-)amnesty decree law allowed the judicial system to continue to ignore perpetrators, the still-powerful armed forces actively threatened insurrection if justice were ever more vigorously pursued, and tensions emerged between relatives and the new authorities. The grassroots historical human rights movement was largely sidelined, with its demands deemed impossible to satisfy given prevailing political conditions. External support – including financial – began to leach away. Although some remains were found, and identifications made, the pace was glacial. In 1991, victims of disappearance were unearthed from unmarked grave sites at the Santiago General Cemetery. Painstaking forensic work by the state forensic medical service attached identities to 90 of the 124 individuals recovered, but some identifications later proved erroneous and remains were reclaimed. The incident took a high emotional toll on relatives, leading to a profound loss of confidence in state-led identification. Other significant finds in this early period served, if anything, only to heighten relatives' frustration at the continued lack of justice and of identification (Avilés, 2018; Medina, 2018).

The next major tipping points, largely unanticipated, came in 1998. Augusto Pinochet's imminent retirement from the army and entry to the senate stimulated renewed efforts to denounce him before domestic courts. In October 1998, he was detained in London by order of a Spanish judge. The resulting international furore put human rights violations in general, and unresolved disappearances in particular, back into the public spotlight. The Chilean authorities made strenuous diplomatic overtures to have Pinochet brought home, thereby giving renewed significance to in-country criminal investigations. The courts were inundated with a slew of additional complaints, many involving disappearance, as relatives and relatives' associations rediscovered their previous traditions of legal activism and 'casebringing'.[24] Administrative stasis began to cede to a new, judicially driven, mode of search,[25] a shift that gathered pace when, as we will see, an ad hoc effort to pre-empt justice innovations administratively came to an ignominious end.

### 1.2.3 *Activist-Driven Judicially Framed Search*

Pinochet returned to Chile in early 2000, having been declared medically unfit to be extradited to Spain. The bravura he displayed exacerbated the outrage felt by many relatives' associations and their supporters. Incoming president Ricardo Lagos, while not reversing the state's hands-off policy regarding justice, convinced Pinochet to leave public life and the armed forces that some additional gesture was needed. The fate of the still-disappeared was unsurprisingly identified as the key remaining sticking point, and a Dialogue Roundtable – the 'Mesa de Diálogo' – was convened. This would supposedly collate information about the fate of the disappeared,

[23] The National Commission on Truth and Reconciliation (Comisión Nacional de Verdad y Reconciliación, CNVR). See CNVR (1991).

[24] The AFEP developed the more comprehensive legal strategy, recruiting law students to draft new complaints. Both AFEP and AFDD, however redoubled their judicially focused activity, especially when the courts took the significant step of recognising the associations, for the first time, as casebringers in their own right.

[25] As we made clear earlier, relatives' resort to legal channels began early and has never ceased. The change reflected by our use of the term 'judicial mode of search' therefore refers not to a novel tactic from relatives but to a breakthrough in court receptivity, as a result of which Chile's primary state action over search came to be located in the judicial branch. That judicially channelled search activity has itself been predominantly activist-driven, while not a given, has in practice been the case: most of Chile's current human rights caseload originates in privately brought complaints (Collins 2010, 2018).

and where they could be found. Although state authorities envisioned relatives sitting at the table alongside military delegates, relatives' associations refused in the end to take part. Some openly doubted the initiative's sincerity. Others opposed its generous anonymity and confidentiality provisions, or the fig-leaf pretence that the armed forces were a good faith broker of information rather than a perpetrating institution. In the end only government and armed forces representatives, and some historic human rights lawyers, took part. The outcome largely vindicated the sceptics, with only a cursory list of names, dates, and places published – some, moreover, demonstrably false.

This highly conciliatory version of state efforts to legitimise or galvanise the administrative mode of search was thereby tested and found wanting. If anything, the judicial route received an unintended fillip: in the expectation that the Mesa would produce larger quantities of useful information than finally proved to be the case, the Supreme Court had assigned additional special investigative magistrates to absorb the anticipated caseload. Political authorities, like the armed forces, were forced to accept both that the 'human rights issue' was back on the front burner and that case-by-case criminal investigations would continue to be the predominant form of action to find the disappeared. This failure of a state-driven attempt at elite conciliation represented both a vindication of relative-driven actions and a blow to the credibility of any future proposals built around administrative modes of search.

### 1.2.4 *The Origins of the National Search Plan*

As we have seen, the turn of the millennium tended to reproduce a familiar pattern, with occasional enforced official revisiting of search taking one of two contrasting, yet equally unsatisfactory, forms. On the one hand, truth-for-justice trade-offs (viz. the Mesa); on the other, faith in the ability and willingness of individual investigative magistrates to find the disappeared while investigating the crimes committed against them.[26] Both alternatives – administrative search without a justice component; or judicial search with no specialised features – became even less palatable after 2006, when historical errors in official forensic identifications were made known.[27] Confidence in judicial-driven processes was particularly shaken, as most of the erroneous results had been produced to judicial order. In practice, however, the ensuing crisis of faith affected all state-ratified solutions, since the underlying scientific analysis was invariably performed by Chile's official forensic service, the Forensic Medical Service (Servicio Médico Legal (SML)).

Substantial restructuring of the latter's human rights work, under a new director who was himself a survivor of political imprisonment, helped create a cautious post-2009 rapprochement between mainstream relatives' associations and the SML. The process however entailed much back-and-forth among and between scientists and associations about where, and by whom, future scientific results should be validated or DNA samples collected and held (Collins 2018; SML 2010). The lived experiences of those who had, and had not, had relatives found, identified, or misidentified began to diverge sharply. So too did the circumstances of relatives and activists whose legal cases had been investigated with alacrity and apparent success, and those still bereft of answers. The capacity of the criminal justice system to generate new finds meanwhile declined – despite real advances in accountability – as easier cases were solved and only

[26] For judicial versus administrative modes of search in Chile, see Sferrazza (2021).

[27] Initially associated with a specific mass gravesite, 'Patio 29' has entered into general parlance as shorthand for the whole issue of scientific error, avoidable and otherwise, and associated harms.

the most intractable remained. The closing of an amnesty-related loophole that had provided a perverse incentive for perpetrators to indicate the location of remains accentuated that decline.[28] This demonstrable lacuna in new finds, with no important discoveries made since 2006,[29] has been perhaps the most persuasive argument for (re-)introducing administrative search measures or features onto Chile's almost exclusively judicial post-1998 pathway.

Politically, 2010 saw the accession of Chile's first right-wing administration since transition, following four successive centre-left presidents at least rhetorically sympathetic to the human rights cause. While the political and social distance between the government and relatives' associations undoubtedly increased as a result, this first right-wing presidency largely allowed existing transitional justice initiatives to continue. The idea of distinguishing search from prosecution continued to gain ground, with search to be given renewed, specialised attention. It is difficult to pinpoint precisely which contributory factor(s) proved decisive, but it is certainly true that the ever-present demands of the AFDD and AFEP came to be echoed and amplified by a range of national and international actors.[30] Concomitantly, Chile acquired international norm commitments in the issue, rendering it beholden to the associated reporting regimes.

The creation of Chile's first-ever Subsecretariat of Human Rights (2016), and the drafting of the country's initial National Human Rights Plan (2018–2022), further served to concentrate minds, as did the inauguration of search offices in a growing list of other Latin American countries (Collins 2022). But, as ever, for non-state actors on the ground the sensation was one of having to chivvy along state officials rather than being able to applaud deft state leadership. In the courts, meanwhile, cases initiated in 1998 began to reach their conclusions. Guilty verdicts and prison sentences were not, however, matched by finds of disappeared persons or their remains, making it increasingly clear that the ordinary criminal justice process could not be relied upon to fill the search gap.[31] The need for a dedicated, interdisciplinary effort gained gradual acceptance.[32] 'Buy-in' from relatives and relatives' associations would, however, be both crucial and difficult to achieve. The twin spectres of Patio 29 and the Mesa de Diálogo – that is, errors of identification, and the prospect of impunity – loomed large.[33] The latter, in particular, left some relatives extremely reluctant

[28] Basically, since 1998 it had been more advantageous for perpetrators at risk of prosecution to admit to (still-amnestiable) homicide than confess to kidnapping someone still disappeared. As homicide charges required the presence of a body, perpetrators had revealed clandestine burial sites. This loophole closed in 2004 with the advent of a crimes-against-humanity interpretation that deemed both crimes equally prosecutable.

[29] No new clandestine burial sites have been detected through judicial investigation since that date. While prospections and exhumations have continued, these have either failed to produce positive results, or have constituted corroboration of previously made identifications or the recovery of posthumous samples from relatives (Observatorio Justicia Transicional 2023).

[30] These actors include the Observatorio de Justicia Transicional, to which one of the present authors belongs. From 2015 the Observatorio began work to encourage fulfilment of outstanding recommendations made by the UN Working Group on Enforced and Involuntary Disappearance after its 2012 mission to Chile. See UN A/HRC/22/45/Add.1, also cited earlier, and rapporteur documents gathered at http://ulster.ac.uk/disappearances.

[31] Even though the judicial branch made efforts, instigating inter-institutional collaboration with the SML and police service to improve responses to accidental finds or anonymous reports (Collins 2020; Sferrazza 2021, 89; see also Lira and Rojas 2022 for a detailed account of how criminal cases involving disappearances proceed through the legal system).

[32] See repeated comments made by the Ministry of Justice and Human Rights in interviews for the transitional justice chapter of the Universidad Diego Portales' annual human rights report, available at https://derechoshumanos.udp.cl/informe-anual/; see also explicit commitments made in Chile's first and second National Human Rights Plans, published respectively in 2018 and 2023 (www.derechoshumanos.gob.cl/plan-nacional-de-derechos-humanos/).

[33] On Patio 29, see supra, n. 28.

to accept any proposal not under explicit judicial direction or oversight. Political feasibility could not be guaranteed either: a second, more hardline, rightist administration took over in 2018, imperilling the parliamentary support and budget needed for any serious initiative. Indeed, exploratory work that had begun under the auspices of the Human Rights Programme of the Ministry of Justice and Human Rights decelerated noticeably (although it was never discontinued).[34]

It therefore fell to incoming president Gabriel Boric to formally oversee the implementation of a search initiative whose groundwork stretched back at least a decade. The incoming government was already conscious of the symbolic weight attaching to the fiftieth anniversary of the coup, due to occur eighteen months hence. A somewhat precipitate scheme to present a draft search plan in a matter of months soon gave way to more realistic assessments, however. On the one hand, numerous technical and legal complexities were yet to be resolved. On the other hand, the new administration quickly gained an appreciation of the potential veto power wielded by the relatives' associations and other long-standing key actors. The language of 'bringing relatives along', or 'getting them on board' – redolent of convincing them to lend credibility to a plan drawn up behind closed doors – was quickly dropped. It was replaced by a greater emphasis on humility, continuous dialogue, and the need to learn from existing expertise, including lived experience.[35] A part-practical, part-strategic decision was also taken to locate the search office under the aegis of the existing Human Rights Programme.[36] The strategic aspects of this choice included reassuring relatives that justice would not be sacrificed on the altar of search, since the bulk of the Programme's activity was, and is, support for criminal prosecution of perpetrators.[37]

## 1.3 FROM 'CONSULTATION' TO 'PARTICIPATION': THE STATE'S APPROACH TO RELATIVES

The early rush to draft a law was abandoned, and time and resources were redirected to a programme of consultation about the design and operational structure and priorities of the plan. Sectorally as well as geographically broad in scope, the consultation would deliberately seek out non-organised relatives as well as the highest profile national associations. Boric's second Justice Minister, in particular, made clear his professional and personal commitment to this deferential yet action-oriented approach, using the language of rights rather than concessions in relation to the role of relatives. His determination produced a favourable

[34] The Programme (https://pdh.minjusticia.gob.cl/) a legacy of Chile's first truth commission, at the time held a brief that covered memory, judicial, and welfare (social assistance) aspects of transitional justice, with an almost exclusive focus on 'absent victims' (the dead and disappeared). A small (three-person) team had been recruited in 2016 to review victim lists and totals, as a prelude to any renewal of efforts in truth, reparations, and/or search.

[35] This paragraph and the one immediately following are based on the close involvement of one of the present authors in many of the dynamics and discussions referred to. Some of its observations were also collated in written form as a memorandum presented by the Observatorio de Justicia Transicional to the UN Committee on Enforced and Involuntary Disappearances during its 129th session, held in Santiago de Chile in February 2023. Memorandum on file with the authors.

[36] One of a range of possibilities including a stand-alone entity, or one incorporated into the SML or the National Human Rights Institute (Instituto Nacional de Derechos Humanos, INDH), Chile's Paris Principles institution.

[37] The downside of this choice has been the perpetuation of a legally driven logic at times in tension with the interdisciplinary vision of the PNB. A swathe of the PNB's new recruits from disciplines other than law left before its first year was up, various of them citing epistemic differences with the prevailing law-driven ethos (Observatorio Justicia Transicional, 2024b).

impression even among dyed-in-the-wool sceptics. Some progress was also made in moving beyond consultation toward a more demanding model of active participation and expanding the latter's theoretical scope beyond relatives to (other) actors with a legitimate interest. In practice, however, the long tradition of political and moral deference to relatives of the disappeared proved hard to break.[38]

Some aspects of this exercise are discussed in greater depth later. We emphasise how the very existence of the process, like the divergent and at times strongly contradictory views to which it gave a voice, reflect important long-standing and emerging realities about disappearance in Chile. One of these is the extent to which relatives were forced from the outset to take on the mantle of search almost single-handed, and at great personal cost. Another is how this obligatory protagonism became, over time, a source of both identity and pride, such that any influx of new actors – perhaps particularly, state actors – has proved difficult to assimilate. Long memories of active mistreatment, errors, and/or neglect by authorities mean relatives and associations are understandably wary or weary of official approaches that promise to finally 'resolve' the problem of search by taking it over. Age cohort, geographical, class, gender, and other differences between and among relatives and other activists have meanwhile come into sharper focus, at times devolving into bitter 'turf wars' with mutual accusations of insensitivity or outright opportunism.[39]

Perhaps divergence among relatives was only to be expected, as family and individual life trajectories over four or five decades diluted the defining power of the early common experience of ambiguous loss. The aging and death of members of the earliest cohort has contributed its own quota of change. Some victims now have no direct family to advocate for them, and are remembered, if at all, by a community of reference made up of friends and political comrades whether within or outside associations. For others, remembrance and commemoration have been moulded and reshaped as they have been passed down through generations of the person's family.[40] Seeing the long-standing desire and demand for official search turned into reality has also created ripples. One lesson that some relatives and associations have acknowledged finding unexpectedly hard is that persuading the state and wider society to take on a share of collective responsibility for search requires the relinquishing of proprietorial attitudes. State search may also need to be 'victim-informed' rather than 'victim-driven', in matters that have a technical or scientific component.[41] Similarly, the state may need to take a position on issues about which there is no consensus – indeed, there may be bitter dispute – within the victim community.

[38] The PNB's current design incorporates a Committee for Participation and Follow-up, which is chaired by relatives' association representatives, although with some spaces for other third sector experts.

[39] An early, and salutary, illustration came in 2020 and 2021, when revised victim lists and totals were presented to the AFDD and AFEP. The AFEP refused to countenance the reclassification into the category of detained-disappeared, of around 400 victims hitherto regarded as politically executed – but the whereabouts of whose remains are not known. Their strenuous objection to having 'their' victims – as they saw it – 'taken from them' and 'given' to the AFDD was one factor in the adoption of an alternative solution: the PNB established a third category of 'victim of enforced disappearance'. The pre-existing socially established categories were mapped onto this, without being thereby subsumed.

[40] Sources include discussions at a 2018 event, co-convened by one of the present authors, bringing together paired members of the same families from different generations. Some site-specific relatives' associations, such as the one attached to the rural settlement of Paine, have explicitly handed the reins to children or grandchildren of the disappeared in recent years, acknowledging that the change, while necessary, has proved difficult.

[41] The 2009 conciliation between relatives and the SML included an agreement to decommission certain DNA samples collected pre-2009: deemed socially necessary to re-establish confidence, the measure was resisted by many forensic staff as entailing the abandonment of perfectly viable, and sometimes irreplaceable, genetic material.

## 1.4 PAVING THE WAY: RELATIVES' VIEWS IN THE RUN-UP TO THE PNB

This section draws on PNB publications including Plan Nacional de Búsqueda (2023) and minutes of preparatory meetings held in early 2023.[42] In total, 775 people took part in one or more of sixty-seven 'dialogues', held across Chile's fifteen regions and structured in advance around five 'critical themes', three of which are of particular interest in illustrating tensions and accommodations between 'activist', 'participatory', and 'resistant' generations of engagement. The themes are, in turn: the relationship between judicial and administratively organised search; incorporation of new cases to official victim registers; and benefits for perpetrators or implicated bystanders who offer information.

Relatives who form part of recognised associations were noticeably more insistent than their non-participating counterparts on the need for continued judicial involvement in search and identification. Even occasional negative experiences of investigations, largely among smaller associations with a local and/or rural purview, did not fully eradicate the distinction between association members and other relatives on this point. The non-organised relatives – perhaps significantly, predominantly second- and third-generation descendants, rather than age cohort peers of the disappeared – tended both to prize rapidity and efficiency, and to see these as incompatible with judicial oversight.[43] Attendees from both categories agreed that any dedicated search team should combine forensic, social, anthropological, and historical expertise: the sticking point remained hands-on state oversight and its location outside the judicial branch. Members of organised, particularly historical, associations were keener to preserve a clear state and judicial character for the PNB.[44] This may well reflect a desire to positively validate their own long-standing option for legal activism, a decision reaffirmed, as we have seen, after 1998. It also however runs at least superficially counter to the decidedly anti-state or at least state-sceptical character that we have attributed to the resistant mode of action with which these groups are primarily identified.[45] This is particularly interesting when combined with the results of discussion about acknowledgement of new victims.

Both organised and non-organised relatives – the latter, as we have established, more likely to belong to more recent age cohorts – agree that previously overlooked victims who disappeared during the dictatorship should be added to official lists. However, only non-organised relatives declared themselves more open than not to (also) including victims from the post-transitional period.[46] Our own view is that this desire to police temporal-definitional boundaries in ways that reaffirm the unique character of dictatorship-era disappearance may shore up associations' historically uncontested claim to primacy in dialogue with the state. In the

[42] Copies of the minutes were obtained by the authors in November 2024 using established access to information channels.

[43] 'With the courts, everything hangs on the criteria of each judge. We need a team that doesn't report to them, that can act more swiftly and effectively' (Minutes number 024, meeting held in Valparaíso, p. 156; authors' translation).

[44] The term 'historical' associations refers here to national or regional 'chapters' of the AFDD and AFEP formed during the dictatorship, and a small number of other groups of similar lineage. The intended contrast is with newer site- or episode-specific associations founded in or after the mid 1990s.

[45] Unless it is read as a relative preference for the judicial branch rather than the executive or legislature, fed by the notably court-led nature of much post-1998 transitional justice progress (Observatorio Justicia Transicional 2023, 2024a, 2024b).

[46] While such cases do exist, they number no more than six people, missing in circumstances suggestive of state agent involvement without systematicity or higher orders.

process, of course, it risks unwittingly or otherwise creating a victim hierarchy, and/or fuelling potentially exclusionary disputation about representativity.[47]

The differences between organised and non-organised relatives were of a secondary order concerning benefits for information: strongly contrasting views were found within and across each category. Members of the nationally organised and urban-based variants of historical associations such as the AFEP and AFDD generally echoed the first-generation, resistant line that no quarter should be given. Members of rural and/or regional chapters of the same associations were however more ready to contemplate exceptions or changes in outlook: 'What I want is to know where s/he is … A pardon for anyone who testifies seems viable to me, if it means we can give [the disappeared] a decent burial.'[48]

These divergences illustrate the evolving nature of search demands and the constantly shifting boundaries of what different groups consider acceptable or negotiable. While historical associations by and large maintain a principled stance against any concessions, the emergence of more pragmatic perspectives among some relatives signals a broader transformation in how disappearance is understood and addressed. A growing tension between rigid moral and political imperatives and the urgency of obtaining information reflects generational shifts but also the cumulative emotional weight of unresolved disappearances.

## 1.5 CONCLUSIONS

The PNB dialogues can be considered, for present purposes, as an example of 'participatory' transitional justice dynamics in the particular sense that this book gives to the term – that is, an invitation extended by the state, to which 'victims' do or do not accede – although in another sense, as we have already explained, we consider their very existence to owe much to relatives' early creation of the terms of the debate. As we have seen, over the course of those dialogues certain strong lines taken by prominent first-generation searchers were nuanced, diluted, or relativised when the views of other relatives were set alongside them. This demonstrates that victim co-creation of transitional justice instances can be 'curated' by state mediation in ways that need not signify co-optation. By instigating a participatory process – in response to victims' wishes and demands – then engineering deliberately broad diversity in engagement with it, the Chilean state created a dynamic that was if anything conducive to expanded protagonism from those victims and/or relatives whose voices were most rarely heard. Indeed, the very strength of combative, resistant historical associations in Chile had made it difficult hitherto for new or dissenting civil society voices to gain a place at the table. Thus we can see how the Chilean state's belated acceptance of a greater share of its responsibilities in relation to the disappeared can be read as an almost wholly victim-impulsed and victim-informed advance, without denying the necessary role of the state in enacting final decisions where victim engagement pulled in mutually incompatible directions. In this instance, the Chilean state preserved or even expanded the range of views that fed into a necessary policy innovation, taking on a 'counterbalancing' function which allowed power imbalances among third sector groups to be moderated and partly redressed. This role is, then, important to consider. State involvement is neither inimical to genuine victim protagonism, nor ineluctably synonymous with a closing down or trammelling of the terms of any particular transitional justice debate.

47 A question that is also, of course, live when associations must determine who to nominate as their rotating representatives on the PNB's consultative committee.

48 Minutes number 23, AFDD member in Copiapó, authors' translation. Anecdotally, more than one member of such associations has told the present authors that they find themselves increasingly personally at odds with the official group line on this matter, while feeling unable to voice this view.

## REFERENCES


Aranda, Gilberto. 2004. *Vicaría de la Solidaridad: una experiencia sin fronteras*. CESOC.

Avilés, R. N. 2018. 'Identification of Skeletal Remains of People Detained Disappeared and Persons Executed for Political Reasons, and Personal Integrity of the Relatives'. *Latin American Legal Studies*, 3, 77–96.

Bastias Saavedra, M. 2013. *Sociedad Civil en Dictadura – Relaciones transnacionales, organizaciones y socialización política en Chile*. Universidad Alberto Hurtado.

Bernasconi, Oriana, and Marcela Ruiz. 2018. 'A Performative and Genealogical Approach to the Liminal Subject's Social Sustenance: The Case of the Disappeared Detainees in Chile'. *Subjectivity*, 11, 228–249.

Bernasconi, Oriana, Loreto Lopez, and Marcela Ruiz. 2020. 'Repertorio de la violencia de Estado: nombrar, definir y clasificar'. In *Documentar la atrocidad: Resistir el terrorismo de Estado*, edited by O. Bernasconi, pp. 209–247. Ediciones UAH.

Bustos, Francisco, and Cath Collins. 2025. 'Justice after Pinochet: Cases in Chile Post-1998'. In *Fifty Years of Human Rights in Chile: Essays in Honour of Alan Angell*, edited by V. Infante-Batiste and Richard Wilkinson, pp. 105–128. Palgrave Macmillan.

Castillo Vergara, Isabel. 2013. *El (im)posible proceso del duelo: Familiares de detenidos-desaparecidos, violencia política, trauma y memoria*. Ediciones Alberto Hurtado.

CNVR. 1991. *Informe de la Comisión Nacional de Verdad y Reconciliación*. http://bibliotecadigital.indh.cl/handle/123456789/170

Collins, Cath. 2010. 'Human Rights Trials in Chile during and after the "Pinochet Years"'. *International Journal of Transitional Justice*, 4(1), 67–86.

Collins, Cath. 2018. 'Transitional Justice from Within: Police, Forensic and Legal Actors Searching for Chile's Disappeared'. *Journal of Human Rights Practice*, 10(1), 19–39.

Collins, Cath. 2020. 'The Reemergence of the Disappeared: The Role of Remains, and the "Forensic Gaze"'. *Memory Studies*, 13(3), 322–336.

Collins, Cath. (ed.) 2022. 'An Innovative Response to Disappearances: Non-Judicial Search for the Disappeared in Asia and Latin America'. *Global Initiative for Justice, Truth and Reconciliation (GIJTR)*. https://tinyurl.com/4e52sdfj

Garibain, Sévane. 2013. 'Buscar a los muertos entre los vivos: dar cuerpo a los desaparecidos de la dictadura argentina por el Derecho'. In *Cadáveres impensables, cadáveres impensados: El tratamiento de los cuerpos en las violencias de masa y los genocidios*, edited by S. Garibain, E. Anstett, and M. Dreyfus, pp. 29–40. Miño y Davila.

Kelly, Patrick. 2015. 'Human Rights and Christian Responsibility: Transnational Christian Activism, Human Rights, and State Violence in Brazil and Chile in the 1970s'. In *Religious Responses to Violence: Human Rights in Latin America Past and Present*, edited by A. Wilde, pp. 95–122. University of Notre Dame Press.

Lira, Elizabeth. 2015. 'Chile. Desaparición forzada: 1973–2015'. In *La verdad nos hace libres. Sobre las relaciones entre filosofía, derechos humanos, religión y universidad*, edited by M. Giusti, G. Gutiérrez, and E. Salmón, pp. 549–573. Fondo editorial de la Pontificia Universidad Católica del Perú.

Lira, Elizabeth. 2017. 'The Chilean Human Rights Archives and Moral Resistance to Dictatorship'. *International Journal of Transitional Justice*, 11(2), 189–196.

Lira, Elizabeth, and Hugo Rojas. 2022. 'El Caso Andrés Pereira Salsberg: La Presencia de la Ausencia de las Desapariciones Forzadas en Chile'. *Revista Austral de Ciencias Sociales*, 43, 261–283.

Medina, Eden. 2018. 'Forensic Identification in the Aftermath of Human Rights Crimes in Chile: A Decentered Computer History'. *Technology and Culture*, 59(4S), S100–S133.

Observatorio de Justicia Transicional. 2023. "Truth, Justice, Reparations, Memory and Guarantees of Non-Repetition in Chile – 25 Years of Criminal Cases." English language version of "Que las promesas se vuelvan ciertas," in Universidad Diego Portales, *Informe Anual: DDHH en Chile* 2023. https://tinyurl.com/4xtxhfns

Observatorio de Justicia Transicional. 2024a. 'Jurisprudential Milestones in Human Rights Cases: Chile 1990–2024'. https://tinyurl.com/5n9yutua

Observatorio de Justicia Transicional. 2024b. '"Para seguir viviendo": Verdad, justicia, reparación, memoria y garantías de no repetición en Chile 2024'. In Universidad Diego Portales, *Informe Anual: DDHH en Chile* 2024. https://tinyurl.com/2pperaux

Plan Nacional de Búsqueda. 2023. 'Resumen Ejecutivo, Informe Final – Proceso de diálogos participativos del Plan Nacional de Búsqueda'. https://tinyurl.com/53yvnncm

Rojas, Hugo, and Miriam Shaftoe. 2022. *Human Rights and Transitional Justice in Chile*. Palgrave Macmillan.

Rosenblatt, Adam. 2015. *Digging for the Disappeared: Forensic Science after Atrocity*. Stanford University Press.

Ruiz, Marcela, and Oriana Bernasconi. 2019. 'Reports on Categorization and Classification of Human Rights Violations in Chile (1974–1978)'. *Discourse & Society*, 30(1), 44–63.

Servicio Médico Legal (SML). 2010. *Memoria: Programa de Derechos Humanos 2007–2010*. Servicio Médico Legal.

Sferrazza, Pietro. 2021. 'La búsqueda de personas desaparecidas en Chile: ¿necesidad de un complemento humanitario?' *Revista mexicana de ciencias políticas y sociales*, 66(243), 79–108.

Wilde, Alexander. 2015. 'The Institutional Church and Pastoral Ministry: Unity and Conflict in the Defense of Human Rights in Chile'. pp. 159–190 in *Religious Responses to Violence: Human Rights in Latin America Past and Present*, edited by A. Wilde. University of Notre Dame Press.

# 2

# Victimhood, Agency, and the Mobilisation of Empathy

*Cheryl Lawther*

## 2.1 INTRODUCTION

This chapter focuses on the case study of Northern Ireland to interrogate the intersection between victimhood, victims' groups as drivers of first-generation transitional justice, and how empathy is mobilised in transitional contexts.[1] The Northern Ireland conflict began in 1969 and lasted over thirty years. Approximately 3,739 individuals were killed, 40,000–50,000 injured, and tens of thousands displaced owing to intimidation and political violence. Legally, over one-third of Northern Ireland's adult population could be classified as a victim or survivor of the conflict. Yet, despite this legacy, Northern Ireland is a transitional jurisdiction characterised by the lack of an overarching transitional justice process. At the time of writing, September 2025, there are no comprehensive processes to provide truth, justice or reparations to all victims and survivors of the conflict.

In this gap, victims' groups have acted as drivers of first-generation efforts at transitional justice, and have consistently campaigned for the provision of truth, acknowledgement, justice, and reparations (Lawther 2025). The 'ways of working' developed by these groups have been shaped by the existence of networks of support, the skills and abilities of their founders, demands of the membership, the availability of funding, and by individual and community experiences of victimhood and relations to the state. Some indicative examples are useful for illustrative purposes at this juncture. Efforts at truth recovery have for example included campaigns for truth and justice into high-profile cases such as Bloody Sunday, the Ballymurphy Massacre, and the Omagh bombing; local truth recovery and storytelling projects; archival work; and the authoring of books and the production of films on a range of conflict related atrocities. WAVE, a cross-community victims' group that operates across Northern Ireland, has been instrumental in both the campaign to recover those disappeared during the conflict and in the delivery of a pension for the seriously injured. Layered on top of these initiatives are a range of therapeutic services, such as counselling, social welfare advice, and befriending services. In the absence of a formal process of transitional justice, the passage of time has not substantially changed the services delivered by victims' groups in Northern Ireland. Moreover, it is victim and survivor groups that continue to lead the call for a comprehensive approach to dealing with the past.

[1] This chapter draws on work funded by the Arts and Humanities Research Council (AH/N001451/) and British Academy (MCFSS22\220018). The arguments made and quotations used in this chapter are explored in full in C. Lawther (2025). *Constructing Victimhood: Beyond Innocence and Guilt in Transitional Justice*. Oxford University Press. I respectfully direct readers to this text for a fuller exposition of these arguments.

Yet, as scholars such as Krystalli and Schulz (2022, 12) remind us, victims' groups should not be 'framed in exclusively positive or romanticized terms'. The moral economy of victimhood can compel individuals and victim group leaders to convey their suffering in particular registers in the attempt to make their losses 'matter' over and above the experience of other victims and survivors and in the quest to achieve resources and status, and 'mobilise empathy' (Golubović 2022; Wilson and Brown 2009). This dynamic is particularly acute in Northern Ireland where in the absence of a formal process of dealing with the past and ongoing contest over the legal definition of a victim or survivor of the conflict, victims' groups often compete for empathy on the basis of diametrically opposed conceptualisations of victimhood. Mirroring the structural fault-lines of the conflict, this has not only led to the reproduction of services in each community, but also to styles of advocacy that are expressed in different and opposing registers – privileging the ideas of innocence and blamelessness in the unionist and loyalist community and inclusivity and the equivalence of grief in the nationalist and republican community. As I argue later, these 'repertories of victimhood' have not only reinforced the politicisation of victimhood, but in certain circumstances have also led to the appropriation of victims' suffering for political ends (de Waardt 2016).

The chapter is structured as follows. The first part of the chapter, 'Victims' Groups as Moral Communities', proposes the ideas of dignity, responsiveness and the creation of spaces of solidarity as lenses through which to understand why victims and survivors choose to become involved in victims' groups. Reflecting these themes, the second part of the chapter, 'Agency, Empowerment and Doing Victimhood Work', uses the example of the campaign for a pension for those seriously injured during the Northern Ireland conflict to illustrate how victims' groups can use their own experiences of physical and psychological injury to leverage profound change in the absence of an overarching process of dealing with the past. The discussion then turns to how victimhood is expressed and empathy mobilised differently within each constituency. The respective framings of 'Victimhood, Agency, and Innocence' as relating to the unionist community and 'Victimhood, Agency, and Inclusivity' as relating to the nationalist and republican community also reflect how victims' groups in the two communities differ in their approach to transitional justice, their understanding of the role of the state as a participant in the conflict and provider of transitional justice, and how their demands for truth and justice have been articulated in different registers. Set against these dynamics, the conclusion points to the risk of the appropriation of victims' suffering for political ends.

## 2.2 VICTIMS' GROUPS AS MORAL COMMUNITIES

The introduction to this chapter alluded to the wide range of activities and advocacy campaigns that have been undertaken by victims' groups in Northern Ireland. In this next part of the chapter, I begin to move our understanding of victims' groups forward by offering a theoretical framework in which to understand the intersection between agency, activism, and individuals' involvement in victims' groups. Situating victims' groups in Northern Ireland as drivers of first-generation efforts at transitional justice is particularly illuminating in this regard. As I demonstrate here, conceptualising victims' groups as 'moral communities' and privileging the themes of dignity, responsiveness, and the creation of spaces of solidarity, it is important to understand why victims and survivors choose to become involved in victims' groups and how such groups may promote agency and empowerment *before* the language and demands of transitional justice are inculcated into their agendas (Durkheim 2019).

For many of the leaders and representatives of victims' groups in Northern Ireland interviewed by the author, their role in establishing victims' organisations or otherwise becoming involved in advocacy and service delivery was an expression of empathy and the practical outworking of an ethical imperative to 'do something' concerning the injustices suffered by family members, friends, and the communities from which they came, as well as the context in which violence was occurring. In this respect, victims' groups can be considered 'moral communities' (Durkheim 2019). The ethical imperative to act, 'of trying to make this place a better place for everybody',[2] and the creation of an embryonic 'moral community' that now runs a high-profile campaign for truth and justice into one particular atrocity in Northern Ireland, is clear in the following statement by a victims' campaigner:

> I could probably tell you the exact date [when began campaign of activism]. It was the thirtieth anniversary [of a specific atrocity], we had the church commemoration, a lovely church commemoration but I got very upset with myself because I'd asked myself the question 'what had I done?', and commemoration is very important, memorialisation is very important but 'what had I done to try and counter their propaganda [of the British state] and to take it further for the campaign and to take them into court?' Just literally the next day I went down to the newspaper archives ...[3]

While such 'ways of working' have evolved over time and are context specific, the fieldwork on which this chapter is based demonstrated the effectiveness and necessity of these moral communities. While space and conceptual clarity prohibit an exhaustive recounting of individual practices, three common themes can be deduced from the Northern Ireland experience which speak to the value of victims' groups and the meaning-making power of grassroots actors. The first of these is *dignification*. Human rights scholars, theologians, anthropologists, and philosophers among others have all discussed the concept of human dignity. During conflict and authoritarianism, humiliation, ill-treatment of victims, and other grave violations of human rights all constitute a fundamental denial of human dignity. The normative emphasis of transitional justice scholarship and practice has thus been to connect the restoration of victims' dignity to the (public) identification of their victimhood, the vocalisation of their experience, and acknowledgement of their plight. This emphasis on the restoration of dignity was apparent in the actions and motivations of victim group leaders and in the praise offered by members of victims' groups themselves. For example, and speaking to the recognition of the moral status of all individuals, a supporter of a victims' group which works predominantly in the nationalist and republican community reflected on how the organisations' campaigning work on behalf of family members of Irish Republican Army (IRA) volunteers who were killed on active service – a community victimised and silenced by the state, constituted a fundamental recognition of their personhood and rights:

> I think their advocacy around that work I think was particularly helpful for the families who felt that their sons or daughters were summarily executed and that they just had to live with that. It was bad enough losing them but they then just had to live with the fact that they were executed and that the people who killed them basically got away with it. So, they changed that for people.[4]

Second is *responsiveness*. As detailed at length elsewhere, much of the theory and practice of transitional justice privileges the concept of being 'victim-centred'. An equal body of literature has interrogated what being 'victim-centred' means and whether transitional justice mechanisms have the ability and will to go beyond this somewhat rhetorical term (see, for example,

[2] Interview, victims' campaigner, 3 May 2017.
[3] Interview, victims' campaigner, 3 May 2017.
[4] Interview, senior republican/senior Republican ex-prisoner, 17 August 2017.

Robins 2017). In Northern Ireland, being victim centred was understood by research participants as being responsive to victims' needs – often in a highly organic and unscripted way. For example, one victim referred to knowing that she could telephone the leader of the group to which she is affiliated 'at any time' and the groups' role in 'keeping her sane'.[5] Likewise, it is well known that where victims' groups have accompanied victims when, for example, receiving cold case reports into the deaths of their loved ones or have guided victims through the process of applying for the pension that is available those seriously injured during the conflict, the outcomes for victims and their families are significantly better (Lundy 2009).[6] These interventions are not only highly thoughtful and sensitive on the part of these different organisations but offer practical illustrations of moral communities in action.

Third is the creation of *spaces of solidarity*. While the scholarship on transitional justice and associated policy directives tends to focus on the ability of victims' groups to advocate for truth, justice, or reparations, for example, or provide therapeutic services, interviewees across the spectrum in Northern Ireland were quick to highlight and appreciate how victims' groups can provide safe spaces in which difficult emotions are recognised, companionship built, and feelings of isolation and loneliness countered (see also Dasli, Chapter 4). Most poignantly, one female interviewee who was involved in the creation of a memorial quilt within her local victims' group reflected on how,[7]

> I found it very enjoyable along with the other ladies and actually looking at the different patches and seeing who was who and what had happened. Because when you don't talk about something you're just apart, you know, and you don't think of anybody else until something like this and you actually see and you see all the different squares, who these people were and the injuries that they received and you know, it kind of broadens it a bit for you instead of being stuck in your own little dark place, you can see there are lots of others.[8]

Offering dignity, responsiveness, and spaces of solidarity, the 'ways of working' developed by certain victims' groups in Northern Ireland may therefore be thought of as offering significant transformative potential for victims and survivors.

## 2.3 AGENCY, EMPOWERMENT, AND 'DOING' VICTIMHOOD WORK

Closely connected to the argument that victims' groups can act as moral communities is the argument that 'taking victimhood seriously requires moving away from the view of it as always synonymous with vulnerability or lack of agency or as entirely reduced to the experience of victimisation' (Krystalli 2020, 1). Over the course of formal interviews and countless informal conversations with this author, members and representatives of victims' groups recounted many positive examples of how feelings of hope, friendship, and empowerment have been cultivated among victims and survivors through their participation in, for example, art projects, the writing of books, and the recording of oral histories that speak to the themes of dignity, solidarity, and responsiveness. Yet what is also apparent is how '*doing victimhood*' – the direct use of individual and collective experiences of harm and the choice to explicitly foreground

[5] Interview, member of unionist victim's group, 9 February 2017, interview 1.

[6] Author's fieldnotes, November 2025.

[7] Victims' groups in both communities in Northern Ireland have created 'memorial quilts' comprised of squares made by loved ones or other group members in memory of deceased family and/or community members. The squares are then sewn together to form a quilt.

[8] Interview, member of unionist victims' group, 9 February 2017, interview 4.

those experiences in campaigning efforts – can be an expression of agency and a form of empowerment (Jeffrey and Candea 2006, 288). Indeed, in the context of victims' groups acting as first-generation drivers of transitional justice, I would argue that at least in Northern Ireland, this approach has been particularly successful.

The campaign for a pension for those seriously injured as a result of the Northern Ireland conflict, authored and driven by WAVE Trauma Centre's Injured Group is illustrative of a creative and nuanced form of 'victimhood work' (Jeffrey and Candea 2006, 288). By way of background, the campaign for a pension grew out of dissatisfaction with the fact that while the Report of the Consultative Group on the Past (CGP) made the recommendation that a Recognition Payment of £12,000 would be paid to 'the nearest relative of someone who died as a result of the conflict', an equivalent acknowledgement of the needs and experiences of the injured was entirely missing from the Report (CGP 2009, 16).[9] Catalysed by this failure to provide material or symbolic reparations, WAVE's Injured Group's 'Campaign for Recognition' began in 2012 and centred on the demand for a pension for those seriously injured during the conflict (see also Bonacker, Chapter 2). The mobilisation and campaigning methods of the group included the publication of the book *INJURED … on that Day*, which details the experiences of individual members of the group, writing letters to relevant stakeholders in politics and civil society, the commissioning of a major research report, presenting a petition of 10,000 signatures to the five major parties in the Northern Ireland Assembly, the filming of a BBC NI *Spotlight* documentary on the pension debate, an active social media campaign (#mentionthepension), and making political alliances in Northern Ireland, Westminster and Dáil Éireann (Breen-Smyth 2012; BBC 2015; WAVE 2009).

At first blush, these campaigning efforts are in keeping with the activities of many other civil society organisations. However, central to the success of WAVE's Injured Group was the self-conscious front and centre positioning of victims and an explicit highlighting of their vulnerability. By actually 'participating' in the campaign to bring about social justice for themselves and others, members of the Injured Group followed Starzyk et al.'s (2014, 121–122) recommendation that victims campaigning for reparations should make that process and the experience of harm as 'real' for outsiders to grasp as possible. For example, when the Injured Group brought the petition of 10,000 signatures to Stormont in May 2012, it was a tightly performed symbolic act. Captured by the print and broadcast media were a group of people in wheelchairs and those using prosthetic limbs and visual aids making their way up the steep driveway of Stormont Estate to the steps of Parliament Buildings (Irish Independent 2012). The signatures were contained in pillowcases made to look like hospital bags, speaking to the time many of the injured spent in hospitals across Northern Ireland. Their positioning was a deliberate and proactive choice on the part of members of the Injured Group in the quest to mobilise empathy for the pension campaign, capture the public imagination, and shame politicians into action (Gallagher 2021; Wilson and Brown 2009).

On one level, the charge of 'victim prostitution' could be levied against the use of such stark imagery (Ashworth 2000). Likewise, and speaking to a sense of disempowerment, the Group's approach could be read as representing one of the 'choiceless decisions' that women and men within settings of conflict are often forced to make in order to survive (Aretxaga 1997, 61). However, as Baines (2015) argues, people do more than navigate to survive – they

[9] The CGP was established in June 2007 by the then Secretary of State Peter Hain and tasked with consulting on how best Northern Ireland could deal with the legacy of its past. The Report and all recommendations fell on the politics of victimhood (Lawther 2014).

contest, resist, and protest gross violations of their person – a point that I would argue is particularly acute in respect to first generation victims' groups. Such negotiations have witnessed victims 'recognising and asserting themselves as particular subjects, in relation to others, to the structures in which they are situated, and to subject positions that may be imposed on them' (Elwood and Mitchell 2012, 4). In respect to the Injured Group, disability aids – often viewed uncritically and as signifiers of damage, vulnerability, and weakness, become tools of 'victimhood work' to be used proactively as any other campaigning tool might (Jeffrey and Candea 2006, 288).

The work of WAVE's Injured Group therefore demonstrates *and* stretches conventional understandings of victim agency and the mobilisation of empathy. De Waardt and Weber (2019) argue that recognising victims' agency in this way requires recognising and building upon victims' pre-existing internal organisational and decision-making processes to create more horizontal ways of relating. The work of the Injured Group fulfilled this brief and can also be thought of as conveying the benefits of belonging to a moral community as discussed previously (Durkheim 2019). However, it also elongates our understanding of agency by reversing the assumption that 'doing victimhood work' is only associated with the denial of agency, the capture of victims' voices, and the inflation of one ethno-national group's claim to greater suffering in the past. The Injured Group demonstrated how victims and survivors can 'do' 'victimhood work' in an entirely unique way – as both a protest of the grave injustices they have suffered, but by simultaneously using their newly reconstituted identities – developed through such agency-enhancing work – to push for change and reclaim their place in society. Not only did the Injured Group achieve their objective with the signing into law of The Victims' Payments Regulations 2020 on 31 January 2020, but many members of the group experienced a profound sense of personal growth (Gallagher 2021).[10] For one Group member, the juxtapositioning of their inability to return to employment after their disability with the sense of achievement brought about by their participation in the campaign was considered tantamount to showing a 'middle finger' to a once disempowering society (cited in Gallagher 2021, 324).

## 2.4 VICTIMHOOD, AGENCY, AND INNOCENCE

These forms of victim mobilisation do, however, stand apart from the politics of victimhood that has dominated the post-conflict landscape in Northern Ireland. Beginning with an examination of how victimhood is framed in the unionist community and then turning to the same in the nationalist and republican community, the following two parts of this chapter point to how, in the absence of a formal process of dealing with the past and ongoing contest over the definition of a victim or survivor of the conflict, victims' groups have mobilised on the basis of diametrically opposed conceptualisations of victimhood. As I demonstrate, the respective mobilisation tactics framed as 'Victimhood, Agency, and Innocence' as relating to the unionist community, and 'Victimhood, Agency, and Inclusivity' as relating to the nationalist and republican community, reflect how victims' groups in the two communities differ in their mobilisation efforts, approach to transitional justice, their understanding of the role of the state as a participant in the conflict and provider of transitional justice, and how their demands for truth and justice have been articulated in different registers.

[10] The Regulations, administered through The Troubles Permanent Disablement Payment Scheme make provision for a pension for those seriously physically or psychologically injured as a result of the conflict related incident between 1 January 1966 and 12 April 2010.

In Northern Ireland, unionist facing victims' groups have long claimed ownership of the 'real' and 'innocent' victims of the conflict (see, for example, Families Acting for Innocent Relatives 2007; South East Fermanagh Foundation (SEFF) 2018; Ulster Human Rights Watch (UHRW) 2018). This approach to victimhood reflects the unionist narrative of the conflict – that the IRA's campaign was illegitimate and unjustified, that state violence was 'law preserving' in this context, and that peace was secured through the sacrifice and service of the security forces (Lawther 2014). Within this hierarchal conceptualisation of victimhood, only 'innocent' victims are considered 'true' victims of the conflict, while members of paramilitary organisations – particularly IRA members – killed in active service (either by the British security forces, other paramilitaries, or by their own actions) sit at the bottom and are considered 'deserving' of their fate (Lawther 2022). To blur these boundaries has been perceived as creating 'moral equivalence' between the 'innocent victim' and the 'guilty perpetrator', 'spreading culpability among all the parties' (Williams and Scharf 2002, 27). Accordingly, unionist victims' groups unanimously reject the (inclusive) statutory definition of a victim contained in the Victims and Survivors (Northern Ireland) Order 2006 and only deliver services to those victims who accept this interpretation of the conflict (Lawther 2025).

This exclusionary approach to victimhood has shaped victim mobilisation efforts and attitudes to transitional justice initiatives within the unionist community. Two manifestations are useful for illustrative purposes. First, it has translated into a succession of unsuccessful calls to change the Victims and Survivors (Northern Ireland) Order 2006. Both SEFF and UHRW, for example, have suggested that the definition of a victim should respectively be based on the European Union (EU) Directive 2012/29/EU of the European Parliament and of the Council, 25 October 2012 on Establishing Minimum Standards on the Rights, Support and Protection of Victims of Crime or the Justice Act (Northern Ireland) 2015 (SEFF and Innocent Victims United 2020; UHRW 2018). Focusing on victims of crime, groups' calls for adopting either of these definitions of a victim are an attempt to reject the explicitly political nature of the Northern Ireland conflict and delegitimise the actions of armed groups and any harm experienced by their members. Daniel Holder from the Belfast based human rights non-governmental organisation the Committee on the Administration of Justice (CAJ) has argued that the latter definition advocated for by UHRW would exclude virtually all victims of state violence from the definition of a victim, including children killed by plastic bullets and cases such as the Bloody Sunday families and John Pat Cunningham, a vulnerable twenty-seven-year-old man with a mental age of seven, who was shot in the back and killed by three bullets fired by a British army patrol in 1974 (CAJ 2019). According to this reading of victimhood, innocence can only relate to those who accept the unionist narrative of the conflict.

Second is a privileging of calls for truth and justice into atrocities of concern for the unionist community and a simultaneous rejection of mechanisms or investigations that are perceived to be unduly 'state-centric', 'biased' in approach, or designed to facilitate a 're-writing' of the past in favour of a Republican narrative of the conflict (Lawther 2014). These arguments have been made in respect to many of the existing, 'piecemeal', mechanisms for truth and justice, including public inquiries, investigations in the coroner's courts, and the findings of Police Ombudsman for Northern Ireland reports on the grounds that these mechanisms have often focused on the actions of state forces during the conflict and, through findings of state responsibility for deaths within the nationalist and republican community, challenge the preferred unionist narrative of the conflict. They also pertain to many unionist victims' groups' opposition to the establishment of a formal process of truth recovery and in respect to many of the proposals for a formal process of truth recovery (Ely 2020; Lawther 2014; SEFF 2020;

UHRW 2018). Underpinning this approach to historical investigations is the narrative that only 'terrorists' and their accomplices, not civilians, were harmed by the state security forces, and a dismissal of campaigns for truth about state violence as republican propaganda (Dawson 2007). In practice, it has translated into a long tradition of rejecting or downplaying the outcome of investigations into atrocities perpetrated by the British state or its agents – and which often resulted in the victimisation of civilian members of the nationalist community – or immediately countering such truth and justice outcomes with calls to investigate atrocities of concern for the unionist community and the role of the Irish state during the conflict (Lawther 2014).

These dynamics could be seen at the time of writing, September 2025, when the Northern Ireland Secretary of State Hilary Benn announced that an independent public inquiry into the death of solicitor Pat Finucane would take place.[11] Mr Benn told members of the House of Commons that he hoped the inquiry would provide information that the Finucane family had 'sought for so long' (BBC 2024). While clearly stating that there was 'no justification' for the murder of Finucane, Kenny Donaldson, leader of the unionist victim's group SEFF critiqued the (perceived) 'continuance of a policy which elevates and empowers the few' and argued that Benn's decision 'has the impact of deeply hurting other families who have been denied any recourse to justice, truth and accountability' (McNabb 2024). In a classic example of deflecting from the attention placed on the actions of the British state during the conflict, and what I have argued previously is a 'truth as trumps' dynamic in which one call for truth or the production of truth is countered by that of a more 'significant' or more 'important' truth, Donaldson went on to highlight the role of the Irish state in providing truth and justice and placed the spotlight on a series of deaths in the unionist community (Lawther 2014, 70):

> The Irish Government has vociferously raised this case with the UK Government, what is its record in regards to representing the interests and cries for justice and accountability for SEFF's families? Whether that be Terence McKeever's family, Ian Sproule's family, the families of The Narrow Water massacre, the families of Harry Breen and Bob Buchanan, the families of so many innocents impacted within their own jurisdiction (McNabb 2024).

It is of course the right and duty of a victims' advocate to make such a call. Indeed, such an intervention relates to the three themes of how victims' groups can promote the themes of dignity, solidarity, and responsiveness discussed earlier in this chapter. However, the very timing and context of Donaldson's words is suggestive of a denial of the victim – Finucane – and is illustrative of how unionist hierarchies of victimhood have translated into hierarchies of truth and justice (Cohen 2001). Grounded in an exclusive interpretation of victimhood, the resulting 'truth as trumps' dynamic in this example is illustrative of how the contest over the definition of a victim is a driver for victim mobilisation efforts and (partial) attitudes towards truth and justice initiatives.

## 2.5 VICTIMHOOD, AGENCY, AND INCLUSIVITY

In contrast to unionist victims' groups, an inclusive conceptualisation of victimhood that prioritises the commonality of grief and rejects hierarchies of victimhood has been supported

[11] Finucane, a solicitor, was killed at home by members of the loyalist paramilitary group the Ulster Defence Association (UDA) in February 1989. Collusion has long been alleged between members of the UDA and the Army Force Research Unit, Royal Ulster Constabulary Special Branch and MI5. The family have long campaigned for a public inquiry: www.gov.uk/government/speeches/statement-by-the-secretary-of-state-for-northern-ireland-on-the-murder-of-patrick-finucane.

by nationalist and republican victims' groups (see, for example, Pat Finucane Centre 2018; Relatives for Justice 2020). As I explore here, this approach to victimhood has informed their approaches to group organisation and mobilisation and advocacy for truth, justice, and material and symbolic reparations (Wilson and Brown 2009).

Inclusivity serves two purposes. First, it has allowed nationalist and republican victims' groups to reject the idea of hierarchies of victimhood and a calibration of victimhood based only on the allocation of innocence and guilt. The Pat Finucane Centre (2018, 6), an advocacy group working in the nationalist and republican community, for example, has argued that the definition of a victim in the Victims and Survivors (Northern Ireland) Order 2006 should be maintained as 'it reflects the wide-ranging and complex nature of the conflict'. In the opinion of Relatives for Justice (2020, 6), one of the largest victims' groups in the nationalist and republican community, 'It is morally inept to advocate for a distinction of victimhood in favour of one political outlook to another; it consists of a calculation of suffering through the lens of an individual's own narrative of the conflict.'

Second, advocating for an inclusive definition of victimhood and the rejection of hierarchies of victimhood speaks to groups' efforts to highlight the criminalisation of members of the nationalist and republican community and emphasise the fact that institutional discrimination under the Stormont regime, oppressive policing, and 'occupation' by the British army was a source of victimisation for the nationalist and republican community (see, for example, Allmand, Harvey, and Burton 2020; Ní Aoláin 2000). This perspective has also allowed groups to expand their campaigning efforts to include the victimisation of those who would ordinarily be considered 'guilty victims' – members of armed groups, principally the Provisional IRA who were injured or killed by State forces, other paramilitary groups, or during incarceration. Highlighting the situational nature of violence and the different roles that people can assume at different times speaks to the existence of the 'complex political victim' – the victim 'who is no longer chained to characteristics of complete innocence and purity but remains a victim nonetheless' (Bouris 2007, 10). As discussed earlier, this approach to victimhood has been fundamental to the restoration of the dignity of such victims and their families and has led to the creation of important communities of solidarity.

Against this backdrop, since their inception in the 1980s and early 1990s, much of the public-facing work of victims' groups working in nationalist and republican communities has been orientated towards seeking truth and justice for those victims who were killed by British state forces during the Northern Ireland conflict. The contrast between the two opposing registers of victimhood in which victimhood is expressed and in which mobilisation efforts take place in Northern Ireland is thus immediately apparent. This work has played out in relation to individual deaths and specific atrocities and in respect to campaigning for a comprehensive truth recovery process. For example, from the 1970s onwards, and reflecting the dearth of official mechanisms for recovering truth and justice, nationalist and republican victims' groups mobilised to organise a series of 'bottom up' truth recovery inquiries into the deaths of members of the nationalist and republican community who were killed by British security forces in controversial contexts or where an element of collusion was alleged (Rolston 1996). More recently and backed by existing victims' groups, organisations such as the Bloody Sunday Truth and Justice Campaign and the Ballymurphy Massacre Campaign have successfully campaigned for truth and justice in respect to these individual atrocities where civilian members of the nationalist and republican community were unlawfully killed by British state forces.

At the time of writing, September 2025, nationalist and republican victims' groups have continued with specific advocacy campaigns, but have also invested significant energy into campaigning for a comprehensive process of justice and truth recovery and opposing the British government's efforts to close down the same. Passed by the then Conservative government in September 2023, the Northern Ireland Troubles (Legacy and Reconciliation) Act 2023 ended all conflict related investigations and legal proceedings, including civil actions, coronial inquests and historical investigations by the police and the Police Ombudsman for Northern Ireland on 1 May 2024.[12] While imperfect and incomplete, each of these mechanisms had been vital to providing some measure of truth and justice for victims and their families (Lawther 2025). The new mechanism of truth recovery, the Independent Commission for Reconciliation and Information Recovery (ICRIR) is mandated to carry out 'reviews' (not investigations) of deaths and other harmful forms of conduct that occurred during the conflict and produce 'final reports'. Aspects of the ICRIR's work have been found by the High Court in Belfast to be incompatible with the European Convention on Human Rights, including in respect to the need for Article 2 (the right to life and duty to investigate killings involving state actors) compliant investigations.[13]

In a series of public demonstrations against the legislation, Relatives for Justice have engaged in haunting and evocative pieces of street theatre that are designed to publicly highlighting the role of the British state during the conflict in Northern Ireland and cast shame on its failure to deliver on its internationally binding commitments to truth, justice, and accountability. Dressed in black suits and wearing white face masks, several of the group have carried a coffin marked 'Justice' while others have held placards designed to look like tombstones which read 'R.I.P. Justice', 'R.I.P. Victims Rights', 'R.I.P. Accountability', 'R.I.P. Rule of Law', 'R.I.P. Truth', 'R.I.P. Investigations', and 'R.I.P. Human Rights' (Lawther 2025). Victims holding pictures of their loved ones have been a visible presence at such rallies. That these campaigning efforts have placed emphasis on the importance of securing state accountability for its role in the conflict in Northern Ireland has reinforced the politics of victimhood and perpetuated division over truth and justice issues.

## 2.6 CONCLUSION

Using Northern Ireland as a case study, the chapter has demonstrated how victims' groups may mobilise and act as drivers and 'doers' of transitional justice in the absence of formal state-sanctioned processes of truth, justice, and reparations. While seeking to meet victims' needs and demands in respect to these variables, victims' groups are also crucial sites for the promotion of dignity and solidarity among group members. Yet, as the example of Northern Ireland also shows, victims' groups often compete for empathy on the basis of opposing conceptualisations of victimhood and differing drivers for truth and justice demands. As I have argued elsewhere, the moral economy of victimhood all too easily translates into competition over whose losses 'matter' the most and how efforts at transitional justice are perceived (Lawther 2025).

While not downplaying the remarkable achievements of victims' groups in Northern Ireland or the extent of their support for victims and survivors of the conflict, over the course of the peace process, two countervailing dynamics have emerged. First, the competing 'repertoires of victimhood' – victimhood as innocence and victimhood as resistance – have reproduced politicised notions of victimhood, which has, on occasion, contributed to rhetoric and practice that denies the victimhood of 'the other' (de Waardt 2016). It has also seen victims and

12 www.legislation.gov.uk/ukpga/2023/41.

13 *Dillon* [2024] NIKB 11.

their needs used to leverage political demands (Lawther 2025). Particularly in the early stages of the peace process, certain victims' groups in Northern Ireland acted in a manner akin to Madlingozi's (2010) conceptualisation of the 'transitional justice entrepreneur', claiming to know and speak for victims in a way that was expressly political and far removed from victims' everyday needs. Second, and as discussed earlier, competition over the definition of a victim has punctuated, disrupted, and curtailed progress on a significant range of issues relating to attempts to respond to the needs of victims and deal with the legacy of the conflict. While both approaches to victimhood respond to the needs and wishes of victims and the approach and methods taken by groups in both communities may offer dignity and solidarity, as this case study of first-generation victims' groups demonstrates, without settled acceptance of or at least mechanisms in place to comprehensively deal with the legacy of a violent past, victims and their needs remain at risk of appropriation for political ends.

## REFERENCES


Allmand, Warren, Richard Harvey, and John Burton. 2020. 'I am Sir, You Are a Number': Report of the Independent Panel of Inquiry into the Circumstances of the H-Block and Armagh Prison Protests 1976–1981. Coiste na nIarchimí.

Aretxaga, Begoña. 1997. *Shattering Silence: Women, Nationalism and Political Subjectivity in Northern Ireland*. Princeton University Press.

Ashworth, Andrew. 2000. 'Victims' Rights, Defendants' Rights and Criminal Procedure'. In *Integrating a Victim Perspective within Criminal Justice: International Debates*, edited by Adam Crawford and Jo Goodey, pp. 185–204. Ashgate.

Baines, Erin. 2015. '"Today, I Want to Speak Out the Truth": Victim Agency, Responsibility, and Transitional Justice'. *International Political Sociology*, 9(4), 316–332. https://doi.org/10.1111/ips.12100

BBC. 2015. 'Spotlight'. BBC, 2 June. www.bbc.co.uk/programmes/b05xgmd7 (recording on file with author).

BBC. 2024. 'Finucane's Fight for Public Inquiry "A Long Journey"'. BBC, 11 September. www.bbc.co.uk/news/articles/cp35e2g254p0

Bouris, Erica. 2007. *Complex Political Victims*. Kumarian Press.

Breen-Smyth, Marie. 2012. *Injured in the Troubles: The Needs of Individuals and Their Families*. WAVE Trauma Centre.

Cohen, Stan. 2001. *States of Denial: Knowing about Atrocities and Suffering*. Polity Press.

Committee on the Administration of Justice. 2019. *Supplementary Written Evidence to Northern Ireland Affairs Committee Consultation on Stormont House Agreement (SHA) Inquiry*. Committee on the Administration of Justice.

Consultative Group on the Past. 2009. Report of the Consultative Group on the Past. Consultative Group on the Past.

Dawson, Graham. 2007. *Making Peace with the Past? Memory, Trauma and the Irish Troubles*. Manchester University Press.

de Waardt, Mijke de. 2016. 'Naming and Shaming Victims: The Semantics of Victimhood'. *International Journal of Transitional Justice*, 10(3), 432–450. https://doi.org/10.1093/ijtj/ijw011

de Waardt, Mijke de, and Sanne Weber. 2019. 'Beyond Victims' Mere Presence: An Empirical Analysis of Victim Participation in Transitional Justice in Colombia'. *Journal of Human Rights Practice*, 11(1), 209–228. https://doi.org/10.1093/jhuman/huz002

Durkheim, Émile. 2019. *Professional Ethics and Civil Morals*. Routledge.

Elwood, Sarah, and Katharyne Mitchell. 2012. 'Mapping Children's Politics: Spatial Stories, Dialogical Relations and Political Formation'. *Geografiska Annaler: Series B, Human Geography*, 94(1), 1–15. https://doi.org/10.1111/j.1468-0467.2012.00392.x

Ely Centre. 2020. *The Ely Centre Submission to the Northern Ireland Affairs Committee on Addressing the Legacy of Northern Irelands Past Monday 1st June 2020*. Ely Centre.

Families Acting for Innocent Relatives. 2007. 'Real Justice for Innocent Victims'. Families Acting for Innocent Relatives Press Release, 14 March. Copy on file with author.

Gallagher, Paul. 2021. 'New social movement theory and the reparations movement in Northern Ireland: The case if the WAVE Injured Group and its Campaign for Recognition'. PhD diss., Queen's University Belfast. Copy on file with author.

Golubović, Jelena. 2022.. 'Beyond Agency as Good: Complicity and Displacement after the Siege of Sarajevo'. *Journal of Refugee Studies*, 35(3), 1344–1363. https://doi.org/10.1093/jrs/feab096

Irish Independent. 2012. 'Troubles Victims Urge More Support'. *Irish Independent*, 17 May. www.independent.ie/news/troubles-victims-urge-more-support/26855164.html

Jeffrey, Laura, and Matei Candea. 2006. 'The Politics of Victimhood'. *History and Anthropology*, 17(4), 287–296. https://doi.org/10.1080/02757200600914037

Krystalli, Roxani. 2020. 'Attendance Sheets and Bureaucracies of Victimhood in Colombia'. *Journal of the Association for Political and Legal Anthropology*. Available at: https://tinyurl.com/3emztca6

Krystalli, Roxani, and Philipp Schulz. 2022. 'Taking Love and Care Seriously: An Emergent Research Agenda for Remaking Worlds in the Wake of Violence'. *International Studies Review*, 24(1), viac003. https://doi.org/10.1093/isr/viac003

Lawther, Cheryl. 2014. *Truth, Denial and Transition: Northern Ireland and the Contested Past*. Routledge.

Lawther, Cheryl. 2022. 'Heroes and Hierarchies: The Celebration and Censure of Victimhood in Transitional Justice'. *The International Journal of Human Rights*, 26(3), 518–540. https://doi.org/10.1080/13642987.2021.1946038

Lawther, Cheryl. 2025. *Constructing Victimhood: Beyond Innocence and Guilt in Transitional Justice*. Oxford University Press.

Lundy, Patricia. 2009. 'Can the Past Be Policed? Lessons from the Historical Enquiries Team Northern Ireland'. *Journal of Law and Social Challenges*, 11, 109–156.

Madlingozi, Tshepo. 2010. 'On Transitional Justice Entrepreneurs and the Production of Victims'. *Journal of Human Rights Practice*, 2(2), 208–228. https://doi.org/10.1093/jhuman/huq005

McNabb, Johnny. 2024. 'Pat Finucane inquiry: "This has the impact of deeply hurting other families who have been denied any recourse to justice, truth and accountability" says SEFF director Kenny Donaldson'. Newsletter, 12 September. https://tinyurl.com/5h2hvxz9

Ní Aoláin, Fionnuala. 2000. *The Politics of Force: Conflict Management and State Violence in Northern Ireland*. Blackstaff Press Ltd.

Pat Finucane Centre. 2018. *Submission by the Pat Finucane Centre – Addressing the Legacy of Northern Ireland's Past*. Pat Finucane Centre.

Relatives for Justice. 2020. *Fulfilling Commitments: Proposals for a Programme of Reparations for the Bereaved Victims of the Conflict in Ireland*. Relatives for Justice.

Robins, Simon. 2017. 'Failing Victims? The Limits of Transitional Justice in Addressing the Needs of Victims of Violations'. *Human Rights and International Legal Discourse*, 11(1), 41–58.

Rolston, Bill. 1996. *Turning the Page without Closing the Book: The Right to Truth in the Irish Context*. Irish Reporter Publications.

South East Fermanagh Foundation. 2018. *Response to the Northern Ireland Office Consultation Paper 'Addressing the Legacy of Northern Ireland's Past'*. South East Fermanagh Foundation.

South East Fermanagh Foundation and Innocent Victims United. 2020. *Submission to the NIAC Consultation on the NIO Legacy Proposals* 2020. South East Fermanagh Foundation.

Starzyk, Katherine, Danielle Gaucher, Gregory Boese, and Katelin Neufeld. 2014. 'Framing Reparation Claims for Crimes against Humanity: A Social Psychological Perspective'. In *Reparations for Victims of Crimes against Humanity: The Healing Role of Reparation*, edited by Jo-Anne Wemmers, pp. 113–125. Routledge.

Ulster Human Rights Watch. 2018. Ulster Human Rights Watch Legacy Consultation Submission. NIO Consultation: Addressing the Legacy of Northern Ireland's Past. Ulster Human Rights Watch.

WAVE. 2009. *INJURED … on that Day*. WAVE Trauma Centre.

Williams, Paul, and Michael Scharf. 2002. *Peace with Justice: War Crimes and Accountability in the Former Yugoslavia*. Rowman and Littlefield.

Wilson, Richard, and Richard Brown. 2009. *Humanitarianism and Suffering: The Mobilization of Empathy*. Cambridge University Press.

# 3

# Victim Engagement in Reparations and the Role of Conflict-Related Classifications

*Thorsten Bonacker*

## 3.1 INTRODUCTION

Reparations are widely seen as a key mechanism for delivering justice to victims and survivors of armed conflicts, largely because they are a central priority for those directly affected (David 2017). Beyond material redress, reparations shape how victims perceive the legitimacy of a post-war order and influence their satisfaction with efforts to address past harms (de Greiff 2006, 454). While compensation was initially regulated at the interstate level in the context of the two world wars, it was the advocacy of victim groups that pushed reparations to the forefront of civil society mobilisation. So, the institutionalisation of an international victims' right to reparations is thus deeply rooted in the persistent activism of those directly affected, who, after World War II, demanded recognition and compensation for the harms they had endured (Torpey 2006).

Victim engagement has always related to a wide range of individual and collective, material and symbolic reparations, often emphasising the collective aspect of suffering. This chapter highlights material reparations such as monetary payments to compensate for past suffering, but also access to special support services such as in healthcare or education as they demonstrate that reparations are a political project (Moffett 2017, 381). This political dimension is expressed in the demands placed on a government, which then must decide politically on the establishment and implementation of reparations programmes. This is primarily because material reparations are costly for post-war governments, which are already in a difficult political and economic situation. They are closely tied to a balancing act over the allocation of scarce financial resources and the uncertain legitimacy of a post-war government. The use of costly resources in transitional justice can increase trust in the new government on the side of victimised groups (Kitagawa 2022). Therefore, demands for compensation and how they are handled are a genuine part of the political process of transitional justice and, in this regard, a central field of victim engagement after the end of violence and repression.

The chapter explores the opportunities and boundaries for victims to articulate and enforce claims for compensation and how these opportunities are shaped by social classifications of certain victim groups that arose during or prior to conflicts. I assume that governments are more likely to consider positively classified groups eligible for compensation as a means of enhancing governments' legitimacy. To illustrate this, the chapter will first show that reparations, as a central element of transitional justice, are often rooted in victim engagement. I then argue that victim engagement is shaped by the nature of the conflict, with social classifications of victim groups serving as a moderating factor. To illustrate this, the chapter analyses three distinct case studies, each representing a different type of conflict. However, these classifications are not fixed; as the transitional justice process unfolds, victims and survivors can actively reshape their classifications.

## 3.2 VICTIMS AS PROTAGONISTS IN REPARATION

Reparations are intended to restore the dignity of victims and compensate them for the suffering they have endured. Individuals and groups, by virtue of their recognised victim status, are the beneficiaries and recipients of reparations, while demands for reparations are primarily directed at states or governments (Moffett 2017). At the same time, victim groups often play a role in shaping these institutional reparations programmes within the context of second-generation victim engagement – for example, by disseminating information about compensation programmes or participating in the victim registration process, which typically precedes individual compensation (Rombouts 2004). Truth and Reconciliation Commissions (TRCs) play a pivotal role in this context. They typically include recommendations for reparations, which victim groups can leverage in their demands toward the government. At the same time, victim groups are often involved in the establishment and operational work of TRCs, though they may also critique these mechanisms (Bangura et al. 2023). However, this chapter takes a step back from the discussion on second-generation victim engagement, for example in TRCs and reparation programmes, and instead examines the factors that drive the emergence of such formal responses. It highlights the crucial role of first-generation victim engagement in this process, as it lays the groundwork for the establishment of administrative reparations programmes.

An important normative reference point for victim engagement in reparations is the international norm of compensating victims for their losses (Bonacker 2013, 2015). A milestone in this norm development was undoubtedly the adoption of the 'Basic Principles and Guidelines on the Right to a Remedy and Reparation for Victims of Gross Violations of International Human Rights Law and Serious Violations of International Humanitarian Law' (hereafter: Basic Principles) by the United Nations (UN) General Assembly in 2005. The international legal institutionalisation of a victim's right to reparations is also closely linked to the Statute of the International Criminal Court (ICC), which gives victim rights a prominent place (García-Godos 2008; van Boven 2013). The Basic Principles operate with a comprehensive understanding of reparations, which primarily aims to assert victims' rights to redress for human rights violations under international law (de Greiff 2006, 452). The reference to the Basic Principles allows victim groups to make their compensation demands heard. However, at the same time, it was victim engagement itself that was crucial to the international institutionalisation of this norm. As shown in norm research, such institutionalisation processes are closely linked to the activism of civil society actors who advocate for the concerns and interests of victims and survivors on the international stage (Sikkink 2011). Organisations working directly with survivors and victims of human rights violations have contributed to the development of the Basic Principles and other key UN documents through reports, testimonies, and hearings (UN Office of the High Commissioner for Human Rights 2008); at the same time, civil society actors representing victims' interests were central to the development of the Rome Statute of the ICC, with its comparatively strong victim focus and affirmation of the right to compensation (Lohne 2018; Törnquist-Chesnier 2007).

Victim groups and civil society organisations representing victim interests are not only protagonists of international norm development in the field of transitional justice and reparations.

They also act in national contexts, seeking to influence administrative reparations decisions even beyond the existence of commissions dealing with past violence. This is partly because victim status is also linked to the expectation of compensation for past wrongs, beyond the narrower scope of transitional justice. Thus, the entire history of demands for redress has been shaped not only by the demand for retribution, but also by the demand for compensation (Elster 2006). However, victim engagement does not take place in a neutral space, but is, as I will show, strongly influenced by the conflict, its causes, as well as its issues and the way it ends.

## 3.3 CONFLICT-RELATED VICTIM CLASSIFICATIONS

Research on transitional justice has repeatedly pointed out that previous conflicts shape the way in which violence is addressed in various ways (David 2017; Duhie and Seils 2017; Fletcher et al. 2009) and that certain tools for conflict resolution are not suitable for all types of conflict (Kostovicova 2019; Sriram and Ross 2007)[1]. It is therefore reasonable to assume that the conflict also influences the possibilities and conditions for victims to successfully demand reparations. In the following, I argue that these possibilities are heavily influenced by conflict-related social classifications, through which groups appear more or less attractive to a government for costly reparations programmes.

Social classifications are collectively shared concepts about groups that play a crucial role in determining their social status. They establish a symbolic order, providing a framework for navigating complex social realities. This symbolic order (re)produces social inequality by elevating or devaluing certain groups. These classifications are often reinforced through everyday actions, but they can also be actively promoted by specific actors or contested in struggles for recognition (Neckel 2003). When linked to demands for reparations from victim groups, these classifications become part of these broader struggles. Negative classifications generally restrict the agency and the ability of social groups to fulfil their needs (Neckel and Sutterlüty 2008, 16), whereas positive classifications enhance agency and increase the likelihood that their demands will be heard.

Social classifications shape how governments evaluate the demands of groups. In times of transitions, governments often face uncertain legitimacy. As a result, they are likely to evaluate costs based on the potential gains in legitimacy, particularly through performance legitimacy. This form of legitimacy arises when the government is perceived as more legitimate by providing welfare to specific groups in need, thereby demonstrating its ability to meet the population's essential needs (Dagher 2018). In this context, compensating positively classified victims becomes more appealing, as it can generate legitimacy gains by addressing the needs of specific groups. However, some victims belong to groups that are stigmatised by negative classifications within a symbolic order of inequality, making them less likely to be prioritised for compensation by governments. A key question for transitional justice is how these negative classifications are perpetuated in a post-conflict society.

Classifications can be either gradual or categorical (Neckel and Sutterlüty 2008). Gradual classifications rank groups based on how much they conform to certain characteristics, creating a hierarchical structure where groups with fewer traits are devalued. In contrast, categorical classifications make qualitative judgements about groups, often based on ascriptive characteristics such as sex, religion, or ethnicity, leading to mutually exclusive evaluations.

[1] The following analysis is based on research conducted in collaboration with Pia Falschebner, Eva Willems, and Kim Baudewijns as part of a project on the reparations policies of victim organisations, funded by the German Research Foundation.

To illustrate the influence of conflict-related social classifications in the context of victim engagement for reparations, in the following I discuss three different case studies on administrative reparations, each corresponding to distinct conflict profiles. This highlights how conflicts shape the classifications of victim groups, thereby affecting their chances of successfully demanding compensation from governments. Since international conflicts primarily differ from internal conflicts in terms of international law and the issue of reparations, the following discussion focuses exclusively on the latter. Three factors can be distinguished when trying to ideal-typically differentiate the nature of internal armed conflicts: (a) the issue of the conflict and (b) the way the conflict was ended. In addition, (c) structural causes of the conflict or the social fabric of the society that experienced armed conflict, play an important role, as they categorise certain groups in a particular, usually negative, manner. It is important to recognise that victim classifications are never determined by a single factor alone but rather by a combination of influences.

Regarding the issue of the conflict, internal conflicts are typically categorised into those that revolve around the control of a specific territory and those that aim for control of the government (Pettersson et al. 2021). The first case includes conflicts over the secession of a state-controlled area (secessionist conflicts) or for increased autonomy in a region (autonomy conflicts). The second case involves conflicts where the authority of a government is contested and challenged with violence (anti-regime conflicts). Even if we assume that armed conflicts are either about territory or government control, identity or intergroup conflicts can play a role to varying degrees. Research on genocides, for example, has shown that genocidal violence, which is always linked to identity constructions as group-based violence, is typically associated with violent conflicts within states (Kiernan 2007). In terms of dealing with past violence, it is crucial whether identity conflicts were a central component of internal conflicts and whether certain groups were particularly affected by violence. In this regard, internal conflicts can be differentiated depending on whether they revolve around territory or political power and to what extent identity conflicts were a central component of these conflicts and the predominantly one-sided violence committed within them. Identity-based conflicts make it more likely that victim groups will be classified categorically, based on ascribed characteristics.

Whether this is associated with positive or negative classifications is closely linked to the way in which a conflict terminates. Armed conflicts can end in different ways, such as through a peace agreement between the parties involved or through the victory of one party. Research shows that the way a conflict ends has a significant influence on transitional justice (Gurses et al. 2008). If conflicts end with the victory of one party, it is likely that the legitimacy of the new government relies on this victory and associated heroic narratives. If it ends in a compromise and later involves the conflict parties in government, the conditions for victim groups fundamentally change, as it is likely that reparations claims will be oriented along the old conflict lines, and reparations are viewed as divisible, meaning that both sides – or alternatively, neither side – would receive compensation. The end of conflicts can also more or less involve international support, such as international mediation of peace agreements and corresponding arrangements for post-war justice. Here, it can be assumed that international actors particularly align with international norms and prioritise the right to compensation.

Even when international actors push for reparations and governments consider certain victim groups suitable for compensation, negative classifications often persist. This continuity is rooted in the ongoing marginalisation of certain groups, whose negative classification, and thus their low social status, is deeply embedded in the social fabric and frequently outlasts the conflict itself. While liberal transitional justice approaches assume that post-war state-building entails structural reforms, research has shown that societal continuities tend to be more enduring than expected (Sriram 2007; Olarte and Franzki 2013).

I will now illustrate how different types of conflict moderate the ways in which the nature of a conflict shapes the opportunities and conditions for victim groups to demand material reparations from the government. To do so, I will examine three distinct conflicts, each characterised by a unique combination of conflict issues, modes of termination, and the persistence of social stratification. These variations result in different types of conflicts preceding transitional justice, in which victims have received administrative reparations.

## 3.4 CASE STUDIES

The following case studies illustrate how conflict-related classifications impact victim groups' opportunities when claiming reparations. They also highlight that, to some extent, these groups have contributed to shaping reparation programmes and the surrounding debates, particularly by discursively challenging the prevailing classifications to which they are assigned.

### 3.4.1 *Guatemala*

The thirty-six-year-long civil war in Guatemala represents an anti-regime conflict that was resolved in 1996 through an internationally mediated peace agreement between the government and the leftist guerrilla group Guatemalan National Revolutionary Unity (Unidad Revolucionaria Nacional Guatemalteca), which was led by ethnic minorities of the Maya Indigenous people as well as Ladino farmers. At the same time, the violence was marked by identity-based, one-sided, and genocidal violence against the Indigenous population. In 2003, the Guatemalan government established the National Reparations Programme (Programa Nacional de Resarcimiento, PNR) to compensate victims of severe human rights violations in the context of the armed conflict. This followed recommendations in the Truth Commission report, which also addressed the structural causes of the violent conflict, including deeply rooted racism against Indigenous groups and the extreme inequality in land distribution. Victim groups such as the more urban Group for Mutual Support (Grupo de Apoyo Mutuo) and the more rural National Coordination of Widows of Guatemala (Confederación Nacional de Viudas de Guatemala) were key protagonists in the debate surrounding reparations before and during the establishment of the PNR (Green 1999; Martínez and Gómez 2019; Simon 1984). They are part of a broad, often locally operating civil society in Guatemala, which played an active role, particularly in place-based transitional justice approaches (Destrooper and Parmentier 2018).

The creation of the PNR was also driven by constant and broad advocacy from civil society and victim groups, who drew on the international norm of victim compensation and previous recommendations from other commissions addressing violence in Guatemala, such as the Commission for Historical Clarification. Three years before the establishment of the PNR, around ninety victim and human rights groups formed the Multi-Institutional Instance for Peace and Concord (Instancia Multiinstitucional por la Paz y la Concordia) to present collective demands to the state for the implementation of the peace agreement. They negotiated the framework of the reparations policy. The reparations programme thus directly reflects the agency and demands of victims as protagonists (Mejía Bonifazi 2022), who were meant to participate in the form of a Victims' Consultative Council at the PNR. However, this was never implemented by the government, leaving victim groups reliant on informal mechanisms. Especially in the context of budget cuts to the PNR, victim groups consistently raised their voices, demanding full implementation of reparations. Activism eventually led to an increase in the budget, thus being somewhat successful in this specific regard (Impunity Watch et al. 2021).

The reparations policy of the PNR included, among other things, economic compensation, psychosocial support, and rehabilitation measures. After more than fifteen years, the PNR had compensated 32,802 victims (Martínez and Gómez 2019, 16). The reparations covered various forms of violence: forced disappearance, extra-judicial executions, physical and psychological torture, forced displacement, forced recruitment, sexual violence, violence against children, massacres, and human rights violations through arbitrary attacks as well as (attempted) arbitrary executions. Notably, the PNR rejected compensation claims from women who had suffered sexual violence, deeming their accounts as uncredible (Martínez and Gómez 2019, 23). Compensation payments within the PNR are explicitly not made to former members of the military or armed groups. However, there has been an intense public debate in Guatemala regarding possible reparations for paramilitaries, as they were often forcibly recruited but also committed crimes against the civilian population. Since 2003, various governments have promised reparations for paramilitaries, some of which have been partially implemented since 2005.

The reparations decisions within the PNR are clearly based on positive classifications of certain victim groups, which the government considered ideal recipients for compensation. The government largely followed the recommendations of the Commission for Historical Clarification and compensated those victims who can be seen as moral exemplars. Since the conflict in Guatemala ended with a peace agreement, the government would have risked losing legitimacy, especially in the eyes of the international community, if it had made a categorical distinction between victim groups, differentiating between innocent, civilian, and other victims. A categorical distinction of victims would have undermined the inclusive character of the peace agreement and raised the question of whose victims mattered more.

In Guatemala, paramilitaries have been seen from the outset as complex victims, which is why they only came into focus for compensation when the government could be relatively sure of its legitimacy or when, during a massive mobilisation of former members of the Civil Defence Patrols (Patrullas de Autodefensa Civil) it had to fear a loss of legitimacy. Two observations from the PNR analyses particularly highlight the persistence of negative classifications. On one hand, categorical gender-specific negative classifications from the conflict context continued, leading to women who were victims of sexual violence, despite their seemingly ideal victim status, receiving reparations less frequently. On the other hand, the armed conflict was characterised by a high degree of genocidal violence against Indigenous peoples, which was based on collective notions of inferiority. The fact that victims from this group were compensated far less frequently points to the continuity of categorical classifications that prevent certain victim groups from receiving reparations (Brett and Malagón 2020, 10). The organisational design of the PNR, which made it difficult for Indigenous groups to prove their victim status, for example through presenting birth or death certificates, also contributed to this (Martínez and Gómez 2019, 24).

Although in the case of Guatemala the focus of the gradual classification of victim roles initially lay on particularly vulnerable groups, the PNR largely ignored the specific needs of Indigenous groups such as the Maya (Aldana 2013; García-Godos 2018, 42) as well as the linguistic challenges in translating PNR terminology into local languages and cultural contexts. Instead of a collective compensation for indigenous groups, individual compensation was initially preferred (Viaene 2010). This is not least due to the fact that the public discussion about

Guatemala's violent past is still highly polarised today, along both identity-based and class-based divides. In the case of groups affected by genocidal violence, the government apparently did not expect to gain legitimacy by addressing and compensating negatively viewed groups.

### 3.4.2 *Timor-Leste*

The conflict in Timor-Leste ended in 1999 with a victory for the Timorese resistance over the Indonesian occupation. At its core, it was an anti-colonial, secessionist conflict about the territory's affiliation with Indonesia or its independence, decided through a referendum conducted by the UN. As part of the transition, the country was administered by the UN. With independence, a Truth and Reconciliation Commission (Comissão de Acolhimento, Verdade e Reconciliação, CAVR) was established to deal with the violent past and the related serious human rights violations between 1974 and 1999. The CAVR report spans 2,000 pages and includes, in addition to a comprehensive review of the events, recommendations for reparations, with a focus on community-based reconciliation (Evans 2012, 191–193; Ottendörfer 2016, 125–142). However, recommendations have not been implemented to this day. The main reason for this was the ongoing resistance from the political leadership, which has only recently begun to subside. The lack of compensation for victims stands in stark contrast to the veterans' pensions, which play a central role in Timor-Leste's social security system (Roll 2018).

Administrative decisions that disregard the recommendations are clearly connected to the decisive outcome of a prolonged secessionist independence conflict. The nation-building process since independence has been strongly focused on the positively evaluated resistance movement, from which the governments have also been recruited. Accordingly, governments primarily relied on the national popularity of the successful resistance to support their legitimacy. Therefore, there was little reason for the government to seek victims whose compensation could promise political legitimacy. Victim groups such as the Association of Ex-Political Prisoners (Associação dos Servidores do Estado de Timor-Leste) or the 12 November Committee, named after the Santa Cruz Massacre in 1991, reinforce the heroic narrative surrounding the resistance movement because they were generally also members of that movement. A significant factor is that the categorical distinction between Indonesian occupiers and the Timorese resistance aligns more with the demands of reconciliation-oriented transitional justice, as it overshadows internal Timorese divisions, particularly between resistance members and collaborators.

Both victim and human rights organisations, as well as the CAVR and its rehabilitation programme, focus primarily on victims of sexual violence and particularly vulnerable groups, using gradual classifications that correspond to varying levels of vulnerability. After the CAVR's mandate ended, various civil society groups continued this focus on vulnerable groups in their advocacy for reparations, including the Chega! Association for Us (Asosiasaun Chega! Ba Ita, ACbit), which successfully demanded support from the Ministry for Social Solidarity (Cross 2021, 155). Timorese victim organisations, human rights groups, and individual parliamentarians have repeatedly tried to bring the issue of reparations into parliament, building on the CAVR's reparations recommendations. In 2009, they initially succeeded: two draft laws addressing the violence between 1974 and 1999 were discussed in parliament. However, they were ultimately rejected. There was no agreement on which victims should receive reparations, as the official narrative claimed that all Timorese were victims. The lack of categorical classification favoured rejection, as on the one hand reparations were deemed too costly and, on the other hand, could no longer be passed as such because they would benefit not specific victim groups, but all citizens, thus aligning more with a general state welfare policy (Cross 2021, 154).

In addition to the absence of categorical classifications on the part of the victims, a continuity of negative classifications of women is striking. Narratives of victims and heroes in Timor-Leste are not only gendered, but also reproduce the lower social status of women (Rothschild 2017). This is reflected in the corresponding role distribution within the Timorese resistance, where fighting men and supporting women were valued differently. As a result, it is primarily the male members of the armed resistance who receive state benefits, while the clandestine resistance, in which women were involved, is marginalised (Kent and Kinsella 2015; Kent and Wallis 2014, 1).

Demands for reparations never fully subsided after the end of the CAVR and have, over time, even gained visibility. This eventually led to the establishment of the successor institution to the CAVR, the National Chega! Center (Centro Nacional Chega!, CNC), in 2016, which is subordinate to the prime minister and thus holds significant political influence. The establishment was triggered by a conference organised by victim and human rights groups, during which the then Prime Minister Araujo met with Timorese 'stolen children' who had been abducted to Indonesia. Interestingly, the Decree-Law of the CNC and its framework replaced the term 'victim' with that of 'survivor' and also avoided using the term 'reparations' (Cross 2021: 156). The CNC is tasked with working with non-governmental organisations (NGOs) and the government to implement certain recommendations from the CAVR, including material reparations, primarily health-related services and psychological support. Again, a gradual classification of victims is applied, focusing on the groups with the greatest vulnerability. Victim engagement remains shaped by the absence of categorical classifications in favour of a national unity discourse closely linked to the way in which the conflict ended.. The conflict type offers few opportunities for categorical distinctions between victims and thus limits the possibilities for making reparations claims.

### 3.4.3 *Northern Ireland*

In Northern Ireland, the violent conflict – similar to Guatemala – ended with a peace agreement, the Good Friday Agreement, in 1998. It resulted in permanent power-sharing between nationalists and unionists. As in Timor-Leste, territorial questions were at the centre of the conflict, although in Northern Ireland, these were more strongly charged with identity politics than in Timor-Leste.

The processing of the civil war remains, to this day, marked by a politicisation of victimhood and essentially mirrors the conflict lines of the civil war (Fay et al. 1999). Administrative definitions of victims regularly face resistance. The public debate around victimhood continues to focus on the question of whether perpetrators can also be victims, and who the 'real' victims of the conflict are. Many Northern Irish parties have their own definitions of victimhood. The politicisation strongly affects decisions on reparations. This was evident in the public responses to the report from the Consultative Group on the Past, which was set up in 2008 to propose comprehensive measures for addressing violence and conflict. Of the thirty recommendations, only one referred to material compensation for survivors. Despite a range of different compensation schemes, Northern Ireland still lacks a comprehensive reparations strategy because the debate remains highly politicised. Many victim compensations are still paid through court rulings, such as the large compensations granted in 2018 to the victims of the Bloody Sunday massacre.

The most important administrative compensation body for a long time was the Compensation Agency, which compensated victims on request based on the Northern Ireland Criminal

Injuries Compensation Scheme. This system avoids political charge by treating applicants as victims of crime rather than political violence and excludes members of armed groups. The Northern Ireland Troubles-related Incident Victims' Payment Scheme of 2020 introduced conflict-related compensation for individuals who suffered serious and lasting physical or psychological injuries because of civil war violence. However, individuals who have inflicted harm on themselves through their own fault are excluded, though it remains unclear how broadly this exclusion will be interpreted by the Victims' Payments Board. Those formally excluded are currently only those who have been legally convicted for crimes related to the Troubles.

Reparations in Northern Ireland 'is a "dirty word", rarely invoked and advocated for' (Moffett 2020, 4). This is largely because reparations claims are seen as part of the still ongoing conflict and thus offer no legitimacy to the government, or at best only highly group-specific legitimacy. In the case of Northern Ireland, victims are initially categorised either as victims of one or the other side of the conflict. This is obviously closely linked to the conflict dynamics of an identity-based territorial conflict that ended with a peace agreement and a power-sharing agreement. Constructions of victimhood largely reproduce the conflict lines. This results in reparations that either operationally address certain groups more or less exclusively or idealise victims of violence by treating them as victims of criminal acts rather than political violence. The exclusion of members of armed groups from compensation measures underscores this.

However, the Victims' Payment Scheme compensates victims of political violence as such for the first time. Although there were already social service programmes for survivors of political violence before, these were generally not understood or discussed as reparations (Moffett 2020). NGOs and victim organisations played an important role in the introduction, particularly the WAVE Trauma Centre, which was a driving force behind the campaign for compensation payments. Other state or civil society organisations, such as Relatives for Justice and The Commission for Victims and Survivors, which represent or include victim interests, were also involved in the consultations and political debates around the Victims' Payment Scheme. By restricting compensation to victims who suffered serious injuries and were not convicted for crimes related to the Troubles, it ensures that perpetrators and victims can be categorically distinguished. Here, gradual classification systems come into play, based either on the severity of the injury or on the victims' needs. In any case, these are group-specific victim identities, whose compensation, however, again offers no prospect of legitimacy for the government. On the contrary: one-sided reparations for victims under power-sharing conditions would lead to a legitimacy crisis. However, since both sides have a responsibility to compensate 'their' victims, group-specific victim organisations are used for this purpose within national reparations programmes.

## 3.5 CONCLUSION

Material compensation for victims is based on victim engagement in multiple ways. First, victim groups often refer to an international norm of the right to compensation, as expressed in the Basic Principles and the Rome Statute of the ICC. The international institutionalisation of this norm, which informs formal transitional justice mechanisms such as reparations programmes, has primarily come about through the transnational mobilisation of victim groups. Second, administrative reparations decisions by governments generally follow, though in a very selective manner, recommendations from truth and reconciliation commissions. Both prior to and following these commissions, organisations representing victim interests play a central role. As a result, governments are continuously confronted with commission recommendations that generally have high national and international legitimacy. The demands of victims and the mobilisation of victim interests are heavily shaped by the type of previous conflict, that is, its subject matter and the manner in which it ended, as well as the continuation of a symbolic order tied to the structural causes of the conflict. These variables shape the classification of victims and the context in which victims articulate their claims. For instance, as a direct consequence of how the conflict over a common territory ended, the absence of categorical victim semantics in Timor-Leste complicates the demands for reparations for certain groups. In Northern Ireland, on the other hand, the persistence of categorical classifications, closely linked to the identity-based nature of the conflict and the type of peace agreement, means that there are few general reparations measures. In Guatemala, as in Timor-Leste, continuities of negative classifications of certain marginalised groups are observed, making reparations policies less attractive for governments. In contrast, the fact that the conflict was state-driven facilitated reparations claims insofar as certain groups could define their victim status, specifically as victims of state and paramilitary violence. This categorical classification also allowed for holding the state accountable.

Thus, classifications play a significant role in how reparations claims can be articulated. However, they are not set in stone and can be altered by the victims themselves. For instance, victim groups may choose to highlight universalist language, such as in the context of human rights discourses, instead of emphasising specific group identities tied to victimhood. Not coincidentally, in many cases of compensation claims, alliances between human rights groups and victim groups are observed, especially where collective identities of victim groups are not divided by the conflict. In Timor-Leste, for example, there is a very close connection between victim and human rights groups, not least to counter the heroic narrative and the accompanying preference for veterans.

Another way to change classifications is through what Rancière (1992) calls 'disidentification', that is, resistance against the prevailing categories through which people are assigned to political or social structures. Here, victim engagement in reparations evidently moves into its third generation, as activism now targets the prevailing victim categories, which are reinforced by existing transitional justice mechanisms. In Rancière's terms, hegemonic identity categories are broken to create new forms of political recognition and agency, such as by rejecting fixed identities or replacing them with new ones that allow for political subjectivities beyond entrenched conflict lines. In Northern Ireland, for example, this applies to organisations working towards the recognition of the diversity of experiences – especially gendered experiences – individuals and groups had during the Troubles (Daşlı and Murphy 2023). In a certain sense, it can be said that in Timor-Leste, local memory practices and the associated victim identity equated to a rejection of the hegemonic heroic narrative (Kent 2011). This rejection opened up the possibility for articulating victim interests that were largely ignored by the government in favour of focusing on veterans and reconciliation with Indonesia. In Guatemala, various studies have shown that a number of groups do not fit into the typical victim identities fixed within the transitional justice process, challenging assumptions of homogeneous victim identities, and that particularly at the local level, complex experiences are articulated that cannot simply be projected onto identities within transitional justice (Willard 2022).

Finally, time also plays a role in changing classifications. A government's need for legitimacy can either diminish or increase over time, thus opening up new opportunities for victims to make reparations claims because they may find it easier to re-code classifications. The complexity of victimhood and the question of whether 'guilty victims' (Moffett 2015) should be compensated can, as shown by the cases of Guatemala and Northern Ireland, develop in different ways over time, bringing forth new victim classifications and potentially making claims for compensation by former paramilitaries or fighters from the opposing side seem more legitimate.

Thus, the political space in which reparations claims are articulated is always characterised by classification struggles in which the recognition and disregard of social groups are negotiated. These classification struggles are always also struggles over the power to interpret (Bourdieu 1989; Neckel and Sutterlüty 2008, 17) – including the interpretation of what defines a victim entitled to compensation.

## REFERENCES


Aldana, Raquel. 2013. 'A Reflection on Transitional Justice in Guatemala 15 Years after the Peace Agreements'. In *Victims of International Crimes: An Interdisciplinary Discourse*, edited by Thorsten Bonacker and Christoph Safferling, pp. 297–316. T.M.C. Asser Press. https://doi.org/10.1007/978-90-6704-912-2_18

Bangura, Ibrahim, Kate Lonergan, and Anders Themnér. 2023. 'Patrimonial Truth-Telling: Why Truth Commissions Leave Victim and Ex-Combatant Participants Aggrieved'. *Journal of Intervention and Statebuilding*, 17(4), 371–393. https://doi.org/10.1080/17502977.2023.2187135

Bonacker, Thorsten. 2013. 'Global Victimhood. On the Charisma of the Victim in Transitional Justice Processes'. *World Political Science Review*, 9(1), 97–129.

Bonacker, Thorsten. 2015. 'The Inclusion of Victims and the Globalization of Criminal Law'. In *From Globalization to World Society. Neo-Institutional and Systems-Theoretical Perspectives*, edited by Boris Holzer, Fatima Kastner, and Tobias Werron, pp. 107–127. Routledge.

Bourdieu, Pierre. 1989. 'Social Space and Symbolic Power'. *Sociological Theory*, 7(1), 14–25. https://doi.org/10.2307/202060

Boven, Theo van. 2013. 'Victim-Oriented Perspectives: Rights and Realities'. In *Victims of International Crimes: An Interdisciplinary Discourse*, edited by Thorsten Bonacker and Christoph Safferling, pp. 17–27. T.M.C. Asser Press. https://doi.org/10.1007/978-90-6704-912-2_2

Brett, Roddy, and Lina Malagón. 2020. *Realising Victims' Rights to Reparation, Truth and Justice in Guatemala in the Midst of a Zero-Sum Game*. Reparations, Responsibility and Victimhood in Transitional Societies. https://reparations.qub.ac.uk/assets/uploads/Guatemalan-Report-.pdf

Cross, Kyoko. 2021. 'The Pursuit of Justice, Truth, and Peace: Reflections on Twenty Years of Imperfect Transitional Justice in Timor-Leste'. *Asian Journal of Peacebuilding*, 9(1), 139–161. https://doi.org/10.18588/202105.00a176

Dagher, Ruby. 2018. 'Legitimacy and Post-Conflict State-Building: The Undervalued Role of Performance Legitimacy'. *Conflict, Security & Development*, 18(2), 85–111. https://doi.org/10.1080/14678802.2018.1447860

Daşlı, Güneş, and Emma Murphy. 2023. 'Moving beyond Binary Identities in Transitional Justice: Recognising the Complexity of Agency in Agonistic Spaces'. *The International Journal of Human Rights*, online first, 1–20. https://doi.org/10.1080/13642987.2024.2430288

David, Roman. 2017. 'What We Know about Transitional Justice: Survey and Experimental Evidence'. *Political Psychology*, 38(S1), 151–177. https://doi.org/10.1111/pops.12395

Destrooper, Tine, and Stephan Parmentier. 2018. 'Gender-Aware and Place-Based Transitional Justice in Guatemala: Altering the Opportunity Structures for Post-Conflict Women's Mobilization'. *Social & Legal Studies*, 27(3), 323–344. https://doi.org/10.1177/0964663917718050

Duthie, Roger, and Paul Seils, ed. 2017. *Justice Mosaics: How Context Shapes Transitional Justice in Fractured Societies*. Research Report, International Center for Transitional Justice. https://tinyurl.com/2s3kjh8e

Elster, Jon, ed. 2006. *Retribution and Reparation in the Transition to Democracy*. Cambridge University Press.

Evans, Christine. 2012. *The Right to Reparation in International Law for Victims of Armed Conflict*. Cambridge Studies in International and Comparative Law. Cambridge University Press.

Fay, Marie-Therese, Mike Morrissey, and Marie Smyth. 1999. *Northern Ireland's Troubles: The Human Costs*. Gardners Books.

Fletcher, Laurel E., Harvey M. Weinstein, and Jamie Rowen. 2009. 'Context, Timing and the Dynamics of Transitional Justice: A Historical Perspective'. *Human Rights Quarterly*, 31(1), 163–220.

Franzki, Hannah, and Maria Carolina Olarte. 2013. 'Understanding the Political Economy of Transitional Justice: A Critical Theory Perspective'. In *Transitional Justice Theories*, edited by Susanne Buckley-Zistel et al., pp. 201–221. Routledge.

García-Godos, Jemima. 2008. 'Victim Reparations in Transitional Justice – What Is at Stake and Why'. *Nordisk Tidsskrift for Menneskerettigheter* 26 (2): 111–130.

García-Godos, Jemima. 2018. 'Victims and Victimhood in Reparation Programs: Lessons from Latin America'. In *The Politics of Victimhood in Post-Conflict Societies*, edited by Vincent Druliolle and Roddy Brett, pp. 25–51. Palgrave.

Green, Linda Buckley. 1999. *Fear as a Way of Life: Mayan Widows in Rural Guatemala*. Columbia University Press.

Greiff, Pablo de, ed. 2006. *The Handbook of Reparations*. Oxford University Press.

Gurses, Mehmet, Nicolas Rost, and Patrick McLeod. 2008. 'Mediating Civil War Settlements and the Duration of Peace'. *International Interactions*, 34(2), 129–155. https://doi.org/10.1080/03050620802043362

Impunity Watch, Christalla Yakinthou, and Manal Sarrouf. 2021. *The Struggle for Truth and Justice in Guatemala: Victim and Survivor Participation in Informal Transitional Justice Processes*. Accessed 14 March 2025. https://tinyurl.com/3934j9c6

Kent, Lia. 2011. 'Local Memory Practices in East Timor: Disrupting Transitional Justice Narratives'. *International Journal of Transitional Justice*, 5(3), 434–455. https://doi.org/10.1093/ijtj/ijr016.

Kent, Lia, and Joanne Wallis. 2014. *Timor-Leste's Veterans' Pension Scheme: Who Are the Beneficiaries and Who Is Missing Out?* ANU Dept. of Pacific Affairs (DPA) Formerly State, Society and Governance in Melanesia (SSGM) Program Working Papers, https://doi.org/10.25911/5f20073ef001b

Kent, Lia, and Naomi Kinsella. 2015. 'A Luta Kontinua (The Struggle Continues)'. *International Feminist Journal of Politics*, 17(3), 473–494. https://doi.org/10.1080/14616742.2014.913383

Kiernan, Ben. 2007. *Blood and Soil: A World History of Genocide and Extermination from Sparta to Darfur*. Yale University Press.

Kitagawa, Risa. 2022. 'From Political Violence to Political Trust? How Transitional Justice Affects Citizen Views of Government'. *International Studies Quarterly*, 67(1), 1–13. https://doi.org/10.1093/isq/sqad013

Kostovicova, Denisa. 2019. 'Transitional Justice and Conflict Studies: Bridging the Divide'. *Journal of Global Security Studies*, 4(2), 273–278. https://doi.org/10.1093/jogss/ogz003

Lohne, Kjersti. 2018. 'NGOs for International Justice: Criminal or Victims' Justice?' In *The Judicialization of International Law: A Mixed Blessing?* edited by Andreas Follesdal and Geir Ulfstein, Oxford University Press, online edition. Accessed 11 March 2025. https://doi.org/10.1093/oso/9780198816423.003.0007

Martínez, Denis, and Luisa Gómez. 2019. 'Report: A Promise to Be Fulfilled: Reparations for Victims of the Armed Conflict in Guatemala'. Reparations, Responsibility & Victimhood in Transitional Societies. 8 August 2019. https://tinyurl.com/mr2v7pj4

Mejía Bonifazi, Gretel. 2022. 'Assessing the State of Reparations for the Victims of the Internal Armed Conflict in Guatemala: Shortcomings and the Outlook for the Future'. *Justice Visions* (blog). Accessed 11 March 2025. https://tinyurl.com/3f4ys5y3

Moffett, Luke. 2015. 'Reparations for "Guilty Victims": Navigating Complex Identities of Victim–Perpetrators in Reparation Mechanisms'. *International Journal of Transitional Justice*, 10(1), 146–167. https://doi.org/10/ggnq4b

Moffett, Luke. 2017. Transitional Justice and Reparations: Remedying the Past? In *Research Handbook on Transitional Justice*, edited by Cheryl Lawther, Luke Moffett, and Dov Jacobs, pp. 377–400. Edward Elgar.

Moffett, Luke. 2020. 'Struggling for Reparations in Northern Ireland'. In *Reparations for Victims of Genocide, War Crimes and Crimes against Humanity: Systems in Place and Systems in the Making. Second Revised Edition*, edited by Carla Ferstman and Mariana Goetz, pp. 678–709. Brill Nijhoff. https://brill.com/edcollbook/title/38931

Neckel, Sighard. 2003. 'Kampf um Zugehörigkeit: Die Macht der Klassifikation'. *Leviathan*, 31(2), 159–167.

Neckel, Sighard, and Ferdinand Sutterlüty. 2008. 'Negative Klassifikationen und die symbolische Ordnung sozialer Ungleichheit'. In *Mittendrin im Abseits*, edited by Sighard Neckel and Hans-Georg Soeffner, pp. 15–25. VS Verlag für Sozialwissenschaften. https://doi.org/10.1007/978-3-531-91157-1_2

Ottendörfer, Eva. 2016. *Die internationale Politik der Vergangenheitsaufarbeitung global-lokale Interaktion in Timor-Leste*. Nomos.

Pettersson, Therése, Shawn Davies, Amber Deniz, Garoun Engström, Nanar Hawach, Stina Högbladh, Margareta Sollenberg, and Magnus Öberg. 2021. 'Organized Violence 1989–2020, with a Special Emphasis on Syria'. *Journal of Peace Research*, 58(4), 809–825. https://doi.org/10.1177/00223433211026126

Rancière, Jacques. 1992. 'Politics, Identification, and Subjectivization'. *October*, 61, 58–64. https://doi.org/10.2307/778785

Roll, Kate. 2018. 'Street Level Bureaucrats and Post-Conflict Policy-Making: Corruption, Correctives, and the Rise of Veterans' Pensions in Timor-Leste'. *Civil Wars*, 20(2), 262–285. https://doi.org/10/gjsrnb

Rombouts, Heidy. 2004. *Victim Organisations and the Politics of Reparation: A Case-Study on Rwanda*. Intersentia.

Rothschild, Amy. 2017. 'Victims versus Veterans: Agency, Resistance and Legacies of Timor-Leste's Truth Commission'. *International Journal of Transitional Justice*, 11(3), 443–462. https://doi.org/10.1093/ijtj/ijx018

Sikkink, Kathryn. 2011. *The Justice Cascade: How Human Rights Prosecutions are Changing World Politics*. W. W. Norton & Co.

Simon, Jean-Marie. 1984. *Guatemala: The Group for Mutual Support*. SSRN Scholarly Paper. Rochester, NY. https://doi.org/10.2139/ssrn.2329201

Sriram, Chandra. 2007. 'Justice as Peace? Liberal Peacebuilding and Strategies of Transitional Justice'. *Global Society*, 21(4), 579–591. https://doi.org/10.1080/13600820701562843

Sriram, Chandra Lekha, and Amy Ross. 2007. 'Geographies of Crime and Justice: Contemporary Transitional Justice and the Creation of "Zones of Impunity"'. *International Journal of Transitional Justice*, 1(1), 45–65. https://doi.org/10.1093/ijtj/ijm001

Törnquist-Chesnier, Marie. 2007. 'How the International Criminal Court Came to Life: The Role of Non-governmental Organisations'. *Global Society*, 21(3), 449–465. https://doi.org/10.1080/13600820701417881

Torpey, John. 2006. *Making Whole What Has Been Smashed: On Reparations Politics*. Harvard University Press.

UN Office of the High Commissioner for Human Rights. 2008. Working with the United Nations Human Rights Programme. A Handbook for Civil Society. Accessed 11 March 2025. https://digitallibrary.un.org/record/653716/files/Handbook_en.pdf?ln=en

Viaene, Lieselotte. 2010. 'Life Is Priceless: Mayan Q'eqchi' Voices on the Guatemalan National Reparations Program'. *International Journal of Transitional Justice*, 4(1), 4–25. https://doi.org/10.1093/ijtj/ijp024

Willard, Emily. 2022. 'Beyond Transitional Justice: Learning from Indigenous Maya Mam Resistance in Guatemala'. *International Journal of Transitional Justice*, 15(3), 490–509. https://doi.org/10.1093/ijtj/ijab021

# 4

# Exploring Relational Agency in Collective Mobilisation for Justice

## *The Saturday Mothers Movement in Turkey*

*Güneş Daşlı*

### 4.1 INTRODUCTION

Although victim movements face growing challenges, including the rise of authoritarianism, increasing illiberal peace projects, and the failures of international mechanisms, they continue to organise, mobilise, and act globally, in diverse contexts such as Syria, Nepal, Sri Lanka, and Turkey. Such obstacles have led to greater resilience and innovation in victim-led mobilisation, for example, in developing new forms of agency and activism, expanding and leveraging networks, and employing a language and vocabulary that blends law and emotion. As several chapters in this book show, families of the disappeared, for instance, have sustained their justice claims over time (see Carrasco and Collins, Chapter 1) and often developed creative protest methods, including artistic performances (see Saeed, Chapter 19, and Ibrahim et al., Chapter 15). The examination of the case of the Saturday Mothers in Turkey in this chapter proves that victims have historically been the driving force behind both formal and informal transitional justice efforts. Victim movements thus continue to shape justice agendas from the ground up, and a closer examination of their mobilisation dynamics is essential for gaining a deeper understanding of genuine victim engagement in transitional justice.

In Turkey, the Saturday Mothers, the relatives of the disappeared in the context of Kurdish conflict, recently marked their 1,000th week of protest with a series of events to reaffirm their demands for justice. Despite police attacks, demonstration bans, the COVID-19 pandemic, and the continuation of the conflict, they remain steadfast in their struggle. In 2018, during their 700th-week demonstration, activist-relatives were taken into police custody, and the Galatasaray Square was subsequently closed to them and banned for protests. After persistently advocating for their right to return, they successfully held their 1,000th-week gathering at the square. Maside Ocak, a relative of the disappeared in the movement, described the experience of returning to the square for their weekly protests as feeling 'like I come to my home, as if I am visiting the gravesites of our beloved ones' (Gazete Duvar 2024).

This chapter employs the concept of relationality to examine victim agency in collective action, focusing on the phenomenon of enforced disappearances in the case of the Saturday Mothers in Turkey. Existing literature in relational sociology, feminist moral philosophy, and communitarian theory highlight that the political is relational (Baines 2015), and political agency is constructed and exercised within social networks and through interactions with others (Burkitt 2016). In the domain of transitional justice, relational understandings of agency have recently gained prominence as a critical lens for exploring the politics of victimhood, victim participation, and collective activism (Daşlı 2024; Kreft and Schulz 2022; Krystalli 2024). Expanding on this scholarship, I propose a relational model of agency as an analytical lens to better understand how agency is formed in collective actions and peer-group relationships and how victims open a social space for (re-)imaginations of justice. This chapter ultimately contributes to the under-explored nexus of victim participation and collective mobilisation in transitional justice, as it helps to explain the resilience of victims-protagonists demanding an institutional response in the face of apparent deadlock.

In line with the framework proposed in this handbook, this chapter views victim engagement not as confined to formal transitional justice mechanisms but as encompassing informal spaces led by victims and grassroots actors, extending beyond institutional frameworks. Such a view encourages us to think beyond engagement or participation in terms of numerical presence or as a procedural box-ticking exercise, and to consider the broader transitional justice ecosystem wherein victims act and mobilise (Selim 2017; Evrard et al. 2021). Within this ecosystem, victim movements and associations – sometimes in collaboration with professional human rights organisations – often begin organising and articulating demands for justice and truth long before formal peace settlements. They shape the complex transitional justice landscape by creating informal spaces, and by advocating for and engaging with formal mechanisms throughout different phases of political violence and transition. Through their sustained mobilisation, the Mothers of the Plaza de Mayo in Argentina, for example, gained the political and moral standing necessary to push international law to recognise enforced disappearance as a unique crime. Their collective mobilisation over generations has profoundly influenced the global transitional justice realm and inspired many families in other countries, including the Saturday Mothers. A closer examination of victim associations and movements reveals that their role extends far beyond merely interacting with or responding to the shortcomings of formal transitional justice processes. Rather, they are the architects of justice struggles, actively shaping and driving the evolution of the transitional justice landscape (Kovras 2017). Like many critical scholars working on victim participation in transitional justice, this chapter therefore takes victims' political agency as its starting point (Bhandari and Robins 2024; de Waardt and Weber 2019; Evrard et al. 2021).

Such an actor-oriented view requires an empathetic engagement with victims' experiences. As Desmet (2014) suggests, one must attempt to 'put oneself in the shoes' of those affected (Evrard et al. 2021, 429). However, this is an ambitious task, as victims' experiences and perceptions of justice are shaped by a complex interplay of identities, temporalities, spaces, forms of victimhood, and socialisation. To gain a deeper, more nuanced understanding, I adopt a relational model of agency to examine how organised victims construct internal relationships, develop shared values, and construct narratives that sustain and empower their justice-seeking efforts. This approach aligns with the idea of 'speaking nearby' rather than 'speaking about' – engaging closely (relationally) with the subject 'without seizing or claiming it' (Trinh T. Minh-ha quoted in Chen 1992, 87). It offers scholars and practitioners an analytical framework for understanding intersubjectivity among *indirect languages* of activism, storytelling, art, and literature projects for justice in conflict settings (Dasli 2024).

This relational lens provides key insights into how victims themselves shape participation within their organisations, actively creating spaces for empowerment and solidarity. A relational approach can thereby support the design of more victim-centred transitional justice processes by providing insights into how organised victims regain a sense of control, mitigate isolation, and articulate their own visions of justice within their socio-political environment.

My findings draw on twenty-two in-depth interviews conducted in 2021 and 2024 with grassroots actors,[1] including eight activists in the Saturday Mothers movement,[2] as well as extant academic and journalistic sources, informal conversations and participatory observations by spending time with activist relatives in the Human Rights Association (İnsan Hakları Derneği, IHD) İstanbul branch – where the movement is organised. The chapter begins by outlining its relational model of agency before introducing the Saturday Mothers. I then present my findings along two key themes: (a) the creation of social networks that foster empowerment and (b) the establishment of social spaces where victims advance their justice agenda and practise a form of justice. Finally, I discuss the relational model of agency which can be used as an analytical framework for enhancing meaningful victim participation in transitional justice.

## 4.2 RELATIONAL AGENCY, SOCIAL SPACES, AND AMBIGUOUS LOSS

In this chapter, political agency refers to capacities of acting and perceiving (Mackenzie 2019). The focus on political agency serves this chapter's twofold aim: unpacking (organised) victim agency and exploring the social space that victims create for justice within the transitional justice landscape. Drawing on the feminist concept of relational autonomy, I offer an analytical lens for analysing political agency in activism for justice. This concept emphasises the importance of social self and socialisation in agency-building processes, in which people renegotiate their values, perform multiple roles, and make meanings of life. Similarly, I view justice not as an abstract legal term but as socially and politically constructed value, underlining the notion that 'justice matters to people who are already in community with each other' (Held 2006, 102). I propose a relational agency model to analyse the work of victim movements mobilising around the crime of enforced disappearance. This embeds the chapter in broader debates about political agency, collective action, and transitional justice.

Relational autonomy challenges the individualistic view of agency, particularly the idealised concept of 'the autonomous man' embedded in Western culture (Mackenzie and Stoljar 2000, 38–39). This critique leads to the metaphysical critique that agents are socially constituted through the social relationships they are part of (Mackenzie and Stoljar 2000, 7). Relational autonomy criticises the individualistic feature of the liberal concept of agency and argues that people are not casually isolated from others and that people advance in relations. It centres social self in its inquiry without exclusion of individual self. It extends its inquiry from feminist care studies, which question the liberal emphasis on independence and self-autonomy. I find it useful to reflect on feminist scholars who highlight relational values – such as loyalty, caring, and friendship – rooted in interdependent relationships. While these

[1] Ethical approval for the PhD research feeding into this chapter was obtained from Friedrich Schiller Universität Jena, Ethikkommission der Fakultät für Sozial- und Verhaltenswissenschaften on 16 July 2021 and permission for the following fieldwork with the victim-activists in the Saturday Mothers was obtained on 18 June 2024.

[2] Those eight interviewees who were members of the Saturday Mothers, including two daughters of the mothers who initiated the movement in 1995, a spokesperson for the movement, and three members who have lived in other cities in the Kurdish region. They were mainly from the second generation consisting of sons and daughters. In accordance with ethical considerations, I anonymised their identities when citing them in the chapter and informed them of this process. I use the labels that they provided during the interviews – such as relative, IHD activist, or other self-identified roles. Since many did not prefer to identify as victims, I use this term only in reference to discussions in the literature. When discussing the Saturday Mothers in the text, I refer to them as family members, relatives or activists.

values are often devalued by liberal conceptions of agency, as they are traditionally associated with femininity (Mackenzie and Stoljar 2000, 9), they are essential to understanding the political agency of victims in the context of political violence. In this framework, relational autonomy also considers memory, imagination, emotional dispositions, and attitudes, which are often overlooked in liberal understanding of agency.

While I focus on informal (claimed) spaces to understand political agency from a relational lens, I prefer the concept of social space – a fluid, dynamic space shaped by social interactions. Social space is 'rooted in the processes of social interaction within specific temporal and spatial locations' (Liu 2024, 2). Drawing from relational sociology (Goffman 1971), it consists of three key elements: (a) actors, (b) spatial locations, and (c) the relationships between actors and spatial locations. The concept of social space also accounts for how emotions and perceptions shape physical spaces over time (Liu 2024). This lens helps me to analyse political agency with socialisation and spatial interactions, which provides a multilayered understanding of victims' agency-building processes.

Given my focus on phenomena of enforced disappearances, ambiguous loss theory provides another layer for understanding agency. Families experience ambiguous loss as an ongoing, chronic trauma, marked by 'a lack of information about the whereabouts or status of a loved one as absent or present, as dead or alive' (Boss 2007, 105). In the context of political violence, enforced disappearance is instrumentalised to terrorise not only families but also the broader oppressed community. The politics of ambiguous loss are inherently relational in their ripple effects, continuing to shape the oppressed socialisation for victims. Using this framework helps illuminate both the enduring emotional burdens of those left behind and the political threats they face, which shape broader social and political relations for victims. Despite its devastating psychological impact, ambiguous loss also fuels emotional motivations for collective mobilisation (Robins 2024). This framework further reveals how mobilised families resist the politics of ambiguous loss and the oppressive socialisation that leaves victims trapped in isolation, and how they can break through it by forging new political relationships.

## 4.3 SATURDAY MOTHERS MOVEMENT IN TURKEY

The Saturday Mothers (Dayikên Şemiyê in Kurdish, Cumartesi Anneleri in Turkish) is a victim-led movement initiated by the families of the forcibly disappeared in Turkey. The movement is the main actor seeking justice in the context of state violence. Despite the absence of transitional justice framework or a formal peace agreement, the Saturday Mothers propose a range of transitional justice measures such as legal accountability and guarantees of non-recurrence, and practices such as truth-seeking and memorialisation. On 27 May 1995, the group held its first gathering in Galatasaray Square, a prominent public location in Istanbul. Since then, the Saturday Mothers have staged weekly vigils and sit-ins, using powerful symbols to sustain their visibility. Inspired by the Mothers of the Plaza de Mayo in Argentina, they have carried out Turkey's longest-running mobilisation of civil disobedience.

Every Saturday at noon, families, along with human rights and feminist activists, sit in silence, holding photographs of their disappeared loved ones. Their protest centres around a banner with the slogan: 'The Perpetrators Are Known, Where Are the Disappeared?' (Failler Belli, Kayıplar Nerede?). Red carnations, symbolising the absence of graves, are placed on the banner and carried throughout the vigil. Each week, a different participant reads the story of a disappeared person before the protesters quietly disperse.

### 4.3.1 *Enforced Disappearance as a Crime of Lingering Harm*

International law recognises families of the disappeared as victims and captures the specificity of the crime thanks to the organised victims' dedicated struggle. The legal and institutional void of the 1980s initially left these crimes unaddressed, but victims' mobilisation eventually helped establish an international legal framework for enforced disappearances (Kovras 2017). Enforced disappearance is a uniquely insidious crime, causing multi-faceted harm. Beyond physical loss, it inflicts enduring psychological distress, fear, and isolation (Robins 2024). The clandestine nature of the crime fosters deep uncertainty, making closure impossible. In Turkey's context, in rare cases where families recover a body, they consider themselves 'fortunate' to at least have a grave. For many, however, the absence of remains leaves them trapped in prolonged grief – which one relative described as 'a never-healing wound'.[3]

This ambiguous loss creates an ongoing state of ambiguity, preventing families from fully engaging with the present. As one relative described: 'We are always on that day. Even if our hair turns white, even if our teeth fall out, even if our skin wrinkles, we are always on that day.'[4] The uncertainty forces them to exist in two opposing realities – clinging to hope that their loved one is alive while fearing they are dead.

This psychological limbo causes doubt and insecurity. Some families recount following strangers on the street, convinced they resemble their missing relatives (Korucu 2024, 82). Others feel uneasy in public, fearing they might unknowingly encounter their loved one's perpetrator.[5] These anxieties extend beyond individual trauma, shaping families' broader sense of safety and belonging in society. The emotional and social toll of ambiguous loss, in turn, fuels their collective mobilisation and commitment to seeking justice in public spaces.

### 4.3.2 *Relational Agency and Justice: Collective Activism, the Evolution of Justice Demands, and Social Space*

#### 4.3.2.1 *Constructing a New Social Network through Collective Mobilisation*

Social movements function as complex networks of individuals who share common values, attitudes, and (constructed) collective identities, linking them within various webs of exchange (Diani and McAdam 2003). The Saturday Mothers exhibit many characteristics of a social movement: they have a clear agenda, create rituals through their collective mobilisations (Can 2022), and share a common grief and experience of victimisation centred around enforced disappearances. They are organised in a non-hierarchical and horizontal manner, employing direct participation in the decision-making process to discuss issues related to gatherings, strategic decisions about protests, and official meetings with the governmental bodies.

Despite their diverse political, social, and economic backgrounds, the movement has persisted for three decades, sustained by transparent communication and direct participation.[6] From the outset, they have collaborated with IHD, exchanging knowledge on human rights activism and utilising its premises for meetings, public statements, and interviews. However, apart from this organic relationship with the IHD, the Saturday Mothers remain an independent movement. They lack legal status as an association and do not rely on external fundings, donors, or donations.

3 Relative of the disappeared, personal interview, conducted online, 24 September 2021.
4 Ikbal Eren, sibling of Hayrettin Eren, disappeared person, quoted in Korucu (2024, 78).
5 Relative of the disappeared, personal interview, conducted in Istanbul, 18 September 2021.
6 Saturday person, personal interview, conducted online, 25 September 2024.

Their internal participation process is not a product of a strategic decision but emerges organically from their close relationships, intimacy, and collective attitude towards decision-making, which function as forms of mutual care. Understanding their political agency and internal participation requires a nearby-speaking approach – one that applies a relational lens to victims' agency and seeks to understand how they socialise, interact with one another, and build relationships and networks, primarily among themselves but also with allied human rights defenders, committed lawyers, and other supporters.

Activist relatives frequently describe the Saturday Mothers as a 'big family', where a process of socialisation – shaped through their collective actions – plays a key role in its formation, alongside their shared experience of victimhood. I interpret this as a 'political family', in which relatives of the disappeared exercise political agency with relational values. Here, the notion of family transcends traditional, biologically determined definition and instead reflects a communal group whose members act as caregivers, capable of understanding one another's wounds. This political family differs significantly from the conventional concept of a nuclear family. A relative explained their experience at the Galatasaray Square sit-ins: 'It's not just a place where we look for our lost loved ones. In fact, we have become a big family there. Everyone lacks one person in that square, but other relatives of missing persons fill that gap to some extent.'[7]

When they gather at Galatasaray Square, they reunite as a family. This is a profoundly performative act, in which families experience a sense of togetherness that helps mitigate the isolation and unbearable grief they endure. The uncertainty of not knowing where the bodies of the missing are located causes an 'ambiguous loss' that hinders the closure process for families. For example, keeping the door open in case the missing father returns home symbolises the lingering and persistent nature of their suffering.[8]

Ambiguous loss, which can be even more distressing than confirmed death, creates lingering fear and uncertainty that contributes to an oppressed form of socialisation for both families and the broader community. It evokes emotions that can be manipulated by states, but it can be also a trigger for mothers and relatives to mobilise through associations (Robins 2024, 9). Collective mobilisation is crucial in this context, as ambiguous loss is relational; it affects not only individuals but also families and broader communities. Collective action works as an antidote for families, embedding relational approaches into the movement's activism.

Collective mobilisation helps families cope with psychological and social isolation by fostering a sense of community, in a social space where they have interacted with others who have experienced similar harm. One relative, who began joining demonstrations with her mother at the age of twelve, recalled: 'When I was little, I thought we were the only ones who had experienced this [enforced disappearance], I thought the worst thing happened to us.'[9] However, as she became a part of the movement, she realised she was not alone – many others had endured similar suffering. Another activist mother shared her story that she moved from Izmir to Istanbul specifically to participate in the protests. 'For twenty years, I went to work. For twenty-nine years, I have regularly gone to Galatasaray Square', emphasising her long-term commitment to the cause, which she described as being even greater than a lifetime job. She justified her dedication simply: 'It feels good to be with people', implying the supportive socialisation that activism has brought into her life.[10]

7 Relative of the disappeared, personal interview, conducted online, 24 September 2021.
8 Relative of the disappeared, personal interview, conducted online, 15 September 2021.
9 Relative of the disappeared, personal interview, conducted in Istanbul, 18 September 2021.
10 Hanife Yildiz, mother of Murat Yildiz, disappeared person, quoted in Korucu (2024, 164).

Within this 'political family', activist relatives practise relational values that shape their social network, the relations between them, their personalities, and their ideas of justice. The bonds that sustain them are no longer solely rooted in shared grief. One relative described these connections as arising from a 'beautiful solidarity', while another emphasised 'empathy' as the glue holding the group together. Two relatives emphasised the uniqueness of their relationship within the Saturday Mothers, with one describing it as extending beyond friendship. He explained how he and another relative who participated developed a sense of intimacy through the movement, maintaining their connection for over twenty-one years. The intimacy fostered through empathy, solidarity, and friendship within the group extends into their personal lives, sustaining the close relationships that underpin the victim movement.

When speaking with activist relatives, many told that they first joined to demand justice for their missing relatives. Over years, they have sought legal accountability and recognition not just for their own families, but for everyone in their 'big family'. They have a holistic understanding of justice, which should be restored for all victims. Many define their activism as a part of a democracy struggle, which aims to re-establish rule of law in Turkey.

In addition to the evolution of their understanding of justice, collective mobilisation has been particularly transformative in the gendered roles for mothers in the 1990s, a chance that has a continuing and relational impact on other families. In Balochistan, for example, women's activism for missing persons has introduced a new dimension to families for participation in a patriarchal society (Ashraf et al. 2023). A similar transformation occurred among the Saturday Mothers. Women who were previously 'only housewives' became political actors contesting state violence in the public sphere.[11] For many, it was their first experience participating in a political demonstration. Some used public transportation independently for the first time to travel to Istanbul's city centre. Collective action and repeated involvement brought a new socialisation to their life, transforming traditional motherhood. One relative recounted her mother's journey: 'My mother transformed from someone who asked my father for permission "Can I go there today?", to a woman who says, "I am going there!"'[12] Men, in turn, began to take on domestic roles, such as cooking, while wives or other women relatives attended the protests.[13] This shift not only altered gender roles within families but also encouraged broader transformations that benefited younger generations in families, particularly women.

#### 4.3.2.2 *Shaping an Evolving Justice Agenda across Generations*

For relatives of the disappeared, the most important and prioritised demand is prosecutions and legal accountability. As Dincer (2020) discussed, this is particularly crucial because enforced disappearance is not legally recognised as a crime in Turkey (Dinçer 2020). Prosecutions, therefore, serve as a means to formalise its recognition and ensure that the crime is acknowledged by national courts. However, this legal focus was not the initial priority for mothers in the 1990s. At the outset, mothers and other relatives mobilised in the hope of finding their missing loved ones alive. As time passed and hope faded, their focus shifted from finding their relatives to at least recovering remains and establishing gravesites where they could mourn.

This evolution in justice demands reflects a broader intergenerational transformation within the Saturday Mothers movement. The first generation of activists, primarily the mothers, clung to the belief that their loved ones might still return. Their slogan, 'You took them

11 Relative of the disappeared, personal interview, conducted online, 24 September 2021.
12 Ikbal Eren, sibling of Hayrettin Eren, disappeared person, quoted in Korucu (2024, 75–76).
13 Spokesperson of the Saturday Mothers, personal interview, conducted online, 25 September 2024.

alive; we ask you to return them alive', embodied their hope and demand for the release of the disappeared. However, as years passed and the realities of state violence became clearer, a second generation – comprising sons, daughters, granddaughters, and grandsons – emerged with a different set of justice priorities, as outlined earlier. By the time the movement resumed its gatherings in 2009 after a decade-long hiatus, this younger generation had taken on more active leadership roles while mothers remained the movement's emotional and moral core.

For the second and recently third generations, legal accountability and truth recovery became the central demands. Unlike their elders, who initially sought the physical return of the disappeared, younger activists emphasised uncovering the full truth about the disappearances and prosecuting those responsible. This shift in justice priorities was poignantly captured by İrfan Bilgin, a relative of the missing Kenan Bilgin, during the 500th-week gathering: 'We knew that they would not give them back alive as they took them. They were taken into custody and disappeared as part of a plan. The decision had been made beforehand' (Kural 2024).

Relationality does not merely sustain activism but actively transforms justice demands over time. Research by Kaya et al. (2024) highlights how growing up in this movement fosters an intergenerational commitment to justice (Kaya et al. 2024). Many children of the disappeared attended protests at Galatasaray Square alongside their mothers, embedding activism into their social and political identities. The responsibility of carrying forward this struggle has had a profound impact on the second and third generations. One activist, reflecting on her decision to join the movement, explained: 'It was awful to witness the mothers' acceptance [that our fathers would never come back]. I told myself, "this is not enough for me. I want to do something more."'[14] This responsibility – carrying a heritage – can be seen as a relational value that is not easily reduced to an individual choice. It is collectively constructed, bringing with it a future-oriented view of justice, aimed at ensuring non-repetition.

The relational values that sustain the Saturday Mothers movement – solidarity, intergenerational responsibility, and friendship – are not just by-products of activism; they actively shape the movement's justice agenda. The relative who grew up at Galatasaray Square recounted:

> I first started searching for my father. It was where I came looking for my father when I was twelve years old, but over time it turned into something else … No, it's not only my father who has been lost. I'm not the only one who has experienced this. Why am I struggling? Not just to find my father. They're all in the same place for me.[15]

Socialisation within the movement has broadened their justice demands beyond individual cases to encompass all victims of enforced disappearances in Turkey. The relational lens reveals that the movement for the disappeared evolved not only in response to political contexts but also through the intimate, lived experiences of families within the victim group.

#### 4.3.2.3 *Practising Restorative Justice, Truth and Memory in Galatasaray Square*

While collective activism has shaped the relatives' justice agenda, evolving towards demanding legal accountability and prosecutions, it has also opened a social space for truth, memory, and healing. This activism fundamentally challenges the assumption that retributive justice and restorative justice are necessarily in tension. Transitional justice literature often misses this point and overlooks the nuances in victims' perspectives, which do not fit neatly into rigid

[14] Relative of the disappeared, personal interview, conducted in Istanbul, 18 September 2021.

[15] Relative of the disappeared, personal interview, conducted in Istanbul, 18 September 2021.

justice categories. Victim groups do not perceive these forms of justice as mutually exclusive; rather, they envision a formal transitional justice by articulating their justice agenda through legal demands while simultaneously engaging in healing, memory-making, and other local forms of justice – independent of the state's will.

In other words, collective mobilisation sustains a social space where victims organically articulate their demands for state-guaranteed justice as a prospect while simultaneously practising alternative forms of justice through diverse tools and actions. For example, the relatives recently organised a series of events and mobilised public figures for memory projects. To honour the 1,000th gathering of the Saturday Mothers in 2024, a famous Turkish rock star was invited to perform a song written for them, and an oral history project, conducted by journalist Serdar Korucu and later published as a book, has served as a crucial resource for this chapter. Both initiatives exemplify how victim movements integrate truth-seeking and memory work with their broader pursuit of justice, demonstrating that legal accountability and restorative practices can coexist and reinforce one another.

When justice processes are dominated by legal frameworks, their relational character is often sidestepped. However, many transitional justice measures, including truth commissions, apology, and amnesty justice are more about rebuilding relationships and trust between victims and communities (Llewellyn and Philpott 2014). The relational element of restorative justice resonates with families' mobilisation, as it enables victim participation in a way that ensures they feel heard, listened, and recognised within newly constructed social networks. The safe space created by the Saturday Mothers has become a refuge for other victims of enforced disappearances who are not actively involved in the movement, contributing to the formation of what is referred to as a 'big family'. Galatasaray Square represents the physical core of this social space, where families find a sense of justice by sharing their stories and raising their voice to demand truth and recognition. Over the course of their activism, the Saturday Mothers have held more than 1,000 weekly sit-ins. Each week, they disseminate the story of a different disappeared person, a number that far exceeds the families actively participating in the movement.

Families who have remained silent for years often approach the Saturday Mothers to dedicate a sit-in to their missing loved one. During the 1990s, many families did not search for their missing relatives out of fear that doing so could lead to further state violence, such as torture in police custody or the loss of another family member.[16] The state strategically wielded the politics of ambiguous loss as a weapon of war. When a family decides to involve in the ritualised demonstrations, a family member reads a detailed account of the person's life, the circumstance of their disappearance, information about the perpetrators, the status of any legal proceedings, and the family's demands. Thus, families who expose these crimes through activism also challenge existing power relations. While not all families become permanent members of the Saturday Mothers, the movement provides them with an opportunity to share their truth in a space where they will be heard. This authentic temporal space allows victims to tell their stories when they are ready, rather than being constrained by a rigid timeline, as is often the case with formal truth commissions.

Truth commissions are considered among the most suitable transitional justice mechanisms for achieving restorative justice and fostering victim participation, as they typically carry fewer institutional and legal restrictions. However, they generally operate for only two or three years. Even the best-funded commissions, such as the one in East Timor, can only include a small number of victims. To address this limitation, Braithwaite (2016) suggests bottom-up

[16] Relative of the disappeared, personal interview, conducted online, 24 September 2021.

practices embedded in communities that are free from donor-driven timelines and function as 'a permanent Truth Commission that keeps its doors open to victim testimony in perpetuity' (Braithwaite 2016, 1). Spaces created by victim movements often fulfil this role, providing a platform for truth and recognition – such as the Saturday Mothers for thirty years – in the absence of a transitional justice framework or in the wake of the failed official practices.

As mentioned earlier, the Saturday Mothers' relationship with Galatasaray Square is central to their sense of justice at a local level. The square holds profound symbolic meaning for them and is often described as a 'healing place'.[17] One relative explained: 'Here [Galatasaray Square] is a memory space for us. Our loved ones do not have gravesites. So, when we come here [to the square] since 1999 and hold the photographs of the people we have lost, it is like we are embracing their gravestones.'[18]

The square has become a space claimed through resistance – a site for mourning missing relatives, preserving memory, demanding justice, and fostering a sense of community through collective action. It is a social space where there are heavy emotions, spiritual meanings, and encounters with others. This deep bond with the square is reflected in the families' justice imaginations. One relative expressed his vision of justice as follows: 'Imagine a big screen turned on at Galatasaray Square in Taksim on a Saturday … The day when, in my home, on TV or on the internet, I see my father's story being told and finally being respected and appreciated. I will no longer hold a grudge against anyone.'[19]

Beyond seeking acknowledgement of the crimes, families engaged in activism also demand the official recognition of the Galatasaray Square as a memory site that honours their decades-long resistance. They view any future transitional justice process as inseparable from the square, advocating for a holistic approach to justice, one that includes both the prosecutions of perpetrators and the recognition of the square as a space of collective memory for society. On the other hand, to understand their political agency better, it is essential to capture the role of Galatasaray Square in the pursuit of justice. This space has been central to helping families navigate ambiguous loss, shaping their justice demands across generations, and fostering an evolving understanding of justice through the interplay of space, collective action, and social relationships. Recognising the deep emotional, social, and temporal connections that families have with the square is crucial to appreciating both their resistance and the justice they envision.

## 4.4 CONCLUSION

Research on victim participation demonstrates that victims' engagement extends well beyond formal transitional justice mechanisms, encompassing informal spaces claimed by victims. Victim associations and movements have created spaces for the principles of transitional justice that can take root even during pre-transitional periods. More conceptual and empirical studies are needed to explore the intersection of victim movements and victim participation within the transitional justice landscape. In this chapter, I examined the Saturday Mothers movement to understand how they construct political agency and how they shape the social spaces they inhabit. Using a relational lens, I analysed their activism to highlight how political agency emerges from collective activism, social networks, and relational values. This

[17] Alkan, 'Keeping Hope in the Neverland through Resistance and Struggle', 160.

[18] Ikbal Eren, sibling of Hayrettin Eren, disappeared person, quoted in Korucu (2024, 82).

[19] İHD activist and the relative of the disappeared, personal interview, conducted online, 3 August 2021.

analytical framework deepens our understanding of how victim movements socialise, interact, develop personal and collective identities, and exercise participation, which can sustain their activism per se, as well as their demands for institutional transitional justice processes.

This approach contributes to transitional justice literature by shedding light on internal decision-making processes, modes of communication, and the evolution of public participation with long-standing victim movements. However, this internal focus has limitations, as it places less emphasis on interaction with broader social structures and systems. By focusing on internal dynamics – such as decision-making, communication, and intergenerational transmission and transformation of justice demands – this analysis contributes to transitional justice literature by offering a nuanced view of long-standing victim movements. The case of the Saturday Mothers demonstrates how victim groups have shaped the transitional justice realm, relationally, even as violence persists. However, political agency deserves further exploration within the relationship between grassroots activism and institutional processes.

The Saturday Mothers exemplify the formation of a resilient social network sustained by shared grief, solidarity, and a redefined sense of family. This *political family*, forged through collective suffering rather than biological ties, creates a communal network of care and support. Members are united through the experience of ambiguous loss and the pursuit of justice for the disappeared. The movement operates horizontally, fostering participation through transparent communication and shared decision-making. Relational values such as empathy, solidarity, and mutual care sustain the group, enabling personal empowerment and challenging traditional gender roles while shaping relational agency. This relational dimension underpins their activism, which sustains a dynamic social space in which restorative justice – healing, memory, and truth-recovery – coexists with the demands for an institutional process. This dynamic has become more visible in recent phase of the movement, led by the second generations.

Intergenerational dynamics have played a crucial role in sustaining the movement and shaping its evolving justice agenda. Over the decades, the demands of the Saturday Mothers have shifted – from searching for their loved ones to demanding prosecutions and truth recovery. These changing demands reflect the enduring impact of ambiguous loss and the evolving interplay of personal and collective needs over time. At the heart of their struggle is Galatasaray Square, a space imbued with symbolic and social significance where memory, resistance, and justice converge. This case demonstrates how victim movements not only demand formal justice but also actively shape the landscape of transitional justice itself. Recognising the interplay of space, memory, and activism offers critical insights into how transitional justice processes can better reflect the lived experiences of victims, ensuring that justice is not only a legal outcome but also a relational and social transformation.

## REFERENCES

Ashraf, Shala, Ikram Badshah, and Usman Khan. 2023. 'The Role of Women's Political Activism against Enforced Disappearances in Balochistan: A Study of the Baluch Missing Persons'. *Inter-Asia Cultural Studies*, 24(6), 979–993. https://doi.org/10.1080/14649373.2023.2265687

Baines, Erin K. 2015. '"Today, I Want to Speak Out the Truth": Victim Agency, Responsibility, and Transitional Justice'. *International Political Sociology*, 9(4), 316–332. https://doi.org/10.1111/ips.12100

Bhandari, Ram Kumar, and Simon Robins. 2024. 'Formal but Local Transitional Justice: Memorialization of the Missing by Local Government in Nepal'. *International Journal of Human Rights Practice*, 1–17.

Boss, Pauline. 2007. 'Ambiguous Loss Theory: Challenges for Scholars and Practitioners'. *Family Relations*, 56(2), 105–110.

Braithwaite, John. 2016. 'Learning to Scale up Restorative Justice'. In *Restorative Justice in Transitional Settings*, edited by Kerry Clamp, pp. 173–189. Routledge.

Burkitt, Ian. 2016. 'Relational Agency: Relational Sociology, Agency and Interaction'. *European Journal of Social Theory* 19(3), 322 339. https://doi.org/10.1177/1368431015591426

Can, Başak. 2022. 'How Does a Protest Last? Rituals of Visibility, Disappearances under Custody, and the Saturday Mothers in Turkey'. *American Anthropologist*, 124(3), 467–478. https://doi.org/10.1111/aman.13749

Chen, Nancy N. 1992. '"Speaking Nearby": A Conversation with Trinh T. Minh–Ha'. *Visual Anthropology Review*, 8(1), 82–91. https://doi.org/10.1525/var.1992.8.1.82

Daşlı, Güneş. 2024. 'Victim Agency, Relational Autonomy and Transitional Justice: Experience of Saturday Mothers'. *International Journal of Transitional Justice*, 18(3), 371–386, https://doi.org/10.1093/ijtj/ijae021

de Waardt, Mijke, and Sanne Weber. 2019. 'Beyond Victims' Mere Presence: An Empirical Analysis of Victim Participation in Transitional Justice in Colombia'. *Journal of Human Rights Practice*, 11(1), 209–228. https://doi.org/10.1093/jhuman/huz002

Desmet, E. 2014. 'Analysing Users' Trajectories in Human Rights: A Conceptual Exploration and Research Agenda Special Issue – Studying Human Rights Law from the Perspective(s) of Its Users'. *Human Rights & International Legal Discourse*, 8(2), 121–141.

Diani, Mario, and Doug McAdam. 2003. *Social Movements and Networks: Relational Approaches to Collective Action*. Oxford University Press.

Dinçer, Hülya. 2020. 'Türkiye'de cezasızlık politikalarının bilançosu: Savaşın gölgesinde "adalete bağırmak"'. *Toplum ve Bilim*, 152(1), 40–71.

Duvar, Gazete, (Ed.). 2024. Cumartesi Anneleri 1000 Hafta Direndi: Kayıplarımızı Bulmuş Kadar Sevindik. www.youtube.com/watch?v=RnDVAr2IdUs

Evrard, Elke, Gretel Mejía Bonifazi, and Tine Destrooper. 2021. 'The Meaning of Participation in Transitional Justice: A Conceptual Proposal for Empirical Analysis'. *International Journal of Transitional Justice*, 15(2), 428–447. https://doi.org/10.1093/ijtj/ijab013

Goffman, Erving. 1971. *Relations in Public: Microstudies of the Public Order*. Routledge.

Held, Virginia. 2006. *The Ethics of Care: Personal, Political, and Global*. Oxford University Press.

Kaya, Orhan, Yasemin Gülsüm Acar, Celal Cahit Agar, and Fergus Neville. 2024. 'Resistance from Generation to Generation: The Saturday Mothers in Istanbul'. *Journal of Community & Applied Social Psychology*, 34(4), e2843. https://doi.org/10.1002/casp.2843

Korucu, Serdar. 2024. *Cumartesi Anneleri: Galatasaray Meydani`nda 1000 Hafta*. Dogan Kitap.

Kovras, Iosif. 2017. *Grassroots Activism and the Evolution of Transitional Justice: The Families of the Disappeared*. Cambridge University Press.

Kreft, Anne-Kathrin, and Philipp Schulz. 2022. 'Political Agency, Victimhood, and Gender in Contexts of Armed Conflict: Moving beyond Dichotomies'. *International Studies Quarterly*, 66(2), sqac022. https://doi.org/10.1093/isq/sqac022

Krystalli, Roxani. 2024. *Good Victims: The Political as a Feminist Question*. Oxford University Press.

Kural, Beyza. 2024. 'Adalete Ulaşıncaya Kadar Galatasaray'da…' Bianet, 25 October 2024. https://bianet.org/haber/adalete-ulasincaya-kadar-galatasaray-da-159444

Liu, Sida. 2024. 'Social Spaces: From Georg Simmel to Erving Goffman'. *The Journal of Chinese Sociology*, 11(1), 13. https://doi.org/10.1186/s40711-024-00217-9

Llewellyn, Jennifer J., and Daniel Philpott. 2014. 'Restorative Justice and Reconciliation: Twin Frameworks for Peacebuilding'. In *Restorative Justice, Reconciliation, and Peacebuilding*, edited by Jennifer J. Llewellyn and Daniel Philpott, pp. 14–37. Oxford University Press.

Mackenzie, Catriona. 2019. 'Feminist Innovation in Philosophy: Relational Autonomy and Social Justice'. *Women's Studies International Forum*, 72 (January), 144–151. https://doi.org/10.1016/j.wsif.2018.05.003

Mackenzie, Catriona, and Natalie Stoljar, eds. 2000. *Relational Autonomy: Feminist Perspectives on Autonomy, Agency, and the Social Self*. Oxford University Press.

Robins, Simon. 2024. 'The Politics of Ambiguous Loss: Missing Persons and Social Ecologies after Armed Conflict'. *Journal of Human Rights Practice*, OnlineFirst https://doi.org/10.1093/jhuman/huae020

Selim, Yvette. 2017. 'The Opportunities and Challenges of Participation in Transitional Justice: Examples from Nepal'. *Journal of International Development*, 29(8), 1123–1148. https://doi.org/10.1002/jid.3001

# Second Generation

# 5

# Searching for the Disappeared

## *Victim Participation, Recognition, and Procedural Justice – Lessons Learnt from Colombia and El Salvador*

*Mina Rauschenbach and Briony Jones*

### 5.1 INTRODUCTION

While the international legal issues related to the search for victims of enforced disappearances (ED) have received considerable attention, limited research has been conducted on how participation in the search impacts victims' lives.[1] In particular, we argue for the importance of inserting victim recognition into these discussions, to improve our understanding about what types of institutional and social responses are needed to ensure effective and victim-oriented search processes. This will include different types of recognition including self-recognition of the victims themselves and recognition of victims by institutional actors and processes. In doing so, we understand the search for disappeared persons as a complex multi-actor and multi-activity process, which ideally only ends when the fate and whereabouts of the disappeared are determined (Ott et al. 2022, 9).

Building on the United Nations Guiding Principles for the Search for Disappeared Persons,[2] which ratifies the right to participation, this chapter explores the intersection between victim participation in both formal and informal search processes and recognition, which is particularly stark in cases of ED and the accompanying ambiguous loss which families face. This includes looking at how participation and recognition may impede or reinforce each other, through an analysis of how family members experience judicial and state-based mechanisms as key justice stakeholders. In doing so we apply the concepts of procedural justice and victim recognition to analyse and understand how families navigate their participation as justice stakeholders within judicial and state-based mechanisms.

Our chapter utilises the concept of 'recognition relationships'. This concept is particularly useful for elucidating the intersection between victim participation and victim recognition because it introduces an understanding of the importance of interactions between the actors which are at the heart of any search process. Specifically, this notion helps address the following elements relevant to our chapter: the complex landscape of formal and informal actors who engage with each other in different ways throughout the course of a search process; the way in which the passage of time shifts relationships between actors and re-shapes processes, victims'

1 ED is a human rights violation which is defined by the International Convention for the Protection of All Persons from Enforced Disappearances (ICPPED) as 'a deprivation of liberty by state agents or by persons acting with the authorization, support or acquiescence of the state, followed by a refusal to acknowledge the deprivation of the liberty or a concealment of the fate of the whereabouts of the person' (ICPPED, art. 2).

2 www.ohchr.org/en/documents/legal-standards-and-guidelines/guiding-principles-searchdisappeared-persons.

needs, as well as possibilities for and spheres of recognition; the in-built power relations between those seeking recognition and those empowered to grant it, or not.

We analyse recognition relationships with reference to two cases: Colombia and El Salvador. We take a fresh look at data from a project which focused on legal and psychosocial aspects in the search for disappeared persons. Our findings provide important insights into what meaningful victim participation and recognition in formal search programmes could look like. The chapter reveals obstacles, resources, and opportunities, highlighting the complex and often cumbersome constraints around this involvement and how it impacts victims' capacity to mobilise for the full and effective recognition of their rights and voices. Most importantly, it illuminates the importance of thinking about recognition relationships in order to capture the dynamics of power, mobilisation, and participation which are central to any successful and just search process.

The first part of the chapter explores the theoretical literature on victim participation in formal transitional justice mechanisms, on different understandings of recognition, on participation and procedural justice, and on the role of voice and power in recognition relationships, with reference to changing norms, guidelines, and legal frameworks. The second part introduces our methodology and the two cases, while the third part moves into the analysis which is focused on the time, spheres, and power dynamics of recognition relationships for the families of the disappeared in the two case study countries. In the final part of the chapter, we draw out some key implications of the recognition relationships concept and framing, and reinforce the importance of seeing families as justice stakeholders.

## 5.2 CONNECTING THE KEY CONCEPTS

### 5.2.1 *Victim Recognition and Participation in Formal Mechanisms*

Recognition of victims is often thought of as a process that can facilitate or hinder victims' participation in the search process while also being generated by this participation. Recognition as a process takes on cumulative forms, and one of its key stages concerns recognising victims' rights and the obligations of states to uphold these rights: 'legal norms are enabling, suggestive, or prohibitive of different modes of intersubjective recognition' (Wilke 2007, 482).

As this quote suggests, fundamental to the realisation of recognition is an intersubjective relationship – between those who seek recognition and those with the power to grant it, or not. In the case of ED, this is the relationship between victims (and more specifically the families of the disappeared) and varied other actors, both formal (lawyers, government officials) and informal (other families, wider society).

Recognition of ED in the legal sphere was born from the relentless struggles of victims and the human rights movement. Building upon the struggles of broader victim movements against impunity and for the recognition of the right to justice, truth and reparation within international norms, families of the disappeared strived for many decades to have ED recognised as a human rights violation per se. This also meant, initially at the international level, then nationally, recognising the distinctive characteristics of ED as a continuous human rights violation, which eventually allowed families themselves to be recognised as victims. This opened up the possibility to recognise that, in virtue of their status as victims, they had various rights and that states had corresponding obligations towards them, including in relation to the search process. Yet even when the state in question takes concrete measures to uphold these rights at the national level, this is only the first step in their struggle for recognition, as these rights need to be effectively enforced within the judicial system and its institutions, leading to meaningful recognition and measures of redress.

The realisation of rights depends on different levels of recognition (Goodey 2005), starting from a victim recognising that one's experience constitutes a victimisation which amounts to a violation (self-recognition), to the possibility of reporting victimisation as a violation, of having it recorded, leading to initiating an investigation and, depending on the case, a search process. As stages of recognition relationships which involve different actors in various decision-making processes, they determine how, when, and why those who are affected by ED are recognised as victims and can realise their rights effectively. While victims may have their rights recognised formally, when rights to effective remedies for victims are enshrined within legal frameworks, they may face many challenges to exercising their rights in reality, creating obstacles and constraints for other levels and forms of recognition to materialise. This speaks to De Greiff's (2012) argument that victims need not only be recognised as having experienced harm, but also as legal rights holders and relevant political actors, citizens, and justice stakeholders. He distinguishes two components to recognition: that a person has been wronged (moral recognition) and that the person is a right-bearer owing to this rights violation (political recognition). The latter component relates to the status of 'recognised victims', which aims to restore their dignity and to contribute to their political (re-)integration into society and is therefore tied to measures of redress. Transitional justice mechanisms which aim to promote truth, reparation, and judicial accountability can thus contribute to victim recognition when they validate the harm suffered by victims, as well as restore their dignity by vindicating them (acknowledging the wrongdoing by someone else) and addressing the violation's impacts.

Yet victims often face obstacles in claiming rights because these rights are invariably interlinked to a corresponding duty of the state to uphold that right. State-level enforcement often reveals relationships dominated by power and political concerns, which inevitably impact victim recognition (Dixon 2015). Victim recognition depends on politics of framing (Fraser 2005), discretionary powers of judicial actors, and administrative processes, which also determine the degree of access victims may have to formal mechanisms. Moreover, the structural positions of victims and the capital they enjoy within the broader justice stakeholders' landscape after mass atrocity also impact their recognition possibilities (Barton-Hronesova 2018) through dynamics of social and cultural constructions of appropriate victimhood (Hearty 2018) and processes of validating or excluding particular voices and experiences.

### 5.2.2 *Participation as a Form of Recognition*

Victim participation has been described as constituting a valuable form of recognition for victims (Correa, Guillerot, and Margarell (2020, 242), when it is 'respectful, knowledgeable, and transparent, and achieved through effective forms of representation'. This description speaks to the significance for victims to be politically recognised as rights-bearing citizens and relevant justice stakeholders. It is also key in linking participation as a form of recognition with the ideas of voice and power. This is in line with Wemmers' (2008) observation that victims' participation is shaped by relative abilities to voice experiences and to have one's experiences recognised. As Correa, Guillerot, and Margarell (2020, 242) stress, participation as a form of recognition, is particularly important for invisibilised and marginal populations, serving 'not only to add value to measures of restitution, rehabilitation, or compensation, but also as a good in itself by opening the space for debate about how to ensure greater inclusion for victims both socially and politically'.

Yet victim participation also depends on discretionary powers and the decision-making of various actors within formal mechanisms. This impacts the degree to which victims have a voice and can have their victimisation experiences and their identity as rights-bearers and relevant justice stakeholders recognised (Correa, Guillerot, and Margarell 2020; Garbett 2013). The public and official recognition of victims' experiences is part of the restoration of their dignity. It constitutes an acknowledgement that societal norms regulating wrongful actions were breached to the detriment of victims. It can help alleviate the stigmatisation of victims within communities by validating publicly the legitimacy of their struggles to have ED recognised as a violation and families to be recognised as victims of a continuing crime. Efforts to standardise search processes and victim participation are important in facilitating such recognition. It is also important to analyse in detail actual search processes and what we can learn from them about the kinds of recognition relationships that sustain or impede actual recognition and its impact in wider society. State-based forms of recognition of harm and injustice do not always resonate in the public sphere, or lead to victims' social (re)-integration. This highly depends on whether state mechanisms' responses reflect a political recognition of victims by providing effective access to different measures of redress, such as truth-seeking measures, the initiation of a judicial investigation, and the possibility of obtaining reparations and psycho-social assistance (De Greiff 2012).

### 5.2.3 *Procedural Justice and the Voices of Victims*

Procedural justice is a concept which can capture, and bring together, the previously discussed threads of the chapter: victim recognition and victim participation. It is also apposite for an approach focused on recognition relationships as it brings in dynamics between different actors in the varied spheres of recognition in which victims engage as part of their search for justice. Developed within social psychology, procedural justice is concerned with how people judge their social experiences and whether the processes they experience in their interactions can be perceived as fair and just (Jones et al. 2023). It is about relationships between people, between people and processes, and importantly about the subjective way in which such experiences can be perceived. Importantly, when applied to the legal sphere, procedural justice literature tells us that the extent to which victims perceive a justice mechanism to be just depends on victims' evaluations of fairness of procedures more than of outcomes (Killean 2016). This has also been identified as important for victims of ED (Robins 2013), most relevantly in terms of relational and informational concerns (Jones et al. 2023).

As such, whether or not victims experience justice processes as just will be directly connected to their experiences of participation as justice stakeholders, and whether they are heard and treated respectfully (Wemmers 2008). In turn, being heard and treated respectfully will be directly connected to the way in which other actors perceive victims, whether they are understood to be credible and valid interlocutors. Being heard requires an audience that is willing to listen and in turn to be influenced by what is said, a dynamic which is further complicated when those in positions of power are unable or unwilling to understand speakers in marginalised or vulnerable positions (Dotson 2011).

## 5.3 CASE STUDIES AND METHODOLOGY

Both Colombia and El Salvador have carried out a series of transitional justice efforts to reckon with their past, including setting up special official mechanisms to search for disappeared persons. They also share some similarities in armed conflict patterns and formal and informal responses to victims' needs: (a) ED was and is still being committed to some extent; (b) civil society organisations (CSOs), including family associations, are active in seeking to either complement or contest the official search. Both contexts differ in terms of the overall legal framework of recognition at the disposal of families of the disappeared ED.

Colombia has endured a long-lasting armed conflict since the mid-1960s. It involved many different actors (i.e., state forces, guerrilla groups, paramilitaries, and criminal actors) and has led to more than 200,000 victims of ED until 2016. The Colombian state's recognition in 2000 of ED as an autonomous crime opened up the possibility to establish various normative frameworks and institutional mechanisms aimed at addressing victims' rights. The Unit for the Search for Persons Presumed Disappeared in the context and by the reason of the armed conflict (henceforth, Search Unit), included in the Comprehensive System of Truth, Justice, Reparations, and Non Repetition, created for all the victims of the conflict following the 2016 peace agreement between the Colombian government and Revolutionary Armed Forces of Colombia, is particularly relevant. It constitutes an extra-judicial institution with a humanitarian approach: the search outcome cannot be used for the purpose of establishing legal accountability in judicial processes. It allows victims to not have to rely on criminal proceedings to seek the truth about the whereabouts of disappeared persons, and the recovery, identification, and dignified return of remains. Official search efforts taking on a judicial approach, with the primary objective of prosecution and which are highly reliant on criminal proceedings' progress and priorities, exist as well. Information and evidence emerging from criminal proceedings may also be used to facilitate search processes. ED victims, as all victims of harms related to armed conflict that were committed after 1 January 1985, can also register with the Victims Unit, an administrative entity established by the 2011 Victims and Land Restitution Law. This registration allows victims to obtain the legal status of victim and to benefit from various reparation measures, including compensation, restitution, and land restitution. Colombia has also ratified the ICPPED). Despite these various efforts, the institutional response to ED in Colombia remains unsatisfactory in practice, with high levels of impunity and a lack of effective access to justice and truth for victims. This is owing to challenges in securing sufficient and sustainable resources to support state institutions' activities, as well as coordination issues between institutional search actors.

In El Salvador, approximately 8,000 persons disappeared during the armed conflict (1980–1992). ED is not included in the domestic criminal code as an autonomous crime but as a crime against humanity. This augments significantly the threshold for judicial procedures and convictions, making it difficult for those who have experienced the disappearance of a loved one to have this victimisation be legally recognised as a crime of ED. El Salvador has not ratified the ICPPED and, until 2016, an amnesty law prevented criminal investigations regarding crimes committed during the armed conflict (including ED). Faced with continued lack of response and denial, as well as criminalisation of victims from the state, civil society-initiated humanitarian searches have existed since the late 1980s. This has led notably to the implementation of DNA databases to help families in identifying the disappeared.

The insights presented in this chapter come directly from research undertaken as part of a larger project, *Connecting Legal and Psychosocial Aspects in the Search for Victims of Enforced Disappearance in Colombia and El Salvador*, which took place in 2019 and 2020, with partners from Colombia and El Salvador.[3] Based on a qualitative approach, this research included

3 www.swisspeace.ch/articles/connecting-legal-and-psychosocial-aspects-in-the-search-for-victims-of-enforced-disappearance-in-colombia-and-el-salvador.

semi-structured interviews conducted with the families of the disappeared, CSO representatives, and representatives or former staff members of official search mechanisms. In total we conducted nine interviews for the case of Colombia and seven for the case of El Salvador. In Colombia, we interviewed five family members of disappeared persons – two of whom also identified as activists – as well as two activists and two officials who had previously worked for different state institutions involved in the search. In El Salvador, we interviewed six family members of disappeared persons – two of whom also identified as activists – as well as an activist working for a state institution and a staff member of an official search mechanism. The selection of the sample of interviewees was determined in great part by the existence of previously established relationships of trust with the local project partners Dejusticia (Colombia) and Pro-Búsqueda (El Salvador). For reasons of anonymity, interviewees are identified with a code designating the number of the interview, the country (C for Colombia and E for El Salvador) and self-identification of positionality (V for victim and A for activist).

## 5.4 THE SEARCH: INITIATION

The initiation of a search process is triggered by different experiences and at different points in time, depending on the information the families have initially and the circumstances surrounding the disappearance, as well as the socio-political and legal opportunities for such participation. These different experiences also have an impact on how they understand their victimhood and may self-recognise as victims.

Some may not know at first that their loved ones were forcibly disappeared, thinking, as 1CV recalls concerning her husband, that he went missing. When her husband did not reappear one day, she did not try to look for him as she assumed he had purposefully left her for someone else. She was forced to move on, taking two family roles to fill the void left, recognising herself in a new identity as 'I'm mom and dad at the same time'. It was only twenty years later, when attending an information session about the Colombian system of registration for victims, following the recommendation of a friend involved in activism, that she realised that she could search for her husband. After registering in a database of unidentified bodies and remains, she discovered her husband was registered as dead, his remains buried many years ago. This realisation shattered her beliefs and plunged her back into painful feelings. It was when her victimhood was validated and vindicated by others, her activist friend and the national registry for victims of ED, that she self-recognised as a victim and started the search.

Other relatives, such as 4EVA, knew that their loved one(s) were disappeared and did not initiate the search owing to fear of stigmatisation and reprisals. When she and her family were desperately looking for their disappeared loved ones, they could not count on support from the community, in particular the church, and suffered threats, rejection, and stigmatisation instead. This lack of recognition and denigration led her family 'to suffer that inner pain' without showing it and stop searching for answers. They had no choice but to accept the disappearance 'as something that had happened'.

When impunity and the state denial of grave human rights violations prevail, self-recognising as victims is not enough for victims to have the possibility to engage in the search. Encounters with state actors who deny and do not recognise their victim status leave relatives powerless and alone with their pain. Without answers or knowing that they have rights, relatives may not be aware of how to advance in their search. 14EV's account illustrates further how this unawareness hinders victims' participation within the judicial sphere in filing a report, and the importance of social resources in providing support. They are less likely to engage in the process of filing a report when they do not have supportive others who can validate their needs as legitimate recognition claims which are attached to rights: 'they don't have a connection, some guide, something that leads them to the search'.

## 5.5 THE SEARCH: PARTICIPATION

Families' search trajectories in connection with state mechanisms often begin with filing a report on the disappearance of their loved ones with a judicial actor. In Colombia, ED victims are assumed to benefit from a political recognition of their status as victims and are theoretically entitled to corresponding rights through the workings of state mechanisms. Yet there is a disconnection between the multiplicity of existing legal frameworks and ineffectiveness at the institutional level in recognising ED victims in practice. This implies difficulties in achieving recognition from the moment of filing a complaint to the other stages of the search process, including investigation and identification of the whereabouts of the victim.

The accounts of our interviewees make it clear that knowing that what they are experiencing is unjust and criminal, and that they are entitled to be recognised as victims with the right to seek help from the state in their search for their loved ones is only the first step in a long trajectory of struggles for recognition. While their experience of harm is understood legally as a violation of the law, the political dimension of this recognition, which entitles them to claim rights to truth and measures of redress, is not always granted in practice in interactions with officials. 11CV, for example, needed to register at the Victims Unit to claim her rights, and recalls being told that neither did she have the right to be recognised, nor did she deserve to be so. She experienced these encounters as denying a recognition of her dignity, and of her right to know and to justice by virtue of her victim status.

Bureaucratisation and its depersonalising effect may also interfere significantly in bringing about meaningful and empowering recognition relationships from the very beginning of victims' institutional trajectories. 5CVA explains how when people were disappeared, 'nobody ever looked for them, and we feel that nobody is looking for them now'. Referring to a police inspector, with whom she was in contact, she explains how 'he didn't care, because that body that was there was of no value'. To him, these were mere depersonalised bodily remains. This exemplifies how an investigation process' bureaucratic functioning may also be 'another way of making the person disappear' (10CO). It also highlights the importance of taking into account the reality of bureaucratisation when reflecting on the implementation of standards of good practice within formal search processes towards improved participation and more effective recognition.

For many participants, there is also a sense that the suffering generated by ED and the devastating impact it has on the lives of families and communities is not recognised in how it affects their access to the rights they are legally understood to enjoy. As 1CV recounts, the disappearance of her husband, which left her alone to take care of her children and which should have constituted enough evidence of her victimhood, did not suffice to obtain recognition of this status. This depended on whether she could provide DNA proof of her children's affiliation to her disappeared husband. She struggled to find information concerning the DNA identification procedure without any psychological or legal accompaniment throughout this cumbersome and painful process. Left with the clinical and impassive responses of judicial actors, she felt no recognition of her suffering and dire need of support.

In order to continue with a search after it has been initiated, the families of disappeared persons with whom we spoke particularly valued feeling supported by relevant officials, who were willing to build rapport, demonstrate sensitivity, and thus engage in a form of relationship-building as part of the search process. Too often this need was not met, as in 5CVA's interactions with civil servants experienced as constrained by a mundane bureaucracy of office life. These officials do not share or even acknowledge the emotional experiences central to victims. They also do not recognise the urgency of victims' organisations to act swiftly upon information concerning a disappearance. Although, during weekends, information on ED cases comes to the attention of organisations, there is no forensic official on duty to follow-up on it. This significantly constrains organisations' agency in searching for the disappeared; they cannot search on their own, as they will be blamed for obstructing justice if they go and dig in a particular location without forensic actors present. Judicial bureaucracy can thus affect recognition by hindering relatives' search for the truth through such relationships of denial and obstruction.

Bureaucratic encounters can also amplify the experience of lack of recognition by generating additional unrecognised structural impacts to the harm suffered, as in 2CV's case. She had to go back and forth between different actors for a year and a half just to obtain the death certificate for her two disappeared children, which she needed to receive minimal financial compensation. She obtained this compensation, but was still left with no information as to whether the report she filed led to an investigation to find the remains of her children. Thus, she had to remain in the capital city, Bogotá, waiting for any news from the prosecutor's office and struggling to pay for her daily expenses. Reflecting on the magnitude of these psycho-social impacts, she would like to receive a state compensation for her unjust circumstances. It would validate her suffering and express the state's recognition of its obligation to repair the wrong done to an innocent citizen: 'that they put themselves in our shoes because we carry the bulge, see, paying rent, (…) To alleviate that weight you carry (…) because of them!'

State actors in dealing with victims' claims also do not recognise the symbolic importance of financial compensation as an expression of societal solidarity and as rights victims have in virtue of their experiences of harm, as highlighted by 10CO. He regrets this situation explaining that 'I don't know if it would hurt less but at least they would feel less badly treated and less alone.'

Mirroring this observation, 1CV recalls her encounters with state search mechanism actors, having felt no recognition for her need for answers and support in relation to the search process. These actors' lack of humanity left her with a sense of profound powerlessness, experiencing 'blow after blow' as they continuously fail to understand her suffering and her relational needs.

Many highlighted the Colombian judicial sector's failings to investigate ED cases thoroughly and engage in effective search processes, owing to a lack of political will to prioritise the issue of ED at the institutional level, in conjunction with insufficient functional resources and bureaucratic factors. An example is the Search Unit for 8CA: a well-intended initiative which is not perceived as having fulfilled its promises for victims, because it was never given the proper, budgetary, administrative, and structural means to do so.

In El Salvador, our findings highlight that recognition may be often limited to its moral dimension. Victims have scarce possibilities to go beyond the mere acknowledgement of the harm they suffered and see their rights enforced through state responses. Even after the significant socio-political transformations that followed the peace agreement, most victims have little to no chance of seeking or obtaining justice, or to know the truth about what happened to their relatives, or to receive reparation. Owing to the enactment of the Amnesty Law, many families, such as 4EVA's, did not have a possibility to seek justice. They 'have no right to be recognised'. Her sister's husband's death at the hands of a guard was not considered a crime by the judge to whom she went to file a report, because the perpetrator was a state agent who had been granted amnesty. 4EVA poignantly expresses how victim recognition cannot occur when state agents' actions are constructed as legitimate responses and victimhood experiences are delegitimised as subversive or political: 'those who the guard kills do not have the right to be recognised because the guard is [fulfilling] his duty'.

For 4EVA, the repeal of the Amnesty Law in 2016 should have opened the door to victim recognition. While, in theory, it opened the possibility for crimes committed during the armed conflict to be investigated and prosecuted, in practice nothing changed for her. Upon reporting the disappearance of her loved one, she is still faced with silence and uncooperative state authorities who refuse to release the archives of the armed forces containing information on the location of remains, leaving her struggling for recognition, answers, and, ultimately, justice.

A political transformation is not a guarantee of improved recognition for victims, when silence and denial are still present, as findings related to El Salvador illustrate. While the existence of violations of ED is now officially recognised, impunity still prevails because of a lack of political will to address victims' claims and fulfil state obligations to ensure their rights to truth, justice and reparation are respected: 'If the authorities had paid attention and said "let's look for them, really, let's look for them (…). I'm going to compensate you", if that happened, it would advance, and people would take more interest' (7EVA). What this quote suggests is that lack of political recognition affects also how ED is recognised within society and citizens' concern for the rights of victims.

Ongoing impunity for ED poses an obstacle to official and state recognition of victims, whether in the form of finding information about the remains and circumstances around the disappearance in archives or through investigations, of reparations, or of criminal justice proceedings aimed at establishing accountability.

4EV recounts the disappearance of her nephew long after the peace agreement. Her sister, who knew of his abduction and detention by a particular state official, was threatened when she started searching for him in places where she thought he might be held. They now know that he was murdered and are searching for his remains, waiting for DNA results confirming that they are buried in a mass grave that was discovered recently. They feel powerless and are continuously struggling to obtain answers and information from judicial actors on the investigation outcome. Their encounters with the police and the prosecutor's office leave them with pain, uncertainty, and disarray, with little trust and hope that they will earnestly put efforts into establishing the truth about the circumstances of the death of her nephew. These interactions fail to bring them a recognition of their dignity or to help them enjoy an effective access to justice and truth.

Impunity, stemming from the state's inability to hold those involved in ED to account for their responsibilities, is another manifestation of this lack of political recognition. 13EA, a Salvadorian activist, explains concretely how impunity implies very few chances of recognition in terms of accountability: 'the majority of cases remain at the administrative level in the Attorney General's Office'. Very few cases make it to the stage of prosecution in national courts. This impunity is also the result of the stigmatisation of victims by law enforcement actors, particularly in cases where they are part of criminalised social groups (e.g., youth from disadvantaged communities). Ideal imageries of victimhood tainting judicial actors' perceptions may clash with the complexity of victims' experiences and identities, leading to biases and selectivity in the handling of cases. Thus, certain cases may end up being given less attention or even being closed by the Attorney General's Office in El Salvador when the disappeared come from criminalised communities.

Experiences of re-victimising and demeaning encounters with state search actors can also historically affect participation. 14EV suggests that lack of political recognition has persisted across regimes of governance, from both sides of the Salvadoran political spectrum, affecting historically excluded and victimised communities, disempowering them further in claiming their rights. These experiences highlight how impunity and stigmatisation generate encounters of dismissal and inaction, epitomising deficient recognition relationships which disengage and disempower significantly relatives' struggles for answers and search efforts.

Acknowledging poor chances of obtaining justice in terms of perpetrators being held accountable and prosecuted, other ways for the state to bring validation and vindication for Salvadorian victims are highlighted. 12EV discusses the possibility of 'a symbolic trial where there is effective recognition that there has been a violation of rights and of life itself'. This initiative, as a measure of political recognition, would symbolically restore victims' moral worth and dignity as citizens, by officially legitimising their claims within their communities. By fostering societal capital for recognition relationships, it could also facilitate their collective mobilisation: 'something that can unite us, because all the survivors who are victims of ED can be united in this search for justice'.

This idea of recognition as an expression of societal solidarity and reintegration connects also to 15EV's critical view of the Salvadoran state project to offer minimal compensation to victims. It should not be a way for the state to silence people or a means to maintain denial and impunity. It should be a right for victims in relation to damage incurred and a 'debt' that the state has and should recognise. Only then may it constitute a meaningful political form of recognition.

## 5.6 THE SEARCH: MOVING FORWARD THROUGH OTHER RECOGNITION RELATIONSHIPS

The disjuncture in recognition relationships between families and official search mechanisms continues to define potential and actual resolutions to search processes. Many victims express the need for supportive recognition relationships, as support which is continuous and throughout their search journey from its initiation to the end. This helps mitigate the various experiences of lack of recognition they may have with state actors, and contributes to recognising the long-term and deeply emotional nature of the search journey.

2CV's experience with forensic actors points to the importance of long-term support. After a long trajectory of search within judicial institutions and experiences of lack of recognition, she had yet another painful encounter with officials during the identification of her son's remains. Having identified him thanks to his missing finger, she still had to convince the officials who had overlooked this personal detail that this was a distinctive feature of his identity. Her experience illustrates the value of psycho-social assistance in encounters with forensic institutions. Our respondents described it as a much-needed support, mostly given by non-governmental organisations (NGOs) in the context of forensic investigations, particularly at the stages of notification (when the relatives are informed of the discovery of their loved one's remains), identification (when the remains are identified by the family), and repatriation (when the remains are returned to the family).

When state recognition is absent, or ineffective, victims employ different strategies to find recognition, which may bring them agency in the search. Faced with silence from state institution actors, 4EVA found collective resolve in engaging within the association of families of disappeared persons to continue the search. As is often the case, the families themselves gather and rely on other networks of recognition and support, grounding their collective mobilisation in shared solidarities, emotional experiences, and objectives. In the case of 4EVA, she went on to lead a victims' association, an evolution from individual search, to collective search, to shared activism. The path of activism can also be a way of coping with the uncertainty and distress of ambiguous loss.

Victim organisations can thus be valuable recognition resources for the participation of families in the search. They can steer victims in the right direction when they feel lost, provide them with the relevant information to know where to go and how to proceed in an often bureaucratic and complex process, as well as offer sympathy.

Recognition relationships with victim organisations can promote participation throughout the search, but importantly also in bringing it to a conclusion, whether by finding the disappeared person alive or identifying where their remains are. For many, Pro-Búsqueda in El Salvador was key in offering recognition where it has been lacking from the state, and also supporting the completion of search processes, notably through its DNA database. Many participants described trusting more such NGOs than the state-run search mechanism, which 'creates a lot of expectations for the victims, it re-victimizes them more', for example because of identification errors (14EV).

## 5.7 CONCLUDING REMARKS

In the stories which we have included in our analysis there is a strong sense of a journey. This journey begins with victims making sense of their suffering and demanding to know what has happened to their loved ones who have been disappeared. Recognition relationships are significant in helping them understand their experience of suffering as being attached to rights and state obligations. At this stage, recognition is required from officials, from peers, and from wider society so that these victims are validated in their demands to know the truth and the basic facts of a disappearance are recognised. Through engagement with official mechanisms as well as civil society actors and fellow victims, the search journey can lead, for some, to activism, and for others, to heightened participation. This involves recognition relationships being developed between victims within collectives, and between victims and official mechanisms, as well as between victims and activists. At each stage, and through each interaction, victims can be recognised or denied as justice stakeholders. We have argued that this recognition is shaped through recognition relationships which in turn determine whether participation can itself be a valuable form of victim recognition.

In the ebb and flow of these recognition relationships being developed over time and in different contexts, we see how each recognition relationship shapes and builds upon others. Societal recognition – from family, friends, peers, wider society – can influence whether and how victims make demands of official processes and how victim activists push official processes to offer what is needed. In turn, recognition from the state of the victims and their rights as well as experiences influences societal recognition. Societal recognition is likely to be challenging, especially if there is continued state denial or lack of political will, which can fuel doubts within the community about the legitimacy of victims' claims and of their struggles in initiating or sustaining a search process. This is where we see the importance of the element of procedural justice which runs throughout the analysis. If victims do not perceive the search process to be fair, if they are re-traumatised and re-victimised through their interactions with officials, if their informational needs are not recognised, then they will not perceive the process to be just. In this sense procedural justice can facilitate recognition relationships which have significant implications for ongoing or future participation of relatives as justice stakeholders. Moreover, as we illustrate in our analysis, procedural justice is directly influenced by recognition relationships, as they determine to what extent victims feel that their experiences and rights are recognised. Impunity and stigmatisation foster conditions which are not fertile for recognition, and which can contribute to disengaging and disempowering relatives in their struggle for answers.

Full and effective recognition may not happen through the judicial process, especially concerning the administrative burdens that characterise initiation and continued participation in a search. In addition, recognition can occur even without a successful search process, as we see in the cases of activists who feel supported in their peer networks and recognised both legally and morally. These dynamics point to the complex ways in which the search process and recognition relationships interact, and either reinforce or limit each other. This is the case not least because of the different meanings that different actors will attach to their experiences and the different ways in which they define recognition. A recognition relationship is as much about resources, contexts, and needs as it is about a static definition of what victim recognition is and should be, and what rights and meanings of justice are attached to it. It demonstrates that recognition is made, shaped, and contested through relationships between actors. Our findings reveal that relationships are experienced as recognising, through meaningful actions of support and redress, which demonstrate genuine understanding, responsibility, and concern for immediate, but also long-term, impacts of ED. Moreover, recognition relationships are not one thing, but may emerge as self-recognition, social recognition, official recognition, political recognition, and moral recognition. Any one of these, or many of these, may be present at a given point in time or in a given context. As our analysis highlights, there is a complex landscape of formal and informal actors who engage with each other in different ways throughout the course of a search process. Whether these engagements form recognition relationships depends on time and place and the associated possibilities for spheres of recognition.

Our chapter underscores the importance of participation as a valuable form of victim recognition. However, we also wish to highlight the importance of recognition relationships for determining both procedural justice and then ultimately participation itself. In order for participation to offer recognition, multiple recognition relationships must be negotiated, managed, built, and challenged. This is both demanding for victims and obstacle-ridden. However, we see in both our cases that victims we have spoken to are constantly finding ways to practise their agency and to participate as justice stakeholders, reshaping recognition relationships as they go. It is incumbent upon transitional justice researchers, policymakers, and practitioners to not forget this complex web of relationships which will influence the success and fairness of any given search process.

## REFERENCES

Barton-Hronešová, Jessie. 2018. *The Struggle for Redress. Victim Capital in Bosnia and Herzegovina.* Palgrave Macmillan.

Correa, Cristian, Julie Guillerot, and Lisa Margarell. 2020. 'Reparations and Victim Participation: Experiences with the Design and Implementation of Domestic Reparations Programs'. In *Reparations for Victims of Genocide, War Crimes and Crimes against Humanity,* edited by Carla Ferstman and Marina Goetz, pp. 383–414. Brill | Nijhoff.

De Greiff, Pablo. 2012. 'Theorizing Transitional Justice'. *American Society for Political and Legal Philosophy,* 51, 31–77.

Dixon, Peter. 2015. 'Reparations and the Politics of Recognition'. In *Contested Justice: The Politics and Practice of International Criminal Court Interventions,* edited by Carsten Stahn, Christian de Vos, and Sara Kendall, pp. 326–351. Cambridge University Press.

Dotson, Kristie. 2011. 'Tracking Epistemic Violence, Tracking Practices of Silencing'. *Hypatia*, 26(2), 236–257.

Fraser, Nancy. 2005. 'Reframing Justice in a Globalizing World'. *New Left Review*, 36, 69–88.

Garbett, Claire. 2013. 'The Truth and the Trial: Victim Participation, Restorative Justice, and the International Criminal Court'. *Contemporary Justice Review*, 16, 193–213.

Goodey, Jo. 2005. *Victims and Victimology: Research, Policy and Practice*. Longman.

Hearty, Kevin. 2018. 'Victims of Human Rights Abuses in Transitional Justice: Hierarchies, Perpetrators and the Struggle for Peace'. *The International Journal of Human Rights*, 22(7), 888–909.

Jones, Briony, Lisa Ott, Mina Rauschenbach, and Camillo Sanchez. 2023. 'Hiding in Plain Sight: Victim Participation in the Search for Disappeared Persons, a Contribution to (Procedural) Justice'. *International Journal of Transitional Justice*, 17, 233–251.

Killean, Rachel. 2016. 'Procedural Justice in International Criminal Courts: Assessing Civil Parties' Perceptions of Justice at the Extraordinary Chambers in the Courts of Cambodia'. *International Criminal Law Review*, 16(1), 1–38.

Ott, Lisa, Ana Julia Escalante, Pamela Favre, Helí Hernandez, Alejandro Jímenez, Briony Jones, Mina Rauschenbach, Camilo Sanchez, Ana Srovin Coralli, and Bronwen Webster. 2022. *The Search for Victims of Enforced Disappearance: A Multidisciplinary Exploration of Current Practices*. Swisspeace working paper 2.

Robins, Simon. 2013. *Families of the Missing: A Test for Contemporary Approaches to Transitional Justice*. Routledge.

Wemmers, Jo-Anne. 2008. 'Victims' Participation and Therapeutic Jurisprudence'. *Victims and Offenders*, 3, 165–191.

Wilke, Christine. 2007. 'Recognising Victimhood: Politics and Narratives of Rehabilitation in Germany'. *Journal of Human Rights*, 6, 479–496.

# 6

# Formal Participation, De Facto Exclusion?

## *The Impact of Transitional Justice Standardisation in Uganda for Affected Communities and Victims*

*Thomas Obel Hansen*

### 6.1 INTRODUCTION

This chapter explores how the international standardisation of transitional justice has impacted domestic transitional justice processes in Uganda. It pays particular attention to the increasingly sanitised involvement and participation of local stakeholders, including victims, thus offering a contribution to the discourse referred to in this volume as 'second generation victim engagement' – and more broadly the literatures around victims, participation, and transitional justice (e.g., Evrard, Bonifazi, and Destrooper 2021; Moffett 2021). The chapter shows how, despite the presence of language such as 'local consultation', 'participation', and 'victims-centeredness' in official transitional justice policy documents in Uganda, affected communities are largely detached from the government-designed transitional justice process, in part reflecting a lack of genuine intention among decision-makers in the country to give meaningful effect to principles of inclusion. As such, formal 'compliance' with ideas about civil society, local community and victim participation and engagement, as endorsed by international standards about transitional justice, has in the case of Uganda generally not resulted in either process or substance that meet the (multi-faceted) expectations and demands of affected communities, victims, and other relevant stakeholders.

The chapter focuses the analysis mainly on the process surrounding the development and adoption of Uganda's National Transitional Justice Policy (hereafter NTJP or the Policy), which has emerged as the central policy document for transitional justice in the country (even if at the time of writing, in early 2025, it is yet to be adopted in law).[1] Where particularly relevant, the chapter also pays attention to other frameworks and processes, including those occurring outside the official state-endorsed transitional justice set-up.

The research for this chapter draws on extensive consultations with relevant stakeholders in Uganda, including community-members and persons directly affected by the operations of transitional justice. In addition, the research consulted government ministers, officials, and other transitional justice decision-makers and policymakers; technical staff working with government bodies responsible for designing or implementing transitional justice; judges and

The author is grateful to the many research participants in Uganda for sharing their views on complex and often sensitive matters.

[1] In August 2024, a private bill seeking to implement the NTJP in law, sponsored by Charles Onen, was proposed for consideration in the Uganda Parliament. www.parliament.go.ug/news/3016/transitional-justice-bill-reconcile-turbulent-past-northern-uganda.

other legal sector personnel; donor representatives and representatives of international organisations; academics; journalists and other representatives of the media; transitional justice practitioners and representatives of local and international civil society organisations working on transitional justice in Uganda. A total of seventy persons were interviewed or consulted through focus groups for this research.[2] The chapter draws on findings and arguments developed by the author in previous and forthcoming publications, but adds to that analysis in the sense that the focus here is specifically on issues relating to engagement with and participation of affected communities and victims.[3]

The chapter proceeds as follows: First, it provides a brief examination of how the 'transitional justice script' – understood as an outcome of the process of international standardisation in the field that has occurred over the last decades – approaches issues relating to engagement with and participation of affected communities and victims. Next, in its main empirical analysis, the chapter turns to an examination of how Uganda's approach to transitional justice formally approaches issues relating to engagement with and participation of affected communities and victims, coupled with an assessment of how this plays out in practice. This involves a review of relevant transitional justice policy documents that, ostensibly, guide transitional justice in the country as well as data collected in field work in Uganda, to understand the dynamics at play in the design of transitional justice solutions in the country, which claim to foster engagement and participation. Based on that analysis, the chapter concludes by questioning whether the international standardisation of transitional justice may not necessarily remedy shortcomings in practice in terms of involving affected communities and victims.

Throughout this analysis, the chapter demonstrates how the transitional justice script, the implementation of which is supported by donors and other international actors, can be associated with a 'tick-the-box approach' to consultation, participation, and other relevant principles relating to inclusion of affected communities and victims. It argues that this challenge can be especially outspoken in contexts such as Uganda where the national political leadership may lack genuine commitment to the underpinning principles and values. The chapter concludes that state-endorsed transitional justice in Uganda remains largely 'empty', detached from reality and unimplemented.

## 6.2 TRANSITIONAL JUSTICE STANDARDISATION AND PRINCIPLES OF INCLUSIVENESS IN THE TRANSITIONAL JUSTICE SCRIPT

The international standardisation of transitional justice has seemingly contributed to a situation where the 'processual understanding' in transitional justice is largely unaffected by developments that mean transitional justice now involves actors at multiple levels (vertical

[2] Approximately half of the respondents were consulted in semi-structured interviews, the other half in focus groups. Interviewees were given the option of citation by name, generically, or anonymously; hence the variation in citation details. All interviews were conducted in English and recorded with the permission of research participants. Focus group participants are cited with reference to the relevant focus group (group 1: local media representatives; focus group 2: ex-combatants; focus group 3: persons born in captivity; focus group 4: persons becoming mothers in captivity). All research activities are approved by the relevant ethics committee at Ulster University, according to UK standards and law.

[3] Previous publications are focused more generally on analysing processes and dynamics surrounding the international standardisation of transitional justice and its impact locally in Uganda (Hansen 2024). The present chapter uses several quotes and other case-specific material referenced in the mentioned works, as they provide helpful insights into the specific theme of engagement with affected communities and victims treated in this chapter.

expansion) and applies to a wide range of contexts outside the field's origin in paradigmatic transitions from authoritarian to democratic rule (horizontal expansion), including semi-authoritarian post-conflict situations such as Uganda (Hansen 2013). Based on a review of transitional justice manuals and toolkits, Gissel (2022, 871) argues that transitional justice standardisation 'circulates an international yet particularistic notion of justice', which has remained fairly consistent over time and takes the form of universal 'liberal-cosmopolitan justice'. These priorities have, in the words of Gissel (2022, 871; see also Lambourne 2014; Subotić 2012), resulted in 'a highly specific model' where four processes – trials, truth-telling, reparations, and institutional reform – are seen to constitute the core elements of transitional justice. However, more recent transitional justice manuals, including the United Nations (UN) Secretary-General's 2023 guidance note, sometimes replace 'institutional reform' with the broader notion of 'guarantees of non-recurrence', seen to encompass institutional reform and vetting but also 'measures in the societal, cultural and individual spheres' (UNSG 2023, 2). Additionally, more recent manuals and guidelines often claim to embrace a more contextual approach to transitional justice, one where the customs and expectations of affected communities are said to be more central to international actors' support to the formulation of transitional justice responses nationally (e.g., UNSG 2023, 6–7).

Accordingly, a transitional justice 'script' has emerged as an outcome of an internationally led standardisation process occurring over the last decades. This script sets relatively clear parameters and boundaries for what transitional justice should achieve; how these goals should be promoted in practice through specific institutional arrangements, design and process; and the principles and values guiding these processes, including ideas about ownership and participation (Gissel 2022). At the same time, contemporary expressions of the transitional justice script increasingly claim to embrace 'innovative solutions that are tailored to the context' (UNSG 2023, 6), for a significant part with a view towards achieving justice that is more meaningful to affected communities and victims. This is likely to be in part the result of the critique of 'top-down' transitional justice that has for long surrounded international actors' involvement in transitional justice design and process (e.g., McEvoy and McGregor 2008), coupled with increased focus in contemporary transitional justice discourse on notions of participation (e.g., Evrard, Bonifazi, and Destrooper 2021).

The standardisation of transitional justice is closely associated with what has been referred to as a broader process of globalisation of transitional justice, whereby international actors, such as UN agencies, international development agencies, international non-governmental organisations (NGOs) and other international actors, are increasingly involved in framing and conceptualising transitional justice (e.g., Teitel 2014). That international involvement centres for significant parts on producing transitional justice manuals, guidelines, and other forms of standard-setting tools, which enables – or, some would say, pushes – national decision-makers to take the starting point in international standards when designing and implementing transitional justice nationally. As scholars such as Miller (2008, 271) observed long ago, international involvement in transitional justice is also associated with a high level of 'consistency of language and terminology employed in a wide diversity of post-conflict contexts', which points to transitional justice as a 'global phenomenon'. As we shall see, this phenomenon is reflected in the case of Uganda, in the sense that national transitional justice policies draw heavily on the vocabulary of the transitional justice script, not least in terms of transitional justice buzzwords suggesting *inclusiveness*, such as a 'victim-centred approach' and 'consultative, participatory and inclusive processes' (NTJP 2019, iii; 2). As we shall also see, commitment to such notions in formal policy documents is no silver bullet to realisation. This raises broader methodological questions concerning how best to examine regimes for participation and engagement, explored by, for example, Evrard, Bonifazi, and Destrooper (2021, 429–430). These concerns are reflected in this chapter through its attention to how matters are perceived by relevant stakeholders in Uganda.

For the purposes of the analysis in this chapter, it is vital to understand the vocabulary of the transitional justice script concerning engagement with and participation of affected communities and victims. Victim participation has for long been treated as a central *procedural criterion* in various transitional justice manuals, for example in the context of criminal trials (Gissel 2022, 866). Broader concepts concerning involvement of and engagement with victims is stressed – and unpacked – in some expressions of the transitional justice script, not only in a procedural but also in a more *substantive* sense. The UN Secretary-General's 2010 guidance note, for instance, has among its 'guiding principles' to ensure the 'centrality of victims in the design and implementation of [transitional justice] processes and mechanisms', adding that 'national consultations, conducted with the explicit inclusion of victims and other traditionally excluded groups, are particularly effective' for achieving sustainable peace and accountability through transitional justice (UNSG 2010, 6).

Notions of *inclusiveness* have evidently become increasingly central to transitional justice manuals over time. One of the most central contemporary transitional justice manuals – the UN Secretary-General's 2023 guidance note on transitional justice (UNSG 2023) – provides useful insight into how key standardisers perceive these themes and their significance contemporarily (although for the purposes of the empirical analysis in this chapter it should be recalled that the main aspects of transitional justice policy development in Uganda predate the 2023 guidance note). Key terms included in the UNSG 2023 guidance note in this regard include 'consultations' with victims, communities, and other specific groups (twenty-one counts); 'participation', relating both to victims and specific groups such as young people (eighteen counts); 'empower' or 'empowerment', including of victims, communities and other specific groups (ten counts); 'victim-centred' (five counts); 'people-centred' (three counts); and 'community ownership' (four counts).[4]

How then are these and related terms understood, and what does that tell us about the current state of the art in the UN's approach to transitional justice in terms of engagement with and participation of affected communities and victims in transitional justice contexts? One of the three 'core objectives' of the 2023 guidance note concern 'contributing to a tangible and transformational impact for people and communities' (UNSG 2023, 3). This reflects the UN's current approach that transitional justice should not only be 'victim-centred' but also 'people-centred' (UNSG 2023, 11).[5] At the same time, 'victim-centred' transitional justice, as a 'stand-alone' objective, remains key in the 2023 guidance note. That concept is used not only to connote the idea that 'the legal rights of victims under international law' must be duly considered (UNSG 2023, 15), but also more broadly in the context of objectives such as promoting an inclusive approach to transitional justice that aims at 'empowering victims' and 'fostering community ownership' (UNSG 2023, 8). The guidance note further stresses that transitional justice being victim-centred means that meaningful *victims' participation* must be facilitated (UNSG 2023, 8). Victims' participation, it is emphasised, should be 'conceived as an ongoing process, not as single initiatives' (UNSG 2023, 8). *Consultation* with victims

4 Counts are approximate, as they in some cases cover closely related terms (e.g., 'participation'/'participate').

5 The term 'people-centred' is invoked, alongside the terms 'strategic', 'integrated', and 'innovative', to counter 'what has at times become an ad hoc, fragmented, formulaic and technocratic approach' to transitional justice (UNSG 2023, 3–4).

and other groups is seen as a central component of participation, because it facilitates 'the acquiring of essential knowledge and specific insights'; increases the likelihood that transitional justice measures will 'capture their diverse views on justice and on what constitutes effective redress'; enables a 'closer congruence between the expressed needs of victims and measures yet to be designed'; 'increase the legitimacy of future [transitional justice] measures because the process of consulting is itself a measure of the recognition and empowerment of victims and communities'; and 'helps them gain or regain a place in the public sphere that they were denied' (UNSG 2023, 13). The 2023 guidance note set out 'four crucial factors', seen to underlie successful consultations, namely (a) 'effective capacity-building and sensitisation among all stakeholders'; (b) 'not [to] be construed as one-off events but as on-going processes'; (c) 'selection of an inclusive and gender-balanced group of stakeholders'; and (d) 'safety, consent and confidentiality are primordial requirements for meaningful consultations' (UNSG 2023, 13).

Accordingly, the transitional justice script, in its contemporary formulation, embraces notions of consultations with victims, local communities, and other specific groups in the design of transitional justice; participation of victims and other specific groups are seen as benchmarks for the legitimacy of transitional justice processes; and empowering victims and local communities are viewed as key objectives of transitional justice. Recent manuals such as the UNSG 2023 guidance note unpack some of these notions and set forth pathways to achieving the broader goals and objectives in practice.

The existence of a transitional justice script may nonetheless present risks that national authorities draw on the language and concepts endorsed, with a view towards legitimising national transitional justice responses without having the necessary thought for giving meaningful effect to these terms in practice, or, possibly, a genuine intent to do so. Whereas language in recent expressions of the transitional justice script concerning inclusion can therefore be seen to reflect growing attention to victims' rights and needs at policymaking level, this may have little real impact on situations where there is no genuine commitment to these principles. These points will be demonstrated in the following through the case of Uganda.

## 6.3 THE INSTITUTIONAL APPROACH IN UGANDA'S TRANSITIONAL JUSTICE POLICY TOWARDS ENGAGEMENT AND PARTICIPATION – AND THE REALITY 'ON THE GROUND'

Ugandan government actors involved in drafting the country's NTJP sometimes argue that the Policy is 'mainly locally driven',[6] and originates in 'an organic consultation process'.[7] However, the research underpinning this chapter demonstrates that 'locally driven' mainly translates into how ministry technocrats have sought to accommodate the demands in the national political leadership (often driving transitional justice *away* from meaningful effects for affected communities and victims) alongside donors' insistence on 'letter compliance' with the transitional justice script. This has resulted in a transitional justice policy and institutional set-up that appears forthcoming to ideas about engagement with affected communities and victims through inclusion of transitional justice buzzwords, but with only limited attention to how to give effect to these principles in practice. These points are unpacked in the

[6] Interview with Jane O'Dongo, lead drafter of NTJP, Uganda Law Reform Commission, Kampala, (16 August 2022).

[7] Interview with national transitional justice advisor to Government of Uganda, online (14 September 2022).

following analysis, first through an assessment of the *process* surrounding the development of Uganda's NTJP and next through an analysis of its *substance*.

### 6.3.1 *Process: A 'Consultative', 'Participatory' and 'Inclusive' Process?*

Uganda's NTJP entails a good portion of transitional justice buzzwords, resembling those found in the transitional justice script outlined earlier, with relevance to engagement of affected communities and victims in the process. By way of example, the Policy speaks to a 'victim-centred approach', including 'consultative, participatory and inclusive processes' (NTJP 2019, 2). Whereas the Policy offers little guidance concerning how to give effect to these principles, consultations, including with local communities and victims, *did* occur in Uganda – and extensively so. The transitional justice consultation process in Uganda, facilitated at government level by the Justice Law and Order Sector (JLOS), involved numerous 'validation meetings' with international partners including donors, civil society groups, and local communities (NTJP 2019, 2). JLOS' consultation work was evidently informed, at least in terms of terminology, by the standards embraced by the transitional justice script. For instance, the transitional justice process in Uganda, JLOS states, 'is one that seeks to be comprehensive, holistic and victim-centred', objectives that are claimed to be achieved 'through a consultative and participatory process involving victims, war affected communities, civil society organizations, cultural and religious leaders, local government, and other stakeholders'.[8] One could hardly imagine a description of transitional justice consultations more in 'harmony' with the transitional justice script's expectations of inclusiveness.

In reality, however, the consultation process appears in several ways to have been counterproductive to creating a timely and meaningful justice response to atrocity crimes in the country. The inclusion of transitional justice buzzwords without a clear pathway towards realisation is pointed to as a key challenge by several respondents. By way of example, a government transitional justice advisor notes: 'while there were a lot of consultations to lead up to the [Transitional Justice] Policy, it is unclear how the information/views shared were actually integrated and used to inform the policy'.[9] A civil society representative similarly explains that victims in Uganda desire a NTJP that is 'transparent', 'participatory', and implemented 'together with victims', but concludes that such inclusion has not been happening in practice:

> we are trying to tell them [i.e. government agencies] they should include victims when they are doing this project, they should not impose. It should be a down-up approach, not an up-down approach. If we don't involve the victims they don't feel the difference; right now we are already seeing a gap. [...] We are worried that victims are [not] aware that the TJ policy has been [adopted]; it will be too late for them to come in and say 'no, we didn't know anything, we are not aware about this'. So they [i.e. government agencies] are doing it, they are imposing it, they are planning it alone, and our worry is some victims will be left out.[10]

Arguably pointing to a lack of genuine interest in government circles to facilitate meaningful inclusion, civil society organisations struggled to even access the final version of the NTJP, as adopted:

[8] JLOS website, https://jlos.go.ug/index.php/about-jlos/priority-focus-areas/transitional-justice.

[9] E-mail from international transitional justice advisor to Government of Uganda (23 January 2023).

[10] Interview with Grace Acan, representative of national civil society organisation Women's Advocacy Network, online (14 September 2022).

> Even when they [i.e. JLOS] announced that the Policy had been approved, it took civil society writing a [petition] to demand that JLOS release the policy officially. I remember that we sat [as] a group of civil society organisations [and] wrote a [petition] and had to take it through the newspaper demanding that JLOS can make this a public document, and also undertake sensitisation so that the public and the community are aware about this policy.[11]

A separate – and more profound – question raised by some is whether the extensive consultation process facilitated by JLOS and funded by donors was even necessary in the first place. Reflections on this note by a transitional justice practitioner consulted in this research are worth citing in detail:

> That is where the problem is, the consultation is to say, 'okay we want to do something for you, what should we do for you'? It took away the power from the people who were affected… So, they spent 10 years consulting; in the meantime, the directly affected victims have all died. By 2007 there was already a framework for TJ in Northern Uganda; JLOS was not involved in the development of that framework. Why did they not implement the framework which was the agreement on accountability and reconciliation in Northern Uganda? […] Why did they have to consult? There was nothing to consult [about]. People had already spoken […] all this was taken away by JLOS.[12]

Pointing to the continued relevance of the concept of 'distance' in transitional justice and international law more generally explored in other contexts by, for example, Clark (2018), the same transitional justice practitioner additionally reflects that actors involved in facilitating consultation often did not 'understand what the premise of transitional justice in the local person's sense of mind is', framing discussions in ways 'that the local person will have to try to make sense [of]'.[13]

Accordingly, government-facilitated transitional justice consultations in Uganda are often perceived negatively by civil society groups and persons affected by conflict. For some this evidently amounts to a form of sham that has mainly aimed at 'ticking the right boxes' to satisfy donors' demands of an inclusive process, as embraced by the transitional justice script, rather than reflecting a genuine desire to understand and accommodate community perspectives and concerns.

JLOS was not the only stakeholder involved in transitional justice consultations with communities and victims in Uganda. For one, the International Center for Transitional Justice (ICTJ) played a key role in 'linking up victims or communities locally or nationally' in the context of NTJP development.[14] The ICTJ's engagement with local communities was, naturally, not devoid of values and perceptions of how transitional justice could be framed. Indeed, as one respondent observes, the ICTJ 'has been very active […] trying to help actors understand what TJ is'.[15] That is to say, the ICTJ apparently came to see its main objective of working in Uganda, at least in the early phases of the process, as informing Ugandans what, in its view, transitional justice is and how it ought to work.[16] Unsurprisingly, that view relied heavily on the transitional justice script, as formulated at the time, including a so-called pillar or

11 Interview with representative of international civil society organisation, Kampala (9 August 2022).
12 Interview with transitional justice practitioner, online (16 September 2022).
13 Interview with transitional justice practitioner, online (16 September 2022).
14 Interview with representative of national civil society organisation (Grace Acan, Women's Advocacy Network), online (14 September 2022).
15 Interview with representative of national civil society organisation, online (18 October 2022).
16 Interview with representative of international civil society organisation, Kampala (19 August 2022).

comprehensive approach to transitional justice,[17] endorsed by key transitional justice funders over time (e.g., EU 2015; UNSG 2004). Without diminishing the value of the ICTJ's consultation efforts, seen by some respondents as crucial for advancing inclusiveness at an early stage, it is worth noting that others express reservations about the ICTJ's approach. For some, it was wrongly based on a perspective, as one transitional justice practitioner phrases it, that 'you have to do comprehensive transitional justice, which means you have to tick all those boxes'.[18] This leads the same transitional justice practitioner to conclude that the ICTJ 'took away the liberty for [Ugandans] to design their own TJ measures according to their situation'.[19] Whether that is an accurate assessment or not, the fact remains that international NGOs such as the ICTJ approached transitional justice 'recipes' for Uganda much along the same line as bilateral donors and UN agencies, informed mainly by a universal transitional justice script.

Beyond the consultation efforts by government agencies and the ICTJ, local NGOs in Uganda have also consulted affected communities and victims on transitional justice matters, in ways that are sometimes experienced as more present and relevant by those involved compared with government-led consultations. Some observe: 'you will never find any government body coming to the grassroots to follow-up [...] you will find that it is the NGOs and the victims who are forming [...] networks' that are most relevant from the perspective of affected communities and victims.[20] The community-based transitional justice work and grassroot mobilisation conducted by the Refugee Law Project (RLP) is often pointed to as a particularly innovative counter-model to the official government approach to transitional justice.[21] That work takes – in the words of the RLP itself – the starting point as what community members see as important, rather than universal understandings reflected in the transitional justice script: 'It's not like we define these processes [...] we trust that victim communities know what they want. So they inform the activities that we actually do. It's about sitting with communities in a memory dialogue for instance and asking communities, "where does healing start for you"?'[22]

One could say that consultation and substantive transitional justice process occur simultaneously here, possibly facilitating more meaningful participation along the lines of what for instance de Waardt and Weber (2019, 223–224) have suggested. Of course, the absence of a formal institutional set-up, official sanctions, and remedies can present challenges for those involved, especially considering their justice preferences discussed elsewhere in this chapter.

In summary, extensive consultations about transitional justice have taken place in Uganda, including with affected communities and victims, reflecting donors' demands of 'compliance' with the transitional justice script's expectations in this regard. It is questionable, however, to what extent these consultations have informed the development of official transitional justice policies in the country. Additionally, the government-sponsored consultation process has been associated with extensive delays putting in place relevant policies – and implementing them. In the view of some, the consultation process has even served to disempower victims and affected communities, in part because it was premised on fixed understandings of what transitional justice should be about.

17 Interview with representative of international civil society organisation, Kampala, (10 August 2022) (interview 2). The ICTJ's work in Uganda and elsewhere has been analysed by, for example, Batanda (2009) and Robins (2009).

18 Author's interview with transitional justice practitioner, online (16 September 2022).

19 Author's interview with transitional justice practitioner, online (16 September 2022).

20 Focus Group 2, Gulu, 30 November 2022, participant 7.

21 E.g., Interview with TJ practitioner (Isaac Okwir), online (25 November 2022).

22 Interview with representative of national civil society organisation (RLP), Kampala (12 August 2022).

### 6.3.2 *Substance: Mismatch between Transitional Justice Policy and (Multi-Pronged) Expectations by Affected Communities and Victims?*

How do the main components of the NTJP, as adopted, correspond with the needs and expectations of affected communities and victims as to what transitional justice in Uganda ought to be about and how it ought to operate? Because there are numerous, often conflicting, views among Ugandans affected by conflict and atrocity crimes, it is self-evidently difficult to say much about this in general terms. However, some basic observations can be made.[23]

The NTJP, adopted in 2019, is framed around five 'policy priority areas', which are elaborated in the following in light of perceptions among respondents.

One priority area involves 'formal justice', which the NTJP frames mainly as a question of witness and victims' protection (NTJP 2019, 18), though, curiously, without detailing how these safeguards should work in practice and, equally puzzling, without clarifying what the relevant justice processes are (criminal proceedings, civil proceedings, or something else). The Policy does, remarkably, not make any explicit connection to the International Crimes Division (ICD) in this regard, although it is the only institution in Uganda specifically set up to pursue 'formal justice' for atrocity crimes, often viewed by commentators through the prism of International Criminal Court complementarity (e.g., Moffett 2016; Nouwen 2013). A related priority area in the NTJP addresses amnesties, but makes no real commitments in this regard, as it simply states that amnesties 'played a role' in transitional justice in Uganda in the past, and that 'accountability challenges' need to be addressed 'if a future amnesty should be considered' (NTJP 2019, 19–20).

There is a question whether the NTJP and Uganda's transitional justice response to date, which in operational terms focuses on criminal justice through the establishment of the ICD and the NTJP's treatment of amnesties, are in line with prevailing perceptions in affected communities concerning what transitional justice ought to be about. Whereas views among Ugandans concerning criminal justice vis-à-vis amnesties are complex, multi-faceted, and not easily reconcilable, it does seem clear that local civil society groups and victims often feel that the categorical rejection of amnesties was unmerited. That rejection reflects at least in part an insistence by international actors on criminal justice along the lines of the transitional justice script (which emphasises criminal justice in general and excludes amnesties for international crimes). But this approach does not necessarily correspond with affected communities' understanding and preferences for post-conflict justice.[24] Questioning of the transitional justice script's demands in this regard can even be met with hostility: A transitional justice practitioner in Uganda explains his view that civil society groups who spoke in favour of amnesties 'became cursed in all kinds of manners' for endorsing impunity, an accusation experienced to be 'very far from the truth'.[25]

Another priority area in the NTJP involves 'nation building and reconciliation', an area which speaks to truth-seeking, notwithstanding that the Policy does not envisage the creation of a formal truth-finding body (NTJP 2019, 19). This presents a departure from the transitional justice script in an institutional sense. However, the research underpinning

[23] Several of the points that follow were originally developed – and are further unpacked – in Hansen 2024.

[24] Interview with TJ practitioner, online (16 November 2022). On the amnesty process and perceptions concerning its legitimacy among international donors, see generally Macdonald (2019, 240–243) and Oola (2015).

[25] Interview with transitional justice practitioner, online (16 September 2022).

this chapter suggests that truth-seeking is deemed a vital component of transitional justice for many Ugandans. The fact that the NTJP does not envisage a formal truth-seeking exercise makes several of the persons consulted in this research observe that transitional justice decision-makers in Uganda have departed from the stated preferences of local communities and victims with a view towards accommodating expectations or demands from the political leadership in the country. Indeed, some suggest that the government is 'against' truth-seeking because 'they know that once you begin that process then you will have to tackle discussions of what happened by all actors', thus potentially countering the existing narrative endorsed by the government that 'the state did nothing [wrong] [...] and that the perpetrators, the bad guys, are basically the LRA'.[26]

Another priority area in the NTJP involves reparations (NTJP 2019, 20), but the commitments set out are so vague that it is entirely unclear how this will be implemented, as the Policy simply makes a vague commitment to 'establish and implement a reparations [programme]' (NTJP 2019, 20). Reparations are regularly pointed to by the respondents in this research as being among the most pressing needs for victims in Uganda.

A last priority area in the NTJP covers 'traditional justice mechanisms', which commits the government to recognise these practices and 'protect [the] rights of parties' in such processes (NTJP 2019, 18), again, however, without giving concrete detail what these processes are or could look like in practice.[27] Respondents in this research often flagged the importance of traditional justice in the Ugandan context, but some were critical of the ambiguity of the Policy in this regard – including uncertainty how it could be implemented and by whom.

Unsurprisingly, a key concern for many with the NTJP is therefore that, as one civil society representative phrases it, 'everything is left vague'.[28] At the same time, however, such ambiguity is pointed to by others as potentially opening the door for further integrating civil society perspectives on transitional justice in the implementation phase: 'the policy is broad, it allows room [...] It is an opportunity in many ways; I know people see [the ambiguity of the Policy] as something that is detrimental', but 'it buys us time to look for funding' and 'to actually input into how do we implement this policy, how do we breathe life into this policy, in a manner that [...] helps us as a country'.[29]

At a broader level, some respondents consulted in this research suggest that Uganda's NTJP has become more of a 'JLOS Policy', rather than a policy for Ugandans, because it has been 'adulterated so much' and is experienced as remote by affected communities around the country, to the extent they are even familiar with it.[30] In sum, although it is impossible to speak in general terms about what victims and affected communities in Uganda demand or expect from transitional justice, there is evidently a level of mismatch between the institutional arrangements and substance envisaged by the NTJP and what for many Ugandans are seen to be the most important elements of dealing with past violence and atrocity. This brings into question the main motivations of the Ugandan government to develop a national transitional justice policy in the first place, issues addressed in the conclusions that follow.

26 Interview with representative of international civil society organisation, Kampala (10 August 2022).

27 While the usual four-pillar approach to TJ does not include traditional justice, some form of reliance on customary or traditional practices is sometimes endorsed, at least to the extent that various safeguards known from human rights law are considered. Gissel's (2022, 864–865) review of TJ manuals point to the consideration of traditional practices in the TJ script as a form of 'second-tier' TJ.

28 Interview with representative of international civil society organisation, Kampala (9 August 2022).

29 Interview with representative of national civil society organisation (RLP), Kampala (12 August 2022).

30 Interview with transitional justice practitioner, online (16 September 2022).

## 6.4 CONCLUSIONS: DUAL DYNAMICS IN TRANSITIONAL JUSTICE POLICYMAKING, DESIGN, AND IMPLEMENTATION

Uganda's approach to transitional justice is on the surface heavily marked by donors' expectations concerning 'compliance' with the transitional justice script, including inclusiveness, while simultaneously reflecting a desire to accommodate the demands of national decision-makers. These dual – and in some ways contradicting – dynamics in transitional justice policymaking, design, and implementation are arguably among the key factors explaining why in Uganda this process in many ways has materialised as a form of 'tick-the-box' exercise.

The result of such dualism in demands has been explained by Macdonald (2019, 227) through the notion of 'isomorphic mimicry', where donors and government recipients are seen to 'have a shared interest in prioritizing institutional form (what an institution looks like) over institutional function (what it achieves and the extent to which it is institutionalized)'. For the purposes of this chapter, the significance of these dynamics is mainly that they may result in transitional justice buzzwords, originating in the transitional justice script and covering inclusiveness, being integrated into relevant NTJP documents, while the outcome in terms of substance and institutional set-up of national transitional justice policies is one that remains largely detached from reality, including the expectations of affected communities and victims.

This outcome is affected not only by donors' insistence on formal compliance with the transitional justice script, but also demands of national political leaders, including avoiding functional processes that could potentially challenge the official narrative of conflict. In Uganda, the dual dynamics described here appear to have resulted in a high level of accommodation of transitional justice script *terminology* relating to inclusiveness, but in a low level of *internalisation* of the underpinning principles and values.

These dual dynamics are also associated with what has in Uganda materialised as a level of accommodation and a level of deviation from the transitional justice script in terms of the institutional set-up of transitional justice, the latter reflected most clearly in the absence of an official truth-seeking body. Comments by staff working in Ugandan government bodies tasked with transitional justice policy design, such as the Law Reform Commission (LRC), are illustrative. In the words of the lead drafter of the NTJP in the LRC, 'right from the onset of this process of TJ in Uganda, the context in which the donor partners were looking at it, was the theoretical context of what TJ is', not primarily preferences among ordinary Ugandans as to what transitional justice should be about.[31] This may help explain how international standards were perceived as what some government advisors refer to as a form of 'check list', albeit a check list that could be deviated from in terms of institutional set-up when deemed desirable, taking into account the policy preferences of national decision-makers.[32] All of this suggests that donor/national decision-maker dynamics are central to consider when seeking to understand how the international standardisation of transitional justice impacts affected communities and victims locally.

This cocktail of interests has in the view of many Ugandans involved with, or affected by, transitional justice been counterproductive for those intended to benefit from transitional justice. In the view of some respondents, blame attaches mainly to the transitional justice script itself. By way of example, a transitional justice practitioner argues that transitional justice in

[31] Interview with Jane O'Dongo, lead drafter of the NTJP, Uganda Law Reform Commission, Kampala (16 August 2022).

[32] Interview with national transitional justice advisor to Government of Uganda, online (14 September 2022).

Uganda has been 'a dismal failure', observing that this 'failure basically [originates in] the standardisation of TJ'; the primary concern here being that promotion of the transitional justice script and its local implementation in Uganda 'took away the demand for justice from the people who are affected like me and made it a subject for people who have no idea on what happened to be the champion of the pursuit of justice'.[33] For others, the blame goes as much to national decision-makers who have been generally uninterested in seeing justice materialise in a meaningful sense for affected communities and victims. A regular comment by these sceptics is that the Ugandan government promoted a transitional justice policy mainly, in the words of one civil society representative, to be able to '[tick] the box so [Uganda would be] the first to have a national TJ Policy', with little care for the expectations by relevant stakeholders as to what are the most pressing transitional justice themes and processes.[34]

The current lack of *implementation* of the NTJP is central to this critique. Lyandro Komakech, a former member of Parliament from Gulu, explains that 'not a single penny has been appropriated for the implementation of the TJ Policy', adding that 'we are not even sure which ministry should be leading [implementation efforts]'.[35] Many respondents reflect along similar lines that, ultimately, lacking political will in Uganda to give effect to the principles underpinning transitional justice inclusiveness remains the main challenge, and may likely result that the NTJP will never be fully implemented in practice.

Whether the finger is mainly pointed one way or the other, the fact remains that in countries such as Uganda, where real commitment in the political leadership to principles of inclusiveness may, at best, be half-hearted or conditional, formal accommodation of the transitional justice script's terminology may easily present an avenue for 'pretending' that genuine and inclusive transitional justice is happening, while in reality it is not. In that sense, the Ugandan example illustrates how transitional justice can be made to look comprehensive on paper and 'tick' what for many standardisers and donors are the 'right boxes', for example concerning consultation with local communities and victim participation, only to materialise as a formalistic and in many ways 'empty' arrangement which is detached from reality and remains generally unimplemented.

## REFERENCES

Batanda, Jackee. 2009. 'The Role of Civil Society in Advocating for Transitional Justice in Uganda'. Institute for Justice and Reconciliation.

Clark, Phil. 2018. *Distant Justice: The Impact of the International Criminal Court on African Politics*, Cambridge University Press.

de Waardt, Mijke, and Sanne Weber. 2019. 'Beyond Victims' Mere Presence: An Empirical Analysis of Victim Participation in Transitional Justice in Colombia'. *Journal of Human Rights Practice*, 11(1), 209–228.

EU. 2015. 'The EU's Policy Framework on Support to Transitional Justice'.

Evrard, Elke, Gretel Bonifazi, and Tine Destrooper. 2021. 'The Meaning of Participation in Transitional Justice: A Conceptual Proposal for Empirical Analysis'. *International Journal of Transitional Justice*, 15(2), 428–444.

Gissel, Line. 2022. 'The Standardisation of Transitional Justice'. *European Journal of International Relations*, 28(4), 859–884.

[33] Interview with transitional justice practitioner, online (16 September 2022).

[34] Interview with representative of national civil society organisation, online (18 October 2022). The NTJP mentions that Uganda 'sets the records as the first [AU] Member State to adopt a National Transitional Justice Policy' (NTJP 2019, 6).

[35] Interview with Lyandro Komakech, former Member of Parliament (Gulu), in Kampala, Uganda (16 August 2022).

Hansen, Thomas. 2013. 'The Vertical and Horizontal Expansion of Transitional Justice: Explanations and Implications for a Contested Field.' In Susanne Buckley-Zistel et al. (eds.), *Transitional Justice Theories*, Routledge, pp. 105–124.
Hansen, Thomas. 2024. 'The Impact of the International Standardization of Transitional Justice Locally: A Case Study of Uganda'. *Georgia Journal of International and Comparative Law*, 53(1), 1–30.
Lambourne, Wendy. 2014. 'What Are the Pillars of Transitional Justice? The United Nations, Civil Society and the Justice Cascade in Burundi'. *Macquarie Law Journal*, 13, 41–60.
Macdonald, Anna. 2019. '"Somehow This Whole Process Became So Artificial": Exploring the Transitional Justice Implementation Gap in Uganda'. *International Journal of Transitional Justice*, 13(2), 225–248.
McEvoy, Kieran, and Lorna McGregor. 2008. *Transitional Justice from Below: Grassroots Activism and the Struggle for Change*, Hart Publishing.
Miller, Zinaida. 2008. 'Effects of Invisibility: In Search of the "Economic" in Transitional Justice'. *The International Journal of Transitional Justice*, 2, 266–291.
Moffett, Luke. 2016. 'Complementarity's Monopoly on Justice in Uganda: The International Criminal Court, Victims and Thomas Kwoyelo'. *International Criminal Law Review*, 16(3), 503–524.
Moffett, Luke. 2021. 'Victims, Victimology and Transitional Justice'. In *Transitional Justice*, edited by Hakeem O. Yusuf and Hugo van der Merwe, pp. 30–53. Routledge.
National Transitional Justice Policy (NTJP). 2019. Ministry of Internal Affairs (Uganda), June 2019.
Nouwen, Sarah. 2013. *Complementarity in the Line of Fire: The Catalysing Effect of the International Criminal Court in Uganda and Sudan*, Cambridge University Press.
Oola, Stephen. 2015. 'In the Shadow of Kwoyelo's Trial: The ICC and Complementarity in Uganda'. In *Contested Justice: The Politics and Practice of International Criminal Court Interventions*, edited by Christian de Vos et al., pp. 147–170, Cambridge University Press.
Robins, Simon. 2009. 'Whose Voices? Understanding Victims' Needs in Transition: Nepali Voices: Perceptions of Truth, Justice, Reconciliation, Reparations and the Transition in Nepal'. *Journal of Human Rights Practice*, 1(2), 320–331.
Subotić, Jelena. 2012. 'The Transformation of International Transitional Justice Advocacy'. *International Journal of Transitional Justice*, 6(1), 106–125.
Teitel, Ruti G. 2014. 'Transitional Justice Globalized', Globalizing Transitional Justice: Contemporary Essays (online edn, Oxford Academic).
UNSG. 2004. 'The Rule of Law and Transitional Justice in Conflict and Post-Conflict Societies: Report of the Secretary-General'.
UNSG. 2010. 'Guidance Note of the Secretary-General: United Nations Approach to Transitional Justice'.
UNSG. 2023. 'Guidance Note of The Secretary-General: Transitional Justice, A Strategic Tool for People, Prevention and Peace'.

# 7

## Why Now, to What End, and How?

### *A Victim-Oriented Examination of the International Criminal Court Office of the Prosecutor's Policy on Complementarity and Cooperation*

*Miracle Chinwenmeri Uche*

### 7.1 INTRODUCTION

The International Criminal Court (ICC), which came into existence on 1 July 2002, stands out from other formal mechanisms for addressing war crimes, crimes against humanity, and genocide ('international crimes') for two main reasons – it is the first permanent international criminal court, and the first of its kind to make room for victims' participation and reparations. The Rome Statute which is the founding instrument of the ICC created a system of complementarity, recognising states' primary responsibility to address international crimes, and the Court's complementary role to address these crimes when states are unable or unwilling genuinely to do so – that is, when warranted (Rome Statute of the International Criminal Court, 2002). This system requires a type of partnership between the ICC and national authorities. Yet the nature of international crimes (their gravity, manner of victimisation, number of perpetrators involved, and massive number of victims) often requires partnership beyond these two key actors to include regional and international governmental and non-governmental organisations, some of which are victims' associations. When the provisions of the Rome Statute are interpreted in light of the Statute's object and purpose to end impunity and do justice for victims, it appears that victims should actively participate in the process and contribute to shaping the outcomes. As the ICC is an international criminal justice institution, proceedings are formal; therefore, victims' participation must be crafted in a way that fits within such processes.

The inclusion of victims' provisions in the Rome Statute was in part due to generations of victims' engagement in international courts and tribunals prior to the ICC's establishment. More than two decades since the ICC opened its investigation into the Uganda situation, there is an ongoing shift in the perception of victims' role within the Rome Statute system, partly in response to victims' mobilisation and demands for accountability, and partly in response to a broader trend in the field of international human rights and transitional justice. This can be seen in the recent move to update the 2012 ICC's Victim Strategy with one of the key objectives being to prioritise a victims-centric approach (ICC Information 2024). Furthermore, the first ever ICC Policy on Complementarity and Cooperation promises to build a community of practice, deliver closer engagement with victims and affected communities, and bring justice closer to victims. This chapter analyses the Office of the Prosecutor's (OTP's) Policy on Complementarity and Cooperation and seeks to answer two questions. First, how can the logic, modalities, and aspirations of this policy be better understood by analysing them through the lens of generations of victim engagement? Secondly, how can the policy contribute to meaningful victim engagement in formal institutions throughout all stages of proceedings? These are pertinent issues which will affect when, where, how, and to what extent victims can participate.

Before proceeding, it is important to make some clarifications. Reference to 'victims' in this chapter means either victims qualified to participate at different stages of ICC proceedings in accordance with Rule 85 ICC Rules of Procedure and Evidence (adopted September 2002), or victims who have suffered an infringement of their rights in other contexts discussed. As the chapter demonstrates, victims are not passive voiceless individuals, but protagonists who endeavour to utilise their agencies in seeking justice. It is also worth mentioning that in formal and complex processes such as the ICC's, victims usually participate through Legal Representatives (Article 68(3) Rome Statute, Rules 90–93 ICC Rules of Procedure and Evidence), but during outreach activities, victims can directly engage with ICC officials and intermediaries.

The chapter is divided into two parts. The first traces generations of victims' engagement in order to examine the evolution of victims' rights and role in international law prior to and following the creation of the ICC. The idea is not to provide a linear narrative or account; rather, there is a degree of flashbacks and flashforwards when discussing developments related to victims' rights. The second scrutinises select OTP and ICC policies and strategies alongside the Policy on Complementarity and Cooperation. It also looks at ways in which the Policy may contribute to meaningful victim engagement throughout all stages of proceedings before the ICC, and before other national, regional, and international mechanisms for addressing international crimes.

## 7.2 GENERATIONS OF VICTIMS' ENGAGEMENT IN INTERNATIONAL LAW

Human rights violations and mass atrocities give rise to international crimes, and addressing these has not always been the priorities of states. Often victims are left to carry the burdens of not only their sufferings but also of seeking justice. At the domestic level, victims as individuals and as groups, and civil society organisations (CSOs) usually set up informal spaces to enable victims to process different forms of injustices, and some mobilise to push for an institutional response and accountability (Doak 2008; also Güneş Daşlı, Chapter 4). From the 1830s–1899 anti-slavery and equality movements in the United States (Resnik 2007; Williams 1994) to the Aba Women's Riots of 1929 (Afolabi and Akeem 2022), and from the adoption of human rights instruments to the post-World War II (WWII) accountability mechanisms and expansion of transitional justice (Bassiouni 2006; Karstedt 2010), victims have navigated challenges and obstacles to national accountability mechanisms by finding ways to amplify their voices on the regional and international scenes. Strategic networking comes into play – something Martinez refers to as 'the importance of transnational ties to successful mobilization' (Martinez 2013, 248; also Hearty 2018). Moreover, the robust approach to victims' participation and reparations within the ICC's Rome Statute system is a result of the combined effects of some relevant events and trends within these periods. Likewise, the OTP's Complementarity and Cooperation Policy did not develop in isolation. The Policy's cornerstone of partnership with vigilance is a reminder that any approach to addressing international crimes cannot be achieved without drawing on victims' historical involvement in international criminal justice and relying on national and regional actors. This helps with understanding the Policy's logic and aspirations and its planned modalities of implementation. Hence, a closer look at some key global events and trends is necessary.

### 7.2.1 *Post-WWII Military Tribunals, Global Discourses, and Victims' Rights*

The scale of criminality in the context of WWII raised the question of accountability which led to the creation of the Nuremberg and Tokyo military tribunals. A common criticism of these tribunals is that victims' participation was almost absent. Documentary evidence was heavily relied upon (Karstedt 2010; Olugbuo and Wachira 2011). This aligns with the perception of victims' role as passive objects in criminal proceedings – relevant to the extent that they may be allowed to narrate their suffering, while active roles are taken up by those who are considered neutral, qualified, and more knowledgeable to 'do justice for victims' or for the society at large (Christie 1977).

The aftermath of WWII up to the 1960s saw the rise in human rights discourse and the incremental adoption of several human rights instruments, including the essential Universal Declaration of Human Rights and Genocide Convention in 1948 (Convention on the Prevention and Punishment of the Crime of Genocide 1948; Viljoen 2009; also Bassiouni 2006; Olugbuo and Wachira 2011). It witnessed the growing awareness of victimisation, the emergence of civil society, and individual and victim group advocacy (Doak 2008). There was a parallel rise in victimology and restorative justice discourse which shone a new light on victims' roles in the quest for justice nationally, but sometimes having impact beyond the national jurisdiction (Doak 2008; Garbett 2017; Hearty 2018; Manikis 2019; Nelson 2007). In 1985 the first universal non-binding instrument addressing various aspects of justice for victims of domestic crimes was adopted (Declaration of Basic Principles of Justice for Victims of Crime and Abuse of Power 1985 ('UN Victims' Declaration')). It covers victims' status, access to justice, their rights and roles in the process, and substantive outcomes such as reparations. The Declaration itself was, as one author puts it, the result of 'the energy and persuasive power of the flourishing "victims' movement" in the 1970s' (Moore 2016, 146), but not all states were convinced about any active role for victims within criminal proceedings (Bassiouni 2006; Holm 2022; Karstedt 2010). Nonetheless, the UN Victims' Declaration influenced further developments of victims' rights, including those in the Rome Statute. For example, Principle 6(b) is similar to Article 68(3) of the Rome Statute, which deals with victims' participation at appropriate stages of proceedings.

The prominence of transitional justice in the 1980s in Latin American transitional societies (Arthur 2009; Encarnación 2024), while not without criticisms (Robins 2017), contributed to the evolution of victims' participation and roles in formal processes (Hoeres 2023; Viebach 2023). Furthermore, the Inter-American Court of Human Rights – an important player in transitional justice in the Americas, has been a source of inspiration for other regional and international mechanisms, including the ICC, when dealing with victims' rights (Antkowiak 2011; McGonigle Leyh 2018; van Zyl 2011).

### 7.2.2 *Victims from the Ad Hoc Tribunals to the ICC: From Witnesses to Independent Actors*

The 1990s and early 2000s saw the emergence of international and hybridised criminal tribunals as formal processes for addressing violations of victims' rights (Williams 2012). The International Criminal Tribunal for the Former Yugoslavia and the International Criminal Tribunal for Rwanda were created following international crimes committed within the context of armed conflicts in these states. These ad hoc tribunals made more room for victims than the Nuremberg and Tokyo tribunals by generally recognising victims' rights (Ferstman 2002; Zegveld 2019). Some victims of crimes within their respective jurisdictions had roles as witnesses and with the right to protection and support (Garkawe 2006). Many victims were disappointed for reasons of lack of participation and reparations (Kamatali 2005; Trumbull IV 2008). This brings to the fore the doubts as to the extent to which institutionalised approaches may meet victims' expectations of justice (Hansen, Chapter 6). Such processes and institutions are imperfect, not that perfection is required. What is important is the commitment to stock-taking geared towards lesson learning and a commitment to as far as possible pursue victim-oriented justice. From the achievements and missed opportunities of the Nuremberg trials and the rise in human rights and victimology discourse to the ad hoc tribunals, there is proof that states' practice, lessons learnt, and victims' engagement resulted in evolution of victims' rights and role in formal processes, including at the ICC (Trumbull IV 2008; Victims' Rights Working Group 2018; Proposal Submitted by Egypt for Article 43 1996).

Victims before the ICC have an independent and distinct role and interests in proceedings, and the main principle guiding their participation is that '[it] shall be meaningful and effective as opposed to purely symbolic' (Representing Victims before the ICC 2020). This should be balanced with the formal nature of the ICC's proceedings, in addition to the requirement of protection of the rights of defendants and the massive number of victims. Therefore, direct participation is rare and collective participation through legal representatives is the norm (Hirst and Sahyouni 2020; Sehmi 2018). Participation under Article 68(3) of the Rome Statute requires a case-by-case assessment of whether victims' personal interests are affected by the subject of the proceeding. Thus, ICC judges play an important role in giving effect to victims' participation, and they may authorise victims to make oral and written representations, make opening and closing statements, question witnesses, and lead evidence (OTP Policy on Victims' Participation 2010; Representing Victims before the ICC 2020).

Having looked at one aspect of generations of victims' engagement in international criminal justice, the following section examines the evolution of victims' participation within the ICC, the impact of the Court's legal framework and policies on such a development, and any external impact the ICC's victims' participation practice may have on victims' access and participation in national proceedings.

## 7.3 MODALITIES AND ASPIRATIONS OF THE OTP'S COMPLEMENTARITY AND COOPERATION POLICY THROUGH THE LENS OF GENERATIONS OF VICTIM PARTICIPATION

### 7.3.1 *The OTP's Policy on Complementarity and Cooperation in the ICC's Third Decade*

As stated in the introduction, the ICC's Rome Statute system is one of complementarity involving mainly states who have the primary responsibility to tackle international crimes and do justice for victims, while the ICC complements such efforts when states are unable or unwilling genuinely to do so (Article 17 ICC Rome Statute). It was necessary to develop a means to determine who between the ICC and states can address such crimes at any given time, hence the complementarity principle. Complementarity is also based on considerations that 'states will generally have the best access to evidence and witnesses'. Moreover, there are '[resource related] limits on the number of prosecutions the ICC can bring' (International Criminal Court 2003). Consequently, national, regional, and other international actors must contribute towards closing the accountability gap and ensuring justice for more victims. Victims were not at the heart of the debate around the development of the regulatory framework for complementarity, but their needs and interests are inevitably impacted by how complementarity is interpreted and applied at all stages of ICC proceedings.

The OTP's Complementarity and Cooperation Policy outlines the OTP's understanding of the principles of complementarity and cooperation, their paramountcy to the success of the Rome Statute system, the legal framework governing these principles, and how the OTP will interpret them in the course of its work. The Policy was published in 2024, over two decades following the establishment of the ICC. Yet victims have been engaging with the ICC from its inception. Therefore, in answering the question of how the logic, aspirations, and modalities of the Complementarity and Cooperation Policy may be better understood, some key antecedent OTP and ICC policies will be discussed. These policies include the Policy Paper on Preliminary Examinations (2013), Policy Paper on Case Selection and Prioritisation (2016), and the Policy on Situation Completion (2021) – all of which describe the life cycle of OTP's operations in a situation (Policy on Situation Completion 2021). Other relevant policy papers are the Paper on Some Policy Issues Before the ICC with its annex (International Criminal Court 2003), the OTP Policy Paper on Victims' Participation (2010), and the Court-wide Strategy in Relation to Victims 2009, revised in 2012. These policies determine how the OTP and the ICC commence and execute their justice mandate and inevitably impact which victims can participate, and when, and how they can do so.

Prosecutor Khan stated that the Complementarity and Cooperation Policy's main aim is to 'deliver a paradigm shift in [the OTP's] relationship with [complementarity stakeholders, i.e.] national authorities and other accountability mechanisms, and, crucially, the victims and survivors of atrocities globally' (International Criminal Court 2024). It is argued that the Policy was mainly inspired by (a) the increase in the ICC's workload with more situations and cases before the Court than when it first started (Office of the Prosecutor 2024b) and (b) new developments on how complementarity is interpreted with states seeking ICC deferral of investigations and victims wanting to participate in these early-stage proceedings. The Policy is grounded on principles of partnership and vigilance; that is, the OTP will partner with other accountability actors and will remain vigilant in carrying out its mandate. The Policy bases its aspirations for partnership and cooperation on four pillars – (a) creating a community of practice, (b) bringing justice closer to communities, (c) technology as an accelerant (not covered here), and (d) harnessing cooperation mechanisms.

The correct explanation of complementarity as requiring partnership and vigilance can be traced to the 2003 OTP Policy Paper, its Annex, and the Informal Expert paper (International Criminal Court 2003), arguably the OTP's first attempt to articulate how complementarity should work in practice. These and the 2024 Policy on Complementarity and Cooperation outline that the ICC should be focused on the most responsible – but only where its intervention is absolutely warranted, while encouraging national authorities to go after lower ranking perpetrators. Such an approach can contribute to closing the impunity gap and increase the chances of more victim engagement and participation in the global pursuit of justice. However, the early practice of the OTP reflects an approach some considered as actively pursuing self-referrals from States Parties (Clark 2011; Nouwen 2013). The first referral was made by Uganda in December 2003 followed by a second referral by the DRC in April 2004 (ICC January Press Release 2004; Schabas 2008). Self-referrals come with an increased risk of manipulations, as self-referring states may wish to ensure that the Court's investigations and prosecutions do not include crimes committed by perpetrators linked to the government (Clark 2011; Nouwen 2013). For example, so far, in the Uganda and DRC situations before the ICC, the focus has been on rebel forces, and in Uganda only one other Lord's Resistance Army (LRA) rebel – Thomas Kwoyelo – has been tried for crimes within the context of the situation. Victims of crimes committed by government forces were unable to exercise participatory rights in the Rome Statute context (Kasande 2024;

Nyeko 2024). Contrasting this with the OTP's 2010 Policy on Victims' Participation and the 2024 Complementarity and Cooperation Policy, both emphasise improved engagement with victims, which can help with uncovering the true extent of criminality and victimisation (OTP Policy on Victims' Participation 2010). This suggests that the OTP and the entire Court are at a place where they see victims as having a distinct and active role in the pursuit of justice – another sign of an evolution of victims' engagement in the ICC's context. However, the extent to which such an engagement with victims may ensure that the OTP and states investigate both government and non-government actors will depend on how the OTP goes about implementing the Complementarity and Cooperation Policy. It may also be limited by the lack of a neutral and inclusive ICC complementarity body (not the OTP) which makes room for better relationship with CSOs, victims, and other stakeholders (see, for instance, FIDH Unpacking the ICC Office of the Prosecutor's New Approach to Complementarity and Cooperation 2024).

The Policy also explains that partnership requires collective effort at all stages of proceedings with states, victims, and CSOs and other stakeholders, mobilising to seek and shape justice on multiple fronts. The Office of the United Nations High Commissioner for Human Rights, Eurojust's Joint Investigative Teams, International Federation for Human Rights (FIDH) and local CSOs including those represented by the Coalition for the ICC (Coalition for the ICC, 'About the Coalition', n.d.), are examples of such stakeholders who are often the first to engage with victims and may be assisting states with transitional justice processes. So how the OTP and the ICC as a whole shape their engagement with stakeholders at each stage of proceeding will increase or diminish the space and type of victims' participation, in judicial and in non-judicial transitional justice processes. It is therefore important to consider the Complementarity and Cooperation Policy in each of these stages with a focus on how a community of practice can help to bring justice closer to victims, while having regard to pre-existing policies.

### 7.3.2 *Early-Stage Proceedings: Preliminary Examinations and Investigations*

It should be recalled that complementarity can be engaged at different stages of ICC processes: during preliminary examinations where the OTP examines whether (a) information it has received suggest that crimes within the ICC's jurisdiction have been or are being committed by nationals of ICC States Parties or on their territories, (b) such crimes are of sufficient gravity to warrant the Court's action, and whether (c) the Court may exercise its jurisdiction over such a situation if warranted by states' unwillingness or inability genuinely to investigate or prosecute. Following the examination, the Prosecutor may decide to investigate, decline to investigate, or decide to collect more information before making a determination (International Criminal Court 2013). Any of these decisions will have implications for victims' engagement locally, regionally, or in The Hague, hence they need to be aware of their rights at this stage and how they can exercise them.

The period before and during preliminary examinations can be the first opportunity for victims to engage with the ICC and actively participate through submission of information to the Court, subsequently being notified of the Prosecutor's decision to investigate or not to investigate (Court's Revised Strategy in Relation to Victims 2012; OTP Policy on Victims' Participation 2010). In such a scenario, their representation can aid the Court in deciding to authorise an investigation into the situation 'within which the same victims claim to have suffered harm as a result of the commission of crimes within the jurisdiction of the Court.' (ICC-02/04-101 2007; ICC-02/11-6 2011; Representing Victims Before the ICC 2020). The OTP's 2013 Preliminary Examination Policy focuses on three main objectives – transparency; ending impunity; and prevention (OTP Policy on Preliminary Examination 2013). To this end, the OTP has published reports on preliminary examinations up to 2020 (OTP Policies and Strategies) and issued reasoned decisions either to proceed or not to proceed with investigations (for example, UK/Iraq Report 2020). These together with effective communication, cooperation, and engagement with victims, states, and other stakeholders can positively affect efforts to tackle impunity. For instance, if the OTP decides not to initiate an investigation, victims and other stakeholders may push for reconsideration (Situation in Colombia 2022a; International Federation for Human Rights 2024) or they may work together to pursue justice at the national and regional levels – the Colombia Situation being an example (Niño 2021). Results of the OTP's approach to preliminary examinations have been mixed. Victims and CSOs have constantly raised issues regarding ineffective communication and outreach activities during this early-stage process (Coalition for the ICC 2021; FIDH Recommendations 2024); ICC-RoC46(3)-01/22-6 2022).

Whether the ICC or national or regional authorities investigate, the scope of their investigation will impact how criminal justice will be shaped, and which victims will eventually participate. ICC Chambers have differed on the extent and nature of victims' participation during the investigations stage, with some finding that victims have broad participatory rights at this stage (ICC-01/04-101-tEN-Corr 2006; ICC-02/04-101 2007; ICC-02/05-111-Corr 2007; Representing Victims before the International Criminal Court 2020). Some of these rulings have been influenced by international human rights law and jurisprudence (McGonigle Leyh 2018); that is, earlier generations of victims' participation outside the ICC. However, the Appeals Chamber in 2008 clarified that victims have no general rights to participate at the investigation stage of a situation, but they are entitled to participate in any judicial proceeding conducted at this stage provided their personal interests are affected (ICC-01/04-556 2008). The OTP agrees with this interpretation, but commits to better engagement with victims and their representatives (OTP Policy on Victims' Participation 2010). This is in line with human rights jurisprudence, which has established that victims' ability to participate and uncover the truth about their harm will eventually contribute to substantive outcomes such as reparations (Dissenting Opinion Judge Ibáñez Carranza 2020, 39–68). This current generation of victims' participation in early-stage proceedings goes even further. Victims have protected their interests to see justice done through an international actor where national authorities fail in this regard as seen in Philippines and Venezuela decisions authorising the resumption of investigations (ICC-01/21-77 2023; ICC-02/18-89 2024). The Venezuela situation also reflects the impact of CSOs (Venezuelan Civil Society Organizations Joint Statement 2024) and regional organisations in the pursuit of justice for victims. The Organization of American States Panel of Independent International Experts played a key role in referring the situation to the ICC (Office of the Prosecutor 2018) and in the appeals process when Venezuela challenged the Pre-Trial Chamber's decision to authorise the resumption of the investigation (ICC-02/18-89 2024).

The OTP's experience with implementing its Preliminary Examination Policy with respect to victims' participation also informed its policies on case selection and prioritisation, and situation completion – how it concludes its work in situations such as the concluded Uganda Situation. The criteria for selecting and prioritising cases are based on the gravity of the crimes, the degree of responsibility of the alleged perpetrators, and the potential charges. The OTP aims to select and prioritise cases in a manner which constitute a representative sample of the main types of victimisation and of the communities which have been affected by the crimes in that situation (International Criminal Court 2016). This approach differs from the approach adopted in the ICC's first case – *Prosecutor v. Thomas Lubanga Dyilo* (ICC-01/04-01/06-803-tEN 2007) – where the OTP's charges were limited to the war crimes of enlisting and conscripting children under the age of fifteen years and using them to participate actively in hostilities. Thus, victims of crimes committed by the child soldiers were negatively affected. Since then, the OTP has widened charges brought against other defendants in the DRC and other situations. Relatedly, the OTP may be required to prioritise or deprioritise investigations or cases at different times depending on prevailing circumstances including those relating to cooperation of states, security, and resource constraints (International Criminal Court 2016). The Kenya situation is a good example of how such issues can ultimately affect victims' participation and their protection; witnesses were intimidated into recanting their testimony and ending their cooperation with the ICC, and Kenya refused to fully cooperate (Office of the Prosecutor 2023b, *The Prosecutor v. Paul Gicheru*, ICC-01/09-01/20, ICC Trial Chamber V(B) refers non-cooperation of the Kenyan Government to the Assembly of States Parties to the Rome Statute 2016).

There are situations where the OTP's approach to prioritisation has been criticised as limiting and excluding some victims. In the situation in Afghanistan, prior to the Taliban takeover, the Afghan government requested that the Prosecutor defer investigations in the situation to Afghanistan to allow it to exercise its jurisdiction in accordance with Article 18 of the Rome Statute (ICC-02/17-139 2020). Following the Taliban takeover, the Prosecutor requested the Chamber's authorisation to resume investigations. However, he released a statement that he had decided to deprioritise some aspects of the investigation and would focus on crimes allegedly committed by the Taliban and the Islamic State–Khorasan province (Office of the Prosecutor 2021). Through their participation, victims contributed to the Chamber's decision to address the Prosecutor's modified focus, (ICC-02/17-29-AnxI-Red 2018; ICC-02/17-39 2019; ICC-02/17-168-AnxA 2021; ICC-02/17-218 2023; ICC-02/17-196 2022). Eventually, the original scope of the investigation was reinstated (ICC-02/17-218 2023).

Completion of a situation indicates that the ICC is winding down some or all its activities in that situation. The Policy on Situation Completion explains how the OTP will do so. This is now a priority for the Court given that it is busier than ever. The Policy highlights the relevance of completion of investigation phase for victims, states, CSOs, regional and other stakeholders as they should better understand the OTP's progress and direct their expectations and justice efforts aright. This may include building capacity of domestic or regional mechanisms which open more avenues for victims to continue their active engagement in the fight for justice and in closing the impunity gap. The OTP has concluded the Kenya, Georgia, Central African Republic (CAR) II, and Uganda investigations (Office of the Prosecutor 2022a, 2022b, 2023a, 2023b). In Kenya, no national proceedings are underway for crimes within the situation's context (International Federation for Human Rights 2023). By contrast, five warrants of arrest were issued in the Uganda situation, one conviction of the LRA commander Domnic Ongwen was achieved – 4,095 victims were granted the right to participate in the proceedings, and implementation of the reparations order is awaited (ICC-02/04-01/15-1762-Red 2021; Kirabira and Uche 2024). The Uganda situation supplied the ICC with its first attempt at confirmation of charges hearing in absentia in the *Kony* case, which took place on 10 September 2025 (ICC-02/04-01/05-633 2025; ICC-02/04-01/05-532 2024). Victims expressed their support for the hearing in absentia as a means of reviving the case, and 5,795 victims were authorised to participate in the proceedings (ICC-02/04-01/05-532 2024; ICC-02/04-01/05-624 2025; ICC-02/04-01/05-466 2023; ICC-02/04-01/05-483 2024).

The foregoing discussions reflect how victims' participatory rights have worked in practice at different stages of ICC proceedings, including those dealing with complementarity issues. They also suggest that the aspirations of the Complementarity and Cooperation Policy could reinvigorate the current generation of active victims' engagement with the ICC, national, and regional mechanisms for addressing international crimes. The Policy speaks of the creation of a community of practice – for example, a complementarity and cooperation forum through which information and ideas can be exchanged with national counterparts, tracking progress of actions being taken at the domestic level with respect to international crimes, and identification of needs and making efforts to address them. In practice, the ICC has played an important role in encouraging, supporting, and monitoring Ukraine, CAR, DRC, Guinea, Colombia, and Uganda situations (International Criminal Court 2024). In CAR's Special Criminal Court, victims participated, and some have been awarded reparations (Benga 2024; Special Criminal Court Press Release September 2024). Victims' push and perseverance contributed to shaping justice in Guinea for crimes against humanity (UNSC S/2009/693 2009, Coalition for the ICC, 'Guinea', n.d.). These suggest that there is indeed a 'coexistence of various generations [of victims' participation] within one context' and which form components of the broader justice ecosystem (to quote this book's Introduction).

## 7.4 CONCLUSION

The discussions around the first question show that the inclusion of victims in the first permanent international criminal court was due to growing national and regional victims' participation practices, public reactions to their exclusion in previous international crimes tribunals, and the work of victims, their advocates, and partners who foregrounded victims' plight as well as their relevance for establishing truth and ensuring justice. With regard to the second question, the OTP's Complementarity and Cooperation Policy reflects an even broader evolution of victims' roles in international law, in part as a response to victims' experiences and engagement with redress mechanisms which have enhanced understanding of their roles in national, regional, and international formal justice processes for addressing international crimes. What commenced as recognising victims' individual rights and the doing of justice in the name of victims has slowly crystallised into doing justice in partnership with victims. Despite the shift, there are still issues with outreach to victims, and some restrictions to victims' ability to meaningfully participate during preliminary examination and investigations stages. The ICC can maximise the potentials of the Policy on Complementarity and Cooperation by moving one step towards creating a neutral and inclusive complementarity body that can pursue a holistic approach to delivering justice in partnership with victims while widening avenues for redress.

## REFERENCES

### CASES AND LEGAL INSTRUMENTS

International Criminal Court Rules of Procedure and Evidence (adopted September 2002).
*Prosecutor v. Thomas Lubanga Dyilo*, ICC-01/04-01/06.
Rome Statute of the International Criminal Court, Rome, 17 July 1998, in Force 1 July 2002, 2187 UNTS 3.
Situation in the Democratic Republic of the Congo, ICC-01/04-101-tEN-Corr, PTC I, 22 March 2006.
Situation in Uganda, ICC-02/04-101, PTC II, 13 August 2007.
Situation in Darfur, Sudan, ICC-02/05-111-Corr, PTC I, 14 December 2007.
Situation in the Democratic Republic of the Congo, ICC-01/04-556, AC, 19 December 2008.
Situation in the Republic of Cote D'Ivoire, ICC-02/11-6, PTC II, 6 July 2011.
Situation in the Islamic Republic of Afghanistan, ICC-02/17-29-AnxI-Red, PTC III, 20 February 2018.
Situation in the Islamic Republic of Afghanistan, ICC-02/17-39, PTC II, 10 June 2019.

Situation in the Islamic Republic of Afghanistan, Dissenting Opinion of Judge Luz del Carmen Ibáñez Carranza, ICC-02/17-137-Anx-Corr, AC, 10 March 2020.
Situation in the Islamic Republic of Afghanistan, ICC-02/17-139, PTC II, 16 April 2020.
Situation in the Islamic Republic of Afghanistan, ICC-02/17-168-AnxA, PTC II, 14 October 2021.
Situation in Colombia, 2022a. ICC-RoC46(3)-01/22-2, PTC I, 6 May 2022.
Situation in Colombia, ICC-RoC46(3)-01/22-6, PTC I, 22 July 2022.
Situation in the Islamic Republic of Afghanistan, ICC-02/17-196, AC 31 October 2022.
Situation in the Islamic Republic of Afghanistan, ICC-02/17-218, AC, 04 April 2023.
Situation in the Republic of the Philippines, ICC-01/21-77, AC, 18 July 2023.
Situation in the Bolivarian Republic of Venezuela, ICC-02/18-89, AC, 1 March 2024.
*The Prosecutor v. Thomas Lubanga Dyilo*, ICC-01/04-01/06-803-tEN, PTC I,14 May 2007.
*The Prosecutor v. Dominic Ongwen*, ICC-02/04-01/15-1762-Red, TC IX, 04 February 2021.
*The Prosecutor v. Joseph Kony*, ICC-02/04-01/05-466, PTC II, 23 November 2023.
*The Prosecutor v. Joseph Kony*, ICC-02/04-01/05-483, PTC II, 11 March 2024.
*The Prosecutor v. Joseph Kony*, ICC-02/04-01/05-532, PTC III, 29 October 2024.
*The Prosecutor v. Joseph Kony*, ICC-02/04-01/05-624, PTC III, 12 August 2025.
*The Prosecutor v. Joseph Kony*, ICC-02/04-01/05-633, PTC III, 6 November 2025.
*The Prosecutor v. Paul Gicheru*, ICC-01/09-01/20.
UN General Assembly, Resolution 217A (III), Universal Declaration of Human Rights, A/RES/217(III) (10 December 1948).
UN General Assembly, Resolution 40/34, Declaration of Basic Principles of Justice for Victims of Crime and Abuse of Power, A/RES/40/34 (29 November 1985).

## OTHER SOURCES

Afolabi, Abiodun, and Oladiti Abiodun Akeem. 2022. 'Change and Resistance: A Reflection on the Aba Women Uprising in Colonial Nigeria'. *Hemispheres*, 37, 41–61.
Antkowiak, Thomas M. 2011. 'An Emerging Mandate for International Courts: Victim-Centered Remedies and Restorative Justice'. *Stanford Journal of International Law*, 47(2), 279–332.
Arthur, Paige. 2009. 'How "Transitions" Reshaped Human Rights: A Conceptual History of Transitional Justice'. *Human Rights Quarterly*, 31(2), 321–367.
Bassiouni, M Cherif. 2006. 'International Recognition of Victims' Rights'. *Human Rights Law Review*, 6(2), 203–279.
Benga, Rodrigue le Roi. (15 October 2024). 'Central African Republic reparations: what victims say about first payments'. *Justiceinfo.net*. https://tinyurl.com/fa6patkm
Christie, Nils. 1977. 'Conflicts as Property'. *The British Journal of Criminology*, 17(1), 1–15.
Clark, Phil. 2011. 'Chasing Cases: The ICC and the Politics of State Referral in the Democratic Republic of the Congo and Uganda'. In *The International Criminal Court and Complementarity: From Theory to Practice*, edited by Carsten Stahn and Mohamed M. El Zeidy, pp. 1180–1203. Cambridge University Press.
Coalition for the ICC. 2021. The Coalition for the ICC delivers ASP20 closing statement, 10 December. https://tinyurl.com/2tmtz5v8
Coalition for the ICC. n.d. 'About the Coalition'. www.coalitionfortheicc.org/about-coalition-0
Coalition for the ICC. n.d. 'Guinea'. www.coalitionfortheicc.org/country/guinea
Convention on the Prevention and Punishment of the Crime of Genocide. 1948. Paris, 9 December, in force 12 January 1951, 78 UNTS 277.
*Cour Penale Speciale Communiqué de presse CPS n°160924* (Special Criminal Court Press Release CPS n°160924). 16 September 2024 (copy on file with the author).
Doak, Jonathan. 2008. *Victims' Rights, Human Rights and Criminal Justice: Reconceiving the Role of Third Parties*. Bloomsbury Publishing.
Encarnación, Omar G. 2024. 'Transitional Justice at 40: A Critical Appraisal'. *Current History*, 123(849), 3–8.
Evrard, Elke, Gretel Mejía Bonifazi, and Tine Destrooper. 2021. 'The Meaning of Participation in Transitional Justice: A Conceptual Proposal for Empirical Analysis'. *International Journal of Transitional Justice* 15(2), 428–447.

Federation for International Human Rights. 2024. Protecting the ICC and Upholding Victims' Rights Amid Crises and Threats: FIDH Recommendations to the ICC Assembly of States Parties, 2–7 December. www.fidh.org/IMG/pdf/asp23_fidh_position_paper.pdf

Ferstman, Carla. 2002. 'The Reparation Regime of the International Criminal Court: Practical Considerations'. *Leiden Journal of International Law*, 15(3), 667–686.

Garbett, Claire. 2017. 'The International Criminal Court and Restorative Justice: Victims, Participation and the Processes of Justice'. *Restorative Justice*, 5(2), 198–220.

Garkawe, Sam. 2006. 'The Role and Rights of Victims at the Nuremberg International Military Tribunal'. In *The Nuremberg Trials: International Criminal Law since 1945: 60th Anniversary International Conference*, edited by Herbert R. Reginbogin, Christoph J. M. Safferling, and Walter R. Hippel, pp. 86–93. K. G. Saur Verlag.

Hearty, Kevin. 2018. 'Victims' of Human Rights Abuses in Transitional Justice: Hierarchies, Perpetrators and the Struggle for Peace'. *The International Journal of Human Rights*, 22(7), 888–909.

Hirst, Megan and Sandra Sahyouni. 2020. 'Effective Legal Representation for Participating Victims: Principles, Challenges and Some Solutions'. In *Advancing the Impact of Victim Participation at the International Criminal Court: Bridging the Gap between Research and Practice*, edited by Rudina Jasini and Gregory Townsend, pp. 4–32. University of Oxford.

Hoeres, Peter. 2023. 'Historical Perspectives on Transitional Justice'. In *After Dictatorship: Instruments of Transitional Justice in Post-Authoritarian Systems*, edited by Peter Hoeres and Hubertus Knabe, pp. 5–19. De Gruyter.

Holm, Fanny. 2022. 'Successful Human Rights Implementation? Victims of Crime and the Swedish Example'. *Nordic Journal of Human Rights*, 40(4), 529–48.

International Criminal Court. 2003. Office of The Prosecutor. Informal expert paper: The principle of complementarity in practice.

International Criminal Court. 2003. Office of The Prosecutor. Paper on some policy issues before the Office of the Prosecutor.

International Criminal Court. 2010. Office of The Prosecutor. Policy on Victims' Participation.

International Criminal Court. 2012. Court's Revised Strategy in Relation to Victims, ICC-ASP/11/38.

International Criminal Court. 2013. Office of The Prosecutor, Policy Paper on Preliminary Examinations.

International Criminal Court. 2016. Office of The Prosecutor, Policy Paper on Case Selection and Prioritisation.

International Criminal Court. 2021. Office of The Prosecutor. Policy on Situation Completion.

International Criminal Court. 2024. ICC publishes questionnaire on Revised Victims Strategy. Information. 15 August. www.icc-cpi.int/news/icc-publishes-questionnaire-revised-victims-strategy

International Criminal Court Press Release. 2004. ICC – President of Uganda refers situation concerning the Lord's Resistance Army (LRA) to the ICC', 29 January. https://tinyurl.com/7cnpdfsx.

International Criminal Court Press Release. 2016. 'ICC Trial Chamber V(B) refers non-cooperation of the Kenyan Government to the Assembly of States Parties to the Rome Statute', 19 September. https://tinyurl.com/7r357hfd

International Federation for Human Rights. 2023. 'Kenya: ICC to encourage Domestic Accountability Efforts Despite Conclusion of Investigation', 21 December. https://tinyurl.com/53fw2fk8.

International Federation for Human Rights. 2024. 'Q&A: Unpacking the ICC Office of the Prosecutor's New Approach to Complementarity and Cooperation', 26 April. https://tinyurl.com/4rzjp3yt

Kamatali, Jean-Marie. 2005. 'From the ICTR to ICC: Learning from the ICTR Experience in Bringing Justice to Rwandans'. *New England Journal of International and Comparative Law*, 12(1), 89–104.

Karstedt, Susanne. 2010. 'From Absence to Presence, from Silence to Voice: Victims in International and Transitional Justice since the Nuremberg Trials'. *International Review of Victimology*, 17(1), 9–30.

Kasande, Kihika Sarah. 2024. 'Uganda's Long Road to Accountability: The Kwoyelo Verdict and Lessons for Future International Crimes Prosecutions', 21 August. *International Center for Transitional Justice*. https://tinyurl.com/45vbnh2h

Kirabira, Tonny Raymond, and Miracle Chinwenmeri Uche. 2024. 'Lord's Resistance Army: ICC Awards Reparations to Victims of Commander Dominic Ongwen – What Happens Next'. *The Conversation*, 7 March. https://tinyurl.com/pyyspnur

Leyh McGonigle, Brianne. 2018. 'Pragmatism over Principles: The International Criminal Court and a Human Rights-Based Approach to Judicial Interpretation'. *Fordham International Law Journal*, 41(3), 697–736.

Manikis, Marie. 2019. "Contrasting the Emergence of the Victims' Movements in the United States and England and Wales'. *Societies*, 9(2), 35.
Martinez, Jenny S. 2013. 'The Anti-Slavery Movement and the Rise of International Non-Governmental Organizations'. In *The Oxford Handbook of International Human Rights Law*, edited by Dinah Shelton, pp. 222–249. Oxford University Press.
Moore, Linda. 2016. 'U'. In *A Companion to Crime, Harm and Victimisation*, edited by Karen Corteen, Sharon Morley, Paul Taylor and Joanne H. Turner, pp. 146–148. The Policy Press.
Nelson, Elizabeth. 2007. 'Victims of War: The First World War, Returned Soldiers, and Understandings of Domestic Violence in Australia'. *Journal of Women's History*, 19(4), 83–106.
Niño, Santiago Vargas. 2021. 'When a Preliminary Examination Closes, a New Era Opens: The OTP's Innovative Support for Transitional Justice in Colombia'. *OpinioJuris*. https://tinyurl.com/49uh7z8d
Nouwen, Sarah M. H. 2013. *Complementarity in the Line of Fire: The Catalysing Effect of the International Criminal Court in Uganda and Sudan*. Cambridge University Press.
Nyeko, Oryem. 2024. 'War Crimes Trial Continues in Uganda after Long Delays'. *Human Rights Watch*, 29 January. www.hrw.org/news/2024/01/29/war-crimes-trial-continues-uganda-after-long-delays
Office of Public Counsel for Victims. 2020. *Representing Victims before the International Criminal Court a Manual for Legal Representatives*. International Criminal Court.
Office of the Prosecutor. 2021. 'Statement of the Prosecutor of the International Criminal Court, Karim A. A. Khan QC, Following the Application for an Expedited Order under Article 18(2) Seeking Authorisation to resume investigations in the Situation in Afghanistan', 27 September. https://tinyurl.com/mr2kh4cm
Office of the Prosecutor. 2022a. 'The Prosecutor of the International Criminal Court, Karim A.A. Khan KC, Announces Conclusion of the Investigation Phase in the Situation in Georgia', 16 December. https://tinyurl.com/3c63zk5c
Office of the Prosecutor. 2022b. 'The Prosecutor of the International Criminal Court, Karim A.A. Khan KC, Announces Conclusion of the Investigation Phase in the Situation in the Central African Republic', 16 December. https://tinyurl.com/3dxa92fe
Office of the Prosecutor. 2023a. 'Statement of ICC Deputy Prosecutor, Nazhat Shameem Khan, Announcing Her Decision to Conclude the Investigation Phase of the Situation in the Republic of Kenya', 27 November. https://tinyurl.com/w264sw26
Office of the Prosecutor. 2023b. 'Statement of the Prosecutor of the International Criminal Court, Karim A.A. Khan KC, Announcing His Decision to Conclude the Investigation Phase in the Situation in Uganda', 1 December. https://tinyurl.com/3b8j3tf2
Office of the Prosecutor. 2024a. Policy on Complementarity and Cooperation, April. www.icc-cpi.int/sites/default/files/2024-04/2024-comp-policy-eng.pdf.
Office of the Prosecutor. 2024b. 'Remarks by ICC Prosecutor Karim A.A. Khan KC at the Opening of the 23rd Session of the Assembly of States Parties', 2 December. https://asp.icc-cpi.int/sites/default/files/asp_docs/ASP-23-STMT-PROS-ENG.pdf
Office of the Prosecutor. n.d. 'Policies and Strategies'. www.icc-cpi.int/about/otp/otp-policies
Office of the Prosecutor. 2018. 'Unofficial Translation of Venezuela Referral', 26 September. https://tinyurl.com/3b2f8kss
Olugbuo, Benson Chinedu, and George Mukundi Wachira. 2011. 'Enhancing the Protection of the Rights of Victims of International Crimes: A Model for East Africa'. *African Human Rights Law Journal*, 11(2), 608–638.
Preparatory Committee on the Establishment of an International Criminal Court. 1996. Proposal Submitted by Egypt for Article 43, A/AC.249/WP.11, 12–30 August (19 August).
Resnik, Judith. 2007. 'Sisterhood, Slavery, and Sovereignty: Transnational Antislavery Work and Women's Rights Movements in the United States during the Twentieth Century'. In *Women's Rights and Transatlantic Antislavery in the Era of Emancipation*, edited by Kathryn Kish Sklar and James Brewer Stewart, pp. 19–54. Yale University Press.
Robert F. Kennedy Human Rights. 2024. 'Venezuelan Civil Society Organizations Present a Joint Statement before the Plenary of the Assembly of State Parties to the International Criminal Court in The Hague.' https://tinyurl.com/3v7mven7
Robins, Simon. 2017. 'Failing Victims? The Limits of Transitional Justice in Addressing the Needs of Victims of Violations'. *Human Rights and International Legal Discourse*, 2017(2), 41–58.

Schabas, Williams A. 2008. '"Complementarity in Practice": Some Uncomplimentary Thoughts." *International Criminal Law Forum*, 19, 5–33.
Sehmi, Anushka. 2018. '"Now that We Have No Voice, What Will Happen to Us?": Experiences of Victim Participation in the Kenyatta Case'. *Journal of International Criminal Justice*, 16(3), 571–591.
The Office of the Prosecutor. 2020. 'Situation in Iraq/UK Final Report', 9 December. https://tinyurl.com/4ertpauc.
Trumbull IV, Charles P. 2008. 'The Victims of Victim Participation in International Criminal Proceedings'. *Michigan Journal of International Law*, 29(4), 777–826.
UN Security Council. 2009. Letter addressed to the President of the Security Council by the Secretary-General, S/2009/693, 18 December.
van Zyl, Paul. 2011. 'Promoting Transitional Justice in Post-Conflict Societies'. In *Transitional Justice Handbook for Latin America*, edited by Félix Reátegui, pp. 45–67. Brazilian Ministry of Justice Amnesty Commission.
Victims' Rights Working Group. 2018. 'Victims' Rights Working Group (VRWG) and the Lunch Talk Series'. https://tinyurl.com/3866xbzk
Viebach, Julia. 2023. 'Rwanda: Transitional Justice after Genocide'. In *After Dictatorship: Instruments of Transitional Justice in Post-Authoritarian Systems*, edited by Peter Hoeres and Hubertus Knabe, pp. 81–148. De Gruyter.
Viljoen, Frans. 2009. 'International Human Rights Law: A Short History'. *UN Chronicle*. www.un.org/en/chronicle/article/international-human-rights-law-short-history
Williams, Carolyn. 1994. 'The Female Antislavery Movement: Fighting against Racial Prejudice and Promoting Women's Rights in Antebellum America'. In *The Abolitionist Sisterhood Women's Political Culture in Antebellum America*, edited by Jean Yellin Fagan and John C. Van Horne., pp. 159–178. Cornell University Press.
Williams, Sarah. 2012. *Hybrid and Internationalised Criminal Tribunals: Selected Jurisdictional Issues*. Bloomsbury.
Zegveld, Liesbeth. 2019. 'Victims as a Third Party: Empowerment of Victims?' *International Criminal Law Review*, 19(2), 321–345.

# 8

# Beyond the Extraordinary Chambers in the Courts of Cambodia

## *Tracing the Nexus between Buddhist Justice and Formal Transitional Justice Approaches*

*Fangyi Li*

### 8.1 INTRODUCTION

The Khmer Rouge (KR) regime, a radical communist group that ruled Cambodia from 17 April 1975 to 6 January 1979, perpetrated extreme violence in Cambodia that led to the deaths of approximately 1.6–1.9 million people through starvation, forced labour, executions, torture, and other forms of violence. On 7 January 1979, the Vietnamese army invaded Phnom Penh – the capital of Cambodia, ousted the KR regime, and installed the pro-Vietnam People's Republic of Kampuchea government. In 2003, after a few years of painstaking negotiations between the government of Cambodia and the United Nations (UN), an agreement was reached on the establishment of the Extraordinary Chambers in the Courts of Cambodia (ECCC) – also known as the Khmer Rouge Tribunal – to respond to the atrocious crimes during the KR period (Gidley 2019). In 2006, the ECCC was set up as a hybrid tribunal, having both international and Cambodian prosecutors, lawyers, and judges, and applying both international and Cambodian law. After sixteen years of operation, the ECCC completed its caseload and transited to residual functions on 1 January 2023. During its tenure, the tribunal has tried and convicted three defendants: Kaing Guek Eav (alias 'Duch') of Case 001, and Nuon Chea and Khieu Samphan of Case 002. The remaining Case 003 and Case 004 that involved more defendants were terminated by the Supreme Court Chamber in December 2021 after thirteen-year long stand-offs in the Tribunal, where the international side of the Court insisted that the cases should proceed to trial and their national counterparts wanted both cases dismissed (ECCC 2011).

Nearly two decades after the creation of the Tribunal, a vibrant body of literature has emerged on how the institution and the form of justice it stands for have been received in Cambodian Buddhist society. Most scholarship focuses either on perceptions of the ECCC held by victims who were involved in its formal processes (Hinton 2018; Killean 2016), or on local justice strategies and practices outside the ECCC as alternatives to the formal institution and narratives it produces (Bennett 2018; Kidron 2021). By bringing both perspectives together in a comparative view, this chapter provides a more nuanced and comprehensive understanding of the (in)compatibilities between two justice frameworks – liberal, retributive justice and Buddhist karmic justice – as experienced by those who participated in the ECCC's proceedings and those who chose not to engage. In doing so, it uncovers divergent perspectives on the dynamics and limitations of the vernacularisation of foreign justice models in the Cambodian transitional justice context.

To address these questions, the chapter is structured as follows. Section 8.2 introduces the place that the ECCC occupies in Cambodia's transitional justice landscape, highlighting its innovative efforts to engage victims through its Civil Party participation mechanism. Section 8.3 examines the group of victims who participated in ECCC proceedings as a means of fulfilling perceived obligations to their deceased loved ones by seeking truth of their fate, restoring dignity to them, and bringing peace to the spirits of the deceased. Section 8.4 shifts focus to non-participating victims who expressed scepticism and resistance towards the Tribunal and non-governmental organisations (NGOs) working in its orbit, and as an alternative participated in everyday justice practices aligned with their Buddhist beliefs. Section 8.5 compares how victims navigate the tensions between the liberal and the Buddhist justice frameworks through two distinct approaches: the insider approach, where individuals engage with formal justice mechanisms while incorporating Buddhist beliefs, and the outsider approach, where victims reject institutional avenues in favour of personal, merit-based practices. By analysing these divergent responses, the section highlights the opportunities and challenges of reconciling externally imported justice models with locally embedded spiritual world views.

## 8.2 THE ECCC AND ITS CIVIL PARTY PARTICIPATION MECHANISM

The ECCC has been widely seen as the most prominent institution in Cambodia to address the legacies of the KR regime (Ciorciari and Heindel 2014). Its centrality in Cambodia's transitional justice landscape is evidenced in various ways, from the statements of Court officials to its substantial budget, as well as its discursive dominance over other competing narratives. Judge Kong Srim, President of the Supreme Court Chamber, reiterated the commitment of the Court at its eighth plenary session to 'expeditiously and effectively deliver justice to all victims of the Democratic Kampuchea' (ECCC 2010). Similarly, Sean Visoth, Director of the Office of Administration, highlighted the mission of the Court to 'seek justice for [KR] victims, and for the entire Cambodian people' (ECCC 2006). The ECCC has been portrayed as the definitive path to justice for Cambodia, monopolising discourse of transitional justice in the post-KR context. If doubts remain about the dominance of the Tribunal, the statistics speak volumes. During a ten-year period between 2002 and 2012, only 9 per cent of international assistance was directed to civil societies, while the ECCC received USD 250 million – approximately 91 per cent of the overall funding (Sperfeldt and Oeung 2019). In addition to being favoured by international donors as a funding priority, the ECCC sets the frame for wider societal efforts to confront the violent past. Destrooper's analysis underscores the normative influence of the ECCC in shaping 'the discourses, priorities, and praxis' of Cambodian NGOs operating in its shadows (Destrooper 2018).

Despite being a formal institution implemented by national and international authorities, the ECCC has made an unprecedented effort to engage victims through its innovative Civil Party participation mechanism. The introduction of the mechanism represents a groundbreaking development in the history of international criminal justice, enabling victims to participate as active parties in the trial process instead of remaining passive observers. As direct victims of crimes within the jurisdiction of the ECCC, Civil Parties are entitled to: (a) participate in judicial proceedings against the charged persons in support of the prosecution and (b) request collective and moral reparations once the accused is convicted (ECCC 2022, Rule 23). However, prior to the start of trial proceedings in Case 002, structural changes were made to the form of victim participation amid concerns of judicial efficiency and the defendants' fair trial rights (Killean 2017). These adjustments resulted in a significant reduction in the scope of victim participation, raising concerns about the symbolic nature of their involvement (Bernath et al. 2022). While the number of Civil Parties admitted by the Court surged from 76 in Case 001 to 3,869 in Case 002, there was a notable decline in the overall percentage of Civil Parties who provided oral testimony during the trial, as well as a decrease in the amount of trial time allocated to them (Cohen et al. 2015). Additionally, the 3,869 Civil Parties in Case 002 were consolidated into a single group represented by two lead co-lawyers during the trial, effectively diluting the representation of diverse interests among the participating victims.

With regard to reparations, in Case 001, the Trial Chamber endorsed two requests, namely the publication of statements of apology issued by Duch throughout the trial, and the inclusion of the names of all Civil Parties in the final judgment. In contrast, in Case 002, Civil Parties were provided with an additional avenue for reparations via financial support and other forms of assistance from external third parties (ECCC n.d.). The Trial Chamber approved eleven projects requested by Civil Parties in Case 002/01 and thirteen in Case 002/02. While some projects aimed at improving the physical and mental well-being of Civil Parties in both severed cases, a closer examination of the endorsed reparation projects reveals that nearly all of them were driven by the imperative of remembrance. The therapeutic and conciliatory values of memory is highlighted in projects ranging from a National Day of Remembrance and the dissemination of ECCC case materials to exhibitions on the KR history and genocide education programmes. This emphasis on remembrance is distinct from the perspectives of many who chose not to participate in institutionalised justice efforts. For them, as will be illustrated in Section 8.4, the past is an illusion, and true peace and freedom can only be achieved by letting go of it.

## 8.3 PARTICIPATION IN THE ECCC PROCEEDINGS AS A FORM OF 'RETURN' TO THE DEAD

In post-KR Cambodia, where over 90 per cent of the population adheres to Theravada Buddhism, conceptions of justice are deeply influenced by long-standing Buddhist traditions embedded in Khmer society.[1] In contrast to the formal approach that constructs trials as a means of determining accountability and punishment, Civil Parties at the ECCC interpret the proceedings and their participation in alternative ways through the lens of their cosmological beliefs. For many victims, the Court provides an opportunity for them to fulfil their obligations to lost loved ones (Hinton 2018). This sense of obligation is rooted in the Khmer concept of *sâng*, meaning 'to return' something, especially in the context of repaying a debt, whether monetary or moral. Cambodian culture places significant emphasis on showing respect and gratitude, as well as repaying the good deeds that one has received (Hinton 2005). Failing to acknowledge and reciprocate such kindness is believed to risk provoking the dead, who might inflict suffering upon the living. During Case 001 at the ECCC, in which Duch – the head of the notorious Tuol Sleng (S-21) detention centre who had overseen the torture and execution

[1] According to the 2022 data from the Cambodian Ministry of Cults and Religions, approximately 93 per cent of Cambodia's population adheres to Buddhism, with 95 per cent of them practising Theravada Buddhism. The remaining 7 per cent includes Christians, Muslims, animists, Baha'is, Jews, and Cao Dai followers. See the US Department of State. 2023. '2023 Report on International Religious Freedom: Cambodia'. www.state.gov/wp-content/uploads/2024/04/547499-CAMBODIA-2023-INTERNATIONAL-RELIGIOUS-FREEDOM-REPORT.pdf.

of more than 12,000 individuals between 1975 and 1979 – stood trial, Civil Parties expressed their desire to honour this obligation through their testimony. Touch Monin, a Civil Party who lost his cousin at S-21, stated that '[m]y intention is to pay my gratitude to my cousin, Chea Khan alias Chin, who had [made] great and kind sacrifice [for] my family' (ECCC 2009d, 98). Similarly, Im Sunthy, the wife of Phung Thon, Duch's former teacher who perished at S-21, remarked that 'I am here to actually pay homage to the dead souls of my husband and my father and the lost family members' (ECCC 2009b, 23).

In an effort to honour and show gratitude to the deceased, many victims brought to the fore the virtues and good deeds of their lost loved ones during trial, seeking to 'preserve the memory of [the deceased] in the court record and in the minds of those listening to their testimonies' (Stover et al. 2011, 522). For them, the Tribunal provided a formal and highly publicised forum to publicly grieve and ensure that their loved ones were not forgotten. Looking back on the moments they spent together, Antonya Tioulong testified about the 'radiant personality' of her sister, Raingsy Tioulong, who was tortured and killed at S-21:

> [She behaved like] an older sister as in the traditional way in the Khmer ... society, where the older siblings must take care of the younger ones ... She took care of my grandfather until the end as well ... She protected her children by sending them to live in France ... She protected us all the time ... but she was not able to protect herself. (ECCC 2009a, 24–28)

Similarly, Phung Guth Sunthary spoke during the trial about her father, Phung Thon, describing him as someone who always protected the family. Her father, she testified, 'was like a great shadow to protect us from the outside world of hatred and problems ... I have spent the entire [childhood and adolescent-hood] to be in the very good care of my father' (ECCC 2009b, 28–32). She noted that it was her duty 'to attest to this Chamber the memory, the dignity, the caring father' (ECCC 2009b, 30). It is as Civil Party Chum Sirath, who lost his brother at S-21 said in an interview outside the ECCC, 'Who could have told their story, if not me? Those stories have to be told to the court so there will be memory and people will not be forgotten ... That is why it is my duty to testify' (Stover et al. 2011, 522).

During the trial, nearly all Civil Parties presented photographs of their lost loved ones, seeking to restore the faces, voices, and dignity that had been stripped from them. Civil Party Neth Phally displayed a photo of his brother, Neth Bunthy, who was detained and killed at S-21, hoping to give his spirit an active presence in the courtroom. By the end of his testimony, Neth was asked by Presiding Judge Nil Nonn whether he had any further questions or requests. He responded, 'I would like to show a photo of my brother', raising a black-and-white photograph in front of him of a young man in a black collared shirt with a youthful face (ECCC 2009a, 109). Neth continued, 'it is like he is now sitting ... next to me ... I believe that my brother will be at peace, having learned that justice is achieved through this Court' (ECCC 2009a, 109–110). Holding up the photo with his only arm – his left arm having been severed in an accident while chopping down a rubber tree, distracted by thoughts of his brother – Neth started to address his brother, pausing every few words:

> At that time you were taken to S-21 while you were being blindfolded and when you were taken out to be killed you remain blindfolded. Now the Court revealed the faces of those people who committed the atrocity. So please, [may] the soul of you be here with me and in the photo forever so that I can pay homage to you and dedicate the offerings whatsoever to you. I can never find the dead body of you and this is [the only] photo, the photo which really represents the ashes and the body of you. (ECCC 2009a, 110)

Neth's testimony sheds light on the importance of the spirits of the dead in the Cambodian cosmological world, where many believe that those who suffered violent deaths may struggle to reincarnate. Civil Party Seang Vandy made a similar prayer for the soul of his brother, Seang Phon, who died at S-21, praying that he might 'detach from this world and to find a peaceful world' (ECCC 2009b, 86). While informing the Court of the documents he found at the Tuol Sleng Genocidal Museum that contain records of his brother's confessions, Seang started to sob, putting his hand on his throat as he found it difficult to continue his speech. After a deep breath, he proceeded to address his brother:

> Brother Phon, I truly believed that you are here to listen to the proceedings before this Chamber because this afternoon I prayed to you to come here and to participate … so that you can witness and hear that I have attempted to find the justice for the criminal act committed upon you. So may your soul receive the peace and that you rest in peace. (ECCC 2009b, 86)

Like Neth and Seang, many victims who decided to testify in the courtroom were driven by desires to help the deceased spirits find peace, release them from a world of limbo, and accelerate their reincarnation into the next being. This process was not solely enabled by the Court's role in putting those once-powerful perpetrators on trial, offering Civil Parties the chance to confront them and, in case of conviction, witnessing their punishment. Notably, the Court also provided opportunities for Civil Parties to uncover the truth about the fate of their disappeared families. During the Case 001 trial, Civil Party Ou Savrith asked Duch what his brother had endured inside S-21 – whether he had been subject to interrogation and torture while being detained (ECCC 2009c, 68). Many Civil Parties also pressed Duch to confirm the locations where their loved ones were killed. As indicated by Judge Nil, President of the Trial Chamber, knowing where the remains of their families had been buried would allow them to gather soil from those places in order to conduct proper death ceremonies dedicated to the dead (ECCC 2009c, 46). Stover et al. (2011) observe that many victims had even built shrines in anticipation of receiving tangible information on the interment of their loved ones.

The highly publicised nature of the trials, the legitimacy they are endowed with as a space for determining criminality, as well as the shifted power dynamic between perpetrators and victims collectively make the courtroom a desired place for families of the deceased to show respect and pay gratitude to their lost loved ones as a way to make the return. It provides a platform for them to bring peace to the deceased spirits by telling their stories, bearing witnessing to the justice process, and seeking the truth about their fate. The way victims utilise the Court space to accommodate their own ideas of justice reflects a process of 'vernacularisation' or 'localisation' of foreign justice models (Merry 2006). This occurs when local communities adapt and instrumentalise universalised discourses, norms, and practices in their pursuit of justice (Viaene and Brems 2017). Often, this process includes integrating local customs, religious beliefs, and traditional dispute resolution mechanisms to make foreign justice models more accessible and meaningful to the affected population. In the context of the ECCC, Civil Parties brought their lived experiences to the Court, often articulated through the lens of Theravada Buddhism, thereby imbuing the Court with new meanings that align with local religious beliefs. Legal proceedings at the ECCC were shaped not just by international criminal law, but also by local Buddhist notions of justice, karma, and the afterlife. This dynamic process of negotiation between global norms and local realities allows for an interaction between victims' retributive desires of seeking punishment for perpetrators, and their religious beliefs in assisting the deceased spirits to reincarnate into a better world.

## 8.4 'PARTICIPATION' IN ORDINARY SPACES THROUGH BUDDHIST BELIEFS

While some victims participated in the ECCC proceedings to honour the spirits of the dead, many others chose not to engage with this hybrid mechanism. Instead, there was a noticeable lack of interest in, or even resistance to, the form of justice provided by vernacularised post-conflict models. Many invoked the Buddhist principle of forgetting, which emphasises that dwelling on the past can stir up difficult emotions such as intense pain, anger, or desire for vengeance. One example of this hybridity is 'testimonial therapy', a practice employed by the Transcultural Psychological Organization Cambodia (TPO Cambodia) to facilitate trauma healing of those most affected by the KR regime. This is, indeed, one of the memory-based reparation projects endorsed by the ECCC for Civil Parties of Case 002/01. The process begins with a series of individual therapeutic sessions, during which victims recount their traumatic memories with the guidance of a TPO counsellor. The counsellor then converts these narratives into a written testimony. In a video posted by TPO Cambodia on YouTube titled 'Testimonial Therapy', the process is illustrated through a structured sequence of rituals. After the individual sessions, victims participate in a group visit to Choeung Ek killing fields, where many of their relatives were executed. Gathered around the memorial *stupa* which contains a large collection of skulls and other exhumed remains of S-21 victims, they light incense and present flowers as act of reverence, seeking peace for the spirits of their loved ones. The final stage of the process takes place in a nearby pagoda, where victims' testimonies were read aloud by TPO counsellors during a Buddhist ceremony attended by survivors, relatives, community members, local authorities, and NGO representatives. Following this emotional reading, victims kneel before the monk and hand in their personal testimonial folder. The monk then ties a red string around their wrist, which is held to provide protection from harmful spirits. As victims chant prayers, the monk sprinkles holy water on their heads, symbolising a transfer of merit to their deceased relatives, ensuring their peaceful passage in the afterlife.

Testimonial therapy, described by TPO Cambodia as a 'culturally adapted and rights-based treatment approach', was originally developed by Lira and Weinstein to address widespread post-traumatic stress among victims of political repression during the Pinochet regime in Chile (Bichescu et al. 2007). This therapeutic technique, which involves narrating and documenting a patient's traumatic experiences in a structured and supportive environment, has been internationally recognised as a healing and empowering process that helps victims process emotions, reduce distress, and restore self-esteem (Cienfuegos and Monelli 1983). Since its development, the treatment has been widely implemented in multiple post-conflict settings, including Bosnia and Rwanda, facilitated by local NGOs. In Cambodia, TPO Cambodia vernacularised this therapeutic method by integrating traditional Buddhist practices facilitated by Buddhist monks and pagodas, marrying memorial practices and human rights discourse with Buddhist beliefs related to reincarnation, family ties, and merit transfer, all of which are integral to Cambodia's spirit-based culture.

According to TPO Cambodia, this hybrid scheme serves multiple purposes: it enhances public acknowledgement of victims' suffering, destigmatises trauma, and restores dignity to victims. At the same time, it allows victims to bring comfort to their ancestors' spirits and pay homage to their deceased loved ones, reinforcing the spiritual and cultural dimensions of healing in Cambodian society. However, ethnographic interviews conducted by Kidron (2021) suggest that this vernacularised model has not gained overall popularity within the local community. When asked about their views on testimonial therapy, some respondents acknowledged that victims do speak about the past but prefer to do so in informal, private, and pressure-free settings.

Moreover, with the passage of time, perspectives on the past evolve. Thirty years later, many feel that resources would be better spent on improving their living conditions, which they now prioritise. Some admitted attending the therapy session for financial incentives, but left feeling overwhelmed by excessive recalling without any tangible benefit. Others, like Kichy, invoked Buddhist teachings as a reason for her reluctance to participate:

> I have no interest in thinking about the past. I forget the past... I think about doing bon [acts that promote merit] behave good actions and give donation to Wat to have merit. I do rituals for my brother [murdered in genocide]. I am a Buddhist. I do not believe in this approach ... [Pushing] survivors to talk about painful past is like pushing them to live again in the sad time. Something that they don't want to remember. (Kidron 2021, 303)

In her statement, Kichy emphasises the Buddhist belief that dwelling on the past arouses difficult emotions such as pain and anger. Arun, a former NGO employee, states that adapting foreign, memory-based post-conflict models to local contexts is not only perceived as a threat to mindfulness and inner peace, which Buddhist teachings seek to foster, but also risks reigniting the very communal tensions these initiatives aim to ease (Kidron 2021, 299–301). Reflecting on his experience with victim outreach activities in rural Cambodia, Arun describes:

> I had two actors present a play to the villagers. One played a KR soldier and the other a victim. The soldier told the victim that he was very sorry for all the bad things he did to the victim and his family. He suffers for his actions hurting and killing people. he says he did it because he was afraid. He asks for forgiveness. The victim then shakes his hand and says he forgives. Me and my co-worker explain to the villagers that we listen to the perpetrator and understand he was afraid like the victim – he is also a victim. If we forgive we can live in peace. (Kidron 2021, 300)

Arun recalls that the idea of victim outreach stemmed from a training trip to European concentration camps, where they were taught that peace could only be achieved through open dialogue about past atrocities. However, when they implemented these outreach activities in Cambodian villages, the results were not as expected. During one performance, an elderly woman broke down in distress after watching the play. Running up to the actor portraying the soldier, she began beating him, crying out: 'You killed you killed! We won't forgive. You didn't suffer like us' (Kidron 2021, 300). Witnessing this reaction cemented Arun's decision to leave his NGO job. He explains, 'This play was what the foreign advisor at the NGO calls peace pedagogy. But it can't work. You can't teach people to forgive when they don't want to, when they don't believe this is the way ... Villagers do not want to speak about the past suffering or hear about it. The foreigner does not understand the Khmer way' (Kidron 2021, 300).

Pich, a lay devotee nun at a local *wat*, further highlights the fundamental incompatibility between the Buddhist approach to peace and healing and the NGO-initiated victim–perpetrator engagement:

> Buddhism teaches us that all life is suffering. We must accept our pain and anger and let it go. You would say – forgive – but this is a mistake. It is not our place to forgive. Each person is on their own path to acceptance of suffering and pain. Our response to those who killed will not change their path or ours. Every day we must decide to release attachment to desire, hunger, creed, evil – it is all an illusion that causes suffering. Only release will give us peace. Shaking hands with the KR is meaningless if in our heart we are attached to anger, If a man is violent in his heart – no ceremony will change the future. (Kidron 2021, 298)

Many victims' reluctance to engage in vernacularised memory work is deeply rooted in Cambodian Buddhist teachings, which emphasise the acceptance of suffering and the release of illusive desires and anger (Harris 2005). Central to this perspective is the concept of karma, a fundamental element of Cambodia's cultural and cosmological frameworks. Karma operates on the principle of 'cause and effect', where the merit a person accumulates in this life determines the nature of existence that they will reincarnate into. In essence, people reap what they sow. It is in this sense that holding onto the past is seen as both pointless and harmful. On the one hand, KR cadre who committed grave sins will inevitably suffer the karmic consequences in their next life. It is believed that individuals who have committed serious wrongdoings may be unable to reincarnate after death or remain trapped in limbo for a long time as *pretas* – hungry ghosts tormented by extreme hunger and thirst. *Preta* can only be freed from their state of misery when they are reborn (Guillou 2012). On the other hand, practices of memorialisation often lead to attachment and bad deeds, which negatively affect one's own karma and reincarnation (Davis 2013). As a result, many victims choose to move beyond the past by focusing on merit-making as a way to honour their deceased loved ones, a personal practice believed to bring peace to both the living and the dead (Pham et al. 2011). Merit-making, a concept at the core of Buddhist practice, is seen as the path to improving one's karma and facilitating a quicker rebirth into a higher state of existence. In Cambodia, the transference of merit typically takes place during Pchum Benh, an annual Cambodian festival for the dead, during which people pay visit to pagodas to make offerings for the spirits of their ancestors.

## 8.5 TWO APPROACHES TO THE TENSIONS BETWEEN THE LIBERAL AND BUDDHIST JUSTICE FRAMEWORKS

The post-KR context has witnessed the co-existence of (at least) two strands of justice efforts to address the legacies of the past: institutional efforts towards liberal, legal justice and grassroots efforts centred on Buddhist karmic justice. Some scholars argue that these two justice frameworks are largely aligned, as both seek to distinguish right from wrong behaviours (Ledgerwood and Un 2003). Others, however, highlight their fundamental differences: while the rights-based framework foregrounds the assignment of accountability and the enforcement of punishment through judiciary and institutional mechanisms, Buddhist karmic justice operates independently of formal justice avenues, focusing instead on the accumulation of virtues and sins over time (Bennett 2018). In navigating these global-local tensions over what constitutes an appropriate response to mass harm, victims in Cambodian society have adopted very different approaches, which essentially manifests an insider–outsider dynamic.

Victims who took the insider approach tapped into the opportunities provided by formal justice avenues while simultaneously infusing them with their own Buddhist conceptions of justice. Many saw the trial proceedings at the ECCC as a platform to restore dignity to their loved ones, bring peace to their deceased spirits, and uncover the truth about their fate. One such example is Civil Party Chhin Navy, who lost her husband at S-21 and participated in Case 001 trial against the defendant Duch. Recognising the significance of the trial in revealing her husband's fate and educating future generations of the cruelty of the KR regime, Chhin frequently invoked Buddhist precepts and principles during her testimony to interpret both past suffering and present justice (ECCC 2009d, 74–77). Chhin's husband was taken away shortly after her sister accused him of being a CIA agent to the KR soldiers, a betrayal that once filled Chhin with anger. However, over time, she reframed her understanding through Buddhist teachings, attributing her sister's actions to ideological indoctrination. Instead of harbouring resentment, she chose compassion, even helping to look after her sister's children. Chhin explained to the Court that her acceptance stemmed from her Buddhist belief in karmic justice: her sister, like the defendant Duch, would inevitably face the karmic repercussions of her actions as an integral part of the continuous cycles of birth, death, and rebirth (*samsara*). As she put it, 'if you plant a hot chili pepper, you'll get a hot chili pepper; if you plant sweet sugarcane, you'll receive sweet sugarcane; if you plant bitter *sdauv* [a plant], your yield will be bitter *sdauv*' (ECCC 2009d, 76; Hinton 2018, 214). By inserting these existing beliefs into the ECCC's legal process, this group of victims essentially integrated local world views into the framework of the Tribunal as a way to make it more culturally resonant.

By contrast, victims who adopted the outsider approach showed a lack of interest in or resistance towards formal justice avenues and their underlying principle of memorialisation. These approaches were viewed as fundamentally incompatible with Buddhist notions of no-self, non-attachment, and acceptance of past suffering. For them, disengagement from formal institutions was not just a passive choice but a necessary step in upholding their own pursuit of Buddhist karmic justice (Husgafvel 2016). Instead of seeking redress through formal platforms, they turned to the ordinary, everyday spaces as the only meaningful forum to seek justice. Motivated by the desire to relieve his brother who died at the hands of the KR regime of his bad karma, Ta Sann, one of Bennett's interviewees, explained that he regularly visits the pagoda to 'practice Buddhism and gain merit' (Bennett 2018, 74–75). Similarly, Pich remarked that 'only meditation and the path of the Buddha can allow us to accept the past and let it go and make a better future' (Kidron 2021, 298–299). Kichy, as previously noted, rejects revisiting the painful past and instead engages in merit-making through good deeds, donations to the *wat*, and religious rituals for her deceased brother (Kidron 2021, 303). These accounts illustrate how Buddhist justice notions shape victims' responses to past atrocities, steering them away from institutionalised justice efforts and towards personal, merit-based practices. For them, attempts to adapt imported justice models to local contexts prove futile, as these frameworks remain fundamentally at odds with Buddhist understandings of suffering, redemption, and the self.

## 8.6 CONCLUSION

Thirty years after the KR period, the Cambodian government and the UN established the ECCC to address the suffering endured by the Cambodian population. However, as Guillou (2012, 212) notes, Cambodians did not remain 'silent, unconcerned, or reluctant' in confronting the violent past during this period. Instead, they developed their own responding mechanisms deeply rooted in Cambodian religious traditions to move forward. Against this background, the ECCC and its vision of justice have been perceived differently among victimised communities, whose ideas of justice are largely informed by Cambodian Buddhist notions. This chapter examines two groups of victims who navigated the tensions between Buddhist and formal justice in different ways. While some engaged with institutional platforms, seeking to carve out spaces there for alternative forms of participation aligned with Buddhist practices, others distanced themselves from these mechanisms, favouring more private, merit-based rituals instead.

Beyond differing views on the compatibility of ECCC-led justice and Buddhist karmic justice, this analysis also raises further questions about the capacity of formal mechanisms to respond to diverse justice demands on the ground. First, the victim participation scheme at the ECCC has already been criticised for its largely symbolic nature, constrained by the legal process which 'cannot hold the complexity of victimization' (Elander 2013, 114). This research raises questions on the extent to which the ECCC accommodated the demands of those who brought different world views into its purview. Were victims adequately informed about the fate of their lost loved ones? Were they given adequate spaces to tell their stories and restore dignity to the dead? To what extent did the Tribunal acknowledge the spiritual harm endured by the participating victims and the deceased spirits?

Second, while the ECCC holds a significant place in Cambodia's transitional justice landscape, scholars such as Hinton (2014) caution against the tendency of transitional justice frameworks to focus on the top-down imposition of mechanisms that decentre local epistemologies. Similarly, Parent (2010, 278–279) argues that 'post-conflict reconciliation revolves not only trust and constructive attitudes or imposed peacebuilding measures but recognizing the humanity of the "other"; that is, the "other's" needs, interests, understandings, and perceptions of war, peace, and even reconciliation'. This raises questions: to what extent can we explore the potential of formal spaces in directing attention to local justice practices that operate alongside the rights-based framework? How can institutional efforts ensure they do not crowd out, but instead make space for, the everyday practices through which communities pursue justice? These questions regarding the strengths and limitations of formal justice approaches in facilitating the complex, multi-layered justice demands on the ground warrant further examination.

## REFERENCES


Bennett, Caroline. 2018. 'Karma after Democratic Kampuchea: Justice Outside the Khmer Rouge Tribunal'. *Genocide Studies and Prevention: An International Journal*, 12(3), 68–82. https://doi.org/10.5038/1911-9933.12.3.1567

Bernath, Julie, Somaly Kum, and Boravin Tann. 2022. 'Symposium on the ECCC: Victim Participation at the ECCC – Final Justice for the Victims of the Khmer Rouge?' Opinio Juris. Published 2 November. https://tinyurl.com/mr3v9dkb

Bichescu, Dana, Frank Neuner, Maggie Schauer, and Thomas Elbert. 2007. 'Narrative Exposure Therapy for Political Imprisonment-Related Chronic Posttraumatic Stress Disorder and Depression'. *Behaviour Research and Therapy*, 45(9), 2212–2220. https://doi.org/10.1016/j.brat.2006.12.006

Cienfuegos, Ana Julia, and Cristina Monelli. 1983. 'The Testimony of Political Repression as a Therapeutic Instrument'. *American Journal of Orthopsychiatry*, 53(1), 43–51. https://doi.org/10.1111/j.1939-0025.1983.tb03348.x

Ciorciari, John D., and Anne Heindel. 2014. *Hybrid Justice: The Extraordinary Chambers in the Courts of Cambodia*. University of Michigan Press.

Cohen, David, Melanie Hyde, Penelope Van Tuyl, and Stephanie Fung. 2015. 'A Well-Reasoned Opinion? Critical Analysis of the First Case against the Alleged Senior Leaders of the Khmer Rouge (Case 002/01)'. East–West Center. www.eastwestcenter.org/sites/default/files/private/cohen-wellreasoned2015_0.pdf

Davis, Leesa S. 2013. 'Mindfulness, Non-Attachment and Other Buddhist Virtues'. In *The Handbook of Virtue Ethics*, edited by Stan van Hooft, pp. 306–317. Acumen Publishing.

Destrooper, Tine. 2018. 'Accountability for Human Rights Violations in Cambodia: Mapping the Indirect Effects of Transitional Justice Mechanisms'. *Asia-Pacific Journal on Human Rights and the Law*, 19(2), 113–139.

ECCC. 2006. 'The Cambodian Approach: Finding the Truth and Reconciliation in Cambodia through ECCC'. Released 28 August. https://archive.eccc.gov.kh/documents/2457076?title=null&matterId=52&page=2

ECCC. 2009a. 'Transcript of Trial Proceedings – Kaing Guek Eav "Duch": Trial Day 60'. Case 001, Doc. E1/64.1, Trial Chamber, 18 August, 0907H. https://archive.eccc.gov.kh/documents/986124?title=E1/64.1&matterId=49&page=3

ECCC. 2009b. 'Transcript of Trial Proceedings – Kaing Guek Eav "Duch": Trial Day 61'. Case 001, Doc. E1/65.1, Trial Chamber, 19 August, 0907H. https://archive.eccc.gov.kh/documents/989342?title=E1/65.1&matterId=49&page=2

ECCC. 2009c. 'Transcript of Trial Proceedings – Kaing Guek Eav "Duch": Trial Day 62'. Case 001, Doc. E1/66.1, Trial Chamber, 20 August, 0905H. https://archive.eccc.gov.kh/documents/988458?title=E1/66.1&matterId=49

ECCC. 2009d. 'Transcript of Trial Proceedings – Kaing Guek Eav "Duch": Trial Day 63'. Case 001, Doc. E1/67.1, Trial Chamber, 24 August, 0907H. https://archive.eccc.gov.kh/documents/985203?title=E1/67.1&matterId=49

ECCC. 2010. 'Opening Speech by the Plenary's President Judge KONG Srim, during the 8th Plenary of the Extraordinary Chambers in the Courts of Cambodia (ECCC) on 13 September 2010'. Released 13 September. https://archive.eccc.gov.kh/documents/2461102?title=null&matterId=52&page=23

ECCC. 2011. 'Decision on International Co-Prosecutor's Appeal of the Pre-Trial Chamber's Failure to Send Case 003 to Trial as Required by the ECCC Legal Framework'. Case 003, Doc. No 3/1/1/1, Supreme Court Chamber, 17 December. https://archive.eccc.gov.kh/documents/1274240?title=3/1/1/1&matterId=49

ECCC. 2022. 'International Rules (Rev.10)'. Revised 27 October. https://tinyurl.com/5n6fdkuu

ECCC. n.d. 'Reparations'. www.eccc.gov.kh/en/organisation/victim-and-witness-support/reparations

Elander, Maria. 2013. 'The Victim's Address: Expressivism and the Victim at the Extraordinary Chambers in the Courts of Cambodia'. *International Journal of Transitional Justice*, 7 1, 95–115. https://doi.org/10.1093/ijtj/ijs028

Gidley, Rebecca. 2019. *Illiberal Transitional Justice and the Extraordinary Chambers in the Courts of Cambodia*. Palgrave Macmillan.

Guillou, Anne Yvonne. 2012. 'An Alternative Memory of the Khmer Rouge Genocide: The Dead of the Mass Graves and the Land Guardian Spirits [*Neak ta*]'. *South East Asia Research*, 20(2), 207–226. https://doi.org/10.5367/sear.2012.0102

Harris, Ian. '"Onslaught on Beings": A Theravada Buddhist Perspective on Accountability for Crimes Committed in the Democratic Kampuchea Period'. In *Bringing the Khmer Rouge Justice: Prosecuting Mass Violence before the Cambodian Courts*, edited by Jaya Ramji and Beth Van Schaack, pp. 59–95. Edwin Mellen Press.

Hinton, Alexander Laban. 2005. *Why Did They Kill? Cambodia in the Shadow of Genocide*. University of California Press.

Hinton, Alexander Laban. 2014. 'Justice and Time at the Khmer Rouge Tribunal: In Memory of Vann Nath, Painter and S-21 Survivor'. *Genocide Studies and Prevention: An International Journal*, 8(2), 7–17. http://dx.doi.org/10.5038/1911-9933.8.3

Hinton, Alexander Laban. 2018. *The Justice Façade: Trials of Transition in Cambodia*. Oxford University Press.

Husgafvel, Ville. 2016. 'On the Buddhist Roots of Contemporary Non-Religious Mindfulness Practice: Moving beyond Sectarian and Essentialist Approaches'. *Nordic Journal for the Study of Religion*, 52(1), 87–126. https://doi.org/10.33356/temenos.55371

Kidron, Carol A. 2021. '"Rebirthing" the Violent Past: Friction between Post-Conflict Axioms of Remembrance and Cambodian Buddhist Forgetting'. *Anthropological Forum*, 31(3), 291–311. https://doi.org/10.1080/00664677.2021.1971512

Killean, Rachel. 2016. 'Procedural Justice in International Criminal Courts: Assessing Civil Parties' Perceptions of Justice at the Extraordinary Chambers in the Courts of Cambodia'. *International Criminal Law Review*, 16(1), 1–38. https://doi.org/10.1163/15718123-01601002

Killean, Rachel. 2017. 'Pursuing Retributive and Reparative Justice within Cambodia'. In *Research Handbook on Transitional Justice*, edited by Cheryl Lawther, Luke Moffett, and Dov Jacobs, pp. 466–487. Edward Elgar Publishing.

Ledgerwood, Judy, and Kheang Un. 2003. 'Global Concepts and Local Meaning: Human Rights and Buddhism in Cambodia'. *Journal of Human Rights*, 2(4), 531–549. https://doi.org/10.1080/1475483032000137129

Merry, Sally Engle. 2006. 'Transnational Human Rights and Local Activism: Mapping the Middle'. *American Anthropologist*, 108(1), 38–51. https://doi.org/10.1525/aa.2006.108.1.38

Parent, Geneviève. 2010. 'Reconciliation and Justice after Genocide: A Theoretical Exploration'. *Genocide Studies and Prevention: An International Journal*, 5(3), 277–292. https://doi.org/10.1353/gsp.2010.0012

Pham, Phuong, Patrick Vinck, Mychelle Balthazard, Michelle Arévalo-Carpenter, and Sokhom Hean. 2011. 'Dealing with the Khmer Rouge Heritage'. *Peace Review*, 23(4), 456–461. https://doi.org/10.1080/10402659.2011.625818

Sperfeldt, Christoph, and Jeudy Oeung. 2019. "The Evolution of Cambodian Civil Society's Involvement with Victim Participation at the Khmer Rouge Trials." In *Civil Society and Transitional Justice in Asia and the Pacific*, edited by Lia Kent, Joanne Wallis, and Claire Cronin, pp. 85–105. Australian National University Press.

Stover, Eric, Mychelle Balthazard, and K. Alexa Koenig. 2011. 'Confronting *Duch*: Civil Party Participation in Case 001 at the Extraordinary Chambers in the Courts of Cambodia'. *International Review of the Red Cross*, 93(882), 503–546. https://doi.org/10.1017/S1816383111000439

Viaene, Lieselotte, and Eva Brems. 2017. 'Transitional Justice and Cultural Contexts: Learning from the Universality Debate'. *Netherlands Quarterly of Human Rights*, 28(2), 199–224. https://doi.org/10.1177/016934411002800204

# 9

# Truth Processes and Victim Participation in the United States of America

## *An Examination of Maryland and California*

*Brianne McGonigle Leyh*

### 9.1 INTRODUCTION

The notion of truth is a powerful one within transitional justice, and truth-telling and truth-seeking are considered to be a necessary part of any justice pursuit. The 'right to truth', rooted in the broader right to a remedy, forms the foundation for both individual and societal efforts in truth-seeking. Formal truth processes can take many different forms. They range from parliamentary or executive bodies seeking to uncover the truth about specific incidents of harm to historical or expert commissions dedicated to examining past events. In traditional or paradigmatic transitional contexts, truth commissions are a widely accepted and frequently implemented response to addressing serious harms (Bakiner 2014; Vella 2014). They have garnered support from states, the UN, regional organisations, international and local civil society, and external donor countries (Shaw and Waldorf 2010; Sriram 2007; UN OHCHR 2011; UN Secretary-General 2004). Generally, truth commissions are officially mandated, temporary, non-judicial bodies tasked with investigating patterns of violence and abuse, exploring their causes and consequences, and producing a final report (Hayner 2011, 11–12; UN OHCHR 2006). Their activities often include gathering and analysing oral and written testimonies, conducting exhumations or forensic investigations, and performing historical research (UN OHCHR 2006). These commissions typically focus on addressing specific harms, such as extra-judicial killings, torture, or destruction of livelihoods (Ochs 2021, 9). While they are not criminal investigative entities, they can recommend cases for prosecution to relevant authorities.

The significance of truth commissions lies in their ability to publicly disclose the truth, create a historical record, and acknowledge victims' suffering. They may also contribute to broader goals such as national healing or provide individuals with a sense of catharsis through participation (Allen 1999; Bakiner 2014). However, there is ongoing debate about their effectiveness in fostering societal reconciliation, addressing victims' needs, or preventing future abuses (Allen 1999; Chapman 2009; Freeman and Hayner 2003). Critics often point to their temporary nature and limited authority as potential weaknesses. Despite these criticisms, truth commissions remain a cornerstone of transitional justice, with over forty state-sponsored commissions established globally since the 1970s (Aciru 2017; Bakiner 2014; Vella 2014).

Also in the United States of America (US), a growing number of officially sanctioned truth commissions (or truth commission-like processes) have been installed at the federal, state, and local levels to deal with a wide range of violent and discriminatory contexts. This chapter explores two such contemporary truth commissions operating at the sub-national level in the states of

Maryland and California. While the US constitutes an aparadigmatic case of transitional justice, in that it is not seen to be transitioning out of a serious conflict or authoritarian rule, the truth processes emerging from within the country are important to evaluate and learn from. This is especially the case since President Trump took office, effectively ending federal transitional justice work, thereby highlighting the increasingly relevant work at the sub-national level.

As earlier research has shown (Destrooper et al. 2023), there is a growing context of stable, democratic states, at both the national and sub-national levels, adopting the language and practice of transitional justice to address historical and present-day harms. Indeed, the field of transitional justice is no longer confined to the traditional typology of cases. Rather, the field has evolved to examine broader situations of harm where communities seek to address their violent pasts and, in most cases, move towards more socially just societies. Language, processes, and underlying beliefs championed by activists, community leaders, and politicians in these new contexts, including among others in Canada, the Netherlands, and Sweden, have led to the development of new insights and ideas within the field (Destrooper et al. 2023). Victims and victim communities play an important role in spearheading truth efforts in these contexts and have effectively leveraged political support to shed light on their harms.

Building on this earlier work, this chapter argues that examining efforts in the US, particularly around agency and empowerment, can shed light on broader developments around formalised participation, thereby contributing to a better understanding of the second generation of victim engagement in transitional justice practices in the US. Doing so can provide a fresh perspective on how the field broadly views participation in formal truth processes. As such, the chapter takes a constructive and normative approach and actively looks for what can be learned from these institutional attempts to create more meaningful and constructive truth-seeking processes. Drawing from scholarship and practice from the broader transitional justice field, particularly from participation scholarship, the chapter highlights how current and future truth processes can better conceptualise and implement victim participation to have deeper engagement and impact with affected communities.

## 9.2 VICTIM PARTICIPATION IN TRANSITIONAL JUSTICE PROCESSES

Participation in transitional justice processes is vital for ensuring that victims and marginalised communities have a voice in shaping the mechanisms that address historical injustices and foster societal healing (UN Guidance Note 2010). Accordingly, critically evaluating participatory practices is essential to avoid tokenism, address power imbalances, and ensure that these processes genuinely empower participants to influence outcomes and drive transformative change. This chapter builds on two relevant lines of scholarship on participation: one focusing on participation in formal processes and another taking a broader perspective, examining how participation has evolved over time within the field and situating participation with a generational framework.

First, Sherry Arnstein's 'Ladder of Citizen Participation', introduced in the late 1960s, remains a foundational framework for understanding the dynamics of civic engagement and power in institutional decision-making processes (1969). Arnstein proposed the ladder as an eight-rung continuum, ranging from non-participation (manipulation and therapy) through tokenism (informing, consultation, and placation) to genuine citizen power (partnership, delegated power, and citizen control). Her work was groundbreaking in highlighting the importance of not just involving citizens in governance but ensuring their participation has real influence and power. She argued that participation risks becoming superficial without authentic power-sharing, serving to placate or manipulate communities rather than empowering them. Her framework remains a critical tool for evaluating participation practices, particularly in formal transitional justice processes, emphasising the need for equitable and meaningful engagement to drive social change (McGonigle Leyh 2011). Because Arnstein's ladder emphasises formal or institutionalised processes of participation, it serves as a useful framework for this chapter's focus on the broader trends concerning formalised participation in the US. While other parallel spaces may also facilitate meaningful participation, a full analysis of non-formal spaces is beyond the scope of this chapter.

Second, this handbook's non-linear concept of 'three generations of victim engagement' offers another valuable framework for understanding the evolving roles of victims in justice processes over time (Destrooper 2024). The first generation of victim engagement involves victim mobilisation, where demands for justice are made. Here, victims are not passive stakeholders but rather finding avenues to voice their interests and concerns. In response to victims' demands and agenda setting, formal institutional transitional justice mechanisms are often created, marking a shift to the second generation of participation.

Traditionally, within the second generation, victims have been regarded as passive recipients of justice. Their agency is often overlooked with limited involvement, such as providing testimony with little influence over the proceedings or outcome. Yet this limited role has evolved in many institutional contexts as victims have demanded more dispositive participatory roles. As a result, it is important to explore formal transitional justice processes to evaluate the range of participatory practices within second-generation contexts. This is especially true because victims remain vulnerable to institutional constraints and capture.

When combined, Arnstein's Ladder of Citizen Participation and Destrooper's and Evrard's framework on the generations of victims' engagement present important frames and insights into agency and empowerment in participatory processes. Arnstein's ladder presents a linear and institutional focus on victim participation, highlighting the risks of tokenism and the necessity of power redistribution for meaningful engagement. In contrast, this handbook's framework adopts a non-linear approach, which zooms out and underscores the evolution of victim engagement over time in driving meaningful and transformative change. Utilising both frameworks to conceptualise the institutional processes of participation can help maintain a pragmatic equilibrium, neither neglecting the agency of victims beyond formal spaces, nor overlooking the role and significance of institutional mechanisms. Together, these approaches reveal that empowerment demands spaces, whether formal or informal, that enable individuals and communities to shape decisions and outcomes meaningfully.

Significantly, both frameworks underline the interplay between agency and systemic power dynamics: true empowerment occurs when those historically marginalised are not only heard but are also able to influence and direct processes addressing their needs and rights. These frameworks challenge practitioners to move beyond symbolic gestures, striving for participatory practices that honour and expand the agency of individuals and communities, particularly in contexts of justice and reconciliation. Accordingly, the concepts of agency and empowerment lie at the heart of both frameworks, offering a deeper understanding of how individuals and groups move from marginalisation to meaningful engagement in decision-making processes. Both concepts are essential to discussions of justice, reconciliation, and societal transformation, as they address how power is shared, exercised, and experienced in participatory settings.

For the purposes of this chapter, agency refers to the capacity of individuals or groups to act independently, make decisions, and effect change in their lives and environments (Sen 1999). In Arnstein's ladder, agency is often constrained at lower rungs, where participation is characterised by manipulation or tokenism, reducing individuals to passive recipients of decisions made by others. Destrooper's (2024) generational framework highlights the critical role of agency throughout each generation but similarly places value on the increased role of victims' agency in mobilising and driving transitional justice. Although both frameworks overlook, to some degree, the agency of victims in making demands for formal justice responses, by placing agency at the centre of participatory processes, these frameworks nevertheless remind us that effective participation is not just about being included but about having the power to co-create and co-decide. This aligns with critical theorists such as Amartya Sen (1999), who argue that fostering agency is fundamental to advancing human freedoms and capabilities.

The concept of empowerment builds on the notion of agency, emphasising the processes through which individuals and communities gain the skills, resources, and authority to act and effect meaningful change. Empowerment is not merely the granting of opportunities to participate; it involves dismantling structural barriers and redistributing power to enable individuals to act on their agency (Rowlands 1997). While empowerment can and does take place in various settings, Arnstein's higher rungs – such as partnership, delegated power, and citizen control – represent the institutional spaces where empowerment is actualised as individuals transition from being consulted to genuinely sharing (some) power. As such, it provides insight into how institutions can support and actualise parallel informal processes of empowerment, ultimately creating institutional spaces to overcome structural barriers and foster processes of meaning-making, agency and action. Similarly, this handbook's framework views victims as transformative actors whose engagement goes beyond consultation to include shaping justice processes and advocating for systemic change across a range of spaces. Empowerment is particularly critical in contexts of transitional justice, where marginalised groups often face systemic disempowerment. Scholars such as Nancy Fraser (2009) emphasise that empowerment must address issues of recognition and redistribution, ensuring that marginalised voices are not only included but also amplified in ways that challenge existing power dynamics. This resonates with Destrooper's call for participatory justice processes that recognise victims' experiences while enabling them to lead transformative societal reforms.

When viewed together, agency and empowerment provide a roadmap for meaningful participation. Participation without empowerment risks becoming hollow or performative, while empowerment without respect for individual agency can be paternalistic or coercive. Arnstein's ladder and the generational framework demonstrate that achieving both requires intentional design, inclusive practices, and a commitment to addressing systemic inequalities. This is especially relevant in transitional justice, where the empowerment of victims and marginalised groups to reclaim agency can transform justice processes into vehicles for long-term societal healing and reconciliation. In the context of formalised processes, the integration of these concepts challenges practitioners and policymakers to: (a) create participatory spaces that enable agency by valuing diverse voices and ensuring all stakeholders have a genuine role in decision-making; (b) foster empowerment by addressing structural inequalities, redistributing power, and providing tools, resources, and opportunities for marginalised groups to influence outcomes; and (c) evaluating participatory efforts through the lens of power. This requires questions such as: are participants merely included, or are they driving the process?

## 9.3 TRUTH PROCESSES IN THE US

As noted in the introduction to this chapter, truth processes can take various forms, ranging from parliamentary or executive bodies tasked with uncovering the truth about specific incidents of harm to historical or other commissions composed of experts dedicated to examining past events. Within the US Context, there have been several federally backed truth processes following World War II (WWII), which took the shape of executive committees or congressional commissions. Among the handful of executive-backed actions, President Truman's 1947 Committee on Civil Rights (President's Committee on Civil Rights 1947) and the 1967 Kerner Commission established under President Johnson stand out (National Advisory Commission on Civil Disorders 1968/2016). Both examples resulted in powerful final reports detailing the racial inequalities facing Black Americans, detailing the causes of that inequality, and making strong recommendations for addressing the structural inequalities. Yet neither process adopted broad or meaningful victim participation. Instead, the commissions were comprised predominantly of white men and were largely driven from the top down (Anderson 2003; Juhnke 1989). For various reasons, both reports had only limited impact, yet a common factor for both was a lack of meaningful participation.

Later Congressional commissions would become more prominent. Two of these truth-seeking commissions did lead to more tangible and concrete results for affected communities. One example is the 1975–1977 Joint Congressional Declaration in relation to Native Americans (American Indian Policy Review Commission 1977),[1] which helped lead to important legal and policy changes in the lives of Native Americans, including the passage of the Indian Child Welfare Act of 1978. The report also proved useful as an official source of authority, documenting the wide array of abuses experienced by Native American populations and providing a basis to call for further attention to specific forms of abuse. For example, in 2015, the Lakota People's Law Project relied on the report to support its calls for a federally backed Truth and Healing Commission aimed at researching the impacts and ongoing effects of the nation's boarding school policy (Lakota People's Law Project 2015). Most recently, in 2020 and again in 2024, senators from across the political spectrum have submitted a bill to establish a Truth and Healing Commission on Indian boarding school policies.[2] However, the process overall was limited in terms of participation, with victim communities acting predominantly as information providers, with little say or input over the shaping of the process.

Another example concerns the Commission on Wartime Relocation and Internment of Civilians in relation to Japanese-American internment during WWII (CWRIC 1982–1983). This commission is particularly significant as it resulted in material reparations and is frequently cited by justice advocates across the US as a model of effective truth-recovery efforts. Although the commission had only one female member and one member with a Japanese background, its approach to participation was greatly improved from previous practice, largely owing to the lobbying effort of affected communities. For instance, the commission travelled to cities across the US to hear from over 750 victims and how they were affected by the internment. These testimonies profoundly impacted the final report and how Congress took it up. More importantly, the commission responded to many of the concerns civil society groups raised, including receiving Japanese testimonies, providing for simultaneous interpretation for first-generation Japanese speakers, and conducting hearings off governmental property (Chin 1981; Michaelson 1981).

Nevertheless, although this was a significant step in documenting their suffering and led to reparations, their role in shaping the Commission's mandate or recommendations was

[1] Public Law 93–580, 93rd Congress, S.J. Res. 133, 2 January 1975, available, along with other relevant materials, at: www.fordlibrarymuseum.gov/library/document/0142/1103353.pdf.

[2] H.R. 8420, 116th Cong. (2020); S. 4752, 116th Cong. (2020).

minimal, underscoring a lack of deeper participatory engagement. Similarly, in processes addressing Native American historical grievances, such as the investigations into Indian boarding schools, victim participation was often constrained to providing testimony rather than influencing the broader truth-seeking or policy-making agenda. These processes largely treated victims as sources of information rather than active collaborators, limiting their agency and the transformative potential of their participation. Such limitations highlight the need for more inclusive frameworks that centre victims as key actors in truth and reconciliation processes.

Since the mid-1980s, increasing political polarisation, particularly on issues related to the nation's legacy of racial inequality, has hindered efforts to establish new truth commissions at the federal level. Nevertheless, the federal examples have inspired civil society groups to lobby for truth commission-like processes at the sub-national level to have officially backed truth processes that recognise and document historical and present-day harms suffered by marginalised communities. The sections that follow outline two state-backed truth processes that have been created at the sub-national level in the US since 2019, including truth processes in Maryland and California. These are just two of five state-backed truth processes presently operating across the US.[3] They were selected because of their differences in terms of their focus as well as the size and geography of their state contexts.

Through the Maryland Lynching Truth and Reconciliation Commission, the state of Maryland has focused on addressing the legacy of racial terror lynchings. This body investigates documented cases of lynchings, provides space for victims' descendants to share their stories, and fosters dialogue aimed at confronting the enduring impact of racial violence. In California, the Truth and Healing Council was established to examine the state's historical treatment of Native American communities. The council focuses on acknowledging the atrocities committed against Indigenous peoples, including massacres, forced removal, and cultural erasure, while working collaboratively with tribal leaders to promote healing and inform policy changes that support tribal sovereignty and justice. Both efforts reflect state-level commitments to truth-telling and reconciliation, addressing distinct yet intersecting histories of systemic violence and marginalisation. Both commissions also prioritise inclusive participation practices by cantering the voices of affected individuals and communities through testimony, consultation, and active engagement. These participatory approaches validate lived experiences and empower communities to shape the narratives and outcomes of the truth-seeking processes.

### 9.3.1 *Maryland*

Maryland is a smaller state located on the East Coast of the US, with a population of 6.1 million. A bill for creating the Maryland Lynching Truth and Reconciliation Commission (hereinafter the Maryland Commission) passed in 2019 with strong bipartisan support. It was drafted with the help of the volunteer-based non-profit Maryland Lynching Memorial Project, which is part of the Equal Justice Initiative's (EJI's) community memorial projects. The EJI is a non-profit organisation dedicated to ending mass incarceration, challenging racial and economic injustice, and protecting basic human rights for the most vulnerable in American society. Its Community Remembrance Project collaborates with local communities to memorialise

[3] Other truth commission-like processes have taken place in Maine, Vermont, and New York (Posthumus and Zvobgo 2021).

victims of racial violence by erecting historical markers and collecting soil from lynching sites, fostering public acknowledgement and dialogue about past injustices.

The Maryland Commission was established to research, rather than investigate (since this term proved too controversial), some of the most egregious acts of racial terror committed against Black Americans in the state's history. Its mandate specifically focuses on researching and reporting racially motivated lynchings that occurred between 1854 and 1933. Lynchings, typically carried out by mobs as extra-judicial killings – often by hanging – were used after the American Civil War to terrorise and control Black communities, with more than 6,500 African Americans lynched nationwide by white mobs during this period (Wells-Barnett 2014; Zvobgo 2019). Those responsible for these acts were rarely held accountable.

The Maryland Commission is composed of eighteen commissioners, including representatives from the state commissions on civil rights and African American history and culture, the state archivist, the head of the state National Association for the Advancement of Colored People, leaders of historical societies and museums, historians from the state's four historically Black colleges and universities, and four public members – a journalist, historian, professor, and museum director – nominated by the Commission. While commissioners are unpaid, a budget is allocated to cover their operational expenses, with staff support provided by Bowie State University in collaboration with the volunteer-based Maryland Lynching Memorial Project. The Commission's work includes holding public hearings, consulting with descendants of lynching victims and impacted communities, issuing subpoenas to compel testimony, producing a final report, and making restorative justice-based recommendations for addressing Maryland's history of racial violence. Initially set to conclude in 2024, the Commission's mandate has been extended to 2026.

Its first session was held in Allegany County together with the civil society-led Allegany County Lynching Truth and Reconciliation Committee (ACLTRC), which is an unofficial truth-telling process supported by non-profit organisations. This collaboration is indicative of the close relationship between the Commission, community organisations, and private justice initiatives. The Maryland Commission's first session, held at the Emmanuel Episcopal Church, focused on the 1907 lynching of eighteen-year-old Robert Hughes (also known as William Burns) and included the local police chief and descendants of those affected. While early meetings were conducted in person, later sessions transitioned online owing to the pandemic, and since then, meetings have often adopted a hybrid format. The Commission's proceedings, though formal with public contributions typically limited to three minutes, begin with 'soul checks' – a reflective moment allowing commissioners and attendees to share their emotions about the mentally and emotionally challenging truth-recovery work.

In 2020 and 2023, the Maryland Commission received additional funding – USD 300,000 and USD 175,000, respectively – from the US Department of Justice's Emmett Till Cold Case Investigations Program. These funds support the study of unsolved lynchings in Maryland through a project titled 'Justice in the Aftermath: Documenting the Truth of Racial Terror Lynching in Maryland to Support Restorative Justice Among Affected Communities'. The Commission also plans to examine government and media roles in lynchings and engage the public to explore ways to restore justice to victims' families and communities. Federal funding has been critical to sustaining the Commission's research and outreach, and the Equal Justice Initiative has played an essential role in drafting legislation, providing staffing, and facilitating the truth-recovery process, alongside the efforts of local justice advocates.

Participation before Maryland's Commission reflects a collaborative and community-driven approach, with civil society playing a critical role in its establishment and early processes. Local justice advocates and organisations crafted the draft legislation to create the commission, ensuring that the initiative was grounded in the needs and priorities of affected communities. Public consultation began immediately, engaging descendants of lynching victims, historians, and community members to shape the focus and scope of the commission's work. Efforts were made to make the process inclusive and representative, including open calls for commissioners to ensure diverse perspectives and close connections to the public. This pre-commission participation helped lay the foundation for a transparent and inclusive approach, centring the voices and experiences of those most affected by Maryland's history of racial terror.

### 9.3.2 *California*

California, which is a larger state on the West Coast of the US with a population of 38 million,[4] has been at the forefront of addressing its history of large-scale abuses, particularly those inflicted on Native American tribes. The state has made significant strides in transitional justice efforts, including truth recovery initiatives. Like many truth-telling processes, California's work began with a formal acknowledgement of harm. In 2019, Governor Gavin Newsom issued a public apology for the state's treatment of Native Americans, explicitly describing the actions as genocide (Oxford 2019).

The apology marked the beginning of a series of new laws aimed at strengthening Native American rights in California (Ochs 2021) and led to the establishment of the California Truth & Healing Council.[5] Created by Governor Newsom through Executive Order N-15-19,[6] the Order acknowledges the resistance and resilience of Native American communities while recognising that the state and Native Americans 'have never jointly formally examined or documented their relationship' to acknowledge and account for historical wrongs committed by California against Native Americans.[7] The Order explicitly identifies the state as a perpetrator of these injustices while laying the groundwork for healing. It tasks the Governor's Tribal Advisor with forming the Truth & Healing Council to bear witness to, document, and examine historical records, and to collect Native American narratives to clarify and acknowledge the historical relationship between the state and its Indigenous communities in the spirit of truth and healing.[8]

The Council was mandated to consult with California Native American tribes to shape its focus and approach, ensuring it 'accurately represents the diversity of experience of California Native Americans within the State'. Operational since 2020, the Council is led by the Governor's Tribal Advisor and overseen by a Governing Council comprising twelve representatives from California Native American tribes, selected with regional representation in mind. Additional participants may include representatives from relevant state and local agencies as well as non-governmental stakeholders.

The functions and powers of the Truth & Healing Council are outlined in its Charter.[9] The Council is responsible for gathering information through activities such as statement-taking,

4 US Census Statistics, available at www.census.gov/quickfacts/fact/table/CA/PST045223.

5 See generally About the California Truth & Healing Council, California Office of the Tribal Advisor, available at https://tribalaffairs.ca.gov/cthc/about/.

6 Executive Department, State of California, Executive Order N-15-19, 18 June 2019, available at www.gov.ca.gov/wp-content/uploads/2019/06/6.18.19-Executive-Order.pdf.

7 Executive Department, State of California, Executive Order N-15-19, 18 June 2019, available at www.gov.ca.gov/wp-content/uploads/2019/06/6.18.19-Executive-Order.pdf.

8 Executive Department, State of California, Executive Order N-15-19, 18 June 2019, available at www.gov.ca.gov/wp-content/uploads/2019/06/6.18.19-Executive-Order.pdf.

9 California Truth & Healing Council, Charter, December 2020, available at https://cthcupdates.files.wordpress.com/2021/05/cthc-charter_final.pdf.

archival research, consulting with experts, and drafting annual reports, culminating in a final written report with recommendations, due by 1 January 2025.[10] To facilitate information collection, the Council holds meetings and listening sessions across the state, both in person and online, with recordings made publicly available. In-person sessions emphasise inclusivity and prioritise Native American voices by establishing speaking orders that favour their participation. The Council has also adopted principles for respectful meetings and emphasises equity, justice, and healing in its Charter.[11] Its processes aim to foster mutual respect among participants while maintaining a focus on serving and prioritising the affected Native American population.

As the first expansive truth commission-like body in California with a broad-based mandate, the Truth & Healing Council has carefully structured its processes through tribal consultations and a thorough review of international mechanisms.[12] The Council highlights key resources on its website, including reports by the UN Special Rapporteur on the promotion of truth, justice, reparation, and guarantees of non-recurrence, UN declarations such as the Declaration on the Rights of Indigenous Peoples, and studies by non-governmental organisations focused on truth commissions.[13] The site also features comparative case studies from countries such as Canada, New Zealand, Guatemala, Mauritius, Peru, and Sierra Leone, showcasing lessons learned from global truth-seeking efforts. Additionally, the Council references other US-state truth commissions, such as the Maine Truth Commission report and archive, to underscore the importance of knowledge exchange and the development of norms in transitional justice. While the Truth & Healing Council's publications themselves do not explicitly use the term 'transitional justice', the comparative resources provided do make use of the term.

Like the Maryland example, participation in the California Truth & Healing Council reflects an inclusive, collaborative, and community-driven approach. Participation prior to the establishment of the Council involved significant government consultation with California Native American tribes, reflecting an effort to ensure that the Council's focus and structure were inclusive and representative. Governor Gavin Newsom's Executive Order N-15-19, which created the Council, explicitly recognised the importance of engaging tribal communities in shaping its mandate and guiding its work. Before the Council's formal operations began in 2020, tribal leaders and community members were consulted to ensure that the process reflected the diverse experiences of California Native Americans and addressed the historical injustices perpetrated by the state. The involvement of tribal voices was integral in defining the scope of the Council's truth-seeking efforts, including its commitment to documenting harms and fostering healing. This participatory groundwork was essential for building trust and ensuring that the Council's processes were grounded in the priorities of those most affected by California's legacy of systemic violence against Native Americans.

[10] California Truth & Healing Council, Charter, December 2020, article 8 available at https://cthcupdates.files.wordpress.com/2021/05/cthc-charter_final.pdf.

[11] California Truth & Healing Council, Charter, December 2020, article 2 available at https://cthcupdates.files.wordpress.com/2021/05/cthc-charter_final.pdf; California Truth & Healing Council, Principles for Respectful Meetings, available at https://tribalaffairs.ca.gov/wp-content/uploads/sites/10/2022/06/CTHC-Respectful-Engagement_Final.pdf?emrc=a6c4c8.

[12] California Truth & Healing Council, Overview Webinar, available at https://tribalaffairs.ca.gov/wp-content/uploads/sites/10/2020/10/CTHC_Overview-Webinar_10-14-20.pdf.; see also the Frequently Asked Questions section of its website: https://tribalaffairs.ca.gov/cthc/faq/.

[13] California Truth & Healing Council, Resources, available at https://tribalaffairs.ca.gov/cthc/resources/.

## 9.4 ANALYSIS: AGENCY AND EMPOWERMENT

As Zenobia Jeffries Warfield observes, 'the United States is a long way from having any sort of national truth-telling, let alone reconciliation' (Jeffries Warfield 2016, para. 6). However, the examples given here demonstrate that state government officials across the US have embraced the design and significance of truth processes. As reflected in their proceedings and online platforms, these commissions share a common belief: truth-telling is an essential first step toward healing and transformation despite its challenges. The two examples of truth processes in Maryland and California illustrate states' capacity to address historical and contemporary harms. Notably, both commissions combine historical analysis with examining current discriminatory policies and practices, highlighting their relevance to present-day, ongoing issues. It is hoped that these commissions will provide actionable policy recommendations aimed at government officials, emphasising their dual focus on acknowledging the past and informing present-day reform efforts.

Importantly, neither Maryland nor California waited on the federal government to take action. They also do not leave truth-process work exclusively to local and municipal actors. Instead, they are responding to justice demands made by their residents and explicitly turning to the field of transitional justice for guidance. These examples show how both smaller and larger states are adopting the truth commission model common within the field of transitional justice. By connecting with transitional justice experts and universities, referencing comparative state practice, and emphasising the human rights norms and best practices from the field, they are creating linkages between their justice work and broader global justice work. Importantly, they are not just 'cut and pasting' truth commission models. They are both unique in how they approach their truth processes. Nevertheless, they are noteworthy for their collaborative and inclusive participatory methods and the unique public–private relationships underpinning their operation. This is especially important given the limited funding available from the states.

Although the two examples differ in context and operation, with Maryland's proceedings being more formalised and academic and California's being more fluid and focused on healing, both demonstrate a departure from earlier federal practice. In fact, both the truth processes are squarely situated within the second generation of this handbook's framework and on the higher rungs of Arnstein's ladder. They illustrate that participation in formal spaces, too, can be genuinely progressive and participatory, allowing for more dispositive decision-making on the part of victims and victim communities. This departure from previous practice at the federal level is important because it highlights how active participation in the creation and early stages of a formal truth process allow for intentional and inclusive practices aimed at addressing historical wrongs as well as systemic inequalities. They demonstrate that even within the second-generation frame, which is often critiqued for its tokenism toward victims, victims are increasingly ensuring their voices are heard in dispositive ways. Indeed, the two examples demonstrate an overall awareness around the importance and value of meaningful participation. It is crucial to underline that both initiatives responded to victims' explicit demands and mobilisation and were, in that sense, state-sanctioned but victim-driven. Civil society groups have been instrumental in the design and implementation of the two truth commissions, with community consultations beginning immediately marking a notable contrast to earlier federal-level truth processes. In Maryland, civil society actors drafted the legislation for the truth commission, and once political support was secured, operational procedures were designed to be inclusive and transparent. Each commission prioritised outreach by creating websites, seeking diverse commissioners, and engaging with relevant communities for representation. California allowed tribal partners to select commissioners, and Maryland even issued open calls for some commissioner spots to ensure a direct connection to the broader public

In their proceedings, both truth commissions emphasise creating inclusive, participatory spaces where community members feel acknowledged and heard. They adopt rules and agreements that stress respect and centre the voices of marginalised groups. Processes are tailored to the needs of their target communities – for example, California refers to its public meetings as listening sessions and incorporates traditional rituals and prayers in opening and closing quarterly meetings and adopting a more informal style suited to the wants of its Native stakeholders. Similarly, Maryland integrates 'soul checks' to provide space for emotional reflection. The commissions also balance dispositive and non-dispositive roles for community members, focusing on amplifying voices historically ignored by the state. The use of technology and online meetings has further enhanced participation, offering a flexibility unavailable to earlier truth processes.

By responding to and partnering closely with civil society, the truth commissions have managed to ensure both official acknowledgement and victim engagement, which is essential to their success. Also in a practical sense, this reliance is particularly evident in these commissions, which depend on in-kind contributions, such as support from universities or tribal actors and volunteer efforts from community members. While truth commissions are generally less costly than other transitional justice measures such as reparation programmes, they still require funding, which may come from state budgets, private donors, federal government support, or a combination of these sources. The availability of human and financial resources greatly influences the scope and outcomes of their work.

Despite their political, geographic, and demographic differences, the two examples are instructive of how institutional participatory spaces enable agency which can lead to further empowerment. The spaces opened up through the truth processes explicitly valued diverse voices and perspectives. Whether formal or informal, the spaces sought to include a wide range of stakeholders. The processes have also sought to empower different communities by discussing and addressing issues around systemic harm, structural inequalities, and power relations (both historical and present day). Through their websites and events, the truth commissions have also sought to provide community members with tools, resources, and opportunities to influence not only the outcomes of the work of the truth commissions but also to take further steps in their communities to bring about change.

Neither of these commissions would operate without the invaluable role played by civil society actors. In both cases, the relevant groups were not simply participating in formal truth-telling processes but rather collaborating in the creation and running of truth-telling processes. As such, participation in formal processes can be seen to be deepened into meaningful collaboration when stakeholders move beyond procedural engagement to actively co-create solutions, fostering mutual trust and shared ownership of outcomes. Volunteers, non-profit organisations, and tribal communities are driving these processes, and these public–private relationships and collaborations are important for many reasons.

Given the budgetary constraints, without these collaborations, the work of the commissions would likely not get funded. And while the communities could likely organise similar types of sessions themselves, they often place great importance on the formal acknowledgement and role played by the state. Official recognition from the state legitimises their grievances.

Formal recognition by the state is crucial for victims participating in transitional justice truth processes because it validates their experiences, acknowledges the harm they have suffered, and establishes a foundation for accountability and systemic change. This recognition symbolises an official acceptance of responsibility for past injustices, helping to restore the dignity of victims who have often been silenced or marginalised. It also provides legitimacy to truth processes, encouraging broader societal acknowledgement and fostering trust between victims, the state, and the wider community. From a practical perspective, formal recognition ensures that truth processes have the institutional support and authority needed to operate effectively. It signals a commitment to addressing historical wrongs, which can empower victims by transforming them from passive recipients of justice to active participants in shaping outcomes. Moreover, formal recognition sets the stage for meaningful reparations, policy reforms, and guarantees of non-recurrence, emphasising the state's role in creating pathways for healing and reconciliation. Without formal recognition, truth processes risk being perceived as superficial or (solely) performative, undermining their ability to deliver justice and lasting societal transformation.

Therefore, collaboration becomes important in order to bring the commission's work home to other community members. Civil society actors play a pivotal role in transitional justice truth processes by initiating, shaping, and sustaining efforts to address past injustices. Their involvement is crucial in informing and mobilising communities. Civil society actors inform communities about the existence and purpose of truth processes, educating individuals about their rights and the mechanisms available to address past harms. This dissemination of information enhances agency by enabling people to make informed decisions and actively engage in the processes that affect them. They also often serve as intermediaries between affected individuals and formal institutions. They help organise forums, collect testimonies, and provide platforms for voices that might otherwise go unheard. Ensuring that marginalised groups are included promotes a more equitable and representative process. They also advocate for the needs and interests of their communities within truth processes. They offer a wide range of assistance and support that empowers individuals to share their stories confidently and safely. By actively engaging with communities and keeping them informed, civil society actors help demystify the workings of truth commissions. This transparency builds trust in the process and holds institutions accountable to the people they serve. However, there are serious concerns about the over-reliance on the unpaid labour of victims and civil society actors. This reliance can become exploitative, as it disproportionately burdens victims – often without adequate recognition or compensation – while reinforcing systemic inequities (Ullrich 2024).

Notwithstanding these valid concerns, when individuals come together to share experiences and seek justice, they build stronger communal ties, which often enhances collective empowerment and the capacity to advocate for systemic change. Importantly, civil society involvement ensures that the insights and needs of the community are reflected in policy recommendations and reforms resulting from truth processes. This influence can lead to long-term changes that address root causes of injustice. For example, in the Maryland Lynching Truth and Reconciliation Commission, civil society groups such as the Maryland Lynching Memorial Project were instrumental in the commission's formation. They not only helped draft the legislation but also engaged in outreach to descendants of lynching victims and affected communities, ensuring their stories and needs were central to the commission's work. In California, civil society actors collaborated closely with Native American tribes in the establishment of the Truth & Healing Council. They facilitated consultations and informed Indigenous communities about opportunities to participate, ensuring that the council's efforts were grounded in the lived experiences of those directly impacted by historical injustices. By informing their communities and fostering active participation, civil society actors enhance agency and empowerment by redistributing power. Community members move from being passive subjects of historical narratives to active agents shaping their own stories and the outcomes of justice processes. The participatory role of civil society actors in informing and engaging communities is essential for transforming truth processes into inclusive, empowering endeavours that address past harms and contribute to building more just and equitable societies.

The examples also point to the fact that the victim communities engaging with these commissions are not necessarily aiming to be subversive or disruptive. They are seeking to draw official attention and recognition through *state-backed* but *community-driven* processes. Although they may ultimately be advocating for substantial reforms, in these two cases, the processes are not challenging the role and functions of the governing authorities per se, which may partly explain the willingness of authorities to engage in the ways that civil society proposed.

## 9.5 CONCLUSIONS

Truth commissions and truth commission-like processes in the US are relatively underexplored in transitional justice scholarship, despite their growing prevalence. Posthumus and Zvobgo (2021) have identified over a dozen such initiatives – past and present – across federal, state, and local levels that align with general definitions of truth commissions. The two examples explored in this chapter illustrate the diverse methodologies, stakeholders, and outcomes at the sub-national level of states. While not exhaustive, these examples highlight the potential of truth commissions at the sub-national level to contribute to building a more socially just society through, first and foremost, collaborative and inclusive participatory processes. Both examples sought the collaboration of victims and affected communities from the outset, allowing relevant stakeholders to have a decision-making role in the mandates and processes of the commissions. While the ultimate impact of their reports remains uncertain, the positive steps taken in the area of participation signal a shift in thinking about how truth processes should take shape – with the victim being the driving force.

## REFERENCES

Aciru, Mercy. 2017. 'Rethinking Post-Truth Commissions: Empowering Local Capacities to Shape the Post-Truth Commission Discourse'. *Human Rights and International Legal Discourse*, 11(1), 71–82.

Allen, Jonathan. 1999. 'Balancing Justice and Social Unity: Political Theory and the Idea of a Truth and Reconciliation Commission'. *The University of Toronto Law Journal*, 49(3), 315–353. https://doi.org/10.2307/826002

American Indian Policy Review Commission. 1977. Final Report Submitted to Congress, 17 May. US Government Printing Office. http://eric.ed.gov/?id=ED164229.

Anderson, Carol. 2003. *Eyes off the Prize: The United Nations and the African American Struggle for Human Rights, 1944–1955*. Cambridge University Press.

Arnstein, Sherry R. 1969. 'A Ladder of Citizen Participation'. *Journal of the American Institute of Planners* 35 (4): 216–224.

Bakiner, Onur. 2014. 'Truth Commission Impact: An Assessment of How Commissions Influence Politics and Society'. *International Journal of Transitional Justice*, 8(1), 6–30. https://doi.org/10.1093/ijtj/ijt025

Chapman, Audrey R. 2009. 'Approaches to Studying Reconciliation'. In *Assessing the Impact of Transitional Justice: Challenges for Empirical Research*, edited by Hugo van der Merwe, Victoria Baxter, and Audrey R. Chapman, pp. 143–172. US Institute of Peace.

Chin, Frank. 1981. 'Unfocused LA Hearings: "A Circus of Freaks"'. *Los Angeles Japanese Daily News*, 21 August. https://tinyurl.com/27w2pv5h

CWRIC (Commission on Wartime Relocation and Internment of Civilians). 1982–1983. *Personal Justice Denied: Report of the Commission on Wartime Relocation and Internment of Civilians*. University of Washington Press.

Destrooper, Tine. 2024. 'Generations of Victim Engagement: Towards an Encompassing Analytical Framework for Understanding Victims' Roles in Transitional Justice Processes'. *Opinio Juris*, September. https://tinyurl.com/2p3d69y7

Destrooper, Tine, Line Engbo Gissel, and Kerstin Bree Carlson, eds. 2023. *Transitional Justice in Aparadigmatic Contexts: Accountability, Recognition, and Disruption*. Routledge.

Fraser, Nancy. 2009. *Scales of Justice: Reimagining Political Space in a Globalizing World*. Columbia University Press.

Freeman, Mark, and Priscilla Hayner. 2003. 'Truth-Telling'. In *Reconciliation after Violent Conflict: A Handbook*, edited by David Bloomfield, Teresa Barnes, and Luc Huyse, pp. 122–144. International Institute for Democracy and Electoral Assistance.

Hayner, Priscilla B. 2011. *Unspeakable Truths: Transitional Justice and the Challenge of Truth Commissions*. 2nd ed. Routledge.

Jeffries Warfield, Zenobia. 2016. 'How to Attempt Racial Healing – Even during a Trump Presidency: America's Past Truth and Reconciliation Processes Show Us What Works'. *Yes Magazine*, 21 December. https://tinyurl.com/434fs95s

Juhnke, William E. 1989. 'President Truman's Committee on Civil Rights: The Interaction of Politics, Protest, and Presidential Advisory Commission'. *Presidential Studies Quarterly*, 19(3), 593–610.

Lakota People's Law Project. 2015. *Truth & Reconciliation in the United States of America*. December. https://tinyurl.com/mr3pd7tw

McGonigle Leyh, Brianne. 2011. *Procedural Justice? Victim Participation in International Criminal Proceedings*. Intersentia.

Michaelson, J. 1981. 'Quiet Americans' Break Silence: Hearings a Catharsis for Internees'. *LA Times*, 9 August. https://ncrr-la.org/NCRR_archives/redresshearings81/press/LAT19810809HearingsACatharsis.PDF

National Advisory Commission on Civil Disorders. (with J. E. Zelizer). 2016. *The Kerner Report*. Princeton University Press (Originally published 1968).

Ochs, Stephen L. 2021. 'A National Truth Commission for Native Americans'. *Wisconsin Journal of Law, Gender and Society*, 36(1), 1–32.

Oxford, Andrew. 2019. 'California Governor Calls Native American Treatment Genocide'. *Associated Press*, 19 June. https://tinyurl.com/29m3pe8c

Posthumus, David, and Kelebogile Zvobgo. 2021. 'Democratizing Truth: An Analysis of Truth Commissions in the United States'. *International Journal of Transitional Justice*, 15(3), 510–532.

President's Committee on Civil Rights. 1947. *To Secure These Rights: The Report of the President's Committee on Civil Rights*. www.trumanlibrary.gov/library/to-secure-these-rights

Rowlands, Jo. 1997. *Questioning Empowerment: Working with Women in Honduras*. Oxfam.

Sen, Amartya. 1999. *Development as Freedom*. Oxford University Press.

Shaw, Rosalind, and Lars Waldorf. 2010. 'Introduction: Localizing Transitional Justice'. In *Localizing Transitional Justice Interventions and Priorities after Mass Violence*, edited by Rosalind Shaw, Lars Waldorf, and Pierre Hazan, pp. 3–26. Stanford University Press.

Sriram, Chandra Lekha. 2007. 'Justice as Peace? Liberal Peacebuilding and Strategies of Transitional Justice'. *Global Society* 21(4), 579–591.

Ullrich, Leila. 2024. *Victims and the Labour of Justice at the International Criminal Court: The Blame Cascade*. Oxford University Press.

UN Guidance Note. 2010. *Guidance Note of the Secretary-General: United Nations Approach to Transitional Justice*.

UN Office of the High Commissioner for Human Rights (UN OHCHR). (2006). *Rule-of-Law Tools for Post-Conflict States: Truth Commissions*. UN Doc. HR/PUB/06/1.

UN OHCHR. 2011. *Report of the United Nations High Commissioner for Human Rights on Human Rights and Transitional Justice*. UN Doc. A/HRC/18/23.

UN Secretary-General. 2004. *Report of the Secretary-General on the Rule of Law and Transitional Justice in Conflict and Post-Conflict Societies*. UN Doc. S/2004/616.

Vella, Louise. 2014. 'Translating Transitional Justice: The Solomon Islands Truth and Reconciliation Commission'. *State, Society and Governance in Melanesia Discussion Paper*, 2014(2), 1–19.

Wells-Barnett, I. B. 2014. *On Lynchings*. Dover Publications.

Zvobgo, Kelebogile. 2019. 'Maryland Has Created a Truth Commission on Lynching–Can It Deliver?' *USC Dornsife*. https://tinyurl.com/3n9jy9cp

# Third Generation

# 10

# Reparations as Resistance

*Luke Moffett*

## 10.1 INTRODUCTION

Reparations are the antipode of violence, being concerned with remedying rather than inflicting harm. In international law, reparations are firmly rooted in the notion of ensuring an effective and adequate remedy for breaches and violations. Yet the practice of reparations in transitional justice and human rights law has arisen not simply out of international legal norms, owing to the lack of compliance, but through the mobilisation and advocacy of victims and their allies to resist the impunity around the atrocities they suffered. As such, reparations are about counteracting the effects and consequences of violence, as well as more socially and politically resisting impunity. Victims as protagonists in transitional justice are critical in understanding how the field has developed and continues to evolve. This can be seen in victims' claims-making around reparations. Accordingly, this chapter argues that understanding reparations through solely a legal lens fails to appreciate that reparations are a political and social struggle as a means to resist the discourses, policies, and practices that gave rise to violence that harmed victims, as well as to reaffirm victims' dignity and right-holder status in society and prevent their repetition.

This chapter explores the place of victims resisting the narratives of the state, coercive tactics, and violence against them in their claims for reparations. It also reflects on the impact of resistance on victims, where claims-making for justice measures such as reparations can take years, decades, even generations. While there is an emerging literature on the benefit of social mobilisation in terms of building solidarity among victims and peer–peer support, this chapter considers the long-term impact of mobilisation for reparations on victims. This also has implications for the purported benefits of reparations in terms of trust, reconciliation, and a sense of satisfaction. Drawing on interviews with over 100 victims in six case studies (Colombia, Guatemala, Nepal, Northern Ireland, Peru, and Uganda), this chapter develops three themes of thinking about victim participation and resistance in terms of: victim participation as a form of resistance; self-repair; and the struggle for reparations. These notions reflect that reparations are part of a political, legal, and social struggle against violence, and the tension around the discourse of reparations where in defending the core value of the concept and legal validity of reparations as a practice we appreciate its limits and contradictions. Before we unpack these issues, it is worth discussing social mobilisation and resistance in relation to claims-making around redress.

## 10.2 REPARATIONS AS A FORM OF NON-VIOLENT RESISTANCE

Reparations at their core are about recognising the harm of past violations, running counter to narratives, policies, and laws that justified and legitimised such violence; at the same time as legal redress, they provide entitlements to those considered as deserving of redress and rights-holders. As such, reparation claims can be seen on the wider spectrum of non-violent resistance, as a means to seek political change in the face of violence or aggression through peaceful means, whether protest, legal institutions, or political mobilisation. In general, resistance can be a public rejection of the government's legitimacy to rule or hold power, where a consent theory of power would suggest that the social contract between people and the State has been broken (Parkin 2016, 261). Pinckney defines non-violent resistance as 'the application of political force outside the normal bounds of politics and without the use of violence' (2021, 211) with others speaking about groups using 'socio-political action' in the midst of conflict (Sharp 1999, 567). Victims, as those often politically marginalised, turn to non-violent resistance as a strategy to counter the dominant narratives in society and state priorities to avoid truth-seeking and dealing with the past (Lawther 2015; Kodikara 2023). That said, while not the focus of this chapter, some victims do engage in violence as the only means for their grievance to be redressed, who identified with personal or collective victimisation as a justification for their resort to arms as a means of resistance (Moffett 2023). However, for victims I have engaged with over the past fifteen years, many express the view that they could never get involved in violence and inflict such suffering on other families. This aversion to, even disgust with violence, means that non-violent resistance is the only pathway for many victims to see change in society that no longer justifies violence against them and tries to redress it. This can be a symbolic way for victims to take the moral high ground and to distinguish themselves from their perpetrators.

Resistance by victims can also take the form of resisting reparations efforts by the state. This can often take on the character of victims campaigning to expand the scope of the forms of reparations and eligibility. This broadening of redress can seek to deepen the penetration of reparations in society, in that such measures are more meaningful, and the state is forced to confront the extent of injustice and the continuing trauma. This can expand the frame of dealing with the past, which initially was not dealt with as it was seen as too politically contentious, such as injured victim-perpetrators in Northern Ireland, or was neglected, such as victims of sexual violence and torture in Nepal. More general victim participation in transitional justice is often marked by adversity through their agonistic stance against perpetrators and the state (whether inactive or unwilling to deal with the past). This often means that victims' role in advocating for justice is a form of resistance, whether that is before any transitional justice processes are established and/or those responsible are still in power, or even when justice mechanisms have been established and victims continue to agitate to strive for more adequate redress, fuller accountability, and comprehensive truth. As one Colombian victim put it, such resistance is their own individual struggle: 'I have received some reparations because I kept insisting so I am like a thorn in their shoe, I don't go away and every day I am pushing a little bit and pushing a little bit.'[1] This was shared by a victim group in Guatemala:

> Our fundamental role was to become the opposition to the [reparation] programme as an actor in demanding the rights of the victims... Here we are, we have a very long process, as well as a contribution to the national reparation program, government after government, because unfortunately, after fifteen years of having constituted the programme, it has not fulfilled its

[1] Interview with civil society actor, Huila, Colombia (C18).

objectives of comprehensively compensating the victims ... So the challenge for us continues to be a struggle for the state to recognize the rights of the victims and repair the damage caused as part of its responsibility.[2]

Before a programme is created, victims need to be given the space to develop their own vision of reparations and have the tools to articulate what redress means to them moving forward. To some extent, victims also need to be 'socialised into special discourse' where they are familiar with reparations, how to apply for funding, and engage with state institutions.[3] Making victims aware of reparations and education on the language of redress so that they can harness its power to their own cause can, to some extent, be useful for driving their claims forward. This can almost be a 'pedagogy' in approaching reparations so that victims are sensitised and conversant in the language of redress.[4] This can complement victims' own efforts to devise their own vision of internal redress and self-repair, discussed further in Section 10.3.

For victims pursuing reparations, non-violent resistance can take different forms. Seeking reparations from a bottom-up perspective through informal mechanisms can be a way to resist state inaction and to shame and stigmatise perpetrators who live in a community (Akello 2019, 253). For other victims, the continuing documentation of violations can be a means of resistance to violence that aims to obliterate their suffering, through collecting evidence to support later claims for reparations around their victimisation (Lira 2017, 192). This can be especially important in the face of continuing impunity where the perpetrators remain in power, leaving no domestic civic space for victims to peacefully campaign for justice or waiting for opportunities for new regimes to spring up. For instance, in Syria, documentation has been a means for victims and civil society in the diaspora to continue to 'fight back' against impunity (Nassar 2022), which before the fall of the Assad regime in December 2024 seemed impossible, but will now play a vital part in supporting truth, justice, and redress efforts. Documentation also reflects a bottom-up/grassroots approach by being a means to counter dominant state narratives by nuancing official accounts of the past and implicating the role of other actors complicit in violence, such as the World Bank, IMF, and France in Tunisia (Aboueldahab 2023). At the same time offers of the state to document harms of the past may not reflect the extent of reparations victims may want. As one victim group in Colombia explained,

> [T]he state came to us, and they promised that they would give us, as reparations, a documentation centre and a monument that would acknowledge the harm that the trade unions had suffered within the university. We felt that the state cannot unilaterally come and impose a project like this, but they should do so in dialogue with the victims ... without an historic memory of what happened inside the university in terms of labour and union movements, the state cannot have a capacity to identify the harms if it's just three people in a room trying to decide what went on...
>
> [During the conflict a paramilitary leader took over the area and] he basically removed everybody from the administration and put his own family and friends in charge of the university. For instance, one of the things that we require was that [these paramilitary leader appointed] staff would be purged and replaced with new staff as an act of reparation. Without this historic memory exercise, it would have been impossible for the government to reach this conclusion of the necessity to do this as reparation. When the state comes and imposes their own view of reparations, it's usually not an overlap with what victims might want.[5]

[2] Interview with victim group leader, Guatemala City, Guatemala (G6).
[3] Interview with peace negotiator, Bogota, Colombia (C25).
[4] Interview with civil society actor, Medellin, Colombia (C10).
[5] Interview with civil society actor, Medellin, Colombia, (C10).

Resistance through reparations is also seen through how victims mobilise and find solidarity with each other.

## 10.3 SOCIAL MOBILISATION, RESISTANCE, AND REDRESS

Reparations and resistance can be better understood in terms of social mobilisation and the literature around social movements. Social movements have long been of interest to political science and sociology as a means to explore political agency beyond the hegemony of the state. As a concept, social movements have increasingly been a focal point for better understanding the practice of reparations (Destrooper 2023; Falschebner et al. 2024; Greenstein 2020). This is not surprising given that victims fit what such movements entail – informal groups working on joint action, engaging in non-violent struggle – based on a 'shared collective identity' (Diani 1992, 1–2). Social movements as a field of study focus on how individuals and groups 'mobilise resources' around a particular social issue, how they 'frame' their demands and take advantage of 'political openings' (Ratner et al. 2014, 231). As a broader extension of grassroots perspectives of transitional justice, a social mobilisation view provides a contrast to the normative and top-down state bureaucracy of reparations through a 'collective political insurgency' of people who feel 'simultaneously aggrieved and optimistic' (Aiyetoro and Davis 2010, 717).

Social mobilisation for reparations provides a particular place for victims to find solidarity in their cause with other individuals who have faced similar experiences, as well as to receive and collectively demand recognition of their suffering, rights, and dignity. Such a collectivity of victim mobilisation is a dynamic process, where the victim group or movement may evolve, fragment, or make strategic links with other groups to advance its goals. This more relational and organic perspective on how reparation demands arise among those most affected by violence contest and add meaning to what form and scope reparations should take (Moon 2012, 190). It is also through victim organisations that victims find solidarity, common purpose, and a safe place to express themselves. As one Colombian civil society actor said,

> one can't understate the role of victim organisations, because what they have done, or NGOs [non-governmental organisations] that are working with victims, is that they have now realised through their engagement with other organisations is that they're not alone, that there are other people in their situation and also these organisations contribute to their recuperation because they are working on those feelings of guilt that people have. They are working on making them understand that they can move on from this and they become political subjects to a degree once they do engage with these organisations.[6]

Being political subjects may mean that victims have to fit into legal collectivities to achieve political goals of redress, such as framing their suffering within international crimes which garner more attention. In Guatemala, we spoke to a number of victim groups about ongoing and successful cases. In the case of Sepur Zarco, where members of the military were convicted for rape and sexual slavery as crimes against humanity, one legal NGO was key in sensitising and consulting with the victims to organise collectively so that the violations were an attack against the civilian population rather than individual violations. As one of their lawyers articulated, 'there are thousands of women and it is never going to be easy to walk alone, because really here the group is strong'.[7] In another case involving the genocide of the Ixil, focusing on this group suffering as genocide was seen as a more productive – as 'paradigmatic [or] emblematic'

6 Interview with civil society actor, Bogota, Colombia, (C4).

7 Interview with civil society actor, Guatemala City, Guatemala (G7).

cases that could establish a precedent for others.[8] This raises a danger for individual murders or singular incidents of rape or torture that their victims will get left behind, as only a few group or massacre cases are successful; this is especially acute when redress is fragmented and piecemeal, and not handled through an administrative reparations programme. In Northern Ireland this tension is particularly acute, whereby human rights law provides continued investigative avenues for state-based violations, including collusion, in particular massacres (Ballymurphy, Bloody Sunday, Omagh bombing),[9] but not for the majority of paramilitary attacks that often involved one or two victims. This has meant that many victims have been neglected and were initially left out of the conversation on reparations.

The mobilisation of victims around reparations as a social movement is increasingly analysed in terms of its political dimensions and advocacy; as a social construct it is embedded in struggles for recognition and redress (Johnston 2009, 13). Whereas grassroot perspectives tend to focus on capacity-building of victims to support official legal institutions or comparable informal transitional justice efforts, such as truth recovery or memorialisation, social mobilisation is a more subaltern and political rallying of victims that values actions outside official state bodies. High-profile social movements focused on reparations include the South Korean Comfort Women claiming reparations from the Japanese government (Soh 1996), the National Coalition of Blacks for Reparations in America (N'COBRA) (Aiyetoro and Davis 2010), or the WAVE Seriously Injured Victim Group in Northern Ireland (Gallagher 2021). Barkan sees such negotiated redress between social movement and political entities as a 'social treaty' rather than justice per se, as it signifies 'social moral theory that binds universal values to social realities' (Barkan 2000, 309). Wolfe categorises a redress and reparation movement as a 'collectivity formed by those that have experienced injustice which mobilises in order to obtain redress' (2014, 5). Such a collectivity is a dynamic process of negotiation among those involved in 'collective identity formation, grievance and justice framing' (Ratner et al. 2014, 231). Such framing 'requires decisions about who is the perpetrator of a wrong, who is the victim, what exactly are the reparations desired' (Howard-Hassmann and Lombardo 2007, 28).

Resistance through reparations claims-making by movements often involves extra-legal demands for redress. Such claims for reparations are typified by acts of resistance through social, demonstration, and artistic claims, which are often required in the face of inaction, reluctance, or limitations of legal measures of 'attending to the social, psychological, and cultural needs of survivors' (Soh 1996, 3–4). Indeed, Moon argues that the focus on reparations' technical aspects or semantic differences, such as symbolic and material forms, neglects how victim groups 'contest' reparation and the 'meaning' to which beneficiaries of such measures impute the state in reparations (Moon 2012, 190). It is this more complex understanding of reparations that helps to shed light on what victims want, what they are claiming, how they achieve an outcome, what they accept, and why.

Such claims-making is not just limited to ethnicity or victim group, but often reflects class dynamics (Aiyetoro and Davis 2010, 719) where well-off victims can be more resilient and move on more easily than those who are impoverished and vulnerable as a result of violations, such as those displaced or seriously injured. In Nepal, there was a 'blurring' of compensation efforts

[8] Interview with civil society actor, Guatemala City, Guatemala (G9).

[9] The first of these was subject to an inquest; the other two are public inquiries, with the latter to begin in 2025. These were all large casualty events (eleven, fourteen, and twenty-nine killed) and involved direct state violence or allegations of collusion (Omagh bombing). Compensation was paid out initially in these cases, but after these investigative processes more adequate compensation was made to victims.

under the Interim Relief Payment scheme, where those affected by the disruption of conflict, such as property owners unable to collect rent, and only select groups, such as disappearances or killings, were able to benefit (Carranza 2012, 4). This also plays into wider structural inequalities, where marginalised and impoverished victims, such as Dalits and Janajatis, who lived as indentured or landless farmworkers, face an uphill struggle to socially and politically mobilise to claim redress (Carranza 2012, 8). Social mobilisation of victim can overcome some but not all of these problems. The power of the movement and collectivity is that it can create the social, political, and legal space to improve the situation of these victims and visibilise their suffering, even if it does not transform broader social inequalities that affect their community, group or people. In Colombia, one former director of the Victims' Unit noted that before the 2011 reparations law was established victims were invisible, but now victims are no longer just 'poor peasants', but those from the upper classes, in particular those affected by bombings in Bogota. They form a 'very visible movement', which can continue to mobilise and resist efforts to shut down the transitional justice process and reparations – making their resistance a 'political cost'.[10]

Social movements around reparations also say something about the law. There are clear power dynamics in claims-making. Aiyetoro and Davis, writing about the claims about reparations for African-Americans, point to the need to understand the nature and expectations of the law by looking 'not only at how the law operated on Black people, but also at the claims Blacks made on the law' (Aiyetoro and Davis 2010, 689). A successful social movement around reparations needs to ensure its framing proffers a 'new, counterhegemonic narrative' that has sufficient 'emotional and moral' resonance among those victimised, those responsible, and society, to mobilise support and 'demobilise antagonists' that can in turn shape the law to provide appropriate redress processes (Howard-Hassmann and Lombardo 2007, 28–29). Indeed, this is not distinct from the notion of struggle within the nature of human rights as giving a vision to the subaltern, to those who suffer, but do so in solidarity with others, to resist 'the abuse of power and of the assertion of right in the face of immoral might' (Gearty 2014, 37). Human rights and social movements have an intertwined relationship at times when it comes to reparations, providing substantive input and motivation to encourage each other. Yet, as Madlingozi highlights, certain movements can fail to find purchase in claiming reparations as they are defined as 'bad' victims in official discourses of the past because they seek to upset the status quo (2007, 125). An example of such a group is the Khulumani support group, which seeks to broaden the scope of Apartheid victims and implicate the role of corporate actors in Apartheid. This is apparent with victim competition, complex victims, and a hierarchy of victimhood that often characterises debates around redress.

Victim movements can transcend a country's borders, encompassing transnational and international formal and informal networks. Social mobilisation of victims is key in making these transnational networks, as they need to pool their resources and be sufficiently organised to connect to other international and national transitional justice, peace-building, or human rights actors. War often creates large, displaced populations who are forced to become refugees or exiles. It may be more politically possible to engage in more proactive and public resistance outside the territory where the violations occurred, owing to the reduced risk of reprisals by perpetrators. Diaspora victimised communities can play an important role in the mobilisation and visibilisation of victim movements in claiming reparations. Diaspora advocacy is not simply international 'lawfare' or 'long-distance nationalism', but a people's 'collective memories of violence, marginalisation, and impunity' that seeks to highlight their truths and transformation of the state (Bala 2015, 21).

[10] Interview with government official, Bogota, Colombia (C26).

Transitional justice that is driven by diaspora can suffer from the power dynamics of elites controlling debates on redress from afar, which may not reflect the realities on the ground in a post-conflict society. Nevertheless, diaspora can continue to break the silence outside a country by continuing memorialisation processes, advocating for change within their new countries to pressurise action on their home state, or to ensure that the next generation is politically astute about what happened (Orjuela 2020, 370). This more nuanced understanding of victim movements helps to shed light on what is being claimed and the issues around which victims are mobilised.

I am reluctant to believe that paying compensation, setting up a memorial, and reforming the police would be enough to rebuild trust between victims and those responsible. This is not to say these measures have no value, but they often reflect hard-won pyrrhic victories, wherein victims have to struggle for decades to get those responsible to recognise and repair the harm they have caused. Reparations are part of the struggle for justice within societies transitioning away from a violent past, where those responsible for violations often maintain power, influence, and political support that perpetuates their impunity. Social mobilisation of collectivities of victims are an integral part of long-term claims-making that is necessary to secure redress. Accordingly, victims' struggle for reparations are about recognition, some measure(s) to remedy their suffering, and importantly changing society and its values, to ensure such violations do not recur. It is here that victims' participation and their struggle for redress adds meaning to the adequacy of reparations and dissent to unresponsive state-led top-down redress, which are unlikely to remedy the harm caused or prevent its repetition. The rest of this chapter turns to look at resistance through social mobilisation in how victims can together open up opportunities for self-repair and collective struggles for reparations.

## 10.4 SELF-REPAIR AS RESISTANCE

Self-repair is the process and outcome of how victims manage to live with their suffering (individually and/or collectively) (Gilmore and Moffett 2021). Self-repair can also be seen as a process through official and unofficial channels for victims to find their own resolution of the past. As one victim said, 'I have been building my own reparation process, as an individual, as a victim in Colombia, because I think one important thing for me is to know what happened. I always wanted to know what happened, why. This is an answer that helps you to heal.'[11]

'Victim' as a fixed identity is a means for individuals to get their basic rights or recognition. It means that individuals or groups have to perform as victims, which in itself can be counter-intuitive with regard to the provisional and directional nature of transitional justice efforts. Ideally transitional justice efforts should allow a victim to get up every day without having to resist and struggle for justice and put their victim hat on in order to be clearly identified as someone with legitimacy to speak on such issues. As one former coordinator of a reparations programme said, forcing victims to remain in a state of resistance in struggling for reparations can have its benefits and disadvantages:

> There is a terrible risk that the victims will become professional victims and that they will not overcome their character as victims and become citizens … [Victim groups] have to organize the victims so that there is solidarity among them, especially among the regional victims, of the same crime, and that they mobilize in favour of their rights and that they disappear as subjects. One will always keep the pain, [and] be a victim for the pain caused.[12]

[11] Interview with Colombia victim, Belfast, Northern Ireland (C2).

[12] Interview with senior reparation official, Bogota, Colombia (C32).

Considering self-repair as part of the practice of reparations (and non-implementation) also reflects that victims have agency and may not always need to brand or identify themselves with the victim-survivor label to manage their suffering. For instance, one trade union group in Colombia spoke about how they, with nineteen other trade unions, developed their own historic memorial project for killed trade unionists through their own solidarity networks with each other and without the support of the state: 'it's about people working through their own history and building their own history from the ground up'.[13]

There are limits to victim groups being sites for repair, as they can also bring their own political and personal baggage that discourage others from being associated with them. As one victim in Northern Ireland said,

> I never had any involvement in any victim's groups at all, I had no interest … [my perception of] victims' groups for victims of IRA violence would have had … a sort of sectarian undertone of 'we are the superior victims, our side did no wrong, the only reason there was a conflict is because of the IRA and they're all bad. And the best thing that we can do is wear poppies and sing the sash.' I know that this is not fair, OK, but that would have been my perception and that was nothing about me.

Resisting can also be a personal and internal bodily experience, as one victim from Colombia commented:

> For me, as a forgiveness process for me is a healing process. I don't want to carry with this the hate. It's too heavy. I have no space in my heart for hatred. I get sick. My body cannot resist that feeling, you know. It's because you feel something I have been talking today in the panel is the sense of the life as a sacred thing. If you lose it then everything is lost, and if you have this sense, if you really know the sense of life being a sacred thing, you don't allow yourself to put your own life in that kind of energy. Why? Because you are holy, you are also sacred, you hurt, your soul is also sacred. And I think I'm very lucky because we are coming from a very indigenous and a very ethnic background in my country, my family is a mix of many things, especially ethnic groups and I think there is something very related to that and in touch with that memory.[14]

As such, self-repair is an agent-centred view of those who are victimised, seeing victims as active citizens who are trying to mitigate and alleviate their suffering in the face of state inaction. This means that repair is more likely to allow victims to find meaning in how they cope with their suffering and rationalise their own sense of self and purpose after such violations. Each victim may find their own path of self-repair through a victim group or alone, perhaps through spiritual introspection. As one victim found, 'you need to really [practise] self-care and work out what you need to leave behind'.[15]

For other victims, being able to engage in resistance or struggle in the public realm is impossible, as they are unable to leave their homes. As one victim whose husband was disappeared in Nepal explained, 'My husband … said that he will come back after five minutes, but he never came back, that's why whenever I leave the house, I think my husband might come back, if he is knocking the door if it is locked then he will just leave and not return back, so I don't want to leave the house.'[16]

13 Interview with civil society actor, Medellin, Colombia (C10).

14 Interview C2.

15 Interview with victim, Fermanagh, Northern Ireland (NI17).

16 Interview with victim, Bardyia, Nepal (N21).

Some victims are unable to engage in the struggle, and may only feel able to speak about such issues or claim redress once the hard work of the struggle has succeeded in seeing reparations delivered. As one Colombian civil society actor explained, 'Victims didn't want to appear as victims because they were afraid, because they were stigmatized, displaced persons often concealed their status as displaced persons. Only with the Law of Victims did they begin to appear, [but other] stigmas were also generated, and the vision of why [does the government] give you if we are equally poor.'[17]

As such when thinking about self-repair, resistance, and reparations, there is a need to be critical of transitional justice itself: it is not the only pathway to live a dignified existence. Transitional justice is often framed through institutions and policy, as this is how the state as the obligation holder under human rights and constitutional law is held responsible to deliver redress for mass atrocities. Yet for victims this framing of responding to their personal violence is too often impersonal, bureaucratic, and slow. Indeed, the constant rebadging as a victim to obtain recognition and support can be debilitating for individuals' personal growth and agency after violence. As one victim support worker said about the fixity of victim identity, 'people stay sick, because if you recover, well then, you're no longer eligible for services ... in a way it's like a perverse cycle where people will maintain a psychological injury, because to give it up they lose that victimhood and access to financial services and means as well'.[18] Accordingly, victims embracing self-repair as the agent of their own repair journey can be engaging in a form of resistance against the state and part of a wider understanding of the struggle for redress.

## 10.5 RESISTANCE AND THE STRUGGLE FOR REPARATIONS

Jones and Bernath argue that transitional justice is a political process and discourse, and that any understanding of resistance as part of it needs to place the struggle for justice within the broader political and social context as well as in relation to long-term efforts by victims and civil society. As such, a subjective approach is needed to understand the place of resistance by such groups as not a binary of them being for or against transitional justice measures, but rather as reflecting their more complex and at times dynamic views on transitional justice that can vary between individuals and change over time (Jones and Bernath 2023). I have seen this myself in Northern Ireland, where over time some groups that were resistant to any consideration of reparations for all injured victims of the Troubles, and others who were for including everyone, both changed their position in the face of state inaction and attempts to gain support or progress. Yet other victim groups chose particular issues on reparations as their red-line in order to maintain their own principles and solidarity, such as resisting calls to endorse a hierarchy of victims by allowing only 'innocent' victims to avail themselves of a compensation scheme in Northern Ireland, and saw any move away from a campaign for all injured victims as a betrayal and weakening of their position: 'if you concede on that then you'll be forced to concede on others'.[19] Despite the success in implementing a reparations programme for injured victims of the Troubles, those who have resisted a hierarchy continue to seek the inclusion of those excluded from the scheme, both through litigation and political advocacy.

A key part of the struggle for redress is being antithetical to silence. A key part of self-repair is for victims to confront the violence they have suffered, to find a way to live with it every

[17] Interview with civil society actor, Bogota, Colombia (C27).
[18] Interview NI17.
[19] Interview with civil society actor, Belfast, Northern Ireland (NI01).

day and not be defined by it. Silence may be the way for some victims to find their own self-repair pathway and deal with the past. Yet there can be no state delivered reparations without victims making 'noise'. This was the view of a former Colombian reparations official: in her view, 'without the strength of victims' organisations there would have been no Victims Law'.[20] Victims as a political issue became mainstream as their struggle became acceptable to dominant discourse, as one Colombian judge said:

> Today no politician says 'I am against the Victims Law.' No one, so that's politically unspeakable. Then it became political because the victims are there and they became a powerful and visible movement, also very plural, today one sees victims, something that did not happen ten years ago, not only the displaced peasants, but for example the lady who lost her children in the club El Nogal. A woman who has enormous visibility, who is a high stratum, and says this cannot continue to happen, and also political victims, they are no longer just poor peasants, she has become a very visible movement and I believe that the political cost she has generated has also mobilised the issue and can continue to mobilise it.[21]

It is clear that the positionality of some victims means that the noise from their voice is louder than that of others. This risks 'celebrity' victims dominating the space on redress for victims and portraying the idea that victims speak with one voice.

Resistance to the state also faces challenges when reparations are being developed and implemented, and victims are asked to come forward. Reparations can be rebranded or framed around the state's narrative of the past or its own beneficence, rather than the struggle by victims. As one Colombian museum curator said, 'the government has this idea that they did [reparations] in order to show solidarity towards victims, but it was really because of their pressure that this actually happened'.[22] This can reflect the diverging perspectives and experiences of mass violence. For the state, atrocities are a political issue that it is often easier to ignore or silence rather than dealing with the difficult past and its continuing reverberations in society. When a state does engage in dealing with the past, it is through a bureaucracy that is concerned with making social life legible and standardised so that it can be administered (Scott 1999), and so the suffering of victims becomes quantifiable data and costs to redress. As 'hegemonic devices', reparations can convey an 'illusion of social progress', without fundamentally addressing the drivers of conflict (Yamamoto 1992, 232). As a bureaucratic process of 'informational accumulation and tabulation' that 'make evident a state's right to power', reparations can designate who is worthy or unworthy (Matsunaga 2021, 26). For victims who are deemed unworthy, their resistance focuses on broadening the scope of eligibility of such reparation programmes. Ultimately such struggles are about forcing society and the state to acknowledge past continuing wrongs and unpick the dominant narrative that some people deserved violence.

While reparations are political, victims' resistance against silence, impunity, and state inaction, the bureaucracy of the state is presented as permanent, impersonal, and hierarchal, portrayed as law-abiding, neutral, and cohesive. Yet participating in a state reparations programme involves victims accepting some risk by complying with its rules as well as risking transferring their 'moral authority' to the state (Ludi 2006, 450). Some victims spoke of engaging with political and state actors in the campaign for reparations, while some politicians used victims to improve their own moral standing. Some political actors 'open doors' to advance their campaign.[23] For other

[20] Interview with former senior judge and reparation official, Bogota, Colombia (C26).

[21] Interview C26.

[22] Interview with civil society actor, Medellin, Colombia (C13).

[23] Interview with victim, Kathmandu, Nepal (N14).

victims, one government 'never received us, they closed the doors, that was a delay of five years, and it was terrible for us'.[24]

At the same time, continuing to resist and refusing to engage with a reparation process can leave some victims worse off than others. Holding onto principles can be costly, and for a victim group risky, with its membership opting to claim redress rather than to live without it, risking disintegration of the group. As one victim who was successful in claiming reparations in the midst of ongoing violence, there were 'narrow windows of legal opportunity'.[25] For others, struggling for redress can be exhausting, and they may feel that their energies are best spent elsewhere. One Colombian political analyst spoke about there being a 'huge bias' towards more recent victims of the conflict being mobilised to claim reparations; those 'victimised long ago are much less likely to be visible at all and are probably part of this resilience story, or the I-give-up story, because the state never really showed up for their needs'.[26]

## 10.6 CONCLUSION

Reparations and claiming redress are in many ways acts of resistance against violence. Victims often have to agitate and mobilise so that together they can seek redress through their common identity and shared values, or at least goals. The struggle for reparations is one of victims' agency in shaping the debates on redressing the past and being the litmus test in the effective implementation of reparation measures. Such a struggle may provide some solidarity with others in the same position and with their own experience of suffering, which can in part self-repair their harm. However, victims cannot redress their own harm, and the good news story of victim solidarity and self-repair cannot provide external validation and alleviation that is needed in their struggle for recognition and remedy. A key aspect that is under-explored in the field of transitional justice is fatigue, resignation, and despair (Meija 2024). Perhaps a liberal, normative view of reparations and transitional justice more generally that emphasises the positivity of such struggles for justice neglects the impact of time, failure, and non-implementation, which causes victims to lose hope that justice is possible in their lifetime. This story is important as it should cause us to reflect on how best to support claims-making in the long term and victims' journey of self-repair in the meantime, and to plan for alternative strategies beyond transitional justice.

While resistance is an important part of the practice of claiming redress, reparations will at some point involve compromise to achieve a settlement, reconciliation, or 'legal peace' (Bazyler 2003, 83–84). Resistance cannot be a complete strategy, and may even be detrimental to claiming reparations in the long term as measures are implemented, causing victims to lose out or continue to live in a state of distrust, suffering, and the disquiet of repeated violence. The focus on resistance and the struggle for reparations can be an important part of the story of victims mobilising as they struggle for redress. Such a struggle can give meaning to reparations, and, importantly, help to create a healthy civic space in society, allowing it to evolve values that protect those who have been victimised.

## REFERENCES

Aboueldahab, Noha. 2023. Transitional Justice as Repression and Resistance Practices in the Arab World'. *Journal of International Criminal Justice*, 21, 701–717.

[24] Interview with civil society actor, Lima, Peru (P17).
[25] Interview C2.
[26] Interview C25.

Acholiland, Northern Uganda. 2019. *The International Journal of Transitional Justice*, 13(2), 249–267.

Akello, Grace. 2019. 'Reintegration of Amnestied LRA Ex-Combatants and Survivors' Resistance Acts in Acholiland, Northern Uganda,'. *The International Journal of Transitional Justice*, 13(2), 249–267.

Aiyetoro, Adjoa, and Adrienne Davis. 2010. 'Historic and Modern Social Movements for Reparations: The National Coalition for Reparations in America (N'COBRA) and its Antecedents'. *Texas Wesleyan Law Review*, 16(4), 687–766.

Bala, Mytili. 2015. 'Transitional Justice in Sri Lanka: Rethinking Post-War Diaspora Advocacy for Accountability'. *International Human Rights Law Journal*, 1(1), 1–47.

Barkan, E. 2000. *The Guilt of Nations: Restitution and Negotiating Historical Injustices* (1st ed). Norton.

Bazyler, Michael J. 2003. *Holocaust Justice: The Battle for Restitution in America's Courts*. New York University Press.

Carranza, Ruben. 2012. *Relief, Reparations, and the Root Causes of Conflict in Nepal*. ICTJ.

Destrooper, Tine. 2023. 'Disruptive Reparations? Tunisia's Victim Regions and the Collective Reparations Dilemma in Transitional Societies'. *Journal of Peacebuilding & Development*, 18(2), 127–141.

Diani, Mario. 1992. 'The Concept of Social Movement'. *The Sociological Review*, 41(1), 1–25.

Falschebner, Pia, Eva Willems, and Thorsten Bonacker. 2024. 'Collective Agency in Reparation Politics: A Contentious Politics Perspective on Victim Mobilisation in Northern Ireland'. *Global Society*, 39(3), 331–358.

Gallagher, Paul. 2021. 'New social movement theory and the reparations movement in Northern Ireland: the case of the WAVE Injured Group and its campaign for recognition'. PhD diss., Queen's University Belfast.

Gearty, Conor. 2014. *Human Rights: The Necessary Quest for Foundations*. Cambridge University Press.

Gilmore, Sunneva, and Luke Moffett. 2021. 'Finding a Way to Live with the Past: "Self-Repair", "Informal Repair", and Reparations in Transitional Justice'. *Journal of Law and Society*, 48(3), 455–480.

Greenstein, Claire. 2020. 'Patterned Payments: Explaining Victim Group Variation in West German Reparations Policy'. *International Journal of Transitional Justice*, 14(2), 381–400.

Howard-Hassmann, Rhoda E., and Anthony P. Lombardo. 2007. 'Framing Reparations Claims: Differences between the African and Jewish Social Movements for Reparations'. *African Studies Review*, 51(1), 27–48.

Johnston, Barbara. 2009. 'Waging War, Making Peace: The Anthropology of Reparations,'. In *Waging War, Making Peace: Reparations and Human Rights*, edited by B. Johnston and S. Slymovics, pp. 11–29. Left Coast Press.

Jones, Briony, and Julie Bernath. 2023. 'Resistance and Transitional Justice'. In *The Oxford Handbook of Transitional Justice*, edited by J. Meierhenrich, A. L. Hinton, and L. Douglas. Oxford University Press.

Kodikara, Chulani. 2023. 'The Office on Missing Persons in Sri Lanka: Why Truth Is a Radical Proposition'. *International Journal of Transitional Justice*, 17(1), 157–172.

Lawther, Cheryl. 2015. 'Peace without the Past? Truth, Transition and the Northern Ireland Case'. In *Theorizing Transitional Justice*, edited by Claudio Corradetti, Nir Eisikovits, and Jack Volpe Rotundi, pp. 29–42. Routledge.

Lira, Elizabeth. 2017. 'The Chilean Human Rights Archives and Moral Resistance to Dictatorship'. *The International Journal of Transitional Justice*, 11(2), 189–196.

Ludi, Regula. 2006. 'The Vectors of Postwar Victim Reparations: Relief, Redress and Memory Politics'. *Journal of Contemporary History*, 41(3), 421–450.

Madlingozi, Tshepo. 2007. 'Good Victim, Bad Victim: Apartheid's Beneficiaries, Victims and the Struggle for Social Justice'. In *Memory and the Legacy of Apartheid: Ten Years after AZAPO v President of South Africa*, edited by W. le Roux and K. van Marle, pp. 107–126. Pretoria University Law Press.

Matsunaga, Jennifer. 2021. 'The Red Tape of Reparations: Settler Governmentalities of Truth Telling and Compensation for Indian Residential Schools'. *Settler Colonial Studies*, 11(1), 21–41.

Mejía Bonifazi, Gretel. 2024. 'The Struggle Continues: Socio-Legal Analysis of Maya Ixil Victims-Survivors' Trajectories of Participation in Transitional Justice in Guatemala.' PhD diss. Ghent University.

Moffett, Luke. 2023. 'Violence as Redress: Armed Groups, the Right to Rebellion and the Resort to Force for Gross Violations of Human Rights'. In *Armed Groups and International Law*, edited by K. Fortin and E. Heffes, pp. 15–42. Elgar.

Moon, Claire. 2012. '"Who'll Pay Reparations on My Soul?" Compensation, Social Control and Social Suffering'. *Social and Legal Studies*, 21(2), 187–199.

Nassar, Habib. 2022. 'Justice as Resistance: How Post-Arab Spring Experiences Are Reshaping the Global Transitional Justice Landscape'. *The International Journal of Transitional Justice*, 16(2), 181–186.

Orjuela, Camilla. 2020. 'Passing on the Torch of Memory: Transitional Justice and the Transfer of Diaspora Identity across Generations'. *The International Journal of Transitional Justice*, 14(2), 360–380.

Parkin, Nicholas. 2016. 'Non-violent Resistance and Last Resort'. *Journal of Military Ethics*, 15(4), 259–274.

Pinckney, Jonathan. 2021. 'Nonviolent Resistance, Social Justice, and Positive Peace'. In *The Palgrave Handbook of Positive Peace*, edited by Katerina Standish, Heather Devere, Adan Suazo, and Rachel Rafferty, pp. 1–16. Palgrave Macmillan.

Ratner, R. S., Andrew Woolford, and Andrew C. Patterson. 2014. 'Obstacles and Momentum on the Path to Post-Genocide and Mass Atrocity Reparations: A Comparative Analysis, 1945–2010'. *International Journal of Comparative Sociology*, 55(3), 229–259.

Scott, James. 1999. *Seeing Like a State: How Certain Schemes to Improve the Human Condition Have Failed*. Yale University Press.

Sharp, G. 1999. 'Nonviolent Action.' In *Encyclopaedia of Violence, Peace, and Conflict*, edited by L. Kurtz and J. E. Turpin, pp. 567–574. Academic Press.

Soh, Chunghee Sarah. 1996. 'The Korean "Comfort Women": Movement for Redress'. *Asian Survey*, 36(1), 1226–1240.

Wolfe, Stephanie. 2014. *The Politics of Reparations and Apologies*. Springer.

Yamamoto, Eric. 1992. 'Friend, or Foe or Something Else: Social Meanings of Redress and Reparations'. *Denver Journal of International Law and Policy*, 20(2), 223–242.

# 11

# Storying Participation

## *Memoir, Victim Engagement, and 'Quiet' Transitional Justice*

*Lauren Dempster and Kevin Hearty*

### 11.1 INTRODUCTION

In this chapter we explore how victims have participated in unofficial transitional justice efforts involving non-state armed groups (NSAGs). Using the memoir of Seamus Kearney in the Northern Ireland (NI) context as an empirical case study, we critically examine how victims can participate in what we call 'quiet' transitional justice (QTJ) efforts (Dempster 2019, 2020) beyond formal or paradigmatic mechanisms. Reading Kearney's memoir through the lens of critical transitional justice scholarship, we centre our discussion around two interlinked foci: (a) the story of how he unofficially engaged with the Irish Republican Army (IRA) in the pursuit of acknowledgement and truth and (b) how his memoir represents a participatory space where Kearney leads the narration of his experience of QTJ. Arguing that his memoir is, and contains, evidence of victim-led transitional justice, we juxtapose Kearney's agency in the QTJ process with the passivity of his engagement with formal truth recovery mechanisms. In doing so, we hope to further expand the transitional justice imagination on the place and role of victims beyond their engagement with formal mechanisms. Here, we follow the lead of Herremans and Destrooper (2021) in exploring how victims' narrated lived experience of alternative transitional justice processes can offer a corrective to the dominant tendency of trying to force a fit with the formal processes that comprise the transitional justice 'toolkit'.

The chapter proceeds as follows: Section 11.2 provides background context to the Kearney case and efforts to deal with the past in NI. Section 11.3 introduces the concept of QTJ, outlining how it speaks to key critiques of transitional justice. Section 11.4 presents the Seamus Kearney case study and in Section 11.5 we interrogate the implications of this case study for transitional justice, examining what this case tells us about: (a) the role of NSAGs in transitional justice processes; (b) victim participation in transitional justice; (c) the value of QTJ; and (d) how the transitional justice imagination might be 'renewed' (following Sharp 2019) in terms of understanding victim engagement in ways that more fulsomely embrace a mosaic of approaches to addressing legacies of past violence. We conclude in Section 11.6.

### 11.2 SETTING THE CONTEXT

The 1998 Good Friday Agreement (GFA) brought an end to decades of tripartite political violence between state security forces (i.e., military, police, and intelligence services), Irish republican NSAGs seeking the national reunification of the island of Ireland, and Ulster loyalist NSAGs seeking to violently maintain the constitutional status quo of NI.[1] Lasting three decades, but with deeper historical roots in colonialism (McVeigh and Rolston 2021; Millar 2014), that violence claimed over 3,700 lives (Bell 2003), left over 40,000 people physically injured and many more psychologically injured (Breen-Smyth 2013), and thousands of families internally displaced (Moffett et al. 2020). Not only did the GFA fail to offer any consensus on the causes or nature of past violence, but it also failed to provide any overarching transitional justice mechanisms to address the legacy of human rights abuses committed by armed actors.

Reflecting NI's status as a 'non-paradigmatic transition' without an obvious winner or regime change (Alvarez-Berastegi 2017; Ní Aoláin and Campbell 2005), the gap left by the absence of overarching transitional justice mechanisms within the GFA was plugged by a 'piecemeal approach' to 'dealing with the past' (Bell 2003, 1097). Rather than taking a macro-level view of events, patterns and trends, this piecemeal approach has involved separate and disparate mechanisms and processes such as public inquiries (Rolston and Scraton 2005), historical police investigations (Lundy 2009), coronial inquests (Hearty 2021), and official apologies (Lundy and Rolston 2016) being held and/or issued in individual cases. Similarly, these official mechanisms and processes have been accompanied by mobilisation by victims through civil litigation (Dempster 2022), grassroots memory activism (Rolston 2020), and campaigns for reparation (Moffett 2020a). As a result of this fragmented approach, consensus on the causes, nature, and consequences of past violence continues to be elusive and an imbalance has materialised between those victims who have accessed truth, justice, and reparation and those who have not.

Although proposals for a 'joined up' approach to addressing the legacy of the conflict were made in 2006, overarching transitional justice mechanisms continue to be a hostage to wider political fortunes in post-GFA NI. Perhaps the closest NI has come to seeing overarching transitional justice mechanisms was the Stormont House Agreement (SHA) proposals for an investigatory police body, an information retrieval body, and an oral history body to provide themes for further exploration by an overarching body tasked with conducting a thematic overview of the conflict (Hearty 2021). However, successive UK governments have unilaterally departed from the SHA arrangements by bringing forward legislation to close down inquests and prevent the prosecution of former state actors for unlawful killings (Bryson and McEvoy 2023; Hearty and McEvoy 2024). Keir Starmer's Labour government of 2024 has since signalled its intention to repeal the Northern Ireland Troubles (Legacy and Reconciliation) Act 2023, beginning the parliamentary process for doing so in December 2024.

While NI has an impressive record of public and collective mobilisation by victims and survivors (Bryson and McEvoy 2023; Dempster 2022; Rolston 2020), this chapter focuses on the individual case of Seamus Kearney and his efforts to recover the truth about the killing of his brother Michael by the IRA in 1979. In what follows, we draw on Kearney's (2021) memoir *No Greater Love* for an insight into the QTJ process that he engaged in with the IRA.[2]

1 Irish republican NSAGs included the Provisional Irish Republican Army (IRA), the Official IRA, the Irish National Liberation Army and the Irish People's Liberation Organisation. Ulster loyalist NSAGs included the Ulster Volunteer Force, Ulster Freedom Fighters, Ulster Defence Association, and Red Hand Commando. Other smaller and localised armed groups also existed, while a number of splinter and spoiler groups continue to exist today.

2 In adopting a wider narrative victimological approach, we also draw directly from two blog posts that Kearney wrote following the publication of his memoir.

## 11.3 INTRODUCING 'QUIET' TRANSITIONAL JUSTICE

The concept of QTJ was developed by one of the authors in the context of their research on the establishment of the Independent Commission for the Location of Victims' Remains (ICLVR) to address conflict-related disappearances perpetrated during the NI conflict (Dempster 2019). Seventeen individuals were disappeared between 1972 and 1985. In most of these cases, the IRA has either acknowledged responsibility, or is suspected of responsibility, for perpetrating these disappearances. Families of the disappeared had for years been publicly campaigning for the return of their loved ones' remains. In 1999, both British and Irish government ministers referred in their respective parliaments to behind-the-scenes negotiations involving the Irish government and an intermediary to the IRA in the development of a process to facilitate the recovery of the disappeared. The result was the establishment of the ICLVR, a body that utilises a limited immunity mechanism to facilitate the provision of information relating to the burial sites of the disappeared (Dempster 2019; Dempster and Knupfer 2023).

QTJ was designed as a practical framework for understanding these 'behind the scenes' type efforts. It involves several components:

> First, given the focus of TJ, it involves an attempt to come to terms with violence and human rights abuses of the past … Second, it is work that is done behind closed doors…[involving] discussion and negotiations between the different actors and the concurrent exclusion of the media and broader public … Third, in some instances, as was the case with the 'disappeared' in Ireland, the outworkings of these deliberations do become public, albeit in a carefully managed and choreographed fashion. In other contexts, the results of such processes might not become known for years or even decades … Fourth, the mechanism is then implemented and at some level delivers what it promised, particularly to the victims. (Dempster 2020, 247)

The concept of QTJ was not introduced as a 'new' element of transitional justice. Rather, it was developed as this type of confidential, secretive, or 'behind the scenes' work, or simply activity that is conducted outside the public gaze, is likely often a key component of transitional justice efforts, however rarely the focus of scholarship. Instead, scholarly focus is often on the more public aspects of transitional justice, such as the process or outcomes of transitional justice mechanisms, victim mobilisation, political contestation around the past, institutional reform, and memorialisation efforts. While – as noted in the quotation – QTJ efforts may become publicly known at a later stage, we argue here that examining the 'quieter' stage(s) is a worthwhile endeavour. QTJ can manifest in various ways. The response to NI's disappeared presents an example of top-down QTJ, where back-channel negotiations between representatives of the state and an intermediary to the perpetrator organisation led to the development of an effective mechanism for recovering the disappeared (Dempster 2019, 2020). In the case study we explore below (Seamus Kearney), QTJ is a form of grassroots or 'bottom-up' transitional justice, in that it is initiated and shaped by those most impacted by harm. As we argue, this case is an example of 'victim-driven' transitional justice (Weis 2022) and unofficial truth recovery (Bellal 2017). While we are in the early stages of exploring the applicability of the concept of QTJ, we suggest that QTJ can be utilised by a range of actors operating at various levels of the transitional justice landscape, including those at the grassroots, political elites, and potentially also those who operate at the 'mid-level' (Collins 2018), who are directly involved in the implementation of transitional justice processes. Across these various manifestations, what makes QTJ distinct is its 'quietness' – that this activity happens behind closed doors, or at least away from the public gaze.

'Publicness' is a key concept in transitional justice, with the broadcasting or reporting of truth commissions and trials associated with the construction of narratives about the past (Karstedt 2009), public or societal acknowledgement of harm (Cole 2010; Kostovicova and La Lova 2024), educating society (Buruma 2009; Douglas 2001), contributing to the 'expressive' function of justice and therefore (purportedly) deterrence (see, e.g., Drumbl 2007; Garland 1990), and supposedly contributing to the 'never again' narrative by demonstrating to a wide audience the horror of past violence (Douglas 2001; Osiel 1999). The focus on 'quiet' efforts arguably runs counter to this prioritisation of publicness. However, as argued earlier, 'quiet' processes and activities *do* happen, and we should seek to understand them. Furthermore, these processes can lay the groundwork for more public expressions of transitional justice that can contribute to addressing the needs of victims (as examined in the Kearney case here) or building political trust between antagonists (as in the case of NI's disappeared (Dempster 2020)). QTJ was therefore developed to identify, conceptualise, and better understand the manifestation and contribution of these quiet types of activities to transitional justice, both in and of themselves and as steps in a more complex process.

The value of 'doing' transitional justice 'quietly' speaks to four challenges in, or critiques of, transitional justice. First is the contribution of this type of work to truth recovery. As one of the UN's four pillars of transitional justice, truth recovery is argued to fulfil a range of aims, including addressing the needs of (some) victims, helping societies and states understand what happened in the past, and providing a basis for institutional or structural reform (e.g., Bakiner 2013; Hayner 2011). However, there are limitations to 'top-down' or elite-led truth recovery efforts that have been well covered by others. These can include, inter alia, insufficient resources, limited remits or powers, challenges in accessing testimonies or other data, selectivity in whose or which truths are captured, and a lack of political will to follow through on recommendations (see, e.g., Brahm 2008; Hayner 2011; Jara et al. 2018; Ugarriza and Peralta 2024). One of the challenges of recovering truth is incentivising those with information to come forward (Mallinder 2008). This has particular relevance for perpetrators of past violence as – depending on the presence or absence of amnesty legislation, or indeed other concerns relating to loyalty to one's comrades or a distrust of state institutions – revealing information about the past may incriminate them or other members of their organisation. Thus, 'behind the scenes' conversations and confidential collaboration between victims and perpetrator organisations can be one way in which information about past violence is passed to the victim. This is exemplified in the Kearney case study in this chapter. Second, QTJ can provide an alternative (as in the Kearney case), or a pathway (as in the case of Ireland's disappeared) to top-down or elite-led transitional justice efforts. These more formal approaches to transitional justice have been critiqued for the provision of 'technocratic and decontextualised solutions' (Nagy 2008, 275) in the form of a 'top-down template-driven toolbox' (Jones and Lühe 2021, 4). The examples of NI's disappeared and Kearney evidence forms of transitional justice that are workable in the specific context of NI, with the particular actors involved. QTJ therefore potentially provides scope for the emergence of more localised or contextualised transitional justice, as has been called for in the field for over a decade (Shaw and Waldorf 2010). We of course acknowledge that these bottom-up efforts are not without their challenges, as hierarchies can exist or emerge within local or grassroots contexts also (Firchow and Selim 2022; Manning et al. 2023). Third, transitional justice has been critiqued for the continued dominance of legalism and legalistic approaches in the field (McEvoy 2007; Rigney 2024). Pursuing truth and/or justice in ways that are quiet or unofficial arguably creates a space for engagement with a wider range of transitional justice efforts that are not confined by the boundaries of more legalistic or institutionalised approaches. Accordingly, as we suggest in the case of Kearney, they can facilitate transitional justice approaches that more comprehensively meet the needs of victims. Fourth, as one of the authors has examined elsewhere (Dempster 2020), such processes can be considered legitimate if they are supported by victims.

While efforts to recover the 'disappeared' of NI were very much led by victims, the QTJ efforts took place between the perpetrator organisation and the state (Dempster 2020). In this chapter, we examine a case study of QTJ that is victim-led – the details of which we turn to next.

## 11.4 THE KEARNEY CASE

Seamus Kearney was an IRA member whose family moved to West Belfast after being displaced from their East Belfast home in 1971. In October 1977 he was sentenced to fourteen years imprisonment after trying to ambush a part-time member of the security forces (Kearney 2021, 49). With the UK government having withdrawn political status from politically motivated prisoners convicted after 1 March 1976, Kearney joined other Irish republican prisoners on a protest that began with them wearing a blanket instead of a prison uniform, escalated into them refusing to wash and slop out, and culminated in hunger strikes in 1980 and 1981.[3]

While Seamus Kearney was imprisoned, his younger brother Michael joined the IRA. Michael was subsequently arrested, yet released without charge, after an IRA explosives cache was discovered in Belfast. Following his release from custody, Michael was debriefed by the IRA. Although Michael had been cleared by the local IRA leadership over the issue, he was taken out of the area for interrogation by members of the IRA's Internal Security Unit responsible for investigating suspected state agents within IRA ranks. Michael Kearney's body was subsequently discovered lying on the border in Co. Fermanagh on 11 July 1979; the IRA had shot him dead as an informer. Despite the stigma surrounding the informer within Irish republican communities (Dudai 2005; 2022), both the Kearney family and local republicans refused to accept that Michael was an informer. They believed, and would subsequently maintain, that he had been set up to protect the identity of the real informer (Kearney 2021, 137).

When Seamus Kearney was released from prison in 1986, his mother asked him to 'help clear my son's [Michael] name and restore his honour before I die' (Kearney 2021, 359). The enormity of this was not lost on Seamus Kearney, who was 'shocked and dismayed at my mother for asking me to do this'. He admits that at the time he 'wouldn't know where to start' with such a task, feeling that it was a 'poisoned chalice' because asking the IRA to exonerate someone shot dead as an informer was 'unprecedented' (Kearney 2021, 360). Despite this, Seamus Kearney obliged to his mother's request and made some tentative queries that yielded little success. However, with the changing socio-political context that the GFA brought about, Irish republicans began to address the issue of intra-communal violence directed at alleged informers and others (Dempster 2019). Circumstances would further help Seamus Kearney in his endeavour when it publicly emerged that one of those tasked with unearthing informers within the IRA was himself an informer. This uncomfortable revelation added impetus to demands from bereaved families of alleged informers who wanted to know whether this person had set up their loved ones (Dudai 2022).

Seamus Kearney privately re-engaged with the IRA to seek a review of his brother Michael's case. The IRA leadership duly directed an internal inquiry into the killing in October 2001.

3 For further discussion of prison-related protests, see Jamieson (2015).

Following an extensive engagement between Seamus Kearney and the organisation, the findings of the inquiry were delivered privately to Kearney in 2003. The 'comprehensive report' that emerged from this inquiry concluded that Michael Kearney was not an informer, thus 'clearing Volunteer Michael Kearney from any suggestion that he was working for the British Forces, or had been a paid informer' (Kearney 2021, 360). Upon Kearney relaying the inquiry's findings to her, his mother said, 'now I can go to my grave knowing that my son's good name has been restored and he can finally rest in peace' (Kearney 2021, 360). The conclusion of the IRA inquiry into the case was subsequently publicised in the local media – the publicness of the conclusion showing that even with 'quiet' processes, expressivism is important for public acknowledgement of past harms, perhaps particularly so whenever perpetrators exonerate their wrongfully accused victims.

## 11.5 LESSONS FROM THE KEARNEY CASE AND IMPLICATIONS FOR TRANSITIONAL JUSTICE

Kearney's engagement with the IRA speaks directly to many relevant discussions within the broader transitional justice literature: the role that NSAGs can and/or should play in truth recovery (by providing information) and reparation (through providing acknowledgement and/or apology), what victim participation in transitional justice processes can or might be, and how adopting alternative approaches such as QTJ can broaden the transitional justice imagination. In the section that follows, we use the empirical insights from the Kearney case study to critically examine where and how QTJ intersects with these debates.

### 11.5.1 *The Role of NSAGs in Transitional Justice Processes*

Owing to the state-centricity of the legalistic mechanisms it has historically relied upon (Robins 2017), transitional justice has traditionally afforded insufficient attention to the role that NSAGs can play in addressing past abuses (Herman 2024). While there has been persistent debate about the legal, political, and practical challenges of involving NSAGs as transitional justice stakeholders, an increasing body of transitional justice scholarship has nevertheless recognised their potential to contribute to truth recovery and reparations processes (Bellal 2017; Dempster 2019; Dudai 2005; McEvoy, Lawther and Moffett 2022; Moffett 2020b). As the Kearney case attests, the argument for including NSAGs as transitional justice stakeholders is particularly persuasive where the group has both the ability and willingness to make amends (Moffett 2020b), with the issue of 'horizontal violence' directed against its own membership and/or support base being a suitable 'entry point' (Dudai 2005). The feasibility of QTJ in the Kearney case stemmed from the IRA retaining their organisational capacity to investigate past killings and being receptive to internal pressures to address the issue as part of the transition out of armed conflict.

As is evident from Kearney's memoir, the necessity for engaging with NSAGs in transitional justice is for practical and symbolic reasons. On a practical level, the successful relocation of the remains of those disappeared by the IRA demonstrates the importance of engaging with NSAGs who have access to information about past abuses (Dempster 2019). Given that the IRA had internal court-like procedures for the interrogation, sentencing, and killing of alleged informers (Dudai 2022), successful truth recovery was contingent on accessing the corporate knowledge held by members involved in the Michael Kearney case. Drawing on this corporate knowledge allowed the IRA to confirm that Freddie Scappaticci, the state agent known as Stakeknife,[4] had been involved in the court martial and execution of Michael, albeit maintaining that he 'had not played a central role' (Kearney 2023). With truth recovery being possible through both official and unofficial channels (Bellal 2017), the Kearney case shows the value of victims using the latter to retrieve information from NSAGs.

On a symbolic level, acknowledgement from the IRA carried what Moffett (2020b) calls an 'added value' beyond any repair the state could afford to the Kearney family. It was, after all, the IRA that was directly responsible for abducting and killing him. More crucially, though, the symbolic importance of acknowledgement from the IRA lay in the fact that it was *only* that organisation that could restore Michael's reputation. The stigma of the informer within republican communities and the suspicion around state prevarication on the matter (Dudai 2005, 2022) gave formal acknowledgement from the IRA significant social, cultural, and political weight. Engaging with the family, conducting an inquiry, and disclosing the exoneration represented the IRA taking 'active responsibility' (McEvoy et al. 2022) by owning past harms and seeking to make amends. Within the specific context of the Kearney case and the stigma endured by families of alleged informers within republican communities, the buy-in from the IRA was also important in helping to restore relationships between the victim (Kearney family), victimiser (IRA), and the wider community (Irish republican support base) (McEvoy et al. 2022). Public acknowledgement from the IRA of Michael's innocence of the informer allegation meant that 'as far as the family were concerned Michael's name was cleared and his honour restored' (Kearney 2021, 360). The restoration of Michael's honour could *not* have been achieved through any state-centric process that precluded IRA involvement.

While the state *could not* provide the kind of acknowledgement that the IRA did, the Kearney family nonetheless sought an admission from the state that Michael's death involved 'state manipulation' (Kearney 2021, 360). In pursuit of this, the family engaged with the Operation Kenova investigation into the deaths of alleged informers attributed to agent Stakeknife. The family learnt from a briefing with the Operation Kenova team that 'Michael's life could and should have been saved by those in authority' because on at least three separate occasions the security forces were informed by at least two different agents that Michael's life was in danger (Kearney 2024). Even if a QTJ engagement with the IRA could provide the Kearney family with admission of Stakeknife's involvement and with a symbolically important exoneration, it could *not* offer them the level of detail about state agent involvement that was retrieved via Operation Kenova.

### 11.5.2 *Victim Participation*

The Kearney case can also broaden our perspective on what victim participation in transitional justice processes can be. While transitional justice processes and mechanisms have long postured as being 'victim-centric', just how much input victims have in the design, implementation, and delivery of them has been increasingly questioned (McEvoy et al. 2022; Robins 2017;). The problem is particularly acute with truth recovery processes where victim participation is limited by mandates, time constraints, and the narrowly legalistic way that institutions frame participation (Bellal 2017; Evrard et al. 2021). As Firchow and Selim

4 Although named in the media and widely believed by victims' families and others to be Stakeknife, Scappaticci maintained until his death in hiding in April 2023 that he was not the agent. The interim report of Operation Kenova (the police investigation into the agent Stakeknife's activities within the IRA's Internal Security Unit) that was published in March 2024 refused to confirm or deny that Scappaticci was the agent.

(2022) have recently pointed out, improving participation is conceived of here as encouraging more victims to engage with these pre-designed processes rather than critiquing whether they even allow for meaningful participation by victims in the first place (see also Firchow and Laplante, Chapter 18).

The Kearney case shows that informal and non-legalistic approaches offer the potential for improving the quality of victim participation. Rather than co-opting victims and pigeonholing them into a typecast role as top-down formal mechanisms and processes tend to, QTJ enables victims to initiate, contribute to, and evaluate informal transitional justice processes. It was, after all, Kearney who set in motion the QTJ process by approaching the IRA with a very specific ask. Approaches of this nature have also been noted in Colombia, where mothers of the disappeared visited imprisoned members of NSAGs to get the necessary information about the location of their loved ones' bodies from them (McEvoy et al. 2022 – for a similar example in the Kurdish/Turkish context see Daşlı, Chapter 4). However, Kearney's participation extended beyond merely approaching the IRA to request a review of his brother's case. Both prior to and after the IRA inquiry, Kearney can be seen to exercise agency within the QTJ process. He had, for example, set up a 'secret strategic think tank' comprising trusted former comrades to help him clarify what exactly his ask of the IRA was and to persuade the IRA to respond accordingly (Kearney 2024). Likewise, not only did Kearney continue to engage with the IRA throughout the process, but he also continued to meet with them after the inquiry findings had been presented as he sought to agree on the text of the public statement the IRA were to issue on the case (Kearney 2024). Finally, as was discussed earlier, Kearney was able to evaluate the success or otherwise of the QTJ process by expressing the family's satisfaction that Michael's name had been cleared and his honour restored.

The agency exercised by Kearney throughout his engagement with the IRA speaks to arguments made within the literature about affording victims input into transitional justice processes and allowing them to shape their outcome (Moffett 2020b). Similarly, it shows the disconnect between the lived reality of victim participation when and where it is encouraged and properly facilitated, and the reductive way that it is conceived of and enacted within legalistic and state-centric mechanisms and processes (Evrard et al. 2021). Echoing the argument of Firchow and Selim (2022) that improvement in victim participation should be premised on *quality* over *quantity*, the Kearney case shows how participation by victims can be made meaningful in bottom-up individualised cases such as QTJ. The Kearney case shows, then, that at the very least QTJ can complement more formal processes such as the Operation Kenova investigation.

### 11.5.3 *Value of 'Quiet' Transitional Justice in the Kearney Case*

The Kearney case demonstrates several benefits to 'doing' transitional justice 'quietly'. In the face of the aforementioned difficulties in identifying, accessing, and engaging with those with the relevant information in any given case it: (a) allows for a pragmatic and victim-driven approach to transitional justice; (b) provides a space for victim agency in a context where an overarching, formal transitional justice mechanism is lacking; and (c) can sidestep potential barriers to progress, such as local victim hierarchies and political contestation.

First, the Kearney case demonstrates how a pragmatic approach can respond to the needs of victims. Pragmatist philosophy encourages us to learn from and listen to those most directly affected by the harm (Sullivan 2007). As discussed earlier, in this case, fulfilling the family's need for the truth required information from the IRA. Furthermore, the process built on a pre-existing relationship between Kearney and the IRA. From a pragmatic perspective, this approach to the pursuit of truth and acknowledgement was potentially the most straightforward way to respond to Kearney's mother's call to have her son's name cleared. Handling the case as Kearney did facilitated the provision of an individualised response that provided the family with the information they wanted. Relatedly, by leading this process himself (rather than via, for instance, an official information recovery mechanism) Kearney was free to pursue this unofficial route, and this can thus be considered an example of victim-driven transitional justice (Weis 2023).

Second, over a quarter of a century after NI's peace agreement, as noted earlier, there is still no overarching transitional justice mechanism. The Kearney case prompts three points of interest here. First, Seamus Kearney's actions can be considered as a response to the lack of state provision with regards to transitional justice – thus as discussed earlier, it is a demonstration of victim agency and arguably resistance against the status quo. Second, the case raises questions over whether any state-led mechanism would have produced the information that the Kearney family wanted – for instance, one can question if this type of detail would have been included within the remit of a top-down transitional justice process, or if the IRA would have provided the same level of information via a formal mechanism. Third – and while there are limitations to this (as we will examine later) – as one of the authors has argued elsewhere (Dempster 2019), as a result of NI's 'piecemeal' approach to the past (see Section 11.2) we arguably know more about some victims and events related to the conflict than we might through a formal process, as a result of the advocacy of individual victims or victim organisations. Top-down understandings of past violence can sideline those who were directly impacted by past violence (Acosta et al. 2018) and 'channel and streamline' their perspectives (Nagy 2008, 276). Engaging quietly with the IRA allowed Kearney to access a level of truth and acknowledgement that may not have been possible with a mechanism led by the external transitional justice 'professionals' who have come to dominate the field (Jamar 2019; Nesiah 2016).

Third, as has been explored by others (see, e.g., Jankowitz 2018, Lawther 2022), efforts to address victims' needs in NI are deeply politicised, and hierarchies have emerged, with some victims considered more 'deserving' than others. As he was an IRA member, not all in NI would sympathise with Kearney's case and any state-led process would potentially be met by opposition from some Unionist politicians or victims' groups (Hearty and Alvarez-Berastegi 2019). By leading this process as an individual, away from the public or media gaze, Kearney sidestepped the potential contestation or controversy that might have emerged in such a case.

## 11.6 CONCLUSION: EXPANDING THE TRANSITIONAL JUSTICE IMAGINATION?

Building on earlier calls to 'localise' transitional justice, Sharp's (2019) 'renewed' transitional justice advocates for a transitional justice that is bottom-up, locally owned, victim-centred, contextually tailored, and politically and culturally grounded in ways that foreground an array of options. As examined here, as an example of 'victim-driven' transitional justice, the Kearney case study arguably speaks to this idea of a 'renewed transitional justice'.

There are, however, limitations with the approach presented here. While – as detailed earlier – the process can be said to be successful for this individual family, we can raise questions about the broader appropriateness of, or capacity for, victims and survivors to pursue truth and acknowledgement at an individual level. We of course do not seek to advise victims on how to pursue justice, but we contend that this pursuit should not be the responsibility of victims. In the aftermath of armed conflict, the state has a responsibility to provide victims with redress (and indeed in cases where there has been a violation of international law, a legal duty to investigate). Furthermore, Kearney had the ability and connections required to pursue the route he did. Many others may lack the access, capacity, or resources to undertake this type of task. For instance, in the case of NI, many relatives of those murdered during the conflict are now quite elderly and may be dealing themselves with physical and/or psychological injuries from the conflict. This creates a risk of adding a further dimension to the hierarchy of victimhood, in which those who have the capacity to pursue transitional justice themselves supersede those who do not.

However, notwithstanding these limitations, we contend that the case study examined here demonstrates that the transitional justice framework has utility for capturing, exploring, and acknowledging the value and contribution of these 'quieter' initiatives on their own terms. From our perspective as authors, transitional justice as a field encompasses a spectrum of approaches, tools, and mechanisms of varying levels of formality and originating from a diversity of individuals, organisations, and institutions. Through re-focusing our attention on the less public-facing aspects of transitional justice, more of this landscape can be brought to light.

By bringing the memoir of Seamus Kearney into conversation with the notion of QTJ (Dempster 2019; 2020), we have argued that the Kearney case serves as an example of victim-led transitional justice and provides evidence that quiet, confidential, or behind-the-scenes efforts can be a valuable vehicle for the pursuit of transitional justice. As demonstrated by both the case study presented here, and the example of NI's disappeared introduced earlier, QTJ arguably has particular potential for engaging with NSAGs – a subject overlooked in transitional justice. In sum, 'quiet' efforts can provide a pathway or an alternative to more formal transitional justice, a space for victim-driven transitional justice that can redefine the boundaries of the field, and may have particular potential in the context of NSAG engagement in transitional justice.

## REFERENCES


Acosta, Mónica, Angela Castañeda, Daniela García, Fallon Hernández, Dunen Muelas, and Ángela Santamaria. 2018. 'The Colombian Transitional Process: Comparative Perspectives on Violence against Indigenous Women'. *International Journal of Transitional Justice*, 12(1), 108–125.

Alvarez-Berastegi, Amaia. 2017. 'Transitional Justice in Settled Democracies: Northern Ireland and the Basque Country in Comparative Perspective'. *Critical Studies on Terrorism*, 10(3), 542–561.

Bakiner, Onur. 2013. 'Truth Commission Impact: An Assessment of How Commissions Influence Politics and Society'. *International Journal of Transitional Justice*, 8(1), 6–30.

Bell, Christine. 2003. 'Dealing with the Past in Northern Ireland'. *Fordham International Law Journal*, 26(4), 1058–1147.

Bellal, Annyssa. 2017. 'Non-state Armed Groups in Transitional Justice Processes: Adapting to New Realities of Conflict'. In *Justice Mosaics: How Context Shapes Transitional Justice in Fractured Societies*, edited by Roger Duthie and Paul Seils, pp. 234–257. International Center for Transitional Justice.

Brahm, Eric. 2008. 'Uncovering the Truth: Examining Truth Commission Success and Impact'. *International Studies Perspectives*, 8(1), 16–35.

Breen-Smyth, Marie. 2013. 'Injured and Disabled Casualties of the Northern Ireland Conflict: Issues in Immediate and Long-Term Treatment, Care and Support'. *Medicine, Conflict & Survival*, 29(3), 244–266.

Bryson, Anna, and Kieran McEvoy. 2023. 'Human Rights Activism and Transitional Justice Advocacy in Northern Ireland'. *International Journal of Transitional Justice*, 17(3), 453–469.

Buruma, Ian. 2009. *The Wages of Guilt: Memories of War in Germany and Japan*. Atlantic Books.

Cole, Catherine M. 2010. *Performing South Africa's Truth Commission: Stages of Transition*. Indiana University Press.

Collins, Cath. 2018. 'Transitional Justice 'From Within': Police, Forensic and Legal Actors Searching for Chile's Disappeared'. *Journal of Human Rights Practice*, 10(1), 19–39.

Dempster, Lauren. 2019. *Transitional Justice and the 'Disappeared' of Northern Ireland: Silence, Memory, and the Construction of the Past*. Routledge.

Dempster, Lauren. 2020. '"Quiet" Transitional Justice: "Publicness", Trust and Legitimacy in the Search for the "Disappeared"'. *Social and Legal Studies*, 292, 246–272.

Dempster, Lauren. 2022. 'Northern Ireland: The Right to Life, Victim Mobilisation and the Legacy of Conflict'. In *International Conflict and Security Law: A Research Handbook*, edited by Sergey Sayapin et al., pp. 1333–1358. TMC Asser.

Dempster, Lauren, and Geoff Knupfer. 2023. 'The Independent Commission for the Location of Victims' Remains'. In *Encyclopaedia of Transitional Justice*, edited by Lavinia Stan and Nadya Nedelsky, pp. 1069–1724. Cambridge University Press.

Douglas, Lawrence. 2001. *The Memory of Judgment: Making Law and History in the Trials of the Holocaust*. Yale University Press.

Drumbl, Mark. 2007. *Atrocity, Punishment and International Law*. Cambridge University Press.

Dudai, Ron. 2005. 'Closing the Gap: Symbolic Reparations and Armed Groups'. *International Review of the Red Cross*, 93(883), 783–808.

Dudai, Ron. 2022. *Penality in the Underground: The IRA's Pursuit of Informers*. Oxford University Press.

Evrard, Elke, Gretel Mejía Bonifazi, and Tine Destrooper. 2021. 'The Meaning of Participation in Transitional Justice: A Conceptual Proposal for Empirical Analysis'. *International Journal of Transitional Justice*, 15(2), 428–447.

Firchow, Pamina, and Yvette Selim. 2022. 'Meaningful Engagement from Bottom-Up? Taking Stock of Participation in Transitional Justice Processes'. *International Journal of Transitional Justice*, 16(2), 187–203.

Garland, David. 1990. *Punishment and Modern Society: A Study in Social Theory*. Oxford University Press.

Hayner, Priscilla. 2011. *Unspeakable Truths: Transitional Justice and the Challenge of Truth Commissions*. Routledge.

Hearty, Kevin. 2021. 'Truth beyond the "Trigger Puller": Moral Accountability, Transitional (In)Justice and the Limitations of Legal Truth'. *International Journal of Transitional Justice*, 15(3), 658–677.

Hearty, Kevin, and Amaia Alvarez-Berastegi. 2019. 'A Context Based Model to Frame Political Victimhood: Experiences from Northern Ireland and the Basque Country'. *International Review of Victimology*, 25(1), 19–36.

Hearty, Kevin, and Kieran McEvoy. 2024. 'Veteran Mobilisation, Prosecutions and the Contested Legacy of the Past in Northern Ireland: Deconstructing the "Witch-Hunt" Narrative'. In *Sights, Sounds and Sensibilities of Atrocity Prosecutions*, edited by Mark Drumbl and Caroline Fournet, pp. 427–447. Brill.

Herman, Olivia. 2024. *Reparations by Non-state Armed Groups under International Law: From Conflict to Repair in Colombia and Beyond*. Routledge.

Herremans, Brigitte, and Tine Destrooper. 2021. 'Stirring the Justice Imagination: Countering the Invisibilization and Erasure of Syrian Victims' Justice Narratives'. *International Journal of Transitional Justice*, 15(3), 576–595.

Jamar, Astrid. 2019. 'The Crusade of Transitional Justice: Tracing the Journeys of Hegemonic Claims'. Violence and Democracy. The British Academy. www.thebritishacademy.ac.uk/documents/242/Violence-and-Democracy.pdf

Jamieson, Ruth. 2015. 'Through the Lens of War: Political Imprisonment in Northern Ireland'. In *Criminology and War: Transgressing the Borders*, edited by Sandra Walklate and Ross McGarry, pp. 94–119. Routledge.

Jankowitz, Sarah. 2018. 'The "Hierarchy of Victims" in Northern Ireland: A Framework for Critical Analysis'. *International Journal of Transitional Justice*, 12(2), 216–236.

Jara, Daniela, Manuela Badilla, Ana Figuieredo, Marcela Cornejo, and Victoria Riveros. 2018. 'Tracing Mapuche Exclusion from Post-Dictatorial Truth Commissions in Chile: Official and Grassroots Initiatives'. *International Journal of Transitional Justice*, 12(3), 479–498.

Jones, Briony, and Ulrike Lühe. 2021. 'Knowledge for Peace: Transitional Justice and the Politics of Knowledge in Theory and Practice'. In *Knowledge for Peace: Transitional Justice and the Politics of Knowledge in Theory and Practice*, edited by Briony Jones and Ulrike Lühe, pp. 1–19. Elgar.

Karstedt, Susanne. 2009. *Legal Institutions and Collective Memories*. Hart Publishing.
Kearney, Seamus. 2021. *No Greater Love: The Memoirs of Seamus Kearney*. Kearney.
Kearney, Seamus. 2023. 'Stakeknife – A Meeting of Minds'. *The Pensive Quill*, 17 April. www.thepensivequill.com/2023/04/stakeknife-meeting-of-minds.html
Kearney, Seamus. 2024. 'The Lonely Death of Michael Kearney'. *The Pensive Quill*, 11 March. www.thepensivequill.com/2024/03/the-lonely-death-of-michael-kearney.html
Kostovicova, Denisa, and Lanabi La Lova. 2024. 'Grandstanding Instead of Deliberative Policy-Making: Transitional Justice, Publicness and Parliamentary Questions in the Croatian Parliament'. *Journal of Intervention and State Building*, 18(5), 1–22.
Lawther, Cheryl. 2022. 'Heroes and Hierarchies: The Celebration and Censure of Victimhood in Transitional Justice'. *The International Journal of Human Rights*, 26(3), 518–540.
Lundy, Patricia. 2009. 'Exploring Home-Grown Transitional Justice and Its Dilemmas: A Case Study of the Historical Enquiries Team, Northern Ireland'. *International Journal of Transitional Justice*, 3(3), 321–340.
Lundy, Patricia, and Bill Rolston. 2016. 'Redress for Past Harms? Official Apologies in Northern Ireland'. *International Journal of Human Rights*, 20(1), 104–122.
Mallinder, Louise. 2008. *Amnesty, Human Rights and Political Transitions: Bridging the Peace and Justice Divide*. Hart Publishing.
Manning, Peter, Jordan Tchilingirian, Somaly Kum, and Tudor Nedelcu. 2023. 'Transitional Justice Networks and the Role of "Local" Actors in Cambodia'. *Journal of Peacebuilding & Development*, 18(2), 158–176.
McEvoy, Kieran. 2007. 'Beyond Legalism: Towards a Thicker Understanding of Transitional Justice'. *Journal of Law and Society*, 34(4), 411–440.
McEvoy, Kieran, Cheryl Lawther, and Luke Moffett. 2022. 'Changing the Script: Non-state Armed Groups, Restorative Justice, and Reparations'. *Journal of Human Rights Practice*, 14(2), 454–477.
McVeigh, Robbie, and Bill Rolston. 2021. *Ireland, Colonialism & the Unfinished Revolution*. Beyond the Pale.
Millar, David. 2014. *Rethinking Northern Ireland: Culture, Ideology & Colonialism*. Routledge.
Moffett, Luke. 2020a. 'Struggling for Reparations in Northern Ireland'. In *Reparations for Victims of Genocide, War Crimes and Crimes against Humanity*, pp. 678–709. Brill.
Moffett, Luke. 2020b. 'Violence and Repair: The Practice and Challenges of Non-state Armed Groups Engaging in Reparations'. *International Review of the Red Cross*, 102(915), 1057–1085.
Moffett, Luke, Cheryl Lawther, Kevin Hearty, Andrew Godden, and Robin Hickey. 2020. *No Longer Neighbours: The Impact of Violence on Land, Housing and Redress in the Northern Ireland Conflict*. Queen's University Belfast Human Rights Centre.
Nagy, Rosemary. 2008. 'Transitional Justice as Global Project: Critical Reflections'. *Third World Quarterly*, 29(2), 275–289.
Nesiah, Vasuki. 2016. 'Theories of Transitional Justice: Cashing in the Blue Chips'. In *The Oxford Handbook of the Theory of International Law*, edited by Anne Orford and Florian Hoffman, pp. 779–796. Oxford University Press.
Ní Aoláin, Fionnuala, and Colm Campbell. 2005. 'The Paradox of Transition in Conflicted Democracies'. *Human Rights Quarterly*, 27(1), 172–213.
Osiel, Mark. 1999. 'Making Public Memory, Publicly'. In *Human Rights in Political Transitions – Gettysburg to Bosnia*, edited by Carla Hesse and Robert Post, pp. 217–261. Zone Books.
Rigney, Sophie. 2024. 'Building an Abolition Movement for International Criminal Law?' *Journal of International Criminal Justice*, 22(1), 211–233.
Robins, Simon. 2017. 'Failing Victims: The Limits of Transitional Justice in Addressing the Needs of Victims of Violations'. *Human Rights & International Legal Discourse*, 11(1), 41–58.
Rolston, Bill. 2020. 'Ambushed by Memory: Post-Conflict Popular Memorialisation in Northern Ireland'. *International Journal of Transitional Justice*, 14(2), 320–339.
Rolston, Bill, and Phil Scraton. 2005. 'In the Full Glare of English Politics: Ireland, Inquiries and the British State'. *British Journal of Criminology*, 45(4), 547–564.
Sharp, Dustin. 2019. 'What Would Satisfy Us? Taking Stock of Critical Approaches to Transitional Justice'. *International Journal of Transitional Justice*, 13(3), 570–589.
Shaw, Rosalind, and Lars Waldorf, eds. 2010. *Localizing Transitional Justice*. Stanford University Press.

Sullivan, Shannon. 2007. 'Pragmatism'. In *The Blackwell Guide to Feminist Philosophy*, edited by Linda Martín Alcoff and Eva Feder Kittay, pp. 64–78. Blackwell Publishing.

Ugarriza, Juan E., and Laly C. Peralta. 2024. 'Ex-combatants and the Truth Commission in Colombia: An Analysis of the Participation of Former Military and Ex-guerrillas'. *International Journal of Transitional Justice*, 18(2), 201–217.

Weis, Valeria Vegh. 2022. 'Who Can Organize and Exercise Effective Resistance? A Southern Criminology Perspective on the Victimology of State Crime'. *Theoretical Criminology*, 27(3), 381–403. https://doi.org/10.1177/13624806221135598

Weis, Valeria Vegh. 2023. 'Exploring the World's First Successful Truth Commission: Argentina's CONADEP and the Role of Victims in Truth-Seeking'. *Journal of Human Rights Practice*, 15(1), 100–117.

# 12

# Victim Mobilisation as Transformative Local Process after Mass Violence

## *Families of the Missing in Nepal*

*Simon Robins and Ram Kumar Bhandari*

### 12.1 INTRODUCTION

In many contexts a normatively driven approach to transitional justice, rooted in human rights law and focused on criminal accountability and truth-telling, frames victim participation in transitional justice solely in terms of its orientation towards a formal process. This resonates with an overwhelming focus on what formal mechanisms can achieve, despite significant empirical data showing that informal approaches can also be effective in addressing victims' needs. Here, we seek to reframe the whole understanding of 'process' and note that action in a range of social spaces that are not labelled as explicit approaches to past violations can be effective in addressing the needs of victims. This resonates with what this volume's Introduction identifies as a 'third generation' of victim engagement in transitional justice, revolving around victim protagonism, which in this chapter is seen as synonymous with the exercise of agency by victims. We discuss how this plays out in the context of Nepal, and will examine the experience of victims' organisations seeking to mobilise some of the poorest and most marginalised people in the country to enable their agency in shaping process to address their needs, with a focus on families of those missing and disappeared from the ten-year civil war. While there is a stuttering formal transitional justice process ongoing, it has been consistently obstructed politically and has yet to deliver anything of substance, to victims or otherwise. As such, the participation we discuss here is independent of both that formal process and of any broader state action.

The mobilisation of victims, often spontaneous and initially at a highly local level, is driven by a need for mutual support, solidarity, and an addressing of everyday challenges in family and community (also see Daşlı, Chapter 4). Here, we use the term *social ecologies*, which has emerged in psycho-social work as a frame for understanding how the social environment is crucial in fostering and sustaining resilience after conflict and violence (Clark and Ungar 2021). Conceptualising social ecologies, such as family, community, and groups of peers, such as victims' groups, as spaces for justice linked to the impacts of rights violations reframes both how to conceive of transitional justice and what participation can mean. This chapter makes several challenges to current practice around the idea of victim participation in transitional justice. First, it notes that most victims gain little benefit from formal transitional justice and acknowledges that there are multiple mechanisms by which victims' needs are addressed beyond what is typically labelled as transitional justice. Second, it shares data that show that victims are constantly renegotiating what victimhood means in their everyday lives, articulating a *critical victimology* (Walklate 1990), where they seek not to leave victimhood behind but rather shape how they experience it. Third, victims are only able to shape agendas, in both their everyday social spaces and beyond, through collective action, meaning mobilisation with others who share their agenda, typically other victims, through which they become political actors. Finally, this prompts an understanding of victim participation as synonymous with the enabling of their agency.

This represents a victim-centred definition of participation in transitional justice, which understands victims' needs as being addressed in multiple spaces, most of them unrelated to what is formally labelled as 'justice', transitional or otherwise. It also highlights how individual victims, particularly when they are from the poorest and most marginalised sectors of society, can most effectively exercise agency collectively. We see that victims naturally seek each other out locally, to build solidarity, create meanings around the incomprehensibility of missing a loved one, and, ultimately, to act collectively as victims. Such action and collectivity are built not on a normative basis of rights or even an explicit politics of resistance, but rather a culture of care from which such perspectives can evolve (Krystalli and Schulz 2022). It seems clear from this analysis that victim mobilisation, particularly for the socially excluded, is a prerequisite to any engagement with the state on victims' terms.

The story of victim mobilisation in Nepal is that of a challenging of the many constraints to such action and the creation of a new victim identity that transcended the long-standing political identities of victims from both sides in the conflict. Despite minimal technical, political, and financial resources, national networks have emerged that link local groups throughout the country; these have been able to articulate the agenda of victims at a national level, and finally become visible internationally.

The focus on collective action represents a challenge to a human rights discourse that largely denies victims' often shared experience. The individualism at the heart of human rights has seen transitional justice practice isolate and atomise victims, in ways that prevent them being seen as a constituency that can act, and be empowered, collectively or for whom solidarity can be a crucial tool. Transitional justice practice denies the social in ways that explain its resistance to an examination of the potential of mobilisation, or collective political action of victims, as a route to change. It is remarkable, for example, how little has been written about victims' groups and their role in transitional justice, although this appears to be changing (e.g., Nassar 2022; Tamayo Gomez 2021, 2022).

## 12.2 THE STRUGGLE FOR TRANSITIONAL JUSTICE IN NEPAL

Nepal's decade-long Maoist insurgency ended in 2006, leaving more than 17,000 dead and some 1,400 disappeared. Maoist former rebels became a constitutional political party, won the first post-war election, and in the years since, a republic has been declared and a new Constitution to underwrite a federal republic created.

While the Comprehensive Peace Agreement that ended the conflict promised both a dedicated commission on disappearances and a Truth and Reconciliation Commission (TRC), these took many years to be created, reflecting political suspicion of any transitional justice process. Government eventually passed an Act in 2014 creating the TRC and the Commission of Investigation on Enforced Disappeared Persons but including provision for amnesty and forced reconciliation. The two Commissions represent the only institutional efforts at transitional justice in Nepal. It quickly became clear that the government had decided to create bodies that would be unable to satisfy their remit, that could constitute an empty ritual visible to the international community, but were not able to address the impunity of political leaders and the security forces. After long years of inaction, however, an amended Act was passed by Parliament in August 2024, at least in part catalysed by the action of victims' groups, that creates new commissions with a four-year mandate and that has been widely welcomed by both local and international stakeholders. It remains to be seen as to what impact they can have.

The absence of any state commitment to transitional justice has seen civil society take up a role as an advocate for such a process, with substantial financial support – at least in the early years of the transition – from international donors. The emergence of a victims' movement, however, showed the transitional justice agenda in Nepal is contested, with divisions between those seeking to represent victims predominantly from rural and marginalised communities, and a professional Kathmandu-based civil society largely drawn from urban ethnic and caste elites (Robins 2012). Human rights non-governmental organisations (NGOs) reflect the global discourse of their international donors, and as such have articulated an approach that prioritises the civil and political as well as criminal accountability over the social and economic, and a national institutional approach over local needs of victims. The diverse range of victims mobilising for justice, in contrast, have a more nuanced agenda, welcoming prosecutions, but also prioritising the issues of poverty and marginality that define their everyday lives and linking violations to historical social exclusion on the basis of their caste and ethnicity (Robins 2011). As a result, victims' organisations, while also demanding accountability, articulate a demand for reparations and livelihood as an essential and urgent component of justice, alongside an addressing of the structural issues that condemn them to poverty. Victims and NGOs are also divided politically, with a majority of victims traditionally linked to the Maoists, since most violations were state perpetrated, while NGOs based in the capital are informally and often formally linked to a political party that was in government during much of the conflict.[1]

## 12.3 CONCEPTUALISING PARTICIPATION IN TRANSITIONAL JUSTICE AS AGENCY

Conceptualisations of participation in transitional justice have largely focused on a model of citizen control of the formal transitional justice process, framed as contestation between the state and citizens (Taylor 2014). Perhaps the most widely referenced framework is that of a 'ladder of participation' (Arnstein 1969), in which 'participation is a categorical term for power' (Arnstein 1969, 216) and conceived as essentially the consequence of a power struggle between citizens trying to move up the ladder and controlling institutions limiting their ascent (Tsai and Robins 2021). This 'zero-sum' understanding of participation has been challenged by scholars in a number of fields with an appreciation of the more complex set of relationships that exist in many ongoing participatory situations, where roles are less easy to define and responsibilities emerge during, and as a consequence of, the participatory process itself (e.g., Baker and Chapin 2018; Collins and Ison 2009). This resonates with the transitional justice space where a linear, hierarchical model of involvement – such as Arnstein's ladder – fails to capture the dynamic and evolutionary nature of citizen and victim engagement. It also challenges the implicit assumption of such models of participation that full citizen – or victim – control of a

[1] The link between the Communist Party of Nepal (Unified Marxist-Leninist) (CPN(UML)) and human rights NGOs arises from their common origin in activism that led to the 1991 People's Movement that established multiparty democracy in Nepal. The CPN(UML) has since become one of the fiercest defenders of the caste and ethnic status quo.

transitional justice process would necessarily be positive, and, by conflating victims' influence over a national transitional justice process with the normative lens, that victims represent the moral authority and legitimacy of that process.

In practice, power is relational and permeates the lives of victims – and others – far beyond the direct action of the state. Concerned constituencies in a transitional context, including victims, will seek to both build and leverage relationships to advance their goals, including through collective action. This view of power as determined through relationships, and indeed as constitutive of social identities (Dyrberg 1997), is particularly relevant for victims' organisations and resonates with the idea of a social movement that actively aids the construction of a victim identity (Gready and Robins 2017). This demands that participation be conceptualised as empowerment beyond the binary of state and victim, to include the many complexities of a particular context and an understanding of how contextual factors shape both the nature and outcomes of participation.

Agency is considered important because it reflects an ethical imperative: 'The doctrine of action has become essential to our recognition of other people's humanity' (Asad 2014, 272). As such, enabling the agency of victims is an essential part of restoring their dignity and humanity, challenged by the violation they have experienced, and where victimhood is at least partly defined in terms of their passivity, as individuals to whom something has happened. Agency is understood primarily as the autonomy of the subject, both as individual and community: the sense in which victims are in control of their own destiny and are agents in processes to address their needs. Victims are subordinate not only because of their victimhood, but also in many cases prior to their victimisation for reasons of marginalisation by poverty, gender, or ethnicity. Their needs, as seen in Nepal, result from the confluence of long-term marginalisation that typically facilitates victimhood through the violations of conflict. Given this understanding, here – in seeking to privilege victims and their empowerment to play a role in addressing their own needs – we persist in using the term *participation*, rather than the term *engagement*, referenced in the Introduction to this volume. This is in an effort to emphasise agency, something the term participation appears better able to do. In the light of this, victim participation in transitional justice is here defined as: 'Enabling the agency of victims, understanding them as social actors able to shape how they experience victimhood, as well as address its impacts, including through influencing processes to address legacies of violations.'

Participation can then be understood as the exercise of agency in any space or process that ultimately addresses victims' needs as they define them. In many cases such needs are best addressed not by state action but by empowerment: this reiterates Arnstein's ladder of participation not at the level of the state but in terms of challenging class, patriarchy, and other forms of hierarchy and discrimination in the everyday lives of victims. It implies that participation is inherently political because it is intimately concerned with power relations, not just a politics of the state but a politics in all the spaces with which victims' lives intersect. It challenges the construction of victims by rights discourse as a set of individuals, enabling acknowledgement of collective agency and mobilisation as a route to enabling justice. One consequence of this definition is an implicit redefinition of transitional justice as something that can unfold in a range of everyday spaces and social ecologies, rather than consisting solely of processes, whether formal or informal, that seek to address rights violations.

Given the challenges of marginalised victims exercising significant agency individually in any social ecology, mobilisation is seen here as the primary route to their doing so. Collective action is empowering and enables an engagement in a range of social ecologies that can address victims' needs. That engagement, a direct result of mobilisation, is here seen as a particular and important form of participation and one of very few ways in which victims can demonstrate agency. This understanding of collective action as inherently agentic resonates deeply with a *relational autonomy* approach, where agency is understood as socially constituted in social relations, as discussed by Daşlı, with reference to victim mobilisation in Turkey (2024). Daşlı shows that mobilisation on the basis of multiple overlapping identities, which are reinforced and reconstructed in the process, is empowering for victims of disappearance and serves to build informal spaces for justice.

The definition of participation given here echoes the actor-oriented approach of Evrard et al. (Evrard et al. 2021), but here we refer not to transitional justice mechanisms, whether formal or informal, but see participation as being relevant for a range of social ecologies with which families, and victims more generally, can engage. Such an approach also recognises that the vast majority of victims never benefit from a transitional justice process and see any addressing of their needs as actually coming from elsewhere, which is why it is crucial to focus on their capacity to change how they experience victimhood, while acknowledging it as central to their claims making, of the state and others. This represents a contrast to transitional justice approaches which typically appear to seek to end victimhood. This resonates with ideas of a victim-centred process which can be conceptualised as challenging priorities and processes that emerge from liberal state-building approaches by maximising the agency of victims, notably through empowerment and mobilisation.

The data discussed here show that the addressing of the needs of victims can occur in a range of spaces and social ecologies. Indeed, for families of the missing in Nepal, the commitment of the authorities to impunity for conflict-era violations has meant that almost no process of relevance to victims has emerged from the state. However, families of the missing have found that elements of their needs can be addressed elsewhere, through solidarity with families in the same position, through their position as objects of patronage for politicians who seek to be seen rewarding them, through local governments that are beginning to acknowledge and support victims, through humanitarian assistance on the basis of their victimhood, and through memory work in various spaces that delivers recognition. We interpret this by referencing the fact that many scholars and others acknowledge that transitional justice process in practice extends far beyond a definition restricted to state-led approaches, as articulated by the idea of *justice in transition* (Gready and Robins 2014). While there has been a significant engagement with 'informal' process, there is still an excessive focus on 'process', the idea that only something that can be identified and labelled as dedicated to justice, and that is separate from the everyday lives of victims, can be considered as transitional justice. Here, we define transitional justice in a victim-centred way, as a set of practices, mechanisms, and concerns that aim to confront and address past violations of human rights and humanitarian law and their legacies. This lays out a range of spaces and actors that can drive processes that address victim needs, typically not labelled as 'transitional justice', including civil society and – as discussed here – victim organisations. Such an understanding also explicitly frames justice as addressing all rights violations, including the social and economic, as seen in the horizontal inequalities that drove Nepal's conflict – a *transformative justice* (Gready and Robins 2014).

Such an understanding of justice in transition extends the possibilities for victim participation, because many of these spaces and actions offer far greater potential for the agency of victims than formal state process, particularly where – as in Nepal – the authorities have enshrined impunity.

## 12.4 VICTIMS AS JUSTICE ACTORS: A CRITICAL VICTIMOLOGY

Victims are defined as such by what has been done to them, and passivity remains a dominant characteristic assigned to them: positivist victimology denies the victim as an actor and makes invisible the many other identities and relationships a victim has (Walklate 2012). The overall impact of these approaches to victimhood in transitional justice is to superficially depoliticise it, to distance the fact of a violation from the identity of the victim that motivated the state to commit the violation, while participation *repoliticises* such discourse.

The conceptual framework with which this chapter seeks to interrogate this potential dual identity – as both victims and activists – is that of *critical victimology* (Mawby and Walklate 1994), which understands victims as sovereigns rather than subjects (Hoondert et al. 2019). In contrast to positivist victimology, an interactionist perspective understands 'victim' as a social role and seeks to interrogate the processes by which such groups are defined as victims, perceiving the assigning of victimhood as subject to questions of power and authority. A critical approach acknowledges that victims are also agents and allows the victim identity to not exclude – and even be defined by – ongoing collective action by groups of victims.

Transitional justice demands that victims *perform* victimhood, emphasising as it does institutional stages where victim testimony both fuels and legitimates a process. Victims are, however, much less visibly also performing victimhood in the communities and societies in which they live: acknowledging this reframes the question one asks of a victim from 'what happened to you', emphasising the victim as passive, to 'what do you do in the light of what happened', emphasising agency, coping, and politics. While transitional justice seeks to leave victimhood behind, as seen in the effort to relabel victims as 'survivors', on the understanding that this enhances agency, victims seek rather to give meaning to victimhood and use their status as a platform to make claims that can drive change in their lives.

Data are presented from Nepal concerning a victims' movement that grew directly from victims' frustration at the absence of formal processes to address their needs and the broader lack of agency they had in efforts to address their victimhood, and that was ultimately able to force victims to be heard. It is presented as a case study of participation in transitional justice, where both participation and justice are understood in novel and transformative ways.

## 12.5 VICTIM MOBILISATION AS A DRIVER OF SOCIAL CHANGE

In a context such as Nepal, victims' groups at the local level do not form from a desire to impact a transitional justice process; indeed, research in Nepal shows that prior to their mobilisation, most victims were unaware of the concept (Robins 2013). Victims come together to address their immediate needs: to express solidarity and to create structures that can offer emotional, psychological, and social support, as well as to advocate for action to address the impacts of violations.

The first such group in Nepal – beyond the confines of the Maoist movement – was the Conflict Victims' Committee (CVC) established in 2006 in Bardiya, the district most affected by disappearances, where an indigenous ethnic group was targeted by the state (OHCHR 2008). CVC was initiated by a schoolteacher whose father, an indigenous land rights' activist, had been disappeared by the army. Similar groups were established elsewhere, largely in more remote and rural districts, where the conflict had been fiercest, and where the success of Maoist mobilisation during the conflict reflected poverty and exclusion. Even as local groups, divorced from national debates and initially unaware of the concept of transitional justice, victims' organisations were able to advance the interests of their members, mobilising them to ultimately become a driving force in the national transitional justice processes.

### 12.5.1 *The Home and Community as Sites of Empowerment*

The lens of ambiguous loss (Boss 2009) permits an understanding of the impact of having a missing relative and can guide approaches to support families. Boss has suggested that effective therapeutic approaches, such as narrative therapy, enable those impacted by ambiguous loss to become the privileged authors of their subjectivities (White and Epston 1990). This demonstrates the importance of the agency enabled by participation in a family association and the unique benefits it can have. Robins outlines how family associations enable social engagement and the generation of new discursive imaginaries that can 'both construct ambiguity and mold social relations that can build resilience … in ways that positively influence the well-being of the families of those missing, as well as on the meanings and identities that affected persons construct from them' (2016, 308).

Given that most of the missing are men, women are the most impacted and these impacts intersect with their broader disempowerment. The traditional Nepalese family is patrilocal, with wives moving to their husband's home on marriage, and in the household there are power relationships, dominated by older men and with the younger wives at the bottom of the hierarchy, expected to be subservient to their mother-in-law. Young women are dependent for their status within the family on their husband, or on their children, notably boys. The ambiguity over a woman's marital status and her persistence in wearing the symbols of marriage – for her a statement of hope for her husband's return – permit a perception that the wives of the missing are somehow predatory in their search for a new husband. Within the family, the wife of a man who is missing will often be perceived as seeking an opportunity to leave, typically through elopement with another man. This often leads to the stigmatisation of wives of the disappeared, with a wife trapped within a family that resents her presence but does not want her to leave owing to the social stigma that would result. In the broader community, the perceived reputation of the wives of the disappeared led to extreme problems in some cases, including sexual assault. This most often, however, took the form of community members telling wives they should simply accept that their husbands were dead and abandon the hope – and the search – that for women represent an effort to honour their absent husband.

The importance of mobilisation in response to these challenges emerged clearly. Peer interaction was widely understood as positive; indeed the most discussed positive coping mechanism among women was to share problems with peers, as seen in testimony from victims:

> When I met CVC leaders at the beginning, I met other members from the community and I feel a group spirit to give us a power of togetherness. CVC has helped many members to become active and strong in their communities. If something happens in the village and members face some problem, they have a place to go and report their problems. (Interview with family member, Bardiya, 6 December 2023)

This emphasised the value of a family association, since it solves the major problem of having access to someone who not only understands but also shares your problem. Contact with a family association promotes resilience by validating the status of women as wives of the missing, women without men, but not widows. As such, the efforts of women to assert an identity as the wife of someone missing represents them demonstrating agency over their own identity, precisely echoing how a critical victimology understands agency as changing how victims experience victimhood. This resonates with the understanding from ambiguous loss approaches that living well with ambiguity demands being able to find meaning and identity despite uncertainty. Just as community attitudes, such as the insistence that the missing are dead, represent a denial of both ambiguity and the agency of the closest family members, so mobilisation created spaces where women could define the meanings they give to their situation and their own identity, on their own terms.

In this way participation in the family association allowed women to understand their own reactions to having a missing husband, having a therapeutic impact that represents self-agency, having control of their life, and being responsible for their actions, thoughts, and feelings. More than this, however, it was empowering in creating and validating meanings and identities that they valued, that could then be articulated outside the family association, in homes and communities. As such, mobilisation was crucial to what might be called the micro-mechanics of empowerment.

One demonstration of these impacts was seen in a community where wives of the missing visited the local school as a group to successfully demand that, as victims of the conflict without husbands, they should be given access to reduced school fees for their children, demonstrating, even at the most local level, the power of collective action (Robins 2013). While such local activism, which renegotiated power relations at multiple levels, was possible from the start of such associations, as they grew and built networks between them their access to experience and resources, both technical and financial, enhanced their capacity for such action.

Victim movements and the empowerment participation in them generates, shows them as tools of personal transformation through conscientisation, and there are many cases of the caricature of the passive victim – reinforced by Nepali stereotypes of women and deferential lower castes – being radically altered by engagement with victims' groups. Challenging isolation by networking with other victims and developing solidarities can create meanings that enlarge the lives victims lead, and in turn allow victims to act together in their communities to change how they are perceived and listened to.

> It was only when we met other families of those disappeared, we felt that we had common problems; we knew that we had the same pain. For this reason, we could share our sorrows. We wept and cried together and that helped us ventilate our sorrows. Then we formed this association. It helped us to meet friends having similar problems. Then we organised the sit-ins. As many friends gathered we felt greatly relieved. From that time onward, we felt courageous to fight for our cause. (Wife of missing man, Kathmandu, quoted in Robins and Bhandari 2012)

This represents the most explicit demonstration of the impacts of mobilisation and explains why, for example, women from the most marginalised communities are able as a result of being a part of a victims' association, to make demands of their traditional superiors, whether mothers-in-law, community leaders, or national politicians.

### 12.5.2 *Victim Movements as Collective Participation*

Victims' groups represent an alternative form of action to that of the human rights NGO, not only in the sense of having a constituency beyond donors and seeking to be representative of those for whom they act, but also in the forms of action in which they engage. As social movements they are identity-based, serving as a source of solidarity among victims with the capacity to create as well as mobilise a victim community, redefining understandings of who is a victim and shaping victim identity. The movement of families of the missing in Nepal has helped to assert the identity of the families of the missing as such, representing the first step in their action having a political salience, and to assuming a political role.

As identity-based movements, however, associations of families of the missing necessarily engage with the complexity of identities people bring to them, and the politics that accompany those identities. This has meant in Nepal that such movements cannot ignore marginality arising from gender, caste, and ethnicity, as rights NGOs in the country who work on transitional justice typically do. Rights NGOs have articulated an agenda focused narrowly on truth and prosecutions, largely ignoring victim communities' demands both for social transformation that challenges their exclusion and for short-term livelihood support. As such, NGO action has been characterised as advancing a liberal politics that reflects global transitional justice practice and centres elite actors in the capital, rather than the demands of victims (Robins 2012).

The impacts experienced by wives of the missing in rural Nepal discussed earlier are necessarily intersectional, with many of the priorities that victims articulate being linked to social and economic exclusions that heighten the impacts of missing a husband or son. The nature of victim participation when it is instantiated in a highly local, and locally owned, praxis such as that of a family association, is not as a victim of violence with a unique and particular experience, but rather as someone who is part of a collective and whose victimhood is a direct consequence of that shared identity. In this sense, victimhood itself is a layered experience reflecting the multiple and dynamic identities – many of them driving disadvantage and vulnerability – that the families articulate. While they are victims of enforced disappearance, they are victims of much else, and their participation will always reference that broader experience.

As a result, while the original victims' groups were firmly rooted in political attachment to one or other side of the conflict, the victims' movement has successfully challenged this polarisation and enabled a cross-cutting victim identity that carries a different political salience. This represents victims finding routes to agency beyond those traditionally privileged in Nepal, such as formal political parties, and has seen activists long committed to the Maoist Party, and whose allegiance had been reinforced by the sacrifice of loved ones to that cause, become activist victims, as critical of Maoist politicians as of those actors who disappeared their family members. This highlights one long neglected aspect of the Nepalese victim movement: its role as a peacebuilder (Robins and Stockwell 2024), challenging identities that use victimhood to reinforce the divisions of conflict through the creation of a new victim identity that campaigns to address the needs of all victims.

In Nepal, however, this radical democratic practice has faced challenges in generalising the model to the national level, with the rural women who are over-represented among the families of the missing unable to play a full role in the movement through poverty and a need to work, through deference to the idea of always having been spoken for, or simply because they live too far from the capital and regional centres to engage fully with the movement. The flat structure of the victims' movement can work at a local level where members are in constant contact. However, a national presence demands a process of representation, and while this is done democratically through elections at multiple levels and regional meetings, this represents the limits of the agency of the typical female, rural, and poor victim. Inevitably, the traditional power relations that define who has access to education, even who can speak Nepali, assert themselves in who leads the national movement.

### 12.5.3 *Victim Movements and Local Governance*

Understanding participation as agency also sheds light on how victims of rights violations become political actors. Mobilisation allows local family associations to emphasise their role as political actors by engaging, beyond the informal, with formal governance structures. In an environment where central authorities have institutionalised impunity, there remains the possibility of an engagement with local government. Decentralisation of governance as a part of the peace agreement led to the creation of local governments in seven provinces and 753 local municipalities. This has enhanced both the representation of the minorities who suffered most in the conflict in governance and the responsiveness of these authorities to their constituents. While both accountability and a comprehensive search for the missing are beyond the remit of local government, such an engagement – between families and the new decentralised authorities – has the potential to advance local democracy by integrating local actors, including victims and survivors, into political processes, and in particular in driving memory work. The presence of family associations in communities, as visible and important social actors, has led in some municipalities to their building relationships, and advocating, with local government. In particular, they have pushed these authorities to engage in memorialisation activities that address needs of both victims and communities.

In Barbardiya Municipality, in Bardiya district, where CVC has been active, the families of the disappeared and martyrs formed a local coordination group led by victims' families, and local government provided them with a formal space to come together and develop victim-centred policies towards memorialisation and other support initiatives in their context. The Kumbher Adda Memorial Park has been created, with the names of the missing written on a 'memory pillar' in the park. Additionally, a local road has been named after Sagunlal Chaudhary, a local school principal who was disappeared by the military. The municipal council also developed a policy to educate a new generation about the history of past atrocities, implementing a new curriculum in local schools for grades five, six, and seven (ages ten to twelve years), including in textbooks consideration of the contribution of martyrs, the disappeared and injured from the conflict. Victims saw this engagement as an extension of the empowerment of mobilisation: 'Family members can organise local activities and have influence in communities and in politics. We realised that we feel empowered now and there is access to local government and administration due to our group identity as CVC. CVC has both advanced local peace and is advancing access to government structures' (Family member, Bardiya, 7 December 2023).

In Marsyangdi Rural Municipality in Lamjung district, in the central west of Nepal in the mid-hills, families of victims have organised, evolving into a strong victim-led group working with both political actors and local government to develop formal policies and advance memory work in the municipality. Following three years of engagement, the Municipal Assembly in 2020 adopted a policy on memorialisation that created a Memory Study Centre, led by victims and funded by the municipality, with the Centre disseminating the narratives of victim families through publishing memoirs, organising public events, and launching a memory hall in the name of victims, as well as making a public commemoration in collaboration with the local authorities.

These interventions are transformative for families of the missing, in acknowledging them and their experience and integrating them both socially and politically. More than this, however, they are also transformative more broadly since they allow the sharing and sanctioning of local narratives that remember the conflict in terms of the excluded and marginalised groups that it often targeted. In Bardiya, for example, the new curriculum allows local government to recognise the long exclusion, socially, politically, and economically of the majority Tharu Indigenous group in the district, and catalyse efforts to address this.

It should be noted that this engagement is as much social as political: victim associations are highly respected in their communities, and the memory initiatives they are advancing are welcomed not only by communities, who see them as addressing legacies of past violence – both structural and physical – but by all sides of the political spectrum. This represents the integration of victims and their narratives into broader social frameworks, with families of the missing becoming actors who can impact their society and community.

## 12.6 CONCLUSION: TRANSFORMATIVE PARTICIPATION IN TRANSITIONAL JUSTICE

We have here conceptualised victim participation in transitional justice in terms of enabling the agency of victims and empowering them to both address their needs in everyday spaces and become political actors through their collective mobilisation. We can seek to revisit the four issues this chapter set out to interrogate, namely: the lack of concrete benefits for victims from formal transitional justice processes, the renegotiation of how victimhood is experienced, the extent to which victims are able to shape agendas that impact them through collective action, and the extent to which such participation can be understood as a form of agency.

It is seen, first, that victims have indeed seen no benefits from a transitional justice process that remains stalled owing to a lack of political will, but that, second, victims can begin to address needs in their own communities and shape their experience of victimhood through mobilisation. The value of a victims' group is that it represents a social ecology of peers that can provide both support and a platform for broader empowerment in other environments, articulating a critical victimology that acknowledges victims as actors. Such an approach recognises victimhood as social and cultural practice and both redefines transitional justice beyond dedicated 'process', as a practice that is social, cultural, and political, and inherently relational, rather than primarily legal.

Third, mobilisation represents a form of participation in transitional justice (and a repoliticisation of it) that most ensures the agency of victims to drive transformative change in their lives, articulating a victim politics at multiple levels. Such movements perceive the communities in which they live as sites of action where they can drive change in their daily lives and prioritise action to address the social and economic rights violations of marginalisation, as well as provide a framework for representative action at the national level. While this chapter does not focus on the national impact of the victim movement, it has been hugely successful in mobilising tens of thousands of people, often the poorest and most marginalised, to register their cases with the transitional justice commissions, despite the United Nations, international NGOs, and national civil society urging a boycott (Billingsley 2019).

Finally, victims' movements challenge what participation means in transitional justice, with family associations representing decentralised approaches to addressing the impacts of victimhood in their communities. The victims' movement has both leveraged and remade the identity of 'victim', from a term indicating passivity and subjection to one that serves as a basis to create solidarities and support claims-making. In a field where the meaning of victim agency remains unclear, victims' groups as local and accessible vehicles for victim agendas represent one route to the empowerment of victims to drive change at a local level that addresses their needs. Defining such participation, in any relevant space, as agency can serve to operationalise 'victim-centred' approaches to transitional justice, and emphasises that engagement must be on victims' terms if it is to resonate with an addressing of their needs.

These approaches have broader implications for the practice of transitional justice. Victims' organisations, as an articulation of agency, challenge the individualisation of victims that underlies liberal rights practice. Victims' movements are an alternative to NGO and advocacy-led approaches to addressing histories of violence, and an effort to resist representation, through social movement-style activism and more engaged and confrontational repertoires of action. While the Nepalese victims' movement is not the first to challenge the ideology and politics of the transitional justice 'industry', it represents an example of a sustained thread of victim mobilisation as participation.

## REFERENCES


Arnstein, Sherry R. 1969. 'A Ladder of Citizen Participation'. *Journal of the American Institute of Planners*, 35(4), 216–224.

Asad, Talal. 2014. 'Comments on Conversion'. In *Conversion to Modernities*, edited by Peter van der Veer, pp. 263–273. Routledge.

Baker, Susan, and F. Stuart Chapin. 2018. 'Going beyond "It Depends:" The Role of Context in Shaping Participation in Natural Resource Management'. *Ecology and Society*, 23(1), 1–11.

Billingsley, Krista. 2019. 'Making Them Accountable: Victim-Activists' Critical Engagement with Truth Commissions in Nepal'. *Journal of Human Rights Practice*, 11(1), 190–208.

Boss, Pauline. 2009. *Ambiguous Loss: Learning to Live with Unresolved Grief.* Harvard University Press.

Clark, Janine Natalya, and Michael Ungar, eds. 2021. *Resilience, Adaptive Peacebuilding and Transitional Justice*. Cambridge University Press.

Collins, Kevin, and Ray Ison. 2009. 'Jumping Off Arnstein's Ladder: Social Learning as a New Policy Paradigm for Climate Change Adaptation'. *Environmental Policy and Governance*, 19: 358–373.

Daşlı, Güneş. 2024. 'Victim Agency, Relational Autonomy and Transitional Justice: Experience of Saturday Mothers'. *International Journal of Transitional Justice*. https://doi.org/10.1093/ijtj/ijae021

Dyrberg, Torben B. 1997. *The Circular Structure of Power: Politics, Identity, Community*. Verso.

Evrard, Elke, Gretel Mejía Bonifazi, and Tine Destrooper. 2021. 'The Meaning of Participation in Transitional Justice: A Conceptual Proposal for Empirical Analysis'. *International Journal of Transitional Justice*, 15(2), 428–447.

Gready, Paul, and Simon Robins. 2014. 'From Transitional to Transformative Justice: A New Agenda for Practice'. *International Journal of Transitional Justice*, 8(3), 339–361.

Gready, Paul, and Simon Robins. 2017. 'Rethinking Civil Society and Transitional Justice: Lessons from Social Movements and 'New' Civil Society'. *The International Journal of Human Rights*, 21(7), 956–975.

Hoondert, Martin J., Paul Mutsaers, and William R. Arfman, eds. 2019. *Cultural Practices of Victimhood.* Routledge.

Krystalli, Roxani, and Philipp Schulz. 2022. 'Taking Love and Care Seriously: An Emergent Research Agenda for Remaking Worlds in the Wake of Violence'. *International Studies Review*, 24(1), 1–25.

Mawby, R. I., and Sandra Walklate. 1994. 'Perspectives on Victimology'. In *Critical Victimology: International Perspectives*, edited by R. I. Mawby and Sandra Walklate, pp. 7–22. Sage.

Nassar, Habib. 2022. 'Justice as Resistance: How Post-Arab Spring Experiences Are Reshaping the Global Transitional Justice Landscape'. *International Journal of Transitional Justice*, 16(2), 181–186.

OHCHR (Office of the United Nations High Commissioner for Human Rights). 2008. *Conflict-Related Disappearances in Bardiya District*. OHCHR.

Robins, Simon. 2011. 'Towards Victim-Centred Transitional Justice: Understanding the Needs of Families of the Disappeared in Postconflict Nepal'. *International Journal of Transitional Justice*, 5(1), 75–98.

Robins, Simon. 2012. 'Transitional Justice as an Elite Discourse: Human Rights Practice Where the Global Meets the Local in Post-Conflict Nepal'. *Critical Asian Studies*, 44(1), 3–30.

Robins, Simon. 2013. *Families of the Missing: A Test for Contemporary Approaches to Transitional Justice*. Routledge.

Robins, Simon. 2016. 'Discursive Approaches to Ambiguous Loss: Theorizing Community-Based Therapy after Enforced Disappearance'. *Journal of Family Theory & Review*, 8(3), 308–323.

Robins, Simon, and Ram Kumar Bhandari. 2012. *From Victims to Actors: Mobilising Victims to Drive Transitional Justice Process*. NEFAD.

Robins, Simon, and Jill Stockwell. 2024. 'Addressing Missing Persons Arising from Armed Conflict as a Driver of Peace: Towards a Research Agenda'. *International Review of the Red Cross*, 927, 1–24.

Tamayo Gomez, Camilo. 2021. 'Victims' Communities as Knowledge Producers in Transitional Justice Processes'. In *The Routledge International Handbook of Public Sociology*, edited by Leslie Hossfeld, E. Brooke Kelly, and Cassius Hossfeld, pp. 287–300. Routledge.

Tamayo Gomez, Camilo. 2022. 'Recognition as Transitional Justice "From Below": Analysing Victims' Grassroots Activism in Postconflict Colombia'. *International Journal of Transitional Justice*, 16(3), 314–330.

Taylor, David. 2014. 'Victim Participation in Transitional Justice Mechanisms: Real Power or Empty Ritual'. Impunity Watch 14.

Tsai, Jennifer, and Simon Robins. 2021. Strengthening Participation in Local-Level and National Transitional Justice Processes. Global Initiative for Justice, Truth, and Reconciliation (GIJTR). https://tinyurl.com/2evb6pv6

Walklate, Sandra. 1990. 'Researching Victims of Crime: Critical Victimology'. *Social Justice*, 17(3 41), 25–42.

Walklate, Sandra. 2012. 'Who Is the Victim of Crime? Paying Homage to the Work of Richard Quinney'. *Crime, Media, Culture*, 8(2), 173–184.

White, Michael, and David Epston. 1990. *Narrative Means to Therapeutic Ends*. Norton.

# 13

# Breaking the Mould?

## *Social Movements and the 'Ideal Victim' of Conflict-Related Sexual and Gender-Based Violence in Colombia's Transitional Justice*

*Daniela Suárez Vargas*

### 13.1 INTRODUCTION

Conflict-related sexual and gender-based violence (SGBV) has been a central issue in Colombia's transitional justice process (Céspedes-Báez 2018). Yet the dominant narrative of ideal victimhood – constructed around gendered, racialised, and political stereotypes – has excluded those who do not conform to it. This includes LGBTQI+ people, Indigenous women, Afro-descendant women, and women fighters, limiting their access to truth, justice, and reparations (Weber 2023). This chapter examines how women and LGBTQI+ organisations have contested these narrow narratives, pushing institutions such as the Truth Commission and the Special Jurisdiction for Peace (JEP) to adopt more inclusive, intersectional approaches. This involves recognising the diverse identities and experiences of SGBV victims across gender, racial, ethnic, and political or military affiliation contexts. It also requires rejecting the false dichotomy between victimhood and agency, that is the notion that victims cannot exercise agency or that those who do are not victims, as is often seen in the case of women combatants who experience SGBV.

The mobilisation of women and LGBTQI+ groups in Colombia's transitional justice has not only diversified representations of SGBV victimhood but also influenced institutional framings, ensuring recognition for marginalised and complex victims. While these groups have also fostered alternative, non-institutional spaces for resisting gendered victimhood (Nieto-Valdivieso 2023), this chapter focuses on their engagement within institutional settings. The chapter also looks at the case of Corporación Rosa Blanca, a group of former women fighters of Fuerzas Armadas Revolucionarias de Colombia (FARC) who suffered gender-based violence within the guerrilla group. Unlike other groups of victims and women fighters, they have chosen to present themselves as 'ideal victims' to achieve greater visibility and legitimation.

The chapter contributes to transitional justice debates on victimhood and social movements in two key ways. First, it critiques how transitional justice mechanisms often privilege 'ideal victims' of SGBV – those perceived as innocent and aligned with cisheteronormative and racial stereotypes – while further marginalising those that do not fit this mould. Second, it highlights the role of social movements in reshaping transitional justice from below in Colombia, demonstrating how victim-led advocacy and participative transitional justice can redefine institutional framings, introducing more complex narratives of victimhood. This resonates with debates on a victim-centred and bottom-up approach to transitional justice, which emphasise the inclusion of traditionally marginalised groups – such as victims themselves – in shaping the frameworks, policies, and narratives of transitional justice institutions (Lundy and McGovern 2008; UN Secretary General 2023). The goal of these approaches is to prevent decision-making in transitional justice from becoming a top-down institutional imposition detached from victims' lived realities, identities, and needs (Robins 2011).

Section 13.2 reviews briefly literature on the politics of victimhood in transitional justice. Section 13.3 explores the politics of victimhood in Colombia, including its gendered aspect. Section 13.4 outlines the evolution of victims' engagement in Colombian transitional justice. Section 13.5 examines how women and LGBTQI+ organisations have challenged the 'ideal victim' of SGBV to gain recognition in the Truth Commission and the JEP. Section 13.6 examines the contrasting case of Corporación Rosa Blanca.

## 13.2 THE POLITICS OF VICTIMHOOD IN TRANSITIONAL JUSTICE

Victim movements around the world have shifted the role of victims from passive bystanders to central players in transitional justice (Méndez 2016). Victim-centredness in transitional justice implies guaranteeing their active participation and consultation in the design, development, and implementation of justice, truth, and reparation measures (UN Secretary General 2023). While the alleged benefits of victim participation in institutional transitional justice processes are manifold, meaningful forms of participation are often difficult to attain owing to logistical constraints, token inclusion of victims, and biases about 'ideal victimhood' (Moffett 2023). Victimhood is often assumed to be a neutral and apolitical claim (Jeffery and Candea 2006). However, the concept of 'victim' is not uncontentious; it is a social construct shaped by the subjective values, beliefs, and rhetoric of different social groups (Walklate 2007). Being recognised as a 'victim' is a powerful rhetorical tool that legitimises certain individuals and experiences in transitional justice settings, granting access to fundamental rights as citizens (Weber 2023). The term 'victim' creates a moral binary, positioning victims as 'innocent' and 'passive' against wholly 'culpable' perpetrators (McEvoy and McConnachie 2012). In conflict settings, the 'ideal victim' archetype, typically associated with blameless civilian women or children, receives greater moral legitimacy and easier access to justice (Christe 2018; Moffett 2023). This construct serves as both a moral condemnation of suffering and a tool for political prioritisation, enabling victimhood hierarchies (Madlingozi 2008). While 'ideal victims' receive institutional support, 'troublesome' victims – those challenging gender, racial or political norms – face marginalisation (Krystalli 2024; Lawther 2025). Considering this framework, we now explore the politics of victimhood in Colombia.

## 13.3 THE POLITICS OF VICTIMHOOD IN COLOMBIA

### 13.3.1 *Who Is a Victim of the Conflict?*

Conflict-related victimhood is highly contested in Colombia. Victims' groups, the state, and armed actors hold differing views on the conflict, the scale of suffering, and questions of innocence or guilt, making it difficult to establish a single narrative of victimhood (Schmidt 2023). In 2011, the Colombian government sought to address this issue through the Victims' Law, defining victims in abstract legal terms. Drawing on the United Nations (UN) Basic Principles on the Right to Reparations (United Nations 2006), the law defines a victim as any individual or collective that suffered harm during the conflict (Victims Law, 2011c, Art. 3). Despite its apparent neutral definition, legislative debates in Congress reveal that the concept of 'victim' was shaped by the political and personal interests of legislators, with some using their privileged positions to influence the definition based on their own experiences of victimisation during the conflict. This marginalised the narratives of rural victims and other disadvantaged communities, prioritising the perspectives of social and political elites, particularly from major cities (Foringer 2023).

Similarly, right-wing legislators used their partisan identities to promote a restrictive notion of the 'ideal victim' tied to the concept of the 'good Colombian', in other words a law-abiding citizen (Bolaño-Pérez 2021). This framing was aimed to exclude victims of the state, who, in the accounts of right-wing legislators, were responsible for their own victimisation owing to their opposition and resistance to the established order (Roche 2022). While some victims were invited to participate in these debates, Congress did not meaningfully engage with them during the Victims Law drafting process (MOVICE 2011). Their interventions were treated solely as factual accounts to reconstruct the attack. However, victims' interpretations, identities, and their broader social, political, economic, ethnic, or gender contexts were not considered valuable in shaping deliberations (Tapia Navarro 2019). As a result, these nuances were overlooked in the official definition of 'victim'. Article 3 of the Victims' Law imposes three controversial restrictions on the definition. First, it only covers victims of incidents occurring after 1985, limiting earlier victims to symbolic reparations (Congress of Colombia, 2010, 2011a). Second, it excludes victims of criminal gangs (Congress of Colombia, 2010), despite the violence of such groups often fuelling the conflict. Third, it denies victim status to combatants, reinforcing their stigmatisation as 'evil perpetrators', except for child soldiers who demobilised before legal age, as they are framed as 'innocent victims' (Congress of Colombia, 2011b).

Following the law's adoption, victim groups filed constitutional actions against the law's definition of victim. They argued that this definition results in discriminatory treatment by excluding certain victims from reparations and humanitarian aid through arbitrary distinctions (Colombian Constitutional Court 2012, 11–16). However, the Constitutional Court rejected this claim, stating the Victims' Law doesn't define who is a 'real victim' of the conflict but selects which ones deserve access to the measures contemplated in it (2012, 59). The Court deemed victims' prioritisation necessary for the law's operability, favouring those victims who acted within the rule of law (2012, 66–75). In this sense, the Court seems to endorse a hierarchy of victimhood that privileges those perceived as legally compliant and innocent in the conflict. The drafting and constitutional review of the Victims' Law reveal how state bodies imposed a hegemonic narrative of victimhood, equating the 'ideal victim' with the 'good Colombian'. As a result, victims who challenged the status quo were marginalised. This framing forces victims who do not clearly fit the labels of 'ideal victim'/'good Colombian' to prove their 'good character' to gain legal recognition and access the benefits that this status entails.

### 13.3.2 *Gendered Victimhood: The 'Ideal Victim' of SGBV*

Victimhood in Colombia is also shaped by gender stereotypes, particularly in conflict-related SGBV. The legal system positions the heterosexual, cisgender civilian woman as the 'ideal victim' of this violence (Céspedes-Báez 2018; Sanchez Parra 2023). This essentialist approach restricts women's agency – whether individual, political, or armed – and overlooks their diverse roles in conflict. Rodriguez-Castro (2021a) further highlights the racialised framing of SGBV victimhood, which portrays Indigenous and Afro-descendant women as particularly vulnerable owing to their 'lack of education' or their 'backward' communities. This is evident in Ruling AU-092/08, in which the Constitutional Court argued that these women are more easily manipulated by armed actors into sexual relations (Colombian Constitutional Court 2008, sec. III.1.9). Such generalised portrayals emphasise their supposed 'gullibility', stripping them of agency and justifying paternalistic state interventions (Rodríguez Castro 2021a).

Another example of gendered victimhood is found in the rulings of the Justice and Peace Tribunal, established in 2005 following the peace process with Autodefensas Unidas de Colombia. Coral-Diaz (2017) explains that the top-down, adversarial system in these tribunals limited women's participation in SGBV cases, often forcing their testimonies to fit hegemonic gendered narratives of civilian women as 'ideal victims', thus preventing full contextualisation of their stories. In cases of SGBV against women fighters, the Justice and Peace Tribunal denied them victim status unless the women were minors at the time of demobilisation (Justice and Peace Tribunal 2011, paras 805–810; 2015, 225). The tribunal resorted to stereotypes of 'innocence' to recognise girl soldiers as victims, arguing that their incorporation into armed groups was due to their 'psychological and emotional immaturity, as well as their ignorance of war' (Justice and Peace Tribunal 2011, para. 621). The reliance on infantilising narratives exhibits how victim recognition, particularly in cases of SGBV, remains tied to perceived defencelessness and lack of agency.

Furthermore, the tribunal argued that girl soldiers were more susceptible to SGBV owing to their gender, and that their victimisation was worsened by a hostile environment that compelled them to adopt masculine values (Justice and Peace Tribunal 2011, paras 807–811). This reasoning relied on reductionist portrayals of SGBV victimhood, framing the victimisation of girl soldiers as more significant because it occurs in a setting that forces them to transgress traditional female roles. Likewise, by asserting that girls suffer more in forced recruitment owing to their gender and experiences of SGBV, the tribunal created a hierarchy that implicitly downplays the suffering of boy soldiers. It wrongly suggests that the harm they endure, including SGBV, is less serious simply because they are men. Such framing is potentially linked to cultural constructs of warrior masculinity, where men's suffering in wartime is often normalised and seen as an expected part of their role as warriors (Truth Commission 2022b). Moreover, drawing on the 2011 Victims Law, the Justice and Peace Tribunals have denied victim status to girl soldiers who suffered SGBV and did not demobilise after turning eighteen, arguing that their involvement in illegal activities undermines their legitimacy to access reparations through this judicial proceeding (Justice and Peace Tribunal 2015, 315–319). For the tribunal, by choosing to remain in the armed group as adults, these women exposed themselves to a foreseeable risk, which disqualifies them from victim status (Justice and Peace Tribunal 2015, 318). This approach places the blame for their victimisation on women fighters, as their decision to stay in the illegal armed group departs from the expectations of a 'good woman' and an 'ideal victim' in Colombia.

In 2019, the Constitutional Court reviewed the exclusion of women fighters who suffered SGBV in illegal armed groups from victim status in the Helena case. This landmark decision recognised them as victims under the Victims' Law and critiqued institutions such as the Victims Unit for revictimising them for transgressing accepted gender norms (Colombian Constitutional Court 2019, 60–67). Despite progress in incorporating a gender perspective in examining this type of cases, it is striking that the Court relied on Helena's forced recruitment as a girl to grant her innocence and legitimise her victimhood. The tribunal could have recognised her victim status based on her specific experience, but the lack of qualification reinforces the assumption that all women fighters were coerced into joining armed groups, overlooking their agency. In fact, many joined out of self-interest, for political reasons, to escape domestic or sexual violence, or to improve their social or economic positions (Anctil Avoine 2024). Furthermore, it perpetuates the idea that a woman fighter must prove she did not choose to be a 'bad woman' to be recognised as a legitimate victim by the legal system.

Associating women with gendered, infantilised, and racialised interpretations of victimhood creates a hierarchy in the recognition of SGBV experiences. Those who don't conform to the 'ideal victim' – such as men, LGBTQI+ individuals, or women fighters – risk being excluded from legal and political recognition as legitimate victims in Colombia. The failure to acknowledge diverse victim identities not only discourages participation in transitional justice processes (Gilmore et al. 2020), but also reinforces gender, racial, and socio-political stereotypes in wartime. Furthermore, hierarchising victimhood may politicise SGBV experiences, perpetuating societal divisions based on gender, race, and socio-political status that favour certain political agendas in the transitional justice process, while discarding or invalidating others. Another risk is the pressure on women victims to 'whitewash' their identities, downplaying their agency to align their experiences with the 'ideal victim' narrative imposed by public institutions, which, in turn, enables them access to resources, services, and support networks (Krystalli 2024; Weber 2023).

## 13.4 ENGAGEMENT OF VICTIMS' MOVEMENTS IN COLOMBIAN TRANSITIONAL JUSTICE

Hegemonic narratives of victimhood have not stopped victims' movements from serving as bottom-up agents for democratisation in Colombian transitional justice. Institutional spaces of transitional justice have been largely controlled by state actors, leaders of illegal armed groups, international organisations, and urban and international non-governmental organisations (Diaz 2010). Some government officials have gone so far as to dismiss victims' groups as 'too radical' owing to their political views, perceiving them as uncommitted to reconciliation (García-Godos and Lid 2010, 495). This perception has often been used as a pretext to avoid collaborating or engaging with these groups. In response to this, victims' movements have used social, political, and legal activism to countering their exclusion, invisibility, or limited involvement in institutional settings. Through their mobilisation, victims have resisted the power of the state and illegal armed groups over their territories, bodies, identities, and narratives (Delgado Barón 2011). Victims' movements have been vocal in expressing their views and criticisms of the institutional processes of truth, justice, and reparation promoted by the Colombian state. Notable examples include their disapproval of the peace process with paramilitary groups (2002–2006). Organisations such as MOVICE criticised the process for lacking genuineness to ensure justice and accountability for the crimes committed by paramilitary groups. They also argued that the state's approach failed to provide a transformative transition of the conflict and excluded recognition of victims of state violence (Diaz 2010). Similarly, as noted earlier, MOVICE strongly criticised the drafting process of the Victims' Law (2010–2011), condemning the lack of meaningful consultation with victims. This omission resulted in an overly restrictive legal definition of victims of the conflict.

In this sense, the peace process between the Colombian government and the FARC (2012–2016) marked a significant change in the inclusion of victims in transitional justice. Responding to victims' demands and seeking broader national and international support, the government and the FARC agreed to include victims in the peace negotiations (Government of Colombia and FARC-EP 2014). Victims participated in regional consultative forums to provide feedback on key aspects of the Agreement, including the one on justice (High Commissioner for Peace of Colombia 2018). Likewise, since 2014, victims' delegations participated in the Havana negotiations, presenting proposals for the design of the comprehensive truth, justice, and reparation system (Brett 2022). Although the delegations did not represent all conflict victims, they reflected the diversity of victim identities. Their participation helped break the silence and denial surrounding marginalised groups, including peasants, women, LGBTQI+ individuals, trade unionists, human rights defenders, and child soldiers (Brett 2022). Their inclusion challenges hegemonic and homogenising narratives of victimhood, by making visible the complex and varied identities of those affected by the Colombian conflict. Furthermore, many victims felt that being heard in the negotiations provided them with a sense of legitimisation and vindication of their status as victims (Brett 2022).

The participation of victims in the peace process, however, was often characterised by controversy and politicisation. On the one hand, including certain victims' groups sparked competing narratives of victimhood, as each group sought greater prominence in the negotiations. For instance, some victims of the FARC, particularly former state agents, prominent political leaders, and those aligned with the conservative right, felt overshadowed by victims of the state and 'leftist' victims' groups (León and Bermúdez Liévano 2014). On the other hand, opponents of the peace process actively sought to spoil it by promoting divisive narratives that distinguished between 'good victims' and FARC members. A notable example occurred in August 2014, when right-wing congresswoman María Fernanda Cabal posted a photo on X of Ángela Giraldo (a victim of the FARC serving as a delegate in the peace talks) greeting a man she falsely identified as a FARC member. Cabal implied that Giraldo's apparent sympathy for the FARC contradicted her status as a victim (Semana 2014). Such rhetoric reinforces a rigid dichotomy between victims and perpetrators, where any perceived rapprochement with aggressors calls into question a victim's authenticity. This not only perpetuates division but also stifles reconciliation by discouraging dialogue and revictimising those who engage with former perpetrators.

The main outcome of victim participation in the peace negotiations was the incorporation of a victim-centred approach into the Peace Agreement. This ensures that any decision, policy, or action by the transitional justice institutions established under the Agreement affecting victims must include their direct and meaningful involvement (Colombian Congress 2017, Articles 5 and 12). This approach enables the JEP, the Unit for the Search for Disappeared Persons, and the Truth Commission to provide normative frameworks and spaces for victims to influence their work. For example, the Truth Commission worked with over 30,000 victims and received more than 1,000 reports from victims representing diverse social, political, gender, ethnic, and racial backgrounds (Truth Commission 2022a). This inclusivity was crucial for incorporating, recognising, and dignifying the diverse identities and experiences of harm endured by victims in its final report.

In the JEP, victims' movements are active parties to the judicial process with a wide range of procedural rights (Colombian Congress, 2019, Articles 15 and 17). They have appropriated the legal tools provided by the JEP. This empowerment has been key in the opening of the eleven macro-cases currently under investigation (JEP 2022). Through their reports, interventions in hearings, and participation in extra-judicial spaces, the victims have influenced the adoption of intersectional and more inclusive criteria to open and prioritise cases that reflect their realities (Suárez Vargas 2024). The macro-case on SGBV, for example, was opened thanks to the activism of women's and LGBTQI+ organisations, despite resistance from some JEP officials and FARC leaders (Castrillón Palacio 2023). This highlights the persistence and influence of victims within the JEP, as they overcome institutional opposition to ensure their interests are upheld. As will be seen in the following sections, the activism of victims' movements in transitional justice following the 2016 Peace Agreement has also been instrumental in pointing out that SGBV is a complex experience that intersects with other structural factors of marginalisation, which implies that SGBV victimhood cannot be homogenised through essentialist narratives.

## 13.5 RESISTING THE 'IDEAL VICTIM' OF SGBV

Women's and LGBTQI+ movements have been key in reframing victimhood for SGBV in Colombia. Initially excluded from the peace negotiations with the FARC in 2012, collectives such as Sisma Mujer, Ruta Pacífica de las Mujeres, Colombia Diversa, and Caribe Afirmativo united to promote a gender focus on transitional justice, seeking to prioritise SGBV without downplaying the political agency of women and LGBTQI+ victims (Mujeres por la Paz 2012). Their push led to the creation of the Gender Sub-Commission in 2014, a technical body dedicated to integrating gender perspectives into the Peace Agreement and engaging with these collectives to incorporate their recommendations on the matter (Fernández-Matos and González-Martínez 2019).

During this time, collectives such as Colombia Diversa stressed that the gender perspective should extend beyond heterosexual and cisgender women (Maier 2020). They emphasised the importance of recognising, for the first time in a peace process, the SGBV and victimhood of LGBTQI+ people in the armed conflict (Maier 2020). These collectives stressed that their victimisation was historically dismissed, further reinforcing their second-class citizenship (Serrano Amaya 2023). They therefore urged the negotiating parties to identify the institutional structures that perpetuate and conceal this violence, as well as to dismantle narratives that uphold discriminatory gender orders against LGBTQI+ victims (Maier 2020). While many proposals from women's and LGBTQI+ groups were included in the Peace Agreement (Serrano Amaya 2023), evangelical and Catholic movements, along with parties such as the Democratic Centre, opposed the gender focus during the 2016 plebiscite. Campaigning against the agreement, they accused it of promoting a 'gender ideology' that threatened traditional values (Corredor 2021). This resulted in a watering down of the gender perspective during the renegotiation of the Agreement (Céspedes-Báez 2017). Thus, despite the efforts of social movements for a broader definition of victimhood for SGBV, the Final Agreement adopted a narrow view, framing once again civilian, cisgender, heterosexual women as the 'ideal victims' of SGBV (Government of Colombia and FARC-EP 2016, 79, 144, and 193).

Grassroots collectives such as Red de Mujeres del Caribe and Matamba y Guasá also criticised the gender perspective adopted in the Peace Agreement, arguing that it was largely shaped by the views of urban Colombian and international elites, which they felt were disconnected from the realities of rural and ethnic women (Paarlberg-Kvam 2019; Rodríguez Castro 2021b). They thus advocated for the decolonisation of hegemonic narratives that persist in Colombia's peacebuilding. Grassroots collectives question the homogenisation of women's victimhood during the conflict, arguing that the framing of SGBV draws on colonial conceptions that reduce the bodies of rural and ethnic women to objects that can be appropriated by men (Rodríguez Castro 2021a). This view obscures the broader impact of the conflict-related SGBV on Indigenous, Afro-Colombian and rural women. It affects not only their physical and emotional well-being but also their connection to their territories, cosmovisions, communities, and families, while undermining their leadership roles (Loperena et al. 2023). Regarding this latter aspect, grassroots collectives criticised that the Agreement juxtaposes the political agency of rural and ethnic women with their victimhood. They insist that recognising their victimhood should not preclude their political and social activism (Zulver 2022). As both victims and political agents, they must be able to challenge oppressive systems without their activism being undermined by societal expectations that victims – especially rural and ethnic women – should not raise their voices (Rodríguez Castro 2021b).

In the current phase of implementation of the Peace Agreement, women's organisations from diverse ethnic, geographical, and political backgrounds, together with LGBTQI+ groups, continue to push transitional justice institutions to broaden the gender perspective and recognise the diverse identities and experiences of SGBV victims. While the Peace Agreement adopted a limited gender focus, the Truth Commission and the JEP have integrated the gender perspective in a comprehensive and intersectional way in their actions (Colombian Congress 2017, art. 8; 2019, art. 18). This has facilitated the active participation of SGBV victims, as well as women's and LGBTQI+ collectives, within these institutions. The ongoing achievements of this advocacy are discussed in Sections 13.5.1 and 13.5.2, as well as how the bottom-up, victim-centred approach of the JEP and the Truth Commission has empowered social and victims' movements, influencing the deconstruction of the prevailing 'ideal victim' in Colombia.

### 13.5.1 *Reshaping Victimhood in the Truth Commission*

Women's organisations (including ethnic and women fighters) and LGBTQI+ organisations engaged with the Gender Working Group of the Truth Commission, presented reports and participated in regional forums to address conflict-related SGBV (Truth Commission 2020). The dialogue facilitated the Commission's adoption of an intersectional approach to SGBV, recognising its diverse forms, causes, and differential impacts on Indigenous and Afro-descendant women, women fighters, and LGBTQI+ people. In its final report, the Truth Commission emphasises the heterogeneous and complex identities of SGBV victims, which cannot be reduced to the figure of the cisgender, heterosexual civilian woman. It emphasises that SGBV victimhood is not uniform, implying the need for tailored processes of truth acknowledgement and reparation that are responsive to victims' diverse contexts (Truth Commission 2022b).

A notable acknowledgement resulting from the dialogue with social movements is the issue of SGBV against women fighters. The Commission notes that their experiences have been ignored and discredited by public institutions, which demonised them for their role in hostilities and disqualified them as 'ideal victims'. The Commission also observes that during the peace negotiations in Havana, some political actors portrayed FARC women exclusively as under-age victims, minimising their political and armed agency (Truth Commission 2022b; 2022c). The Commission thus adopts a more complex view of victimhood, recognising the overlap of victim-combatant identities in women fighters. It also exposes how institutional narratives have re-victimised these women, either by blaming them for transgressing gender and 'ideal victim' stereotypes or by infantilising them to fit the mould of innocent victims.

### 13.5.2 *Reshaping Victimhood in the JEP*

By actively involving social movements and a normative framework favouring a differential approach, the JEP has adopted an intersectional and contextualised approach to SGBV. It has recognised that conflict-related SGBV responds to power dynamics of armed groups, imposing gender roles rooted in patriarchal, heteronormative, and cisnormative values (JEP 2021, paras 624–647). When it comes to women and LGBTQI+ people from ethnic communities, the JEP recognises SGBV not only as a physical attack, but also as an attack on their communities, territories, and leadership roles. It also notes that ethnic and racial discrimination within armed groups and wider society aggravates and normalises SGBV against Indigenous and Afro-descendant people (JEP 2023a, paras 837–843; 2023b, paras 326–328). The JEP's perspective is a nascent but significant step towards contextualising the differential experiences of ethnic groups, who have criticised the lack of public recognition that SGBV against their communities also builds on systemic violence and colonial legacies.

In October 2024, the JEP issued a landmark decision holding senior FARC commanders responsible for SGBV against child soldiers. Here, the JEP acknowledged the significance of social movements and victims' participation, which were fundamental in identifying patterns of violence and contextualising victimhood (JEP 2024, paras 52–56). The JEP adopted a broad vision of child recruitment and SGBV, analysing these events as part of a continuum of violence and socio-economic vulnerability experienced by child soldiers (JEP 2024, paras 699–709). This approach provided an understanding of how the decisions made by children before, during, and after their recruitment were, in some cases, ways of resisting violence or improving their living conditions within the armed group and the conflict. The JEP also took an intersectional approach when examining child recruitment and SGBV, comprehensively examining childhood, gender, and ethnicity. For the tribunal, this approach enables to address 'the complexities of childhood experiences and the stereotypes associated with it' (JEP 2024, para. 23). The JEP concluded that SGBV in the FARC arose from gender hierarchies deeply rooted in the group's military culture, but also noted that these hierarchies alone could not explain the violence. Factors such as rank, family ties to leaders, and the political or educational background of the women fighters all played a role in reducing their vulnerability to SGBV (JEP 2024, paras 632–698).

A highlight of this decision was the recognition, for the first time in Colombia, that LGBTQI+ child soldiers also suffered SGBV, facing discrimination and punishment for their sexual orientation and gender identity (JEP 2024, para. 950). This recognition challenges the heteronormative and cisnormative stereotypes of the 'ideal victim' and fighters. The JEP questioned FARC commanders' claim that banning homosexuality was meant to 'protect' LGBTQI+ individuals, arguing that the fighters' traditional rural values made them unprepared to include them (JEP 2024, paras 955–957). Ironically, this narrative legitimised homophobic and hyper-masculine behaviour within the group instead of preventing it. The JEP clarified that, while its decision focuses on the victimisation of child soldiers, it does not seek to generalise the experience of all women fighters. It recognised that some women did not suffer SGBV and were able to exercise autonomy over their reproductive and sexual decisions (JEP 2024, paras 649 and 689). This approach reflects a commitment to a more nuanced understanding of the experiences of SGBV of girl soldiers, without pretending to universalise their experiences or forcing them to 'whitewash' their agency.

These developments set a positive precedent for the macro-case on SGBV. This macro-case represents one of the most significant achievements of women's and LGBTQI+ groups within the JEP. Their input led the JEP to recognise the justice system's failure to acknowledge diverse SGBV victims (JEP 2023c, paras 116–118). Therefore, the JEP stresses that, in this macro-case, it will reflect the complexities of both of civilians and members of state and non-state armed groups (JEP 2023c, para. 119). This approach represents an important change from the stereotypical and gendered perspectives of 'ideal victimhood'. Furthermore, the work carried out by social movements in other macro-cases lays the foundations for recognising in the future of this macro case a more nuanced and diverse understanding of SGBV, one that considers how factors such as gender, race, social class, and political and military affiliation intertwine with conflict-related SGBV.

## 13.6 CORPORACIÓN ROSA BLANCA: REPRODUCING 'IDEAL VICTIMHOOD'

Just as victim identities cannot be universalised, neither can social movements. While some question the narrative of 'ideal victimhood', organisations such as Rosa Blanca – a collective of FARC women who experienced forced recruitment and SGBV inside the group – have embraced it to gain visibility in Colombia and distance themselves from their past as guerrilla fighters. For them, 'rosa blanca' (white rose in English) symbolises the 'innocence' and 'purity' of FARC women (Corporación Rosa Blanca 2022). To frame their victimhood, Rosa Blanca emphasises the portrayal of FARC women as girls, whose innocence was stolen by the FARC (Corporación Rosa Blanca 2022). The 'ideal victimhood' narrative and the infantilisation of FARC women has been rejected by groups such as Mujeres Farianas. They believe that framing FARC women as victims depoliticises them and minimises their political and armed agency. For them, a FARC woman is a figure of resistance, whose militancy is a source of pride (Schmidt 2023). They claim that being a guerrilla was an emancipatory experience where they found their political voice (Anctil Avoine 2024). For this reason, they criticise Rosa Blanca, accusing them of spreading malicious rumours to discredit the FARC (Ehasz 2020). Likewise, figures such as Victoria Sandino – former FARC commander – question the occurrence of SGBV in FARC, claiming that it was prohibited, and that the abortion policy represented an achievement of insurgent feminism (Saura 2018). These conflicting narratives highlight the difficulty of constructing a unified account of women's experiences in armed groups. While Rosa Blanca presents FARC women as 'ideal victims', other organisations promote a more empowering vision of insurgent womanhood. However, there is concern that this perspective may be used to downplay or deny the victimisation of some FARC women. Differing experiences within the armed group do not negate the occurrence of SGBV. Moreover, fear of challenging the dominant narrative within the FARC and the risk of re-victimisation by former comrades may discourage other victims from speaking out.

Another key difference between Rosa Blanca and other victim groups is their outspoken opposition to the Peace Agreement, which they accuse of whitewashing the FARC's crimes (Corporación Rosa Blanca 2022). Unlike most victim organisations, Rosa Blanca has aligned with political opponents of the agreement, such as Centro Democrático, and federations such as FEVCOL, which represents FARC victims from the country's political, social, and economic elites, including military personnel, legislators, and businesspeople (Centro Democrático 2020; NTN24 2018). This affiliation has helped them gain greater visibility in the media and legitimise their victim status despite their past involvement in the FARC. Rosa Blanca's distrust of the Peace Agreement also led them to reject participation in the Truth Commission, despite the institution's efforts to include them. They argued that its methodology distorted victims' testimonies and changed the traditional narrative on the FARC (Agudelo 2022). Instead, they collaborated with the National Centre for Historical Memory (2019–2022) under Darío Acevedo, a historian aligned with Centro Democrático, resulting in the publication of *Testimonios de la Rosa Blanca*. This report strongly emphasises the 'innocence' of Rosa Blanca's 'girls'. Rosa Blanca's engagement with the JEP has taken a different turn. Despite their initial opposition to the tribunal, in recent years, they have actively participated, submitting reports on forced recruitment and SGBV (JEP 2023c, para. 224; 2024, para. 52). Their participation suggests the JEP's intention to examine diverse perspectives on SGBV victimhood, though the challenge remains in balancing traditional narratives with the demands of other victims advocating for a more progressive understanding of SGBV victimhood.

In sum, Rosa Blanca's case illustrates how victim groups navigate between complex identities and traditional victimhood narratives. By embracing the 'ideal victim' identity, Rosa Blanca members have distanced themselves from the stigma of their past as combatants and gained legitimacy among conservative political actors who push for more traditional notions of victimhood.

## 13.7 CONCLUSION

The chapter explored how social movements influence narratives of conflict-related victimhood in Colombia, focusing on SGBV. In Colombia, there is a hegemonic narrative associated with political, gender, and racial stereotypes, where the civilian, heterosexual, and cisgender woman is seen as the 'ideal victim', excluding non-normative victim identities. Racialised and infantilised representations are also used to confer 'innocence' on certain victims, minimising their agency, as in the case of Indigenous, Afro-descendant, and fighter women. Thus, the activism of LGBTQI+ and diverse women's groups has been key in the 2016 Peace Agreement's implementation, questioning these stereotypes and demanding that institutions such as the Truth Commission and the JEP adopt more inclusive perspectives on victimhood. These efforts have influenced the decisions of these institutions, which have sought to recognise the diversity of victim identities. These achievements may also result from the victim-centred legal framework that facilitates the bottom-up impact of social movements on outcomes of the JEP and the Truth Commission.

## REFERENCES


Agudelo, Oscar Felipe. 2022. '¿Por qué los testimonios de Rosa Blanca no salieron en el informe de la Comisión de la Verdad?' Colombia Check.

Anctil Avoine, Priscyll. 2024. 'Liminal Bodies and Spaces: Farianas' Gendered Contestations in Northeast Colombia'. *Geopolitics*, 29(5), 1659–1693.

Bolaño-Pérez, Laura. 2021. 'Análisis de Los Mecanismos de Desconexión Moral En El Discurso de Álvaro Uribe Vélez'. *Forum. Revista Departamento de Ciencia Política*, 21.

Brett, Roddy. 2022. 'Victim-Centred Peacemaking: The Colombian Experience'. *Journal of Intervention and Statebuilding*, 16(4), 475–497.

Castrillón Palacio, Elisa. 2023. 'Delitos sexuales: la JEP abrirá el caso más difícil de investigar'. *La Silla Vacía*. https://tinyurl.com/2s936t6p/

Centro Democrático. 2020. 'No existen los exvioladores'. Centro Democrático. www.centrodemocratico.com/opinion/no-existen-los-exvioladores_15193

Céspedes-Báez, Lina. 2017. 'En Los Confines de Lo Posible'. In *Utopía u Oportunidad Fallida*, edited by Lina Céspedes-Báez and Enrique Prieto-Ríos, pp. 295–326. Editorial Universidad del Rosario.

Céspedes-Báez, Lina. 2018. 'Creole Radical Feminist Transitional Justice'. In *Truth, Justice and Reconciliation in Colombia*, edited by Fabio Andres Diaz Pabon, pp. 133–152. Routledge.

Christie, Nils. 2018. 'The "Ideal Victim"'. In *Revisiting the 'Ideal Victim': Developments in Critical Victimology*, edited by Marian Duggan, pp. 1–24. Bristol Policy Press.

Colombian Constitutional Court. 2008. Auto 092.

Colombian Constitutional Court. 2012. C-253A/12.

Colombian Constitutional Court. 2019. SU-599/19.

Colombian Congress. 2010. *Gaceta 1004*.

Colombian Congress. 2011a. *Gaceta 98*.

Colombian Congress. 2011b. *Gaceta 253*.

Colombian Congress. 2011c. Victims' Law (Law 1448).

Colombian Congress. 2017. *Decree Law 588*.

Colombian Congress. 2019. *Law 1957*.
Coral-Díaz, Ana Milena. 2017. *Cuerpo femenino en transición*. Editorial Universidad del Rosario.
Corporación Rosa Blanca. 2022. *Testimonios de La Rosa Blanca*. Centro Nacional de Memoria Historica.
Corredor, Elizabeth. 2021. 'On the Strategic Uses of Women's Rights: Backlash, Rights-Based Framing, and Anti-Gender Campaigns in Colombia's 2016 Peace Agreement'. *Latin American Politics and Society*, 63(3), 46–68.
Delgado Barón, Mariana. 2011. 'La Ley de Justicia y Paz en Colombia: La Configuración de un Subcampo Jurídico-Político y las Luchas Simbólicas por la Inclusión'. *Revista de Relaciones Internacionales, Estrategia y Seguridad*, 6(2), 179–194.
Diaz, Catalina. 2010. 'Challenging Impunity from Below: The Contested Ownership of TJ in Colombia'. In *TJ from Below: Grassroots Activism and the Struggle for Change*, edited by Kieran McEvoy and Lorna McGregor, pp. 189–216. Hart.
Ehasz, Ashley. 2020. 'Political Reincorporation of Female FARC-EP Ex-Combatants: The Creation of Victims, Heroes, and Threats'. *Cornell International Affairs Review*, 13(2), 39–93.
Fernández-Matos, Dhayana, and Maria González-Martínez. 2019. 'La Paz Sin Las Mujeres ¡No va! El Proceso de Paz Colombiano Desde La Perspectiva de Género'. *Revista CIDOB d'Afers Internacionals*, 121, 113–134.
Foringer, Kristin. 2023. 'Defining Victimhood: The Political Construction of a "Victim" Category in Colombia's Congress, 2007–2011'. *Comparative Studies in Society and History* 65(1), 219–241.
García-Godos, Jemima, and Knut Andreas O. Lid. 2010. 'TJ and Victims' Rights before the End of a Conflict: The Unusual Case of Colombia'. *Journal of Latin American Studies*, 42(3), 487–516.
Gilmore, Sunneva et al. 2020. *Beyond Silence and Stigma: Crafting a Gender-Sensitive Approach for Victims of Sexual Violence in Domestic Reparation Programmes*. Queen's University Belfast.
Government of Colombia, and FARC-EP. 2014. 'Declaración de Principios Para Discusión Punto 5'. BAPP. https://tinyurl.com/4rm7znp7
Government of Colombia, and FARC-EP. 2016. 'Final Peace Agreement'.
High Commissioner for Peace of Colombia. 2018. 'Tomo VII.'. BAPP. https://tinyurl.com/5t352raw
Jeffery, Laura, and Matei Candea. 2006. 'The Politics of Victimhood'. *History and Anthropology*, 17(4), 287–296.
JEP. 2021. Caso No. 01. Auto para Determinar Hechos y Conductas.
JEP. 2022. 'Comunicado 039 de 2022'. https://tinyurl.com/3s8syu2x
JEP. 2023a. Caso No. 02. Auto para Determinar Hechos y Conductas.
JEP. 2023b. Caso No. 05. Auto para Determinar Hechos y Conductas.
JEP. 2023c. Caso No. 11. Auto de Apertura.
JEP. 2024. Caso No. 07. Auto para Determinar Hechos y Conductas.
Justice and Peace Tribunal. 2011. Judgment against Fredy Rendón Herrera.
Justice and Peace Tribunal. 2015. Judgment against Olimpo de Jesús Sánchez Caro et al.
Krystalli, Roxani. 2024. *Good Victims: The Political as a Feminist Question*. Oxford University Press.
Lawther, Cheryl. 2025. *Constructing Victimhood: Beyond Innocence and Guilt in TJ*. Oxford University Press.
León, Juanita, and Andrés Bermúdez Liévano. 2014. 'El pulso entre las víctimas por ir a La Habana'. *La Silla Vacía*. https://tinyurl.com/3ussmem6
Loperena, Ana et al. 2023. 'Reparations for Indigenous Women Subjected to Sexual and Environmental Violence in the Colombian Post-Peace Agreement'. *The International Journal of TJ*, 17(1), 32–53.
Lundy, Patricia, and Mark McGovern. 2008. 'Whose Justice? Rethinking TJ from the Bottom Up'. *Journal of Law and Society*, 35(2), 265–292.
Madlingozi, Tshepo. 2008. 'Good Victims, Bad Victims: Apartheid Beneficiaries, Victims and the Struggle for Social Justice'. In *Law, Memory and the Legacy of Apartheid*, edited by Wessel Le Roux, pp. 107–126. Pretoria University Press.
Maier, Nicole. 2020. 'Queering Colombia's Peace Process: A Case Study of LGBTI Inclusion'. *The International Journal of Human Rights*, 24(4), 377–392.
McEvoy, Kieran, and Kirsten McConnachie. 2012. 'Victimology in TJ: Victimhood, Innocence and Hierarchy'. *European Journal of Criminology*, 9(5), 527–538.
Méndez, Juan E. 2016. 'Victims as Protagonists in TJ'. *International Journal of TJ*, 10(1), 1–5.

Moffett, Luke. 2023. *Reparations and War. Finding Balance in Repairing the Past.* Oxford University Press.
MOVICE. 2011. 'Declaración Pública'. https://tinyurl.com/dt3tsez8
Mujeres por la Paz. 2012. 'La paz sin las mujeres ¡No va!'. https://tinyurl.com/yt4knjvd
Nieto-Valdivieso, Yoana. 2023. 'Victim-Survivors as Co-Facilitators of Repair and Regeneration in Colombia'. *Journal of Gender Studies*, 32, 731–742.
NTN24, 2018. "*Farc Prepara Una Campaña de Desprestigio Contra Corporación Rosa Blanca y Contra Mí: Herbin Hoyos*"
Paarlberg-Kvam, Kate. 2019. 'What's to Come Is More Complicated: Feminist Visions of Peace in Colombia'. *International Feminist Journal of Politics*, 21(2), 194–223.
Robins, Simon. 2011. 'Towards Victim-Centred TJ: Understanding the Needs of Families of the Disappeared in Postconflict Nepal'. *International Journal of TJ*, 5(1): 75–98.
Roche, Fabio. 2022. 'Álvaro Uribe Vélez: el negacionismo del conflicto armado y de los crímenes estatales'. *Contenciosa*, 12, 1–16.
Rodríguez Castro, Laura. 2021a. *Decolonial Feminisms, Power and Place*. Palgrave Macmillan.
Rodríguez Castro, Laura. 2021b. '"We Are Not Poor Things": Territorio Cuerpo-Tierra and Colombian Women's Organised Struggles'. *Feminist Theory*, 22(3), 339–359.
Sanchez Parra, Tatiana. 2023. 'The Colombian Truth Commission's Work on Reproductive Violence: Gendered Victimhood and Reproductive Autonomy'. *Feminist Review*, 135(1), 28–44.
Saura, Gemma. 2018. 'Nadie firma la paz apara acabar en una cárcel'. *La Vanguardia*, https://tinyurl.com/rb54txkf
Schmidt, Rachel. 2023. *Framing a Revolution: Narrative Battles in Colombia's Civil War.* Cambridge University Press.
Semana, 2014. 'El insultante trino que puso en aprietos a Cabal'. *Semana*, 19 August. www.semana.com/nacion/articulo/maria-fernanda-cabal-denunciada-en-la-fiscalia/399724-3/%3E/
Serrano Amaya, J. F. 2023. 'Inclusiones, Exclusiones y Reducciones: Sectores LGBT en el Acuerdo de Paz y Su Implementación'. In *Después Del Acuerdo ¿Cómo va la Paz en Colombia?*, edited by Angelika Rettberg and Laura Betancur Restrepo, pp. 111–121. Universidad de los Andes.
Suárez Vargas, Daniela. 2024. 'The subversive victim: victimhood and sexual and gender-based violence inside non-state armed groups in Colombia'. PhD diss., Belfast: Queen's University Belfast.
Tapia Navarro, Nadia. 2019. 'The Category of Victim "From Below": The Case of MOVICE in Colombia'. *Human Rights Review*, 20(3), 289–312.
Truth Commission. 2020. 'La participación de organizaciones de mujeres y personas LGBTI en la Comisión de la Verdad'. https://tinyurl.com/9h9nwyfk
Truth Commission. 2022a. 'Call for a Great Peace'.
Truth Commission. 2022b. 'Tomo 7. Mi Cuerpo Es La Verdad'.
Truth Commission. 2022c. 'Tomo 8. No Es Un Mal Menor'.
United Nations. 2006. 'Basic Principles on the Right to Reparations'.
UN Secretary General. 2023. 'Guidance Note. A Strategic Tool for People, Prevention and Peace'.
Walklate, Sandra. 2007. *Imagining the Victim of Crime.* Open University Press.
Weber, Sanne. 2023. *Gender and Citizenship in TJ: Everyday Experiences of Reparation and Reintegration in Colombia.* Bristol University Press.
Zulver, Julia. 2022. *High-Risk Feminism in Colombia: Women's Mobilization in Violent Contexts.* Rutgers University Press.

# 14

# Archives of Desire

## *Listening to Bottom-Up Consultations on the Design of Transitional Justice Mechanisms in Sri Lanka*

*Chulani Kodikara*

### 14.1 INTRODUCTION

Ensuring participation of both men and women victim-survivors in transitional justice mechanisms has emerged as a key tenet of transitional justice theory and practice. Moreover, the United Nations (UN) toolkit on transitional justice insists that this norm now extends to a right vested in victim-survivors to be consulted on the *design* of transitional justice mechanisms. But what happens when these norms are transported to a specific local context? In this chapter, I explore this question through a case study of the engagement of Tamil women next of kin of those forcibly disappeared during Sri Lanka's civil war with the Consultation Task Force on Reconciliation Mechanisms (CTF).

The CTF was appointed by the newly elected United Front government in 2016, following years of denial of war crimes, as part of an internationally supported transitional justice process, inaugurated at the UN Human Rights Council. The CTF was tasked with conducting consultations on the design of four transitional justice mechanisms including an Office on Missing Persons (OMP) with a mandate to address thousands of disappearances in Sri Lanka. I show that the CFT expended a considerable amount of time, energy, and financial resources with support from the UN Office of the High Commissioner for Human Rights (OHCHR) in Colombo, the capital city, to implement these consultations. Yet the government refused to seriously engage with the findings of the consultations; that is, it initiated the consultation process in bad faith as a box-ticking exercise for the benefit of the international community. In this chapter, rather than merely critiquing the state for implementing participation in bad faith, I engage with the two reports submitted by the CTF – its interim report of August 2016 and its final report of December 2016 (CTF 2016a, 2016b). In so doing, I argue that such consultations on transitional justice processes can generate significant archives that can be probed as 'archives of desire' to understand not only the demands of victims-survivors in relation to what form of justice (truth, accountability, reparation, etc.) or what kind of mechanisms they believe can deliver justice (local, hybrid, or international), but also the depth of affective feelings and investments, whether grief, hope, disappointment, frustration, or rage, animating such demands. In post-war Sri Lanka, the existence of this 'archive of desire' continues to challenge and resist dominant narratives of denial and efforts to entrench impunity for forced disappearances while illuminating how the post-colonial, post-war state continues to deny citizenship rights to the war-scarred Tamil population. Moreover, such archives can equally serve as a resource to build solidarity across differences; to cultivate practices of listening to the 'Other', and to refigure the state towards recognising and redressing its sovereign violence.

The CTF as an archive of desire is particularly salient at this time given the shift in political power in Sri Lanka that took place in 2024. The National People's Power party (NPP), which swept to power, following elections held in 2024, with an unprecedented mandate, received the votes of both the numerical majority and minority communities. They now have a historic opportunity to address the long-standing demands of ethnic minorities, including the matter of justice for war-related atrocities. There is, however, lack of clarity about the NPP's stand on this matter (Uyangoda 2024). The NPP also lacks adequate knowledge about the history of the long struggle for justice and failed efforts of the past. The CTF as an archive can play an important role in addressing this knowledge gap.

I worked with the CTF as one of its senior researchers from April to August 2016. Thus, I write as someone who had first-hand access to and knowledge of the CTF process. In foregrounding survivor engagements with the CTF, I hope I can contribute to the efforts to keep their demands alive and amplify their voices, particularly at a moment when the democratic space to raise the question of truth and justice for disappearances has opened up following the election of a new president and a new government in 2024.

## 14.2 CONSULTATIONS AS AN INVITED SPACE

The principle of victim participation, which has emerged as a key tenet of transitional justice, has many different layers and aspects. In this chapter, I foreground that it is not limited to ensuring that victim-survivors, including women, participate in the conduct or implementation of transitional justice processes. Rather this norm now extends to a right vested in victim-survivors to be consulted on the design of transitional justice mechanisms (OHCHR 2009). The normative value of participating in the design of transitional justice processes has been emphasised by several different UN officials and agencies including Kofi Annan, the former UN Secretary General, The Commission on Human Rights, and the OHCHR (OHCHR 2009, 1). It is now part of the UN tool kit on transitional justice with its own set of guidelines: *National Consultations on Transitional Justice* (2009).[1] The guidelines list the many benefits of consultations, while emphasising that they are not a form of outreach, a one-way information channel, or a public relations exercise. Rather, they are considered a 'dialogue' (OHCHR 2009, 2–3) that will enable transitional justice mechanisms to be tailored to the needs of victim-survivors and trigger important debates in the community (OHCHR 2009, v, 2–3).

The Oxford English Dictionary defines the word consultation as a 'conference in which the parties consult and deliberate' or 'a meeting for deliberation and discussion.' According to the Cambridge English Dictionary, consultation is 'the act of exchanging information and opinions about something in order to reach a better understanding of it or to make a decision, or a meeting for this purpose'. However, all these words – deliberation, discussion, decision, and dialogue – mask or do not convey adequately the unequal relations of power and constructions of citizenship that invariably permeate consultations initiated by the state in a transitional justice setting (Cornwall 2017, 1; Thompson 2007). Following scholars working on participatory democracy, it is possible to think of consultations initiated by the state, such as the one analysed in this chapter, as an invited spaces of participation (Cornwall 2002, 2017; Evrard et al. 2021; Gaventa 2002; Thompson 2007). They invite the 'address of the survivor' (Ballengee 2001, 225).

[1] The *Rule of Law Tools* cover a range of themes such as truth-seeking, prosecutions, and vetting procedures. These guidelines consolidate best practices on establishing, implementing, and exemplifying the operational preoccupations of the transitional justice field (Nesiah 2023, 282).

Implicit in this invitation to speak is a promise to record and to listen to those who are invited; implicit also is a recognition of the historical marginalisation of the survivors' voice, views, and demands from the national discourse and a promise to be more responsive in the future. It goes without saying that those who accept the invitation to participate in state-led consultations expect to be treated with respect and to be heard, and their views given serious consideration in the decisions taken by the government.

Even though such consultations are transient in character, and the rules of engagement often delimit what can be said, they open up the public space for communication and perhaps even deliberation. Following Cornwall (2017, 1), such spaces 'offer the potential to reconfigure relations of rule, and the practice of democracy beyond the ballot box'. Democratic theorists would cast such invitations as efforts to address democratic deficits, deepen democracy, recognise survivors as citizens, and move towards more direct forms of citizen engagement in governance. In Cornwall's words, 'Some might even interpret such invitations as representing a radical reconfiguration of relationships and responsibilities – one that extends beyond citizen-state interactions to encompass complex alliances of actors and networks across permeable institutional boundaries and an expanded vision of the public domain' (2017, 1).

However, participatory processes, even when based on invitation, do not always live up to their normative promise or potential. Indeed, they can take the form of tokenism or empty ritual (Evrard et al. 2021, 432; Taylor 2014) or even epistemic violence (Grewal 2023, discussed later in this section). Self-interested states can feign commitment to the value of participation owing to international pressures, without incurring an obligation or a commitment to listen or to respond to the address of the survivor (see also Thorsten Bonacker, Chapter 3). To think of consultations as an invited space is to recognise that the host still controls this space and makes all the decisions. Invitees can be asked to leave, treated shabbily, or made to feel unwelcome. Or the address of the survivor can be ignored and made marginal to the national discourse once again.

As anthropologists writing at the intersection of transitional justice and the translation and vernacularisation of international norms in particular local contexts have illuminated, there can be very wide gaps between international norms and their local implementation (Kelly and Dembour 2007; Shaw 2007; Shaw and Waldorf 2010; Subotic 2009). Local actors can appropriate, adapt, and even reject international norms in unexpected ways. For this reason, the toolkit approach to transitional justice, of which victim consultations are only one aspect, has been roundly critiqued.

Sri Lanka is a case study in the failure to localise the international tool kit of transitional justice. One of the most compelling critiques of the failure of the internationally supported transitional justice process of 2015 including the CTF process has come from Kiran Grewal (2023).[2] Grewal posits that transitional justice is a story of epistemic violence, which is not necessarily specific to Sri Lanka, but one that is 'built into the very nature of transitional justice as a global enterprise' (323). Despite efforts at 'localising' transitional justice, she states that the 'portable toolkit' approach fails to grapple with the complexities and diversities of specific locations and also undermines the ability of those most affected to actively engage and take ownership of such processes (323). Thus, even when local civil society and victim populations are included in accordance with the new mantra of participation, such processes uncritically draw on the universalist

[2] See also Mihlar's (2024) critique of the CTF and the global project of transitional justice. Mihlar found her interviewees to be disconnected from and distrustful of the United Front's transitional justice process and disregarded by it. Her analysis does not, however, adequately account for survivor agency and why they still engage with such processes.

categories of 'civil society' and 'citizens' that exist within liberal political theory, without giving due attention to the historical and socio-political specificity of these concepts, what can be heard and from whom, or the conceptual framework within which participation takes place. The subaltern in her view simply serves to 'legitimate structures and processes that are already decided and over which they have no say' (331). In line with this critique, she argues that the CTF was limiting as it was 'ultimately structured around a pre-determined and fairly standard set of transitional justice recommendations and mechanisms' (333).

Nevertheless, Grewal (2023) recognises that victim-survivors engage with these processes on their own terms as citizens expressing resistance and wanting to be heard, but very aware of the limitations of these processes. But ultimately, she interrogates why victim-survivors should engage with these state-initiated processes, and what may be missed in the process of so doing, even if they are able to engage creatively and productively. As you will see, part of this chapter also grapples with this question and attempts to offer a response. But first, let me outline the circumstances in which the CTF archive came to be created.

## 14.3 WAR CRIMES AND TRANSITIONAL JUSTICE IN SRI LANKA

Fifteen years since Sri Lanka's civil war between the state and the Liberation Tigers of Tamil Eelam (LTTE) ended in May 2009, there is now ample evidence to show that state military forces violated both international human rights and humanitarian law during the final phase of the war, including through indiscriminate killings of civilians, bombings of civilian sites such as schools and hospitals, torture, sexual violence, and forced disappearances. In terms of the scale and magnitude of violence, forced disappearances were among the most serious of crimes committed by the state, linked to a much longer history of its use as a counter-insurgency strategy in Sri Lanka. The Office of the UN High Commissioner for Human Rights, based on an investigation conducted by it in 2014/2015, concluded that there are grounds to believe that enforced disappearances may have been committed as part of 'a widespread and systematic attack' against the civilian population by the state (OHCHR 2015, 221).

Since the end of the war in 2009, Tamil women whose family members disappeared during the war have been waging a struggle for truth and justice. While they are not a homogenous group, and their demands can vary considerably, a group of them now occupy the vanguard of the struggle for truth and justice for war-related atrocities in Sri Lanka and have become perhaps its most visible face. In the immediate aftermath of the war, former President Rajapaksa and his government, which presided over the defeat of the LTTE, denied disappearances. However, a successor regime called the United Front, which was elected in 2015, six years after the end of the war, acknowledged that the previous government may have committed war crimes including forced disappearances and co-sponsored a UN Human Rights Council resolution (now infamous as Res. 30/1) committing to establish four transitional mechanisms including an Office on Missing Persons to address disappearances. Operative Paragraph (Op. Para.) Three of Res. 30/1 also recognised that the government would engage 'in broad national consultations with the inclusion of victims and civil society, including non-governmental organizations from all affected communities, which will inform the design and implementation of these processes, drawing on international expertise, assistance, and best practices'.[3]

[3] 'Promoting Reconciliation, Accountability and Human Rights in Sri Lanka, A/HRC/ 30/1', adopted by the UN Human Rights Council on 1 October 2015.

As a first step in implementing Op. Para. Three of Res. 30/1, the United Front government in January 2016 appointed the CTF on Reconciliation Mechanisms comprising eleven eminent representatives of civil society organisations and academics. The CTF in turn appointed fifteen Zonal Task Forces (ZTFs) at district level in the north and east of the country and at provincial level in the south of the country. ZTF members were drawn from an array of people including local civil society activists, professionals, clergy, and victim-survivors, including family members of the disappeared. More than half the ZTF's were chaired by women. As Mirak Raheem (2024, 9) has pointed out this was a unique feature of the CTF process, especially as gender quotas have very little support in Sri Lanka and women continue to be under-represented in elected political bodies. The CTF also tried as far as possible to ensure ethnic and sectoral representation, as well as language proficiency within each ZTF. Moreover, 50 per cent of all ZTFs was made up of women. The premise was that people would trust and feel more comfortable expressing their opinions to those from their community and area, and in the language of their choice (CTF 2016b, vii). Once the ZTFs were established, submissions were solicited from the public (citizens, survivors, civil society organisations, and professional groups) relating to the design of the four mechanisms promised by Res. 30/1. Solicitations took the form of written submissions, community level consultations through thematic focus group discussions, and town hall-like meetings which were reported back to the CTF.

At the end of the CTF process, which took approximately twelve months, the CTF received a total of 7,306 submissions of which 4,872 were received at public meetings, 1,386 were received through focus group discussions, and 1,048 were written submissions. Among these were handwritten letters from family members of the disappeared (CTF 2016a). Based on the analysis of these submissions, the CTF submitted a comprehensive report with 'explicit recommendations on each mechanism' including the OMP in December 2016.

The CTF was guided by and strived to implement a victim-centric consultative process (Raheem 2024). Thus, even as the CTF encouraged wide participation, the consultation process paid particular emphasis to the voices of affected persons (CTF 2016b, 10). A training programme that was conducted for ZTF members before the commencement of district/provincial level consultations sought to impart the importance of dealing with those coming before it in a sensitive and dignified manner (CTF 2016b, 17). The CTF also expended considerable time and energy to faithfully and meticulously document the oral submissions made at sectoral consultations at national level and at focus group discussion, thematic consultations, and town hall meetings at district and provincial levels. Each meeting was covered by two note-takers who were tasked with the responsibility to generate a full word-for-word transcript of the meeting. The note-takers were trained and provided with formats and guidelines. Each meeting was recorded to aid this process. These transcripts were subsequently manually coded and analysed by the team of researchers responsible for writing the final report (CTF 2016b, 29–30).

Even though victim-survivors who came before the CTF no doubt had 'commission fatigue' (HRW 2024) in the context of a long history of broken promises by the Sri Lankan state, they (and other citizens) robustly engaged with it. However, even as the consultation process was unfolding, it became clear that the United Front government's commitment to hold consultations in terms of Res. 30/1 was a mere box-ticking exercise for the benefit of the international community. Indeed, parallel to the CTF process, the government appointed a steering committee to draft legislation on the OMP, which finalised its draft bill before the CTF process was completed. The bill was placed on the order paper of Parliament in July 2016. It was passed and enacted into law on 11 August 2016. When the CTF learnt of this parallel process, it called on the OMP drafting committee to meet with a group of family members on 5 July 2016 to make sure that the former could be briefed about emerging concerns. Furthermore, the CTF commenced work on an interim report on forced disappearances to ensure that the views of next of kin of the disappeared received until that point were in the public domain to help in the drafting process. Unfortunately, these efforts were of no avail. The government undermined the whole consultation process by bringing forward the OMP debate in Parliament without prior announcement. The CTF was then forced to hurriedly release the interim report on the day the OMP parliamentary debate was taken up in the hope that some parliamentarians would raise concerns expressed by family members, but as far I am aware no parliamentarian had the time to read the report before the vote was taken up.

One person who made a submission to the CTF once the OMP Act was passed expressed their sense of frustration with the government relating to the timeline of the CTF process as follows: 'The establishment of the OMP, the first mechanism to see the light of day, has been rushed and failed to consult those most affected … this urgency would only make sense if it were driven by a desire to provide redress to families' (CTF 2016b: 198). These words also capture the frustration that was felt within the CTF. Given this reality, the final report of the CTF completed in December 2016, presents the recommendations made by family members of the disappeared as recommendations to amend the OMP Act. Thus, the CTF remains a poignant representation of the expectations, dreams, and hopes of a credible truth and justice mechanism as articulated by Tamil next of kin of those who were disappeared during the civil war.

## 14.4 PARTICIPATORY PROCESSES AND THE ARCHIVE

The relationship between formal transitional justice, archives, and the state has received much attention in recent years (Harris 2002b; Viebach 2021). Viebach's (2021) formulation of the transitional archive refers to archives used in, recuperated for, and generated by transitional justice processes. As she suggests, much of this work has focused on the role of human rights archives: 'Without the documentation of abuses by civil society organisations, private collections or states themselves, the formal theatre of transitional justice would be deprived of an important evidentiary foundation' (426). For Harris (2002b, 85), the archival record 'like all repositories of memory, is an extraordinary creation of remembering, forgetting and imagining', which shapes social memory. Its power tends to be laid bare 'in the extreme circumstances of oppression and in the heady processes of rapid transition to democracy'. At these times, those who have been historically marginalised have the opportunity to enter and refigure the archive, and in turn rewrite history and reshape social memory (Harris 2002b).

However, this scholarship has little to say about the relationship between consultations on the design of transitional justice processes and the archive. Consultations on design ideally democratise, pluralise, and refigure the archive in a somewhat different way. When survivors enter consultative processes, they do so not merely to bear witness to mass atrocity or as wounded victims, but to articulate survivor imaginaries of justice mechanisms. In meaningful consultations, survivors – most often ethnic or religious others who have been discriminated against, marginalised, and treated as second-class citizens – enter these spaces as citizens, as 'protagonists' with agency (Mendez 2016), and with the intention of shaping transitional justice institutions.

Given the magnitude of the problem of disappearances in Sri Lanka, of all the mechanisms promised by Res. 30/1, survivors of the war in the north and east had much to say about the OMP. Based on both oral and written submissions received from war-affected communities, the CTF final report (2016b, 176) observed that 'disappearances constituted the most recurrent and pressing issue brought before the CTF'. It also noted that, strikingly, a higher number of persons affected by disappearances came before the CTF than persons affected by other violations (177). In the CTF, forced disappearances appear as a cross-cutting theme that straddles all four mechanisms promised by Res. 30/1.

In testimony after testimony given before it, family members of those disappeared during the war detailed their expectations of the OMP, even when they struggled to comprehend that their testimonies had to be structured around the aforementioned four pillars of transitional justice. These expectations related to the scope and powers of the OMP; its structure and membership; what relationship it should have with other transitional justice mechanisms; witness and victim protection needs; and even the name of the proposed office.

Such demands made by the next of kin of the disappeared in relation to the OMP were often underscored by the grave and pervasive nature of disappearances, the types and patterns of disappearances, the inordinate lengths to which family members had gone to find their kin, sometimes putting their own lives at risk, and the barriers they faced in taking cases to the police and pursuing justice. Moreover, their practical and material suggestions were rooted in a profound yearning for truth and justice, shaped in turn by a multitude of other feelings and emotions: grief, hope, anger, frustration, and disappointment. Thus, in arguing that the CTF process generated an 'archive of desire', I want to foreground the CTF archive as a list of demands and equally as a 'repository of feelings and emotions' (Cvetkovich 2003). Indeed, these reports bristle and brim with a multitude of contradictory feelings and palpable emotions, conveyed through the text but also through the unedited words of survivors who are quoted directly within the text.

Here, I briefly outline three demands out of many made by the next of kin in relation to the OMP, which were not considered when drafting the OMP.

**Name of the OMP**: Family members were very emotional about the name of the OMP. The CTF interim report records the different ways in which people were disappeared and the need to recognise that people were deliberately disappeared. For this reason, many family members found the word 'missing' objectionable. As one mother pointed out, 'my child didn't suddenly grow wings or fall out of someone's pocket to go missing, they were taken' (mother at Kandavalai public meeting: CTF 2016a, 17). Thus, some submissions called for the replacement of 'missing persons' with the term 'disappeared' or 'involuntary or enforced disappeared' to the existing title. However, for family members of LTTE cadres and leaders who disappeared following their surrender to the Army during the final phase of the war based on the assurance that they would be released following a rehabilitation process, neither the word 'missing' nor 'disappeared' captured their experience; they called for the inclusion of 'surrendees' to the title of the OMP. The wife of a person who surrendered told the CTF, 'when I hear the word disappearances, I get unconsciously very angry. I went and surrendered them with … with my own hands' (wife of a surrendered person at focus group discussion held in Kilinochchi: CTF 2016a, 17).

The CTF in its interim report noted that the naming of the Office would be an important step to give the issue of disappearances explicit and public acknowledgement and focus the mandate of the OMP, while increasing public confidence that the views of the next of kin were being heard by the government (CTF 2016b, 200). However, the Act was named the OMP in disregard of these views.

**Investigations**: Disappointed by the lack of investigations by previous commission processes, participants at CTF consultations expected the OMP to be equipped with a strong investigation unit which could consider their evidence afresh. Disappearances in Sri Lanka sometimes followed in the wake of search and arrest procedures conducted in the full view of the public and where the perpetrators were known to family members. One mother told the

CTF that she had given the names of the officers who took her son away, but to no avail (CTF 2016a, 22). Thus, submissions suggest that investigations by the OMP must be informed by the context within which disappearances took place; the extent of evidence already available within families, communities, and organisations working on this issue, but not recorded in official complaints in the past. The Batticaloa Peace Committee, which has worked with the next of kin of the disappeared in Batticaloa district, in a submission to the CTF envisaged the need to facilitate testimonies from those who know about and those who were eyewitnesses to acts of abduction and surrender, including a role for the next of kin: 'In the context of identifying appropriate mechanisms, we would suggest that active members of the community make presentation to the OMP from given areas where abduction and disappearances took place. These community members could be those who are well versed in the history of the area … The families of the disappeared themselves could provide input into this process' (CTF 2016a: 23). Families were enthusiastic to provide information which could be useful in investigations such as links and patterns related to the history, context, and responsibility for patterns of disappearances (CTF 2016b, 216–217). In the Act that was passed, family members have no role in investigations.

**International participation**: Some family members who came before the OMP repeatedly stressed the need for international involvement in the OMP, especially in the membership, staff responsible for tasks such as investigations and forensics, and to fulfil an oversight function. In both written and oral representations made to the CTF, family members were unequivocal that international involvement was critical to the legitimacy, credibility, and practical efficacy of the OMP. The demand for international involvement in a local truth and justice mechanism was based on their experience of commissions of inquiry and their complete lack of faith in yet another local process.

Among the myriad suggestions that family members made to the CTF, this last, relating to international involvement, was one of the most recurring themes made in the most impassioned manner. One mother from Mullaitivu who attended a consultation on the OMP said: 'We can't trust local mechanisms.' Yet another stated: 'It is extremely difficult for victims to place faith in the OMP and it is difficult to conceive how the OMP made exclusively of Sri Lankans will have the moral and practical courage to enter camps and prisons and properly investigate alleged acts of disappearances' (CTF 2016a, 48; 2016b). When the government failed to take this suggestion seriously, some family members began demanding a purely international justice mechanism. They are saying they no longer have faith in any domestic justice process.

## 14.5 A RESOURCE TO RECONFIGURE THE STATE

Before the CTF was appointed, two commissions appointed by the Rajapaksa regime – the Lesson Learnt and Reconciliation Commission and the Presidential Commission for the Investigation of Complaints into Missing Persons solicited the testimonies of victim-survivors but gave them limited time and space and little or no empathy to narrate their stories on their own terms. By contrast, the CTF allowed survivors who came before it greater space to pour their hearts out. In the pages of the CTF reports, there is grief, sorrow, and despair at the loss of loved ones, often mixed with hope; deep devotion to loved ones to keep searching, and yet weariness and exhaustion from searching; frustration with past commissions, and rage at how family members were treated by government officials and bureaucrats in the past; and scepticism of the Sri Lankan state and its capacity to deliver justice (Salih and Samarasinghe 2017). This is illustrated in the following statements:

> I am dying bit by bit. Sometimes when I set off on the road, I wish that a vehicle would hit me. But she [pointing to the other lady next to her] says don't die, we will see them again … we will. (mother at Kandavalai public meeting: CTF 2016a, 13)

> When you see us you see people who are going about life but we are living with extreme pain in our hearts unable to cry in front of children. We cry when we walk on the street. (wife of a person who surrendered: CTF 2016a, 13)

> People call us mad. Sometimes they laugh at us saying don't you know *peyaikatturanga* [they are just taking you for a ride] … We are always on the road trying to find our children. How can we give up? That would be a betrayal to them. (mother at Kandavalai public meeting: CTF 2016a, 13)

The survivors who came before the CTF did so despite their scepticism and frustration, which brings us back to the question posed by Grewal: why do and why should survivors engage with these mechanisms, when the subaltern is simply called upon to 'legitimate structures and processes that are already decided and over which they have no say' (Grewal 2023, 331)?

Extending as well as responding to Grewal, I would argue that the women next of kin of the disappeared who came before the CTF were engaging in a purposefully, determinedly, insistently, and explicitly state-facing project to learn the fate of the disappeared and to hold the state accountable. They recognised this labour would require 'tweaking', adapting and translating the globalised language of transitional justice. They did so not merely as individuals, but as members of collectives organised to specifically express their demands in the public sphere, hyper-aware of the political context in which they were interpellated as participants of a globalised transitional project. Not only that, they recognised that as citizens they were also negotiating or bargaining with a state that was historically hostile to them, and which has never held state agents accountable for forced disappearances. They recognised that not engaging with the state and not reframing their own demands, would mean that they would die without ever knowing what really happened to their loved ones.

Families often understand bearing witness to state violence as an ethical/mnemonic duty to the disappeared, and in fulfilling this duty they transmit their private memories beyond their families and communities to the wider world. In turn they impose a duty on the state to respond. When such testimony is faithfully documented and made sense of in a written document, this text can be recalled, read, studied, and addressed, long after these processes are over. According to Brent Harris (2002a, 161), the archive in these moments represents 'the end of epistemological instability'. The state can no longer feign ignorance of the demands that survivors are making.

Yet, in the eight years after the enactment of the OMP law, despite its strong legislative mandate, the OMP has failed the vast majority of survivors of forced disappearances in Sri Lanka for it has only conducted a handful of investigations. Much of the work of the OMP at the time of writing in early 2025 was focused on awarding compensation to family members who have expressed a willingness to accept compensation offered by the government. Many family members have, however, refused to engage with the OMP or accept compensation until they are told the whereabouts or fate of their loved ones.

The impassioned call for international participation in the OMP by family members now seems prophetic. The subsequent call for a purely internationalised truth and justice mechanism illuminates their mistrust of the Sri Lankan state as well as the OMP. As Alpa Shah (2024, 559) puts it, this demand reveals that the colonised are themselves divided and include those who subordinate their own people where 'those internally colonized feel the process is ongoing'. Thus, even as we recognise increasing calls to decolonise transitional justice and privilege local justice traditions, following Shah, we need to be attuned to the internal divisions within communities, largely ignored in contemporary decolonisation debates, which draw a simplistic binary between coloniser and the colonised (560). Shah is talking about the upper caste and Dalit divide within the Indian democracy, but her words are equally applicable in relation to transitional justice Sri Lanka where the Sinhala majority has historically wielded hegemonic power over its minority communities including Tamils and Muslims. More than fifteen years after the end of the war, successive governments in Sri Lanka have failed to or refused to deliver justice because a majority of the Sinhala community has refused to recognise and acknowledge that the Sri Lankan military committed war crimes including forced disappearances. Let alone prosecute perpetrators of war-related atrocities, consecutive post-war governments have failed to even implement a meaningful truth-seeking process, because truths relating to the war challenge the majoritarian narrative of the nation. Minority leaders themselves have mobilised survivors to serve their own political agendas and interests rather than responding to their demands.

However, this call for international justice is not an unproblematic demand. It circles us back to the critiques not just of transitional justice but of international law more broadly as a site of domination, hypocrisy, empire, and so on. More materially, as Lori Allen (2020) points out, it is a site of false hope which ultimately does not deliver for victim-survivors and diverts attention and energy away from the work required for political change at the local level. In a similar vein, Nikita Dhawan (2013) has argued that the struggle for justice in the era of neoliberal globalisation does not lie beyond the state but in its reconfiguration.

This may be no truer than at the current moment, when international law is facing an unprecedented crisis in the wake of the genocide in Gaza. In Dhawan's (2013) words we have no choice but to treat the state as pharmakon; that is, as both poison and medicine. In such a context, it is important to think of the CTF as a bridge across differences and a resource for dialogue. The CTF conceptualised as an archive of desire can help us listen and learn from those who have been marginalised from the structures of citizenship. It can be a tool for dialogue. Elsewhere, archives have formed the basis for a dialogue between victims and perpetrators, and between former adversaries at a political level. Viebach et al. (2022) argue that archives are destined to be in a long-term discourse with the collective memory of atrocities or periods of injustice. Academics and activists can play an important role by opening up a dialogue and conversation by revisiting questions that have not been answered yet or asking questions that have not been asked before.

## 14.6 CONCLUSION

This chapter focused on a consultation process initiated by the United Front government in 2016, which sought views relating to the design of four transitional justice mechanisms including an office on missing persons in Sri Lanka. Even though the government was unserious about the consultation process, I show that the CTF, which was responsible for conducting the consultations, made every effort to faithfully record the oral and written submissions made by citizens and survivors into a coherent road map for peace and reconciliation in post-war Sri Lanka. Its members, the Zonal Task Force members, the staff of the CTF, and the expert committee members appointed to advice the CTF did constitute a powerful, if provisional, affective community committed to listening to and documenting the demands of the survivors over the months during which the consultation process unfolded. In its final report, the CTF states that it stands committed to advocate on the proposals when its term ends on the submission of the Reports (CTF 2016b, 10). Indeed, some members and researchers still continue to work and advocate on the issue of forced disappearances in Sri Lanka. However, the CTF failed to ensure that the report was received and implemented by the government. It also failed to ensure that this consultation led to a robust debate about the need for transitional justice in Sri Lanka. Nevertheless, the CTF process generated a significant archive with continuing salience in post-war Sri Lanka, whose value is not only historical. In Appadurai's words, 'documentation does not simply precede intervention but is its first step' (Appadurai 2003, 24). The CTF report is not a simple representation of the past; rather it continues to intervene in the present (Kennedy 2004, 49) by making visible sovereign violence and state apathy and indifference to an accounting of such violence. Engaging with such archives can provide insights into not only the demands of survivors of sovereign violence but also the depth of feelings and emotions that inspire demands at the core of survivor struggles for justice. However, how such archives can be made into resources for reconfiguring the state in contexts of impunity and denial remains one of the most vexed questions facing the contemporary global transitional justice project.

## REFERENCES


Allen, Lori. 2020. *A History of False Hope: Investigative Commissions in Palestine*. Stanford University Press.

Appadurai, Arjun. 2003. 'Archive and Aspiration'. In *Information Is Alive–Art and Theory on Archiving and Retrieving Data*, edited by Joke Brouwer et al., pp. 14–25. V2_NAi Publishers.

Ballengee, Jennifer. 2001. 'Witnessing Video Testimony: An Interview with Geoffrey Hartman'. *Yale Journal of Criticism*, 14(1), 217–232.

Consultation Task Force on Reconciliation Mechanisms (CTF). 2016a. *The Office on Missing Persons Bill and Issues Concerning the Missing, the Disappeared and the Surrendered*. August.

Consultation Task Force on Reconciliation Mechanisms (CTF). 2016b. *Final Report of the Consultation Task Force on Reconciliation Mechanisms*. Vol. 1. 17 November.

Cornwall, Andrea. 2002. 'Locating Citizen Participation'. *IDS Bulletin*, 33(2), i–x.

Cornwall, Andrea. 2017. 'Introduction: New Democratic Spaces? The Politics and Dynamics of Institutionalised Participation'. *IDS Bulletin*, 35(2), 1–10.

Cvetkovich, Anne. 2003. *Archive of Feelings*. Duke University Press.

Dhawan, Nikita. 2013. 'Coercive Cosmopolitanism and Impossible Solidarities'. *Qui Parle*, 22(1), 140.

Evrard, Elke, Gretel Mejía Bonifazi, and Tine Destrooper. 2021. 'The Meaning of Participation in Transitional Justice: A Conceptual Proposal for Empirical Analysis'. *International Journal of Transitional Justice*, 15(2), 428–447.

Gaventa, John. 2002. 'Introduction: Exploring Citizenship, Participation and Accountability'. *IDS Bulletin*, 33(2), 1–14.

Grewal, Kiran Kaur. 2023. 'The Epistemic Violence of Transitional Justice: A View from Sri Lanka'. *International Journal of Transitional Justice*, 17(2), 322–338.

Harris, Brent. 2002a. 'The Archive, Public History and the Essential Truth: The TRC Reading the Past'. In *Refiguring the Archive*, edited by Carolyn Hamilton, Verne Harris, Jane Taylor, Michele Pickover, Graeme Reid, and Razia Saleh, pp. 161–178. Kluwer Academic Publisher.

Harris, Verne. 2002b. The Archival Sliver: Power, Memory, and Archives in South Africa'. *Archival Science*, 2(1–2), 63–86.

Human Rights Watch. 2024. 'Sri Lanka: New Transitional Justice Process Lacks Credibility'. *Human Rights Watch Website*, 29 January. https://tinyurl.com/3pvwye8z

Kelly, Tobias, and Marie-Benedicte Dembour. 2007. 'Introduction: The Social Lives of International Justice'. In *Paths to International Justice: Social and Legal Perspectives*, edited by Marie-Benedicte Dembour and Tobias Kelly, pp. 1–25. Cambridge University Press.

Kennedy, Rosanne. 2004. 'The Affective Work of Stolen Generations Testimony: From the Archives to the Classroom'. *Biography*, 27(1), 48–77.

Méndez, Juan E. 2016. 'Victims as Protagonists in Transitional Justice'. *International Journal of Transitional Justice*, 10(1), 1–5.

Mihlar, Farah. 2024. 'Global Models, Victim Disconnect and Demands for International Intervention: The Dilemma of Decoloniality and Transitional Justice in Sri Lanka'. *Journal of Human Rights Practice*, 16(3), 945–963.

Nesiah, Vasuki. 2023. 'Disappearing Political Analysis in Transitional Justice'. In *Book of the Disappeared: The Quest for Transnational Justice*, edited by Jennifer Heath and Ashraf Zahedi, pp. 277–295. University of Michigan Press.

Office of the United Nations High Commissioner for Human Rights (OHCHR). 2015. *Report of the OHCHR Investigation on Sri Lanka* (OISL), 16 September. A/HRC/30/CRP.2, (OISL Report).

Office of the United Nations High Commissioner for Human Rights (OHCHR). 2009. *The Rule of Law Tools for Post-Conflict States: National Consultations on Transitional Justice*, United Nations.

Raheem, Mirak. 2024. 'Challenging Practices of Victim-Centeredness in Consultations on Transitional Justice: Creating Space for the Voices of the Disappeared in Sri Lanka'. *Journal of Human Rights Practice*. Online.

Salih, Maleeka, and Gameela Samarasinghe. 2017. 'Families of the Missing in Sri Lanka: Psychosocial Considerations in Transitional Justice Mechanisms'. *International Review of the Red Cross*, 99(2), 497–517.

Shah, Alpa. 2024. 'When Decolonisation Is Hijacked'. *American Anthropologist*. Online first.

Sharp, Dustin. 2014. 'Addressing Dilemmas of the Global and the Local in Transitional Justice'. *Emory International Law Review*, 29(1), 71–118.

Shaw, Rosalind. 2007. 'Memory Frictions: Localizing the Truth and Reconciliation in Sierra Leone'. *The International Journal of Transitional Justice*, 1(2), 183–207.

Shaw, Rosalind, and Lars Waldorf, eds. 2010. *Localizing Transitional Justice: Interventions and Priorities after Mass Violence*. Stanford University Press.

Subotic, Jelena. 2009. 'The Paradox of International Justice Compliance'. *The International Journal of Transitional Justice*, 3(3), 362–383.

Taylor, David. 2014. *Victim Participation in Transitional Justice Mechanisms: Real Power or Empty Ritual?* Impunity Watch.

Thompson, Lisa. 2007 '"Created" and "Invited" Spaces'. In *Participatory Governance? Citizens and the State in South Africa*, edited by Lisa Thompson, pp. 95–116. African Centre for Citizenship and Democracy.

Uyangoda, Jayadeva. 2024. 'NPP in Power: Possibilities for Post-War Reconciliation through Civic Nationalism'. *Midpoint*, 14 December. https://midpoint.lk/2024/12/14/3679

Viebach, Julie. 2021. 'Transitional Archives: Towards a Conceptualisation of Archives in Transitional Justice'. *The International Journal of Human Rights*, 25(3), 403–449.

Viebach, Julie, Dagmar Hovestadädt, and Ulrike Lühe. 2022. *Beyond Evidence: The Use of Archives in Transitional Justice*. Routledge.

PART II

# Intersecting Justice Struggles and How to Understand Them

# 15

# Intersecting Injustices

## *Diasporic (Dis-)Engagement in Syrian Justice Struggles*

*Mina Ibrahim, Maria Hartmann, and Susanne Buckley-Zistel*

### 15.1 INTRODUCTION

This chapter contributes to research on the generations of victims' engagement in transitional justice by examining the experiences and activism of the Syrian diaspora in Germany. Using the three-generation model presented in this handbook, we highlight various aspects of engagement across various justice processes. We show that, although successful, first- and second-generation engagement in mobilising and participating in transitional justice measures led to a sense of alienation and disengagement from formal justice struggles, particularly in the context of courtrooms in Germany. In response, however, alternative forms of victim engagement in justice processes have emerged, offering a more fulfilling approach to intersecting struggles of those involved.

While Syrian migrants' narratives are deeply rooted in the post-2011 revolution and subsequent displacement, they reveal a complex diasporic identity that transcends conventional notions of victimhood and activism in post-revolutionary and post-migration contexts. For over a decade – and even before arriving in Germany – the Syrian diaspora has been navigating a turbulent journey, marking a first generation of justice struggles which demanded an institutional response to state violence and displacement. In Germany, which hosts one of the largest Syrian diasporic communities, the principle of Universal Jurisdiction (UJ) has opened pathways for legal accountability, epitomised by the landmark Koblenz trials in 2020. Yet these formal mechanisms (and victims' formal roles in them), representing a second generation of victim engagement, often fail to capture the full breadth of diasporic experiences and justice aspirations.

Between the home country they fled and the host country where they seek refuge, Syrians pursue justice that addresses both the violent past endured in Syria and the marginalisation faced in exile. This duality underscores the complex interplay of past, present, and future in their justice initiatives and narratives, revealing that the quest for justice is a reaction to past violence and a multi-faceted struggle for recognition, equality, and political agency. Disillusionment with the outcomes of legal mechanisms, coupled with the challenges of everyday life in Germany and ongoing violence in and outside Syria, has intertwined with what we term *post-revolutionary diasporic consciousness*. This consciousness reflects overlapping and persistent experiences of

This chapter was written in the context of the DFG-research group Menschenrechtsdiskurse in der Migrationsgesellschaft/ Human Rights Discourses in Migrant Societies (MeDiMi www.medimi.de/en/). We are grateful to the German Research Foundation (DFG) for funding our research.

oppression tied to the contexts of the 2011 revolution and subsequent migration to Europe. Thus, Syrians face the multi-layered challenges of struggles in their home and host countries.

This chapter explores how various groups of Syrian diaspora activists have tapped into earlier generations of engagement, initially mobilising and campaigning for the legal prosecution of human rights violations committed by the Syrian regime in German courts. In response – and sometimes independently of the trials – many (including those who initially mobilised for them) have disengaged from institutional transitional justice frameworks. While some Syrian legal activists continue to file cases against regime members within and outside Germany, others have shifted their justice efforts to community-based and vernacular justice sites, which are often characterised by or rooted in resistance against the shortcomings of these institutional responses, and which are more capable of containing the complexities of the multiple lived injustices. For those unable or unwilling to engage with formal institutions, this third generation of creative and alternative forms of agency has emerged, building on earlier literary and artistic practices that predate the 2011 revolution. This shift, while not entirely rejecting legal and political frameworks, reveals a tension between engagement with state-sanctioned justice processes and the pursuit of justice through localised, personal practices that resonate more deeply with the lived realities of exile.

This shift also reveals a temporal co-existence, where elements of different transitional justice approaches are mobilised and demobilised simultaneously rather than following a linear progression. Rather than framing justice contention as a singular cause against a specific structure or regime, it highlights the complex and intersecting ways in which these actors engage with justice processes. Their narratives encompass past atrocities committed by the Syrian regime, ongoing repression following the 2011 revolution, and constraints faced in their host country. These experiences coalesce into a broader assemblage of oppression, reflecting the inherent multiple facets of their justice struggles.

In the following, we situate diasporic consciousness – and particularly after revolutions – in the broader framework of diasporic identity and activism. Afterwards, we present engagement with German legal proceedings through the Universal Jurisdiction trials as well as critiques of various forms of marginalisation encountered in Germany. Subsequently, we show how the latter, among other factors rooted in everyday experiences and encounters, have spurred the Syrian diaspora to adopt innovative practices, such as artistic interventions, as alternative forms of agency within the realm of justice broadly understood. By situating their struggles within the framework of the three generations model, this chapter sheds light on the migration of the transitional justice paradigm to new forums. It explores its broader implications for justice struggles in exile.

## 15.2 APARADIGMATIC JUSTICE AND SYRIAN DIASPORA IN GERMANY

For over a decade of ongoing war, persecution, and human rights violations in Syria, the realisation of transitional justice had been thwarted by the inviolate rule of the Bashar al-Assad regime before its fall in December 2024, which allowed victims to imagine new pathways for justice. In this chapter, we illustrate that the particular situation of Syrians living in the diaspora with an ongoing conflict back home leads to the oscillation of engagement and disengagement with a range of justice processes. In the past, scholars have emphasised the relevance of diasporic engagement in aparadigmatic cases of transitional justice (Aboueldahab 2023; Saeed 2023), which the Syrian case was categorised as at times (Destrooper et al. 2023). However, the engagement of Syrian diaspora communities with justice processes, especially those involving atrocities committed by the Assad regime, has been an increasingly complex case within transitional justice discourse, in particular before the fall of the regime in December 2024. In the following pages, we argue that their engagement reflected not only their pursuit of accountability for crimes committed in Syria but also the oppression they faced as migrants in their host countries. As our field research shows, the diasporic position between these two societal contexts has led to the emergence of a post-revolutionary diasporic consciousness that influences their engagement with and definitions of the (legal) transitional justice processes and practices.

Since the empirical study for this research was carried out before the regime's fall, it captures diaspora members' experiences during a time when the regime's political dominance remained in place, and the prospects for significant change through structural, formal transitional justice processes seemed distant. We draw on fieldwork conducted between 2019 and 2024, including interviews in Arabic, German, and English, participatory observations, and reflections on artistic performances. Life story interviews and informal talks have been carried out with members of the Syrian diaspora in Germany.[1] Some of them were directly involved in the Koblenz trials as legal practitioners, witnesses, or activists mobilising for their proceedings; others were either unable or unwilling to join the procedures.

Our understanding of the term victim is broad, encompassing not only Syrians directly affected by violence but also their relatives and those who, under the Assad's regime's restrictions, were unable to express themselves freely while in Syria yet also in Germany for fear of surveillance. Many participated in the 2011 Revolution and continue their struggles in the diaspora. This post-revolutionary diaspora – which Helberg (2021) refers to as the 'New Syrian Diaspora' – has been profoundly shaped by the challenges of flight and asylum, complicating their sense of injustice and victimhood. Our findings highlight how Syrian migrants' justice-seeking trajectories are informed by their hybrid positioning between 'here' (Germany) and 'there' (Syria). This transnational positioning serves as a catalyst for reimagining justice, influencing their engagement and disengagement with transitional justice processes. Encounters with state authorities, migration policies, and socio-political challenges in Germany intersect with memories of political violence in Syria, deepening their diasporic consciousness.

## 15.3 POST-REVOLUTIONARY DIASPORIC CONSCIOUSNESS

It is not unique to the Syrian situation that diaspora members have to navigate multiple identities, feelings of exile and alienation, hybrid forms of culture and being, and various levels and degrees of global connectivity. In that regard, diasporic consciousness refers to the awareness of people living in the diaspora while they negotiate their identities between the 'here' and 'there' of two homes – in relation to one another, as well as individually (Brah 1996, 18–20; Hall 1990, 225, 235; Orjuela 2018). While it reflects the complex relationship of displacement and belonging, and sometimes of neither feeling at home here or there, it is a contingent and dynamic rather than a static way of being.

Yet beyond this more general diasporic phenomenon, this chapter focuses on members of the Syrian diaspora existentially shaped through a revolutionary experience. It is important

[1] Giving that our fieldwork for this chapter was carried out while the Syrian regime was in power and for the security of our interlocutors, we anonymised the names of our interlocutors, mentioning them in full or as initials based on their preferences. With their consent, we refrained from providing the exact locations and dates of the interviews. Instead, we indicate the year, the month, and/or the country of the interview, respecting each interlocutor's concern for anonymity.

to remember that the 2011 Syrian revolution, which ignited hopes for change, was met with unprecedented violence. Widespread arrests, torture, and killings intensified what Baker and Üngör (2023) describe as the 'Syrian Gulag' under the Assad-Ba'ath regime (1970–2024),[2] forcing millions into exile and giving rise to a global Syrian diaspora.[3] This displacement has been marked by broken bodies and souls, alongside memories of lost homes, cities, and loved ones, but also by the memory of resistance and uprising. In the course of such post-revolutionary diasporas, Hartmann and Oghalai (2023, 130) emphasise how the subjectivities of its members are shaped by social and political struggles both in their home country and in host countries. In this regard, Ragab points to the impact of the revolutionary experience for Syrian diaspora mobilisation in Germany (Ragab 2020, 143).

As we will illustrate in this chapter, regarding our interview partners, post-revolutionary diasporic consciousness has emerged as a product of several interwoven experiences while encountering the ongoing repression in Syria, the rise and collapse of revolutionary hopes, and the challenges of life in exile in times of anti-migrant sentiments. Increasingly, this consciousness has linked everyday experiences outside the courtroom to official justice mechanisms. Within this context, many Syrians have grown sceptical of UJ trials, seeing them as insufficient and disconnected from their lived experiences of violence and displacement, both before and after migration.

This scepticism has prompted a reimagining of justice rooted in personal and collective experiences. As a result, many diaspora members have shifted away from institutionalised justice systems, gravitating instead toward more informal, community-based approaches that resonate more deeply with their realities and allow them ownership over their stories (Hartmann and Ibrahim 2026). While this chapter highlights one of such expressions through art, our field research reveals a variety of different forms: some have involved themselves in political struggles trying to entangle claims for justice in Syria with those for migrant rights in Germany;[4] others have founded community-based dialogue projects from exile,[5] or engaged with street protests, trying to keep notions of the 2011 experience alive.[6] What these alternative forms of justice have in common is that Syrians can claim spaces, talk and reflect about their experiences, and discuss and engage with other Syrians or people from their host country.

Importantly, for many of our interlocutors, the 2011 revolutionary remains the compass that directs their understanding, their current positioning, and future aspirations. Even with the 'failure' of the revolution in fulfilling its objectives for more than a decade, that is the fall of the regime, 'this political defeat did not stop the ruptures that had already affected the social field' (Al-Khalili 2023, 156). In this regard, one interlocutor expressed the ongoing impact of revolutionary experiences on diasporic activism:

> Me realising within the revolution that I have certain rights, that are unmet from the state, created as well a critical thinking that followed me in diaspora. And I am still being critical about my rights in this country that I am in now. This [...] empowered lots of Syrians in diaspora to also create their movements [...] and to claim their rights as refugees – coming from movements where they were active actors.[7]

2 After the so-called 'Corrective Movement', a bloodless coup in November 1970, Hafez al-Assad officially became president in March 1971.

3 In 2023, the number of Syrians living in Germany had risen from 32,000 (in 2010) to 970,000 (https://tinyurl.com/2p6yyvnu).

4 Field results show how Syrian activists have emphasised this aspect during panel discussions in Marburg in December 2023 and in Berlin in November 2024.

5 Interview with Syrian diaspora activist M.H. in October 2022 in Halle, Germany.

6 Participant observation in Syrian-led community places during spring 2024 in Berlin.

7 Interview with Syrian diaspora activist M.K. in May 2020 in Berlin, Germany.

This statement, echoed by others we talked with during our fieldwork, highlights how the awareness of rights – initially triggered by the revolution – propelled Syrians into advocating for justice in the diaspora. However, this process is not unambiguous. As this chapter illustrates, the diaspora's engagement involves navigating complex dynamics between visibility and invisibility, where public advocacy may conflict with personal and familial concerns. This duality is evident in how our interlocutors reflect on their own roles in both individual and collective justice struggles.

For instance, many Syrians in the diaspora, including those we met during our fieldwork in Germany, find themselves balancing their political activism with other life pursuits. These individuals are not only pushing for justice in Syria but also striving to secure their future within the German context and, therefore, juggle the urgency of justice struggles with the practicalities of survival and stability. As is typical for diaspora communities, securing employment, accessing scholarships, gaining citizenship, or obtaining other forms of residency permits are key objectives. These goals underscore a complex, multifaceted diasporic existence where individuals juggle the urgency of justice struggles with the practicalities of survival and stability.

Especially regarding Germany's stance on the Gaza conflict, one Syrian legal advocate openly illustrated:[8] 'Palestine has been always my lifetime struggle, but if I would use the same techniques and slogans while I was an activist in the streets of Berlin a few years ago, I would not be able to help Syrians in achieving justice through the German legal system [...] One has to be wise.' These tensions reflect an important aspect of post-revolutionary diasporic consciousness, that is, a deep awareness of how their actions may impact their futures, both personally and within the context of their families, communities, and activist networks. Their engagement with justice and political activism is often weighed against the potential consequences of being too visible or vocal.

Notably, this sensibility is not new; it is rooted in experiences of suppression under authoritarian rule, namely of staying quiet to protect oneself. Functioning like an inner alert system, it persists even in exile. Though the consequences would never compare to experiencing the 'Syrian Gulag', many interlocutors recognise that criticising Germany's foreign policy could still have repercussions – not only for their immediate safety but for their long-term prospects in the country and their participation in formal justice processes. This awareness shapes their strategies of engagement and disengagement, leading some to selectively contribute to discussions in ways that align with their broader goals of securing stability in Germany while still contributing to the pursuit of justice for Syria. The intersecting forms of oppression create a continuity of experience that shapes the post-revolutionary diasporic consciousness. However, while the absence of human rights in the past creates a sensitivity towards human rights being threatened, it is exactly the experience of rising up for these rights during the revolution that mobilises diasporic engagement in some cases.

As we move further into the dynamics of post-revolutionary diasporic consciousness, it becomes clear that the justice being sought by these individuals is not limited to the prosecution of perpetrators of violence in Syria. Rather, it extends to the broader political, socio-economic, and diplomatic realities that shape their lives in Europe. Post-revolutionary diasporic consciousness, we illustrate in this chapter, is shaped by the tension between past experiences of violence and the complex realities of living in exile. This consciousness is not static; it evolves as individuals navigate the intersection of activism, survival, and the pursuit of justice. For Syrians in the diaspora, the question of justice is not simply about the past – about punishing perpetrators of

[8] Interview with A.J. in summer 2024 in Germany.

violence – it is about their present and future, which are shaped by both the legacies of conflict and the challenges of adaptation in new political, social, and legal environments. As such, their consciousness reflects their understanding of what is just, what is dangerous, and what is necessary as they consider how, when, where, and to what extent they can speak out as they mobilise their will to contribute to the broader conversation about justice, both for Syria and for their own futures.

In the following sections, we further trace Syrian engagement and disengaging in justice struggles over the three generations: mobilising for justice, participating in doing justice, and resistance to justice, leading to finding alternative modes of justice. We show how this affected the diasporic consciousness and open questions regarding what justice is about and how to achieve it. We also show how these engagements, at times, run parallel to each other, and, at times, emerge in response.

## 15.4 (DIS-)ENGAGEMENT IN LEGAL JUSTICE STRUGGLES FROM DIASPORA

To begin, there was a strong first victim engagement in the pursuit of transitional justice that preceded and pushed for legal justice from Syrians' positioning in the diaspora. Many Syrians arrived in their new host countries with ideas about transitional justice mind (Al Jazairi 2015; Charney and Quirk 2014; Dawlaty 2014, 2016; Herremans and Bellintani 2023). Early attempts to mobilise for transitional justice were based on the hope that the Assad regime would fall shortly after the uprising and that a future after Assad needed to be prepared. Yet, faced with the ongoing war in Syria, these hopes for a transition eventually vanished, and with it, the drive to strive for holistic transitional justice.

As a consequence, from 2016 Syrian diaspora groups increasingly focused on retributive justice as one of the few options to achieve some form of justice (Stokke 2021). At the time, there was much hope that the trials could deliver some form of justice (Human Rights Watch 2017). Victims' second-generation engagement in Germany, in collaboration with national and transnational human rights norm entrepreneurs, led to the first cases against the Assad regime in the city of Koblenz in 2020. The trial at the Higher Regional Court is also known as the Al-Khatib trial, with Al-Khatib (or Branch 251) being a prison in Damascus run by the Syrian General Intelligence Service. Under the principle of UJ, Syrian government officials were tried for crimes against humanity committed during the Syrian civil war. The trials focused on a former senior official in charge of Syria's General Intelligence Directorate – sentenced to life imprisonment for killing, torture, serious deprivation of liberty, rape, and sexual assault as crimes against humanity – and a lower-level operative – sentenced to a four-and-a-half-year prison sentence for aiding and abetting the torture and serious deprivation of liberty as a crime against humanity. Since the trials in Koblenz, other cases, such as at the Higher Regional Court in Frankfurt and in other European cities, followed.

Initially, there was some sense of justice after Koblenz (Karkoutly 2023, 35), something many Syrians had not experienced inside or outside Syrian courtrooms. Against all the injustices in Syria, at least something was done, even when small and with limited impact. As Syrian-German journalist Hannah el-Hitami stressed, '[f]or many survivors, the trial was also an important starting point to regain their ability to act after many years of powerlessness' (El-Hitami 2023, 55). Thus, the Syrian diaspora has an important role in setting the scene for accountability and transitional justice (Arab Reform Initiative 2021).

And yet, despite these achievements, the second-generation experience of the trials, as well as with the German legal sector, led to some disillusion among members of the Syrian diaspora

(Hartmann and Ibrahim 2025). The main points of contention were inadequate witness protection, including poor psychological support for witnesses, no translation of the court proceedings from German to Arabic, no recording of the court proceedings, as well as the selective choice of charges which excluded sexual violence and enforced disappearance (Aboueldahab and Langmack 2022; SJAC 2022). While all these aspects were in line with German law and practices, they were difficult to align with expectations of people from the country in which the crimes occurred and who were searching for justice for Syria. So even though the legitimacy of UJ and the Koblenz trials were initially not contested but welcomed, in response to the court's decision and the prosecution in the course of the proceedings, many Syrian diaspora members gradually reduced their support.

Moreover, one notable aspect of the Koblenz trials and other UJ trials is their reliance on strategic litigation (Buckley-Zistel 2020; Doumit 2020; Herremans and Bellintani 2023; Stokke and Wiebelhaus-Brahm 2019). Prosecuting individuals involved in crimes against humanity requires not only the presence of empirical evidence against the prosecuted individuals but also legal expertise and the cultivation of skills to present victimhood narratives, whether through lawyers or witnesses. However, not all Syrians involved in these trials possess this expertise. Additionally, many former detainees and survivors of torture live far from the trial locations, making it difficult to physically attend proceedings or testify against their torturers. Others felt intimidated by the courtroom setting or the prospect of facing their torturers in person. For some members of the Syrian diaspora, leaving their country does not necessarily mean escaping the violence of the Syrian regime, and there continues to be a strong sense of insecurity. As a consequence, the Koblenz trials led to a moment of rupture in pursuing formal transitional justice processes for (some yet not all) members of the Syrian diaspora.

The Koblenz trials illustrate the challenges of aparadigmatic transitional justice processes in ongoing conflicts in which no real transition can take place (Destrooper et al. 2023). Owing to these challenges, diasporic engagement, particularly through legal mechanisms such as UJ trials, has been fraught with contradictions. While these trials offered a form of accountability, they could not contribute to political change in Syria, nor did they alleviate the pain or oppression felt by diaspora members both in exile and within Syria. As the coming sections will illustrate, the forms of justice achieved in these and other subsequent trials remained detached from the lived heterogeneous experiences of those who were directly involved or detached from the courtroom proceedings. We argue that this rupture is intertwined with a diasporic consciousness developed not only in relation to the limitations of the courtroom but also owing to everyday experiences and relationships that supersede the capacity of the German legal system.

## 15.5 DIASPORIC (DIS-)ENGAGEMENT AND VIOLENT CONTINUITIES

As Syrians fled across the world, they encountered new yet also highly challenging forms of violence and marginalisation in their host countries. While these different experiences of injustice from home country to diaspora collide, this significant complexity extends perceptions of injustice and approaches throughout the three generations. Structural inequalities – ranging from xenophobia to precarious migration policies – exacerbated the trauma of displacement, often mirroring the oppressive conditions they sought to escape. Consequently, Syrians' consciousness and modes of engagement – shaped by critiques of various authorities and ruling powers – have not only expanded and overlapped but, as this section and the following emphasise, have also taken on forms that may be labelled as hidden, complicit, or innovative. These expressions are deeply embedded in everyday aspirations, encounters, and relationships, reflecting resilience, adaptation, and creativity in navigating their realities. One Syrian, who refused to provide testimony in one of the trials, voiced his frustration with what he perceived as Germany's 'double standards': 'How could I be beaten by the police one day [in Berlin during a protest against Israel's war on Gaza] and then give my witness to a courtroom on another day? This is insane.'[9] His statement, shared during an interview conducted after 7 October 2023, reflects Güdück and Desmet's (2022) argument that public policies and discourses in host countries significantly influence diaspora perspectives. External factors – such as interactions with authorities and power structures – play a crucial role in shaping justice struggles (Graca 2021, 295). Since the challenges of living in Germany as migrants – compounded by precarious social and economic conditions and unresolved issues surrounding residency permits – often intersected with the international 'normalisation' of the Assad regime before December 2024, their notions of justice are rendered profoundly complex.

In addition, the immigration to Germany and the asylum processes are difficult to manoeuvre for Syrians (and other newcomers). Bureaucratic processes are strongly based on documents that Syrians who fled the government have difficulties obtaining. Even before December 2024, ironically, Syrian dissidents would be forced to expose themselves to the regime-controlled embassy in Germany, risking arrest and threats for their relatives back in the country. It has thus been argued that 'the interconnectedness between the Syrian and German citizenship regimes imply that the legal production of legality [...] in Germany is achieved through legally ambiguous, if not so-called illegal, practices in Syria' (Ferreri 2022, 818).

To return to the topic of Gaza, for Hannah El-Hitami (2023), Germany's stance could do lasting damage to its reputation as a champion of international law with trials on crimes such as in Syria. Germany's support for the Israeli government's military actions against Gaza, the reprisals against pro-Palestinian protesters in Germany, and the German government's rejection of the South African genocide complaint to the International Court of Justice undermine the trust in Germany's sense of justice. Some Syrian activists (some of them Palestinian refugees who had lived in Syria or are of Palestinian descent) who had to flee because their freedom of speech, freedom of expression, and freedom of assembly were infringed, felt that this right was again curtailed when German police disbanded pro-Palestine demonstrations and sought to, for instance, criminalise wearing a *keffiyeh* as a symbol of solidarity (Alkousaa and Foroudi 2023).

Importantly, in the eyes of many Syrians, these injustices intersect. Rather than viewing them as separate challenges in distinct sectors, our interviewees framed them as part of a broader sense of not feeling welcomed or respected in Germany, coupled with a deep mistrust of public institutions. As noted earlier, the acceptance of formal transitional justice is often shaped by wider social, political, and economic contexts in both the host and home countries (Koinova 2017). The growing anti-immigrant sentiment in Germany, struggles with asylum policies, and German foreign policy, on the one hand, and the ongoing violence and repression in Syria, on the other, shape interpretations of and perspectives on daily life in the diaspora, including transitional justice. As an expression of post-revolutionary diasporic consciousness, our field study reveals that some diaspora activists see their street activism in Germany – driven by dissatisfaction with Western legal proceedings against members of the Syrian regime – not only as a response to Germany's foreign policy but also as a continuity of the activism they chose to engage with during the 2011-revolution.[10] Thus, the silence adopted by some Syrians toward

9 Interview with N.D. in spring 2024 in Germany.

10 Findings of participant observation between February and September 2024 including private discussions in Syrian-led community places in Berlin.

activist causes, exemplified by the refusal to engage with a UJ case in a German courtroom or with a partial engagement as will be noted in the coming section, reflects a politics of repression that extends from Syria to Europe.

Against this backdrop, the complex and ambiguous modes of engagement within the Syrian diaspora – shaped by a continuity of negative encounters both in Syria and Germany – have broadened the lens through which Syrian justice struggles are understood today. Whether or not they initially contributed to them, diasporic agents have moved beyond earlier generations of victims' engagement, which focused primarily on the legal prosecution of a limited range of human rights violations by the Syrian regime in German courts. Their frustration with the outcomes of these court cases and sentences, coupled with the challenges of their everyday lives in Germany and the ongoing violence in Syria, has led to a broadening of the injustices they address. This expanded focus now encompasses not only past atrocities in Syria but also their present-day experiences in the host country. As a consequence, their engagement with formal transitional justice, and more generally cooperation with state authorities, is largely interrupted.

In line with the idea of the third generation as central to this edited volume, we thus observe resistance to or at least the different means of engagement with legal justice in the form of the Koblenz trials. Especially before the fall of the Assad regime in December 2024, seeking justice for past and ongoing crimes in their home country while confronting forms of marginalisation in their new home can be understood as intersecting justice struggles. Past experiences of physical violence, ongoing bureaucratic complications to secure a status in a foreign country, thinking about potential repercussions of mobilising around certain political causes, and the 'wise' choice to remain silent about one justice struggle to pursue another – these are snapshots that bridge various times, locations, and memories. They encapsulate the intricate nature of everyday diasporic realities with the justice process.

## 15.6 ALTERNATIVE ENGAGEMENT THROUGH ART

Against the backdrop of alienation from legal justice and disengagement from the trials, alternative modes of advancing justice are emerging. They include fighting against other forms of injustice, such as residence permits or naturalisation, taking to the streets for Gaza, empowerment work in civil society organisations, critical journalism, and the like. Zooming into one of such alternative modes, this chapter highlights diasporic engagement in artistic projects as an approach that provides a sense of ownership over justice struggles for those involved. Our fieldwork explored vernacular artistic projects that extend and grapple with justice processes both geographically and temporally. Despite their diverse forms, these artistic projects are particularly significant for engaging Syrians from varying social and educational backgrounds while highlighting crimes committed by the Assad regime during Hafez al-Assad's rule (1970–2000). They also strengthen connections between former detainees and the families of those who disappeared in the regime's prisons. Many stakeholders involved in these initiatives were based in countries where formal justice processes have been largely absent, such as Turkey, Lebanon, and north-west Syria (Idlib).[11] Indeed, this third generation has provided an opportunity for a larger number of Syrians to engage with vernacular justice processes beyond the reach of formal institutions.

[11] Since 2016, the Syrian regime has lost and regained control of various parts of north-west Syria, but significant areas, particularly in Idlib province and parts of northern Aleppo, remain outside its control and are held by opposition forces, including Hay"at Tahrir al-Sham and Turkish-backed groups.

For instance, *The Clerk* podcast, co-created by Syrian novelist and former detainee Jaber Baker, writer Bushra Joud, and other former detainees, presents a fictionalised account of the Koblenz trials, in collaboration with the Heinrich Böll Foundation – Beirut, Middle East.[12] It engages audiences with the complex realities of justice, memory, and accountability, offering Syrians a platform to reflect on their inability or unwillingness to engage with legal proceedings in Germany. The project provides an alternative narrative space, filling gaps left by institutional trials and offering insight into Syrians' interactions with justice processes abroad. Notably, through a fictional marriage between Seif, a Syrian in exile in Germany post-2011, and Elda, a German clerk at Koblenz, *The Clerk* vernacularises and humanises the courtroom. The podcast does so not only by making the court sessions accessible in the Syrian Arabic dialect but also by relating the courtroom encounters to the everyday experiences and challenges faced by Syrian migrants in their workplaces, households, and with friends and family members.

Beyond their direct engagement with the Koblenz trials, the team behind *The Clerk* also produced *The Impossible Stage* podcast series. Created in collaboration with the MENA Prison Forum – an interdisciplinary regional project based in Beirut and Berlin – this ten-episode series combines creative expressions such as art, theatre, and music to reflect on atrocities committed by the Syrian regime in Seydnaya prison during the 1980s.[13] Drawing on human rights reports, testimonies from the podcast's protagonists, and literary works such as novels, poetry, and music by former detainees, *The Impossible Stage* uncovers acts of agency that predate the accumulation of evidence for UJ trials. In other words, the series sheds light on forms of activism in Syria that existed before the 2011 uprisings and their aftermath. By amplifying prisoners' stories beyond the Koblenz trials – focused on crimes post-2011 – the podcast not only highlights a drawback in the UJ trials but it also captures a period when both first- and second-generation justice struggles were entirely 'impossible' to be 'staged' inside and outside Syria.

Efforts to expand the Koblenz moment continue in the theatrical play *Palmyra, the Torturers* (Palmyre, Les Bourreaux), directed by Ramzi Choukair and premiered in Naples, Italy, in July 2022.[14] Part of Choukair's trilogy on Syrian detention, the play opens and closes with debates among former detainees from different generations and different ideological backgrounds. These debates reflect on justice, accountability, and memory surrounding the Syrian regime's prisons, questioning whether justice can be achieved outside Syria, especially in light of the ongoing Koblenz trials. The play opens by referencing the trials, but as it progresses, it moves beyond the confines of the courtroom's rigid demands for legal evidence. This shift allows the play to address broader questions of justice and memory, illustrating how institutional trials often fall short in capturing the extent of lived heterogeneous experiences and the particularities of the collective trauma resulted from the Syrian carceral regime, albeit without solely commenting on the proceedings in Koblenz or other ongoing UJ trials in Europe.

These projects offer a glimpse into how Syrians engage with the justice process beyond the constraints of formal legal institutions and beyond the efforts to reform them from inside. They serve as powerful, creative tools for collective remembrance and resistance, nurturing informal communities where participants reflect not only on the ongoing Universal Jurisdiction trials but also on the future of the Syrian regime and their own memories of repression. By addressing everyday challenges – both connected to and beyond the prosecution of Assad regime members – these spaces provide platforms for exploring post-revolutionary diasporic

12 Episodes of the podcast are available in Arabic at https://podtail.com/podcast/–syria-podcast/–2023-02-09/.
13 Episodes of the podcast are available in Arabic with English subtitles: www.menaprisonforum.org/radio/.
14 A trailer of the theatre play is available at www.menaprisonforum.org/blog_detail/41/.

identity. Through a blend of metafictional storytelling and artistic expression,[15] these projects destabilise the rigid narrative structures of legal documentation (Taleghani 2021, 155). As literary scholar Shareah Taleghani argues in relation to Syrian prison literature, 'victims and survivors of human rights violations [...] articulate their stories in narrative form, and these stories must be simultaneously narratable and readable to meet the requirements of legal documentation' (17). Indeed, these artistic interventions, alongside the dialogues occurring during backstage rehearsals, create moments where Syrian migrants can present their stories – not merely as victims of imprisonment and torture but as active agents shaping their narratives and expanding their relevance beyond the courtroom and its legal proceedings.

## 15.7 CONCLUSIONS

In this chapter, we showed how the limitations of the UJ trials exacerbated the sense that diasporic engagement was insufficient, as Aboueldahab (2023) also highlights. With no genuine transition in sight, the pursuit of criminal accountability in the UJ trials was perceived as a limited and somewhat hollow form of justice, particularly as Syrians were simultaneously grappling with the realities of life in exile. The trials did not address the diaspora's broader social, political, and psychological needs. Thus, their diasporic engagement in the quest for justice became not only a response to Syria's violence but also a reaction to their lived experiences of exclusion, discrimination, and marginalisation in Germany. Before the fall of the regime, the engagement of the Syrian diaspora with both formal and informal routes of justice can be understood as a form of activism against their oppressing powers. This activism was intricately linked to the complex and multifaceted nature of their marginalisation by authorities in their host countries. These individuals sought justice not only for the crimes committed in Syria but also for the ongoing oppression they experienced in Germany. Realising that UJ trials were unable to meet these broader diasporic needs led many to disengage from official justice processes, instead turning to vernacular justice mechanisms that more closely reflected their lived realities. Thus, Syrians' engagement with justice processes became a negotiation between the pursuit of criminal accountability and the need for more meaningful, transformative justice that addressed both past violence and present struggles.

Syrian migrants' actions against the disillusionment reflect consecutive injustices arising from a particular (and continually evolving) interpretation of the past. Shaped by a growing diasporic consciousness, this past is currently accompanied by the concrete living conditions of victims of the Assad regime in Germany. In this sense, past injustices become relevant in the present when they hold particular significance for current circumstances – whether in relation to living conditions, everyday challenges, aspirations, or setbacks.

Following the dynamics of diasporic (dis-)engagement, we conclude that striving for justice involves more than narrating a formal truth of victimhood within legal, social, and political frameworks. For post-revolutionary Syrian migrants, justice is intertwined with their changing ability and willingness to act within a global context where the Syrian regime's existence is normalised, if not strengthened. Additionally, one should consider how the legal framing of the transitional justice paradigm often fails to address victims' needs fully and is compounded by Europe's complicated and unjust migration policies. These policies thus not only challenge the inherent limitations of legal institutions but can also foster a diasporic consciousness that shapes

15 Metafiction refers to a type of fiction that self-consciously addresses its own creation, often by drawing attention to the fact that it is a fictional work.

conditions of further engaging in or refraining from justice processes. Within this context, this chapter highlighted the multiple individual and relational experiences of Syrian migrants while grappling with both continuity and rupture in their involvement with different forms of justice processes.

As we draw this conclusion to a close, in December 2024, German streets are filled with Syrians celebrating the fall of the Assad regime – for us, too, a moving moment. As the true horror of the regime, in particular its incarceration policy, becomes more and more visible to the entire world, there is already much talk of transitional justice, truth commissions, and tribunals. While the fall of the Assad regime may eventually broaden the scope of these trials, Syrian researchers, archivists, former detainees, and artists have already been compiling evidence with a broader strategic focus. These efforts not only aim to prosecute individual members of the Syrian regime but also to document and preserve memories of its crimes. They seek to highlight aspects of the regime's history unlikely to be examined within trials, creating a foundation for future justice and accountability efforts, particularly in a post-Assad context.

## REFERENCES


Aboueldahab, Noha. 2023. 'Diasporic and Domestic: Leveraging Criminal Accountability for Transitional Justice in the Middle East'. In *Transitional Justice in Aparadigmatic Contexts: Accountability, Recognition and Disruption*, edited by Tine Destrooper, Line Gissel, and Kerstin Carlson, pp. 22–35. Routledge.

Aboueldahab, Susann, and Fin-Jasper Langmack. 2022. 'Universal Jurisdiction Cases in Germany: A Closer Look at the Poster Child of International Criminal Justice'. *Minnesota Journal of International Law*, 31(2), 1–34.

Al Jazairi, Rania. 2015. 'Transitional Justice in Syria: The Role and Contribution of Syrian Refugees and Displaced Persons'. *Middle East Law and Governance*, 7(3), 336–359.

Al-Khalili, Charlotte. 2023. *Waiting for the Revolution to End: Syrian Displacement, Time and Subjectivity*. University College Press.

Alkousaa, Riham and Layli Foroudi. 2023. 'Palestinian Keffiyeh Scarves – A Controversial Symbol of Solidarity'. Reuters, 15 December. https://tinyurl.com/4rsst4fz

Arab Reform Initiative. 2021. 'Getting to Accountability: The Role of Diasporas in Transitional Justice in MENA'. 25 February. https://tinyurl.com/ed92r62e

Baker, Jaber, and Uğur Ümit Üngör. 2023. *Syrian Gulag: Inside Assad's Prison System*. Bloomsbury.

Brah, Avtar. 1996. *Cartographies of Diaspora: Contesting Identities*. Routledge.

Buckley-Zistel, Susanne. 2020. 'Gerechtigkeit für Syrien aus der Distanz? Das Weltrechtsprinzip und die strafrechtliche Aufarbeitung von Völkerrechtsverbrechen in Deutschland'. *Zeitschrift für Friedens-und Konfliktforschung*, 9(1), 179–187.

Charney, Craig, and Christine Quirk. 2014. 'He Who Did Wrong Should Be Accountable: Syrian Perspectives on Transitional Justice'. *Transitional Justice Research Series* 1. Syria Justice and Accountability Centre, The Hague.

Dawlaty, 2014. *Transitional Justice in Syria*. Dawlaty.

Dawlaty. 2016. *Transitional Justice from the Perspective of Syrian Youth*. Dawlaty.

Destrooper, Tine, Line Engbo Gissel, and Kerstin Bree Carlson, eds. 2023. *Transitional Justice in Aparadigmatic Contexts: Accountability, Recognition and Disruption*. Routledge.

Doumit, Jessica. 2020. 'Accountability in a Time of War: Universal Jurisdiction and the Strive for Justice in Syria'. *Georgetown Journal of International Law*, 252, 263–287.

El-Hitami, Hannah. 2023. 'Die Glaubwürdigkeit endet mit Gaza'. dis:orient. www.disorient.de/magazin/die-glaubwuerdigkeit-endet-mit-gaza

Ferreri, Veronica. 2022. 'The Invisible Hard Work of Retrieving Papers: Syrians and the Paradoxes of Integration in Germany'. *Citizenship Studies*, 26(6), 816–833.

Graca, Sofia. 2021. 'Resistance and the Paradox of Legal Entitlement – A Theoretical Analysis of Migrant Women's Responses to Domestic Abuse in the Host Country'. *Journal of Legal Pluralism and Unofficial Law*, 53(2), 290–314.

Güdük, Ayse, and Ellen Desmet. 2022. 'Legal Consciousness and Migration: Towards a Research Agenda'. *International Journal of Law in Context*, 18(2), 213–228.

Hall, Stuart. 1990. 'Cultural Identity and Diaspora'. In *Identity: Community, Culture, Difference*, edited by Jonathan Rutherford, pp. 222–237. Lawrence & Wishart.

Hartmann, Maria, and Mina Ibrahim. 2026. 'Decolonising Syrian Justice: The Koblenz Trials inside and beyond the Courtroom'. *Journal of Intervention and Statebuilding*.

Hartmann, Maria, and Bahar Oghalai. 2023. 'Jenseits von Migration. Zur Wiederverwendung des Diasporabegriffs'. *Movement Journal for Critical Migration and Border Studies*, 7(2), 125–137.

Helberg, Kristin. 2021. 'Engagiert und zersplittert. Die Syrische Diaspora in Deutschland als neue gesellschaftliche Kraft'. *Blätter für deutsche und internationale Politik*, 66(4), 113–120.

Herremans, Brigitte, and Veronica Bellintani. 2023. 'Overcoming the Justice Impasse in Syria'. In *Transitional Justice in Aparadigmatic Contexts: Accountability, Recognition and Disruption*, edited by Tine Destrooper, Line Gissel, and Kerstin Carlson, pp. 36–51. Routledge.

Human Rights Watch. 2017. 'These Are the Crimes We Are Fleeing'. https://tinyurl.com/fpjbkep9

Karkoutly, Mariana. 2023. 'Case number 1 St 9/19. Syrians' Perceptions of Justice vs. German Legal Procedure'. In *Syrian State Torture on Trial*, edited by Wolfgang Kaleck and Patrick Kroker, pp. 31–45. Bundeszentrale für politische Bildung.

Koinova, Maria. 2017. 'Critical Junctures and Transformative Events in Diaspora Mobilisation for Kosovo and Palestinian Statehood'. *Journal of Ethnic and Migration Studies*, 44(8), 1289–1308.

Orjuela, Camilla. 2018. 'Mobilising Diasporas for Justice. Opportunity Structures and the Presencing of a Violent Past'. *Journal of Ethnic and Migration Studies*, 44(8), 1357–1373.

Ragab, Nora Jasmin. 2020. 'Diaspora mobilization in a conflict setting: the emergence and trajectories of Syrian diaspora mobilisation in Germany'. PhD diss., Maastricht University.

Saeed, Huma. 2023. 'Transitional Justice in Afghanistan. A Hegemonic Power Discourse'. In *Transitional Justice in Aparadigmatic Contexts: Accountability, Recognition and Disruption*, edited by Tine Destrooper, Line Gissel, and Kerstin Carlson, pp. 68–85. Routledge.

SJAC. 2022. *Between Hope and Despair: A Way Forward after the Koblenz Trial*. Syria Justice and Accountability Centre,

Stokke, Espen Ringkjøb. 2021. 'Diaspora mobilisation for justice during conflict: the case of Syria'. PhD diss., University of Bergen.

Stokke, Espen, and Eric Wiebelhaus-Brahm. 2019. 'Syrian Diaspora Mobilisation: Vertical Coordination, Patronage Relations, and the Challenges of Fragmentation in the Pursuit of Transitional Justice'. *Diaspora Mobilizations for Transitional Justice*, 42(11), 1930–1949. https://doi.org/10.1080/01419870.2019.1572909

Talegani, R. Shareah. 2021. *Readings in Syrian Prison Literature: The Poetics of Human Rights*. Syracuse University Press.

# 16

# Lots to Gain and Little to Lose

## *Mobilising Transitional Justice as a Means to Connect Various Justice Struggles in the Democratic Republic of the Congo*

*Kim Baudewijns*

> Victims are the reason why transitional justice comes to life. They are the ones who have lived atrocities and abuses in their flesh and their experiences as human beings. That's why far from being confined in a simple witness role, they are key players [...] the powerful voice of the community.
>
> Leader of the Coalition of Victims' Groups (North Kivu), from 'People power building justice – survivors speak up from Congo' panel, 16 November 2024

### 16.1 INTRODUCTION

Transitional justice is increasingly being mobilised in a broader range of spaces, also in contexts where we might least expect it. This includes spaces where limited formal transitional justice activities are rolled out, where recently no political transition took place or where no peace agreements were signed. In these contexts, too, references to transitional justice are being made by different groups on the ground to support broad justice-seeking efforts. In these contexts, these references function as an organising principle to formulate new claims, which often surpass the original scope of standardised transitional justice. This is, for example, the case in the eastern part of the Democratic Republic of the Congo (DRC), a highly volatile context, where a range of local actors, including victims-survivors,[1] tap into transitional justice across a diverse range of struggles for justice.

For more than three decades, the eastern provinces of the DRC have been and continue to be marred by cycles of violence and conflict. Against this background, transitional justice has been mobilised in this part of the country to confront deep-rooted legacies of violence and facilitate a shift toward a more just and peaceful future. This has been happening in spite of critiques regarding transitional justice's typical focus on recent and direct violence (McAuliffe 2021). While there have been attempts at institutional transitional justice mechanisms, such as a Truth and Reconciliation Commission, this is a context that underscores the obvious challenges of implementing formal transitional justice in contexts of ongoing conflict. On the ground, however, as this chapter will show, transitional justice continues to be invoked in a number of ways by different actors. This creates an *aparadigmatic* scenario, meaning that transitional justice

[1] I employ the terms 'victims' and 'survivors' throughout this chapter, acknowledging that individuals may self-identify differently, some preferring the term 'victim' while others identify as 'survivor'.

language and tools are invoked in the absence of a political transition, and more specifically, within a context of cyclical violence. Critical and empirical scholarship is increasingly interested in understanding the dynamic adoption and adaptation of transitional justice in such contexts, the protagonist role of victims and civil society in driving such aparadigmatic transitional justice practices, and the broader question of what this means for the field of transitional justice (Destrooper et al. 2023; Nagy 2008).

In eastern DRC, the deeply rooted conflict and cyclical, multi-level, and multi-directional violence has led to a wide range of formal and informal, judicial and non-judicial, local and international justice responses. These include informal and customary forms of justice, as well as institutional and judicial processes at various administrative levels, for example in the form of mobile courts. At the international level there has been the Katanga case before the International Criminal Court with rewarded reparations. Additionally, individual and collective interim reparative measures have been implemented by the international organisation, the Global Survivors Fund. Jointly, this range of justice initiatives could be argued to constitute an ecosystem of interconnected and – ideally – mutually reinforcing avenues for seeking justice (Evrard et al. 2021).

Many of these initiatives have explicitly used the rhetoric of transitional justice. Others did not use the rhetoric of transitional justice, but the proposed actions followed the logic and/or objectives of transitional justice – often in relation to justice struggles that seemingly have no direct relation to the kinds of harms that have been central in more paradigmatic transitional justice contexts such as Chile or Guatemala. In this chapter the intersections between transitional justice language and practice on the one hand and other justice struggles on the other is discussed from three different vantage points. These concern three different trends on the ground. It can notably be observed that (a) specific groups of actors, such as youths, are making transitional justice claims, (b) specific demands are put forward, for example regarding gender-based violence, and (c) transitional justice is being mobilised in entirely new struggles, such as the struggle for environmental justice. Across these struggles, innovation and experimentation – often in response to the need for contextualisation or to institutional limitations – is often crucial. This raises questions about the boundaries of transitional justice and how the expansion of the practice challenge these. This chapter examines these questions by analysing the perspectives of those who 'do transitional justice' in eastern DRC.

This chapter is based on a decade of practice and research in the (eastern) DRC. Conversations with a wide range of justice actors active in an equally wide range of justice struggles show that references to transitional justice enter the justice conversations from a number of different angles. There has, for example been both engagement with and resistance against the process of developing a national transitional justice policy by civil society and victim groups. Interestingly, irrespective of whether they embrace or resist formal proposals for and approaches to transitional justice, the existence of a formal framework means that the language and organising logic enters many justice debates – sometimes in unexpected ways. In practice, victim-survivors – in constant conversation with civil society and (inter)national allies – have turned to the language and organising logic of transitional justice as one of many plausible mobilising frameworks or justice avenues in a context that is otherwise marred by institutional deadlock, ongoing insecurities, and cyclical violence. Their practical experience across a range of different justice struggles and their experimentation with a range of different justice paradigms significantly shapes how they engage with transitional justice practice and language.

The aim of this chapter is to show how the language and practice of transitional justice shape a range of justice struggles in eastern DRC, and foster connections that are useful for victims in furthering their struggles. I will use the three previously mentioned vantage points to explore how victim-survivors as protagonists have engaged with transitional justice. Across each of these three cases, I explore how justice actors adopted the standardised transitional justice framework; then rethought and redefined these principles in ways that support their specific justice struggles; and finally how they reapplied these newly emerging conceptualisations.

In the remainder of this chapter I will first situate transitional justice in the context of the DRC, then elaborate on three cases where it has been used in aparadigmatic ways, namely (a) the struggle for social and political rights by the youth organisation Lutte pour le Changement (Struggle for Change, LUCHA), (b) struggles that foreground demands related to conflict-related sexual violence (CRSV) and gender justice (including women's rights), and (c) actors using transitional justice in broader environmental justice struggles. In the discussion I zoom out from these three cases and reflect on how the dynamic of adopting, rethinking, and reapplying standardised transitional justice in this context are relevant beyond the case of the DRC, by foregrounding how the transitional justice language and framework serve as a connector across a range of intersecting justice struggles, and thereby inscribing transitional justice more soundly in a dense justice ecosystem where it operates as an organising principle and mobilising tool for a range of grassroots actors.

## 16.2 SITUATING THE PRESENCE OF TRANSITIONAL JUSTICE RHETORIC IN THE DRC

The first remarkable transitional moment in the DRC was in 1992 when transitioning from a one-party rule to a multi-party democracy. However, the transitional justice discourse became integral to national political processes considering reconciliation and peace-building purposes after the inter-Congolese dialogue, where warring factions signed the Sun City (Peace) Agreement in 2002. After years of violence and two wars, this agreement allowed for a transition period and specific resolutions focusing on, among other things, the establishment of a Truth and Reconciliation Commission (La Commission de Verité et de la Réconciliation). International actors and experts, such as the International Centre for Transitional Justice (ICTJ), national civil society actors and the United Nations (UN) Mission in the DRC (MONUC) have played a key role in advising the Congolese government on transitional justice in this period (Borello 2004).[2] All in all, the highly politicised Truth and Reconciliation Commission gained limited traction in its four-year mandate.

In the decade that followed, President Kabila attempted to bring together political parties and civil society actors inclined to think about consolidating national cohesion and the peaceful development of the country in a national consultation (République Démocratique du Congo 2013; Tunamsifu 2018). However, after years of continuing violence, human rights violations, and impunity for war crimes, it was President Tshisekedi who specifically signalled interest in the establishment of transitional justice mechanisms in 2020 during a Council of Ministers (Arnould 2021), which was welcomed by civil society actors and the UN mission in the DRC. Following this formal expression by the President, transitional justice was on the political agenda in the DRC again. With support of the UN joint Human Rights Office, the Congolese government set up a scientific committee in charge of developing a national transitional justice policy at the end of 2022. In January 2023, the committee presented its report containing, among other things, a draft national transitional justice policy. Besides the national transitional justice policy,

[2] As of 1 July 2010, the UN Organisation Mission of the Congo (MONUC) in the DRC since 1999, was renamed the UN Organisation Stabilisation Mission in the DRC (MONUSCO) in accordance with the adoption of Resolution 1925 by the Security Council on 28 May 2010.

also in December 2022, the government promulgated a reparations law, and two national bodies were established in 2023: the National Reparations Fund for Victims of Conflict-Related Sexual Violence and Other Crimes Against the Peace and Security of Humanity (Fonds National des Réparations des Victimes des violences sexuelles liés aux conflits et des victimes des crimes contre la paix et la sécurité de l'humanité, FONAREV), and the Inter-Institutional Commission for Victim Assistance and Support for Reforms (Commission Interinstitutionnelle d'Aide aux Victimes et d'Appui aux Réformes). Additionally, recently the Ministry of Human Rights created a National Transitional Justice Policy (Politique Nationale de Justice Transitionnelle) (Kasongo 2024; Ministère des Droits Humains 2024). This shows that the state has embarked on a new national transitional justice enterprise, and that there has been significant institutional attention for transitional justice, at least in a formal sense. In practice, several of these initiatives have not been implemented yet, owing to multiple challenges, including lagging political will and lack of resources (Ellemers 2023), as well as, in a more general sense, the uncertain and violent climate. In general, the state-led transitional justice initiatives were not originally intended to be aparadigmatic, but rather to serve as a continuation of the Peace Agreement. However, owing to the persistence of violence, their formal relevance is continuously challenged.

While formal processes such as FONAREV are still under deliberation and far from fully implemented, and for many citizens practical as well as financial barriers continue to hinder access to regional formal justice systems (Jacobs 2018), there have been and still are other initiatives which cater to resolving conflicts at community level. In informal justice spaces, such as the community resolution mechanisms Barza Intercommunautaire,[3] justice is strongly intertwined with truth-telling and reconciliation to rebuild broken relationships and mend social and community bonds (Tunamsifu 2022). While primarily being an approach to resolve small-scale disputes in communities (including discussions on land boundaries, debt, and marriage issues, which are known to become violent and escalate rapidly in the wider context of violence and access to arms in eastern DRC), Barza have also been framed as a transitional justice initiative because of how their focus on addressing community-level difficulties, disputes, and conflict is relevant at the end of conflict or in relation to the return of ex-combatants to the community (Dunn 2017). For many, especially in communities, these kinds of spaces are still the primary route to justice, and a mechanism to prevent escalation of existing or new conflicts, formulate claims for reparations, propose measures for non-repetition, and address re-integration. However, there are limits to what these mechanisms can achieve, especially in a context of mass-scale harms and limited availability of other (criminal) justice spaces at various levels.[4]

## 16.3 THE ADOPTION OF TRANSITIONAL JUSTICE LANGUAGE ACROSS A WIDE RANGE OF JUSTICE STRUGGLES

This section zooms in on how transitional justice references have been made in eastern DRC, by different kinds of actors, to make certain kinds of demands and to address different types of struggles. The three cases serve as examples to demonstrate how actors do not simply adopt transitional justice 'as is' from a national level initiative, but problematise, rethink, and reapply it in line with these shifting positionalities, demands, and struggles. What emerges from the analysis is that transitional justice is seen as a plausible framework for mobilisation that is integrated into

[3] Or Baraza La Wazee in North-Kivu, literally translated from Swahili as a gathering of the elders or wise from the community, who are considered to speak on behalf of others (expert interview, 8 January 2025).

[4] Expert interview, 8 January 2025.

a broader repertoire of action, in which elements of the discourse and practice are re-situated in line with these specific contexts.

### 16.3.1 *The Struggle for Social and Political Rights by Youths*

A first vantage point for exploring the transformation of transitional justice is having a look at which actors are invoking it. Whereas most of the mainstream transitional justice literature sees institutions as drivers of transitional justice, critical scholarship has focused more on the role of civil society organisations (CSO). In the context of eastern DRC, a particular CSO actor that has engaged explicitly with the language of transitional justice is the youth organisation LUCHA. The case of LUCHA represents an aparadigmatic and innovative use of transitional justice – not only because of the interweaving of claims for social rights with those for political rights, but also because these claims are advanced by an atypical transitional justice actor, a youth movement, operating in an atypical context of cyclical violence and continued oppression.

LUCHA is a youth-led, non-violent movement that originated in the capital of North Kivu province in 2011. Over the years, LUCHA has expanded its influence nationwide. With its own explicit manifesto that can be found on its website (LUCHA 2017), it has become a front runner in critically and openly addressing the governance system in the country and continuously holding the government to account by means of advocacy and manifestations. The movement actively intertwines its activism for better governance and social and political rights with broader struggles for justice and accountability. One way in which it does this is by mobilising the rhetoric and building blocks of transitional justice. In doing so, it inserts references to transitional justice in a broader struggle that also draws on other mobilising frameworks, including a more general discourse about fundamental rights. It is notably the context of intersecting rights violations that inspires this utilisation of a wider range of mobilising frameworks that each speak in their own reality to these compound harms.

LUCHA, together with other citizen movements, leverages transitional justice language explicitly during events and protests. An example is the celebration of the formalisation of a national Remembrance Day. In this context the claim 'transitional justice should be applied in the DRC' was made by Duc Mbuyi, the representative of LUCHA. The following statement was also made in relation to the moment when President Felix Tshisekedi officially marked 2 August as a national Remembrance Day: 'We congratulate the President of the Republic on making 2 August a day of commemoration for the Congolese genocide. We are here for this reason, to remember, for this commemoration to tell the whole world that we need justice and that the Mapping Report should be analysed and that transitional justice should be applied in our country.'[5] The statement was specifically made in relation to victims of atrocities as documented in the Mapping Report. This report, spearheaded by the UN, was a large documentation effort of crimes committed in the eastern provinces between 1993 and 2003. Here, transitional justice is suggested as an accountability mechanism for these crimes, but also as a tool for commemoration and outreach about what has happened.

In addition to this, by drawing on transitional justice, the movement highlights its commitment to memory, accountability, and reparative justice. The rhetoric of 'Nous n'oublions pas'

[5] Author's translation. Fragment from the news article 'RDC: des mouvements citoyens réclament "une justice transitionnelle" pour les victimes du genocide.' Retrieved from: https://7sur7.cd/index.php/2023/08/03/rdc-des-mouvements-citoyens-reclament-une-justice-transitionnelle-pour-les-victimes-du

('We will not forget') on 23 November 2019, for example, commemorates victims of state violence, such as Obadi Muhindo, who was killed during peaceful protests in Beni in eastern DRC. This language reflects transitional justice's focus on acknowledgement and memorialisation. Similarly, LUCHA's 19 November 2024 call for President Tshisekedi to abide by constitutional limits reflects a broader demand for rule of law and democratic accountability, linked to the pillar of institutional reform in the framework of transitional justice.

These examples show how LUCHA explicitly draws on transitional justice language, and also how it connects and operates across different claims. On the one hand, by inserting transitional justice rhetoric into their broader advocacy for social justice, LUCHA highlights the interconnectedness of past, present, and future struggles for citizens, and moreover specifically for many who are also victim-survivors. On the other hand, in doing so, LUCHA deviates from standardised transitional justice approaches by interweaving demands for civil and political rights with demands for social rights: for example, by underlining the continuing interlinked struggle for civilians' social rights such as access to water, health, education, and security combined with the cross-cutting indispensable struggle for peace.

This revisiting of mainstream approaches is consequently also put into practice in terms of how demands are made during public appearances, where LUCHA makes claims for justice for victims, memorialisation, and institutional reform, and links these claims to their social and political struggles that connect demands in the realm of social and economic rights (such as access to basic needs such as water, health, and access to education) with demands for state and democratic accountability. The movement's efforts are often intertwined with the struggles of victims in claiming justice for human rights abuses, ending impunity for war crimes, and demanding reparations, alongside demands related to governance and corruption, and advocacy for basic social rights.

As such, LUCHA simultaneously inserts the language of transitional justice into other struggles, and focuses its transitional justice language on issues that are often overlooked in standardised transitional justice, such as social rights. In doing so, it allows transitional justice language and logic to coexist and interact with other justice narratives and frameworks in ways that highlight the porous borders between these frameworks.

### 16.3.2 *Claims Regarding Conflict-Related Sexual Violence and Gender Justice*

A second vantage point for examining innovative approaches to transitional justice in eastern DRC is by looking at the claims that are made. Here it can be observed that transitional justice has become a significant rhetorical and advocacy for those addressing the pervasive issue of CRSV. While CRSV is typically part of a broader transitional justice agenda following conflict, what is striking here is that the actors framing their claims related to CRSV and gender justice through the lens of transitional justice do so in a way that is exclusively focused on this topic, without necessarily embedding it in an overarching narrative of a broader transition away from conflict, thus turning transitional justice into a tool for single-issue justice struggles in ways that are not typical for standardised transitional justice approaches

The primary actors employing transitional justice language include local victim-survivor networks including the Synergy of Women (Synergie des Femmes), but groups such as the Movement of Survivors of Sexual Violence in the DRC (Mouvement des Survivant.e.s de Violences Sexuelles en RDC) – part of a transnational network supported by Mukwege Foundation – also play a leading role in applying the language of transitional justice in these highly specific struggles. They explicitly invoke elements of the transitional justice framework to demand justice, reparations, and recognition for survivors of sexual violence. Central to their framing is the idea that impunity for such crimes perpetuates violence, and the movement's declaration that 'Transitional justice is the answer' highlights the centrality of transitional justice rhetoric in their advocacy. In an open letter to the Congolese government, the Mouvement des Survivant.e.s demands the Congolese government explicitly for transitional justice mechanisms to be put in place for victims of sexual violence: 'The Government of the Republic must do everything in its power to ensure that the Democratic Republic of Congo has all the mechanisms for transitional justice, including reparations for the victims of rape and sexual violence.'[6] In this letter they structure their call around three priorities, which they continue to advocate for until present, framed in terms of transitional justice including: the fight against impunity, reparations for victims of sexual violence, and non-recurrence through providing security of the population and enforcing the rule of law. As such, the state is often turned to as responsible for the violence they survived, and women consider the state responsible to guarantee peace and assure the non-recurrence of mass violence (Mouvement des Survivant.e.s 2018). Furthermore, they refer to a day of solidarity, in memorialisation of victims of crimes committed in 2018 in the eastern provinces. The fight against impunity and sexual violence is considered a priority; it has an impact not only on women, but also indirectly the whole of society.[7]

Interestingly, while these demands are atypical for mainstream transitional justice conceptualisation in the sense of pertaining to a single-issue movement, the case also illustrates how the use of the transitional justice framework allows for connections to be made between demands related to the very specific topic of CRSV and the broader struggle for gendered justice, notably by pointing to the root causes of this CRSV. Victim-survivors and representatives of victim groups often express the need to be able to rebuild their daily lives in a context of structural insecurity and violence, which is facilitated by structures of impunity and lacking realisation of democratic values and the rule of law by the Congolese state (Bihamba 2024). In many instances sexual and gender-based violence (SGBV) leads to stigmatisation or social exclusion. Frequently, after becoming victims of SGBV, women become – financially – responsible for the household when their husband leaves them. This adds pressure to be able to sustain their families. Women account that they fear that their children will become part of an armed group for economic reasons, if they do not manage to make a livelihood. As the consequences of gender and sexual violence are multi-dimensional, survivors often face multiple physical, psychological, social, and economic challenges, exacerbated by gendered social expectations (Kyamusugulwa et al. 2019). As such, victim-survivors not only refer to CRSV related to mass atrocities, but also interconnected forms of SGBV, such as domestic violence, as part of their lives in a highly volatile context. Using the transitional justice framework gives rise to broader emancipatory claims that surpass demands related to CRSV specifically, focusing on the structural nature of (conflict-related) sexual violence in advocating for reparative measures such as holistic care and national reparations initiatives.

In addition to applying transitional justice to single issue campaigns, organisations such as the Panzi Foundation, led by Nobel laureate Dr Denis Mukwege, who advocates strongly against conflict-related sexual violence as a weapon of war, also add to more standardised understandings of transitional justice by bridging local and international transitional justice frameworks

6 Mouvement des survivant.e.s, www.mukwegefoundation.org/wp-content/uploads/2018/04/Memo_Journee-de-solidarite-26-avril-2018.pdf (author's translation).

7 Mouvement des survivant.e.s, www.mukwegefoundation.org/wp-content/uploads/2018/04/Memo_Journee-de-solidarite-26-avril-2018.pdf (author's translation).

and approaches. On the one hand, these victim-survivor and civil society groups are supported by international actors who align with global transitional justice standards to amplify calls for justice and reparations for victims of sexual violence; on the other hand, they have deep roots in local communities and practices that form the basis for the work they do.

As an outcome of these multiple reinterpretations, victim-survivors have, for example, redefined their demands for reparations, but also broader conceptions of what (transitional) justice is by mobilising it as part of a broader agenda for gender justice, in which justice is thought of not only as punitive measures but also more holistically as restorative and reparative processes, including the need for psycho-social and socio-economic reparations or support. These are all elements that are considered to be critical to reintegration and participation in society. For example, conceptions of and demands for reparations and justice go beyond financial compensation; they also include socio-economic and psychological support measures (de Waardt et al. 2023) that allow, for example, female victim-survivors to recover their social status and re-establish their roles in their family and community after having become victims of sexual violence (Meger 2010). In this, victim-survivors approach gender justice from a transformative perspective, in which they also address and challenge root causes of violence and structural inequalities.

These multiple reinterpretations also shape practice. Women's groups working on issues such as savings, literacy, or protection, for example, sometimes combine very concrete workshops with discussions about reparations and justice after experiences with sexual violence. In these collectives, victim-survivors often deliberate upon broader expectations and dimensions of justice, including gender equality, women's rights and emancipation, holistic reparations, and leadership in decision-making spaces (Kyamusugulwa et al. 2019; Maubert et al. 2022).

Here, too, it is relevant to point out that victim-survivor organisations and their support networks in civil society do not rely solely on transitional justice rhetoric but simultaneously draw on other frameworks to strengthen their advocacy. These include universal human rights norms, women's rights, gender justice discourses, socio-economic justice, and the right to participation. By combining transitional justice rhetoric with other frameworks within a single-issue campaign, they forge a multi-dimensional approach to gender justice, challenging the limitations of formalised mechanisms and ultimately advocating for more holistic and emancipatory demands within their specific realm.

### 16.3.3 *Mobilising Transitional Justice for Environmental Justice*

A third vantage point for exploring the expansion of and innovations within the transitional justice framework is by looking at its mobilisation in different kinds of broader justice struggles that are not typically part of transitional justice.

Climate change and environmental degradation in eastern DRC interact with existing insecurities, human rights violations, and socio-economic and political challenges, which increase the likelihood of resource-related and intercommunal conflicts, further compounding existing obstacles to peace and human security (Seyuba 2025). Because of the multi-faceted challenges of human rights abuses, environmental degradation, and resource exploitation, local organisations and actors have been drawing on the holistic ambitions of transitional justice, often in combination with other discourses.

Actors such as the Centre de Recherche sur l'Environnement, la Démocratie et les Droits de l'Homme (CREDDHO) typically focus on environmental and socio-economic dimensions of harm caused by, for example, resource extraction, to address violations related to land rights (*droits fonciers*), labour rights, environmental rights, but also broader socio-political rights. As such, they interweave the struggle for human rights, democracy, and environmental protection/sustainability in eastern DRC (CREDDHO 2025). They notably advocate for accountability and governance around natural resource extraction – community mobilisation to claim social, economic, and cultural rights near mining sites such as those in Virunga National Park.

In doing so, they leverage transitional justice language in this multi-faceted struggle as an avenue to frame accountability issues while advocating for reparations and systemic changes to prevent recurrence of violence fuelled by resource extraction. Victim-survivors and human rights defenders emphasise the importance of integrating local understandings of land, territory, and justice, particularly where environmental degradation and community displacement intersect with violence. As such, the transitional justice rhetoric is not only used in relation to direct mass-scale human rights violations but also in relation to broader – violations of – land and environmental rights. Organisations such as CREDDHO thus use transitional justice to link resource extraction to cyclical violence and environmental degradation, demanding reparations and preventive measures for communities affected by resource extraction. When environmental destruction is framed as a violation of fundamental rights – such as the right to life and a healthy environment – it extends transitional justice's focus on (guarantees of) non-recurrence to ecological contexts. Land rights are framed within transitional justice rhetoric as essential to socio-economic stability and justice. CREDDHO, for example, emphasises the systemic connections between resource extraction, violence, human rights violations, and displacement in the DRC, and proposes a discourse that intertwines human rights, environmental rights, and sustainability through a transitional justice rhetoric.

Interestingly, despite transitional justice's typical focus on the state as a central interlocutor, organisations such as CREDDHO often also advocate for holding other actors such as corporations accountable for environmental crimes.

Another important component of CREDDHO's reliance on transitional justice has been its foregrounding of victims as the drivers of the struggle against impunity and for long-term societal healing, as well as their focus on reparations as a mechanism to facilitate the latter and to recognise victims' experience. Their reparation proposals have notably looked beyond individual reparations, given the extensive number of victims and the structural nature of environmental and human rights violations. The widespread violence in the country results in both direct and indirect victimisation, complicating efforts to clearly delineate individual cases. Consequently, they advocate for collective reparations, asserting that, within a transitional justice framework, such an approach also contributes to community-wide reconciliation by recognising entire groups as victims (Steinberg 2012).

In practice, this multi-faceted rethinking and contextualisation of transitional justice as a more integral approach to address a complex struggle has driven how advocacy is organised. Advocacy efforts are victim-centric and notably focus on reparations and on restoring land access to displaced communities while ensuring fair governance of natural resources. This has also resulted in increased attention for how such an approach can drive and mediate community resistance against extractive industries (Cirhigiri 2022).

Here, too, it should be noted that transitional justice is only one of the many frameworks adopted in the face of complex and intersecting injustices. Other frameworks include the human rights framework, victims' rights, environmental and socio-economic justice, environmental sustainability and climate justice, and global resource governance. In addition, feminist and gender-sensitive perspectives emphasise the impact of resource-related violence on women, children, and marginalised groups (Bashwira et al. 2014), advocating for inclusive justice mechanisms. Additionally, advocacy for human rights and environmental justice ties elements of the transitional justice framework to demands for reparations and reforms to guarantee a sustainable peace for both citizens and nature.

## 16.4 SITUATING TRANSITIONAL JUSTICE IN THE BROADER ECOSYSTEM OF INTERSECTING JUSTICE STRUGGLES

By starting from different actors, demands, and struggles, the previous section sought to show how transitional justice language and practice is adopted, reinterpreted, and reapplied across different justice struggles.

Across these three cases, the picture that emerges is one in which various victim groups and CSOs in eastern DRC are leveraging but also re-signifying elements of transitional justice language, practice, and objectives. They are doing so amid a pattern of cyclical – and currently intensified – insecurity and violence in the region,[8] and where significant barriers to accessing criminal justice (Jacobs 2018), especially in rural and under-served urban areas, where informal (transitional) justice initiatives such as community-based reconciliation programmes are the only accessible spaces for seeking justice. The transitional justice rhetoric thus also draws heavily on informal initiatives and related justice efforts.

Importantly, in none of these cases transitional justice is the only mobilising framework. In the face of ongoing violent conflict, people are pragmatically tapping into any opportunity to further the struggle for justice. 'We have lots to gain, and little to lose,' stated the leader of the Coalition of Victims' Groups (North Kivu).[9] While this eclecticism of frameworks may be pragmatically driven, what emerges is a reality in which various justice frameworks, often rooted in different logics, co-exist, interact, and influence one another in unexpected ways that enable victim-survivors to address the compounded structural inequalities faced in this context (as highlighted by Sifris and Tanyag 2019) through integrated efforts that not only focus on justice but also incorporate more transformative and emancipatory demands such as socio-economic and political dimensions of inequality.

It is furthermore important to underline that across these various cases victim-survivors are the ones adopting the transitional justice framework as part of their struggles, and they are also the ones rethinking and reapplying it in creative ways. This pragmatic and creative engagement with the logic of transitional justice means that transitional justice language and principles come to penetrate a broad range of struggles, but also that elements from these struggles are proposed as important additions to the transitional justice framework. Whereas this chapter has focused on the former dynamic, others zoom in on the latter (see, for example, Paricio Montesinos, Chapter 17).

The interweaving of transitional justice rhetoric in broader justice struggles underlines the permeability of the transitional justice framework, and the intersection of justice struggles more broadly. 'Atypical' actors, demands, and struggles blur the boundaries of seemingly diverse struggles and point to the need for considering transitional justice not just as a self-contained eco-system, but also as part of a broader eco-system (Destrooper 2025). As transitional justice inherently operates in (a priori) highly complex and volatile contexts – especially given the

8 'General assessment of the situation in Goma' by the coordinator of the Coalition of Victims' Groups (North Kivu), 10 February 2025 and 24 February 2024.

9 Panel presentation 'People power building justice – Survivors speak up from Congo' with leader of the Coalition of Victims' Groups (North Kivu), Amsterdam, 16 November 2025.

expansion to contexts such as the eastern DRC with ongoing conflict – the diversity of justice spaces and processes ought to be increasingly recognised. Given the circumstances in which transitional justice is put into practice, we might be at a point to consider a new definition – one that is more embedded in victims' everyday practices. When embarking upon this exercise, it is crucial to safeguard that victims' voices and agency remain at the forefront, ensuring that their practice and conceptualisations drive how the field evolves – rather than rejecting what victims do in practice under the banner of transitional justice if it does not fit pre-defined parameters such as language, definitions, and pillars of the transitional justice framework.

## 16.5 CONCLUSION: MEANINGFUL EVERYDAY JUSTICE

In the volatile and conflict-ridden context of eastern DRC, grassroots movements and justice actors working across a range of justice struggles draw upon elements of the transitional justice framework as one of their action repertoires. By adopting, rethinking, and reapplying transitional justice language and principles to new issues such as social justice, gender justice, and environmental rights, these actors pragmatically innovate and adapt transitional justice principles to become a tool in their struggle for justice, and to better reflect their everyday lived experiences.

This use of transitional justice language in broader justice struggles, by new actors, with new demands and including new topics, blurs challenges taken for granted including assumptions about what transitional justice is or should do. Rather than seeing this as an existential threat, the chapter seeks to open the conversation and ask how this can be considered as an opportunity for rethinking the framework. If transitional justice is to be truly victim-centred, it must be inclusive of victims' definitions and practices rather than rejecting them based on preconceived parameters about what constitutes 'real' transitional justice. Given its inherent operation in volatile and complex environments, inclusion of the increasing diversity of justice spaces and mechanisms is deemed essential. This is particularly true for a context of cyclical violence such as eastern DRC.

Redefining transitional justice as a framework that is not merely institutional but deeply rooted in and emerging from the lived realities and justice struggles of victims takes us back to the revolutionary roots of transitional justice and recentres the conversation on how everyday experiences, needs, and actions of victims can become the foundation for meaningful and lasting peace and justice – especially in times of increased violence, and thus intensified pressure on and threats to those promoting intersecting (human) rights and (transitional) justice.

## REFERENCES

Arnould, Valerie. 2021. 'Reflections on a Decentralized Approach to Transitional Justice in the DR Congo'. *Africa Policy Brief*, 33.

Bashwira, Marie-Rose, Jeroen Cuvelier, Dorothea Hilhorst, and Gemma Van Der Haar. 2014. 'Not Only a Man's World: Women's Involvement in Artisanal Mining in Eastern DRC'. *Resources Policy*, 40(June), 109–116. https://doi.org/10.1016/j.resourpol.2013.11.002

Bihamba, Justine Masika. 2024. *Femme Debout Face à la Guerre*. Éditions de l'Aube.

Borello, Federico. 2004. 'A First Few Steps: The Long Road to A Just Peace in the Democratic Republic of the Congo'. ICTJ report.

Cirhigiri, Christian. 2022. 'Youth on the Frontlines: Preventing Human Rights Abuses in Violent Contexts, a Case Study of LUCHA in the DR of Congo'. *International Journal of Transitional Justice*, 16(1), 133–150. https://doi.org/10.1093/ijtj/ijab036

Centre de Recherche sur l'Environnement, la Démocratie et les Droits de l'Homme (CREDDHO). 2025. https://creddho-rdc.org

de Waardt, Mijke, Dora Georgiou, and Kim Baudewijns. 2023. 'Examining Effects of the Interim Reparative Measures of the Global Survivors Fund on Survivors of Conflict Related Sexual Violence in Guinea and the DRC'. NSCR factsheet.

Destrooper, Tine, Line Engbo Gissel, and Kerstin Bree Carlson. 2023. 'Introduction'. In *Transitional Justice in Aparadigmatic Contexts*, edited by Tine Destrooper, Kerstin Bree Carlson, and Line Engbo Gissel, 1st ed., pp. 1–21. Routledge. https://doi.org/10.4324/9781003289104-1

Destrooper, Tine. 2025. 'Thick Accountability in Contemporary Justice Struggles: An Actor-Centered Re-appraisal of Innovations in Transitional Justice Practice'. *Journal of Human Rights*, 24(4), 424–439. https://doi.org/10.1080/14754835.2025.2517158

Dunn, Holly. 2017. 'The Transitional Justice Gap: Exploring "Everyday" Gendered Harms and Customary Justice in South Kivu, DR Congo'. *Feminist Legal Studies*, 25(1), 71–97. https://doi.org/10.1007/s10691-016-9335-7

Ellemers, Mirjam. 2023. 'Democratic Republic of the Congo Truth and Reconciliation Commission (2003–2007)'. African Transitional Justice Hub article. https://tinyurl.com/578nzjjn

Evrard, Elke, Gretel Mejía Bonifazi, and Tine Destrooper. 2021. 'The Meaning of Participation in Transitional Justice: A Conceptual Proposal for Empirical Analysis'. *International Journal of Transitional Justice*, 15(2), 428–447. https://doi.org/10.1093/ijtj/ijab013

Jacobs, Carolien. 2018. 'Seeking Justice, Experiencing the State: Criminal Justice and Real Legal Uncertainty in the Democratic Republic of Congo'. *The Journal of Legal Pluralism and Unofficial Law*, 50(3), 280–293. https://doi.org/10.1080/07329113.2018.1546421

Kasongo, Gentil. 2024. 'Victim & Survivor expectations of the national transitional justice policy in the DRC. Communities in South Kivu, North Kivu & Ituri speak out'. Impunity Watch Policy Brief.

Kyamusugulwa, Patrick M., Dorothea Hilhorst, and Sylvia I. Bergh. 2019. 'Pathways to Women's Empowerment: Navigating the Hybrid Social Order in Eastern DRC'. Working Paper 76.

Lutte pour le changement (LUCHA). 2017. 'Manifesto of the New Congo'. www.luchacongo.org

Maubert, Camille, Jeremy Allouche, Irene Hamuli, Eustache Kuliumbwa Lulego, Gauthier Marchais, Ferdinand Mushi Mugumo, and Sahela Nazneen. 2022. 'Women's Agency and Humanitarian Protection in North and South Kivu, DRC'. IDS Working Paper 578, Brighton: Institute of Development Studies.

McAuliffe, Pádraig. 2021. 'Transitional Justice, Institutions and Temporality: Towards a Dynamic Understanding'. *International Criminal Law Review*, 21(5), 817–847. https://doi.org/10.1163/15718123-bja10060

Meger, Sara. 2010. 'Rape of the Congo: Understanding Sexual Violence in the Conflict in the Democratic Republic of Congo'. *Journal of Contemporary African Studies*, 28(2), 119–135. https://doi.org/10.1080/02589001003736728

Ministère des Droits Humains. 2024. 'l'Objectif Stratégique Spécifique 1 (OSS1): Implémenter la Justice Transitionelle'. www.droits-humains.gouv.cd/ova_sev/justice-transitionnelle/

Mouvement des survivant.e.s RDC. 2018. 'Memorandum du movement des survivant(es)'. https://tinyurl.com/fnnbcfs6

Nagy, Rosemary. 2008. 'Transitional Justice as Global Project: Critical Reflections'. *Third World Quarterly*, 29(2), 275–289. https://doi.org/10.1080/01436590701806848

République Démocratique du Congo. 2013. 'Les Concertations Nationales: Rapport Général des Travaux'. Palais du Peuple.

Seyuba, Katongo. 2025. 'Climate, Peace and Security in Eastern Democratic Republic of the Congo'. SIPRI Insights Paper on Peace and Security. https://doi.org/10.55163/TCSW2134

Sifris, Ronli, and Maria Tanyag. 2019. 'Intersectionality, Transitional Justice, and the Case of Internally Displaced Moro Women in the Philippines'. *Human Rights Quarterly*, 41(2), 399–420. https://doi.org/10.1353/hrq.2019.0031

Steinberg, Richard. 2012. 'Reparations in the Democratic Republic of Congo'. Sanela Diana Jenkins Human Rights Project UCLA report.

Tunamsifu, Shirambere Philippe. 2018. 'Memorialisation as an Often Neglected Aspect in the Consolidation of Transitional Justice: Case Study of the Democratic Republic of the Congo'. *African Journal on Conflict Resolution*, 18(2), 33–57.

Tunamsifu, Shirambere Philippe. 2022. 'Victim and Survivor Participation in Informal Transitional Justice Processes in the Democratic Republic of Congo'. Impunity Watch report.

# 17

# Bridging the Gap

## *Transitional Justice, Victims, and Business and Human Rights in Colombia*

*Marta Paricio Montesinos*

### 17.1 INTRODUCTION

Businesses have a long-standing record of involvement in severe human rights violations, a trend that continues today and is likely to persist into the future. Several examples, from the Holocaust to the authoritarian regimes and armed conflicts in Africa, Asia, and Latin America, demonstrate how economic actors have been implicated in serious violations both before and during conflicts, as well as in the aftermath of transitions to democracy.

Traditionally, the primary focus of transitional justice has been direct perpetrators for specific sets of crimes, that is, gross violations of civil and political rights and criminal acts. In this narrow approach, structural violence and social injustice are peripheral, and corporate actors have been typically excluded from transitional justice mechanisms (Nagy 2008, 284).

Despite this exclusion, corporate accountability for human rights violations during conflict is not a novel concept in transitional justice. Its roots can be traced back to the Nuremberg trials, where the so-called Industrialist cases sought to hold economic collaborators of the Holocaust accountable. Notably, while corporations were not prosecuted as legal entities, cases such as the conviction of Bruno Tesch by a British military court for supplying Zyklon B gas to Nazi Germany's extermination camps underscored the legal and moral imperative of addressing corporate responsibility (Pietropaoli 2020, 18–49). However, despite the insights gained from these trials, which underscored the role of businesses in conflict and laid the groundwork for corporate accountability, the momentum faded. Subsequent transitional justice frameworks largely excluded corporate actors from scrutiny (Ramasastry 2002).

At present, corporate accountability remains elusive; business enterprises are seldom the subject of law enforcement and criminal sanctions. Although human rights violations resulting from business activities can give rise to legal claims in various jurisdictions, such claims frequently fail to reach a judgment, and when legal remedies are awarded, they are often insufficient to address the harm suffered (OHCHR 2016). It is within this persistent dynamic of impunity that emerging approaches both in the transitional justice and the business and human rights (BHR) field seek to confront corporate abuses.

Since the early 2000s, scholars have increasingly criticised the shortcomings of traditional transitional justice models and have called for the inclusion of economic actors in these processes. This shift, known as the corporate turn in the transitional justice field, has prompted researchers to explore innovations and future opportunities – often driven by the efforts and demands of victims and local organisations – for addressing corporate crimes through transitional justice mechanisms in various countries, including Myanmar, Sierra Leone, Brazil, Colombia, Uruguay, and Argentina (Lai 2024, 387; Pereira et al. 2023).

Parallel to this shift, the BHR field has gained prominence, with corporate due diligence legislation emerging as the future framework for advancing corporate accountability. The 2011 United Nations Guiding Principles on Business and Human Rights (UNGPs), together with the Organisation for Economic Co-operation and Development guidelines on multinational enterprises, remain the primary global frameworks guiding states and corporations in preventing and addressing business-related human rights abuses. More recently, the European Union Directive on Corporate Sustainability Due Diligence (CSDDD) is set to introduce binding obligations for corporations, promising to expand accountability mechanisms.

However, these developments have not been without criticism. The UNGPs, being non-legally binding, rely on the voluntary commitment of businesses, limiting their enforceability and effectiveness. Meanwhile, the CSDDD, despite its potential to create legal obligations, has faced scrutiny for its narrow personal scope, concerns about the extra-territorial effects of its provisions, and the limited involvement of Global South countries and communities in its development (Dehbi and Martin-Ortega 2023).

Furthermore, the BHR field often emphasises the global dynamics of corporate power, focusing on the influence of multinational corporations from the Global North on communities and the environment in the Global South. This perspective tends to overlook the abuses committed by companies within the Global South and underestimates the significant role played by local actors, such as victims and their advocates, in driving accountability (Payne et al. 2020).

In this context, recent and still limited literature has sought to bridge the transitional justice and BHR fields so that they inform each other. On the one hand, BHR scholars emphasise how the UNGPs and other BHR initiatives can influence and inform transitional justice mechanisms, particularly in the area of institutional reform (Pietropaoli 2020, 1–17). On the other hand, the lessons learned from transitional justice experiences can inform international legal developments in BHR, shaping them to better hold corporations accountable in conflict-affected areas and high-risk zones (Van Ho 2020).

This chapter seeks to contribute to both strands of literature by analysing the role and mobilisation of victims' organisations during and after the development of the transitional justice model in Colombia, and by shedding light on their efforts to include corporate accountability into the emerging transitional justice framework there. It aims to demonstrate how their positions and actions shaped debates on transitional justice and corporate accountability, as well as how these actors perceived developments in the BHR field following the Peace Agreements. By offering critical insights into both transitional justice and BHR and their intersection, the chapter highlights the synergies between the two fields and underscores the urgent need for their more effective interaction. Specifically, it argues that including economic actors in transitional justice processes and holding them accountable – whether before judicial mechanisms or through participation in truth commissions – and designing context-sensitive BHR legislation are not merely academic exercises but demands rooted in the lived experiences of those directly affected by corporate abuse.

This chapter draws on a desk study of primary sources, secondary literature, and reports, communications, and news produced by victims' organisations, as well as background interviews with academics. The analysis is structured around three key phases in the development of Colombia's transitional justice process: before the Peace Agreements, including the Justice and Peace Process of 2005 and the Victims and Land Restitution Law of 2011; during the Negotiations in Havana and the creation of the Special Jurisdiction of Peace (JEP) and the

Truth Commission; and, finally, the Post-Agreement Period, with the resurgence of violence and the development of Colombia's National Action Plans on Business and Human Rights (NAPs). In each section, the chapter identifies and analyses some mobilisation efforts and formal participation of victims, focusing on their positions regarding corporate accountability. A subsequent section discusses the implications of these positions for the transitional justice and BHR fields. Finally, the chapter concludes with a synthesis of its findings.

## 17.2 LINKING TRANSITIONAL JUSTICE AND BHR IN COLOMBIA: VICTIMS' MOBILISATION IN SEARCH FOR CORPORATE ACCOUNTABILITY

### 17.2.1 *Pre-Peace Agreements: The Justice and Peace Process and the Victims and Land Restitution Law*

The war in Colombia, experienced since the 1960s, was rooted in disputes over political power, democracy, state governance, land ownership, territorial control, and resource distribution. It resulted in more than 9 million victims, 90 per cent of whom were civilians, with rural communities bearing the brunt of the violence. Among these victims were peasants, Indigenous peoples, and Afro-Colombian communities, who not only suffered significant loss of life but also widespread displacement and dispossession of their land (CEV 2022).

This conflict did not emerge in a vacuum, nor was it the impulsive result of isolated groups initiating violence. Instead, it unfolded within a complex interplay of political, institutional, economic, cultural, military, and drug trafficking interests. In its final report, the Commission for the Clarification of Truth, Coexistence, and Non-Repetition (Truth Commission) highlighted the critical role of economic actors in the paramilitary network. While some businesses were direct victims of violence or coerced into collaboration to maintain operations in conflict zones, others actively supported paramilitary groups. Local and regional economic powers, along with productive sectors, forged alliances with paramilitaries to protect private property and expand wealth through violent means, dispossession, and the strategic clearing of territories (CEV 2022).

The collaboration between economic actors and paramilitary groups became undeniable during Colombia's first transitional justice experience: the Justice and Peace Tribunals, established under the 2005 Justice and Peace Law (Law 975). This law allowed members of the paramilitary group Autodefensas Unidas de Colombia (AUC) to demobilise and receive reduced sentences in exchange for *versions libres* (testimonies) detailing their actions. Through these testimonies, paramilitary commanders revealed the names of companies and businessmen who collaborated with, financed, or supported them. By 2009, prosecutors in the Justice and Peace process had gathered substantial evidence about the AUC's civilian support networks and the infrastructure that sustained their operations (Marín López 2023).

Despite the rulings issued by the Justice and Peace Tribunals often referencing links to politicians and economic actors, this tribunal was limited in scope. The Tribunals were only competent to try members of paramilitary and other armed groups, and the confessions implicating political and economic actors were instead referred to the Attorney General's Office for investigation within the ordinary criminal justice system. This created fragmentation between transitional justice and the ordinary justice system, with the latter proving incapable of addressing the scale of the phenomenon owing to significant legal and practical barriers. For example, ordinary justice tribunals must initiate investigations without the same in-depth knowledge of the collaborations and structures acquired by the Justice and Peace magistrates, and referrals often lack sufficient information to establish economic actors' legal responsibility effectively. Additionally, proving corporate criminal responsibility presents major challenges, including establishing *actus reus*, *mens rea*, and a clear causal link between their involvement and the crimes committed (Michalowski 2024, 463–464). As a result, most cases remain in the preliminary stages, and only a few have progressed to criminal trials (Marín López 2023; Tobar Torres 2019).

Nevertheless, the collaboration networks among the state, the economic sector, and paramilitary groups were far from hidden, especially to victims, grassroots organisations, and ethnic communities that brought public complaints before state bodies (CEV 2022). As shown throughout this section, their efforts reflect a continuous mobilisation that takes diverse forms in the pursuit of justice – both by exposing corporate complicity and by demanding accountability mechanisms. In fact, the role of businesses in past atrocities began surfacing in public discourse as victims' grievances moved from the private sphere into claims made in public forums (Bernal-Bermúdez 2022, 146).

A notable example is the Urapalma case. In the mid-1990s, paramilitary groups entered the Urabá region in the Department of Chocó. While justifying massacres, torture, rapes, killings, and forced displacements as part of a strategy to eliminate the guerrilla influence, these groups also pursued economic interests. They colluded with palm oil businesspeople to seize lands belonging to the communities of Curvaradó and Jiguamiandó for large-scale monoculture plantations (Bernal-Bermúdez 2017). The Comisión Intereclesial de Justicia y Paz (CIJP), alongside the Diocese of Quibdó, supported these communities on the ground. Together, they pursued accountability by filing complaints before local and regional courts, as well as with the Inter-American Commission and Court of Human Rights. In 2014, a Medellín court convicted fifteen businesspeople for their role in the forced displacement of these communities. Thus, as early as the 1990s, local non-governmental organisations (NGOs) such as the CIJP began advocating for broader accountability frameworks – ones that extended beyond armed actors to include economic and other non-armed actors who had facilitated or benefited from violence in the territories (Bernal-Bermúdez 2022, 146).

Apart from pursuing accountability through legal claims, grassroots and victims' organisations began creating their own spaces for advocacy and action, seeking to influence Colombia's political and social realities. These efforts often involved the production of knowledge as a strategic tool, with victims and organisations documenting abuses, framing their narratives, and challenging dominant discourses (Tamayo Gomez 2021). Two examples of such knowledge-production and mobilisation efforts prior to the 2016 Peace Agreement are the 2008 international Permanent People's Tribunal (PPT) in Colombia and the 2011–2012 mobilisations against land dispossession in the context of the new Victims and Land Restitution Law.

From 21 to 23 July 2008, the two-and-a-half-year-long fact-finding process convened by the PPT concluded with its final session and ruling in Bogotá. This non-state forum of international opinion, composed of a panel of international judges, had received a 2005 petition from various social organisations, many grassroots-based, requesting an investigation into the role of transnational corporations in the country. The tribunal's process involved gathering knowledge from individuals' narratives during pre-hearings, making this information actionable for political or legal use during the final session in Bogotá. Between 2006 and 2008, six thematic hearings were conducted at strategically chosen sites across Colombia, supplemented by numerous locally organised pre-hearings and associated events. Testimonies presented during these hearings often named specific companies and, in some cases, included documentary evidence of the harm suffered by victims or their families.

At the final session in 2008, the jury issued a ruling citing extensive violations of social, political, and labour rights, as well as environmental standards, committed by more than thirty multinational companies. The ruling also accused the Colombian and US governments of complicity in these violations and proposed recommendations to combat the pervasive impunity in the country (Brunnegger 2016, 123–124; Tribunal Permanente de los Pueblos 2008). Although the ruling lacked binding legal force, it served as a powerful moral denunciation. As Brunnegger (2016) argues, the PPT's work can be understood as a political act that invokes authoritative knowledge of legal and moral wrongdoings. This process serves specific political, moral, and legal purposes, such as legitimising the organisations involved, identifying accountability, and authoritatively establishing the facts of rights violations.

Another significant example of civil society mobilisation to make victims' realities visible and contest state policies is the resistance against land dispossession. Land dispossession, deeply intertwined with economic motives, involved the active participation or complicity of various economic actors who directly contributed to or benefited from the process. One notable initiative was the National Congress of Lands, Territories, and Sovereignties held in Cali in September 2011.

This congress was convened by grassroots and civil society organisations, including the Movimiento Nacional de Víctimas de Crímenes de Estado (MOVICE), Movimiento Nacional en Defensa del Agua y de la Vida, Congreso Nacional de los Pueblos, and Minga de Resistencia Social y Comunitaria, among others. Its purpose was to provide a platform for victims, peasants, Afro-descendant, Indigenous, and urban communities to analyse, deliberate, and define a collective strategy for defending land and territorial rights. Participants also sought to propose alternative solutions in response to legislative initiatives, norms, and policies that threatened their rights (MOVICE 2011).

This congress occurred against the backdrop of the Victims and Land Restitution Law of 2011 (Law 1448), the second main transitional justice development in the country which aimed to provide a legal framework for land restitution. While progressive in multiple aspects, especially its focus on victims (de Waardt and Weber 2019), grassroots organisations criticised the law as insufficient given the magnitude of land dispossession in Colombia. This mobilisation also unfolded within the broader context of Colombia's National Development Plan, which prioritised foreign investment and facilitated land use for agribusiness, the financial sector, and large-scale mining, energy, and infrastructure projects.

In addition to organising discussions, these organisations engaged in demonstrations, demanding a comprehensive land restitution system. A notable example was the demonstration called by MOVICE on 6 March 2012 (MOVICE 2012a). These actors also worked – and continue to work – to denounce ongoing threats and violence against land defenders and leaders of land claimant organisations, who are often targeted by economic actors and paramilitary groups (MOVICE 2012b, 2017).

### 17.2.2 *The Peace Agreements: The Havana Negotiations and the Formation of the Special Jurisdiction of Peace and the Truth Commission*

The progress in uncovering the role of businesses and their patterns of complicity set a significant precedent. When the Fuerzas Armadas Revolucionarias de Colombia (FARC), the oldest and largest guerrilla group in Colombia, entered peace negotiations with the government in 2012, discussions about accountability for past atrocities extended to economic actors (Bernal-Bermúdez and Sánchez 2022).

Generally, the Havana peace talks between the Colombian government and the FARC receive widespread international praise for their efforts to include victims' voices. From the early stages of the negotiations, the Round-Table established three mechanisms to facilitate engagement. These were: a process allowing citizens or groups to submit proposals physically or electronically, regional and thematic forums held across Colombia, and direct consultations in Havana. By the end of the process, over 3,000 victims participated in three regional forums held in Villavicencio, Barranquilla, Barrancabermeja, and a national one in Cali; sixty victims, selected to represent the diversity of experiences and perspectives of the armed conflict, travelled to Havana to provide testimonies and recommendations directly to the negotiating parties; and approximately 67,000 proposals addressing various agenda items had been submitted (La Oficina del Alto Comisionado para la Paz 2016).

In the reports resulting from the three regional forums, participants consistently called for the inclusion and clarification of the responsibility of non-armed actors for violations committed during the armed conflict, including state officials, political leaders, and economic entities implicated in forced displacement, land dispossession, homicides, and forced disappearances (Universidad Nacional de Colombia and UN 2014a). In Barranquilla, participants specifically urged cattle ranchers, palm growers, and agricultural and industrial entrepreneurs to acknowledge their roles in the escalation of the conflict and commit to achieving peace with social justice (Universidad Nacional de Colombia and UN 2014c). Similarly, in Barrancabermeja, forum participants proposed that transnational companies involved in human rights violations be banned from operating in Colombia and required to provide full reparations to victims. They advocated for revising international treaties or enacting national legislation to hold corporations and business leaders, including multinationals, accountable under the Colombian justice system. Furthermore, participants outlined key functions for a future Truth Commission, emphasising the need to explicitly identify the origins of the armed conflict and investigate the relationships between multinational companies, megaprojects, and armed groups – particularly in cases where such alliances caused displacement in certain regions (Universidad Nacional de Colombia and UN 2014b).

On the other hand, the selection of the sixty victims to directly participate in the Round-Table discussions was a challenge and significant gaps remained, including the under-representation of certain territories and crimes, such as land dispossession and the loss of movable and immovable property. Notably, among the sixty selected victims, only one case – Francia Márquez – focused on a community affected by multinational mining companies. While this representation was limited to a single voice, it carried immense significance (VerdadAbierta 2014).

Francia Márquez, now Vice President of the Republic of Colombia, has long been an Afro-Colombian community activist from La Toma, a town in the department of Cauca. She emerged as a prominent leader in the fight against both illegal and legal mining in her territory. In November 2014, she led the renowned Marcha de los Turbantes, during which eighty women marched for ten days and camped outside the Colombian parliament until they secured a meeting with the Deputy Minister of the Interior. The march began with fifteen women from La Toma and expanded as they passed through other communities, raising awareness about the urgent need for the national government to address illegal mining in their territory. Their determination yielded results, but it also made Francia a target of serious death threats, forcing her to leave her town and officially become a displaced person owing to the violence in Colombia (Olano Duque 2022).

In the end, these negotiations resulted in an institutional framework for transitional justice, which included the creation of the JEP. This independent court was tasked with investigating, judging, and sentencing both armed actors and third parties – referred to as 'civilian third parties' – who bore responsibility for serious crimes committed during the conflict. Additionally, a Truth Commission was established with the mandate to provide the most comprehensive account of the armed conflict, including the role of economic actors (Marín López 2023, 383).

President Santos and the FARC signed the first version of the Peace Agreement on 26 September 2016, which was subsequently put to a plebiscite on 2 October 2016. However, the inclusion of provisions addressing the accountability of business actors sparked organised opposition from segments of the business community, which feared it could lead to a 'witch hunt'. This opposition materialised in various forms, including financial and public support for the 'No' campaign in the plebiscite. When the 'No' campaign prevailed, the government was forced to renegotiate parts of the agreement with the opposition. Nevertheless, while certain adjustments were made, the tribunal retained its competence over economic actors implicated in the armed conflict (Bernal-Bermúdez 2022).

As part of the agreement's implementation, Congress was tasked with issuing laws to operationalise its provisions. On 4 April 2017, it passed Legislative Act No. 01 of 2017, which formally established the JEP. Article 16 of the Act empowered the JEP to summon third parties to the conflict, including businesspeople. However, the legislative Act was subsequently reviewed by the Constitutional Court, which declared the second paragraph of Article 16 unconstitutional, citing a violation of the natural judge principle. This principle ensures that individuals are judged only by a pre-established, competent court, meaning that judges must be designated by law before a case arises and cannot be appointed ad hoc or ex post (Michalowski 2024, 481). The Court argued that third parties, having not participated in the peace negotiations, had not waived their right to be tried under the ordinary jurisdiction. Consequently, the JEP's jurisdiction over third parties became voluntary, leaving victims with significant challenges in holding economic actors accountable.

This decision received criticism for maintaining the fragmentation in the transitional justice narrative that characterised the Justice and Peace Process (Marín 2023; Tobar Torres 2019) and for failing to provide real incentives for business actors to voluntarily appear before the JEP. As Philippe Wesche (2019) anticipated, the success of this voluntary system depends on the existence of a credible threat of regular criminal sanctions in the ordinary justice system. However, given the significant difficulties and poor outcomes of ordinary prosecutors' investigations – particularly in cases involving business actors – there is little incentive for businesspeople to accept the JEP's jurisdiction or contribute to the country's truth-seeking process.

### 17.2.3 *Post-Peace Agreements: The Recurrence of Violence and the National Action Plans on Business and Human Rights*

Meanwhile, in what appeared to be a separate initiative, the Santos administration launched its first NAP in 2015, covering a three-year period; and in 2020, the government, now under the Duque administration, announced a second NAP for the years 2020–2022. These plans, designed to implement the UNGPs, aimed to ensure that Colombia protects human rights while encouraging businesses to respect them and contribute to sustainable development.

Colombian organisations strongly opposed both NAPs. They argued that the plans were characterised by vague goals and ineffective measures, offering no guarantees that the state would fulfil its obligations. They also highlighted the absence of a proper diagnosis of the context and the imbalance of power between actors. Notably, the plans omitted any reference to the Peace Agreement or the role of businesses in the conflict and its aftermath, particularly regarding territorial issues such as dispossession, forced displacement, and socio-environmental damage (Ambiente y Sociedad 2016; Mesa Nacional de Organizaciones de la Sociedad Civil sobre Empresas y Derechos Humanos 2019).

In this sense, Colombian organisations have also criticised the UNGPs and the broader due diligence framework for their lack of effectiveness, non-binding nature, and detachment from local realities. They argue that the framework was developed in an international and elitist process, failing to account for the specific needs and challenges of local communities. Additionally, these organisations perceived the UNGPs as having an economic rather than legal orientation, enabling corporations to appropriate them for mere marketing purposes (Bobbio et al. 2019; Knöpfel 2017; Thomas 2022).

Despite this context and the escalating violence following the Peace Agreements – that disproportionately affected communities, social leaders, and human rights defenders (INDEPAZ 2020) – victims and civil society have continued their fight against corporate impunity, employing a variety of strategies.

One notable example of civil society collaboration in pursuing corporate accountability is the creation of the Mesa por los derechos humanos frente al poder empresarial (CSO Human Rights Round-Table to address corporate power) in 2016. This initiative emerged as a response to shared concerns among various organisations about the shortcomings of the 2015 NAP. The Round-Table has since produced numerous documents and statements analysing policies and legislative initiatives, while also advocating for improvements in Colombia's legal human rights framework. Beyond collective efforts, member organisations of the Round-Table pursue diverse objectives, including establishing forums for civil participation, providing legal assistance to victims, investigating corporate human rights abuses and environmental harm across territories, and raising awareness about these issues (Paricio Montesinos 2024).

Moreover, grassroots and civil society organisations continue to be actively engaged with the transitional justice model, submitting proposals, petitions, and recommendations to both the JEP and the Truth Commission. One notable example is the 2022 document produced by MOVICE and the José Alvear Restrepo Lawyers' Collective (CAJAR), presented to the Truth Commission. This document sought to contribute to a broad, polyphonic understanding of the truth and propose measures to ensure non-repetition and accountability (MOVICE 2022).

Among others, specific proposals regarding business actors included: constitutionally prohibiting the formation, support, and financing of paramilitary groups by the state and companies; establishing mechanisms to prevent land accumulation and demanding reparations from multinational companies involved in serious human rights violations; regulating Corporate Social Responsibility as distinct from business ethics; annulling resource exploitation concessions in Indigenous and Afro-Colombian territories conducted without prior consultation and revoking the licences of companies proven responsible for land dispossession (CAJAR and MOVICE 2022).

On 21 April 2022, the presentation of this document was accompanied by a sit-in in front of the Truth Commission, during which victims and social organisations displayed memory galleries showcasing crimes committed by the state (MOVICE 2022). Another similar mobilisation was the painting of the mural 'Who Gave the Order to…' in 2023 as part of the #CampañaPorLaVerdad. This initiative, organised by the Espacio de Litigio Estratégico, victims' groups, and urban artists, aimed to shed light on military and state agents – both within and outside the security forces – implicated in paramilitarism. The campaign called for their appearance before the JEP as part of the investigations into Macro-Case 08: Crimes Committed by the Security Forces. Among those depicted were Jaime Blanco Maya, a former businessman linked to Drummond, and Enilce López, a former gambling magnate (MOVICE 2023).

In the realm of legal claims through state and non-state judicial mechanisms, victims and organisations have pursued various avenues, including strategic litigation, achieving notable victories in corporate accountability both within and beyond Colombia. Internationally, the most recent and emblematic case involves Chiquita Brands International, a US based banana company accused of financing the AUC in the regions of Urabá and Magdalena. After seventeen years of litigation in the US, driven by the unwavering determination of victims and the human rights organisations supporting them, Chiquita was found liable in 2024 for providing substantial assistance to the AUC and was ordered to pay 38.3 million USD in damages to the families of eight Colombian men killed by the paramilitary group (Tripathi 2024). This case marks the first time a US jury has held a major American corporation accountable for human rights abuses committed abroad. While it establishes a potentially powerful precedent, its broader implications for future cases and the evolving discourse on corporate accountability within the framework of transitional justice in Colombia remain to be seen (Devia and Marín López 2024).

## 17.3 WHO BRIDGES THE GAPS? INSIGHTS FROM VICTIMS' MOBILISATION

When examining the role of victims, there remains a risk that the visibility of many social movements in public and academic debates is limited to headline-grabbing mobilisations or tangible, measurable victories (Casas-Cortés et al. 2008, 51). However, this chapter's portrayal of victims' mobilisation to achieve corporate accountability seeks to demonstrate that their struggle is a continuous pursuit of everyday justice. The practices highlighted – ranging from judicial victories such as those in the Urapalma and Chiquita cases, to opposition or calls for more comprehensive regulations such as in the Victims and Land Restitution Law and the NAPs, as well as demands through formal and informal channels for the inclusion of economic actors in transitional justice – reveal the heterogeneous forms this struggle takes. These efforts also underscore how these diverse organisations, often differing in their specific objectives, collaborate in the shared goal of achieving social justice and shaping an alternative reality in Colombia.

In the realms of transitional justice and BHR, these mobilisations provide critical insights. In the context of transitional justice, the sustained efforts of victims underscore that the accountability of economic actors cannot be treated as peripheral or external to the transitional justice model. Victims' organisations have consistently articulated a clear understanding of the role economic actors played in the conflict, demanding acknowledgement of their responsibility alongside appropriate sanctions and reparations. They have emphasised that Colombia's conflict was not merely a clash between armed groups but was deeply rooted in social injustice and entrenched networks of political and economic power. Moreover, economic actors significantly contributed to the creation, promotion, and sustenance of paramilitarism. Therefore, achieving corporate accountability is essential for uncovering the truth, addressing structural inequalities, and preventing future violence.

Although Colombia is often identified as a post-conflict country following the peace agreements, the persistence of violence – particularly against human rights and land defenders, and social leaders – highlights that significant challenges remain. Many of these threats are linked to opposition of economic interest related to large-scale agro-industry, forestry, energy, infrastructure investments, and mining projects (CIEDH 2020, 9). Including economic actors in transitional justice sheds light on the political and economic power structures underlying past and present violence, exposing how elites collaborated to violently consolidate and perpetuate socio-economic inequalities and ensure the non-repetition of these grave violations (Bowsher 2018). It also strengthens trust in the system and the corporate sector. By contributing to truth and accountability, economic actors can help repair relationships with civil society and victims.

This approach avoids indiscriminate accusations or the 'witch hunts' that many businesses feared, while ensuring meaningful engagement with the past (Sánchez 2018).

Similarly, BHR legislation in Colombia must not develop in isolation, disconnected from the country's conflict and its enduring impacts. The integration of international standards into national frameworks must be context-specific, with a focus on contributing to Colombia's pursuit of social justice rather than serving as a tool for business marketing or international recognition. NAPs and future BHR legislation must address the power imbalances between actors, acknowledge the role of businesses in the conflict, incorporate the truths uncovered through transitional justice processes, and establish specific mechanisms to prevent recurrence and impose sanctions where necessary.

What is more, the development of international BHR frameworks, particularly regarding due diligence requirements for companies operating in conflict-affected areas, should draw on lessons from grassroots mobilisations and transitional justice experiences. Ensuring meaningful and robust participation by victims is essential for such frameworks to be both legitimate and effective. By integrating the insights of victims and their advocates, BHR initiatives can more effectively promote accountability and align with the lived realities of those most affected by corporate misconduct.

The question, therefore, is no longer whether economic actors should be included in transitional justice processes or whether BHR legislation, alongside administrative and judicial mechanisms, should be strengthened to end corporate impunity. Instead, the critical issue is how to achieve these objectives within the prevailing context of systemic impunity. On the one hand, the Colombian transitional justice model, despite its advancements and progressive elements, remains fragmented in its judicial construction of truth, with the JEP's jurisdiction over third parties remaining voluntary and corporate accountability relying heavily on the country's limited ordinary criminal justice system (Tobar Torres 2019). On the other hand, this accountability deficit is deeply embedded in a global economic model that perpetuates impunity (Marín López 2023, 354).

This model manifests in the 'race to the bottom', where Global South countries lower business conduct standards to attract foreign investment. This includes the establishment of de facto legal mechanisms and judicial practices – such as investment arbitration, transactional contracts, and liability exemption clauses – that shield economic actors from accountability, and a lack of political will at the highest levels to advance normative frameworks to protect human rights. This reluctance is often driven by the symbiotic relationship between economic actors and the state, with corporations frequently portrayed as 'stabilising agents' essential for achieving national and global policy objectives (Marín López 2023, 354–355; Payne et al. 2020, 63).

While the efforts of victims and civil society offer invaluable insights and have achieved significant victories, they continue to face immense challenges. Addressing these structural dynamics is essential to ensuring corporate accountability for atrocity crimes and preventing the recurrence of such violations.

## 17.4 CONCLUSIONS

This chapter began by highlighting the recent 'corporate turn' in transitional justice scholarship and the growing body of literature seeking to connect the transitional justice and BHR fields. Building on this foundation, it aimed to contribute to the discussion by analysing the role and position of victims and grassroots organisations in the development and integration of corporate accountability within Colombia's transitional justice model.

From the 1990s Justice and Peace Process onwards, local NGOs advocated for expanding accountability frameworks to include not only armed actors but also those who facilitated or benefited from the conflict, such as economic actors. As victims' grievances transitioned from private struggles to public demands, cases such as Urapalma brought the role of businesses in atrocities into national discourse. Victims mobilised through various avenues, including the PPT and public demonstrations, to push for corporate accountability, holistic social justice, and structural reforms. Notable examples include the National Congress of Lands and protests demanding a stronger Victims and Land Restitution Law.

These mobilisations helped uncover the role of businesses and their patterns of complicity, making it impossible to ignore the involvement of economic actors during the peace negotiations in Havana. However, despite victims' demands to hold economic actors accountable, the Constitutional Court ultimately ruled that the JEP over third parties, including business actors, would be voluntary, thereby hindering efforts to achieve accountability.

Separately, Colombia developed two NAPs on BHR, but these non-binding instruments faced strong opposition from grassroots organisations, which argued that the NAPs failed to account for the conflict's context, the roles businesses played, and the stark power imbalances between companies and victims. Civil society also contested the limitations of the UNGPs, deeming them overly abstract, non-binding, and disconnected from Colombia's realities. Nonetheless, victims pursued alternative avenues for accountability, with landmark cases such as Chiquita before US courts.

With this exposition, this chapter argues that victims' mobilisations provide essential insights for both the transitional justice and BHR fields. These diverse efforts underscore the pivotal role of economic actors in Colombia's conflict and post-conflict violence, demonstrating the urgent need for accountability frameworks that address this reality. Importantly, victims' struggles emphasise that corporate complicity is not confined to the past but reflects ongoing structures of violence and entrenched economic and social injustices. Their persistent demands challenge criticisms of the so-called overstretching of transitional justice by showing that corporate accountability is not an unnecessary expansion of the framework but a necessary condition for achieving meaningful justice. Thus, the inclusion of economic actors in transitional justice processes is not merely an academic ambition but a demand deeply rooted in victims' lived experiences, which highlights the profound links between economic complicity, paramilitarism, and the country's entrenched structural injustices.

For the BHR field, these insights underscore the need for national regulations to align with local contexts rather than operating as isolated frameworks. They also suggest that international standards such as mandatory due diligence must draw lessons from transitional justice and victims' experiences to ensure legitimacy and effectiveness.

Ultimately, while these lessons point to the necessity of collaborative, context-specific approaches that bridge transitional justice and BHR to foster structural change and social justice, significant questions remain. Chief among them is how to establish a comprehensive accountability system in a global economic order that perpetuates corporate impunity.

## REFERENCES

Ambiente y Sociedad. 2016. 'Comunicado de la sociedad civil colombiana frente a la política pública sobre Derechos Humanos y Empresa del Gobierno de Colombia'. 13 July. https://tinyurl.com/569xh8rc

Bernal-Bermúdez, Laura. 2017. 'The power of business and the power of people: understanding remedy and corporate accountability for human rights violations. Colombia 1970–2014'. DPhil. thesis. University of Oxford.

Bernal-Bermúdez, Laura. 2022. 'Backlash against Corporate Accountability for Grave Human Rights Violations in Colombia'. In *The Limits of Judicialization. From Progress to Backlash in Latin America*, edited by Sandra Botero, Daniel M. Brinks, and Ezequiel A. Gonzalez-Ocantos, pp. 139–163. Cambridge University Press.

Bernal-Bermúdez, Laura, and Nelson Camilo Sánchez. 2022. 'Innovation from the Bench: Judges, Prosecutors and Analysists Advancing Truth and Accountability for Conflict-Related Corporate Complicity in Colombia'. In *Economic Actors and the Limits of Transitional Justice: Truth and Justice for Business Complicity in Human Rights Violations*, edited by Leigh A. Payne, Laura Bernal-Bermúdez and Gabriel Pereria, pp. 96–121. Oxford University Press.

Bobbio, Magali, García Naranjo, Luciana Cumpa and Mario Urueña Sánchez. 2019. 'Algunas reflexiones sobre la doctrina de la responsabilidad de proteger'. *REDIC*, 2(2), 52–54. https://dialnet.unirioja.es/servlet/articulo?codigo=7467665

Bowsher, Josh. 2018. "Omnus et Singulatim': Establishing the Relationship between Transitional Justice and Neoliberalism'. *Law Critique*, 29, 83–106. https://doi.org/10.1007/s10978-017-9198-3

Brunnegger, Sara. 2016. 'The Craft of Justice-Making through the Permanent Peoples' Tribunal in Colombia'. In *A Sense of Justice: Legal Knowledge and Lived Experience in Latin America*, edited by Sara Brunnegger and Karen Ann Faulk, pp. 123–146. Stanford University Press.

CAJAR and MOVICE. 2022. 'Cinco mínimos de verdad sobre la criminalidad estatal y su configuración como práctica social genocida cometida en Colombia'. https://tinyurl.com/yf69aut8

Casas-Cortés, María Isabel, Michal Osterweil, and Dana E. Powell. 2008. 'Blurring Boundaries: Recognizing Knowledge-Practices in the Study of Social Movements'. *Anthropological Quarterly*, 81(1), 17–58. https://doi.org/10.1353/anq.2008.0006

CEV. 2022. 'Hay futuro si hay verdad. Informe Final de la Comisión para el Esclarecimiento de la Verdad, la Convivencia y la No Repetición'. www.comisiondelaverdad.co/hallazgos-y-recomendaciones

CIEDH. 2020. 'Asimetrías, estrategias, y posibilidades del litigio estratégico en materia de derechos humanos en el contexto de las actividades empresariales'. https://tinyurl.com/r4dudyea

de Waardt, Mijke, and Sanne Weber. 2019. 'Beyond Victims' Mere Presence: An Empirical Analysis of Victim Participation in Transitional Justice in Colombia'. *Journal of Human Rights Practice*, 11(1), 209–228. https://doi.org/10.1093/jhuman/huz002

Dehbi, Fatimazahra, and Olga Martin-Ortega. 2023. 'An Integrated Approach to Corporate Due Diligence from a Human Rights, Environmental, and TWAIL Perspective'. *Regulation & Governance*, 17(1), 927–943. https://doi.org/10.1111/rego.12538

Devia, Tatiana, and Daniel Marín López. 2024. 'Insights from the Chiquita trial (1): 25 years of struggle'. Justice Info, 12 September. www.justiceinfo.net/en/135749-insights-chiquita-trial-25-years-struggle.html

INDEPAZ. 2020. 'Informe: Líderes y Defensores de Derechos Humanos'. 21 December. https://tinyurl.com/3wjm9rbx

Knöpfel, Laura Dominique. 2017. 'Contesting the UN Guiding Principles on Business and Human Rights from Below'. Working Paper 4/2017, Swiss Peace.

La Oficina del Alto Comisionado para la Paz. 2016. 'Proceso de Paz. Acuerdo sobre las Víctimas del Conflicto'. www.refworld.org/es/leg/trat/pleg/2016/es/127317

Lai, Daniela. 2024. 'Beyond Context: Taking Political Economy Seriously in the Study of Corporate Accountability'. *New Political Economy*, 29(3), 385–399. https://doi.org/10.1080/13563467.2023.2268018

Marín López, Daniel. 2023. 'Justicia transicional fragmentada: entender la complicidad corporativa con actores armados desde la construcción judicial en Colombia'. In *Justicia Transicional en Colombia. Una mirada retrospectiva*, edited by Juana Acosta-López, and María del Rosario Acosta López, pp. 351–394. Universidad de La Sabana.

Mesa Nacional de Organizaciones de la Sociedad Civil sobre Empresas y Derechos Humanos. 2019. 'Pronunciamiento público de las organizaciones no gubernamentales ambientales, sociales y de derechos humanos rechazando nueva versión del plan nacional de acción sobre empresas y derechos humanos'. 10 December. https://tinyurl.com/2mhwdefz

Michalowski, Sabine. 2024. 'Approaches to Criminal Responsibility of Economic Actors in Transitional Justice Processes: Lessons from Colombia'. *Columbia Human Rights Law Review*, 55(2), 444–508. http://repository.essex.ac.uk/id/eprint/38234

MOVICE. 2011. 'Se instala el Congreso Nacional de Tierras Territorios y Soberanías'. 30 September. https://tinyurl.com/bdexxbeh

MOVICE. 2012a. 'Comunicado de Prensa: Movice convoca a movilización nacional por una restitución integral de las tierras'. 8 February. https://tinyurl.com/yvnmk673

MOVICE. 2012b. 'Comunicado Público: Asesinato de líder de tierras demuestra falta de garantías para reclamantes de tierras'. 30 March. https://tinyurl.com/3sj6rfk3

MOVICE. 2017. 'Asesinan al líder Mario Castaño Bravo, integrante de Conpaz en Chocó'. 27 November. https://tinyurl.com/ycxrf6v2

MOVICE. 2022. 'Víctimas entregan propuestas de garantías no repetición a la CEV'. 18 April. https://tinyurl.com/2v8kxfdu

MOVICE. 2023. 'Organizaciones, víctimas y artistas lanzan mural exigiendo verdad sobre paramilitarismo'. 12 October. https://tinyurl.com/4rh99bsh

Nagy, Rosemary. 2008. 'Transitional Justice as Global Project: Critical Reflections'. *Third World Quarterly*, 29(2), 275–289. www.jstor.org/stable/20455040

OHCHR. 10 May 2016. 'Improving Accountability and Access to Remedy for Victims of Business-Related Human Rights Abuse'. A/HRC/32/19.

Olano Duque, Iván. 2022. 'Francia Márquez: de la resistencia al poder'. CTXT, 6 August. https://ctxt.es/es/20220801/Politica/40472/francia-marquez.htm

Paricio Montesinos, Marta. 2024. 'Corporate Due Diligence in Post-Conflict Settings: The Role of Civil Society and Victims in Advancing Environmental and Human Rights Protection in Colombia'. *Revista Española de Empresas y Derechos Humanos*, 2, 47–63. https://doi.org/10.69592/3020-1004-N2-ENERO-2024-ART3

Payne, Leigh A., Gabriel Pereira, and Laura Bernal-Bermúdez. 2020. *Transitional Justice and Corporate Accountability from Below. Deploying Archimedes' Lever*. Cambridge University Press.

Pereira, Gabriel, Leigh A. Payne, and Laura Bernal-Bermúdez. 2023. 'Corporate Accountability Is Reshaping Transitional Justice'. OpenGlobalRights, 10 August. https://tinyurl.com/3xb6w4mk

Pietropaoli, Irene. 2020. *Business, Human Rights and Transitional Justice*. Routledge.

Ramasastry, Anita. 2002. 'Corporate Complicity: From Nuremberg to Rangoon – An Examination of Forced Labor Cases and Their Impact on the Liability of Multinational Corporations'. *Berkeley Journal of International Law*, 20(91), 91–159. https://digitalcommons.law.uw.edu/faculty-articles/741

Sánchez, Nelson Camilo. 2018. 'Comisión de la verdad y actores económicos'. Dejusticia, 10 April. www.dejusticia.org/column/comision-de-la-verdad-y-actores-economicos/

Tamayo Gomez, Camilo. 2021. 'Victims' Communities as Knowledge Producers in Transitional Justice Processes. The Case of Post-Conflict Colombia'. In *The Routledge International Handbook of Public Sociology*, edited by Leslie Hossfeld, E. Brooke Kelly, and Cassius Hossfeld, pp. 287–299. Routledge.

Thomas, Fréderic. 2022. 'Estudio sobre el deber de debida diligencia en Colombia'. CETRI, Brussels. www.cetri.be/Estudio-sobre-la-diligencia-debida?lang=fr

Tribunal Permanente de los Pueblos. 2008. Dictamen final del Tribunal Permanente de los Pueblos: Empresas Transnacionales y Derechos de los Pueblos en Colombia, 2006–2008.

Tripathi, Salil. 2024. 'What Guards the Guardians: Lessons from the Chiquita Case'. IHRB, 13 August. www.ihrb.org/latest/lessons-from-the-chiquita-case

Tobar Torres, Jenner Alonso. 2019. 'Responsabilidad corporativa en procesos transicionales de paz: entre la judicialización y la autorregulación. Elementos de análisis desde el caso colombiano'. *Estudios constitucionales*, 17(2), 121–140. http://dx.doi.org/10.4067/S0718-52002019000200121

Universidad Nacional de Colombia and UN. 2014a. Informe Preliminar de las Mesas de Trabajo. Foro Regional sobre las víctimas – Villavicencio.

Universidad Nacional de Colombia and UN. 2014b. Informe general de las Mesas de Trabajo. Foro Regional sobre las víctimas – Barrancabermeja.

Universidad Nacional de Colombia and UN. 2014c. Informe General de las Mesas de Trabajo. Foro Regional sobre las víctimas – Barranquilla.

Van Ho, Tara. 2020. 'Business and Human Rights in Transitional Justice: Challenges for Complex Environments'. In *Research Handbook on Human Rights and Business*, edited by Surya Deva and David Birchall, pp. 379–401. Edward Elgar.

VerdadAbierta. 2014. 'Víctimas en La Habana: los que fueron y los que faltaron'. 18 December. https://tinyurl.com/29j4yuew.

Wesche, Philipp. 2019. 'Business Actors, Paramilitaries and Transitional Criminal Justice in Colombia'. *International Journal of Transitional Justice*, 13, 478–503 https://doi.org/10.1093/ijtj/ijz016

# 18

# Advancing Relational Justice through Meaningful Participation in Reparations Processes

*Pamina Firchow and Lisa J. Laplante*

## 18.1 INTRODUCTION

Reparation programmes constitute a central pillar of transitional justice – a field of study and practice focused on the approaches taken by countries attempting to redress violent and repressive pasts marked by large-scale human rights violations (Arthur 2009, 321; Roht-Arriaza and Mariezcurrena 2006). Administrative reparation programmes occur through non-judicial mechanisms to more efficiently provide redress to hundreds, and sometimes thousands, of individuals and communities. Resorting to reparation programmes has grown in popularity, and it has become common for governments to create administrative victim reparation programmes pursuant to the recommendations of a truth commission (Dixon 2017, 175–176; Laplante 2015, 570).[1] Indeed, according to the Transitional Justice Research Collaborative, there have been approximately forty-five reparation programmes established in thirty-one countries to date (Dancy et al. 2014; Olsen et al. 2010; Transitional Justice Research Collaborative n.d.).

There is a common assumption that victims of war and armed conflict demand retributive justice; however, empirical evidence often challenges this narrative. Studies indicate that while criminal trials remain important, many affected communities express a stronger preference for practical needs such as employment, infrastructure, education, and development initiatives (Shaw and Waldorf 2010; Firchow et al. 2025). These measures are sometimes provided through reparations for conflict-affected populations through collective reparations, even when perhaps they may not technically correspond to the narrow legally prescribed definition of harm associated with human rights violations. Traditionally reparations programmes focus on civil and political rights violations and thus attend to the harms caused by instances that violate physical integrity while overlooking underlying socio-economic harms that should also be redressed (Laplante 2008). Thus, reparations are viewed as essential for responding to the devastating human harm caused by both political and structural violence and are a critical step in acknowledging fractured societies of families mourning loved ones who were killed or disappeared as well as survivors of torture, rape, unjust imprisonment, or other serious harms.

Demands for reparations gain strength when international law recognises the right to redress, positioning reparations as an essential form of justice (Laplante 2015, 544). Reparation programmes contribute to the broader, more ambitious transitional justice goals

[1] Throughout this chapter we use the term 'victim' in its legal sense as an individual who suffered a human rights violation, while recognizing, however, how this term can be contested as a general term of reference for potentially undermining the agency of the person.

of (re-)establishing the rule of law, ensuring accountability of perpetrators, building democratic institutions and a culture of rights, and fostering national reconciliation, all with an eye towards lasting peace and the prevention of new cycles of violence (United Nations Secretary General 2010, 3). In this way, the law of reparations asserts that reparation programmes not only repair individualised harms but also serve societal interests by helping to prevent the repetition of similar harm in the future as recognised in the principle of non-recurrence (De Greiff 2014).

Yet, despite the importance of reparations, and the demands that they be included in transitional justice programmes, scholars and practitioners have consistently revealed the failures of these programmes and how they are rejected by the very people they seek to serve: the victims (Aguilar 2008; Johnston and Slyomovics 2009; Miller and Kumar 2007; Rubio-Marin 2006). Some observers voice concern that reparation programmes may even re-victimise their intended beneficiaries owing to flawed conceptualisation or implementation and unsatisfactory outcomes (Waterhouse 2009). In response, some argue that the fault lies not as much with the *results* of these programmes (the reparations themselves) as with the *process* (or lack thereof or flawed in nature) used in the determination and delivery of these outcomes (Laplante 2010; Firchow 2013). Thus, a common call for victim-centred approaches rests on the idea that the solution lies with *more* participation of the intended beneficiaries of these programmes, without a deeper understanding of what exactly this involvement should entail (Butti and Leyh 2019; Engole 2012; Laplante 2013, 230). A recent scoping of the literature conducted by Firchow and Selim confirms that even if there exists a consensus that reparation programmes must include more victim participation, more needs to be done to better theorise and problematise how to ensure that beneficiary participation is not just 'greater' but also more 'meaningful' (Firchow and Selim 2022).

With the aim of contributing to this exploration, we present *a relational justice framework* to guide the design, implementation, and evaluation of reparation programmes. We hope to move the conversation beyond simply agreeing that more participation is needed, and to instead ask what such participation should look like in order to be successful. We argue that a theoretical framework provides better guidance to develop inclusive processes that effectively integrate the victims and survivors it means to benefit. At the same time, it may reveal what policy choices more appropriately respond to the observed failures of reparation programmes. While institutional spaces and state-backed processes are central to reparations, acknowledging victims' agency, activism, and resistance broadens the perspective beyond a technocratic approach to participation, therefore fostering a more comprehensive understanding of their engagement across transitional justice spaces. The framework we present may have relevance to policymakers, practitioners, and scholars as both a practical guide for a human rights approach to engaging victims in reparation processes as well as a theoretical presentation for future engagement by others writing on this theme.

We draw from already developed accounts of Relational Theory to show its relevance in establishing standards and criteria for inclusive participatory reparation processes that can lead to more satisfactory outcomes, both in terms of the immediate delivery of reparations but also the more durable democratic culture that is associated with the principle of non-repetition. While we acknowledge that a relational perspective may be relevant in other spaces that engage victims and survivors, including as part of their own mobilisation, we focus on the specific processes that governments follow when implementing reparation programmes. Indeed, we argue that attending to the relational in reparations is a necessary form of justice required to achieve full satisfaction. We describe four criteria we believe are fundamental for taking a relational justice approach to reparations, an Ethic of Care, Non-domination and Equality, Mutual Recognition and Respect and Deliberation and Dialogue, and illustrate these primarily drawing on examples from Colombia. Ultimately, relational theory helps carve out legal recognition of a form of justice that should be an explicit goal of reparation programmes. Specifically, *relational justice* offers a more coherent theoretical framework for re-orienting our understanding of what constitutes appropriate and effective reparations by widening our scope of understanding to include what Laplante and Reyes call 'reparative processes', which refers to the idea that the process of designing and delivering reparations itself forms part of reparations and the reparative act (Laplante and Reyes 2024).

## 18.2 BACKGROUND: THE RELEVANCE OF RELATIONAL THEORY TO REPARATION PROGRAMMES

Relational theory is a framework for understanding human behaviour and social dynamics that emphasises the significance of relationships, processes, and interconnectedness in shaping individuals' experiences, identities, and development. It is multi-disciplinary, drawing insights from fields such as psychology, sociology, legal theory, and feminist theory. Indeed, a review of the literature reveals a diversity of fields engaging with relational theory, especially when tackling social justice issues and the processes designed to facilitate solutions to these problems (Donati 2010). Yet there are only a handful of accounts related to the field of transitional justice generally, and none which address the specific focus of the inclusive engagement of victims in reparation programmes (Kent 2020; Murphy 2017).

We draw from these existing accounts of relational theory to emphasise the fundamental importance of process rather than just outcomes when it comes to successful reparations policies. Here, our proposal synergises with what Thomas Pogge critiques as a 'purely recipient oriented' idea of justice (Pogge 2004). As explained by Schemmel, this concept presents a view of social justice 'as a matter of what individuals are entitled to get, rather than of how social and political institutions are to treat those to whom they apply' (Schemmel 2012, 124). In contrast, when applied to reparations, relational theory emphasises the ways in which the engagement of victims in the design, implementation, and evaluation of reparations includes opportunities for repairing and transforming relationships harmed by Apartheid, armed conflict, and authoritarian repression, as well as historical injustices such as slavery and colonisation. Alternatively, the failure to consider these relationships during such a process risks further harm and entrenchment of historically damaging relationships, thus undermining the very purpose of reparations. At a practical level, we view relational theory as an important yardstick for better understanding and attending to the needs of victims to achieve justice after conflict since it recalibrates a focus on context and relationships. Walker refers to this focus as moral repair that involves restoring, stabilising, and in some cases creating relationships that permit more focus on the 'mode of relating' that can account for 'responses, feelings, and attitudes' that shape the disposition of people toward each other (Walker 2006, 23).

For example, scholars of relational theory advocate for a contextual analysis of 'the embodied diversity of individual persons, and appreciation for the centrality of social relationships in defining justice problems and crafting responses' (Eisen et al. 2018, 6). In particular, these solutions are 'forged in relation to other persons, and realised through relations with other persons' (Eisen et al. 2018, 26). In this manner, relational theory has been viewed as a feminist critique of classical liberal theories by offering a 'relational vision of persons as inherently situated, embodied, interconnected, and interdependent' as opposed to the liberal vision of an 'unsituated, disembodied, isolated, and freely-contracting individual' (Eisen et al. 2018, 27). Typically, most reparation programmes follow the latter approach, often calculating a set of legalistically constructed reparation outcomes (such as compensation in lump sum or pension plans in addition to other social programming) without directly engaging with the intended beneficiaries to learn about the context in which they live and whether these measures are truly appropriate or effective.

Moreover, these programmes ignore the way in which the administrators of these processes *relate* to the victims in making such determinations. This approach ignores 'that the person whose rights and well-being are at stake are constituted by their relationships such that it is only in the context of those relationships that one can understand how to foster their capacities, define and protect their rights, or promote their well-being' (Nedelsky 2011, 121). Those responsible for designing and implementing reparations may overlook how their approach to engaging with victims, literally how they *treat* them, can replicate the original experiences of harm. As Raines observes, '[t]he most basic form of marginalizing people is simply to ignore them, to treat them as if they were not there, or to treat them as if their being there is a problem for us for which they are responsible' (Raines 1989, 137).

Replicating this erasure in a reparation process can reinforce the erasure itself. As Colleen Murphy observes, 'one function of violations of basic rights in the form of rape, torture, and mutilation is precisely to humiliate and degrade the individual whose rights are violated, and by extension the groups or communities of which these individuals are a part' (Murphy 2017, 154). Thus, these same people can experience processes that invoke memories of being dehumanised, erased, or otherwise devalued in a process that is supposed to repair them. Alternatively, a process that attends to these impacts by effectively including and engaging the victim may help to restore a sense of well-being and dignity. The relational becomes a form of justice to guide governments as they develop programmes with participatory and inclusive processes for designing and implementing administrative reparation programmes within transitional justice contexts. These programmes necessarily involve relationships of many kinds and the relational provides a recognition that the repairing act is one that requires reflection about the complex relationships between the state, international actors, victims, perpetrators, and the wider society affected by war. For example, there is the immediate relationship between the government agents and the beneficiaries of reparation programmes in the course of designing, implementing, and evaluating programmes; there are also the past relationships with the government and their representatives, or lack thereof, that contributed to the human rights violations giving rise to the need to be repaired; finally, there are the future relationships between the government and the victim who must continue to rely on the official institutions to protect and fulfil their rights. With the latter, the relationship-focus between the government and the governed directly implicates the broader goals of transitional justice, such as a robust culture of rights, democracy, and the rule of law.

We propose that relational theory offers an important conceptual framework for designing reparation processes that optimise repairing and strengthening relationships to ensure not only better success of reparation programmes but also, in the end, better fulfilment of the more general aspirational aims of transitional justice which support the principle of non-repetition. Indeed, relational theory aligns with transformative justice approaches, which seek not only to address individual harms but also to transform the systems and structures that perpetuate inequities (Gready and Robins 2014). In this manner, we align with the observation made by Colleen Murphy who asserts:

> one rough way of defining the overarching aim of societal transformation is to transform relationships among citizens and between citizens and officials such that they are no longer pervasively structurally unequal. It is rough because relational transformation is not restricted to institutional transformation. It also requires attention to the broader attitudes and ethos that characterize relations and interactions. That is, the interpersonal dimensions of institutionally defined and structured political relationships must also be incorporated. (Murphy 2017, 121)

We believe it is through the process of engaging with victims that this transformation begins.

## 18.3 RELATIONAL JUSTICE RE-ORIENTS PROCESS AND PARTICIPATION

The relational justice account supports what Laplante and Reyes have proposed as a reconceptualisation of victim participation as 'a reparative process that, in itself, is a part of the reparations owed to the victims of human rights violations and an additional right of victims' (Laplante and Reyes 2024, 119). The *reparative process* framing renders participation as more than just good (but discretionary) policy that may be done poorly or not at all into 'a standard against which governments can be held accountable for such deficient implementation processes' (Laplante and Reyes 2024, 119).

Victims have the right to a reparative process as part and parcel to their right to reparations, which requires minimum standards for ensuring the quality of the approach used when involving victims in the design, implementation, and evaluation of reparation programmes. These standards would, in turn, generate the evaluation criteria used to evaluate participatory processes. While we recognise the importance of a relational framework for understanding victims (see Daşlı, Chapter 4, and Robins and Bhandari, Chapter 12), in this chapter we focus on how relation directly impacts how governments engage with the intended beneficiaries of official reparation programmes. That said, it may be that the evaluation criteria we share may have relevance in the general ecosystem of engagement with victims in transitional justice.

While the relational justice approach does not demand the selection of only one methodology or set of procedures, it does guide which participatory approaches will more likely amount to achieving the ideals of a *reparative process*. Notably, while the relational focus may appear similar to the tenets of procedural justice, it differs in its orientation, although it may still be complementary. Specifically, while procedural justice calls for the fairness of processes associated with the administration of justice through both judicial and non-judicial mechanisms, it is more attentive to the presence or absence of legal hallmarks of due process, such as the opportunity to speak, be represented by a lawyer, and so on (Solum 2004). Thus, procedural justice may be satisfied if these aspects of process are present, even if the beneficiaries of these users feel dissatisfied with the process and outcome owing to the failure of the process to meet relational needs. Moreover, procedural justice tends to be more focused on judicial proceedings, overlooking non-judicial administrative processes (Cody and Alexa 2018). While some scholars argue that 'perceptions of fairness' motivate procedural justice, this focus still looks for only the presence or absence of certain procedural requirements typically associated with Western notions of justice (Röhl and Machura 2019).

In contrast, relational justice brings additional focus on the affective components and impacts of the process of designing and implementing reparations. In particular, it focuses on relations formed between the people administering the procedures and the end-users of these procedures. Even if a beneficiary receives the optimal features of due process, they may still be left dissatisfied if the administrator failed to align with the principles of relational justice. Yet a government will claim it met its obligation to provide a robust system of procedure even if there is a less than ideal impact of the relational process on the user.

Thus, relational justice supplies criteria that can be used to determine what procedural approaches most effectively engage participants with an eye towards constantly evaluating the way that the providers of reparations, such as governments, *relate* to the intended beneficiaries. While we do not subscribe to one procedural methodology, we recognise that some methodologies may better satisfy the criteria informed by relational justice. For example, Jennifer Llewelyn has already provided a relational theory account of restorative justice and its methodology (Llewellyn 2012b). Certainly, other practices such as transformative mediation, facilitation, co-design, participatory mapping, and other alternative dispute resolution modalities or participatory design processes could contribute to ensuring reparative processes which satisfy the relational justice criteria we present. For us, the key is not so much in the specific inclusive method as an emphasis on implementation that is meaningful for those who are meant to be 'repaired'.

Thus, the guidelines provided here serve three important functions. First, they offer parameters and benchmarks for designing a process of engaging victims that will be effectively inclusive and offer a reparative process. Second, they are useful guideposts for those engaged in reparative processes to constantly check and moderate how they engage in the process during implementation to allow recalibration when needed to ensure compliance with relational values. Finally, they provide important indicia for evaluating the process once it has concluded, which necessarily calls for the active participation of the victims.

Ultimately, a framework of relational justice better adjusts the focus on the victims engaged in the reparation process to help transform their role to being active agents in not only the immediate task of determining the scope of reparations but also ideally in future engagement with governments over matters that directly impact their lives. Here, Dixon et al. recognise how a relational focus helps to 'put the lived, victim experience at the centre of the implementation of the transitional justice project instead of the institutional struggles and logics that lie at the heart of most post-conflict processes' (Dixon et al. 2024, 28). Relatedly, Murphy argues that the relational justice approach focuses on the type of respect and reciprocity for local agency that places more importance on everyday people to choose the appropriate course of action and govern their own lives, which in turn forms the terms of accountability between state actors and citizens (Murphy 2017).

We now turn to defining and illustrating the four criteria we believe are fundamental for taking a relational justice approach to reparations, while recognising they are non-exclusive: an Ethic of Care, Non-domination and Equality, Mutual Recognition and Respect, and Deliberation and Dialogue. For each, we offer a general overview of each of these criteria and examples from practice.

## 18.4 CRITERIA FOR RELATIONAL JUSTICE AND REPARATIONS

Drawing from relational theory and justice literature, we suggest affective criteria that can guide the behavioural interactions between the entities delivering reparations and the recipients of reparations. In presenting these criteria, we do not propose that this is an exclusive list. Rather, there may be other relational values that could be recognised as useful guideposts in ensuring a truly reparative process. Rather, we offer these already recognised criteria as a starting point to further develop a robust understanding of relational justice and inclusive reparative processes. We also recognise that although we are presenting each as a distinct category, they may in fact overlap and blend. Indeed, many of the examples we share from practice could meet more than one of the criteria outlined.

### 18.4.1 *Ethic of Care*

An ethic of care is a moral framework that emphasises the importance of interpersonal relationships, empathy, and responsibility in ethical decision-making. It focuses on the moral significance of care and connection in human interactions, contrasting with more abstract, rule-based ethical systems such as utilitarianism or deontology. Originating from feminist philosophy and psychology, the ethic of care challenges traditional views of morality that prioritise impartiality, autonomy, and universal principles. Koggel and Llewellyn both stress the importance of an ethic of care for relational justice (Koggel et al. 2022), emphasising that care and concern for one another is fundamental to being since we are connected to others and therefore unable to respect ourselves without such a concern (Koggel 1997; Llewellyn 2012a). An ethic of care is important for reparations processes since it recognises the symbolism of a reparative act, moving away from more transactional approaches to reparations which involve simple payments.

To illustrate the complexity of administering reparations with an appropriate ethic of care, we present an example from Colombia. The village of El Salado, in the Montes de Maria region, has been the recipient of extensive reparations following two massacres in 1997 and 2000 in which sixty-six community members were murdered over a six-day period between 16 and 21 February. Afterwards, the village was abandoned and only a fraction of the population returned. In 2007, El Salado began receiving reparations programmes when it was chosen as one of the pilot sites for the Colombian government's Integral Plan of Collective Reparation (PIRC) (Firchow 2017). The PIRC was the Colombian government's first collective reparations programme, and was implemented with support from the United States Agency for International Development (USAID) and the International Organization for Migration. Once the programme ended, El Salado continued receiving reparations, administered by the Colombian Unidad para las Víctimas (Victims' Unit), established under Law 1448.

Through these programmes, El Salado received administrative, collective, and judicial reparations in the form of development aid, individual compensation, and symbolic reparations, all of which have contributed to rebuilding the village (Firchow 2013). Material reparations included the construction of infrastructure such as a paved road, a community centre and library, aqueduct infrastructure, agricultural programmes, and housing. Individual reparations have largely been dispersed in the form of monetary compensation. As will be described in the following sections, an ethic of care as needed to achieve relational justice was integrated into these reparations' programmes, mainly by establishing three criteria for determining and carrying-out reparations: accompaniment, meaningful consultation, and symbolic reparation.

#### *18.4.1.1 Accompaniment*

Accompaniment describes the psycho-social, de-hierarchised process of supporting those who are seeking justice in a dialogically, mutually respectful manner (Watkins 2019, 2). Attention to proper accompaniment ensures a sustained commitment to the community's recovery, facilitates effective and equitable implementation of reparation programmes, helps to build trust between the community and the state, and promotes a more holistic approach to reparations that addresses both material and symbolic needs. Fundación Semana played a crucial role in coordinating and facilitating the reparations process in El Salado, effectively acting as an *acompañante* (companion) for the community. Fundación Semana is a private, non-profit foundation based in Bogotá, and affiliated with *La Semana* magazine. It previously played a prominent role in supporting peace-building and development initiatives in El Salado. They began working in El Salado in around 2009 with a team and an office in the village, aiming to raise awareness of the community's needs and the devastating impact of the paramilitary violence in the early 2000s. Fundación Semana coordinated the efforts of various actors to carry out projects, which was fundamental to their success (Firchow 2013).

Fundación Semana's work involved a long-term commitment to supporting a community throughout the entire reparations process, from the initial assessment of needs to the implementation and evaluation of programmes. It emphasised a continuous presence and engagement with the community, ensuring that their voices were heard and their needs prioritised. Accompaniment is key to an ethic of care since it fosters community participation and ownership of the reparations process as well as recognising that reparations must go beyond material assistance and also address the psychological and symbolic dimensions of harm.

The case of El Salado exemplifies both the benefits and the challenges of accompaniment in reparations. Fundación Semana, a private foundation, played a crucial role as an *acompañante* in El Salado by coordinating efforts, advocating for the community, and establishing a permanent presence. However, the presence of many actors, including Fundación Semana, USAID, and the Colombian government, created confusion about who was responsible for providing and distributing reparations and obscured the symbolic importance of government reparations and the role of state presence in the community. In other words, it was unclear why a non-governmental organisation (NGO) was administering reparations programmes when the harms had been caused by the state and illegal armed actors. Furthermore, the choice by Fundación Semana to focus on material assistance and compensation overshadowed the need for more reconciliation-targeted interventions to address the psychological and symbolic damages of the massacres.

#### 18.4.1.2 *Meaningful Consultation*

Consultation is often seen as a token participatory mechanism, but it can also be seen as a broad umbrella term for participatory approaches to involving communities in policy processes. Consultation can be effective if it is carried out in a meaningful, high-touch manner. Consultation of the community shaped the reparations process in El Salado, ensuring that the community's needs and priorities were incorporated into the planning and implementation of projects. This approach required the participation of community members and was facilitated by Fundación Semana, which acted as a key intermediary between the community and external actors involved in the reparation programme. The PIRC implemented a five-step process for collective reparations, which began with community assembly discussions that provided a platform for community members to voice their needs, concerns, and aspirations regarding reparations, grounding the plan in local perspectives (Firchow 2017).

The Comités de Impulso, also known as Comités de Víctimas (Victims' Committees), were groups of community representatives formed as part of the collective reparations process in Colombia. They collaborated with the Comisión Nacional de Reparación y Reconciliación (CNRR) – which translates to National Commission for Reparation and Reconciliation (and later the Unidad para las Víctimas) – to formulate El Salado's collective reparations plan, ensuring that it reflected the community's vision for recovery and reconciliation. The Comités also played a role in monitoring the implementation of the reparations plan, ensuring that projects were carried out in a timely and efficient manner and addressed any challenges that arose.

By involving community representatives in the process, Comités empowered communities to shape their own recovery and contribute to building a more sustainable peace. However, although the consultation process was highly successful in El Salado, it also had the effect of generating hope and expectations that later were not met by the Colombian state. Colombia's constantly changing norms and laws surrounding reparations made it difficult for implementers to adequately address the needs of communities and fully carry out their reparation plans. Consultations and accompaniment prepared El Salado for reparations, but the Colombian government's delay in carrying out the reparations caused disillusionment and frustration among community members, potentially causing additional harm. This experience cautions that performative consultation can undermine the value of relational justice if it does not move beyond simply listening without action.

#### 18.4.1.3 *Symbolic Reparation*

Finally, symbolic reparation is key to establishing an ethic of care in reparations processes since payments alone are insufficient. Symbolic reparations are non-monetary actions aimed at acknowledging and addressing the harms suffered by victims of conflict and human rights violations. They focus on restoring dignity, promoting healing, and fostering reconciliation. While some focus on symbolic reparations as end results, such as monuments, we suggest that a relational approach would integrate symbolic acts and ceremonies throughout the process of designing and delivering reparations (Laplante 2012, 217). Integrating ceremonies and symbolic acts into the delivery of reparations communicates to recipients the reasons for the reparations, and brings the provider and recipients closer together in a relational capacity.

In El Salado, symbolic reparations played an important role in the community's recovery process. Here, we move away from a static view of symbolic reparations being merely a reparation 'outcome' such as a memorial. Rather, we recognise that many symbolic acts, especially drawing from performative and healing arts, can be integrated into the process of reparation deliberations to communicate an ethic of care. By supporting approaches to mourn, memorialise, and provide psycho-social support, the reparations process demonstrated care about the community's well-being and cultural and historical importance.

For example, every February, the massacre in El Salado is publicly mourned, with participation from local and national government agencies, security forces, NGOs such as Fundación Semana, and the media. This annual event serves as a symbolic acknowledgement of the community's suffering and a reminder of the importance of preventing future violence. Several books and reports have been written about El Salado. For example, the Centro Nacional de Memoria Histórica (Historical Memory Centre) documented and published a report on the El Salado massacre (Centro Nacional de Memoria Histórica 2009). This helped to bring the community's story to a wider audience, ensuring that the truth about what happened was not forgotten. Addressing psychological trauma, court-ordered psycho-social support was provided to the community by another Colombian NGO, the Fundación Mi Sangre. This support addressed the psychological and emotional trauma suffered by residents because of the violence. Finally, the Unidad para las Víctimas implemented a programme called 'Entrelazando', which focused on dialogue, mourning, and rebuilding the social fabric of the community. This aimed to promote healing and reconciliation among residents (Pabón and Mellizo Rojas 2022).

### 18.4.2 *Mutual Recognition and Respect*

Mutual recognition and respect refer to the process by which individuals, groups, or nations acknowledge each other's inherent value, dignity, and rights while honouring their unique identities, perspectives, and contributions. Mutual recognition is integral to reparative justice, as it involves acknowledging the harm done and the humanity of those who suffered. Respect is demonstrated by taking action to address and repair the harm in meaningful ways (Haldemann 2008).

One of the more salient examples of mutual recognition may come from apologies and recognition of wrongdoing. Although very important, we offer a more expansive view of the concept. Some scholars distinguish between thin and thick recognition, where thin recognition is a legal distinction that acknowledges someone as an independent subject within a larger legal eco-system, whereas thick recognition is concerned with self-esteem and being appreciated for what makes someone unique (Söderström et al. 2021; Strömbom 2014). Our approach is more aligned with thick recognition, which acknowledges the importance of individuals and communities in legal and administrative processes around justice and how the method of engagement can either reinforce or undermine mutual recognition and respect.

For example, a dialogical process serves to avoid reaffirming hierarchical relations to instead foster intersubjective exchanges or parity to balance the relationship between the state and the victims and allows them to be co-creators of reparative measures. As Laplante and Reyes observe, 'Dialogics can be understood as a form of generative collaboration where equals come together to formulate solutions to problems' (Laplante and Reyes 2024). When the state respects victims as empowered citizens with rights and agency, it fosters trust, recognition, and respect. An example shared by Laplante and Reyes looks at how the memorial process following the Oklahoma City bombing in the US engaged in crafting a mission statement together to form the blueprint for participants to navigate the negotiation process, especially in times of indecision, uncertainty, and divisiveness (Linenthal 2003). This co-created guide reaffirmed the recognition of the survivors and mutual respect between the providers and recipients of reparations.

### 18.4.3 *Non-domination and Equality*

Justice involves creating structures that empower all individuals to participate equitably in society and protect them from structural domination. Individuals and groups should be free from arbitrary or unchecked interference, oppression, or control by others. Non-domination and equality are central concepts in *republican theories of justice* and emphasise the importance of creating systems and relationships in which power is exercised in a fair, accountable, and non-oppressive manner (Pettit 1997). Relational justice takes equality of relationship as its goal, therefore it is more concerned with the role of equality in relationships between people and institutions and the role power dynamics play in those engagements. As Koggel explains, 'Achieving this equality requires attention to the particular contexts, the parties involved, and to what will be required to ensure respect, concern, and dignity in the relations between and among parties' (Koggel 1997, 299).

When applied to reparations, this means carefully considering what consequences administrative or collective reparations might have for the power dynamics and hierarchies within communities and the relationships between neighbours, local government, armed actors, and others with a stake in community relations. It can also mean taking into consideration socio-economic dynamics and understanding the consequences of giving money or goods to certain groups and not others. Taking into consideration power dynamics is crucial here because more powerful actors may determine the conditions 'under which the weaker party is forced to act' (Young 2005, 145).

We return to the case of El Salado to illustrate an example of attempts to follow principles of non-domination and equality. To ensure that communities had a basic level of subsistence before participating in the reparations process, the national government introduced the *mínimos vitales* (minimum living standards), fundamental social services and economic conditions necessary for individuals to live with dignity and have a sense of well-being, but also to be able to participate in reparative processes (Firchow 2014). These measures encompass access to essential services and resources, such as food, healthcare, education, housing, and even recreation. The Colombian Constitutional Court, in a judgement from 2009, recognises minimum living standards as a fundamental right, emphasising that people require economic resources to meet their basic needs and live with dignity and justice (Corte Constitucional 2009).

The initial collective reparations pilot projects, launched in 2007, included the provision of 'minimum living standards packages', funded by USAID; these were administered to qualifying communities and individuals before collective and administrative reparations. These humanitarian packages and reconstruction efforts aimed to quickly address the critical deficiencies in basic services in the communities selected for the pilot programmes (Firchow 2017). Because these communities sometimes had never seen a major development project before, the government's *mínimos vitales* were often the first formal interaction these communities had with the national government.

Ensuring minimum living standards in El Salado and other conflict-affected communities was also seen as a necessary first step *before* implementing administrative reparations. This was because the Colombian government recognised that communities severely impacted by violence often lacked access to basic social services, hindering their ability to effectively participate in and benefit from reparations processes.

While conceptually distinct, the line between minimum living standards projects and reparations often became blurred in practice (Laplante 2007). Minimum living standards projects often resembled traditional development initiatives, leading to confusion among community members about whether they were receiving reparations or simply development aid. This became especially confusing since there had been little or no previous contact between the national government and the communities. The significant delays between the implementation of minimum living standards and the subsequent phases of the reparations process further fuelled this confusion.

Finally, although well intentioned, providing minimum living standards only to communities or individuals designated as 'victims' created resentment and a sense of exclusion among other communities or individuals with similar needs that may not have experienced the same level of violence. In El Salado, even within groups designated officially as 'victims' by the state, there was tension because victims in a better socio-economic situation were given reparations before those who had been determined as in need of still meeting their *mínimos vitales*. Uneven or perceived favouritism in the allocation of reparations can lead to resentment and conflict, and undermine peace-building efforts. This is consistent with findings from all the CNRR pilot programmes, which noted that uneven payment of reparations caused conflict and tension within communities (Firchow 2014).

### 18.4.4 *Deliberation and Dialogue*

Deliberation and dialogue involve open, inclusive, and reasoned communication among individuals or groups to address issues of fairness, resolve conflicts, and promote mutual understanding. Deliberation is a process of thoughtful discussion whereby participants critically evaluate ideas, evidence, and arguments to make collective decisions; it is a form of non-violent political engagement (Söderström et al. 2021). Dialogue is an open exchange of ideas and experiences aimed at fostering understanding and building relationships; it is more concerned with the dynamics underlying the relationships between actors involved in the dialogues (Maddison 2015, 1023). Whereas deliberation seeks decisions based on mutual agreement, dialogue focuses on empathy, mutual recognition, and exploring shared values.

The Special Jurisdiction for Peace (JEP) is the main restorative justice mechanism in Colombia created by the Peace Agreement in 2016 between the Colombian government and the Fuerzas Armadas Revolucionarias de Colombia – Ejército del Pueblo (Revolutionary Armed Forces of Colombia – People's Army). It includes hearings on the recognition of truth and responsibility as part of its restorative mechanisms. These processes are based on the dialogic construction of truth, which aims to create communication spaces mediated by the JEP between victims and perpetrators. In these dialogues, the aim is for perpetrators to assume responsibility for the actions committed within the framework of the armed conflict and for the victims to express the damages suffered and their expectations of truth and reparation.

The hearings are broadcast live on different communication channels, with the purpose of having a broad impact on the country's citizens, by hearing directly from the victims the consequences of the war on their lives and the reasons for the violence committed from those responsible, assuming responsibility for the facts and providing truth about the facts. Victims receive these processes in different ways: some feel disappointed and dissatisfied, maintaining distrust of the perpetrators, while others find tranquillity and rest. In any case, they are voluntary spaces, and victims have the right to challenge the version that is told by perpetrators.

However, public hearings are preceded by a preparation process for the parties involved. This occurred in the *Huila* case concerning murders and forced disappearances presented as casualties, known colloquially as 'false positives'. Specifically, a Hearing for Recognition and Acceptance of Responsibility occurred in August 2024 six months before a preparation process began; it included several workshops with victims and defendants separately, in which they prepared for the face-to-face meetings.[2] In addition, a private meeting took place between victims and perpetrators as a prelude to the hearing, where, amid strong emotions, they were able to exchange words directly, always mediated by the JEP. These meetings included deliberation through a restorative justice process and resulted in sanctions imposed on the perpetrator. Without proper facilitation, there is the risk that this communication on such delicate topics opens wounds and recalls a painful past without sufficient satisfactory return, which again may result in a distance between expectations of justice and reparation.

## 18.5 CONCLUSION

This chapter introduces a relational justice framework to guide the design, implementation, and evaluation of reparation programmes, arguing that the process of providing reparations is as important as the outcomes. It critiques the purely outcomes-oriented view of justice, advocating instead for a focus on inclusive processes that repair and transform relationships harmed by conflict and injustice. The chapter emphasises that engaging victims and survivors in the design, implementation, and evaluation of reparations can repair relationships damaged by past injustices, while failure to do so risks further harm. Relational theory recalibrates the focus to context and relationships, viewing justice as something forged and realised through interactions with others, including state actors. The relational justice account supports reconceptualising victim participation as a reparative process that is, in itself, a part of the reparations owed to victims. Ultimately, this framework aims to transform relationships between citizens and institutions and foster lasting peace and non-repetition of violence.

[2] Fieldwork carried out in coordination with the Special Jurisdiction for Peace by Daniel Ortega and Luisa Moreno.

We share examples from Colombia, such as a reparations programme in El Salado and the development of sanctions by the JEP, to illustrate how the relational justice criteria might be applied in practice, but also to demonstrate the potential pitfalls of well-intentioned projects that integrate these benchmarks. A main lesson here for transitional justice policymakers is that universal, template approaches are not a panacea for designing reparations programmes. Instead, taking a relational approach to reparations means tailored, contextual knowledge and integration of the cultural and historical contexts of the communities and individuals receiving reparations. The chapter ultimately advocates for a shift towards recognising victims as active agents in shaping reparations and future engagements with governments, fostering a more comprehensive and transformative approach to transitional justice. Consideration of these relational dynamics can transform relationships among citizens and between citizens and government, addressing broader attitudes and interpersonal dimensions of political relationships. A relational approach to justice aligns with transformative justice, seeking to transform the systems and structures that perpetuate inequities.

## REFERENCES


Aguilar, Paloma. 2008. 'Transitional or Post-Transitional Justice? Recent Developments in the Spanish Case'. *South European Society and Politics*, 13(4), 417–433.

Arthur, Paige. 2009. 'How "Transitions" Reshaped Human Rights: A Conceptual History of Transitional Justice'. *Human Rights Quarterly*, 31(2), 321–367.

Butti, Elena, and Brianne McGonigle Leyh. 2019. 'Intersectionality and Transformative Reparations: The Case of Colombian Marginal Youths'. *International Criminal Law Review*, 19(5), 753–782.

Centro Nacional de Memoria Histórica. 2009. 'La masacre de El Salado: esa guerra no era nuestra'. *Bogotá: Memoria Histórica*. https://centrodememoriahistorica.gov.co/el-salado-esa-guerra-no-era-nuestra/

Cody, Stephen, and Alexa Koenig. 2018. 'Procedural Justice in Transnational Contexts'. *Virginia Journal of International Law*, 58(1), 1–31.

Corte Constitucional. Accion de Tutela para obtener reconocimiento o reliquidación de pension-Reiteración de jurisprudencia Sentencia T-184/09 (2009). www.corteconstitucional.gov.co/relatoria/2009/t-184-09.htm

Dancy, Geoff, Francesca Lessa, Bridget Marchesi, Leigh A. Payne, Gabriel Pereira, and Kathryn Sikkink. 2014. 'The Transitional Justice Research Collaborative Dataset'. www.transitionaljusticedata.com

De Greiff, Pablo. 2014. *Report of the Special Rapporteur on the Promotion of Truth, Justice, Reparation and Guarantees of Non-recurrence*. No. A/HRC/27/56/Add. 1. United Nations.

Dixon, Peter. 2017. 'Transitional Justice and Development'. In *Research Handbook on Transitional Justice*, edited by Cheryl Lawther and Luke Moffett, pp. 159–182. Edward Elgar Publishing Limited.

Dixon, Peter, Pamina Firchow, and Fiorella Vera-Adrianzén. (2024). 'The Paradox of Justice: From Transitional to Everyday Justice'. *Law & Social Inquiry*, 49(1), 26–41.

Donati, Pierpaolo. 2010. *Relational Sociology: A New Paradigm for the Social Sciences*. Routledge.

Eisen, Jessica, Roxanne Mykitiuk, and Dayna Nadine Scott. 2018. 'Constituting Bodies into the Future: Toward a Relational Theory of Intergenerational Justice'. *UBC Law Review*, 51(1).

Engole, Martha. 2012. *Reparations for Women Victims of SGBV in Situations of Armed Conflict: The Case of Northern Uganda*. Lambert Academic Publishing.

Firchow, Pamina. 2013. 'Must Our Communities Bleed to Receive Social Services? Development Projects and Collective Reparations Schemes in Colombia'. *Journal of Peacebuilding & Development*, 8(3), 50–63.

Firchow, Pamina. 2014. 'The Implementation of the Institutional Programme of Collective Reparations in Colombia'. *Journal of Human Rights Practice*, 6(2), 356–375.

Firchow, Pamina. 2017. 'Do Reparations Repair Relationships? Setting the Stage for Reconciliation in Colombia'. *International Journal of Transitional Justice*, 11(2), 315–338.

Firchow, Pamina, and Yvette Selim. 2022. 'Meaningful Engagement from the Bottom-Up? Taking Stock of Participation in Transitional Justice Processes'. *International Journal of Transitional Justice*, 16(2), 187–203.

Firchow, Pamina, Julianne Funk, and Roger Mac Ginty. 2025. 'After War Ends: Aid Paradigms and Post-Conflict Preferences'. *World Development*, 189, 106916.
Gready, Paul, and Simon Robins. 2014. 'From Transitional to Transformative Justice: A New Agenda for Practice'. *International Journal of Transitional Justice*, 8(3), 339–361.
Haldemann, Frank. 2008. 'Another King of Justice: Transitional Justice as Recognition'. *Cornell International Law Journal*, 41, 675.
Johnston, Barbara Rose, and Susan Slyomovics, eds. 2009. *Waging War, Making Peace: Reparations and Human Rights*. 1st ed. Routledge.
Kent, Lia. 2020. 'Introduction: Transitional Justice in Law, History and Anthropology'. In *Transitional Justice in Law, History and Anthropology*, edited by Lia Kent and Melissa Demian, pp. 1–11. Routledge.
Koggel, Christine M. 1997. *Perspectives on Equality: Constructing a Relational Theory*. Rowman & Littlefield Publishers.
Koggel, Christine M., Ami Harbin, and Jennifer J. Llewellyn. 2022. 'Feminist Relational Theory'. *Journal of Global Ethics*, 18(1), 1–14.
Laplante, Lisa J. 2007. 'On the Indivisibility of Rights: Truth Commissions, Reparations, and the Right to Develop'. *Yale Human Rights and Development Law Journal*, 10, 141.
Laplante, Lisa J. 2008. 'Transitional Justice and Peace Building: Diagnosing and Addressing the Economic Roots of Violence through a Human Rights Framework'. *International Journal of Transitional Justice*, 2(3), 331–355.
Laplante, Lisa J. 2010. 'Evaluating Truth Commissions and Reparations through the Eyes of Victims'. *L'Observateur des Nations Unies*, 28, 167–176. https://ssrn.com/abstract=3001511
Laplante, Lisa J. 2012. 'Negotiating Reparation Rights: The Participatory and Symbolic Quotients'. *Buffalo Human Rights Law Review*, 19, 217.
Laplante, Lisa J. 2013. 'Negotiating Reparation Rights: The Participatory and Symbolic Quotients'. *Buffalo Human Rights Law Review*, 19, 217–259.
Laplante, Lisa J. 2015. 'Just Repair'. *Cornell International Law Journal*, 48(3), 513–578.
Laplante, Lisa J., and Ana María Reyes. 2024. 'Measuring Up: A Dialogical Model for Assuring a Reparative Process'. *Law & Social Inquiry*, 49(1), 118–147.
Linenthal, Edward T. 2003. *The Unfinished Bombing: Oklahoma City in American Memory*. Oxford University Press,
Llewellyn, Jennifer J. 2012a. 'Integrating Peace, Justice and Development in a Relational Approach to Peacebuilding'. *Ethics and Social Welfare*, 6(3), 290–302.
Llewellyn, Jennifer. 2012b. 'Restorative Justice: Thinking Relationally about Justice'. In *Being Relational: Reflections on Relational Theory and Health Law*, edited by Jocelyn Downie and Jennifer J. Llewellyn, pp. 89–108. University of British Columbia Press.
Maddison, Sarah. 2015. 'Relational Transformation and Agonistic Dialogue in Divided Societies'. *Political Studies*, 63(5), 1014–1030.
Miller, Jon, and Rahul Kumar, eds. 2007. *Reparations: Interdisciplinary Inquiries*. 1st ed. Oxford University Press.
Murphy, Colleen. 2017. *The Conceptual Foundations of Transitional Justice*. Cambridge University Press.
Nedelsky, Jennifer. 2011. *Law's Relations: A Relational Theory of Self, Autonomy, and Law*. Oxford University Press USA.
Olsen, Tricia D., Leigh A. Payne, and Andrew G. Reiter. 2010. *Transitional Justice in Balance: Comparing Processes, Weighing Efficacy*. United States Institute of Peace.
Pabón, Marysol Rojas, and Wilson Herney Mellizo Rojas, eds. 2022. *Sujetos de reparación colectiva y construcción de territorios de paz. Después de la Estrategia Entrelazando: experiencias de reparación colectiva en comunidades campesinas en Colombia*. Universidad Externado de Colombia.
Pettit, Philip.1997. *Republicanism: A Theory of Freedom and Government*. Oxford University Press.
Pogge, Thomas. 2004. 'World Poverty and Human Rights'. *Ethics & International Affairs*, 19(1), 1–7.
Raines, John C. 1989. 'Toward a Relational Theory of Justice'. *CrossCurrents*, 39(2), 129–160.
Roht-Arriana, Naomi, and Javier Mariezcurrena, eds. 2006. *Transitional Justice in the Twenty-First Century: Beyond Truth versus Justice*. Cambridge University Press.
Röhl, Klaus F., and Stefan Machura, eds. 2019. *Procedural Justice*. Routledge,
Rubio-Marín, Ruth, ed. 2006. *What Happened to the Women? Gender and Reparations for Human Rights Violations*. SSRC.

Schemmel, Christian. 2012. 'Distributive and Relational Equality'. *Politics, Philosophy & Economics*, 11(2), 123–148.
Shaw, Rosalind, Lars Waldorf, and Pierre Hazan, eds. 2010. *Localizing Transitional Justice: Interventions and Priorities after Mass Violence*. Stanford University Press.
Söderström, Johanna, Malin Åkebo, and Anna K. Jarstad. 2021: 'Friends, Fellows, and Foes: A New Framework for Studying Relational Peace'. *International Studies Review*, 23(3), 484–508.
Solum, Lawrence B. 2004. 'Procedural Justice'. *Southern California Law Review*, 78, 181–323.
Strömbom, Lisa. 2014. 'Thick Recognition: Advancing Theory on Identity Change in Intractable Conflicts'. *European Journal of International Relations*, 20(1), 168–191.
Transitional Justice Research Collaborative. n.d. https://transitionaljusticedata.com/
United Nations Secretary-General. 2010. "Guidance Note of the Secretary-General: United Nations Approach to Transitional Justice'. United Nations, March.
Walker, Margaret Urban. 2006. *Moral Repair: Reconstructing Moral Relations after Wrongdoing*. Cambridge University Press.
Waterhouse, Carlton. 2009. 'The Good, the Bad, and the Ugly: Moral Agency and the Role of Victims in Reparations Programs'. *University of Pennsylvania Journal of International Law*, 31, 257–263.
Watkins, Mary. 2019. *Mutual Accompaniment and the Creation of the Commons*. Yale University Press.
Young, Iris Marion. 2005. 'Self-Determination as Non-domination: Ideals Applied to Palestine/Israel'. *Ethnicities*, 5(2), 139–159.

# 19

# Victims' Bottom-Up Participation through the Theatre of the Oppressed in an Aparadigmatic Transitional Justice Context

## *The Case of Afghanistan*

*Huma Saeed*

### 19.1 INTRODUCTION

Afghanistan's prolonged war – spanning decades – has left a devastating impact on its people. From Soviet occupation in the 1980s, to the Mujahideen devastating civil war, the rise of the Taliban, the US invasion in 2001, and the eventual withdrawal of foreign forces in 2021, the country has endured continuous conflict that has shaped the lives of millions. The consequences of this war are not only seen in the destruction of cities and infrastructure but also in the deep psychological and social wounds carried by its victims and survivors. Afghanistan's war victims include not just those physically injured but also millions suffering from the invisible scars of trauma, displacement, and loss.

Despite this, Afghans have been deprived of their rights to demand justice, the truth, and accountability for past wrongdoings through formal and institutional responses because they are caught up in a geopolitical game. When a window of opportunity for transitional justice measures opened in Afghanistan in early 2000, the US-led international community chose to pursue a strategy of stabilisation believed to facilitate a superficial- peace at the expense of justice rather than justice and peace as mutually reinforcing measures, despite the strong desire for justice among Afghan war victims. Afghan civilians, who still bear the burden of the bloody war and re-victimisation, have suffered greatly as a result, and Afghanistan has neither attained peace nor justice (Saeed 2023).

Nevertheless, civil society and human rights organisations continued to advocate for accountability for gross human rights violations and justice to victims. A bottom-up and victim-centred justice process had begun to take shape in the Afghanistan socio-political landscape, which was smothered domestically with the Taliban's return to power in August 2021 and has since continued to be a demand of Afghan justice actors in exile. This chapter argues that in the early days, when activism was still mostly domestic, initiatives such as Theatre of the Oppressed, and specifically the Memory Box project, with war victims in Afghanistan offered a space for participation, mobilisation, and empowerment as an example of multi-faceted justice struggles in the absence of formal transitional justice mechanisms.

The Theatre of the Oppressed is a set of theatre practices and games created to enable underprivileged groups to reflect on their circumstances, confront oppressive structures, and come up with alternative solutions to social and political problems. Theatre of the Oppressed is participatory and interactive, in contrast to traditional theatre, where performers perform for an audience. By taking on the roles of actors and co-creators, participants interact with their own narratives and provide different approaches to pressing problems in the real world.

This chapter highlights the frequently overlooked epistemological and methodological aspects of involving victims, emphasising the crucial role of the performative, emancipatory, and collective elements in art-based initiatives. These factors are essential for rethinking how victims engage with the justice system and for exploring new ways of conducting research alongside them using participatory and action research approaches. The chapter will first discuss literature on human rights, activism, and performance, which will be followed by a discussion of Theatre of the Oppressed, including some relevant methodologies. It will then offer insight on transitional justice and victims of war in Afghanistan, the development of Theatre of the Oppressed in Afghanistan, and the Memory Box project, including its impact on memorialisation, participation, mobilisation, and empowerment.

## 19.2 HUMAN RIGHTS, ACTIVISM, AND PERFORMANCE

Performance, activism, and human rights have always had a dynamic and transformative relationship. Performance – whether in the form of theatre, art, cinema, poetry or public demonstrations – has proven to be a potent tool for expressing human rights abuses, questioning social mores, and promoting change in the face of injustice. When used in this way, performance transcends the realm of entertainment and can be used to mobilise communities, raise awareness, and even influence policy (Boal 2000; English 2023; Green 2001; Jones 1998).

By showcasing individual stories and experiences of resistance, resilience, and suffering, performance may humanise abstract political issues and call for action. In the words of a scholar, 'There are complex patterns that link artistic experience with the pedagogy of sensibility and emancipation. Art cannot be held ransom by political agendas, though it intrinsically lives and breathes politics and promotes diversity. It is not the role of art to chart the course that emancipation should take; it will, however, provide a venue for emancipation for diverse audiences' (Bittar 2020, 84).

Protest theatre's contribution to the struggle against Apartheid in South Africa is one such example. Street theatre was used by artists and activists to dramatise the harsh realities of injustice and segregation in order to spur awareness and encourage group action (Hutchison 2013; Royal Shakespeare Company n.d.;). Similarly, in recent years, performances at demonstrations and rallies – such as the well-known 'Vagina Monologues' given in support of victims of sexual and gender-based violence – remain a means of amplifying voices that are frequently ignored or ostracised (Ensler 2007; Halligan 2014).

In essence, performance is a form of resistance, particularly in authoritarian and conflict-ridden societies. The act of performing inevitably challenges the systems of power that aim to silence dissent or violate human rights, particularly when it questions the status quo (McPherson and Mazza 2014, 946). Through immersive art installations, experimental theatre, or direct political protests, performance can challenge hegemonic narratives and present alternative viewpoints.

The symbolic effect of performance is a crucial component of this resistance. As demonstrated by performance artists such as Marina Abramović, whose works have challenged notions of endurance, vulnerability, and the politics of public space, the body itself becomes a place of protest (Demaria 2004; Hessel 2023). In a similar vein, feminist and queer performances frequently entail reclaiming the body as an expression of power, challenging patriarchal systems and conventional gender stereotypes through performance (Kruger 2021; Zychowicz 2015).

Performance also has the power to elevate the voices of under-represented groups that are frequently left out of the political and media mainstreams (Puvaneyshwaran 2024). The work of Chicano performance artists serves as one illustration of this; they have utilised theatre and performance art as a means of expressing their cultural identity and challenging the prevailing narratives of immigration and assimilation in the US (Acosta and Curlee 1995).

Human rights advocacy through performance has shown itself to be a powerful and persuasive force for social change. Performance, whether in the form of theatre, cinema, public protests, or visual arts, offers a special means of addressing human rights concerns, opposing repressive power structures and elevating under-represented voices. When it comes to addressing the suffering of war victims as protagonists, theatre is particularly powerful and unique in the context of transitional justice, where survivors can seek justice and resist impunity. Survivors can reclaim their stories, process trauma, and interact with their communities through storytelling and performance. Theatre can humanise the effects of conflict by enabling victims to communicate their suffering, resiliency, and need for justice. By bringing these stories to the stage, it promotes public memory, accountability, healing, and understanding on a collective level. In particular, art and theatre can become important platforms for marginalised voices and communities, including women and minorities. In this sense, theatre in post-conflict context becomes a vehicle for societal and personal transformation (Destrooper 2019; Saeed 2015a; Siddiqui et al. 2014; Simić and Milošević 2014).

## 19.3 THEATRE OF THE OPPRESSED

In the 1960s, Brazilian director and activist Augusto Boal created a groundbreaking theatre technique known as the Theatre of the Oppressed, which has since become a vital instrument in the fields of social activism and performance. Boal's approach to theatre was directly influenced by the Brazilian educator Paulo Freire's Pedagogy of the Oppressed, which placed a strong emphasis on critical thinking and dialogue in the educational setting. In his landmark 1979 book *Theatre of the Oppressed*, Boal criticised the mainstream theatre's function as a tool of ruling-class control, splitting the arena into actors and spectators. He contended that the primary goal of the Theatre of the Oppressed is to transform the audience from passive beings into subjects and actors, or 'spect-actors'. Additionally, he proposed that by taking on the position of the protagonist, the 'spect-actor' 'tries out solutions' and 'discusses plans for change', thus employing theatre as a vehicle to confront and alter power.

A transformative weapon for social and political change, Theatre of the Oppressed is more than just a performing technique. By encouraging active discussion between participants and audiences, Theatre of the Oppressed moves theatre away from entertainment and toward action. It offers an environment where people, especially those who have been historically marginalised and oppressed, can examine the oppressive systems that influence their lives and try out collective strategies towards liberation. This is the point at which the relationship between theatre and activism becomes most obvious as a political tool for change. Thus, Theatre of the Oppressed can also be a vehicle for external engagement. It not only addresses trauma or raises people' awareness but it also inspires action and transformation.

The Theatre of the Oppressed has been used in a variety of settings around the world to address topics such as environmental justice, gender-based violence, and racial inequity (Brigell 2010; Singhal et al. 2003). In order to address certain societal issues and spark public discussion, activists, educators, and community leaders have modified Theatre of the Oppressed techniques. For instance, Theatre of the Oppressed has been applied to trauma processing and peace-building in conflict areas. It has aided communities in promoting fundamental human rights such as access to housing, healthcare, and welfare access, including in the developed world (Gallant 2004).

Theatre of the Oppressed includes many different methods, strategies, and games (Boal 2002). There is no obligatory method or technique, but instead 'there is a built-in and continuous interplay between the exercises, games, and techniques of all the forms of the Theatre of the Oppressed: Newspaper Theatre, Image Theatre, Forum Theatre, Invisible Theatre, etc' (Boal 2002, 176).

Games playing is a central technique in the methodology of Theatre of the Oppressed. According to a practitioner of the Theatre of the Oppressed, game playing 'allows participants to stretch the limits of their imaginations, de-mechanise habitual behaviours and deconstruct and analyse societal structures of power and oppression' (The Forum Project 2014). Practitioners choose from among many different types of games, depending on the circumstances and the topic, in order to initiate and facilitate the Theatre of the Oppressed workshops with selected participants. Each game is designed in a way that it will afterwards lead to discussions and reflections about self and the social phenomenon in question. Games can begin with confidence-building (primarily for new participants), followed by storytelling, which can strengthen bonds between workshop participants, picture-building, where participants can create different scenes, and creating a play based on various social issues that have been brought up during the workshops. The play, which often reflects a significant socio-political and/or legal problem, may afterwards be shared with larger audiences (Saeed 2015a).

Forum Theatre is one of the most well-known and frequently used methods whereby a play is shared. In addition to seeing the action on stage, this type of participatory theatre lets the audience actively participate in the story as it unfolds. By allowing the audience to enter the play's universe and offer solutions to the problems or conflicts being depicted, Forum Theatre essentially establishes a dialogue between the players and the audience. Instead of offering a single, conclusive conclusion, the objective is to investigate several options. The community can produce ideas, consider various strategies, and gain a deeper comprehension of the complexities of social issues through this interactive process.

The 'Joker', a facilitator who leads the audience through the play, is a crucial component of forum theatre. The fundamental responsibility of the Joker is to keep the audience's attention on the current problems and to give them the confidence to step in without worrying about being judged. The Joker is an impartial character who frames the conversation, seeks ideas, and stimulates reflection. The Joker serves as an intermediary between the audience and the stage during the performance, eliciting insights and promoting the exploration of potential solutions.

The application of Forum Theatre in social justice movements and political campaigns is a noteworthy illustration of its utilisation. For example, Theatre of the Oppressed was applied in South Africa in the 1980s to combat racial inequality and Apartheid. Members of marginalised communities were invited to participate in performances in townships, where they were urged to rethink their social reality. In these situations, Forum Theatre emerged as a crucial instrument for mass resistance, empowering people to envision and act out a world devoid of institutionalised tyranny and racial division. Similar to this, Forum Theatre has been utilised in community workshops to help men and women learn how to step in when they see sexual assault, harassment, or domestic abuse in the context of gender-based violence. By letting individuals try out answers and solutions, Forum Theatre not only raises awareness, but it can also be used as an outward-facing tool to translate into action and changes in individuals' lives and communities.

Similarly, in areas ravaged by violence and atrocities, Theatre of the Oppressed has been utilised as a tool for conflict transformation. For instance, Search for Common Ground (SFCG) in the Democratic Republic of the Congo has used participatory theatre, putting on more than

600 Forum Theatre performances over two years in front of over 500,000 'spect-actors'. In light of this experience, the organisers created a training booklet titled 'Participatory Theatre for Conflict Transformation' in light of this experience (SFCG 2009). In other conflict-affected countries, including Afghanistan, the Theatre of the Oppressed has been used as a vital tool for pursuing justice and accountability.

## 19.4 TRANSITIONAL JUSTICE AND THE VICTIMS OF AFGHANISTAN'S WAR

Transitional justice in Afghanistan has been a complex and challenging process, hindered by ongoing conflict, political instability, and a lack of political will and institutional capacity. Despite initial efforts to address past human rights violations, including the establishment of the Afghanistan Independent Human Rights Commission (AIHRC) and the creation of an Action Plan for Peace, Justice and Reconciliation (2005), progress has been limited. The US-backed government faced significant obstacles in holding perpetrators accountable, and key transitional justice measures, recommended in the Action Plan, were never fully realised. Following the Taliban's return to power in 2021, the prospects for any meaningful formal transitional justice have become even more uncertain, as the new regime, mired in committing grave human rights violations as an insurgent group prior to assumption of power, has reversed many human rights advancements, particularly for women. As a result, the culture of impunity has been further entrenched and the pursuit of justice for victims of war crimes, forced disappearances, and other human rights abuses remains an elusive goal.

Under these circumstances, the role of civil society has been pivotal in advocating for accountability, creating public awareness, and pushing for long-term peace and justice. In particular, the methodologies of Theatre of the Oppressed have been significant in directly engaging Afghan war victims in the process of seeking justice. After Taliban's return to power in August 2021, many civil society organisations, including those working with war victims, were forced into exile; nevertheless, some organisations continue their work with war victims among the Afghan diaspora in Europe and North America as a way to keep victims' quest for justice alive and on the agenda.

Among conflict-affected countries, Afghanistan presents one of the largest war victim populations. It is therefore important to examine the Afghan conflict's victims and survivors, who make up the country's largest constituency, before discussing Theatre of the Oppressed work with war victims in Afghanistan.

> Anyone who came to power carried out all sorts of injustices. Killings, lootings, confiscation of people's properties, sexual violations, bombardment of civilian homes, destruction of agricultural land and orchards, and finally, forced migrations have all taken place. – Man from Helmand.
>
> People were damaged physically and mentally. Physical damages include loss of family members, property and the right to education. Mental damage was more severe because that destroyed our souls, our psyche. For example, as a result of sexual violations, many have lost their sanity. – Woman from Parwan.

These quotations are derived from the ground-breaking document *A Call for Justice* (2005), which was based on a thorough survey with 4,151 respondents and 200 focus group with over 2,000 Afghans in thirty-two (out of thirty-four) provinces and Afghan refugees in Iran and Pakistan conducted by the former Afghanistan Independent Human Rights Commission. The consultation aimed to gauge perception of Afghans on victimisation, human rights violations and transitional justice. The document stated:

> The atrocities that were committed in Afghanistan are of an enormous scale, and the sense of victimization among the people we spoke to is widespread and profound. Almost everyone had been touched by violence in some way. When we asked 4151 respondents as part of the survey whether they had been personally affected by violations during the conflict, 69% identified themselves or their immediate families as direct victims of a serious human rights violation during the 23-year period. Out of over 2000 focus group participants, over 500 referred to killings among their relatives. Almost 400 had experienced torture or detention either themselves or in their immediate family. These are staggering statistics, in comparison to any other conflict in the world Afghanistan's prolonged war – spanning decades – has left a devastating impact on its people. (AIHRC 2005, 8)

The AIHRC study covered only twenty-three years of the Afghan conflict (1978–2001); nonetheless, the war in Afghanistan persisted long after the NATO-led international intervention, which continued to claim the lives of Afghan civilians (UNAMA 2019). Over a period of twenty years, the War on Terror is thought to have claimed the lives of an estimated 241,000 people (Gul 2021). US and NATO-backed Afghan government-led military operations were the primary source of civilian deaths in the conflict in the final years prior to the Taliban's second takeover (Nelson 2019). In addition to the millions of Afghans who have been internally and globally displaced, innumerable more have suffered from all the usual after-effects of war, such as malnutrition, illnesses, and lack of access to clean water.

The victims of Afghanistan's wars are many and varied – civilians, refugees, children, women, and the elderly, in addition to those who have been attacked for political beliefs, each with their own unique stories of survival, suffering, and resilience. Furthermore, Afghanistan faces the victim/perpetrator dilemma, whereby an individual may have been a victim under one regime while a perpetrator under another (Saeed 2015b).

Since 1978, Afghanistan has experienced several regime changes with shifting political ideologies. In the absence of justice and accountability, each regime has targeted its political opponents, particularly during the rule of the Soviet-backed People's Democratic Party of Afghanistan. This has included arbitrary killing, enforced disappearances, torture, and other inhumane acts. According to a former Ministry of Planning official, 25,000 missing persons had been registered in the three weeks following his employment in 1980 (The Afghanistan Justice Project 2005). These were professionals and educated individuals between the ages of eighteen and sixty, including students, physicians, government representatives, members of the armed forces, and religious leaders (Gossman and Kouvo 2013). In the absence of documentation, the fate of most of the missing persons continues to remain unknown. In 2013, the Dutch Office of the Prosecutor published a list of about 5,000 names of those had been killed during the first twenty months following the 1978 *coup d'état*. This was merely a small portion of the total number of people who were forcibly disappeared and/or subsequently killed in this period or in the later phases of the war (Clark 2013).

Afghanistan has one of the largest displaced and refugee populations in the world. Over the course of the conflict, millions of Afghans have fled their homes to escape violence, seeking refuge in neighbouring countries such as Pakistan and Iran, and even further abroad. Many have been forced to live in overcrowded refugee camps, often for decades, with limited access to education, healthcare, or economic opportunities. These displaced individuals face a future marked by uncertainty and a constant struggle to rebuild their lives.

Afghan women and girls have long borne the brunt of the devastating consequences of war in their country. Over decades of conflict, including the Soviet invasion, the Mujahideen civil war, the rise of the Taliban, and the prolonged US-led war, Afghan women have faced violence, displacement, and systemic gender-based crimes. They have suffered from bombings, forced migrations, and the loss of family members, while also enduring severe restrictions on their rights, particularly under Taliban rule. The destruction of infrastructure, healthcare, and education systems has disproportionately affected women and girls, limiting their access to basic needs and opportunities for empowerment (RWI 2024; Saeed 2021a). Despite these hardships, Afghan women have shown remarkable resilience, often serving as caregivers, educators, and activists in their communities, striving for a better future in the face of adversity.

Civilians have suffered greatly as a result of the conflict. There have been an incredible number of casualties from airstrikes, roadside bombs, landmines, and attacks on settlements. Thousands of women and children have been killed or maimed by bombings, gunfire, and explosives in Afghanistan over the decades of conflict (RWI 2024). Since the stress of losing loved ones or seeing violence leaves lifetime scars, many people suffer emotional as well as physical impairments. Psychological trauma is therefore one of the war's most enduring effects, affecting both people and entire communities. Children who have been raised in conflict areas might never experience peace, and the memories of violence may follow them for the rest of their lives. Adults who have experienced or witnessed violence are particularly susceptible to depression, anxiety, and Post-Traumatic Stress Disorder. Many victims lack access to the necessary therapy or assistance because mental healthcare in Afghanistan remains underdeveloped.

The victims of war in Afghanistan are not simply statistics – they are survivors, storytellers, and justice actors who carry the future of their country. By acknowledging their struggles and amplifying their voices, we can contribute to a more supportive and just world for Afghanistan's war victims and survivors.

## 19.5 THEATRE OF THE OPPRESSED AND THE MEMORY BOX PROJECT IN AFGHANISTAN

Oral storytelling and poetry have a long tradition in Afghanistan. They have been used to not only preserve history in a nation with low literacy rates but also to express societal concerns, particularly those related to injustice and inequality, and to demand change. Realising this significant tradition, in 2008, the former Afghanistan Independent Human Rights Commission and the United Nations Assistance Mission in Afghanistan (UNAMA) began theatre projects centred on transitional justice concerns. These efforts were carried out with assistance from the International Center for Transitional Justice. Around this time, Afghan human rights advocates interested in creating cultural approaches to transitional justice in the country were introduced to both traditional and participatory theatre techniques, including Theatre of the Oppressed (Siddiqui et al. 2014).

Specifically with regards to war victims, the Afghanistan Human Rights and Democracy Organisation (AHRDO) employed Theatre of the Oppressed from 2009 to 2021, when the Taliban seized control of Afghanistan and AHRDO was no longer able to carry out its work inside Afghanistan. Through Theatre of the Oppressed, AHRDO was able to engage Afghan war victims from across the country, who represented different ethnic groups, language and geographical diversities, different generations, and men and women, in memorialisation, dialogue, mobilisation, and other initiatives. The work encompassed many challenges, including security threats and opposition from conservative elements of the society, but with persistent and committed work, AHRDO overcame them and managed to reach out to tens of thousands of war victims. The most tangible outcome of Theatre of the Oppressed work with Afghan war victims was the Memory Box project.

Following years of working with Afghan war victims using a variety of Theatre of the Oppressed techniques, AHRDO used Aesthetics of the Oppressed to support a victims-led approach to addressing Afghanistan's violent past and present through the Memory Box initiative. Aesthetics of the Oppressed is considered another technique of the Theatre of the Oppressed. Theatre of the Oppressed, in Boal's view, is like a tree with expanding branches (owing to its numerous techniques and methods) that adapts to new needs without abandoning any of the previous ones while consistently upholding strict relationships within this diversity (Boal 2006). Aesthetics of the Oppressed 'seeks to develop in those that practice it a capacity for perceiving the world by means of all the arts, centring around three human faculties: the Word, the Sound and the Image' (AHRDO 2013, 2). In other words, Aesthetics of the Oppressed employs also other means, such as poetry, singing, and creative writing, and not just the theatre (Boal 2006).

### 19.5.1 *The Process of Creating the Memory Boxes*

Through various artistic games and exercises conducted by a facilitator, participants could choose the moments of their lives they wanted to focus on and how to represent those moments in their personal boxes using specific images or objects. The process typically lasted three to five days and included activities that could help the participants gradually rediscover their long-forgotten creative abilities in addition to a full day of trust-building and group-building exercises. Every activity created chances for more conversations and reflection regarding the conflict and peace in Afghanistan (AHRDO 2013). Participants could produce their own words, sounds and images in the 'form of poems, declarations of identity, photos, drawings, songs, etc' (AHRDO 2013, 2).

This programme targeted survivors who had experienced severe trauma, such as losing a loved one, being physically uprooted, or directly witnessing violence. Every participant in the Memory Box project constructed a symbolic 'box' filled with objects that symbolised their memories, whether they were simple objects with particular meaning, photographs, or remembrance. These artifacts conveyed an account of their suffering and perseverance, of what was lost and what survived. However, the Memory Box served purposes beyond memory preservation. The goal was to give participants an opportunity to define their own history and choose how their stories would be told in the future, thus making them 'the main protagonists in the creation of public memory about the country's long history of violence and human rights abuses' (AHRDO 2013, 4).

Over the course of one decade (2011–2021), family members and relatives of war victims constructed 700 Memory Boxes that contain more than 15,000 personal objects and stories of their loved ones (AHRDO n.d.). This effort culminated in the establishment of the Afghanistan Centre for Memories and Dialogue in 2019, which was regarded as the country's first museum dedicated to war victims. The Centre, which was housed in the basement of AHRDO's Kabul office,[1] included Memory Boxes and provided a forum for communication and dialogue between war victims, academics, civil society, and the international community. With the Taliban regaining control in August 2021, the Centre was forced to close overnight. Digitalised Memory Boxes are on display at the Afghanistan Memory Home.[2]

1 Initially, the Centre was meant to be housed in Kabul's historic Behzad cinema. However, owing to the pressure from warlords who served in the then Afghan government, former President Hamid Karzai did not authorise the location, despite the Kabul mayor's office agreement. For more on this, see www.afghanistan-analysts.org/en/reports/rights-freedom/commemoration-in-the-basement-kabuls-hidden-war-victims-museum-2/.

2 Afghanistan Memory Home: https://afghanistanmemoryhome.org/en/page/cuh5bcdp15u/home.

### 19.5.2 *The Impact of the Memory Box Project on Victims' Participation, Mobilisation, Empowerment, and Memorialisation*

The foundation of Theatre of the Oppressed is the idea of participation, in which viewers are turned into engaged participants. In contrast to conventional theatre, Theatre of the Oppressed invites individuals to examine their challenges and envision novel approaches to overcoming obstacles. Theatre of the Oppressed provides a forum for war victims in Afghanistan, to consider their personal experiences and comprehend the larger dynamics of violence, injustice, and displacement that have influenced their life.

The Memory Box strengthened the group as a whole and provided them with the means to take charge of telling their own narratives, particularly after Memory Box was displayed at public exhibitions, which was seen as a form of acknowledgement of victims' pain and suffering (AHRDO 2016). Participants were invited to tell the group about their boxes and the story of the objects. By doing this, they began to move past being defined just by their trauma and regain control over their stories. It was a ritual of group healing rather than merely a narrative exercise, and they felt proud of this achievement. As a result of these common experiences, participants bonded and took comfort in the realisation that they were not suffering alone (VOA Dari 2018). The Memory Box project offered a potent means of mobilising people by granting participants control over how they communicated their pain and what they wished to express to others; It thus became a form of 'collective truth-telling' (AHRDO 2013).

This approach was not a passive way to engage families of Afghanistan war victims in a bottom-up initiative. It was the embodiment of a victim-centred approach whereby Afghan victims and survivors 'reclaim their voices, honour their losses and offer a glimpse into the human experiences marred by decades of different regimes, wars and internal conflicts that have shaped the life of Afghan society' (Kaiser 2024). The process empowered survivors by granting them the autonomy and agency to write their own narratives and take action as agents of change. Participants co-created the process rather than merely receiving assistance. Through training sessions and workshops led by AHRDO facilitators, war survivors were able to recreate trauma scenes, share personal stories, and work with others to consider alternative solutions and ways of thinking. One of the main Theatre of the Oppressed techniques, Forum Theatre, gave participants the opportunity to act out traumatic events and adopt new personas, allowing them to investigate various approaches to trauma and oppression (Etilaat Roz 2016). By doing this, individuals experienced empowerment in addition to some level of catharsis.

The participatory nature of Theatre of the Oppressed allowed participants to interact with one another in a space where their voices were central to the process. This sense of community was crucial, particularly in a country such as Afghanistan, where social structures have been fractured by years of war (AIHRC 2005). In Theatre of the Oppressed workshops, people who had suffered similar forms of violence – from the loss of loved ones to physical injuries – could bond together in a unique way. Together, they reimagined their situations through the theatre, acting out solutions and offering support for one another in the process. The mobilisation effort, in which healing was not simply an individual act but a communal movement for recovery and justice, leaned on this community empowerment. Such initiatives played a critical role in the establishment of the first National Victims Network in Afghanistan in 2020, in which Afghan war victims and survivors were mobilised in a victim-centred justice process. The victim-centred justice process was 'based on the idea that victims of gross violations of human rights and war crimes have a fundamental right to mobilise for justice and accountability for past harms' (Saeed 2021b).

Another significant impact of this approach was the way it engaged and empowered marginalised groups – particularly women and youth – to speak out. In Afghanistan, women and girls are often the most silenced in society, and their trauma is frequently overlooked. However, participatory theatre – especially legislative theatre – showed that these venues provide opportunities for Afghan women and girls to participate in socio-political processes and gain empowerment (Saeed 2015a). An important contribution of the Memory Box project was the engagement of women, particularly war widows, in the process. Women were given the opportunity to actively participate in sharing and advancing the war narrative from the viewpoint of women through workshops and public platforms, such as Forum Theatre.

The Afghanistan Memory Box's emphasis on gathering oral histories from Afghans across many generations and geographical areas is among its most beneficial features. Those who have seen or survived significant events including the Soviet invasion, the Mujahideen civil war, the Taliban's first period, and the post-Taliban reconstruction phase are included in this. These first-hand reports aid in documenting not just social and political events but also individual experiences of displacement, resiliency, and survival. The personal stories behind the headlines are preserved thanks to oral histories, which in a context such as Afghanistan is significant towards memorialisation efforts. It was thus also a victim-driven form of documentation that drew on their own voices and lived experiences.

## 19.6 CONCLUSION

Through the use of Theatre of the Oppressed, this chapter has shown how participatory theatre may be used to involve war victims in Afghanistan in a victim-centred, bottom-up justice process even in the lack of an official transitional justice apparatus. The Memory Box project created a forum for war victims and survivors to reclaim their narratives, share their experiences, and come together to heal. In a country that has endured decades of war, these initiatives offer a glimmer of hope for a future in which survivors can actively engage in the justice process, promote social change, empowerment, and a feeling of belonging.

Theatre of the Oppressed offers the potential to transform vulnerability into group strength and suffering into action. It signifies a major shift in our understanding of theatre's capacity to effect social change. From its beginnings in Brazil during a period of political persecution to its current global influence, Theatre of the Oppressed keeps empowering people and communities to stand up to oppression, combat injustice, and imagine new futures. It turns theatre from an art form into a potent instrument for social change and collective emancipation through strategies such as Forum Theatre.

The Theatre of the Oppressed continues to be as relevant as ever as we move forward. Given the current state of social unrest, political polarisation, and growing inequality, the Theatre of the Oppressed emphasis on empowerment, engagement, and discussion provides a potent framework for tackling our problems. Engaging with these techniques serves as a reminder that, in its finest form, theatre is a call to action that uses our shared imagination and unity to create new realities rather than merely reflecting the world.

On a larger scale, these initiatives support peace-building initiatives by providing a voice to under-represented populations that are frequently left out of political and social debate, particularly women, young people, and survivors of violence. In addition to aiding in personal recovery, the practice advances the larger objective of social justice and reconciliation. As demonstrated by the example of Afghanistan and other contexts, Theatre of the Oppressed is not just crucial for involving victims as protagonists in activities such as memorialisation, documentation, and other locally driven justice efforts. It also offers important epistemological and methodological insights for transitional justice research, enhancing our understanding of the role and agency of victims. This approach reshapes our perception of what constitutes activism and engagement, and it influences how we engage with research participants through more empowering methods, such as Theatre of the Oppressed.

## REFERENCES


Acosta, Teresa Palomo, and Kendall Curlee. 1995. 'Chicano Art Networks'. *Texas State Historical Association*. August. www.tshaonline.org/handbook/entries/chicano-art-networks

AHRDO. 2013. 'The Memory Box Initiative'. *Afghanistan Human Rights and Democracy Organization*. https://tinyurl.com/4cdnezjv

AHRDO. dir. 2016. *Memory Box Exhibition*. www.youtube.com/watch?v=fMhShk4ROYo

AHRDO. n.d. 'Afghanistan Memory Home'. https://afghanistanmemoryhome.org/en/page/g7pd5ah8js/our-voices

AIHRC. 2005. 'A Call for Justice: A National Consultation on Past Human Rights Violation in Afghanistan'. Kabul: Afghanistan Independent Human Rights Commission. www.refworld.org/pdfid/47fdfad50.pdf

Bittar, Eduardo C. B. 2020. 'Art, Human Rights Activism and a Pedagogy of Sensibility: The São Paulo Human Rights Short Films Festival-Entretodos'. *Human Rights Education Review*, 3(1), 69–90. https://doi.org/10.7577/hrer.3743

Boal, Augusto. 2000. *Theatre of the Oppressed*. Pluto Press.

Boal, Augusto. 2002. *Games for Actors and Non-Actors*. 2nd ed. Routledge.

Boal, Augusto. 2006. *The Aesthetics of the Oppressed*. Routledge.

Brigell, Madeline. 2010. 'Participatory Theatre and the Prevention of Gender-Based Violence'. Advocates' Forum: University of Chicago School of Social Service Administration, 2010. https://tinyurl.com/mr377z39

Clark, Kate. 2013. 'Death List Published: Families of disappeared end a 30 year wait for news'. Afghanistan Analysts Network – English. 26 September. https://tinyurl.com/4a2ws37z

Demaria, Cristina. 2004. 'The Performative Body of Marina Abramović'. *European Journal of Women's Studies*, 11(3), 295–307. https://doi.org/10.1177/1350506804044464

Destrooper, Tine. 2019. 'Performative Justice? The Role of Theatre and Performance in Facilitating Transitional Justice'. *South African Theatre Journal*, 32(3), 199–214. https://doi.org/10.1080/10137548.2018.1556115

English, Gary M. 2023. 'Theatre and Human Rights: The Politics of Dramatic Form'. *Human Rights Quarterly*, 45(1), 1–31.

Ensler, Eve. 2007. *The Vagina Monologues*. Villard.

Etilaat Roz. 2016. 'صندوق خاطرات قربانیان؛ تلاشی غیرسیاسی برای به‌خاطر سپاری پیامدهای جنگ'. اطلاعات روز 16 February. www.etilaatroz.com/34158/صندوق-خاطرات-قربانیان؛-تلاشی-غیرسیاس/

Gallant, Carrie. 2004. 'Recommendations to Vancouver City Council'. Gallant Solutions Inc. https://council.vancouver.ca/20040506/pe1.pdf

Gossman, Patricia, and Sari Kouvo. 2013. 'Tell Us How This Ends: Transitional Justice and Prospects for Peace in Afghanistan'. 2/2013. AAN Thematic Report. Kabul: Afghanistan Analysts Network. https://tinyurl.com/3kp8n2d5

Green, Sharon L. 2001. 'Boal and Beyond: Strategies for Creating Community Dialogue'. *Theatre*, 31(3), 47–61.

Gul, Ayaz. 2021. 'Afghan War Has Claimed 241,000 Lives, Report Finds'. 16 April. https://tinyurl.com/yvkzp6hn

Halligan, Benjamin. 2014. 'Raunch Culture, Third Wave Feminism and the Vagina Monologues'. *Theory & Event*, 17(1). https://muse.jhu.edu/pub/1/article/539136

Hessel, Katy. 2023. 'Marina Abramović's Shocking Rhythm 0 Performance Shows Why We Still Cannot Trust People in Power'. *The Guardian*, 25 September, Art and Design section. https://tinyurl.com/2zubu4h5

Hutchison, Yvette. 2013. *South African Performance and Archives of Memory*. Manchester University Press. www.jstor.org/stable/j.ctt18mbfgr

Jones, Amelia. 1998. *Body Art: Performing the Subject*. University of Minnesota press.
Kaiser, Alejandra. 2024. 'Afghanistan Memory Home Museum: Documenting and Honouring the Human Cost of War'. *HURIDOCS* (blog). 24 January. https://tinyurl.com/ycyybwuz
Kruger, Loren. 2021. 'Participatory Theatre and The Urban Everyday in South Africa: Place and Play in Johannesburg by Alexandra Halligey, and: Prismatic Performances: Queer South Africa and The Fragmentation of the Rainbow Nation by April Sizemore-Barber (Review)'. *Theatre Journal*, 73(3), 451–453.
McPherson, Jane, and Nicholas Mazza. 2014. 'Using Arts Activism and Poetry to Catalyze Human Rights Engagement and Reflection'. *Social Work Education*, 33(7), 944–958. https://doi.org/10.1080/02615479.2014.885008
Nelson, Craig. 2019. 'Afghan and U.S. Forces, Not Taliban, Killed More Civilians This Year'. *Wall Street Journal*, 24 April, World section. https://tinyurl.com/3ybasn5f
Puvaneyshwaran, David. 2024. 'Empowering the Marginalised: Exploring the Potential of Theatre of the Oppressed as an Intervention for Youth Offenders in Social Work Practice'. *Journal of Social Work: JSW*, 24(3), 375–396. https://doi.org/10.1177/14680173231222614
Royal Shakespeare Company. n.d. 'Theatre and Apartheid | Royal Shakespeare Company'. www.rsc.org.uk/news/archive/theatre-and-apartheid
RWI. 2024. 'Accountability for Human Rights Violations and Violations of International Humanitarian Law'. Raoul Wallenberg Institute. https://tinyurl.com/vhwzmsvw
Saeed, Huma. 2015a. 'Empowering Unheard Voices through "Theatre of the Oppressed": Reflections on the Legislative Theatre Project for Women in Afghanistan – Notes from the Field'. *Journal of Human Rights Practice*, 7(2), 299–326. https://doi.org/10.1093/jhuman/huu028
Saeed, Huma. 2015b. 'Victims and Victimhood: Individuals of Inaction or Active Agents of Change? Reflections on Fieldwork in Afghanistan'. *International Journal of Transitional Justice*, December, ijv032. https://doi.org/10.1093/ijtj/ijv032
Saeed, Huma. 2021a. 'The Rights of Afghan Women Must Not Be the 'Sacrificial Goat' in a Male Dominated Peace Process'. *Security Praxis* (blog). 14 April. https://tinyurl.com/2ew5au3e
Saeed, Huma. 2021b. 'What Happens to the Victims of Afghanistan's War?' Inkstick. 24 May. https://inkstickmedia.com/what-happens-to-the-victims-of-afghanistans-war/
Saeed, Huma. 2023. 'Transitional Justice in Afghanistan: A Hegemonic Power Discourse'. In *Transitional Justice in Aparadigmatic Contexts*, edited by Tine Destrooper, Kerstin Bree Carlson, and Line Engbo Gissel, pp. 68–85. Routledge.
SFCG. 2009. 'Participatory Theatre for Conflict Transformation: Training Manual'. Search for Common Ground. https://tinyurl.com/ypm2cunn
Siddiqui, Nadia, Hadi Marifat, and Sari Kouvo. 2014. 'Culture, Theatre and Justice: Examples from Afghanistan'. In *The Arts of Transitional Justice: Culture, Activism, and Memory after Atrocity*, edited by Peter D. Rush and Olivera Simić, pp. 113–134. Springer. https://doi.org/10.1007/978-1-4614-8385-4_7
Simić, Olivera, and Dijana Milošević. 2014. 'Enacting Justice: The Role of Dah Theatre Company in Transitional Justice Processes in Serbia and Beyond'. In *The Arts of Transitional Justice: Culture, Activism, and Memory after Atrocity*, edited by Peter D. Rush and Olivera Simić, pp. 99–112. Springer. https://doi.org/10.1007/978-1-4614-8385-4_6
Singhal, Arvind, Michael J. Cody, Everett M. Rogers, and Miguel Sabido. 2003. *Entertainment-Education and Social Change: History, Research, and Practice*. Routledge.
The Afghanistan Justice Project. 2005. 'Casting Shadows: War Crimes and Crimes against Humanity, 1978–2001'. Open Society Foundations. 2005. https://tinyurl.com/4y3juwnj
The Forum Project. 2014. 'What Is Theatre of the Oppressed?' http://theforumproject.org/whatisto
UNAMA. 2019. 'Afghanistan: Protection of Civilians in Armed Conflict'. United Nations Assistance Mission for Afghanistan. https://tinyurl.com/42h7rp26
VOA Dari, dir. 2018. Afghanistan War Memory Boxes – VOA Ashna. www.youtube.com/watch?v=eqhD98l70KU
Zychowicz, Jessica. 2015. 'Performing Protest: Femen, Nation, and the Marketing of Resistance'. *Journal of Ukrainian Politics and Society*, 1(1), 79–104.

# 20

# Participatory Research in Postwar El Salvador

## *Co-creation of Community History Books with Civil War Survivors and Local Youth*

*Adriana Alas, Amanda Grzyb, and María Helia Rivera Castillo*

### 20.1 INTRODUCTION

Blanca Tirsa Varela Mátir was just seven years old in 1979 when she and her mother, Teresa Varela, joined a group of women travelling from Arcatao to Chalate to sell their animals amid escalating violence against civilians by the Salvadoran Armed Forces. On their way back from the market, the group paused to rest in the canton of Hacienda Vieja in the municipality of San José Las Flores. It was there that members of the National Guard approached them, targeting Varela Mátir's mother. In a recent interview with our research team, Varela Mátir recounted her memories of the event:

> They already had my mother at gunpoint, and I stayed by her side. I saw when they shot her. Then, a guard turned to me and said, 'Are you going to run or not? If you don't run, I'm going to kill you.' So, I ran alone down the street. They shot at me twice, but I only felt the heat near my back. The bullets burned my loose dress, and thank God, they didn't catch me because I ran away. When I reached the last houses on the street, I stopped and looked back. I saw my mommy walking and waited, hoping she could catch up. But she couldn't.
>
> At the last house, I saw the other women [who had been with us] and they said to me, 'Girl, come here.' I entered that house and I said, 'Give me water, give me water.' A man replied, 'Don't give her water, just wet her lips.' I asked, 'What about my mommy?' They told me, 'No, Teresa went ahead.' 'But why did she leave me?' I asked. They said, 'So that you would go with us.' They didn't want to tell me [the truth]. At that moment, I was scared. I remember up to that point, but nothing after.
>
> Later, around five in the afternoon, I woke up lying in a hammock. [The women] hadn't left me, they were still there. I said to them, 'Give me water,' and they gave me some. Then they said, 'Look, we're going to leave now.' I asked, 'But what about my mommy?' They said, 'No, your mommy already went ahead. She's at the house.' I stayed seated, and after a while I remembered. 'No,' I told them, 'They killed my mommy. My mommy is dead.' [...]
>
> I arrived home around six in the evening. I told my brother, and he went to inform the family. They wanted to go and retrieve [my mother] that same night, but they couldn't because [the guards] were watching her, waiting to see who would come for her. She stayed there for the entire day and night. The next night, they were finally able to bring her back. At that time, it was no longer possible to bury people in the cemeteries, so we half-buried her in the little plot of land where we lived. To this day, she is still there. We visited to make sure she was still resting there, and she is.

> I am fifty years old now, and it's still very hard for me. I tell my children, 'Look how much time has passed and I still feel a deep sadness in my heart. Me, my mother ... Do you see how old I am and yet sometimes I still cry at night when no one sees me.' (Alas et al. 2024, 328–332)

Varela Mátir's testimony – recounting brutal state violence against civilians, the provisional burial of her mother, enduring post-traumatic stress, and impunity for the perpetrators – is a sadly common one, echoed in the experiences of hundreds of thousands of Salvadoran civilians who suffered through a cruel and prolonged armed conflict that began in 1970 and escalated into a full-scale civil war a decade later. As the war ebbed and flowed from 1980 to 1992, approximately 75,000 people were killed, 8,000 were disappeared, and one-third of the entire population of El Salvador was forcibly displaced (Comisión de la Verdad para El Salvador 1993). This chapter examines how – in a context that lacks formal mechanisms to address war crimes – some Salvadorans, including Varela Mátir, are engaging in alternative forms of justice through community-based research and commemoration activities with an international research initiative called Surviving Memory in Postwar El Salvador (Surviving Memory).[1] Using *Experiences and Memories of Arcatao* (2024) as a case study, we highlight Surviving Memory's collaborative methodology, which includes – among other projects – documenting victims' names, mapping massacres, co-creating local community history books, and erecting local memorials. Additionally, we emphasise the long-standing tradition of popular education in Chalatenango and the role of international solidarity actors in these efforts. In doing so, we explore more open-ended ways of engaging alongside victim-protagonists that are available to researchers and practitioners, and that shift the power balance underlying the interactions.

During its post-conflict investigation, the United Nations Commission on the Truth for El Salvador received 22,000 complaints of violence and ultimately held state agents responsible for 85 per cent of wartime violations, attributing 5 per cent to the FMLN guerrilla forces (Comisión de la Verdad para El Salvador 1993). The Commission's final report, *From Madness to Hope*, recommended reparations and the creation of memorials to recognise the victims of state violence. Days after the report was released, the Salvadoran legislature passed a general amnesty law that prevented prosecutions for any war-related crimes, a move that the Inter-American Commission of Human Rights deemed a violation of international law (Inter-American Commission on Human Rights 1999). Although the amnesty law was eventually overturned in 2016, not one post-war government – right or left – has adequately complied with the Truth Commission's directives.

A culture of impunity continues to dominate the national landscape and, in the wake of the state's negligence, efforts to document and commemorate victims of the civil war – the 'fifth pillar' of transitional justice – reside primarily with survivor groups, local communities, civil society organisations, and their international collaborators. This dynamic is symbolically reflected in Varela Mátir's testimony when she describes the local women who stayed by her side, supporting and protecting her after the death of her mother in a context of total impunity. It is also reflected in the makeshift burial of her mother's body, a memorial that is tended only by members of her family. As with thousands of other massacres and assassinations, there is still no justice for the killing of Teresa Varela: no investigation, no exhumation, no state intervention, no apology, no official acknowledgement, and no prosecution. Emotional support for survivors of state violence comes predominantly from local health promotors and survivor groups

[1] Surviving Memory in Postwar El Salvador is supported in part by funding from the Social Sciences and Humanities Research Council of Canada's Partnership Grant programme, the Canadian Foundation for Innovation, the Ontario Research Fund, Western University.

in a context where there is widespread intergenerational trauma and few pathways to professional mental health services. Similarly, the care for mass graves, provisional burial sites, and clandestine cemeteries remains with local survivors who organise commemorations, construct memorials, and file applications for exhumations.

As survivors and perpetrators age and the possibilities for traditional forms of justice are ever further out of reach, some communities are embracing alternative modes of transitional justice and post-conflict reconstruction. The Surviving Memory in Postwar El Salvador research initiative – an international, cross-sector partnership that includes survivors, scholars, artists, lawyers, museums, architects, community organisers, civil society organisations, and mental health professionals – is one such effort to address the gaping wound left open by the state's mass atrocities and subsequent inaction. Founded in 2017 and rooted in a long tradition of popular education in rural El Salvador, Surviving Memory's community-based projects include historical memory workshops, video testimonies, massacre mapping, light detection and ranging (LiDAR) and virtual reconstructions of destroyed villages, the architectural co-design and construction of memorials, a music archive, public art (including murals, ceramics, sculptures, and embroideries), exhibitions, theatrical performances, digitisation of vulnerable documents and photographs, and the co-authorship of local history books.

Using one of Surviving Memory's recent community books, *Experiences and Memories of Arcatao* (2024), as an example, this chapter explores the team's participatory methodologies and public-facing orientation as an alternative way of doing research in collaboration with war-impacted communities, one that prioritises grassroots memory, justice, reconciliation, and resilience. *Experiences and Memories of Arcatao* documents the lives of 230 people from the Arcatao Valley – including Blanca Tirsa Varela Mátir's mother, Teresa Varela – who died as a result of the armed conflict between 1970 and 1992. We situate our discussion of the Arcatao book project within the robust tradition of local community organising in the department of Chalatenango, emphasising the urgency of documenting the war from a bottom-up perspective that illuminates the histories that the Salvadoran state has buried, obscured, and 'forgotten'. We also explore how community books address the requests of youth to be incorporated into civil war memory projects, opening up spaces to rethink their communities and strengthen their solidarity with the older generation of survivors.

## 20.2 BACKGROUND: THE ARMED CONFLICT IN EL SALVADOR

The department of Chalatenango, bordered by the Republic of Honduras, was one of the regions in El Salvador most affected by human rights violations during the war, which were carried out predominantly by the state military and paramilitary forces with substantial support from the US (Comisión de la Verdad para El Salvador 1993). Over the course of the conflict, the Salvadoran Army, the National Guard, the Treasury Police, the National Police, government 'death squads', and the paramilitary group Organización Democrática Nacionalista (ORDEN) perpetrated more than seventy civilian massacres in Chalatenango (Surviving Memory in Postwar El Salvador Massacre Map 2024). In an effort to terrorise the rural populations who were perceived as sympathetic to revolutionary guerrilla groups, the Salvadoran Armed Forces engaged in a scorched earth strategy that included burning houses, farm animals, and crops; destroying infrastructure; committing rape, torture, and other extreme acts of physical violence; brutally killed infants, pregnant women, and elderly people; abducting young children and facilitating illicit adoptions; and deliberately driving civilians out of El Salvador and into refugee camps in neighbouring countries.

To understand the roots of this violence, it is important to recognise the economic, political, and social factors that contributed to conflict in rural communities in the decades prior to the civil war. Salvadoran wealth – related mainly to its productive land – was monopolised by a small number of elite landowners at *haciendas* dedicated to the coffee, cotton, and sugarcane industries. The land scarcity among *campesino/a* (subsistence farming) communities, limited access to basic resources such as health services and education, labour exploitation during harvests at the *haciendas*, and an infamous alliance between the Salvadoran elite and the Armed Forces created the conditions for an oligarchic military regime, electoral fraud, and frequent *coups d'état* that dominated the Salvadoran political landscape during most of the twentieth century (Ching 2016). Salvadoran workers, students, and peasants organised into a range of leftist political organisations – including many Catholic groups inspired by 'liberation theology' – to demand their rights to democracy, better working conditions, education, healthcare, land ownership, and other necessities (Alas López et al. 2025; Montgomery 1982; Pearce 1986). In response, the Salvadoran government turned to violence (Sprenkels and Melara Minero 2017), just as they had during previous periods of political organisation and rebellion, including the 1932 genocide of Indigenous people known as *La Matanza* (Gould and Lauria-Santiago 2008; Lindo Fuentes et al. 2007). In response to this increasing repression, five leftist political-military organisations emerged in rural regions during the 1970s, later uniting under one name: Frente Farabundo Martí para la Liberación Nacional (FMLN).

Other regional movements grew alongside the armed revolutionary groups. In Chalatenango, a strong peasant movement arose through grassroots Catholic 'peasant universities' oriented around liberation theology (Chavez 2010). According to Joaquin Chávez, 'nearly 15,000 peasant leaders studied at these institutions between 1967 and 1977' (Chavez 2010, 132). These institutions were antecedents to the formation of the Union of Rural Workers in 1974, whose members were persecuted, tortured, and killed by state forces. After the Sumpul River Massacre in May 1980 – which claimed the lives of 600 civilians – some of the first communities were forcibly displaced (Pearce 1986, 198; Zamora 2014). The Salvadoran state continued their scorched-earth counter-insurgency measures in communities across Chalatenango, targeting people they considered to be supportive of the insurgent movement. In 1981, dozens of communities in northeast Chalatenango were depopulated, and villagers fled to San Salvador, to refugee camps in Honduras (Grzyb et al. 2021), or started to wander in small groups through the Chalatenango mountains in a precarious state known regionally as *las guindas* (fleeing and hiding). The latter groups of civilians created the Poderes Populares Locales (PPL).

## 20.3 POPULAR EDUCATION AND ORGANISATION IN CHALATENANGO COMMUNITIES

Peasant families founded the PPL to cover their necessities – such as food, health, and education, but also, in the war context, the need for security – in a very precarious environment (Pearce 1986, 244–246). According to Salvadoran philosopher Roberto Deras, 'the functions of the PPL were not limited to protection work; they also constituted a practice of solidarity and revolution, an exercise of power and autonomy. […] its development indeed occurred in a disputed geographical area, controlled by the Fuerzas Populares de Liberación Farabundo Martí (FPL); however, despite the ideological affinity, it had its own ideology and the conviction to transform reality' (2023, 2, our translation). The PPL's organising structure functioned through 'popular assemblies' where the community gathered to reflect on their realities, express their views, cast a leadership vote, and look for ways to meet their collective needs. Through time, the PPL also developed experience in diplomacy, advocating for humanitarian aid and international solidarity throughout the PPL's sub-regional government (Salazar and Cruz 2012, 49).

The PPL was dismantled in 1986 owing to military persecution and the capture of their leadership (Salazar and Cruz 2012, 56). However, the collective experience gained during the PPL era continued to inform new organisations, starting with the repopulation of the municipality of San José las Flores, Chalatenango, in 1986 by PPL-aligned peasant families. Subsequently, one of the most impressive peasant movements in El Salvador and Latin American history was born: a repopulation movement that was motivated by the desire of persecuted civilians to return to their 'places of origin' (Edwards and Tovar Siebentritt 1991). The repopulation movement consisted of thousands of peasant families who lived in Mesa Grande refugee camp in Honduras, and who decided to return to El Salvador and repopulate the communities abandoned between 1980 and 1982 (Grzyb et al. 2021; Lara Martínez 2018).

The Salvadoran Civil War officially ended on 16 January 1992 when the Salvadoran government and the FMLN leadership signed the Chapultepec Peace Accords in Mexico. The civilian victims of the Salvadoran Civil War were never at the centre of the peace negotiations or post-war policies (Deras 2023), but the peasants who repopulated Chalatenango communities continued to organise themselves with a goal of collective solutions to local problems. They established committees to assess their needs, gathered in general assemblies to support reconstruction of Chalatenango communities, and engaged in solidarity efforts with international actors who had accompanied the refugee crisis and the repopulation movements. After the war ended, the FMLN became a political party and the Salvadoran Armed Forces were no longer in political control of the country. However, aggressions by right-wing militias continued, and Chalatenango communities engaged in protests to demand respect for their human rights and end the political persecution of their leadership (Alas López et al. 2025). This baseline of self-organisation illustrates the protagonism and agency of civil war survivors, and provides a strong foundation for the work of the Surviving Memory team.

## 20.4 SURVIVING MEMORY IN POSTWAR EL SALVADOR: AN INTERNATIONAL RESEARCH PARTNERSHIP

Surviving Memory in Postwar El Salvador emerged out of this historic context of grassroots organising, progressive social movements, and local memory work after a series of serendipitous encounters between Salvadorans and international solidarity actors between 2011 and 2016. Officially launched in August 2017, the founding members included survivors, social movement leaders, scholars, architects, and documentarians from El Salvador, Canada, Belgium, and Venezuela. Asociación Sumpul – an all-volunteer organisation of massacre survivors in Chalatenango – has been at the heart of the project since the beginning, providing direction and guidance for Surviving Memory's historical memory interventions, which are also supported by Salvadorans in the diaspora. Scholars, architects, and artists from Western University (Canada), KU Leuven (Belgium), and the University of El Salvador provided academic, technical, and financial support for the first pilot projects, including the architectural co-design and construction of the 1980 Sumpul River Massacre memorial, video documentation of survivors testimonies, and the co-creation of an online interactive map with precise GPS data for massacres across the department of Chalatenango. The Social Sciences and Humanities Research Council of Canada has supported Surviving Memory since 2016, providing the core research funding necessary for the initial pilot projects and later awarding the team a seven-year, 2.5-million-dollar Partnership Grant (2021–2028) to finance the expansion of the initiative.

Today, Surviving Memory has twenty-one formal partners, more than 150 active community and university researchers and artists, and engages in diverse historical memory projects in Chalatenango, Cuscatlán, Cabañas, Morazán, and the Salvadoran diaspora.

The founding members shared a common vision of participatory, community-led, bottom-up historical memory research with rural communities, grounding Surviving Memory's projects in the still unmet recommendations of the Truth Commission (1993). The team grew quickly and – through broad consultations at frequent general assemblies that were inspired by the modalities of the PPL and repopulated communities – Surviving Memory identified eight core research themes to guide the development and execution of its research and artistic projects: Documentation and Testimony; Art, Music, and Theatre; Intergenerational Education; Justice; Mental Health and Healing; Commemoration; Environmental Reparation; and Local Economic Reconstruction (see Figure 20.1). However, the objective is not to work in thematic silos, but to explore how these themes intersect and resonate across sectors, regions, and populations. For example, a commemoration activity could involve music, theatre, and testimony, while also promoting healing, intergenerational knowledge, and an alternative form of justice. Similarly, the project teams are deliberately diverse – including a mix of survivors, local leaders, youth, scholars, artists, architects, scientists, and mental health professionals – to promote holistic and innovative approaches to projects that prioritise the needs of local communities.

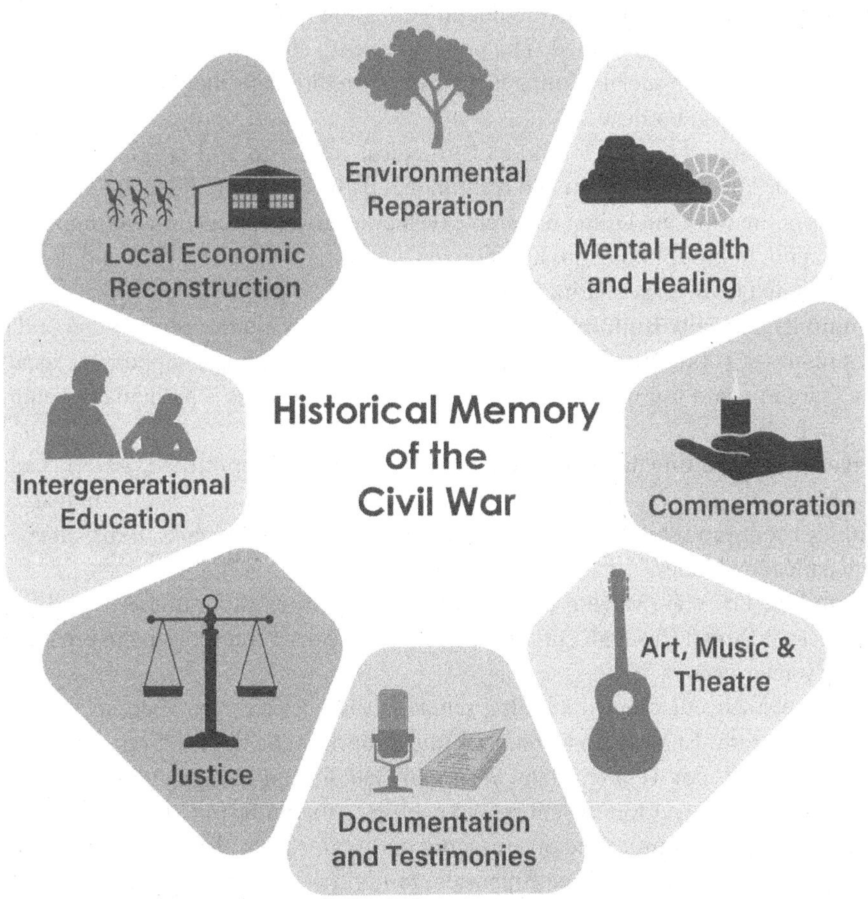


FIGURE 20.1 Surviving Memory in Postwar El Salvador: eight core themes.

As Surviving Memory's momentum grew and additional individuals, communities, and formal partners joined the initiative, the team conducted a series of consultation workshops with diverse stakeholders at general assemblies to develop a set of 'Guiding Principles of Partnership' that are grounded in respect, equity, and sustainability (Surviving Memory in Postwar El Salvador Guiding Principles 2024). They include:

**Horizontal Governance:** The overarching governance structure of the research initiative is horizontal, consultative, cooperative, and consensus based. All partners, partner communities, collaborators, and co-applicants are equal partners and have agreed to share in decision-making about research and research-creation priorities, knowledge sharing activities, and resource allocation.

**Participatory Methodology:** As a community-based research initiative, it employs participatory and decolonial methodologies. All participants are respected as knowledge-holders, co-researchers, and co-creators, and the team accompanies communities through collaborative research processes that amplify the voices of survivors and meet local community needs.

**Equity, Diversity, and Inclusion:** Equity, diversity, and inclusion are promoted in all activities and practices, which should be free of discrimination based on gender, age, race, religion, ethnicity, sexual orientation, ability, education, reading/writing skills or economic status. Three committees focused on the interests of youth, women, and students provide feedback on issues of particular concern to their constituencies.

**Holistic Approach:** The approach to documenting the history of the Salvadoran Civil War is holistic and trauma informed. The project strives to collaborate in innovative ways, with sensitivity to psycho-social contingencies, across traditional scholarly disciplines, sectors, communities, and borders.

**Student Training:** Training for students, medical residents, and postdoctoral scholars is prioritised. The research team and institutional partners strive to integrate trainees into all aspects of the work, including research development, field research, workshop design and facilitation, transcription and translation, co-authoring and co-creation, and development of integrated knowledge sharing activities.

**Community Capacity-Building:** Capacity-building in Salvadoran communities and partner organisations is prioritised, including skills training workshops, support for local strategic planning, and the incorporation of community members – particularly youth – into research teams.

**Intergenerational Education:** Intergenerational education is prioritised, actively facilitating the bi-directional exchange of knowledge between youth and civil war survivors at community events, in school settings, and through the creation of books, films, artistic works, and education guides.

**Accessibility:** There are varying levels of literacy in partner communities, so all outcomes are accessible orally through community meetings, videos and films, radio broadcasts, and audio voiceovers.

**Open Access:** All outcomes, including scholarly publications, are open access and available in Spanish, English, and French through journals, books, the Surviving Memory in Postwar El Salvador website, Maps and Open Data site, and digital archive projects.

**Project Sustainability:** Over the course of the project, the Surviving Memory team will work with partner communities and organisations on sustainability plans and strategic planning. Grant writing initiatives will be supported, to fortify local capacity to continue historical memory projects beyond the tenure period of the SSHRC grant.

**Reducing our Carbon Footprint:** The team is committed to reducing the carbon footprint of the project by balancing the importance of face-to-face meetings and field research with environmentally responsible travel. Video conferencing will be used whenever possible, and research plans that require fewer international flights and longer stays, including long-term internships and fieldwork placements for our trainees, will be privileged.

Surviving Memory's horizontal governance model means that decision-making about the project is consultative, cooperative, and consensus based. By treating all collaborators as equal contributors, Surviving Memory fosters an inclusive environment that prioritises shared authority and mutual respect. Five governance committees representing the interests of youth, women, students, the Salvadoran diaspora, and the founding members ensure that the priorities of these constituencies are addressed and the project remains faithful to the vision of the founding members. This collaborative framework allows diverse voices to shape research priorities and encourages outcomes that reflect the lived experiences and needs of partner communities. By emphasising participatory and decolonial methodologies, Surviving Memory moves beyond extractive research models, positioning participants as co-researchers and co-creators whose knowledge and perspectives are integral to the process.

This ethos of inclusivity is reinforced by a deep commitment to equity, diversity, and accessibility. Surviving Memory actively works to dismantle barriers based on identity, education, or socio-economic status, ensuring that everyone – including youth, women, and survivors – has a central voice in the research and its outcomes. Recognising that knowledge-sharing must accommodate varying levels of literacy and different modes of understanding, the team also employs oral, visual, and multimedia methods to make its outputs universally accessible. In practice, this means prioritising public-facing outcomes, co-authoring scholarly publications with community members, and amplifying the voices of survivors in a global context. These guidelines enable communities to retain ownership of their histories while fostering intergenerational and international understanding of the Salvadoran Civil War through education, commemoration, and creative expression. The Surviving Memory initiative also emphasises a vision of sustainability and ethical collaboration. By building local capacity through skills training, strategic planning, and grant-writing support, the team plans to maintain historical memory activities in communities beyond the end of Surviving Memory's funding period. Its trauma-informed, holistic approach to historical documentation also acknowledges the complex interplay of memory, justice, and community healing in a context where there are few pathways to mental healthcare.

In these ways, the Surviving Memory research initiative posits an alternative mode of justice in communities as well as new forms of collaborative transitional justice research. Traditional models of transitional justice often centre on institutional mechanisms such as courts or reparations programmes. While these approaches could have played a crucial role in the immediate aftermath of the Civil War, El Salvador's culture of impunity has situated Surviving Memory's projects within the localised, relational, and cultural dimensions of healing and justice. By treating participants as co-researchers and knowledge-holders, the initiative also addresses structural imbalances that sometimes define transitional justice processes, fostering a more inclusive and equitable approach to confronting the legacies of oppression, human rights violations, and massacres. This approach aligns with critiques of transitional justice that call for greater attention to cultural specificity, grassroots participation, and long-term social transformation (Lundy and McGovern 2008).

## 20.5 COMMUNITY HISTORY BOOKS AND TRANSITIONAL JUSTICE IN EL SALVADOR

Surviving Memory's community books are aligned with the *educación popular* (popular education) approach to knowledge sharing and skills training developed by the PPL, repopulated communities, and the Catholic Church. Popular education involved developing a curriculum that was based on the reality in which rural Salvadorans found themselves during the war. Carlos Quintanilla Morales, a popular teacher from the community of Guarjila, narrates:

> It is important to mention that popular education created its own programmes. We did not have contact with the Ministry [of Education], but we did them with the technical team. We made our own programmes, and, for example, the brainstorming prompts we used to begin the class discussions were words such as *guindas*, ambush, and massacre. In other words, we contextualised what was happening at the time. Also, in popular education, students were encouraged with songs. Don Tito created the songs, and sometimes he would sing.[2] I remember that the songs 'Nosotros somos igual' (We Are Equal) and 'El carrito azul' (The Blue Car), which were also by Don Tito, as well as 'Cinco Letras' (Five Letters) were the fundamental ones that we sang with the students. It was a better kind of learning because one lives in the context and not in a situation the students do not know. (Alas López et al. 2025)

In keeping with this tradition, as well as with Surviving Memory's Guiding Principles, the community history books complement the inter-related activities of the research team. Grounded in archival photos from solidarity actors and community collections, survivor testimonies, workshop discussions, music, and historic documents, they illuminate collective memories of traditional knowledge, everyday life during the war, the refugee crisis and the *guindas*, the repopulation process, and the immediate post-war recovery period. In other words, they remember civilian war experiences that are 'forgotten' by the state and contribute to an alternative conceptualisation of justice. All the book projects are oriented around the priorities of the collaborating communities and employ participatory methodologies at every step: determining the themes, scopes, and objectives of the book; selecting co-editors, co-authors, and workshop leaders; organizing the necessary fieldwork, community workshops, and archival research; data processing, interpretation, and analysis; and cover art, graphic design, and layout.

Surviving Memory's inaugural book, *Memoria Viva: Photographs and Testimonies about Life in La Virtud and Mesa Grande Refugee Camps, 1980–1992* (2021),[3] documents the experiences of Salvadoran refugees who took refuge in United Nations High Commissioner for Refugees camps in Honduras during the war. The book was one of the outcomes of a series of 'refugee memory workshops' organised in January 2017 by several of Surviving Memory's founding members prior to its formal inception as a research collective. Based on archival photographs from Oxfam Canada and its founding director, Meyer Brownstone, as well as American journalists Steve Cagan and Adam Kufeld, the book includes more than fifty photos that represent the collective experience of the Civil War from the perspective of forcibly displaced civilians

[2] Don Tito is the nickname from Norberto Amaya, a singer and songwriter from Cabañas who fled the Salvadoran Armed Forces in 1980 and found refuge in the refugee camps in Honduras before returning to support the insurgent movement in Chalatenango as an entertainer. The Surviving Memory team made a short documentary about Amaya in 2018: https://www.youtube.com/watch?v=Z1uLxuKzesk.

[3] Memoria Viva was supported in part by a Social Sciences and Humanities Research Council of Canada Insight Development Grant, Montana State University, and Western University. The idea for the workshops that inspired this book was jointly developed by Amanda Grzyb (Western University), Rosa River Rivera (Surviving Historical Memory Committee of Arcatao), and Molly Todd (Montana State University) in November 2015.

now living in repopulated communities in Suchitoto, in the department of Cuscatlán. Selected over three days by a community curation team of ten people elected to represent the workshop participants, the photos reflect on state violence, the departure from El Salvador, daily life in the refugee camps, popular political organisation, and the repopulation movement.

After the success of the *Memoria Viva* pilot project, members of the Surviving Memory team conducted consultation workshops and general assemblies with community members in Chalatenango, and with Salvadorans living in the diaspora (Canada, the Netherlands, and Australia), to develop ideas for a series of community history books that address the various communities' unique but interconnected stories, including their memories, their struggles, their identities, their political positions, their claims to truth and justice, their hope for new generations of Salvadorans, and – undergirding all these themes – the continuity of organisation as the backbone of the communities. As a result of these consultations, the Surviving Memory team developed twelve community history book ideas that include local community histories, documentation of victims, songbooks, recovery of traditional knowledge about local plants and their medicinal uses during the war, migration experiences, cultural and artistic expressions, repopulation and the immediate post-war reconstruction period, graphic novels for youth, and an atlas of the *guindas* (Surviving Memory Community Books 2024).

Surviving Memory recently completed the first four books in the series. *La rebúsqueda: Historias de plantas y resiliencia en Chalatenango* (*La Rebúsqueda: Stories of Plants and Resilience in Chalatenango*) (Carretero et al. 2024) documents the uses of plants and animals before, during, and after the civil war in Chalatenango. It is an effort to highlight the contribution of traditional knowledge to Chalatenango people's survival and healthcare. *Chalatenango: luz y sombra. Fotografías de Ralph Sprenkels y memorias de las comunidades repobladas* (*Chalatenango Light and Shadow: Photographs by Ralph Sprenkels and Memories of the Repopulated Communities*) (Alas López et al. 2025) addresses the memories of the Civil War in repopulated Chalatenango communities, the transition from war to peace, and the current state of the communities to strengthen local organisation as a core value. *Cancionero sobre Memoria Histórica: Las Vueltas* (*Songs about Historical Memory: Las Vueltas*) (Abrams Ansari et al. 2024) documents songs that the Las Vueltas community still sings to remember their struggle during the armed conflict, the repopulation movement, and the peace process. Finally, *Vivencias y memorias de Arcatao* (*Experiences and Memories of Arcatao*) (Alas López et al. 2024) – which is discussed in more detail in Section 20.6 – documents the names and local memories of people who died because of the armed conflict in the community of Arcatao.

Each book employs a participatory methodology that is specifically tailored to the collaborating community and that incorporates the various materials the team can access (e.g., photo collections, archival documents, song lyrics, community poems, plants, testimonies, paintings, or embroideries). A fundamental aspect of this community-based method is the incorporation of local youth into the research process. As part of their strategic priorities, survivors are interested in conveying their historical memories to new generations and creating spaces of intergenerational knowledge exchange for the youth to acknowledge their interests in historical memory and their own family legacies. The community books have become a tangible way to integrate local youth into the Surviving Memory initiative as co-facilitators and co-authors. As part of the Surviving Memory's horizontal governance structure, the team founded an intercommunity youth committee, which has received training in community curation techniques, cinematography and video editing, interview strategies, psychological first aid, and Surviving Memory's research ethics protocol to ensure participants' rights in the research process.

As with the *Memoria Viva* pilot book project, the team's overarching methodology is based on community curatorial practices. To undertake this work, survivors, youth, international scholars, students, researchers, and project partners gather for intensive workshops over two or three days. During the workshops, the cross-sector team decides which photos and artistic pieces to use and establishes criteria to select testimonies for inclusion in the book. After the first intensive workshops, there are consultation meetings and broad feedback from the community to develop thematic book sections, such as the preface (which is usually written by community members), the chapter structure, the historical discussion for framing the testimonies, the photos and artistic pieces, and the epilogue.

## 20.6 EXPERIENCES AND MEMORIES OF ARCATAO

The Surviving Historical Memory Committee from Arcatao (Comité de Memoria Histórica Sobreviviente de Arcatao, hereafter the Arcatao Comité) brings together war survivors from the region to document Civil War violence, honour the victims based on the Catholic tradition, and prevent massacres, political violence, or war crimes from happening again in their communities. The Committee began documenting survivors' war testimonies in 2003, and built a small provisional museum containing war objects, documents, books, and photos that had been collected over many years. They were among the founding partners of Surviving Memory in 2017, and they are active collaborators on several projects, including the documentation of victims' names, the architectural co-design of a permanent community history museum, massacre mapping, and the co-creation of a pilot phone app that provides a guided tour of the historic mountain of La Cañada.

Like Teresa Varela – whose story opened this chapter – most of the civilians killed during the armed conflict by the Salvadoran Armed Forces, their allied militias, or the guerrillas were not properly buried in cemeteries, and the surviving families did not have a communal place for mourning and remembering. For many years, the Arcatao Comité has advocated for the exhumations of hundreds of bodies buried in the Chalatenango territory. Their intense advocacy work has been successful in many cases and the human remains recovered by exhumation teams now rest in the 'Sanctuary of Martyrs', a house built by the Arcatao Comité with the support of the Catholic Church, the community, and international allies. Nonetheless, there are several limitations to recovering the bodies, such as unverified locations of clandestine graves, minimal state resources, the deaths of witnesses, and the possibility that the bodies of victims were consumed by animals and disappeared. To address the limitations, the Arcatao Comité proposed a research project to document the names of all the people killed during the armed conflict (1970–1992) in the Arcatao and neighbouring Nueva Trinidad communities.

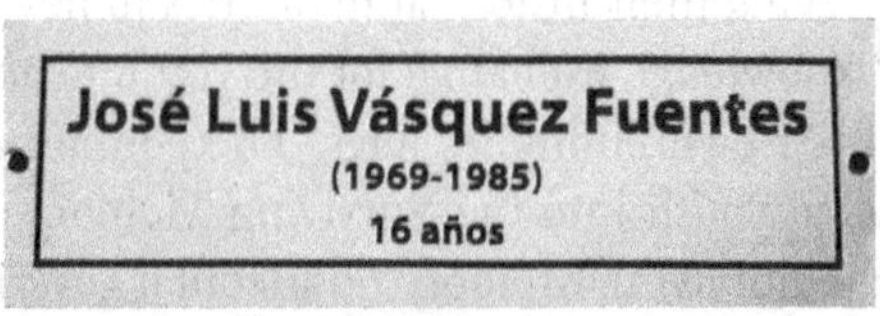


FIGURE 20.2 Plaques with the names of the victims were installed in the Arcatao Sanctuary by Surviving Memory collaborator and Art Professor Miguel Mira (University of El Salvador) and his student, Milton Gabriel Garay, in December 2024.
(From the Surviving Memory Project photo archive)

As one of Surviving Memory's major fieldwork initiatives, the Arcatao Comité proposed that the recovered names would be displayed on plaques in the Sanctuary to provide the community with a central place of mourning (see Figure 20.2), and that the international research team should collaborate on an accompanying community history book that narrates the stories of the people on those plaques as told by their surviving relatives. The resulting book, *Vivencias y memorias de Arcatao* (*Experiences and Memories of Arcatao*, Alas López 2024) (see Figure 20.3), represents three years of collaborative work between the Surviving Historical Memory Committee from Arcatao, the Surviving Memory in Postwar El Salvador research team, ninety people from Arcatao who participated in interviews in May 2023, the local youth association of Arcatao, and Surviving Memory's Youth Committee. As part of the intergenerational knowledge component, the team carried out a research-creation (art-based) one-day workshop with youth and Civil War survivors in Arcatao to finger paint all the victims' names that are documented in the book (see Figure 20.4). The artistic result became the basis for the book's graphic design led by Western University PhD student, Talia Méndez.

Unlike many historical memory projects in Chalatenango, *Experiences and Memories of Arcatao* documents violent stories from both sides of the Civil War on the same pages, opening a new and important dialogue about who qualifies as war victims and how we can begin acknowledging them based on the Arcatao Comité's Catholic faith and a strong motivation for community reconciliation. The book begins with a reflection by an Arcatao Comité member named Rosa Rivera Rivera, which she dedicates to all the youth killed during the Civil War. In her text, Rivera Rivera poetically imagines who those dead children might be today if the army or the war conditions hadn't killed them. She writes: 'Pastor Serrano, if he had not been murdered, would surely be a professional who fought for social transformations or fought for the defence of children's rights. With Pastorcito, we say, "Yes to life, no to violence against children!"' (2024, 1). Rivera Rivera's reflection set the tone for the rest of the book, which

TOMASA LÓPEZ RIVERA
RECUERDA A

Antonio López Rivera
Cruz López Rivera
Roberto Rivera López
María Angelita
Rivera López

180

**Antonio López Rivera**

Él [mi hermano] no estaba viviendo en la misma casa donde yo estaba, él vivía con la mujer que tenía. Iba a comprar unos encargos a la cuesta, había mandado a traer unos encargos a la cuesta, si no me equivoco dicen que unas libras de cacao y azúcar. Iba a traerlos y cuando ya iba llegando se encontró con militares de Honduras.

**Cruz López Rivera**

De la Cruz, mi hermana, yo lo que recuerdo [es] que andábamos juntas, pasamos el río Sumpul juntas y en la quebrada de Acapate fuimos sorprendidas a balazos. Hubo la tirazón y salimos por toda la quebrada corriendo. Yo llevaba a mi niño peladito de los pies, yo no podía caminar porque el niño lo llevaba agarrado de la mano y no podía caminar. Entonces, ella... allí nos desaparecimos en esa quebrada. Ella cargaba dos niños, uno en los brazos, otro en el lomo. El papá de los niños cargaba otros dos porque eran cuatro y allí nos desapartamos [separamos]. Ella salió por un lado y yo por otro. Ya cuando salimos yo esperaba verla a ella, pero ella ya no regresó, fue asesinada. No nos volvimos a ver.

**Roberto Rivera López**

Yo lo que puedo compartir es que él fue incorporado [a la guerrilla] en el 87, pero él no anduvo mucho. Él se incorporó como en febrero [d]el 87 y murió en septiembre del 87, eso es lo que puedo compartir.

**María Angelita Rivera López**

Pues que era una niña y que la cargaba en los brazos. De hambre la niña murió, es lo que yo puedo decir.

181

FIGURE 20.3 Inside *Experiences and Memories of Arcatao*.
(From *Experiences and Memories* of Arcatao by Alas López et al. 2024. Copyright 2024 by Museo de la Palabra y la Imagen)

FIGURE 20.4 A research-creation (art-based) workshop in Arcatao. (From the Surviving Memory Project photo archive)

explores wondering, imagining, and acknowledging how much the communities lost, particularly the loss of people who could have contributed to contemporary life and struggles for justice in Chalatenango. *Experiences and Memories of Arcatao* honours the lives of the victims, aiming to prevent future political violence. The book ends with an epilogue that addresses the younger generations written by the Catholic priest Miguel Vásquez, who accompanied the community of Arcatao for decades. In a universal message that resonates for any post-war community, he pleads: 'We must overcome indifference. May our martyrs' spirit of love, struggle, and song accompany us today and always.' (2024, 341) Thus, following the popular education tradition in Chalatenango, *Experiences and Memories of Arcatao* not only remembers the dead, but also fosters critical thinking about reconciliation, peace, human rights, and equality in a context of continued impunity for war crimes.

## 20.7 CONCLUSION: PARTICIPATORY RESEARCH, INTERGENERATIONAL EDUCATION, AND INTERNATIONAL SOLIDARITY WITH SURVIVORS OF WAR AND CONFLICT

In addressing the unheeded recommendations of the Truth Commission, the Surviving Memory research initiative does not replace the important role of the state in addressing war crimes and fostering reconciliation, but it does open up new modalities, methodologies, and collaborations as an alternative form of justice in a context of chronic impunity and official indifference. By approaching the documentation of war violence from a bottom-up perspective, the team demonstrates how interdisciplinary, cross-sector research, and knowledge mobilisation collaborations with communities can make positive contributions to intergenerational education, capacity-building, healing, reconciliation, and prospects for a lasting peace. Community books such as *Experiences and Memories of Arcatao* are an important part of this collective memory work. Not only do they help to disseminate the research to broad audiences, but they also bind together Surviving Memory's other projects related to geo-spatial data, testimonies, workshops, artistic projects, performances, commemorations, museums, and memorials. This approach ultimately rejects traditionally extractive, territorial, and hierarchical modes of research activity which can – often inadvertently and with good intentions – re-traumatise survivors, prevent communities from accessing the outcomes of documentation efforts, and privilege scholarly reputations over community priorities. At the heart of the Surviving Memory initiative is a strong assertion by survivors and repopulated communities that they remain at the centre of efforts to document their experiences of the war, and a corresponding commitment by accompanying scholars and practitioners to embrace anti-oppressive, decolonial, and truly collaborative ways of doing research and for reimagining the very practice of transitional justice.

## REFERENCES


Abrams Ansari, Emily, Maria Dina Alas, Heidi Calderón, Joel Martinez-Lanzana, Manuel Menjívar, Teresa de Jesús Menjívar, and Román Torres, eds. 2024. *Cancionero sobre Memoria Histórica: Las Vueltas*. Las Vueltas community. www.elsalvadormemory.org/songbooks-eng

Alas López, Adriana, Marisol Zarceño, Felipe Quetzalcoatl Quintanilla, and Comité de Memoria Histórica Sobreviviente de Arcatao, eds. 2024. *Vivencias y memorias de Arcatao*. Museo de la Palabra y la Imagen.

Alas López, Adriana, Lidice Michelle Melara Minero, and Irina Carlota Silber, eds. 2025. *Chalatenango: luz y sombra. Fotografías de Ralph Sprenkels y memorias de las comunidades repobladas*. Museo de la Palabra y la Imagen.

Carretero, Alain, Adriana Alas López, Rosa Lilian López, and Carlos Alberto Elías Ortiz, eds. 2024. *La rebúsqueda: Historias de plantas y resiliencia en Chalatenango*. Museo de la Palabra y la Imagen.

Chávez, Joaquín M. 2010. 'The pedagogy of revolution: popular intellectuals and the origins of the Salvadoran insurgency, 1960–1980'. PhD diss., New York University.

Comisión de la Verdad para El Salvador. 1993. *De la Locura a la Esperanza: La guerra de 12 años en El Salvador. Informe de la Comisión de la Verdad para El Salvador*. Naciones Unidas.

Ching, Erik. 2016. *Stories of Civil War in El Salvador: A Battle over Memory*. University of North Carolina Press.

Deras, Roberto. 2023. "Los Poderes Populares Locales: ¿una experiencia de organización comunitaria sin reconocimiento político?" *Política y Sociedad* (Madrid), 60(1), 79454. https://doi.org/10.5209/poso.79454

Edwards, Beatrice, and Gretta Tovar Siebentritt. 1991. *Places of Origin: The Repopulation of Rural El Salvador*. Lynne Rienner Publishers.

Gould, Jeffrey, and Aldo Lauria-Santiago. 2008. *To Rise in Darkness: Revolution, Repression, and Memory in El Salvador, 1920–1932*. Duke University Press,

Grzyb, Amanda, Jaime Brenes Reyes, and Ángela Velasco, eds. 2021. *Memoria viva: fotografías y testimonios sobre la vida en los campamentos de refugiados en La Virtud y Mesa Grande, 1980–1992*. Museo de la Palabra y la Imagen.

Inter-American Commission on Human Rights. 1999. 'Report No. 1/99: Case 10.480'. Organization of American States.

Lara Martínez, Carlos Benjamín. 2018. *Memoria histórica del movimiento campesino de Chalatenango*. UCA Editores.

Lindo Fuentes, Héctor, Erik Ching, and Rafael Lara Martínez. 2007. *Remembering a Massacre in El Salvador: The Insurrection of 1932, Roque Dalton, and the Politics of Historical Memory*. University of New Mexico Press.

Lundy, Patricia and Mark McGovern. 2008. 'Whose Justice? Rethinking Transitional Justice from the Bottom Up'. *Journal of Law and Society*, 35(2), 265–292.

Montgomery, Tommie Sue. 1982. *Revolution in El Salvador: Origins and Evolution*. Westview Press.

Pearce, Jenny. 1986. *Promised Land: Peasant Rebellion in Chalatenango, El Salvador*. Latin America Bureau.

Salazar, Armando, and María del Carmen Cruz. 2012. *CCR: Organización y Lucha Popular en Chalatenango*. Asociación de Comunidades para el Desarrollo de Chalatenango.

Sprenkels, Ralph, and Lidice Michelle Melara Minero. 2017. 'Auge y declive de la persecución violenta en El Salvador: patrones, variaciones y actores (1970–1991)'. In *La revolución revisitada: Nuevas perspectivas sobre la insurrección y la guerra en El Salvador*, edited by Mauricio Menjívar Ochoa and Ralph Sprenkels, pp. 79–148. UCA Editores.

Surviving Memory in Post War El Salvador. 2024. www.elsalvadormemory.org

Zamora, Marcela, dir. 2014. *Las Aradas: masacre en seis actos*. El Faro. www.youtube.com/watch?v=zfsIx79MpLQ

# 21

# Technology for Justice in Latin America

## *A (Partial) Account of the Awkward Interaction between Technology and Human Rights in the Quest for Justice*

*Michael Reed-Hurtado*

### 21.1 INTRODUCTION

Technology can inject efficiency and dynamism into human rights work and transitional justice efforts; but the use of technology in the human rights field in Latin America has been laden with suspicion, unfamiliarity, and tensions. As in other fields of practice, fear of and fascination with technology qualify an ambivalent relationship with human rights and the pursuit of justice. Notwithstanding, intersections can be identified and fertile interactions between human rights and technology, rooted in bottom-up processes, have taken place starting in the 1980s. Given that the future practice of human rights is inevitably tied to technology, this reflexive detour to examine the past and explore the challenges can assist in identifying areas of interaction and carve out some parameters that could support the role of victims and other protagonists active in the transitional justice realm.

This account is focused on the Latin American context, where I have worked as a practitioner for three decades. Owing to the scarcity of documentation on the intersection of human rights, transitional justice and technology in the region, my reflections are necessarily partial and shaped by my professional experience. While some observations may resonate beyond Latin America, I intentionally avoid generalisation, urging readers not to transpose these insights elsewhere. Given that technological design embeds values and norms that often homogenise experiences, I centre this exploration on Latin America to highlight the unique dynamics of human rights work and the traits of transitional justice in the region. Technology does not operate in a vacuum – context and power structures matter. With these considerations, this chapter seeks to ignite a much-needed discussion on more effectively integrating technological advancements into human rights and transitional justice efforts in Latin America.

As a contribution to this goal, I first track what seems to be the outset of a regional reflection, in the late 1980s, on the use of information technology (IT) in the human rights field in the Southern Cone of the Americas and extract some of the considerations presented at that moment. Section 21.2 historicises and situates the (symbolic) start of the interaction between technology and the human rights field in the region. Following, Section 21.3 posits three factors that slowed and continue to weigh down – perhaps to a lesser degree in the present, but not to a negligible degree – the integration of technology in the human rights field in Latin America, namely: the effects of a legally-centric domain; a language barrier generated by the predominant use of English in the technology field; and a generalised lack of knowledge of technology and the risks it engenders, which turn into suspicion and rejection. In Section 21.4, some breakthrough moments are identified, sometimes linked to transitional justice efforts where greater levels of interdisciplinarity and external cooperation take place. In a cursory fashion, this section provides concrete examples of effective and creative integration of technology in the human rights field. Lastly, in Section 21.5, a few thoughts are offered on how to facilitate the future use of technology in the human rights field in Latin America.

## 21.2 TRACES OF THE EARLY USES OF TECHNOLOGY IN THE HUMAN RIGHTS FIELD IN LATIN AMERICA

Human rights work in Latin America emerged partly as resistance to abusive regimes, aiming to protect victims and confront state denial of atrocities. While early human rights activity existed throughout the region, the struggle against Southern Cone dictatorships in the late 1970s and 1980s – especially in Argentina and Chile – sparked significant activism and gave rise to transitional justice practices (Cardenas 2022; Cleary 1997; Sikkink 2015). These efforts combined grassroots mobilisation, radical lawyering, religious resistance, and both local and diasporic political activism. The Southern Cone's human rights movement and victim groups benefited from higher professional capacity owing to greater education, political participation, and pre-existing cultures of resistance, particularly in Argentina. As a result, technological tools were first integrated into the human rights struggle and the quest for justice in these countries.

During one of the first recorded meetings of the Latin American human rights movement to reflect on the use of IT (*informatica*), the organisers of the event affirmed in 1989:

> The conviction that the struggle for human rights is fundamental forces us to recognize the need to be efficient in that struggle. We believe that IT and the computer should be put at the service of man and not against him. The computer has served in war, in limiting human freedoms, in business. We believe that it should serve humanitarian causes. (Orellana 1989, v)[1]

The participants further reflected on the need to integrate IT into the human rights struggles and use its power to promote justice. In justifying the need to 'modernize' the human rights struggle, they posited:

> The powers of the state that violate the dignity of man have modernized and use the latest technological advances for war and repression on their peoples. Dictatorships use the most sophisticated scientific and technological advances. On the other hand, to defend the rights of the poor, the humiliated, and the offended, resources are scarce, the means are backward and inefficient. (…)
>
> Power must be erected to protect the weakest and if it does not fulfil this function, it must be denounced. To condemn we must report efficiently. (…) To do this, we need the help of IT and thus better fulfil this role of defending the dignity of the human being in the face of the violations carried out by an apparently impersonal and irresponsible state. (Orellana 1989, v–vi)

These statements (made decades ago) continue to reflect existing challenges for human rights struggles and transitional justice processes in Latin America. As we will examine, the integration of technology was not a smooth ride; though purpose and intentions were aptly identified, early on, the human rights movement did not adapt to technology's fast pace.

In the early stages of IT integration, victim-based and human rights organisations prioritised developing information systems and databases to document violations. In Argentina, a few

[1] The non-inclusive language is a sign of the times and the culture. The translation reflects the Spanish framing.

pioneering groups adopted basic IT tools to organise records and compile lists of abuses. They relied on Perfect Filer, a simple DOS-based database bundled with early computers, and dBase, a more advanced database management system by Ashton-Tate that enabled data manipulation and queries but required specialised programming. When dBase III Plus launched in 1986, it quickly became the go-to system for human rights organisations across the Southern Cone, largely owing to HURIDOCS, which actively promoted its standardised format for documenting human rights violations (Orellana 1989). By consolidating records of abuses and safeguarding this critical information, technology became an essential tool for Latin America's victim-based groups seeking justice.

As Raul Alfonsín's transitional government took office in Argentina, victim-based groups and human rights organisations took decisive action to consolidate information on victims, offenders, and violations. Six human rights organisations – including Abuelas de Plaza de Mayo and Centro de Estudios Legales y Sociales (CELS) – formed an ad hoc technical commission that structured and analysed data and identified gaps. Their collaborative efforts produced key documents that laid the groundwork for early transitional justice initiatives, including victim tracing and the pursuit of prosecutions. Their work produced lists identifying 800 military perpetrators, 5,400 victims of forced disappearance, and 1,000 people detained in clandestine centres. These efforts sparked one of the most impactful grassroots movements demanding truth and justice, driven by the relentless protests by the mothers of the disappeared. Their collective achievement is reflected in the official record created by the National Commission on Disappeared Persons, whose 'Never Again' report became a pivotal tool in tracing victims and securing the conviction of powerful perpetrators.

These were the early days of computing, at least in the Latin American human rights movement. Rafael Mazzella, an Argentine activist, recalls that the technical commission disbanded, in part, because of its high costs, but celebrates that 'the saved information was not lost, as it was transferred from a main-frame (computer) to a PC (personal computer) and incorporated into a dBase III plus database' (Orellana 1989, 303). This moment, *circa* 1984, marks the introduction of PCs in the work of human rights organisations in Argentina. Previously, lists were kept in manual form. Mazzella recalls that CELS was the first organisation in Argentina to incorporate a PC, followed shortly thereafter by the Abuelas de Plaza de Mayo, and in 1987 by another innovator in the human rights field, the Equipo Argentino de Antropología Forense.[2]

Though some Argentinian and Chilean organisations stand out in their integration of these tools, most other national civil society counterparts in the region were lagging. For example, Joaquín Caceres of the Comisión de Derechos Humanos de El Salvador remarked in 1989 that they lacked the economic and technical resources to use IT in their documentation efforts, and that their computers were used for word editing and had limited memory (less than 640 kilobytes!) (Orellana 1989, 360). This example is representative, at the time, of most realities in Latin America.

When I began work in the early to mid-1990s in Colombia, the organisation for which I worked, one of the most well funded, only had a few PCs for its staff to use. Only one of them connected via modem to the outside world, which a few of us used to send emails. Almost everyone opted for the telefax for immediate communication. Another of the personal computers was of restricted use, as it housed a FoxPro database that only one person in the organisation

[2] As a matter of reference, in 1984, Europe and the US each housed about 30 per cent of the world's computers, Japan approximately 15 per cent, while only 3 per cent were found in Latin America (Orellana 1989, 284).

knew how to use. The rest of the staff shared the computers and kept the files in mostly poorly organised floppies and diskettes. Losing files and misplacing diskettes was more common than we would like to admit.

The superficial description of my personal experience is intended to make a few simple but fundamental points: first, the use of computers, mostly as a substitute for the typewriter, was not extended until the latter half of the 1990s in human rights organisations in Latin America; second, databases, if used, were treated as mystical maths machines and; third, IT use overall was scant and left to a few technically inclined folk.

In the following section, I explore three reasons that help to explain the slow integration of technology in the human rights and transitional justice fields. Unfortunately, these reasons are as good an explanation for the past as they are factors that continue to pose obstacles for greater integration of technology in the human rights field in Latin America, even if they have subsided with the passage of time.

## 21.3 SOME FOUNDATIONAL AND ONGOING SOURCES OF TENSION AND LIMITS IN THE TECHNOLOGY–HUMAN RIGHTS EXCHANGE

The human rights field in Latin America is not monolithic, but some common factors can be identified throughout the region that have hindered a more successful integration of technology into the practice. I choose to underscore three factors because, unfortunately, they not only account for past difficulties but also continue to bear weight on the troubled relationship between human rights and technology. With time and the inclusion of new generations in the human rights field and transitional justice processes, the impact of these factors has lessened, but they remain as obstacles to be overcome.

### 21.3.1 *No English Spoken Here!*

English is the language of technology; technology is referenced and taught mostly in English. This fact excludes many in the Latin American human rights field from easily exploring developments. The language gap encumbers exchanges and disqualifies many in the movement from taking an active role in the 'human rights technology' debates (Piracés 2018, 290–291).

Despite the US' significant influence in Latin America, English proficiency remains limited, primarily confined to privileged sectors. While bilingual education exists, most students receive only basic exposure, and in professional settings, fluency is largely restricted to the private sector. Even in Mexico, the closest neighbour to the US, only about 5 per cent of the population speaks English fluently, with Colombia reporting an even lower rate of 3 per cent. Most human rights activists in Latin America come from diverse backgrounds outside elite circles, meaning few have had access to high-quality bilingual education. Additionally, in the early 1980s, as the human rights movement took shape, English was rarely spoken within activist circles. Over time, resistance to English – once tied to ideological and anti-imperialist sentiments – has softened.

Moreover, the fact that Spanish is the mother tongue in Mexico and most Central and South American countries led to the structuring of networks that did not require another common language (English). With Spanish as a shared language and some common cultural aspects and similar problems to tackle, strong human rights networks developed with a Latin American flavour, producing an undesired effect of withdrawal from more global networks that tended to operate in English, including those exploring technology.

The fact that English is not used leads to reduced access to the literature and materials that exist on technology. Again, with time, this gap has reduced. Though more materials on IT are available in Spanish, English is still the favoured language of the tech industry, and this continues to pose an obstacle for greater integration.

### 21.3.2 *Fear of the Unknown and Reason to Worry: A Mix Leading to Disintegration*

As the human rights field rolled out (in the 1980s) in Latin America, technology was more the subject of science fiction than knowledge; thus, its use was laden with speculation and confusion. Human rights activists in Latin America were, undoubtedly, subject to persecution and covert operations. The state and its agents were the oppressors, and they ostensibly held control of the technology. How much technology was used in spying and harassing on human rights activists in the 1980s is unclear, but given the portrayal of eavesdropping and wiretapping capabilities in movies and television of the time, activists were weary and suspicious that the surveillance side of technology was reaching them.

Far from embracing technology, many in the human rights movement – shaped by experiences of surveillance and other risks encountered – developed a wary relationship with it, marked by suspicion and caution. This separation formula extends to later moments; for example, as cell phones in Latin America popularised (in the mid 1990s). Though the first cell phones were embraced as tools for convenient telecommunications and security schemes, suspicion of tracing and tapping capabilities spiralled. Fear of surveillance is undoubtedly warranted because of the repressive dynamics and the dirty tactics that state agents have used against many human rights activists. Unfortunately, this fear not only marked potentially intrusive technology but also extended to most forms of technology.

Various forms of technology are inextricably linked to the modern lives of citizens in Latin America, including human rights activists. Connected computers and smartphones are used habitually and are accepted as a source of efficiency and convenience. However, these tools and cyber-connectivity are also experienced as sources of vulnerability and exposition; for example, because of wide-reaching surveillance operations, such as those conducted in Mexico, El Salvador, and Colombia, using NSO Group's spyware Pegasus (Marczak et al. 2018, 2023; Scott-Railton et al. 2022).

Though consciousness of cybersecurity has grown in Latin America, both because of general public awareness as well as targeted campaigns (ACNUDH 2024; R3D n.d.), the prevailing attitudes continue to be marked by fear of the unknown and suspicion. Regardless, most human rights activists remain actively hooked into the network, via their phone, with doubtful security practices (and wilful ignorance) reflecting an ambivalent or naïve relation with IT.

### 21.3.3 *A Legally-Centric Field That Sidelines Other Disciplines*

The structure of the Latin American human rights field was deeply shaped by legal frameworks, positioning lawyers as its primary architects and leaders. This legal-centric foundation, reinforced by judicial and institutional traditions, led to limited engagement with social sciences and other disciplines that more readily adapt to technological advancements. As a result, systemic reliance on legal strategies has constrained the ways in which the human rights field integrates and leverages technology.

The strong legal framing derived, in part, from the need to claim legitimacy in the face of state deviance and abuse of power. As in other parts of the world, international law offered an objective and righteous tool to demand rights and confront wrongful behaviour by state agents (Heupel 2014). However, the degree with which the law and lawyers took hold (*circa* 1980) of the human rights field in Latin America was extreme.

To this day, it is common to be in human rights meetings where people excuse themselves for not being lawyers, as if that condition lessened their ability to provide an opinion on a human rights matter or contribute to a solution. Legal formalism and the role taken by and granted to lawyers paved the way to a flattening of other disciplines, such as sociology or political science, and of other dimensions of the movement, such as political or artistic manifestations. Succinctly, the human rights field in Latin America is characterised by a grammar, semantics, and pragmatics that are principally derived from the law and its practice.

Though the overall assessment of this trend is beyond the reach of this chapter, two repercussions of the legal focus on the way technology is used are underscored, as they continue to bear some weight on today's practice. The first is rather obvious: as (human rights) lawyers in Latin America in the 1980s were largely ignorant of IT, those dominating the field did not prioritise technology. Though most lawyers today coincide on the importance of technology, their legal training does not open them to exploration. Even today, (human rights) lawyers in Latin America are not generally inclined to explore the uses of IT.

Secondly, the dominance of the legal profession, particularly in the 1980s and 1990s, subordinated contributions from other disciplines. The reduced influence of social sciences in methodological and substantive decisions in the early stages restricted interdisciplinarity and the use of non-legal tools, including IT. The human rights field turned (and still turns) to law and its prescriptive categories to document and analyse complex dynamics. As documentation and analytical processes adopted a legal logic, richer descriptive options were mostly set aside. This decision alone led most information systems to get structured in a way as to stockpile and count violations in a rather flat manner, sidelining fuller and more complex understanding of events and their causes, as Hugo Frühling warned in the late 1980s (Orellana 1989, 55–56). Mockery aside, this approach initially reduced tech to a convenient instrument that aggregated violations of the same type and applied simple maths to produce tallies that could be used to denunciate mass scale violations.

With the passage of time, growing application of interdisciplinarity is allowing the exploration of analytical angles offered by other disciplines, and more lawyers are espousing critical and constructive approaches to the law and growing interaction with IT. Nonetheless, the effects of legal centredness continue to be experienced in the human rights field in Latin America.

As stated at the outset, though historic, these factors continue to hold true (granted, to a lesser degree) and offer partial explanations as to why the relationship between human rights, the quest for justice, and technology in Latin America continues to be an awkward one.

## 21.4 AREAS OF INTEGRATION OF IT IN THE HUMAN RIGHTS FIELD IN LATIN AMERICA

In the context of the past and ongoing (though decreasing) resistance to IT, the human rights field in Latin America has progressively used technology in creative and effective ways that strengthen human rights causes and promote justice. Some of the incorporation of these tools and methods has occurred in the context of formal transitional justice mechanisms. As truth commissions or special prosecutorial initiatives are implemented, international actors have utilised and shared ways of using IT that have introduced innovation into the human rights field at the local level. A few of these instances will be highlighted in the following sub-sections.

However, most of the examples draw from national initiatives that seek to document, memorialise, make claims, and demand justice, including archiving and dissemination of declassified documents or graphic and virtual representation of human rights violations, as occurs in other parts of the world (Destrooper and Herremans 2024). The concentration on national practices within the human rights field in Latin America responds to a conscious effort to reflect on transitional justice not as a particular period or a special kind of justice but rather as localised practices and social processes that are conducted, generally from the bottom up, to seek justice or demand rights.[3]

In the past decade, several national organisations have sprouted throughout Latin America that are serving as innovators and developers of human rights technology. These include Data Civica in Mexico, Internet Lab in Brazil, Fundación Karisma in Colombia, ADC in Argentina and R3D in Mexico. I am certain I have excluded other groups that are doing extraordinary work; these are just examples. Likewise, international organisations, such as HURIDOCS, Human Rights Data Analysis Group (HRDAG), Freed Object, Citizen Lab, Forensic Architecture, and Bellingcat (just to name a few and diverse examples), partner with Latin American counterparts to conduct innovative initiatives that harness the power of different strands of IT.

These organisations and their work illustrate that human rights actors are diversifying and that local players not only have the capacity to adapt to rapid technological advancements but also to leverage IT in support of human rights and the pursuit of justice. While challenges remain, forerunners in technology play a crucial role in tackling human rights and justice issues while driving innovation. Understanding their work is essential, but it is equally important to recognise that their advancements do not represent the overall capacity of the broader field.

To ground the discussion, in the following sub-sections, a few areas of integration of IT in the Latin American human rights field are surveyed. The examination is illustrative and will be particularly useful to the reader who is not familiar with the regional dynamic. In addition to plotting some examples, ongoing challenges are also highlighted.

### 21.4.1 *Information Gathering and Technology*

Not too long-ago (even in the early 1990s), having easy access to a photocopier was a game changer for human rights activists in Latin America. The copy granted a mirror image of documents that could otherwise be denied. Lawrence Weschler depicts the early use of the photocopier in his description of the way Brazilian activists gathered the information on the torture regime applied in their country (Weschler 1998). Those copies would substantiate the *Tortura Nunca Mais* report that would later serve as a basis for accountability efforts in Brazil.

With technological advances, image capture was facilitated and increased; first with the use of bulky scanning machines, then with amazingly portable digital scanners, and, of course, now through camera-enabled phones. Moreover, activists in Latin America are using technology options to swiftly gather information – such as tools for web scraping. And the accumulation of information grows. Being able to hold copies of public records has greatly reduced the

3 In the Latin American context, transitional justice was originally linked to practical attempts aimed at realising human rights in the contexts of transitions to democracy to confront the legacies of extreme state repression, for example in Argentina and Chile in the 1980s (Arthur 2009). These attempts were a means to an end and included official and non-official initiatives. This conception is far from the mechanistic approach that thrives today, which stands on shaky ground as results are slim and appears to be caught in the quicksand of lofty aspirational goals that cannot be satisfied. Criticism of the tool-kit approach to transitional justice is not new; it has been expressed in unequivocal terms for at least fifteen years (Bell 2009; McAuliffe 2010).

governments' control of information and its capacity to deny or hide information. The growing capacity to gather and store information is driven by technology: whether for investigations or legal representation, digital copies of documents and data are invaluable assets.

As Latin American human rights organisations amass vast amounts of information, they face growing challenges in managing, securing, and utilising these records effectively. The ease of capturing images and saving documents often leads to incomplete records, lost sources, and decontextualised data. Additionally, large volumes of unprocessed information accumulate across hard drives, flash drives, and unsecured cloud services, making retrieval and verification difficult. Some organisations are tackling challenges posed by accumulated data by implementing data recovery from outdated formats, deduplicating and flattening repositories, adopting standardised naming conventions, and using text exploration tools. Expanding these efforts and actively sharing best practices through training and collaboration are essential steps to ensuring that documentation is both preserved and available to be used in justice-seeking processes.

Organisations and victim-based groups are strengthening their ability to record, archive, and verify information, recognising that well-maintained records are critical to exposing abuses and demanding justice. The challenge remains in maintaining consistency and security amid digital threats and resource constraints. Some have introduced rigorous verification protocols and secure digital archives to enhance reliability. Many are now scaling their impact by training others, fostering cross-network collaboration, and advocating for stronger evidence preservation standards. Expanding these initiatives will be key to ensuring that critical documentation contributes to accountability and long-term justice efforts.

Information gathering is facilitated by IT, and many local human rights groups are obtaining greater volumes of information. This gain requires additional steps that many have not taken in Latin America, including the development of local capacity to effectively store and use the data. As others have warned in relation to the expanding information environment: 'Information on human rights violations is generated faster than it can be processed by advocates and activists' (Gavshon and Gorur 2019, 72).

### 21.4.2 *Human Rights Investigations in the Information Age*

Technological developments have greatly increased the value of open-source investigations in the human rights field in Latin America. As reflected on the global scale, camera-enabled phones, increased publicly accessible data, information exchanged in social networks, and satellite imagery, among others, have qualitatively and quantitatively bolstered human rights investigative activity (Koettl et al. 2019, 14–18). To drive the point home: imagine the difference between investigations based on manually selecting and clipping news stories, sometimes snippets, from a limited number of newspapers that were unsystematically filed, versus investigations applying open source investigations methodologies and tools that span the World Wide Web and use tools to capture information (including metadata on all sources, facial recognition to identify all photographed subjects, transcription of audio records, systematic compilation of multiple formats, automated geo-referencing, just to name a few). Put simply: human rights investigations are no longer the same. The methods and the standards have shifted because of technology.

These tools have facilitated reconstruction of complex events – such as protests and anti-protest violence in Chile (2019–2020) or Colombia (2021), as registered by Amnesty International and Temblores, respectively – that would not have been possible without IT (Amnesty International

2020; Temblores 2021). Another example of IT infused human rights investigation and reporting can also be gleaned from the Mexican context. Commissioned by Centro Prodh and Equipo Argentino de Antropología Forense, Forensic Architecture conducted an investigation using, among others, 3D modelling, photogrammetry, pattern analysis, data mining, and fieldwork to reconstruct the events of one night in late September 2014, when forty-three students from Ayotzinapa were disappeared (Forensic Architecture 2017). They examined thousands of videos, phone records, and testimonies that were transformed into data-points and graphically represented. In their words, 'Working with the families of the disappeared, and NGOs [non-governmental organisations] within Mexico, Forensic Architecture developed an interactive cartographic platform to explore that narrative and its conflicts and inconsistencies. Our goal was to provide a forensic tool for researchers, to strengthen civil society's capacity to investigate the Mexican state's involvement in an historic crime' (Forensic Architecture 2017). However, replicating this type of exercise is difficult, in part because reconstruction of this sort is costly and requires high level technical capacity.

Also complicating the transfer of technology and methods, risks of manipulation and mistakes grow exponentially with the abundance of information on any incident or situation; thus, human rights organisations need to proportionally develop their capacity to verify and control the information they are using. Purposeful misinformation campaigns and doctoring of public records have already been recorded in social protest contexts, for example in Venezuela and Nicaragua.

Regardless of the noted risks, open-source investigation methods and tools offer a repertoire that is progressively being explored by human rights organisations in most Latin American countries.

### 21.4.3 *Archiving and Memorialisation*

Advancements in technology combined with creative communication have been used by human rights activists in Latin America to memorialise, confront denial, and disseminate truth-seeking initiatives. Examples abound, but to illustrate this simple but powerful use of technology, I refer to a couple of initiatives executed in Mexico.

The first goes back to the basics: gathering, declassification, archiving and publishing. Archivos de la represión is an effort led by Mexican civil society to contribute to the right to truth and memory of the repression and systematic violence conducted by the state between 1950 and 1980 in Mexico ('Archivos de la Represión – Memoria y Verdad' 2022). In addition to publishing all documents, the project dynamically conveys analytical findings, multi-media explainers, and soundbites, and memorialises victimised persons. It reflects the power that truth, simplicity, and technology can convey. As stated in the portal, 'the documents made public do not contain all historical truth, but they constitute an important part of the truth'.

Another illustrative example of storytelling aided by simple technology was produced by a group of journalists in Mexico that broke the silence around executions committed by the Mexican armed forces. 'Cadena de mando' (Chain of command) was a daring initiative that unveiled the killing spree that had received little attention in Mexico, through recorded testimonies, animation, and graphic representation of the organisational offending patterns, and depictions of some of the killers and exposition of the chain of command in the military. I describe the project in the past tense to underscore that its footprint continues to be available only through the Internet Archive's Wayback Machine capture (Cadena de Mando (WayBack Machine) 2023). I selected this example not only to acknowledge its daring and innovative contribution to the human rights field but also to highlight the risks associated with the temporality of information on the internet.

Lastly, I bring to mind a recently finalised research and memorialisation project that seeks justice in Veracruz, México. Led by the Mexico office of Article 19, Veracruz de los silencios, it combines investigative journalism, social science, law, community activism, and IT to produce a dynamic record of criminal offending against journalists in the state of Veracruz (Veracruz de los silencios 2024). Timelines, photographs, documents, profiles and analytical findings are vibrantly displayed and shared to engage and memorialise.

Examples of this type are found throughout the region and demonstrate the power of integrating rather simple technology to storytelling and memorialisation.

### 21.4.4 *Information Systems, Databases, and Data Analysis*

Databases and information systems were used as a point of entry to illustrate that technology has been a part of the human rights field in Latin America since the 1980s. However, with that early recognition comes a proviso: not everything that is termed a database is a database. It is likely that, owing to lack of technical literacy, most human rights activists identify any information recorded on a spreadsheet as a database. To illustrate the point, a Swedish cooperation agency commissioned in 2005 a technical study of human rights information systems implemented in Colombian organisations (Roth 2005). The report (on file with the author) found that many information systems lacked conceptual and definitional clarity, and that many compiled information on human rights violations but did not classify or codify it in a systematic fashion. The analyst also found that many documentation initiatives lacked technical support and did not apply minimum security protocols. The report also indicates that many 'databases' are used to stockpile cases, with little substantiation and used mostly for the purpose of producing aggregate sums of violations. Lastly, the report also underscores that documentation initiatives lacked financial resources to be properly implemented. This evaluation was conducted twenty years ago and was partial (as it surveyed only a sample of all documentation projects in Colombia); nonetheless, it is useful to contextualise and situate this type of use of IT.

Formal transitional justice mechanisms gave way to the development of specialised information systems. In addition to greater availability of resources during the operation of these mechanisms, increased engagement by social scientists and activists that seek to transcend the case-by-case approach to address a period of manifest violations motivates the exploration of other bodies of knowledge, methods, and tools to more effectively document and analyse human rights situations.

The achievements of human rights information systems in the context of the Guatemalan and Salvadoran truth commissions were conveniently documented by an American Association for the Advancement of Science initiative (Ball et al. 2000). More recently, the Colombian context gave way to the use of information systems both in the context of the Truth Commission and the Special Jurisdiction for Peace ('Analítica de datos (información y recursos) | Informe Final Comisión de la Verdad' n.d.). HRDAG, once again, played an important part in that process.

In addition, many human rights organisations have now implemented ambitious information systems. The 'Who Did What to Whom' model has been adopted by most straightforward projects that tend to keep a register of violations (Ball 1996). Some organisations use the tools provided by HURIDOCS (Dueck et al. 2001). A few other documentation initiatives, national and sub-national in scope, have turned to Narra, 'a free and open-source tool for organizing and reporting on narrative-driven information promoting human rights' (Narra n.d.). Again, the examples provided are merely illustrative. In addition to producing dynamic databases, these information systems serve as repositories of key human rights information that will substantiate justice claims in the future. They are fundamental to demonstrate patterned violence and engage the responsibility of perpetrators removed from the crime scenes.

To close, the availability of intuitive and inexpensive information systems has not got rid of the practice that relies on lists recorded on spreadsheets. In fact, in the past five years, documentation initiatives using basic spreadsheets to document and store information on human rights violations continue to thrive.

### 21.4.5 *Exploring Big Data*

The last block of this succinct exploration of the use of IT in the Latin American human rights field takes us full circle to the first sub-section on information gathering. It relates to the tools and methods needed to explore large quantities of data. Large language models and machine learning are now the talk of the town; however, owing to the English language barrier and the specificities of human rights work in Latin America, many obstacles still need to be surpassed.

I first used IBM's Watson analytics on a Spanish language human rights project *circa* 2015 – ten years ago. At that moment of sale, it was pitched smoothly by the vendor; the product seemed magical. As implementation started, it was clear to our team that we were in for one of the rockiest roads we had ever travelled. The tool was ready to operate in Spanish only in certain fields, particularly healthcare and finance (given the need that had been established by the private sector to comb through voluminous archives). Human rights and repressive bureaucracies were not in reach. We had to start from scratch. We fumbled through the process of constructing the reference terminology (controlled vocabulary and thesaurus), machine training and manually running many processes (including a very clunky start of optical character recognition). Results were useful, after investing much time, effort, and financial resources. The learning curve was extraordinary and helped some of us understand the logic behind the tools. However, for most in the human rights field in Latin America, this type of investment was and is out of reach, and the technology remains a mystery box.

In the face of today's popularity of IT tools, and to dispel any illusion regarding the ease of the feat, the definitions, training, and adjustments required to implement a large-scale data mining operation that is effective demand time, know-how, and resources. Fortunately, some organisations in Latin America are now using this type of technology for the benefit of the human rights field. A public example can be gleaned from the military records that were made public in 'Con copia occulta' (With Blind Copy), an initiative led by Mexico's Data Civica together with Intersecta, which organises and publishes information gained from an email server of the Mexican military. It literally presents the 'account of the war according to the Secretary of Defence' (*La guerra que cuenta la Sedena*).

Artificial Intelligence (AI), experienced as a mainstream phenomenon *circa* 2020, has been purposefully left out of this review. This trend is far reaching, and its implications are immense; however, as the tools and their use are only rolling out, the review offered here can serve to contextualise future assessments of AI in the human rights field. Undoubtedly, natural language processing, processing of images and videos, machine learning and predictive analytics, decision support and expert recommendations, virtual assistance, and generative models are being used by individuals and groups throughout Latin America. I have highlighted some examples in the cursory review, and others have more systematically reflected on the use of AI in the human rights field (Gavshon and Gorur 2019, 84–87; Piracés 2018, 296–299). Reflections on ethical use and the need to regulate the power of AI are taking place; but most use continues to be largely irreflexive. The potential for transformation of the human rights field in Latin America is immense: the potential for improvement and destructiveness are equally great. The field needs to ensure that it can navigate the hype, and move to programmatic and intentional integration.

IT tools are getting better at working with languages other than English; however, the idiomatic limitation continues to generate difficulties (Gavshon and Gorur 2019, 82, 86). Moreover, once the initial hype is surpassed, the costs of secure and effective exploration of information and big data will remain high. In their piece on 'How Technology Can Help Convert Raw Data into Rich Information for Transitional Justice Processes', Gavshon and Gorur (2019) illustrate several technology options for automated content gathering and content analysis, insisting, though, that these tools do not substitute the human element, but simply aid it (81, 84). Undoubtedly the technology is readily available, and progressively 'the sky is the limit'; the question, however, remains: will the Latin American human rights field be able to adapt and integrate, or will it be left behind as technology booms?

## 21.5 A WORD IN CONCLUSION

To understand the present and look to the future, I have purposefully gone to the past (not so distant) – but given the speed of change, turning to the 1980s and 1990s and examining photocopying as a technological advance seems antediluvian. The relevance of technological development for the future of the human rights movement in Latin America requires that we critically observe the past, and understand how we have incorporated and neglected IT in our practice. The fast pace of technological development and technology's disturbing but enchanting ubiquity demand that we take stock of the road travelled and reflexively seize opportunities brought by IT in human rights practice, but also prepare to confront its risks.

Latin American practitioners and grassroots initiatives, such as those mobilised to search for the disappeared persons in Argentina, demonstrated vanguard use of technology and paved a route that should inform how technology is deployed today. As depicted at the outset of this chapter, Latin American human rights organisations espoused in the late 1980s avant-garde positions and set out to 'dominate technology in order to liberate' (Orellana 1989, 3). Pressed to respond effectively to state sponsored repression, human rights activists sharply leveraged the power of new technologies at the time and implemented documentation techniques that, with minor adjustments, continue to be used today. Regrettably, the spark of that moment did not translate into steady adaptation and evolution.

The razor-sharp focus on learning and staying on top of the IT ascent dwindled, in part, because of the three factors that I have underscored, coupled with others, including the prevailing lack of resources, dangerous working conditions, and competing priorities. Fear of technology's use for intrusion and surveillance remains high (and with good reason, in some cases), but growing awareness and use of cybersecurity protocols assist those in the field to continue doing their work and using IT tools. A few (but a growing number of) organisations have tapped into the power of technology to defend the rights of the powerless, the marginalised, and the oppressed (Orellana 1989). The achievements are valuable, and pave the way for future improvement.

As technology evolves at lightning speed, the ability of the human rights field in Latin America will have to grow substantially – not only to catch up and keep up, but to not be drowned. Craig Mundie of Microsoft is credited with stating, in 2007: 'When the rate of change eventually exceeds the ability to adapt you get "dislocation". "Disruption" is what happens when someone does something clever that makes you and your company look obsolete. "Dislocation" is when the whole environment is being altered so quickly that everyone starts to feel they can't keep up' (Friedman 2016, 28).

For now, regional pioneers and international partners aiding in technological transfer have contributed to avoid obsoleteness and dislocation. The bulk of the human rights actors are treading slowly, and many appear bogged down or simply avoid integration of IT beyond the use of office computers and phones. However, initiatives such as the ones highlighted in this chapter demonstrate that bottom-up efforts to develop greater computer literacy, and to understand IT developments and use their potential to promote justice and human rights, are in place and effectively leveraging technology. Those seeking to deploy creative ways to make use of locally grounded technological design and implementation can benefit from the experiences in the Latin American human rights field.

Through willingness, intentionality, knowledge, and creativity, the future holds an open road for the exploration of IT to reinvigorate the struggle for justice and human rights in Latin America. Technology is not a silver bullet, but it does offer tools and mechanisms that can greatly enhance the capacity of human rights activists and grassroots organisations claiming justice. That local human rights practitioners in Argentina, Colombia and Mexico, among others, are not only active users of IT but are also directly involved in the development of technology, and are ensuring that technological tools respond to local conditions, provides room for optimism (Piracés 2018, 291, 307). Active collaboration avoids unidirectional learning and knowledge transfer that lacks roots. It also ensures that Latin American actors with technological expertise participate and contribute to ethical, epistemological, and practical debates confronting the use of technology around the world. IT will only continue to grow in relevance: it is our responsibility to not only avoid dislocation but also to actively leverage its potential.

## REFERENCES


Alto Comisionado de las Naciones Unidas para los Derechos Humanos (ACNUDH). 2024. 'Caja de herramientas para la seguridad en el entorno digital'. *Seguridad digital* (blog). 8 March. https://seguridad-digital.oacnudh.org/

Amnesty International. 2020. 'Ojos sobre Chile: Violencia policial y responsabilidad de mando durante el estallido social'. Chile: Amnesty International. www.amnesty.org/es/documents/amr22/3133/2020/es/

'Analítica de datos (información y recursos) | Informe Final Comisión de la Verdad'. n.d. www.comisiondelaverdad.co/analitica-de-datos-informacion-y-recursos

'Archivos de la Represión – Memoria y Verdad'. 2022. 16 September. https://archivosdelarepresion.org/

Arthur, Paige. 2009. 'How "Transitions" Reshaped Human Rights: A Conceptual History of Transitional Justice'. *Human Rights Quarterly*, 31(2), 321–367.

Ball, Patrick. 1996. *Who Did What to Whom? Planning and Implementing a Large Scale Human Rights Data Project*. American Association for the Advancement of Science. https://hrdag.org/whodidwhattowhom/contents.html

Ball, Patrick, Herbert F. Spirer, Louise Spirer, and American Association for the Advancement of Science. 2000. *Making the Case: Investigating Large Scale Human Rights Violations Using Information Systems and Data Analysis*. American Association for the Advancement of Science.

Bell, Christine. 2009. 'Transitional Justice, Interdisciplinarity and the State of the "Field" or "Non-Field"'. *International Journal of Transitional Justice*, 3(1), 5–27. https://doi.org/10.1093/ijtj/ijn044

Cadena de Mando. 2023. Cadena de Mando. 27 September. https://tinyurl.com/28fsuzxn

Cardenas, Sonia. 2022. *Human Rights in Latin America: A Politics of Transformation*. 2nd ed. Pennsylvania Studies in Human Rights. University of Pennsylvania Press. https://doi.org/10.9783/9781512822663

Cleary, Edward L. 1997. *The Struggle for Human Rights in Latin America*. Praeger.

Destrooper, Tine, and Brigitte Herremans. 2024. 'Re-Imagining Memorialization and Documentation in Afghanistan'. Justice Visions. https://tinyurl.com/4mkw2drw

Dueck, Judith, Manuel Guzman, and Bert Verstappen. 2001. *HURIDOCS Events Standard Formats: A Tool for Documenting Human Rights Violations*, 2nd ed. https://huridocs.org/wp-content/uploads/2020/11/HURIDOCS_ESF_English1.pdf

Forensic Architecture. 2017. 'The Enforced Disappearance of the Ayotzinapa Students'. 26 September. https://tinyurl.com/3tm83dk6

Friedman, Thomas. 2016. *Thank You for Being Late: An Optimist's Guide to Thriving in the Age of Accelerations*. Farrar, Straus and Giroux.

Gavshon, Daniela, and Erol Gorur. 2019. 'Information Overload: How Technology Can Help Convert Raw Data into Rich Information for Transitional Justice Processes'. *The International Journal of Transitional Justice*, 13(1), 71–91. https://doi.org/10.1093/ijtj/ijy029

Heupel, Monika. 2014. 'The Extension and Legalization of Human Rights'. In *The SAGE Handbook of Human Rights*, vol. 2, edited by Anja Mihr and Mark Gibney, pp. 733–748. SAGE Publications, Limited. https://doi.org/10.4135/9781473909335.n40

Koettl, Christoph, Daragh Murray, and Sam Dubberley. 2019. 'Open Source Investigation for Human Rights Reporting: A Brief History'. In *Digital Witness: Using Open Source Information for Human Rights Investigation, Documentation, and Accountability*, edited by Sam Dubberley, Alexa Koenig, and Daragh Murray, pp. 12–31. Oxford University Press. https://doi.org/10.1093/law/9780198836063.003.0002

Marczak, Bill, John Scott-Railton, Sarah McKune, Bahr Abdul Razzak, and Ron Deibert. 2018. 'HIDE AND SEEK: Tracking NSO Group's Pegasus Spyware to Operations in 45 Countries'. Citizen Lab Research Report No. 113. University of Toronto. https://tinyurl.com/39eb32th

Marczak, Bill, John Scott-Railton, Bahr Abdul Razzak, and Ron Deibert. 2023. 'Triple Threat: NSO Group's Pegasus Spyware Returns in 2022 with a Trio of iOS 15 and iOS 16 Zero-Click Exploit Chains'. Citizen Lab, University of Toronto. https://citizenlab.ca/2023/04/nso-groups-pegasus-spyware-returns-in-2022

McAuliffe, Padraig. 2010. 'Transitional Justice and the Rule of Law: The Perfect Couple or Awkward Bedfellows?' *Hague Journal on the Rule of Law*, 2(2), 127–154. https://doi.org/10.1017/S1876404510200015

'Narra'. n.d. www.getnarra.com/

Orellana, Patricio, ed. 1989. *Derechos humanos e informática: La experiencia latinoamericana*. 1st ed. Fundación de Ayuda Social de las Iglesias Cristianas, FASIC.

Piracés, Enrique. 2018. 'The Future of Human Rights Technology: A Practitioner's View'. In *New Technologies for Human Rights Law and Practice*, edited by Molly K. Land and Jay D. Aronson, 1st ed., pp. 289–308. Cambridge University Press. https://doi.org/10.1017/9781316838952.013

Red en defensa de los derechos digitales (R3D). n.d. '10 principios sobre ciberseguridad y derechos humanos'. Ciberseguridad. https://r3d.mx/ciberseguridad/

Roth, Françoise. 2005 (unpublished). 'Proyecto sobre sistemas de información en materia de derechos humanos y derecho inernacional humanitario'. *Infome final de consultoría*. Bogotá, Colombia.

Scott-Railton, John, Bill Marczak, Paolo Nigro Herrero, Bahr Abdul Razzak, Noura Aljizawi, Salvatore Solimano, and Ron Deibert. 2022. 'Proyecto Torogoz: Hackeo Extensivo de Los Medios de Comunicación y La Sociedad Civil En El Salvador Con El Programa Espía Pegasus'. Citizen Lab, University of Toronto. https://tinyurl.com/bdz9zz9w

Sikkink, Kathryn. 2015. 'Latin America's Protagonist Role in Human Rights'. *Sur International Journal on Human Rights*, 12(22), 207–219

Temblores. 2021. 'Bolillo, Dios y Patria'. Temblores. https://tembloresong.gumroad.com/l/bolillo-dios-y-patria?layout=profile

Veracruz de los silencios. 2024. Veracruz de los silencios. https://veracruzdelossilencios.org/

Weschler, Lawrence. 1998. *A Miracle, a Universe: Settling Accounts with Torturers*. University of Chicago Press.

# Concluding Thoughts

## *A Future Outlook on the Study and Practice of Victim Engagement in Transitional Justice*

*Elke Evrard and Tine Destrooper*

### C.1 THINKING ALONGSIDE VICTIM-PROTAGONISTS

This handbook has provided a framework for understanding the evolving role of victims in transitional justice, alongside a comparative perspective on the realities of victim engagement today. It thereby seeks to establish a shared frame of reference for researchers and practitioners across diverse orientations, and to lay the groundwork for a forward-looking agenda in both scholarship and practice. We started from the observation that, despite deep self-reflective critiques dominating the field, individuals and communities affected by diverse human rights violations are increasingly turning to transitional justice language and practices for resisting injustices and challenging harmful structures. In doing so, they not only adapt transitional justice to their specific struggles but also introduce innovative and creative approaches, reshaping how the paradigm is conceived and practised. While this victim-driven expansion is transforming transitional justice, it also sparks fundamental debates among scholars, practitioners, and policymakers about its evolving scope, purpose, and the central role of victims in shaping its trajectory.

Although different strands of existing scholarship on victim activism and participation – from technical-legal to critical perspectives – offer distinct normative and substantive vantage points to engage with these key questions, meaningful exchanges across these strands of writing have been limited. This handbook has aimed to facilitate such cross-cutting exchanges by offering a more holistic and historically grounded understanding of victim engagement. In doing so, it provides both newcomers to the field, as well as experts, with the conceptual tools needed to navigate and position themselves within contemporary debates. To support this goal, the handbook's proposed framework moves beyond a normative hierarchisation or rigid demarcation when studying varying forms and spaces of participation. Instead, it emphasises that victims themselves often do not draw categorical distinctions between their engagement with various modalities and forums of justice, and that their justice-seeking often takes a more trajectorial approach, involving sequential or parallel engagement across multiple sites.

As such, throughout the handbook and in this Conclusion, we are not proposing a new normative paradigm, nor do we formulate goalposts for where victim engagement *should* be heading. Rather, the contributors to this volume describe and analyse what has occurred and is occurring on the ground, recognising the fluid, interconnected, and innovative nature of victims' actions across different contexts. In keeping with this view, they examine how victims themselves have played an agentic role in driving the trends in the field, and also build on this protagonism to theorise where the field is moving next. Structurally, we organised these contributions around two interconnected conceptual principles: a generational framework that traces the evolution of victim engagement over time, and an exploration of how victims' justice struggles intersect with and reshape the boundaries of transitional justice today.

In this concluding chapter, we integrate the contributions from both sections of the handbook, highlighting how the core tenets of each generation help explain the dynamics of contemporary intersecting struggles. We then explore how these contemporary victim-led practices, in turn, give rise to a future-oriented agenda that truly (re-)centres victims as the drivers of transitional justice theory and practice.

## C.2 SURFACING GENERATIONAL DYNAMICS

The chapters in the first half of this handbook have illustrated the value of analysing victims' engagement in transitional justice through a generational lens, not only for deepening our historical understanding of how different modalities of victim engagement (across formal, grassroots and everyday justice processes) developed over time and in response to institutional and societal opportunities and obstacles, but also for making sense of the contemporary justice landscape and future directions of transitional justice. Applying this generational framework to a range of case studies has highlighted fundamental dynamics and characteristics of victims' protagonism, including how demands and practices emerge, evolve, persist, coexist, or periodically recur. While there is a degree of linearity – mobilisation often precedes the establishment of institutional mechanisms, and participation in those mechanisms can lead to new engagement models rooted in resistance against their limitations – these generational developments do not unfold in strictly sequential or universally applicable phases (see also Destrooper and Evrard 2025). Rather, different generations of victim engagement typically overlap and interact, both globally and within specific contexts.

### C.2.1 *Mobilisation, Norm-Setting, and Capacity Building*

A focus on first generation engagement underscores the extent to which victim protagonism has always been formative in formulating the normative objectives and vocabulary of transitional justice. Chapter 1 by Carrasco and Collins, for example, evocatively described the 'denunciatory activism' in Chile, where relatives of the disappeared exposed state-sponsored disappearances, demanded a state response that would ensure truth and justice, and called for the return of their loved ones, crafting the archetype of the 'detained-disappeared person', a concept that shaped the discourse around human rights violations and influenced international legal frameworks. The persistence of this vocabulary and these demands across time and place (and throughout the chapters in this handbook) demonstrates, on the one hand, how the foundational claims of victim groups continue to inform contemporary justice debates and institutional frameworks; and, on the other hand, encourages us to consider how the expansion of transitional justice to new contexts and issues is likewise shaped by victims' agency in (re)defining the narrative and terminology of transitional justice for understanding the violence they experience and the kind of justice they propose.

Analysis of first generation engagement also accentuates the preconditions necessary for victims to engage in the sustained pursuit of justice, for instance, in terms of capacity-building, social solidarity, and the creation of spaces for collective agency. These are dynamics that have too often been overlooked in discussions of (especially institutionalised) victim participation. In Chapter 4, on the Saturday Mothers, Daşlı emphasised the importance of social networks in fostering solidarity and sustaining long-term activism, describing how grassroots movements form 'political families' while providing spaces for truth-telling, healing, resistance, remembrance, and advocacy through collective action and shared values. In Chapter 2, Lawther similarly viewed the establishment of victims' groups as 'moral communities' that centre dignity, responsiveness, and solidarity. In many contexts described across this handbook, these dynamics have enabled victims to articulate evolving justice claims over time, and across different spaces, and to maintain their struggles despite shifting political contexts. Daşlı's chapter has also pointed to the long temporality and intergenerationality that characterise contemporary struggles (discussed later).

At the same time, as Lawther's chapter shows, the early stages of victim mobilisation – when groups organise and advocate before their demands are formally recognised in transitional justice frameworks – are crucial for understanding the emergence of multiple (and at times competing) constructions of victimhood and registers through which truth and justice are articulated, shedding light on how victims, often in diverse ways, come to understand and invoke the state's role as both perpetrator and justice provider. In a complementary way, Chapter 3 by Bonacker draws attention to the specific conflict context and the nature of its cessation, for understanding the demands victims make from the earliest stages onwards, and for mapping how they appeal to and are varyingly recognised by the state in institutional responses and practices.

### C.2.2 *Participation, Co-optation, and the Proliferation of Justice Spaces*

Studying second generation victim engagement reveals how early (scholarly and political) attention to social movements gradually shifted towards emphasis on 'formal' victim participation, aligning with the emerging discourse of inclusion, participation, and victim-centredness as part of a global, institutionalised transitional justice blueprint and network. This institutionalisation has sparked urgent concerns about the co-optation of victim voices within predefined frameworks – a central line of inquiry in critical transitional justice scholarship. Chapter 6 by Obel Hansen and Chapter 8 by Li illustrated how top-down frameworks often employ victim-centred rhetoric and universal justice appeals while failing to ensure meaningful participation or local relevance, especially where genuine political will is absent. This perspective remains crucial to understand why victims contest the reduction or assimilation of their agency and protagonism to 'participation' in institutional spaces only, and why the opening of institutional avenues has, on the ground, certainly not led to a diminishing but rather to a proliferation of parallel and alternative spaces and strategies.

Yet, in this sense, Li's research on the Extraordinary Chambers in the Courts of Cambodia (ECCC) also offers insights that caution against a simplistic binary of either acquiescence to, or rejection of, state-imposed transitional justice. Li shows how victims may strategically engage with institutional mechanisms while reshaping them to reflect their own justice needs and frameworks. While some Cambodians chose to disengage from the Court and the non-governmental organisations operating in its orbit, viewing their work as incompatible with community-based and spiritually grounded justice perspectives, others opted to participate in ways that injected Buddhist beliefs into the ECCC's proceedings, thereby imbuing these processes with new meanings. This offers a valuable vantage point for understanding how pre-existing justice beliefs shape victims' engagement across different justice arenas, and for conceptualising multi-pronged justice-seeking trajectories that may unfold through institutional mechanisms, in parallel to them, or entirely outside their mandates – collectively constituting a broader justice ecosystem.

Within this multi-layered justice ecosystem, a sound understanding of second generation victim engagement also offers much-needed insights for developing more responsive legal frameworks. Chapter 5 by Rauschenbach and Jones, Chapter 7 by Uche, and Chapter 9 by McGonigle-Leyh urge us to rethink victim participation in International Criminal Court proceedings, to reconceptualise institutionalised engagement in 'aparadigmatic' contexts (including at the subnational level), and to shift the focus from outcomes to the processes of engagement themselves, by examining the relationships that shape the fairness and effectiveness of transitional justice efforts. These chapters illustrate that victims continue to demand and utilise legal and institutionalised mechanisms, in spite of their shortcomings, and that they retain their significance in an encompassing justice ecosystem, encouraging a move to a more critical-constructive research practice, that explores how more meaningful victim engagement in formal institutions can be ensured.

### C.2.3 *Resistance, New Justice Imaginaries, and Moving beyond the State*

What this handbook calls the third generation of transitional justice shares similarities with the first in its focus on victims as disruptive protagonists with agenda-setting power. However, while the first generation often involves activism aimed at calling on the state to act against impunity and inaction, the third generation does not necessarily centre the state. As illustrated in Chapter 11 by Dempster and Hearty and Chapter 12 by Robins and Bhandari, victims may seek to pursue grassroots justice efforts that neither rely on state intervention nor take place in highly visible public spaces. These chapters shifted attention to non-state actors, local social ecologies, and community-based solutions, highlighting the home and community as sites where victims mobilise and advance their interests in the context of everyday life, or illustrating how engaging quietly with non-state armed actors can allow victims to access a level of truth and acknowledgement that may not have been possible through a state or institutional mechanism. Rather than taking these forms of engagement as a wholesale rejection of the state or institutional mechanisms, we suggest that they call for a more expansive theorisation – one that acknowledges how justice can emerge and be pursued outside, and sometimes alongside, the realm of public appeals to the state or society. This requires us to broaden the conversation around victim engagement to include practices that have traditionally not qualified as 'participation' or 'transitional justice'.

Indeed, this kind of resistance and boundary-pushing that characterises third-generation victim engagement can occur both within and outside institutional frameworks, sometimes even simultaneously, as victims re-imagine who, what, and where justice can be sought. Chapter 14 by Kodikara illustrates the power of victim-driven imaginaries in this process, using the concept of 'archives of desire' to examine the demands of Tamil women next of kin of who disappeared in Sri Lanka in the context of flawed state mechanisms. This critical engagement is also evident in Chapter 13 by Suarez Vargas, which illustrates how social movements of women, Indigenous, Afro-descendant, LGBTQI+, and former female fighters in Colombia actively resist the homogenising 'ideal victim' narrative that has shaped traditional transitional justice frameworks, particularly in relation to conflict-related sexual and gender-based violence. By challenging restrictive portrayals of victimhood and asserting more complex, intersectional identities, these groups pushed the Colombian formal and informal transitional justice initiatives to become more inclusive. Both chapters demonstrate how third-generation efforts see victims re-imagine the definitional boundaries of justice from outside institutional frameworks but also reshape these from within.

Lastly, while resistance has been crucial for advancing justice, long-term activism also carries significant emotional, social, and political costs. This book's conceptualization of the third generation of transitional justice acknowledges that prolonged justice struggles can lead to fatigue, resignation, and despair, making it difficult for victims and activists to sustain their engagement, as Chapter 10 by Moffett illustrates. The potential for civic space to shrink once again poses a serious threat, making justice-seeking efforts even more precarious. As fatigue and disillusionment set in, some victims may lose hope in the existing transitional justice framework, and turn to other paradigms and mobilising frameworks. These dynamics, too, are important for exploring and explaining why and how alternative justice strategies and paradigms may become enmeshed – and potentially displace – the transitional justice paradigm.

## C.3 TRACING INTERSECTING STRUGGLES

We argue that studying these generational dynamics, not only from a temporal but also and especially from a conceptual point of view, is essential for understanding today's intricate justice ecosystem and the growing intersection of justice struggles and repertoires across an ever-increasing range of contexts. The chapters in the second half of the book highlighted how, as victims move across and between spaces that pertain to different generations of engagement, the coexistence of different modes of victim agency in waging increasingly diverse justice struggles challenges the very boundaries of transitional justice and pushes new actors and issues to the centre of the debate. These chapters analysed instances where transitional justice is invoked in 'aparadigmatic' justice struggles, as well as instances where new issues and debates are foregrounded in more paradigmatic struggles. This contemporary justice landscape also challenges us to rethink our ethical, epistemic and methodological approaches for how, as researchers, practitioners, or policymakers, we engage in ways that acknowledge victims' protagonism and agenda-setting agency when accompanying and intervening in this multi-layered context.

### C.3.1 *The Return of Disruptive Ambitions*

The previously mentioned prominence of resistance (whether in explicit or implicit forms) as a defining feature of contemporary victim engagement takes us back to the radical roots of transitional justice. The first generation of victim mobilisation was inherently disruptive, with demands for truth, justice, and recognition directly challenging state inaction and impunity. This ethos of resistance remains prominent today. Yet its forms and objectives have evolved. Rather than solely demanding institutional accountability, contemporary victim initiatives often seek to challenge the very structures and paradigms that shape transitional justice. Critical transitional justice scholarship has extensively documented how these demands for disruption, throughout the second generation, were sanitised out of most institutional approaches to transitional justice, but this does not mean that these demands have ceased to exist.

The third generation, in particular, illustrates how contemporary justice struggles increasingly see resistance as a core feature of transitional justice – not merely through demands to disrupt acute situations of violence, but also, and increasingly, through demands to disrupt and resist sanitised modes of action and participation that invisibilise lived realities; to disrupt and resist institutional non-action; to disrupt and resist a more generalised harmful status quo that may inflict both structural and direct violence upon certain groups and individuals (Destrooper 2023). This renewed emphasis on disruption and resistance also reflects an urgent response to contemporary threats such as democratic backsliding, anti-rights discourse, and shrinking civic space (Dancy and Thoms 2025). These justice struggles are then not only about reckoning with past violence but also about resisting ongoing and emerging forms of oppression, and reaffirming victims' protagonism in shaping justice agendas beyond transitional justice's traditional scope.

Many of these dynamics were captured tellingly in Chapter 15 by Ibrahim, Hartmann and Buckley-Zistel on the justice-seeking efforts of Syrian diaspora in Germany. The chapter describes how diaspora justice actors, seeking to disrupt ongoing impunity in a context of – at the time – non-transition in Syria, urged for and engaged with (innovative) institutional avenues such as universal jurisdiction processes, and also how many of them eventually began to complement or shift away from these formal avenues, as they proved insufficient in addressing the lived realities and additional layers of injustice experiences by diaspora justice actors living exile. In response, alternative forms of justice-seeking have emerged, including artistic and localised initiatives that allow diaspora actors to articulate their demands on their own terms. These approaches foreground the intersection between the harms endured in Syria and the structural injustices encountered by these diaspora actors in their host countries. In doing so, they are seeking, once again, to disrupt by resisting the tendency to confine justice claims to a specific timeframe, place or political transition.

### C.3.2 *Experimentation and the Blending of Justice Frameworks*

This growing constellation of struggles in which transitional justice is both mobilised and expanded to encompass new demands has further exposed the structural roots of harm and oppression. And it has become increasingly evident that transitional justice alone is unlikely to fulfil the multi-faceted disruptive and transformative aspirations embedded in many of these struggles. More and more, transitional justice is being employed alongside and as a complement to other justice frameworks, ranging from social justice to decolonisation. The chapters in the second part of this handbook demonstrated that each of these justice frameworks brings its own repertoire of actions, and that these are increasingly beginning to blend.

Much as the demands and vocabulary of the first generation played a formative role in shaping the field of transitional justice and its institutional contours as we know them today, the third generation sees a growing blending and convergence of justice and rights repertoires under the broad banner and normative objectives of transitional justice. This development may well influence the field's future direction, once again positioning grassroots engagement as a potential driver of transformation. Instead of becoming mired in debates over whether such practices should be classified as 'real' transitional justice, the chapters in the second part of this handbook have shifted the focus back to the agentic and creative strategies of a broader set of grassroots actors who are actively enacting justice. In doing so, they reveal how innovation and experimentation across justice frameworks can serve as a productive lens for re-imagining and futureproofing transitional justice.

This is aptly illustrated both in Chapter 16, where Baudweijns explores how in the context of the Democratic Republic of Congo youth movements are turning to transitional justice rhetoric to connect past and present struggles for democratic accountability and human rights, and in Chapter 17, where Paricio Montesinos discusses how transitional justice frames are mobilized in the context of business and human rights in the Columbian context. At the same time, victim-survivor organisations use transitional justice principles to challenge the boundaries between 'everyday' and conflict-related gendered and sexual violence to push for deeper, systemic change. And, similarly, human rights defenders working on environmental and resource exploitation draw on transitional justice language to emphasise structural links between violence and resource extraction, bringing new topics into the framework and expanding the framework to new territory. This creative invocation of transitional justice fosters innovation in a context where efforts to implement a comprehensive national transitional justice policy coexist and interact with grassroots initiatives that reinterpret and reshape transitional justice objectives, principles, and mechanisms to fit specific struggles.

### C.3.3 *Ecosystemic Engagement as Adaptive and Multi-Sited*

Third, the handbook emphasised the extent to which these intersecting struggles (both different approaches to transitional justice narrowly understood, as well as the intersection of various justice struggles) produce a far more complex portrait of what engagement in justice struggles looks like, and also of how the complexity of this ecosystem requires us to adopt a more fine-grained approach to thinking about both the enabling and constraining effects that various types of actions in the institutional and grassroots realm may have upon one another. One of the key insights emerging from this handbook is therefore the importance of analysing victim engagement as long-term, adaptive trajectories.

The handbook explicitly refrained from reducing victim engagement to participation in invited spaces. Instead, the generational framework helps to make visible and to explain when, where, how, and why victims have navigated and created a multitude of justice spaces; and how this often involves implicit or explicit interactions with institutions: at times through collaboration, at other times through acknowledgement or critical engagement, and occasionally through outright rejection. The case studies in this handbook underscored the importance of developing a more nuanced understanding of how different justice avenues intersect and interact within the broader justice ecosystem. While some forms of engagement may reinforce and strengthen each other, others can generate tensions or prompt strategic shifts. Attending more closely to the long-term, adaptive trajectories of victim engagement, both individual and collective, is therefore essential.

In Chapter 18, Firchow and Laplante underscored, for example, the importance of relational justice in repairing conflict harm. They proposed concrete criteria – such as mutual recognition, deliberation, and an ethics of care – for evaluating victims' role in transitional justice processes in ways that look for more meaningful engagement with institutional justice spaces as part of encompassing trajectories. Complementing this, Saeed focused in Chapter 19 on art-based initiatives, particularly the Theatre of the Oppressed, as an alternative space for victim engagement outside formal legal and political mechanisms. These art-based methods acknowledge that victims are the protagonists in their own justice efforts, fostering agency through memorialisation, documentation, and locally driven justice practices. Saeed argued that such approaches offer valuable epistemological and methodological insights for transitional justice research, emphasising the importance of long-term, adaptive engagement beyond institutional timelines.

### C.3.4 *Rethinking Ethics and Epistemics*

Finally, both the complexity and the nature of these intersecting justice struggles make it blatantly clear that current ways of engaging in transitional justice research, policy, or practice need to be revisited. There is a need for epistemological and methodological pluralism in studying victim engagement and for addressing the critical importance of ethical reflexivity, including as they relate to issues of power, representation, and positionality (Jones 2021; Lühe and Baines 2025).

How do we study complex justice ecosystems in ways that reflect their porous boundaries, dynamic networks, and the agency of victims across multiple spheres? And building on that, how do we meaningfully engage with the new themes, practices, and perspectives that emerge from these intersecting struggles? This includes questions of relationality, social repair, the role and politicisation of (victim) identities, and the coexistence of diverse agendas, practices, objectives, and epistemologies. It invites reflection on how these evolving dynamics shape not only what we study but also how we conduct research, and develop our own practice within the field.

In response to these questions, several authors underlined the importance of participatory methodologies, grassroots innovation, and the need to recognise diverse forms of engagement within a justice landscape with porous borders. Similar to Saeed's chapter on Afghanistan, Alas, Grzyb and Rivera Castillo outlined in Chapter 20 participatory and decolonial methodologies that position participants as knowledge-holders, co-researchers, and co-creators rather than subjects of research, and underscored the importance of ethical reflexivity and the prioritisation of local needs and perspectives in justice efforts to foster intergenerational education, healing, and reconciliation. Their work with the Surviving Memory project in El Salvador demonstrates how collaborative documentation practices, such as the co-creation of community history books, can serve as meaningful justice mechanism.

In Chapter 21, Reed-Hurtado, in turn, explored the promises and pitfalls of new technologies in supporting grassroots justice efforts, through a historical lens. His chapter called for a rethinking of traditional research and engagement methods, advocating for methodological flexibility that reflects how justice is pursued. While digital tools and new data technologies can vastly enhance information gathering, documentation, and networking, Reed-Hurtado also identified key challenges, including an overly legal-centric focus, language and accessibility barriers, and communities' cautious relationship with technology. Yet the chapter simultaneously highlighted promising examples of local innovation, where human rights practitioners and victim collectives co-develop technology-based tools tailored to local realities. These efforts are illustrative of a more adaptive, responsive approach to methodology and engagement in transitional justice.

## C.4 IDENTIFYING FUTURE DIRECTIONS

In many ways, the second part of this handbook captures where we currently find ourselves in the evolving landscape of transitional justice: in the midst of ongoing transformations shaped by diverse and intersecting justice struggles. Against this backdrop, the contributions by, and conversations with, the authors brought to light several recurring themes that signal important directions for the field. These themes were not imposed a priori but emerged through the conceptual reflections and real-world practices described across the chapters, and invite us to further build on both the generational and intersecting understanding of victim engagement. What follows, then, is a snapshot of a field in motion – a starting point for thinking about how transitional justice can be future-proofed by responding to the complexities of contemporary justice struggles. We outline three emergent themes here that resonate throughout the handbook and which we consider central to a forward-looking agenda for research and practice.

### C.4.1 *Relationality and Relational Justice Models*

Throughout the handbook, relationality recurred as a significant conceptual lens in understanding victim engagement in transitional justice, acting both as a driver and an outcome of that engagement. This lens emphasises the interconnected nature of victims' roles within dynamic (webs of) relationships – whether familial, communal, institutional, or societal. Relationality intersects with the understanding of people's agency, challenging the notion of victims as isolated individuals and instead highlighting their embeddedness within broader social networks that varyingly shape engagement.

Focusing on bottom-up collective actions and victim peer-group relationships through a relational model of agency demonstrates how solidarity and empathy within victim movements shape political agency, emphasising that victims' engagement is influenced by their relationships with others in their community. Similarly, the concept of social ecologies homes in on family, community, and victims' groups as spaces that contribute to resilience and support after conflict. At the same time, a focus on relational dynamics can also reveal how victimhood hierarchies and competing or exclusionary practices can emerge, potentially leading to fragmentation within and between victim groups or communities. When focusing on relationality in formal modes of participation, a relational justice model argues for reparative processes that aim at repairing and rebuilding relationships – particularly between affected populations and state actors, whereby the process of delivering reparations is relational in itself, with interactions between administrators and recipients playing a crucial role in restoring dignity and well-being.

The notion of 'recognition relationships' similarly emphasises the role of interactions between victims and both formal and informal actors in processes such as the search for the disappeared. Recognition, in this view, is crucially shaped by intersubjective relationships and the power dynamics, time, and engagement contexts characterising these. These discussions raise important questions for research and practice, particularly around how to better acknowledge relationality in transitional justice frameworks both in practice and in scholarship. A central question is how to imagine victim participation in ways that foster not just individual agency but also acknowledge and support the work of broader networks of social actors, highlighting the significance of relationality in shaping both justice processes and outcomes.

### C.4.2 *The Sustainability of Long-Term Struggles*

A second emergent theme is the growing focus on sustainability, resilience, and long-term justice strategies. The temporal stretching that characterises contemporary thinking and practice in transitional justice envisions victim engagement – and indeed transitional justice itself – not as a one-off intervention, but as sustained and evolving processes that often stretch across decades. This long-term perspective reflects the reality that transitional justice, by its very nature, must continuously adapt to shifting socio-political contexts. While several scholars have already problematised the field's conventional temporal assumptions (e.g., Miller 2021), the chapters in this handbook point to an urgent need to reconceptualise its temporality in ways that reflect current innovation and expansions of the paradigm.

Central to this rethinking is not only an awareness that the nature and demands of justice activism are changing, but also a recognition of intergenerational inheritance within justice struggles, to children and grandchildren as well as to youths more broadly. The enduring efforts of movements such as the Saturday Mothers or the Tamil families of the disappeared reveal how justice claims are passed on, adapted, and re-energised over time, while remaining rooted in collective memory and the struggle for accountability. This intergenerational continuity underscores the importance of sustaining justice activism not only through political and legal channels but also through emotional and social support structures that ensure the longevity of these efforts. In addition to relationality, the growing attention to memory work further complements this vision of sustainability, whereby memory initiatives allow for building long-term justice practices, creating spaces where past injustices are not forgotten, and fostering a culture of remembrance that supports ongoing justice struggles.

Yet the chapters also illustrate the emotional, psychological, and physical toll of sustained engagement in justice-seeking, particularly when faced with ongoing violence, systemic repression, dwindling donor aid, or lack of institutional support. On the one hand, the challenge of maintaining momentum over decades complicates the continuity of justice movements. On the other hand, it also helps explain the contemporary transformations in transitional justice practices and demands, as these struggles evolve intergenerationally. New actors often mobilise a broader range of strategies to achieve both initially unmet and newly evolving objectives of the struggle, fostering innovation, experimentation, and transformation along the way.

### C.4.3 *Concurrent De-centrality and Trans-locality*

Finally, a range of contemporary developments, such as the emergence of new media and technologies, have further shaped victims' engagement trajectories, for example, by fostering cross-border solidarity, enabling new modes of documentation and information dissemination, and facilitating more decentralised, networked movements with a global resonance (Pham and Aronson 2019; Teo 2025). The chapters in this handbook allude to the many transnational (and often also cross-generational) linkages between localised justice struggles, and how this also inspires South–South learning through mirroring and adopting justice demands and repertoires, rather than relying solely on largely Global North-inspired legal and institutional frameworks. This is reflected, in particular, in the dominance of non-hierarchical and grassroots organising, such as artistic expressions and community dialogues, which are placed on an equal footing with, or pursued in parallel to, formal justice, thereby creating greater visibility for bottom-up justice needs and demands.

At the same time, some victim-led initiatives and justice practices intentionally operate outside the public gaze. A focus on 'quiet' transitional justice highlights how private or behind-the-scenes efforts can be key components of justice-seeking trajectories, including back-channel negotiations or unofficial truth recovery initiatives driven by victims themselves. On the contrary, a focus on non-participation, subtle resistance, or 'everyday' transitional justice foregrounds agency beyond conventional understandings of victim engagement. Both, however, push back against the current preoccupation with highly public and visible practices of participation and mobilisation. As several contributions to this handbook have shown, this prompts attention not only to new technologies to support justice struggles but also to new methodologies for studying and understanding them – including attentiveness to the non-verbal, the affective, the embodied, and the performative dimensions of victim agency.

These concurrent dynamics of de-centrality and trans-locality, as well as the varying degrees of (in)visibility they may involve, not only emerge from but also foster experimentation. Victim-driven efforts and movements are increasingly exploring innovative approaches to accountability, memory work, and reparation that resonate with broader transnational justice struggles. It is precisely these dynamics that can underpin a power shift within the transitional justice landscape, whereby local actors lead and define justice processes, engaging with global networks and the global resonance of the transitional justice discourse, while staying grounded in local realities, and can promote a more inclusive, networked model of justice pursued collectively across various communities and organisations.

### C.4.4 *An Agenda for Moving Forward*

Jointly, these three dimensions paint the picture of transitional justice as an ongoing victim-driven experiment, rather than a fixed, prescriptive or state-centric model. Such an approach holds appeal in the current geopolitical context: in times of democratic backsliding, even across a wide range of allegedly consolidated democracies, it may seem logical – even necessary – to reject the state as a credible driver of transitional justice. However, contemporary practice need not signal abandonment, but rather a reframing of where agency, legitimacy, and transformation reside. This book has shown that victims engage with transitional justice not because it is a neatly defined field, but because it can be mobilised alongside other paradigms, from human rights to social justice, from local resistance to transnational advocacy. Efforts to seal it off as a self-contained discipline often serve to reinforce professional authority rather than address the realities of those affected by harm.

When we move past the anxiety of coherence and embrace transitional justice as part of a broader ecosystem, its true potential emerges. Victim engagement across generations and geographies reveals an approach to justice that is flexible, open-ended, and disruptive, not through an adherence to preordained models, but rather because of an ability to remain responsive to shifting socio-political conditions and challenges. The task, then, is to increasingly acknowledge and theorise this practice, which constitutes an adaptable, dynamic, and generative force that can foster resistance, sustain memory, and advance justice in ways that are neither prescriptive nor predetermined. This handbook offers a framework for making this exercise the foundation of our ongoing and future research and practice.

## REFERENCES

Dancy, Geoff, and Timo Thoms. 2025. 'Transitional Justice and the Problem of Democratic Decline'. *International Journal of Transitional Justice*, 19(1), 36–59.

Destrooper, Tine. 2023. 'Disruptive Accountability? Temporal Regimes and Social Change in Decolonization Struggles in Belgium'. *Journal of Law and Society*, 50(1), 59–76.

Destrooper, Tine, and Elke Evrard. 2025. 'The (Many) Afterlives of Transitional Justice: Practice-Based Insights on Continuity, Impact and Evolving Justice Struggles'. *International Journal of Transitional Justice*, 19(1), 151–171.

Jones, Briony. 2021. 'The Performance and Persistence of Transitional Justice and Its Ways of Knowing Atrocity'. *Cooperation and Conflict*, 56(2), 163–180.

Lühe, Ulrike, and Erin Baines. 2025. 'Difficult Stories that Haunt: Towards Research Otherwise in Transitional Justice'. *International Journal of Transitional Justice*, 19(1), 118–134.

Miller, Zinaida. 2021. 'Temporal Governance: The Times of Transitional Justice'. *International Criminal Law Review*, 21(5), 848–877.

Pham, Phuong N., and Jay D. Aronson. 2019. 'Technology and Transitional Justice'. *International Journal of Transitional Justice*, 13(1), 1–6.

Teo, Sue Anne. 2025. *Artificial Intelligence and Transitional Justice: Framing the Connections*. Impunity Watch.

# Index

Printed by Integrated Books International,
United States of America